Women in Culture

Women in Culture

A Women's Studies Anthology

Edited by Lucinda Joy Peach

American University

BLACKWELL
Publishers

Copyright © Blackwell Publishers Inc., 1998

Introduction, apparatus, selection, and arrangement copyright © Lucinda Joy Peach, 1998

First published 1998

2 4 6 8 10 9 7 5 3 1

Blackwell Publishers Inc.
350 Main Street
Malden, Massachusetts 02148
USA

Blackwell Publishers Ltd
108 Cowley Road
Oxford OX4 1JF
UK

Library of Congress Cataloging-in-Publication Data
Women in American culture : a women's studies anthology / edited by Lucinda Joy Peach.
p. cm.
Includes bibliographical references and index.
ISBN 1-55786-648-1 (hbk. : alk. paper).—ISBN 1-55786-649-X
(pbk. : alk. paper)
1. Women—Miscellanea. 2. Women in popular culture. 3. Sex role.
4. Social values. 5. Feminist criticism. I. Peach, Lucinda J.
HQ1233.W596 1998
305.4'07—dc21   97-24516
CIP

British Library Cataloguing in Publication Data
A CIP catalogue record for this book is available from the
British Library.

Typeset in 10 on 12½ pt Galliard
by Graphicraft Typesetters Ltd., Hong Kong
Printed in Great Britain by MPG Books Ltd, Bodmin, Cornwall

This book is printed on acid-free paper

Contents

Preface

This anthology provides an introduction to women in American culture. Although there are a number of women's studies textbooks available, most of them focus on issues relating to women in society generally. Little attention has been paid to the specific ways in which American culture has shaped, and been shaped by, women's experience. Yet, as Gloria Anzaldúa (1995: 43) has pointed out, "culture forms our beliefs. We perceive the version of reality that it communicates." This includes our beliefs about women. Thus, there is a need for a text that addresses specifically the topic of women's relationship to culture. This volume attempts to address that need.

The field of women's studies has grown exponentially since it began in the early 1970s. The amount of literature on the subject is far too vast to be encompassed in a single work. For that reason, the readings included here reflect a diverse set of perspectives, but by no means a comprehensive one. Instead, the readings are drawn from a number of different academic disciplines as well as from the mass media and popular culture. Some of the readings are now considered to be "classics" in women's studies or feminist theory; others are less well known. A deliberate effort has been made to include essays reflecting the life experiences of women from different cultural backgrounds, as well as different racial, ethnic, and class backgrounds, and sexual orientation. Readings were selected for their ability to shed light on the contemporary status of women in American culture from a feminist perspective or a perspective of relevance to feminism.

Each of the chapters includes an introductory overview of the subject, current developments in women's studies and feminist thinking on the topic, and some background on the readings. The readings for each chapter provide a representative, but necessarily partial, perspective. Following the readings are several suggested activities, including a series of questions for discussion. These can provide the basis for individual written assignments and small group discussions as well as class-wide discussions. A list of films and videos relevant to the subject follows. Finally, a Bibliography at the end of each chapter provides additional perspectives as well as a source for further research.

Reference

Anzaldúa, Gloria (1995) "Cultural tyranny," in Amy Kesselman, Lily McNair, and Nancy Schniedewind (eds), *Women: Images and Realities. A Multicultural Anthology* (Mountain View, CA: Mayfield).

Acknowledgments

The editor and publishers wish to thank the following for permission to use copyright material:

Aunt Lute Books for material from Papusa Molina, *Making Face, Making Soul/Haciendo Caras: Creative and Critical Perspectives by Feminists of Color*, ed. Gloria Anzaldúa, pp. 326–31. Copyright © 1990 by Gloria Anzaldúa;

Center for Media Literacy for Jean Kilbourne, "Beauty and the Beast of Advertising," *Media & Values: Redesigning Women* (Winter 1990);

The Crossing Press for Marilyn Frye, "Oppression" in *The Politics of Reality*. Copyright © 1983 by Marilyn Frye; and Audre Lorde, "Age, Race, Class and Sex: Women Redefining Difference" in *Sister Outsider*. Copyright © 1984 by Audre Lorde;

Dialogue for material from Susan Sherwin, "Abortion through a Feminist Ethics Lens," *Dialogue*, 30 (1991), pp. 327–42, edited by Alison Jaggar;

Terry K. Diggs for her article "No Way to Treat a Lawyer," *California Lawyer*, December 1992;

Feminist Studies, Inc. for Shirley Glubka, "Out of the Stream: an Essay on Unconventional Motherhood," *Feminist Studies*, 9: 2 (Summer 1983) pp. 223–34;

The Free Press, a division of Simon and Schuster, for material from Johnnetta B. Cole, *All American Women: Lines that Divide, Ties that Bind*, ed. Johnnetta B. Cole, pp. 1–6. Copyright © 1986 by The Free Press;

HarperCollins Publishers, Inc. for material from Kim Chernin, *The Obsession: Reflections on the Tyranny of Slenderness*. Copyright © 1981 by Kim

Chernin; Starhawk, *The Spiral Dance*. Copyright © 1979 by Miriam Simos; and Ellen Bass and Louise Thornton, "Introduction" to *I Never Told Anyone: Writings by Women Survivors of Child Sexual Abuse*. Copyright © 1983 by Ellen Bass, Louise Thornton, Jude Brister, Grace Hammond, and Vicki Lamb;

Houghton Mifflin Company for material from Shari L. Thurer, *The Myths of Motherhood*, pp. 286–301. Copyright © 1994 by Shari L. Thurer;

Douglas Kellner for his essay, "Madonna, Fashion and Identity" in *On Fashion*, eds Shari Benstock and Suzanne Ferris, Rutgers University Press (1994);

Little Brown, with Random House, Inc., for Maya Angelou, "Still I Rise" in *And Still I Rise*, Virago. Copyright © 1978 by Maya Angelou;

Media Studies Journal for Linda M. Scott, "Fresh Lipstick: Rethinking Images of Women in Advertising," *Media Studies Journal*, 7: 1–2 (Winter–Spring 1993) pp. 141–55;

The Michigan Law Review Association and the author for material from Martha R. Mahoney, "Legal Images of Battered Women: Redefining the Issue of Separation," *Michigan Law Review*, 90: 1 (October 1991) pp. 2–19;

William Morrow & Company, Inc. for material from Naomi Wolf, *The Beauty Myth*, pp. 9–19. Copyright © 1991 by Naomi Wolf;

The New Lexington Press for material from Carol Bohmer and Andrea Parrot, *Sexual Assault on Campus: the Problem and the Solution*, Lexington Books, pp. 18–40. Copyright © 1993 by Jossey-Bass Inc., Publishers;

Newsweek, Inc. for Farai Chideya with Melissa Rossi and Dogen Hannah, "Revolution, Girl Style," *Newsweek*, 23 November 1992. Copyright © 1992 Newsweek, Inc.;

Penguin UK and Viking Penguin, a division of Penguin Books USA, Inc., for material from John Berger, *Ways of Seeing*, BBC/Penguin Books Ltd, pp. 45–64. Copyright © 1972 by Penguin Books Ltd;

Sierra Club Books for Ynestra King, "Healing the Wounds" in *Reweaving the World*, eds Irene Diamond and Gloria Feman Orenstein (1990);

South End Press for bell hooks, "Feminism: a Transformational Politic" in *Thinking Feminist, Thinking Black* (1989) pp. 19–27; and Elayne Rapping, *Media-tions: Forays into the Culture and Gender Wars* (1994) pp. 183–91;

Stanford University Press for Sherry B. Ortner, "Is Female to Male as Nature is to Culture?" in *Woman, Culture and Society*, eds Michelle Zimbalist

Rosaldo and Louise Lamphere, pp. 67–87. Copyright © 1974 by the Board of Trustees of the Leland Stanford Junior University;

University of Calgary Press for M. Friedman, "Beyond Caring: the Demoralization of Gender," *Canadian Journal of Philosophy*, suppl. vol. 13 (1987) pp. 87–105;

The University of Chicago Press for material from Carroll Smith-Rosenberg, "The Female World of Love and Ritual: Relations between Women in Nineteenth-century America," *Signs: Journal of Women in Culture and Society*, 1: 1 (Autumn 1975) pp. 1–29;

Yale University Press for material from Patricia Hill Collins, "Shifting the Center: Race, Class and Feminist Theorizing about Motherhood" in *Representations of Motherhood*, eds Donna Bassin, Margaret Honey and Meryle Mahrer Kaplan (1994) pp. 56–74.

Every effort has been made to trace the copyright holders but if any have been inadvertently overlooked the publishers will be pleased to make the necessary arrangement at the first opportunity.

Introduction

This anthology of readings in women's studies is designed to introduce readers to some of the more significant ways in which American culture has shaped women's lives and American women have contributed to shaping their culture. Women's studies is still a relatively new field of study. It began in the early 1970s, but has grown rapidly since that time. Originally, most women's studies research and teaching focused on "retrieval," that is, on uncovering buried evidence of women's contributions to culture that had been ignored or suppressed by the dominant male culture. Since that time, women's studies research has focused more on the causes and conditions of women's oppression, and on how sex and gender differences have been manipulated to justify this oppression. In the past few years, more work has focused on what is called "gender studies." Sometimes, this is just another label for women's studies. Other times, it is intended to signify a shift away from the study of women in isolation from men to the study of women within the context of the social construction of gender. As the focus of this anthology is on women's relationship to culture rather than gender *per se*, it is more properly considered within women's studies than gender studies.

This introductory chapter will provide a kind of map of the territory to be covered by the readings collected in this volume. We will attempt to locate women in relation to American culture before moving on to explore particular aspects of that culture. The term *culture* is difficult to define precisely because it encompasses so many different aspects, and has been interpreted in so many different ways. Most broadly, the term "culture" refers to the practices and products of human civilization. This encompasses images, symbols, myths, values, ideas, language, the arts, folklore, philosophy, and religion. Culture constructs meanings, images, belief systems, and identities. As Stuart Hall explains, culture is "the sum of the available descriptions through which societies make sense of and reflect their common experiences."

It thus includes both the meanings and values of distinctive social groups, and the way they confront and respond to the conditions of their existence. Culture also includes lived traditions and practices which express and embody these understandings (Hall, 1994: 521–2).

In other words, culture shapes who we are as human beings. Some would go so far as to say that culture *constitutes* women's (and men's) lives, especially through *language*. In turn, men and women shape culture. Yet women's contributions to American culture have been largely invisible, at least until recently. In this volume, we will be exploring some of the reasons for this invisibility, as well as some of the often-unrecognized ways that women have contributed to American culture.

Because our subject is *culture*, less attention will be given in this volume to certain topics that are typically covered in women's studies textbooks: gender socialization and the development of sex/gender roles in families, the difference between sex and gender, and the psychological and socio-logical implications of sex roles. While these topics are undoubtedly important, they have already been given extensive coverage elsewhere.

Although this volume is devoted to the topic of women in *culture*, the theoretical perspectives used cannot generally be labelled *cultural studies*, at least not understood as theoretical perspectives derived from Marxism, influ-enced heavily by postmodernism and poststructuralism and other critical theories that challenge traditional understandings of knowledge and power. None the less, certain of the readings are informed by cultural studies per-spectives. In addition, certain approaches common to feminism and cultural studies perspectives, such as an interest in the cultural dimensions of power and inequality, the production of knowledge, the reproduction of social inequality, and relations of dominance and subordination (see Franklin et al., 1991: 7) will be addressed here.

A fundamental characteristic of American culture is the sharp division between males and females along gender lines. *Gender* refers to ideas about the appropriate behaviors and roles of males and females. As Joan Scott (1986: 1056) says, gender is "a social category imposed on a sexed body." *Sex* is generally used here to refer to biological sex, that is, to the sexual organs, hor-mones, and other physiological differences that differentiate males and females.

Gendered aspects of American culture include the greater value attributed to males than females, especially at birth, and all of the consequences that have followed from this cultural inequality. Because gender is a primary determinant of a person's social status, it plays a significant role in shaping the opportunities that a person has for education, employment, and social and political status. Gender or gender differences are also responsible for sexism, employment discrimination, the exclusion of women from the *public sphere* of politics, government, law, paid labor, and religious leadership, the use of male-gendered language as universal (that is, as supposedly referring to both males and females), the tendency to use male terminology as generic (that is, as referring to both males and females), the manner in which women's lives and contributions have been devalued, ignored, or dismissed as irrelevant or unimportant to history and culture, and the portrayal of women in stereotyped or one-dimensional fashion (when they are considered at all).

Essentialist views tend to emphasize biological differences between men and women, especially characteristics such as women's (general) capacity for child-bearing and typically lesser physical strength. These differences often provide the basis for arguments that women are less intelligent, more emotional, and more nurturing than men. Increasingly, scholars have recognized that men and women do not passively adopt the gender characteristics that are associated with their sex. Inclusion of the term "gender" in feminist scholarship and women's studies in the past several years signifies a shift away from the notion that biology is destiny, that is, that sex differences determine what men and women are. Instead, sex differences modify and shape gender norms in accordance with other considerations, including race, ethnic and cultural background, geographical location, educational attainment, socio-economic privilege, and sexual orientation, as well as individual personality and temperament. In this *non-essentialist* view (adopted in this text) gender is *culturally constructed* rather than biological or innate.

As anthropologist Sherry Ortner explains in the first reading in chapter 1, biological facts and differences only take on significance as "superior" or "inferior" within the framework of value systems that have been culturally defined. That is, women's biological differences are not inherently, or in and of themselves, inferior or secondary, but are *deemed* to be so by cultural ascription or designation. Thus, contrary to earlier understandings of gender as primarily determined by biological sex differences, here we take the view that culture is the primary determinant of gender and *gender identity*, that is, how we define ourselves and are defined by others as male or female.

In exploring *American* culture, our focus will be primarily on the United States, but will occasionally extend both north and south of the border to examine how aspects of American culture outside the US influences, and has been influenced by, American women. As there are a multiplicity of different cultures in the US, it is difficult to speak of "American culture" in the singular. Rather, there are many types of cultures that overlap and intersect with one another in significant ways, yet also have a distinctiveness and independent integrity. These cultures have resulted from various factors: racial and ethnic privilege or oppression, social and economic class, educational attainment, political outlook, religious affiliation, sexual orientation, age, disability, and so on. As we will see in later chapters, some scholars have even argued that there is a distinctive women's culture that exists separately from the dominant male culture. Consequently, it is more accurate to think of American culture as plural rather than singular.

None the less, there is also a dominant culture in the United States that is, in significant part, the product of those who have dominated the political, social, economic, intellectual, and artistic institutions of society. This has traditionally been, and continues to be, mainly middle- to upper-class white males, usually well educated, generally of European descent, and most often Christian. The dominant culture has had a tremendous influence on every aspect of American women's lives, regardless of their race, class, ethnicity, religious, or sexual orientation. As we will see in the following chapters, the dominant culture has been a powerful shaper of social attitudes about women, including how women think about themselves, their bodies, intellectual capabilities, expected social roles, and opportunities for self-expression and fulfillment. In recent years, some recognition has been given to the cultural contributions of women, members of minority groups, and others outside the mainstream of intellectual and artistic dominance, but such recognition remains partial and radically incomplete.

Because our subject is *women* in American culture, we will be most interested in exploring how culture has shaped women's lives, and, in turn, how women have shaped culture. In particular, many of the readings deal explicitly with *popular culture*, that is, popular expressions of art, music, fashion, film, and television that are often transmitted through media-generated sounds and images. In addition, some of the readings address culture in the sense of "*high*" or "*civilized*" culture. These expressions include fine art, classical music, and "great" works of literature. A significant part of our inquiry will be devoted to understanding gender as a cultural construction, and the female-gendered identities that are the products of a distinctively American culture. Another significant focus will be on the ways in which women have contributed to shaping contemporary culture.

Several factors have contributed to women's status in American culture. The readings in this anthology reflect a variety of different perspectives on women in American culture from writers representing a diversity of backgrounds and experiences. As a women's studies text, most of the readings included here are feminist in orientation. However, women's studies and feminism are not synonymous. Women's studies is an academic discipline focused on the study of women. It contests the androcentric (male-centered) character of traditional scholarship, and seeks to rectify the omission of women from traditional disciplines by focusing on women's experiences and contributions.

Feminism itself is not monolithic, but encompasses a wide variety of different perspectives. Very generally, feminist perspectives share a commitment to improving the status of women's lives by working to eliminate sexism, patriarchy, and sexual or gender inequality. Some understandings of feminism are much broader. For example, the African-American feminist scholar bell hooks defines feminism as a social movement dedicated to ending the oppression of *all* people, not only women, and thus directed against racism, classism, homophobia, and other forms of oppression, as well as sexism (see hooks, 1990: 189).

Contrary to right-wing media portrayals of feminists as a single, monolithic group of "feminazis" or "man haters," there are radical differences in feminist approaches beyond this basic definition, including liberal, Marxist, socialist, psychoanalytic, postmodern, cultural, lesbian, Mujerista, Womanist, ecofeminist approaches, and so on. We will see examples of some of these types of feminist perspective in the readings in subsequent chapters, and will look at some of them in more detail in chapter 10 in the discussion of feminist politics.

For now, it is important to recognize that feminists have divergent, even conflicting, approaches to a number of different issues. Feminists disagree about what women want and should want: equality or equity; equal opportunity or protection from harm; recognition as being fundamentally like men or significantly different from them; a radical restructuring of the economy or only an equal right to compete within the existing one. Some feminists (sometimes labeled "cultural feminists") criticize the whole notion of women seeking *equal rights*, contending that *rights* are a male conception based on male values of autonomy, independence, liberty, separateness from others, and designed to benefit men. The following issues are among the most controversial in contemporary feminist debates about the cultural situation of women:

1   *Sameness/difference*   Are women like men or different from them? The assumption underlying this question (the same one that underlies the foundation of our liberal political system) is that similar entities should be treated alike, whereas those that are dissimilar may be treated differently. Some, including most liberal feminists, contend that women should strive for *equal* rights on the grounds of their fundamental and essential sameness to men. In their view, the secondary status and subordination of women has resulted from the belief that women are essentially different from men. Others, like cultural feminists, argue that women should be accorded special or different treatment from men on the grounds that they *are* different. From this perspective, women's biological differences,

especially their reproductive capacity, and the child-rearing labor that is usually entailed by it, result in women being disadvantaged when they are treated identically to men.

2 *Essentialism/relativism* A second source of lively contention among feminists today is in some senses a continuation of the first. Focused on similarities and differences *among* women rather than *between* men and women, this debate revolves around whether women are sufficiently similar to one another to warrant making generalized assumptions about "women" as a category or class. Feminists before the 1980s generally assumed that being female gave all women certain shared or universal experiences that were more significant than the racial, class, religious, cultural, and other differences that divided them. Consequently, early feminist scholarship tended to stress commonalities among women in order to stress the universality of women's experience and subordination in sexist and patriarchal societies. As many of the feminists holding this view were white, middle class, and from relatively privileged backgrounds, they tended to ignore differences among women based on race, class, sexual orientation, and so on.

Since the 1980s, these assumptions have been increasingly challenged, first by women of color, and more recently by feminists employing post-modern frames of reference. These critics have pointed out that female gender is only one of several aspects of identity. Persons are *socially con-structed* by a range of different attributes in addition to gender. For women of a privileged race and class, gender may be the most significant form of oppression they experience. For other women, however, racist or classist oppression may be more relevant. For these women, the earlier view, which led to feminist writing that assumed that women's commonalities outweighed their differences, is deemed to be *essentialist*, in contrast to *constructionist* perspectives.

As we shall see in chapter 2, women are *both* similar to and different from one another. There are both commonalities and differences among women that make *essentialist* perspectives too simplistic. However, the abandon-ment of essentialist perspectives has also created problems for feminists. Without a category "woman," of which all females are members, some feminists ask how there can be a women's movement or a feminist politics dedicated to eliminating the oppression of women. This question will be addressed in chapter 10 in relation to feminist politics.

"Patriarchy" is a term derived from the Latin root meaning "rule of the father" or *paterfamilias* (male head of the household). The meaning of the term has been expanded by feminists to include male domination of females more generally. The term "sexism" is used here to refer to forms of cultural expression that discriminate against women on the basis of their sex or gender, or reflect the attitude, belief, or value that women are secondary, inferior, or naturally or appropriately subordinate to men. As we will see in chapter 2, it is frequently difficult to separate out sexism from other forms of discrimination and subjugation of women based on race, socioeconomic class, ethnicity, sexual orientation, or other salient characteristics, and sometimes indefensible even to attempt to do so. None the less, because virtually all women share *some* experience of sex discrimination or gender oppression, even if it is not the *same* experience, it is useful to focus on sexism apart from other forms of discrimination.

"Sexual or gender inequality" is used here to refer to the cultural, legal, and other social disadvantages women experience as a result of their female sex or gender. *Gender systems* or *sex–gender systems* oppose male to female in a hierarchical pattern in which males are dominant and superior and females are subordinate and inferior. They operate to establish, among other things, a gendered division of labor in the home and the outside economy. Since gender is itself a product of culture, gender differences are not permanently fixed or established, but change and shift over time. For this reason, some feminist scholars have determined that it is more appropriate to speak of "genders" rather than a singular gender (see Lorber and Farrell, 1991: 1).

Even within American history, we can see how gender roles have shifted dramatically over different time periods, from the colonial period, where both men and women had domestic tasks, to the industrial era in which work in the public sphere was prescribed for men and proscribed for women. Then, during World War II, women were encouraged to work in the factories to supply the labor lost when men went off to war. In the post-war period, women were again encouraged to return to their domestic duties to make room for the men returning from war. The past few decades have seen the public spheres of work and politics become increasingly open to women, and domestic duties more acceptable for men. None the less, feminist scholars like Susan Faludi have argued that the 1980s witnessed a "backlash" against these gains for women and an effort to return women to their traditional domestic and child-bearing roles (see Faludi, 1991).

The history of the women's movement has also shaped women's contemporary place in American culture. This includes the "first wave" of the women's movement, which culminated in the passage of the Nineteenth Amendment to the US Constitution, granting women the right to vote in 1920. The two world wars finally provided a response (even if only a temporary one) to women's demands to be allowed to work in traditionally male-only occupations. Struggles of the "second wave" of the women's movement of the 1960s and 1970s ended many formal restrictions on women's participation in spheres of public culture such as the traditional male professions of politics, the law, and the arts. This era saw the passage of many laws that have had an influence on bringing women further into the mainstream of American society and culture.

Despite these achievements, which have unquestionably improved the status of many women in American society, the *cultural* status of women remains distinctly secondary and subordinate to that of men. In the chapters that follow we will examine how women's experiences continue to be shaped by gender inequalities in the mainstream culture, as well as how women have developed strategies for resisting and changing mainstream culture, as well as shaping their own cultural traditions.

As the readings illustrate, women continue to struggle for recognition and full participation in every sphere of American culture. One reason for women's continued exclusion from and/or subordination in cultural arenas is that the culture itself is both still largely dominated and controlled by men and biased against women. As we will see, the very ways that women are represented in culture illustrates this bias. We will see this evidenced in images and stereotypes of women, portrayals of women in popular culture, in advertising, fashion, print media, film and television, music and art, and so on. These representations become the texts through which both males and females learn what women "are."

As chapters 4–6 describe, these representations have real effects on women's lives, motivating some to disregard their physical health in the pursuit of cultural ideals of female beauty. These images have encouraged other women to become sexually active in ways that are coerced, more or less overtly, or contrary to the prescribed script for females in American culture. These representations also function to pressure women, subtly or coercively, to become wives and mothers, and to devote themselves selflessly and completely to their husbands and children.

This volume is divided into three parts. Part I, "The Cultural Construction of Gender," investigates how cultural traditions have constructed sexual differences into gender differences, making females women and males men. Chapter 1 examines the seemingly universal cultural oppression of girls and women in American society. Chapter 2 challenges essentialist notions of women by focusing on the differences as well as the commonalities among women. Chapter 3 explores some of the dominant cultural images and stereotypes of women in American culture. The readings here provide a foundation for examining how media and popular culture shape cultural understandings of women.

Part II, "Cultural Institutions Defining Women," considers significant institutions in society that shape cultural understandings of women. Chapter 4 examines the advertising industry, and chapter 5 explores the television and film industries. Chapter 6 investigates how cultural images of female beauty influence women's relationships to their own bodies, including their health and responses to "fashion." Chapter 7 turns to consider motherhood as a cultural institution, and the images, stereotypes, and gender ideology that represent women as naturally or inherently mothers. We will explore how cultural understandings of women as mothers have shaped women's ability to control their reproductive lives and limited the alternatives to traditional motherhood, including access to abortion. We will also look at how the new reproductive technologies are reshaping cultural meanings of motherhood and family.

Chapter 8, the final chapter of Part II, looks at sexual harassment and sexual abuse. The chapter gives special attention to the institution of violence in society, one of the most powerful cultural mechanisms for perpetuating the oppression of women, focusing on three of the more prevalent forms of violence against females in American society today: domestic violence, rape, and childhood sexual abuse.

Part III, "Opportunities for Women in Culture," explores some of the ways that women have used cultural modes of expression to empower their lives. Chapter 9 addresses some of the many ways in which women have contributed to the creation of culture, both a distinctively women's culture as well as artistic and literary standards of the dominant culture. Finally, chapter 10 takes an all too brief look at the prospects for feminism in the future, examining both the backlash against feminism in recent years, as well as ways in which feminists committed to creating positive social change for women are working toward a new culture conducive to the empowerment of women.

General resources in women's studies

Journals and periodicals

Feminist Studies   Women's Studies Program, University of Maryland, College Park, MD 20742. Publishes feminist scholarship in literary criticism, history, and social science, and provides a forum for political analysis and creative work.

Feminist Teacher   Ballentine Hall 442, Indiana University, Bloomington, IN 47405. A non-profit, multidisciplinary magazine committed to combatting sexism and other forms of oppression in the classroom. Published by an editorial collective three times a year, and designated for teachers at all grade levels, preschool through graduate school.

Frontiers: a Journal of Women's Studies University Press of Colorado, PO
    Box 849, Niwot, Colorado 80544. Journal "links the community and the
    academy by publishing scholarly, literary, and artistic work," and focuses
    on how the interaction of gender, race, class, and sexual orientation shapes
    the diversity of women's lives. Particularly emphasizes the work of women
    of color and women in the West.

Ms. PO Box 5304, Harlan, IA 51593-4804. The most prominent journal of
    the second-wave feminist movement, founded by Gloria Steinem. Contains
    national and international news, essays, articles, reviews of books, films,
    health and art, photographs, and reader contributions on issues of rel-
    evance to women.

Off our Backs 2423 18th Street NW, Washington, DC 20009. OOB is the oldest
    feminist news journal featuring coverage of conferences, critical essays,
    international news, and in-depth reporting of issues affecting women and
    the women's movement.

On the Issues: the Progressive Women's Quarterly PO Box 3000, Dept
    OTI, Denville, NJ 07834. Up-to-date coverage of the issues relevant to
    women's lives and fostering positive social change.

Sage: a Scholarly Journal on Black Women PO Box 42741, Atlanta, GA 30311.
    Informative articles, interviews, book reviews, notices of films and exhibits,
    and resource materials for students, teachers and researchers on black
    women's lives.

Signs: Journal of Women in Culture and Society University of Chicago Press,
    Chicago, IL 60657. Leading feminist journal with articles by prominent scholars.

Sojourner 42 Seaverns Avenue, Boston, MA 02130. A national feminist journal
    of opinion, featuring news, essays, articles, interviews, fiction, poetry, and
    reviews of books, films, and music.

Women: a Cultural Review Oxford University Press, 2001 Evans Road, Cary,
    NC 27513. Explores the role and representation of women in arts and
    culture, past and present, including the debates over gender and sexuality.

Women's Review of Books The Women's Review, Inc., 828 Washington Street,
    Wellesley, MA 02181. Valuable source of in-depth reviews of current books
    across the spectrum of women's studies, feminist theory, and gender studies,
    published monthly. Policy is "to represent the widest possible range of
    feminist perspectives both in the books reviewed and in the content of the
    reviews." Includes monthly exchange of letters, and a monthly list of new
    books received.

Women's Studies Abstracts Rush Publishing Co. Inc., PO Box 1, Rush, NY
    14543. Includes over 3,000 abstracts and listings of articles and book
    reviews from 50 women's studies and other feminist journals.

Women's Studies: an Interdisciplinary Journal Gorden and Breach Publishers,
    c/o STBS Order Department, PO Box 786 Cooper Station, New York, NY
    10011. Forum for the presentation of scholarship and criticism about women

in the fields of literature, history, art, sociology, law, political science, economics, anthropology, and the sciences. Also includes poetry, short fiction, film and book reviews.

Women's Studies Quarterly The Feminist Press at CUNY, 311 East 94th Street, New York, NY 10128. Focuses on teaching and research useful to teachers on thematic issues that are disciplinary and interdisciplinary. Contains essays, national and international news, course descriptions and syllabuses, notices of grants and fellowships, and reviews of new books.

Electronic resources

WMST-L: Electronic Forum for Women's Studies Includes a wealth of information of relevance to those concerned with teaching, research, and program administration in women's studies. Includes periodically updated lists of other lists that are relevant to women's studies, including those specializing in a particular field such as H-WOMEN (history) and SWIP-L (Society of Women in Philosophy). Subscribe by sending a message to LISTSERV@UMDD.UMD.EDU: SUBSCRIBE YOUR NAME WMST-L.

Inform Online Women's Studies Database Contains an interesting cross-section of information and on-line texts, including materials on women in politics, education, sexual harassment and employment discrimination, violence against women, and more. To access, telnet or gopher to INFORM.UMD.EDU. Hit return to set the default terminal or type "?" for a list of choices. Select "Women's Studies."

University of Wisconsin-Madison Libraries Gopher Server. Contains core lists – bibliographies – in women's studies on the subjects of feminist movements, health, language, mental health, philosophy, politics, reference works, religion, science, sexual abuse, sociology, sports, and women of color in the United States. To access, gopher or telnet to Wisc.INFO.wisc.edu and select successively Library Catalogs and Services/Journal and Information Databases/UW System Women's Studies Librarian's Office/Core Lists in Women's Studies.

General reference works

Brennan, Shawn, *Women's Information Directory* (Gale Research, 1993).
Ries, Paula and Stone, Anne J. (eds), *The American Woman 1992–93: a Status Report* (Washington, DC: Women's Research and Education Institute, 1993). Special focus on women in electoral politics.
Tierney, Helen, *Women's Studies Encyclopedia* (Westport, CT: Greenwood Press, 1989–91).
Watson, G. Llewellyn, *Feminism and Women's Issues: an Annotated Bibliography and Research Guide* (New York: Garland, 1990).

Film and video distributors for films on women

Alternative Media Information Network, *In her own Image: Films and Videos Empowering Women for the Future.* Media Network, 29 West 14th Street, Suite 403, New York, NY 10011. Catalogs and reviews of alternative-to-mainstream visual productions by and about women.

Filmaker's Library, 124 East 40th Street, New York, NY 10016 (tel. 212-808-4980; fax: 212-808-4983).

First Run Icarus Films, 153 Waverly Place, New York, NY 10014.

New Day Films, 121 West 27th Street, Suite 902, New York, NY 10001 (tel. 212-645-8210).

WAVE: Women's Audio-Visuals in English: a Guide to Nonprint Resources in Women's Studies (1993). Available from Women's Studies Librarian, University of Wisconsin-Madison, 728 State Street, Madison, WI 53706.

Women Make Movies Inc., 462 Broadway, Suite 500, New York, NY 10013 (tel. 212-925-0606). Probably the biggest US distributor of films and videos on women. Contains a wide selection of films, many of them award winning, organized under the headings "Sex Equity," "Health," "Gender," "Global Perspectives and Cultural Identity," and "Arts." Their holdings encompass far more films and videos than the few that are listed in the following chapters.

Bibliography

Anzaldúa, Gloria (1995) "Cultural tyranny," in Amy Kesselman, Lily McNair, and Nancy Schniedewind (eds), *Women: Images and Realities. A Multicultural Anthology* (Mountain View, CA: Mayfield).

Bock, Gissela and James, Susan (eds) (1992) *Beyond Equality and Difference: Citizenship, Feminist Politics, and Female Subjectivity* (New York: Routledge).

Conway, Jill, Bourque, Susan and Scott, Joan (eds) (1987) *Learning about Women: Gender, Politics, and Power* (Ann Arbor, MI: University of Michigan Press).

Denmark, Florence, Nielson, Karen and Scholl, Kristina (1993) "United States of America," in Leonore Loeb Adler (ed.), *International Handbook on Gender Roles* (Westport, CT: Greenwood Press).

Faludi, Susan (1991), *Backlash: the Undeclared War against American Women* (New York: Doubleday Press).

Franklin, Sarah, Lury, Celia, and Stacey, Jackie (1991) *Off-centre: Feminism and Cultural Studies* (New York: HarperCollins).

Hall, Stuart (1994) "Cultural studies," in Nicholas Dirks, Geoff Eley, and Sherry Ortner (eds), *Culture/Power/History: a Reader in Contemporary Social History* (Princeton, NJ: Princeton University Press).

hooks, bell (1990) "Feminism: a transformational politic," in Deborah Rhode (ed.), *Theoretical Perspectives on Sexual Difference* (New Haven, CT: Yale University Press).

Lorber, Judith and Farrell, Susan (eds), *The Social Construction of Gender* (Newbury Park, CA: Sage).

Scott, Joan (1986) "Gender: a useful category of historical analysis," *American Historical Review*, 91 (5), pp. 1053–75.

PART I

The Cultural Construction of Gender

This part of the volume investigates how sex differences between males and females have been culturally constructed into gender differences between men and women. Chapter 1 provides an introduction to women in culture. It explores the status of girls and women in American society. Chapter 2 goes beyond commonalities among women, focusing on the significant differences based on classifications of race, class, and sexual orientation. Chapter 3 explores some of the dominant cultural images and stereotypes of women in American culture. The readings included in Part I provide a foundation for examining how media and popular culture shape cultural understandings of women.

1
Women in Culture

Introduction

Why are men and women treated so differently in American culture, as though they were two different species? Gender differentiation begins at birth (and sometimes even *before*, now that medical technology allows expectant parents to know the sex of their offspring even before they are born). Baby boys and girls are treated differently, from the clothing and toys they receive to the way they are spoken to and touched. Female infants and toddlers are often treated as though they were more fragile and delicate than boys.[1] Boys are more often physically punished than girls, who receive verbal reprimands instead. Mothers also communicate verbally more with their sons than their daughters. Boys are often given more freedom to explore their physical environments at a younger age than are girls. Boys and girls are typically given different household chores, taught different types of play deemed appropriate for their sex, and so on. Parents also tend to dress their children in sex-typed clothing. This cultural practice encourages or discourages certain kinds of play by children, and also sends implicit messages to others about how they should be treated.

The toys that parents provide for their children are also significant influences on gender-differentiated development. Boys are usually given toys like trucks, guns, and building sets that encourage activity, competition, exploration, construction, invention, and aggression, whereas girls typically are given toys like dolls and playhouses that encourage more quiet, domestic play and traits such as creativity, nurturance, and attractiveness. Even when boys are given dolls, they tend to be action-hero types rather than infants or "playhouse" dolls. Providing boys and girls with gender-differentiated toys prepares them for separate roles as adults. Until recently, most children's books ignored females. Many children's books still reflect gender stereotypes of males and females that rigidly define roles and activities based on traditional gender stereotypes (see Renzetti and Curran, 1989: 70–71).

Children also receive messages about appropriate gender behaviors from sources other than their parents, especially once they begin school. Teachers tend to praise boys more than girls, encourage them to speak more often, and tolerate their noisy, disruptive behavior. Girls are responded to less often. Boys are encouraged to be athletic, while girls are expected to have attractive personalities and appearances. These gendered distinctions carry forward into occupations, as males are encouraged to find careers involving competitiveness and achievement-oriented skills, while females are encouraged into the so-called helping professions, such as "sales girls," clerks, secretaries, social workers, and teachers. In sum, as Renzetti and Curran (1989: 74) explain, "Little boys are taught independence, problem solving abilities, assertiveness, and curiosity about their environment – skills that are highly valued in our society. In contrast, little girls are taught dependence, passivity, and domesticity – traits that our society devalues." This kind of socialization results in children viewing the world in terms of gendered distinctions and engaging in *sex typing*, what psychologist Sandra Bem (1993: 598) describes as "the acquisition of sex-appropriate preferences, skills, personality attributes, behaviors, and self-concepts." The problem is not with gender differences *per se*, but with the way these differences are valued as superior and inferior, dominant and subordinate.

As we will see in the following chapters, cultural institutions also contribute to the construction and maintenance of gender roles and the gendered hierarchy that privileges males over females. Again, these gender divisions are intersected by other significant differences such as race, ethnicity, socioeconomic status, religious and political affiliations, and so on, resulting in different experiences of gender. Many different explanations have been given by males in support of women's secondary social status. As feminist philosopher Simone de Beauvoir (1953) stated, "Legislators, priests, philosophers, writers, and scientists have striven to show that the subordinate position of women is willed in heaven and advantageous on earth. The religions invented by men reflect this wish for domination."

In contrast to male-derived explanations of women's inferiority, this chapter will focus on feminist understandings of women's subordinate cultural status. Anthropologist Sherry Ortner explores this question in the first reading "Is Female to Male as Nature is to Culture?". Written in 1974, this classic attempt to shed light on the seemingly universal phenomenon of women's secondary status in culture presents a still-intriguing and provocative thesis. Ortner's article is also a useful site from which to begin our exploration of women in culture because she draws on the work of significant women scholars from a diversity of fields, particularly de Beauvoir, the anthropologist Margaret Mead, and the psychologist Nancy Chodorow.

Ortner's basic thesis is that women are universally subordinated to men because females are identified with nature and males with culture. Ortner insists that this identification is universal, even though there are a diversity of particular conceptions and symbols of women in specific cultures. Indeed, following the earlier work of the anthropologist Margaret Mead, Ortner makes the important point that there is no necessary connection between a particular culture's *imagery, symbols,* and *gender ideology* of women and the actual social status and/or treatment of women in that culture.

The Ortner reading exemplifies the tendency of early second-wave feminist scholarship to emphasize the commonalities rather than the differences in women's experiences. Ortner's article is also significant as representing one of the early articulations of the distinction between *sex* and *gender,* a distinction that has been central to most feminist theorizing since. A second set of distinctions Ortner refers to, which we will see repeatedly in our exploration of women in culture in subsequent chapters, is between the "public" male sphere of social relations and government and the "private" female sphere of family and domesticity.

The division is more than a symbolic one in American culture (and many others as well) because women, until recent decades, were largely excluded, either legally or customarily, from participating in the public spheres of paid employment, politics, government, law, and other aspects of civic life. In addition, gender ideology in various periods of Western history has relegated women to the home and to the roles of wife and mother. When we turn to Carroll Smith-Rosenberg's reading on "The Female World of Love and Ritual" in chapter 9, we will see how the public/private division developed into an ideology of "separate spheres" in the nineteenth century.

The public/private division is not a universal one, however, since some women (especially African-American women) have historically worked outside the home from necessity, and a few women have always managed to participate in public life. None the less, this gendered division of labor – which is sometimes called *"the sex–gender system"* – has remained the prevailing cultural ideal for many.

Since Ortner's article was first published, several scholars have challenged aspects of her thesis. The claims of critics are summarized here to provide some issues to consider while reading "Is Female to Male." First, critics have accused Ortner of being *essentialist* in claiming that the devaluation of women is a universal phenomenon, found everywhere and at all times, one of the "universals of the human condition." Despite Ortner's insistence that the secondary status of women is itself a cultural rather than an inherent fact about femaleness, the first reason she gives for the universal identification of women with nature is women's biological functions of child bearing. The third reason is based on claims about a universal female "psyche." These claims can easily be interpreted as reflecting an essentialist understanding of sex and gender.

In addition, Ortner's claims that the secondary status of women is one of the "true universals" has been criticized as overly broad. Careful ethnographic study of certain cultures suggests that there are exceptions to the general rule that women are *universally* considered to be secondary to men, especially in precolonial American cultures (see MacCormick and Strathern, 1980; Cole, 1986). The accuracy of Ortner's definition of *culture* in terms of "civilization" opposed to nature has also been criticized as inaccurate, since not all cultures devalue nature as Ortner contends. Carol MacCormick and other anthropologists have pointed out that the terms "nature" and "culture" themselves are culturally constructed, and do not represent universal or naturally existing phenomena. For example, MacCormick points out that some cultures do not understand nature to be mutable and transformable as Western culture does, but have different systems of meaning that do not link male to culture and female to nature (MacCormick and Strathern, 1980: 7). In addition, feminist biologist Ruth Hubbard, and other feminist critics of science, have called the stark contrast between culture and nature into question, contending that nature is shaped by culture just as culture is based upon, and thus is, in some respects, a product of nature (see Harding and Hintikka, 1983; Harding, 1986; Hubbard, 1988).

In addition, women in many cultures would deny that they were inferior to males in many respects. But because most anthropology has traditionally been done by males who used other males as their authoritative sources, women's existence, and thus their status within the culture under investigation, has been largely ignored. Rather than linking women with nature, MacCormick suggests that ethnographic accounts instead demonstrate that women are *mediators* between nature and culture and between kinship groups (via marriage). She also argues that women are much less passive in culture than Ortner's model presupposes, and points out that women are not universally restricted to the private sphere of domesticity (MacCormick and Strathern, 1980: 14).

Thirdly, more recent feminist thinking has recognized the significant differences among women that an exclusive emphasis on commonalities obscures. As noted in the Introduction, assuming that women all share certain characteristics or experiences ignores how women's identities and experiences are shaped, not only by gender, but by a variety of interrelated characteristics, especially race, class, and sexual orientation. Thus, recent feminist scholars have recognized that there is no generic "woman" separate and apart from these constituents of gendered identity (see Spelman, 1988).

Lastly, Ortner's argument that the universality of women's subordination is so entrenched and stubborn that it cannot easily be changed, "even by reordering the whole economic structure," has been challenged. Many feminist theorists, especially those who subscribe to Marxist and/or socialist views of society, have pointed to radical economic change as the basis for ending the oppression of women.

Like Ortner, Marilyn Frye seeks to explain women's subordination and second-class status relative to men, but within a philosophical rather than an anthropological framework. The reading by Frye, called "Oppression," is another classic feminist essay that has had a significant impact on subsequent feminist thinking. Frye is less concerned than Ortner with the universality of the oppression of women. However, like Ortner, she seeks to understand the dynamics of women's subordination. Her use of the birdcage metaphor provides a creative illustration of why it is so difficult to recognize women's oppression, especially for women themselves.

In addition to Ortner's and Frye's perspectives about the way in which culture establishes and perpetuates the oppression of women, a number of other scholars have offered alternative views of this issue. Space does not permit an exhaustive analysis of these perspectives here; however, a few of the more prominent theories offered in recent years deserve mention. They are discussed in roughly the chronological order in which they emerged.

Simone de Beauvoir

Ortner draws on the theories of this mid-twentieth century philosopher, considered by many to be the mother of second-wave feminism. De Beauvoir published her much-acclaimed *The Second Sex* in 1953 (originally published in French in 1949), which galvanized feminists throughout Europe and America throughout the 1960s and 1970s. As one commentator has described it, "*The Second Sex* is to Western feminism as the Bible is to Western culture: it's been an undeniably powerful text" (Altman, 1996: 9). *The Second Sex* is best known for two propositions. First, de Beauvoir explained women's subordination in terms of how they are viewed as "the Other," that is, as what men are not. Like Ortner, de Beauvoir assumes that culture is universally considered to be the opposite of nature, that culture is identified with males, and nature with females, and that the former are considered to be superior to the latter. This dichotomy has resulted in *productive* work, historically more the province of men, being valued more highly than *reproductive* work, which only women can do, because it involves a transcendence of nature.

More specifically, de Beauvoir contends that men fear women's power as creators of life while disdaining their biology. Like Sartre, she believed that unless human beings engage in activities that "transcend" their (biological) animal nature, we might as well be wild animals. The goal of life is to *exist*, not merely to *live*. *Existing* entails creative production, not mere reproduction, of the species. Yet men view women as incapable of this transcendence and cultural creation because of their relationship to biological reproduction and the caretaking and domestic labor associated with it. Because men want to deny their own immanence and bodily existence, they regard women as "*Other*." Men cannot regard women as completely or wholly Other, however, because they are dependent on women as social and sexual partners.

Secondly, de Beauvoir is famous for her frequently quoted statement: "One is not born, but rather becomes a woman." This statement reflects her recognition that "woman" is a cultural construction, rather than a product of biology.

She recognizes the disparity between actual women and the cultural ideal of "woman," which is a male myth about the nature of femininity. Even though women may be closer to nature because of their biology, de Beauvoir thought that women could transcend this lower status through productive labor, which would bring them more into the world of culture. Indeed, she believed that how we understand our bodies as male or female is shaped by our cultural context. For de Beauvoir, an essential characteristic of being a woman is considering oneself to be Other to men.

As we will see in chapter 2, de Beauvoir's theories, like Ortner's, have been criticized by subsequent feminists as being "essentialist" in presuming that all women share a commonality by virtue of their gender that transcends other significant differences among them, especially those based on race and class (see, for example, Spelman, 1988). De Beauvoir's views about women's ability to transcend their natural status through productive labor have also been criticized as unreflectively accepting male valuations of nature and culture, rather than recognizing that those valuations are themselves culturally determined, and not inherent.

Betty Friedan

In *The Feminine Mystique* (originally published 1963, second edition 1983), Friedan described "the problem that had no name," referring to the amorphous sense of many 1950s suburban housewives that there was something unfulfilling and unsatisfying about their lives, despite the "experts" and the media telling women that the way to female fulfillment was through being a successful wife and mother. The book appealed to millions of American women, and is regarded by many as a primary impetus for the second wave of the women's movement. Friedan's analysis was based on white, middle-class suburban housewives. The lack of attention to the lives of other women is reflected in her statement that the problems American women were facing "cannot be understood in terms of the age-old material problems of man: poverty, sickness, hunger, cold. The women who suffer this problem have a hunger that food cannot fill" (Friedan, 1983: 26).

Friedan became one of the founders of the National Organization for Women (NOW). Her more recent book, *The Second Stage* (1991), has generated a good deal of controversy for its thesis that feminists have gone too far in rejecting traditional family life.

Nancy Chodorow

Following a second trajectory of thinking about the status of women in culture that Ortner refers to, the work of feminist psychologist Nancy Chodorow has been a significant influence on the development of feminist theories about the seemingly universal subordination of women in culture. In *The Reproduction of Mothering* (1978), Chodorow develops the psychological theory of object relations to explain the social construction of gender. Object-relations theorists believe that the self is constructed out of social relationships. The process of becoming a self is one of differentiating oneself from others, becoming an individual. Since the mother is generally the primary caretaker of infants of both sexes, upon whom the infant is totally dependent, early gender development begins with the infant's relationship with its (usually female) mother. The infant must differentiate itself from the mother in order to develop an individual self.

The development of an individual self is more difficult for boys since they need to differentiate themselves from the female mother in order to adopt male gender role models that can provide the basis for their male selves. This need for differentiation is frequently accompanied by male rejection of the mother, symbolizing females in general, including aspects of themselves that are gendered female, such as tenderness and emotionality. In contrast, since girls share the same sex as their mothers, female gender development requires less of a sharp break from the mother, and permits more continuity.

Mothers contribute to this social construction of gender by tending to treat their sons as other than or different from themselves, while treating their daughters as similar, or even as continuations of, themselves. Consequently, females are generally more concerned with relationships to and connection with others, whereas males are more concerned with independence and autonomy. Thus, it is the fact of women's mothering or primary child rearing that Chodorow claims is responsible for the particular construction of gendered identities we find in society. Her proposed strategy for changing the current configuration of gender relations is to involve fathers more in primary parenting or caretaking, removing the emphasis on the mother as *the* significant parent in the child's (especially early) upbringing.

Chodorow's approach is closely paralleled by the gendered moral psychology developed by Carol Gilligan in her work *In a Different Voice* (1982). Here, Gilligan proposes that men and women have different approaches to morality. Based on research conducted with adolescents, Gilligan found that, while men are more concerned about individual rights, justice, autonomy and independence, women are more concerned about relationships and principles of caring for, and connection with, others. Gilligan's thesis about women's different moral voice has generated a tremendous amount of scholarship, both constructive and critical.

One target of attack on this "cultural feminist" approach has been its unsubstantiated generalizations about the social construction of gender, made without regard to cultural, racial, class, and other significant differences. Chodorow, in particular, has been criticized for assuming that a single model of parenting and family life is universal, rather than recognizing its character as a product of contemporary Western, industrialized societies. None the less, Chodorow's explanation of the reproduction of mothering has been persuasive to many feminists seeking to understand how gendered identities are established and perpetuated from one generation to the next.

Susan Faludi and Naomi Wolf

Two significant, but less academic, analyses of the contemporary second-class status of women in American culture are recent works by Susan Faludi and Naomi Wolf. These authors offer somewhat related, but distinct, analyses of the reasons for women's secondary status in contemporary American culture. Since a selection from Wolf's book *The Beauty Myth* (1991) is included in chapter 6, and Faludi's *Backlash: the Undeclared War against American Women* (1991) is described in chapter 10, only a nutshell description of their arguments is included here.

In *Backlash* (1991), Faludi describes how women's strides toward equality in the 1960s and 1970s have been met with negative reactions from men, especially those in Hollywood, business, and other institutions of power in the contemporary United States – what she calls a "backlash" against women. Although the backlash has not completely succeeded in driving women back to stereotypical female roles as full-time housewives and mothers, it has been successful in increasing occupational segregation. Faludi also contends that the backlash holds women back by mistreating those who dare to challenge traditional roles for women as dependent upon, and subordinate to, men.

Faludi's book received a warm response, especially by women who felt that Faludi had identified the problem they had been experiencing, but had been unable to pinpoint themselves. However, Faludi's book has also received its share of criticism. For example, in *Beyond the Double Bind*, Kathleen Hall Jamieson (1995) disputes Faludi's backlash hypothesis that women's gains have been lost in recent years. Although she admits that women's fight for equality has not made steady improvement, she contends that the progress made is cause for optimism, in contrast to Faludi's pessimism. Jamieson offers the "double bind" as a more appropriate metaphor for women's recent experience than the "backlash," and discusses a number of prominent double binds that have made women's struggle for equality more difficult and costly.

In *The Beauty Myth* (1991), Wolf describes women's place in American culture as defined and limited in large part by standards of beauty. Wolf's basic argument is that standards and expectations for women's beauty control women today just as legal and other social restrictions controlled women in earlier generations. These standards, which are applied to women but not to men, establish expectations for women's physical appearance. Although these expectations are impossible to fulfill, many women nevertheless struggle to satisfy them. The effort to fulfill this unattainable standard of female beauty (the "beauty myth") is fueled by the cultural messages that women's value and worth is determined by how closely they approximate the standards of the beauty myth.

The beauty myth is a myth, according to Wolf, because beauty is culturally relative and variable, changing over time and varying from culture to culture. It is also a myth because it portrays a very narrow set of images of what female beauty is, one that excludes the majority of women, and especially those who are of color, heavy set, disabled, or otherwise "different." According to Wolf, the beauty myth is a product of capitalist industry and advertising that is used as a political weapon against women's advancement. Rather than directing their energies and attention to their social, political, and economic power, Faludi argues, women are instead consumed with trying to live up to the standards of the beauty myth, through spending their time, energy, and money on diet and exercise regimens, health-club memberships, cosmetics, fashionable clothing, and other beauty products.

The preceding discussion demonstrates the variety of theories that have been developed to explain women's subordination and second-class status in American culture. While none of these approaches has avoided criticism, none of them has been completely dismissed either. Perhaps it is fitting to consider each of these theories as providing a *partial* understanding of the problem, one that provides a significant critical perspective, although not a completely adequate or comprehensive one, of women's subordinate status in American culture.

Note

1 For example, parents tend to engage in more physical, and physically rougher, play with their infant sons than with their daughters (Renzetti and Curran, 1989: 67; Denmark et al., 1993: 452).

Is Female to Male as Nature is to Culture?
Sherry B. Ortner

Much of the creativity of anthropology derives from the tension between two sets of demands: that we explain human universals, and that we explain cultural particulars. By this canon, "woman" provides us with one of the

This reading first appeared in *Woman, Culture and Society*, eds M. Z. Rosaldo and L. Lamphere (Stanford, CA: Stanford University Press, 1974), pp. 67–87.

more challenging problems to be dealt with. The secondary status of woman in society is one of the true universals, a pan-cultural fact. Yet within that universal fact, the specific cultural conceptions and symbolizations of woman are extraordinarily diverse and even mutually contradictory. Further, the actual treatment of women and their relative power and contribution vary enormously from culture to culture, and over different periods in the history of particular cultural traditions. Both of these points – the universal fact and the cultural variation – constitute problems to be explained.

My interest in the problem is, of course, more than academic: I wish to see genuine change come about, the emergence of a social and cultural order in which as much of the range of human potential is open to women as is open to men. The universality of female subordination, the fact that it exists within every type of social and economic arrangement and in societies of every degree of complexity, indicates to me that we are up against something very profound, very stubborn, something we cannot rout out simply by rearranging a few tasks and roles in the social system, or even by reordering the whole economic structure. In this paper I try to expose the underlying logic of cultural thinking that assumes the inferiority of women; I try to show the highly persuasive nature of the logic, for if it were not so persuasive, people would not keep subscribing to it. But I also try to show the social and cultural sources of that logic, to indicate wherein lies the potential for change.

It is important to sort out the levels of the problem. The confusion can be staggering. For example, depending on which aspect of Chinese culture we look at, we might extrapolate any of several entirely different guesses concerning the status of women in China. In the ideology of Taoism, *yin*, the female principle, and *yang*, the male principle, are given equal weight; "the opposition, alternation, and interaction of these two forces give rise to all phenomena in the universe" (Siu, 1968: 2). Hence we might guess that maleness and femaleness are equally valued in the general ideology of Chinese culture.[1] Looking at the social structure, however, we see the strongly emphasized patrilineal descent principle, the importance of sons, and the absolute authority of the father in the family. Thus we might conclude that China is the archetypal patriarchal society. Next, looking at the actual roles played, power and influence wielded, and material contributions made by women in Chinese society – all of which are, upon observation, quite substantial – we would have to say that women are allotted a great deal of (unspoken) status in the system. Or, again, we might focus on the fact that a goddess, Kuan Yin, is the central (most worshiped, most depicted) deity in Chinese Buddhism, and we might be tempted to say, as many have tried to say about goddess-worshiping cultures in prehistoric and early historical societies, that China is actually a sort of matriarchy. In short, we must be absolutely clear about *what* we are trying to explain before explaining it. We may differentiate three levels of the problem:

1 The universal fact of culturally attributed second-class status of woman in every society. Two questions are important here. First, what do we mean by this; what is our evidence that this is a universal fact? And, secondly, how are we to explain this fact, once having established it?
2 Specific ideologies, symbolizations, and sociostructural arrangements pertaining to women that vary widely from culture to culture. The problem at this level is to account for any particular cultural complex in terms of factors specific to that group – the standard level of anthropological analysis.
3 Observable on-the-ground details of women's activities, contributions, powers, influence, etc., often at variance with cultural ideology (although always constrained within the assumption that women may never be officially pre-eminent in the total system). This is the level of direct observation, often adopted now by feminist-oriented anthropologists.

This paper is primarily concerned with the first of these levels, the problem of the universal devaluation of women. The analysis thus depends not upon specific cultural data but rather upon an analysis of "culture" taken generically as a special sort of process in the world. A discussion of the second level, the problem of cross-cultural variation in conceptions and relative valuations of women, will entail a great deal of cross-cultural research and must be postponed to another time. As for the third level, it will be obvious from my approach that I would consider it a misguided endeavor to focus only upon women's actual though culturally unrecognized and unvalued powers in any given society, without first understanding the overarching ideology and deeper assumptions of the culture that render such powers trivial.

The universality of female subordination

What do I mean when I say that everywhere, in every known culture, women are considered in some degree inferior to men? First of all, I must stress that I am talking about *cultural* evaluations; I am saying that each culture, in its own way and on its own terms, makes this evaluation. But what would constitute evidence that a particular culture considers women inferior? Three types of data would suffice:

1   Elements of cultural ideology and informants' statements that *explicitly*
    devalue women, according them, their roles, their tasks, their products,
    and their social milieux less prestige than are accorded men and the male
    correlates.
2   Symbolic devices, such as the attribution of defilement, which may be
    interpreted as *implicitly* making a statement of inferior valuation.
3   Social-structural arrangements that exclude women from participation in
    or contact with some realm in which the highest powers of the society
    are felt to reside.[2]

These three types of data may all, of course, be interrelated in any particular system, though they need not necessarily be. Further, any one of them
will usually be sufficient to make the point of female inferiority in a given
culture. Certainly, female exclusion from the most sacred rite or the highest
political council is sufficient evidence. Certainly, explicit cultural ideology
devaluing women (and their tasks, roles, products, etc.) is sufficient evidence. Symbolic indicators, such as defilement, are usually sufficient, although
in a few cases in which, say, men and women are equally polluting to one
another, a further indicator is required – and is, as far as my investigations
have ascertained, always available.

   On any or all of these counts, then, I would flatly assert that we find
women subordinated to men in every known society. The search for a
genuinely egalitarian, let alone matriarchal, culture has proved fruitless. An
example from one society that has traditionally been on the credit side of
this ledger will suffice. Among the matrilineal Crow, as Lowie (1956: 61)
points out, "Women . . . had highly honorific offices in the Sun Dance; they
could become directors of the Tobacco Ceremony and played, if anything,
a more conspicuous part in it than the men; they sometimes played the
hostess in the Cooked Meat Festival; they were not debarred from sweating
or doctoring or from seeking a vision." None the less, "Women [during
menstruation] formerly rode inferior horses and evidently this loomed as a
source of contamination, for they were not allowed to approach either a
wounded man or men starting on a war party. A taboo still lingers against
their coming near sacred objects at these times" (Lowie, 1956: 44). Further, just before enumerating women's rights of participation in the various
rituals noted above, Lowie mentions one particular Sun Dance Doll bundle
that was not supposed to be unwrapped by a woman (1956: 60). Pursuing
this trail we find: "According to all Lodge Grass informants and most
others, the doll owned by Wrinkled-face took precedence not only of other
dolls but of all other Crow medicines whatsoever . . . This particular doll
was not supposed to be handled by a woman" (1956: 229).[3]

In sum, the Crow are probably a fairly typical case. Yes, women have certain powers and rights, in this case some that place them in fairly high positions. Yet ultimately the line is drawn: menstruation is a threat to warfare, one of the most valued institutions of the tribe, one that is central to their self-definition; and the most sacred object of the tribe is taboo to the direct sight and touch of women.

Similar examples could be multiplied *ad infinitum*, but I think the onus is no longer upon us to demonstrate that female subordination is a cultural universal; it is up to those who would argue against the point to bring forth counter-examples. I shall take the universal secondary status of women as a given, and proceed from there.

Nature and culture[4]

How are we to explain the universal devaluation of women? We could, of course, rest the case on biological determinism. There is something genetically inherent in the male of the species, so the biological determinists would argue, that makes them the naturally dominant sex; that "something" is lacking in females, and as a result women are not only naturally subordinate but in general quite satisfied with their position, since it affords them protection and the opportunity to maximize maternal pleasures, which to them are the most satisfying experiences of life. Without going into a detailed refutation of this position, I think it fair to say that it has failed to be established to the satisfaction of almost anyone in academic anthropology. This is to say, not that biological facts are irrelevant, or that men and women are not different, but that these facts and differences only take on significance of superior/inferior within the framework of culturally defined value systems.

If we are unwilling to rest the case on genetic determinism, it seems to me that we have only one way to proceed. We must attempt to interpret female subordination in light of other universals, factors built into the structure of the most generalized situation in which all human beings, in whatever culture, find themselves. For example, every human being has a physical body and a sense of non-physical mind, is part of a society of other individuals and an inheritor of a cultural tradition, and must engage in some relationship, however mediated, with "nature," or the non-human realm, in order to survive. Every human being is born (to a mother) and ultimately dies, all are assumed to have an interest in personal survival, and society/culture has its own interest in (or at least momentum toward) continuity and survival, which transcends the lives and deaths of particular individuals. And so forth. It is in the realm of such universals of the human condition that we must seek an explanation for the universal fact of female devaluation.

I translate the problem, in other words, into the following simple question. What could there be in the generalized structure and conditions of existence, common to every culture, that would lead every culture to place a lower value upon women? Specifically, my thesis is that woman is being identified with – or, if you will, seems to be a symbol of – something that every culture devalues, something that every culture defines as being of a lower order of existence than itself. Now it seems that there is only one thing that would fit that description, and that is "nature" in the most generalized sense. Every culture, or, generically, "culture," is engaged in the process of generating and sustaining systems of meaningful forms (symbols, artifacts, etc.) by means of which humanity transcends the givens of natural existence, bends them to its purposes, controls them in its interest. We may thus broadly equate culture with the notion of human consciousness, or with the products of human consciousness (i.e. systems of thought and technology), by means of which humanity attempts to assert control over nature.

Now the categories of "nature" and "culture" are, of course, conceptual categories – one can find no boundary out in the actual world between the two states or realms of being. And there is no question that some cultures articulate a much stronger opposition between the two categories than others – it has even been argued that primitive peoples (some or all) do not see or intuit any distinction between the human cultural state and the state of nature at all. Yet I would maintain that the universality of ritual betokens an assertion in all human cultures of the specifically human ability to act upon and regulate, rather than passively move with and be moved by, the givens of natural existence. In ritual, the purposive manipulation of given forms toward regulating and sustaining order, every culture asserts that proper relations between human existence and natural forces depend upon culture's employing its special powers to regulate the overall processes of the world and life.

One realm of cultural thought in which these points are often articulated is that of concepts of purity and pollution. Virtually every culture has some such beliefs, which seem in large part (though not, of course, entirely) to be concerned with the relationship between culture and nature (see Ortner, 1973, 1974). A well-known aspect of purity/pollution beliefs cross-culturally is that of the natural "contagion" of pollution; left to its own devices, pollution (for these purposes grossly equated with the unregulated operation of natural energies) spreads and overpowers all that it comes in contact with. Thus, a puzzle – if pollution is so strong, how can anything be purified? Why is the purifying agent not itself polluted? The answer, in keeping with the present line of argument, is that purification is effected in a ritual context; purification ritual, as a purposive activity that pits self-conscious (symbolic) action against natural energies, is more powerful than those energies.

In any case, my point is simply that every culture implicitly recognizes and asserts a distinction between the operation of nature and the operation of culture (human consciousness and its products); and, further, that the distinctiveness of culture rests precisely on the fact that it can, under most circumstances, transcend natural conditions and turn them to its purposes. Thus culture (i.e. every culture) at some level of awareness asserts itself to be not only distinct from but superior to nature, and that sense of distinctiveness and superiority rests precisely on the ability to transform – to "socialize" and "culturalize" – nature.

Returning now to the issue of women, their pan-cultural second-class status could be accounted for, quite simply, by postulating that women are being identified or symbolically associated with nature, as opposed to men, who are identified with culture. Since it is always culture's project to subsume and transcend nature, if women were considered part of nature, then culture would find it "natural" to subordinate, not to say oppress, them. Yet although this argument can be shown to have considerable force, it seems to oversimplify the case. The formulation I would like to defend and elaborate on in the following section, then, is that women are seen "merely" as being *closer* to nature than men. That is, culture (still equated relatively unambiguously with men) recognizes that women are active participants in its special processes, but at the same time sees them as being more rooted in, or having more direct affinity with, nature.

The revision may seem minor or even trivial, but I think it is a more accurate rendering of cultural assumptions. Further, the argument cast in these terms has several analytic advantages over the simpler formulation; I shall discuss these later. It might simply be stressed here that the revised argument would still account for the pan-cultural devaluation of women, for even if women are not equated with nature, they are none the less seen as representing a lower order of being, as being less transcendental of nature than men are. The next task of the paper, then, is to consider why they might be viewed in that way.

Why is woman seen as closer to nature?

It all begins, of course, with the body and the natural procreative functions specific to women alone. We can sort out for discussion three levels at which this absolute physiological fact has significance:

1 Woman's *body and its functions*, more involved more of the time with "species life," seem to place her closer to nature, in contrast to man's physiology, which frees him more completely to take up the projects of culture.

2 Woman's body and its functions place her in *social roles* that, in turn, are considered to be at a lower order of the cultural process than man's.

3 Woman's traditional social roles, imposed because of her body and its functions, in turn give her a different *psychic structure*, which, like her physiological nature and her social roles, is seen as being closer to nature.

I shall discuss each of these points in turn, showing first how in each instance certain factors strongly tend to align woman with nature, then indicating other factors that demonstrate her full alignment with culture, the combined factors thus placing her in a problematic intermediate position. It will become clear in the course of the discussion why men seem by contrast less intermediate, more purely "cultural" than women. And I reiterate that I am dealing only at the level of cultural and human universals. These arguments are intended to apply to generalized humanity; they grow out of the human condition, as humanity has experienced and confronted it up to the present day.

Woman's physiology seen as closer to nature

This part of my argument has been anticipated, with subtlety, cogency, and a great deal of hard data, by de Beauvoir (1953). De Beauvoir reviews the physiological structure, development, and functions of the human female and concludes that "the female, to a greater extent than the male, is the prey of the species" (1953: 60). She points out that many major areas and processes of the woman's body serve no apparent function for the health and stability of the individual; on the contrary, as they perform their specific organic functions, they are often sources of discomfort, pain, and danger. The breasts are irrelevant to personal health; they may be excised at any time of a woman's life.

> Many of the ovarian secretions function for the benefit of the egg, promoting its maturation and adapting the uterus to its requirements; in respect to the organism as a whole, they make for disequilibrium rather than for regulation – the woman is adapted to the needs of the egg rather than to her own requirements. (de Beauvoir, 1953: 24)

Menstruation is often uncomfortable, sometimes painful; it frequently has negative emotional correlates and, in any case, involves bothersome tasks of cleansing and waste disposal; and – a point that de Beauvoir does not mention – in many cultures it interrupts a woman's routine, putting her in a stigmatized state involving various restrictions on her activities and social contacts. In pregnancy, many of the woman's vitamin and mineral resources are channeled into nourishing the fetus, depleting her own strength and energies. And, finally, childbirth itself is painful and dangerous (1953: 24–7). In sum, de Beauvoir concludes that the female "is more enslaved to the species than the male, her animality is more manifest" (1953: 239).

While de Beauvoir's book is ideological, her survey of woman's physiological situation seems fair and accurate. It is simply a fact that proportionately more of a woman's body space, for a greater percentage of her lifetime, and at some – sometimes great – cost to her personal health, strength, and general stability, is taken up with the natural processes surrounding the reproduction of the species.

De Beauvoir goes on to discuss the negative implications of woman's "enslavement to the species" in relation to the projects in which humans engage, projects through which culture is generated and defined. She arrives thus at the crux of her argument:

> Here we have the key to the whole mystery. On the biological level a species is maintained only by creating itself anew; but this creation results only in repeating the same Life in more individuals. But man assures the repetition of Life while transcending Life through Existence [i.e. goal-oriented, meaningful action]; by this transcendence he creates values that deprive pure repetition of all value. In the animal, the freedom and variety of male activities are vain because no project is involved. Except for his services to the species, what he does is immaterial. Whereas in serving the species, the human male also remodels the face of the earth, he creates new instruments, he invents, he shapes the future. (de Beauvoir, 1953: 58–9)

In other words, woman's body seems to doom her to mere reproduction of life; the male, in contrast, lacking natural creative functions, must (or has the opportunity to) assert his creativity externally, "artificially," through the medium of technology and symbols. In so doing, he creates relatively lasting, eternal, transcendent objects, while the woman creates only perishables – human beings.

This formulation opens up a number of important insights. It speaks, for example, to the great puzzle of why male activities involving the destruction of life (hunting and warfare) are often given more prestige than the female's ability to give birth, to create life. Within de Beauvoir's framework, we realize it is not the killing that is the relevant and valued aspect of hunting and warfare; rather, it is the transcendental (social, cultural) nature of these activities, as opposed to the naturalness of the process of birth: "For it is not in giving life but in risking life that man is raised above the animal; that is why superiority has been accorded in humanity not to the sex that brings forth but to that which kills" (de Beauvoir, 1953: 59).

Thus, if male is, as I am suggesting, everywhere (unconsciously) associated with culture and female seems closer to nature, the rationale for these associations is not very difficult to grasp, merely from considering the implications of the physiological contrast between male and female. At the same time, however, woman cannot be consigned fully to the category of nature, for it is perfectly obvious that she is a fully fledged human being endowed with human consciousness just as a man is; she is half of the human race, without whose cooperation the whole enterprise would collapse. She may seem more in the possession of nature than man, but having consciousness, she thinks and speaks; she generates, communicates, and manipulates symbols, categories, and values. She participates in human dialogues not only with other women but also with men. As Lévi-Strauss says, "Woman could never become just a sign and nothing more, since even in a man's world she is still a person, and since insofar as she is defined as a sign she must [still] be recognized as a generator of signs" (1969a: 496).

Indeed, the fact of woman's full human consciousness, her full involvement in and commitment to culture's project of transcendence over nature, may ironically explain another of the great puzzles of "the woman problem" – woman's nearly universal unquestioning acceptance of her own devaluation. For it would seem that, as a conscious human and member of culture, she has followed out the logic of culture's arguments and has reached culture's conclusions along with the men. As de Beauvoir puts it (1953: 59):

> For she, too, is an existent, she feels the urge to surpass, and her project is not mere repetition but transcendence towards a different future – in her heart of hearts she finds confirmation of the masculine pretensions. She joins the men in the festivals that celebrate the successes and victories of the males. Her misfortune is to have been biologically destined for the repetition of Life, when even in her own view Life does not carry within itself its reasons for being, reasons that are more important than life itself.

In other words, woman's consciousness – her membership, as it were, in culture – is evidenced in part by the very fact that she accepts her own devaluation and takes culture's point of view.

I have tried here to show one part of the logic of that view, the part that grows directly from the physiological differences between men and women. Because of woman's greater bodily involvement with the natural functions surrounding reproduction, she is seen as more a part of nature than man is. Yet in part because of her consciousness and participation in human social dialogue, she is recognized as a participant in culture. Thus she appears as something intermediate between culture and nature, lower on the scale of transcendence than man.

Woman's social role seen as closer to nature

Woman's physiological functions, I have just argued, may tend in themselves to motivate[5] a view of woman as closer to nature, a view she herself, as an observer of herself and the world, would tend to agree with. Woman creates naturally from within her own being, whereas man is free to, or forced to, create artificially, that is, through cultural means, and in such a way as to sustain culture. In addition, I now wish to show how woman's physiological functions have tended universally to limit her social movement, and to confine her universally to certain social contexts which *in turn* are seen as closer to nature. That is, not only her bodily processes but the social situation in which her bodily processes locate her may carry this significance. And in so far as she is permanently associated (in the eyes of culture) with these social milieux, they add weight (perhaps the decisive part of the burden) to the view of woman as closer to nature. I refer here, of course, to woman's confinement to the domestic family context, a confinement motivated, no doubt, by her lactation processes.

Woman's body, like that of all female mammals, generates milk during and after pregnancy for the feeding of the newborn baby. The baby cannot survive without breast milk or some similar formula at this stage of life. Since the mother's body goes through its lactation processes in direct relation to a pregnancy with a particular child, the relationship of nursing between mother and child is seen as a natural bond, other feeding arrangements being seen in most cases as unnatural and makeshift. Mothers and their children, according to cultural reasoning, belong together. Further, children beyond infancy are not strong enough to engage in major work, yet are mobile and unruly and not capable of understanding various dangers; they thus require supervision and constant care. Mother is the obvious person for this task, as an extension of her natural nursing bond with the children, or because she has a new infant and is already involved with child-oriented activities. Her own activities are thus circumscribed by the limitations and low levels of her children's strengths and skills:[6] she is confined to the domestic family group; "woman's place is in the home."

Woman's association with the domestic circle would contribute to the view of her as closer to nature in several ways. In the first place, the sheer fact of constant association with children plays a role in the issue; one can easily see how infants and children might themselves be considered part of nature. Infants are barely human and utterly unsocialized; like animals they are unable to walk upright, they excrete without control, they do not speak. Even slightly older children are clearly not yet fully under the sway of culture. They do not yet understand social duties, responsibilities, and morals; their vocabulary and their range of learned skills are small. One finds implicit recognition of an association between children and nature in many cultural practices. For example, most cultures have initiation rites for adolescents (primarily for boys; I shall return to this point below), the point of which is to move the child ritually from a less than fully human state into full participation in society and culture; many cultures do not hold funeral rites for children who die at early ages, explicitly because they are not yet fully social beings. Thus children are likely to be categorized with nature, and woman's close association with children may compound her potential for being seen as closer to nature herself. It is ironic that the rationale for boys' initiation rites in many cultures is that the boys must be purged of the defilement accrued from being around mother and other women so much of the time, when in fact much of the woman's defilement may derive from her being around children so much of the time.

The second major problematic implication of women's close association with the domestic context derives from certain structural conflicts between the family and society at large in any social system. The implications of the "domestic/public opposition" in relation to the position of women have been cogently developed by Rosaldo (1974), and I simply wish to show its relevance to the present argument. The notion that the domestic unit – the biological family charged with reproducing and socializing new members of the society – is opposed to the public entity – the superimposed network of alliances and relationships that *is* the society – is also the basis of Lévi-Strauss's argument in the *Elementary Structures of Kinship* (1969a). Lévi-Strauss argues not only that this opposition is present in every social system, but further that it has the significance of the opposition between nature and culture. The universal incest prohibition[7] and its ally, the rule of exogamy (marriage outside the group), ensure that "the risk of seeing a biological family become established as a closed system is definitely eliminated; the biological group can no longer stand apart, and the bond of alliance with another family ensures the dominance of the social over the biological, and of the cultural over the natural" (Lévi-Strauss, 1969a: 479). And although not every culture articulates a radical opposition between the domestic and the public as such, it is hardly contestable that the domestic is always subsumed by the public; domestic units are allied with one another through the enactment of rules that are logically at a higher level than the units themselves; this creates an emergent unit – society – that is logically at a higher level than the domestic units of which it is composed.

Now, since women are associated with, and indeed are more or less confined to, the domestic context, they are identified with this lower order of social/cultural organization. What are the implications of this for the way they are viewed? First, if the specifically biological (reproductive) function of the family is stressed, as in Lévi-Strauss's formulation, then the family (and hence woman) is identified with nature pure and simple, as opposed to culture. But this is obviously too simple; the point seems more adequately formulated as follows: the family (and hence woman) represents lower-level, socially fragmenting, particularistic sorts of concerns, as opposed to interfamilial relations representing higher-level, integrative, universalistic sorts of concerns. Since men lack a "natural" basis (nursing, generalized to child care) for a familial orientation, their sphere of activity is defined at the level of interfamilial relations. And hence, so the cultural reasoning seems to go, men are the "natural" proprietors of religion, ritual, politics, and other realms of cultural thought and action in which universalistic statements of spiritual and social synthesis are made. Thus men are identified not only with culture, in the sense of all human creativity, as opposed to nature; they are identified in particular with culture in the old-fashioned sense of the finer and higher aspects of human thought – art, religion, law, etc.

Here again, the logic of cultural reasoning aligning woman with a lower order of culture than man is clear and, on the surface, quite compelling. At the same time, woman cannot be fully consigned to nature, for there are aspects of her situation, even within the domestic context, that undeniably demonstrate her participation in the cultural process. It goes without saying, of course, that except for nursing newborn infants (and artificial nursing devices can cut even this biological tie), there is no reason why it has to be mother – as opposed to father, or anyone else – who remains identified with child care. But even assuming that other practical and emotional reasons conspire to keep woman in this sphere, it is possible to show that her activities in the domestic context could as logically put her squarely in the category of culture.

In the first place, one must point out that woman not only feeds and cleans up after children in a simple caretaker operation; she, in fact, is the primary agent of their early socialization. It is she who transforms newborn infants from mere organisms into cultured humans, teaching them manners and the proper ways to behave in order to become fully fledged members of the culture. On the basis of her socializing functions alone, she could not be more a representative of culture. Yet, in virtually every society, there is a point at which the socialization of boys is transferred to the hands of men. The boys are considered, in one set of terms or another, not yet "really" socialized; their entrée into the realm of fully human (social, cultural) status can be accomplished only by men. We still see this in our own schools, where there is a gradual inversion in the proportion of female to male teachers up through the grades: most kindergarten teachers are female; most university professors are male.[8]

Or again, take cooking. In the overwhelming majority of societies cooking is the woman's work. No doubt this stems from practical considerations – since the woman has to stay home with the baby, it is convenient for her to perform the chores centered in the home. But if it is true, as Lévi-Strauss has argued (1969b), that transforming the raw into the cooked may represent, in many systems of thought, the transition from nature to culture, then here we have woman aligned with this important culturalizing process, which could easily place her in the category of culture, triumphing over nature. Yet it is also interesting to note that when a culture (e.g. France or China) develops a tradition of *haute cuisine* – "real" cooking, as opposed to trivial ordinary domestic cooking – the high chefs are almost always men. Thus, the pattern replicates that in the area of socialization – women perform lower-level conversions from nature to culture, but when the culture distinguishes a higher level of the same functions, the higher level is restricted to men.

In short, we see once again some sources of woman's appearing more intermediate than man with respect to the nature/culture dichotomy. Her "natural" association with the domestic context (motivated by her natural lactation functions) tends to compound her potential for being viewed as closer to nature, because of the animal-like nature of children, and because of the infrasocial connotation of the domestic group as against the rest of society. Yet at the same time her socializing and cooking functions within the domestic context show her to be a powerful agent of the cultural process, constantly transforming raw natural resources into cultural products. Belonging to culture, yet appearing to have stronger and more direct connections with nature, she is once again seen as situated between the two realms.

Woman's psyche seen as closer to nature

The suggestion that woman has not only a different body and a different social locus from man but also a different psychic structure is most controversial. I will argue that she probably *does* have a different psychic structure, but I will draw heavily on Chodorow (1974) to establish first that her psychic structure need not be assumed to be innate; it can be accounted for, as Chodorow convincingly shows, by the facts of the probably universal female socialization experience. None the less, if we grant the empirical near universality of a "feminine psyche" with certain specific characteristics, these characteristics would add weight to the cultural view of woman as closer to nature.

It is important to specify what we see as the dominant and universal aspects of the feminine psyche. If we postulate emotionality or irrationality, we are confronted with those traditions in various parts of the world in which women functionally are, and are seen as, more practical, pragmatic, and this-worldly than men. One relevant dimension that does seem pan-culturally applicable is that of relative concreteness versus relative abstractness: the feminine personality tends to be involved with concrete feelings, things, and people, rather than with abstract entities; it tends toward personalism and particularism. A second, closely related, dimension seems to be that of relative subjectivity versus relative objectivity: Chodorow cites Carlson's study (1971), which concludes that "males represent experiences of self, others, space, and time in individualistic, objective, and distant ways, while females represent experiences in relatively interpersonal, subjective, immediate ways" (Chodorow, 1974: 56, quoting Carlson, 1971: 270). Although this and other studies were done in Western societies, Chodorow sees their findings on the differences between male and female personality – roughly, that men are more objective and inclined to relate in terms of relatively abstract categories, women more subjective and inclined to relate in terms of relatively concrete phenomena – as "general and nearly universal differences" (1974: 43).

But the thrust of Chodorow's elegantly argued article is that these differences are not innate or genetically programmed; they arise from nearly universal features of family structure, namely that "women, universally, are largely responsible for early child care and for (at least) later female socialization" (1974: 43) and that "the structural situation of child rearing, reinforced by female and male role training, produces these differences, which are replicated and reproduced in the sexual sociology of adult life" (1974: 44). Chodorow argues that, because mother is the early socializer of both boys and girls, both develop "personal identification" with her, i.e. diffuse identification with her general personality, behavior traits, values, and attitudes (1974: 51). A son, however, must ultimately shift to a masculine role identity, which involves building an identification with the father. Since father is almost always more remote than mother (he is rarely involved in child care, and perhaps works away from home much of the day), building an identification with father involves a "positional identification," i.e. identification with father's male role as a collection of abstract elements, rather than a personal identification with father as a real individual (1974: 49). Further, as the boy enters the larger social world, he finds it in fact organized around more abstract and universalistic criteria (see Chodorow, 1974: 58; Rosaldo, 1974: 28–29), as I have indicated in the previous section; thus his earlier socialization prepares him for, and is reinforced by, the type of adult social experience he will have.

For a young girl, in contrast, the personal identification with mother, which was created in early infancy, can persist into the process of learning female role identity. Because mother is immediate and present when the daughter is learning role identity, learning to be a woman involves the continuity and development of a girl's relationship to her mother, and sustains the identification with her as an individual; it does not involve the learning of externally defined role characteristics (Chodorow, 1974: 51). This pattern prepares the girl for, and is fully reinforced by, her social situation in later life; she will become involved in the world of women, which is characterized by few formal role differences (Rosaldo, 1974: 29), and which involves again, in motherhood, "personal identification" with *her* children. And so the cycle begins anew.

Chodorow demonstrates to my satisfaction at least that the feminine personality, characterized by personalism and particularism, can be explained as having been generated by social-structural arrangements rather than by innate biological factors. The point need not be belabored further. But in so far as the "feminine personality" has been a nearly universal fact, it can be argued that its characteristics may have contributed further to the view of women as being somehow less cultural than men. That is, women would tend to enter into relationships with the world that culture might see as being more "like nature" – immanent and embedded in things as given – than "like culture" – transcending and transforming things through the superimposition of abstract categories and transpersonal values. Woman's relationships tend to be, like nature, relatively unmediated, more direct, whereas man not only tends to relate in a more mediated way, but in fact ultimately often relates more consistently and strongly to the mediating categories and forms than to the persons or objects themselves.

It is thus not difficult to see how the feminine personality would lend weight to a view of women as being "closer to nature." Yet, at the same time, the modes of relating characteristic of women undeniably play a powerful and important role in the cultural process. For just as relatively unmediated relating is in some sense at the lower end of the spectrum of human spiritual functions, embedded and particularizing rather than transcending and synthesizing, yet that mode of relating also stands at the upper end of that spectrum. Consider the mother–child relationship. Mothers tend to be committed to their children as individuals, regardless of sex, age, beauty, clan affiliation, or other categories in which the child might participate. Now any relationship with this quality – not just mother and child but any sort of highly personal, relatively unmediated commitment – may be seen as a challenge to culture and society "from below," in so far as it represents the fragmentary potential of individual loyalties *vis-à-vis* the solidarity of the group. But it may also be seen as embodying the synthesizing agent for culture and society "from above," in that it represents generalized human values above and beyond loyalties to particular social categories. Every society must have social categories that transcend personal loyalties, but every society must also generate a sense of ultimate moral unity for all its members above and beyond those social categories. Thus, that psychic mode seemingly typical of women, which tends to disregard categories and to seek "communion" (Chodorow, 1974: 55, following Bakan, 1966) directly and personally with others, although it may appear infracultural from one point of view, is at the same time associated with the highest levels of the cultural process.

The implications of intermediacy

My primary purpose in this paper has been to attempt to explain the universal secondary status of women. Intellectually and personally, I felt strongly challenged by this problem; I felt compelled to deal with it before undertaking an analysis of woman's position in any particular society. Local variables of economy, ecology, history, political and social structure, values, and worldview – these could explain variations within this universal, but they could not explain the universal itself. And if we were not to accept the ideology of biological determinism, then explanation, it seemed to me, could only proceed by reference to other universals of the human cultural situation. Thus the general outlines of the approach – although not, of course, the particular solution offered – were determined by the problem itself, and not by any predilection on my part for global abstract structural analysis.

I argued that the universal devaluation of women could be explained by postulating that women are seen as closer to nature than men, men being seen as more unequivocally occupying the high ground of culture. The culture/nature distinction is itself a product of culture, culture being minimally defined as the transcendence, by means of systems of thought and technology, of the natural givens of existence. This, of course, is an analytic definition, but I argued that at some level every culture incorporates this notion in one form or other, if only through the performance of ritual as an assertion of the human ability to manipulate those givens. In any case, the core of the paper was concerned with showing why women might tend to be assumed, over and over, in the most diverse sorts of worldviews and in cultures of every degree of complexity, to be closer to nature than men. Woman's physiology, more involved more of the time with "species of life"; woman's association with the structurally subordinate domestic context, charged with the crucial function of transforming animal-like infants into cultured beings; "woman's psyche," appropriately molded to mothering functions by her own socialization and tending toward greater personalism and less-mediated modes of relating – all these factors make woman appear to be rooted more directly and deeply in nature. At the same time, however, her "membership" and fully necessary participation in culture are recognized by culture and cannot be denied. Thus she is seen to occupy an intermediate position between culture and nature.

This intermediacy has several implications for analysis, depending upon how it is interpreted. First, of course, it answers my primary question of why woman is everywhere seen as lower than man, for even if she is not seen as nature pure and simple, she is still seen as achieving less transcendence of nature than man. Here intermediate simply means "middle status" on a hierarchy of being from culture to nature.

Secondly, intermediate may have the significance of "mediating," i.e. performing some sort of synthesizing or converting function between nature and culture, here seen (by culture) not as two ends of a continuum but as two radically different sorts of processes in the world. The domestic unit – and hence woman, who in virtually every case appears as its primary representative – is one of culture's crucial agencies for the conversion of nature into culture, especially with reference to the socialization of children. Any culture's continued viability depends upon properly socialized individuals who will see the world in that culture's terms and adhere more or less unquestioningly to its moral precepts. The functions of the domestic unit must be closely controlled in order to ensure this outcome; the stability of the domestic unit as an institution must be placed as far as possible beyond question. (We see some aspects of the protection of the integrity and stability of the domestic group in the powerful taboos against incest, matricide, patricide, and fratricide.)[9] In so far as woman is universally the primary agent of early socialization and is seen as virtually the embodiment of the functions of the domestic group, she will tend to come under the heavier restrictions and circumscriptions surrounding that unit. Her (culturally defined) intermediate position between nature and culture, here having the significance of her *mediation* (i.e. performing conversion functions) between nature and culture, would thus account not only for her lower status but for the greater restrictions placed upon her activities. In virtually every culture her permissible sexual activities are more closely circumscribed than man's, she is offered a much smaller range of role choices, and she is afforded direct access to a far more limited range of its social institutions. Further, she is almost universally socialized to have a narrower and generally more conservative set of attitudes and views than man, and the limited social contexts of her adult life reinforce this situation. This socially engendered conservatism and traditionalism of woman's thinking is another – perhaps the worst, certainly the most insidious – mode of social restriction, and would clearly be related to her traditional function of producing well-socialized members of the group.

Finally, woman's intermediate position may have the implication of greater symbolic ambiguity (see also Rosaldo, 1974). Shifting our image of the culture/nature relationship once again, we may envision culture in this case as a small clearing within the forest of the larger natural system. From this point of view, that which is intermediate between culture and nature is located on the continuous periphery of culture's clearing; and though it may thus appear to stand both above and below (and beside) culture, it is simply outside and around it. We can begin to understand then how a single system of cultural thought can often assign to woman completely polarized and apparently contradictory meanings, since extremes, as we say, meet. That she often represents both life and death is only the simplest example one could mention.

For another perspective on the same point, it will be recalled that the psychic mode associated with women seems to stand at both the bottom and the top of the scale of human modes of relating. The tendency in that mode is to get involved more directly with people as individuals and not as representatives of one social category or another; this mode can be seen as either "ignoring" (and thus subverting) or "transcending" (and thus achieving a higher synthesis of) those social categories, depending upon the cultural view for any given purpose. Thus we can account easily for both the subversive feminine symbols (witches, evil eye, menstrual pollution, castrating mothers) and the feminine symbols of transcendence (mother goddesses, merciful dispensers of salvation, female symbols of justice, and the strong presence of feminine symbolism in the realms of art, religion, ritual, and law). Feminine symbolism, far more often than masculine symbolism, manifests this propensity toward polarized ambiguity: sometimes utterly exalted, sometimes utterly debased, rarely within the normal range of human possibilities.

If woman's (culturally viewed) intermediacy between culture and nature has this implication of generalized ambiguity of meaning characteristic of marginal phenomena, then we are also in a better position to account for those cultural and historical "inversions" in which women are in some way or other symbolically aligned with culture and men with nature. A number of cases come to mind: the Sirionó of Brazil, among whom, according to Ingham (1971: 1098), "nature, the raw, and maleness" are opposed to "culture, the cooked, and femaleness";[10] Nazi Germany, in which women were said to be the guardians of culture and morals; European courtly love, in which man considered himself the beast and woman the pristine exalted object – a pattern of thinking that persists, for example, among modern Spanish peasants (see Pitt-Rivers, 1961; Rosaldo, 1974). And there are no doubt other cases of this sort, including some aspects of our own culture's view of women. Each such instance of an alignment of women with culture rather than nature requires detailed analysis of specific historical and ethnographic data. But in indicating how nature in general, and the feminine mode of interpersonal relations in particular, can appear from certain points of view to stand both under and over (but really simply outside of) the sphere of culture's hegemony, we have at least laid the groundwork for such analyses.

In short, the postulate that woman is viewed as closer to nature than man has several implications for further analysis, and can be interpreted in several different ways. If it is viewed simply as a *middle* position on a scale from culture down to nature, then it is still seen as lower than culture and thus accounts for the pan-cultural assumption that woman is lower than man in the order of things. If it is read as a *mediating* element in the culture–nature relationship, then it may account in part for the cultural tendency not merely to devalue woman but to circumscribe and restrict her functions, since culture must maintain control over its (pragmatic and symbolic) mechanisms for the conversion of nature into culture. And if it is read as an *ambiguous* status between culture and nature, it may help account for the fact that, in specific cultural ideologies and symbolizations, woman can occasionally be aligned with culture, and in any event is often assigned polarized and contradictory meanings within a single symbolic system. Middle status, mediating functions, ambiguous meaning – all are different readings, for different contextual purposes, of woman's being seen as intermediate between nature and culture.

Conclusions

Ultimately, it must be stressed again that the whole scheme is a construct of culture rather than a fact of nature. Woman is not "in reality" any closer to (or further from) nature than man – both have consciousness, both are mortal. But there are certainly reasons why she appears that way, which is what I have tried to show in this paper. The result is a (sadly) efficient feedback system: various aspects of woman's situation (physical, social, psychological) contribute to her being seen as closer to nature, while the view of her as closer to nature is in turn embodied in institutional forms that reproduce her situation. The implications for social change are similarly circular: a different cultural view can only grow out of a different social actuality; a different social actuality can only grow out of a different cultural view.

It is clear, then, that the situation must be attacked from both sides. Efforts directed solely at changing the social institutions – through setting quotas on hiring, for example, or through passing equal-pay-for-equal-work laws – cannot have far-reaching effects if cultural language and imagery continue to purvey a relatively devalued view of women. But, at the same time, efforts directed solely at changing cultural assumptions – through male and female consciousness-raising groups, for example, or through revision of educational materials and mass-media imagery – cannot be successful unless the institutional base of the society is changed to support and reinforce the changed cultural view. Ultimately, both men and women can and must be equally involved in projects of creativity and transcendence. Only then will women be seen as aligned with culture, in culture's ongoing dialectic with nature.

Acknowledgments

The first version of this paper was presented in October 1972 as a lecture in the course "Women: Myth and Reality" at Sarah Lawrence College. I received helpful comments from the students and from my co-teachers in the course: Joan Kelly Gadol, Eva Kollisch, and Gerda Lerner. A short account was delivered at the American Anthropological Association meetings in Toronto, November 1972. Meanwhile, I received excellent critical comments from Karen Blu, Robert Paul, Michelle Rosaldo, David Schneider, and Terence Turner, and the present version of the paper, in which the thrust of the argument has been rather significantly changed, was written in response to those comments. I, of course, retain responsibility for its final form. The paper is dedicated to Simone de Beauvoir, whose book *The Second Sex* (1953), first published in French in 1949, remains in my opinion the best single, comprehensive understanding of "the woman problem."

Notes

1   It is true, of course, that *yin*, the female principle, has a negative valence. None the less, there is an absolute complementarity of *yin* and *yang* in Taoism, a

recognition that the world requires the equal operation and interaction of both principles for its survival.

2 Some anthropologists might consider this type of evidence (social-structural arrangements that exclude women, explicitly or *de facto*, from certain groups, roles, or statuses) to be a subtype of the second type of evidence (symbolic formulations of inferiority). I would not disagree with this view, although most social anthropologists would probably separate the two types.

3 While we are on the subject of injustices of various kinds, we might note that Lowie secretly bought this doll, the most sacred object in the tribal repertoire, from its custodian, the widow of Wrinkled-face. She asked $400 for it, but this price was "far beyond [Lowie's] means," and he finally got it for $80 (1956: 300).

4 With all due respect to Lévi-Strauss (1969a,b, and *passim*).

5 Semantic theory uses the concept of motivation of meaning, which encompasses various ways in which a meaning may be assigned to a symbol because of certain objective properties of that symbol, rather than by arbitrary association. In a sense, this entire paper is an inquiry into the motivation of the meaning of woman as a symbol, asking why woman may be unconsciously assigned the significance of being closer to nature. For a concise statement on the various types of motivation of meaning, see Ullman (1963).

6 A situation that often serves to make her more childlike herself.

7 David M. Schneider (personal communication) is prepared to argue that the incest taboo is not universal, on the basis of material from Oceania. Let us say at this point, then, that it is virtually universal.

8 I remember having my first male teacher in the fifth grade, and I remember being excited about that – it was somehow more grown-up.

9 Nobody seems to care much about sororicide – a point that ought to be investigated.

10 Ingham's discussion is rather ambiguous itself, since women are also associated with animals: "The contrasts man/animal and man/woman are evidently similar . . . hunting is the means of acquiring women as well as animals" (1971: 1095). A careful reading of the data suggests that both women and animals are mediators between nature and culture in this tradition.

References

Bakan, David (1966) *The Duality of Human Existence* (Chicago: Rand McNally).

de Beauvoir, Simone (1953) *The Second Sex* (originally published in French in 1949) (New York: Knopf).

Carlson, Rae (1971) "Sex differences in ego functioning: exploratory studies of agency and communion," *Journal of Consulting and Clinical Psychology*, 37: 267–77.

Chodorow, Nancy (1974), "Family structure and feminine personality," in M. Z. Rosaldo and L. Lamphere (eds), *Woman, Culture and Society*, pp. 43–66. (Stanford, CA: Stanford University Press).

Ingham, John M. (1971) "Are the Sirionó raw or cooked?" *American Anthropologist*, 73: 1092–9.
Lévi-Strauss, Claude (1969a) *The Elementary Structures of Kinship*, trans. J. H. Bell and J. R. von Sturmer; ed. R. Needham (Boston: Beacon Press).
Lévi-Strauss, Claude (1969b) *The Raw and the Cooked*, trans. J. and D. Weightman (New York: Harper and Row).
Lowie, Robert (1956) *The Crow Indians* (originally published in 1935) (New York: Farrer and Rinehart).
Ortner, Sherry B. (1973) "Sherpa purity," *American Anthropologist*, 75: 49–63.
Ortner Sherry B. (1974) "Purification rites and customs," *New Encyclopaedia Britannica: micropaedia*, 15th edn (Chicago, IL: Encyclopaedia Britannica).
Pitt-Rivers, Julian (1961) *People of the Sierra* (Chicago: University of Chicago Press).
Rosaldo, Michelle Z. (1974) "Women, culture and society: a theoretical overview," in M. Z. Rosaldo and L. Lamphere (eds) *Woman, Culture and Society*, pp. 17–42. (Stanford, CA: Stanford University Press).
Siu, R. G. H. (1968) *The Man of Many Qualities* (Cambridge, Mass.: MIT Press).
Ullman, Stephen (1963) "Semantic universals," in Joseph H. Greenberg (ed.), *Universals of Language* (Cambridge, Mass.).

Oppression
Marilyn Frye

It is a fundamental claim of feminism that women are oppressed. The word "oppression" is a strong word. It repels and attracts. It is dangerous and dangerously fashionable and endangered. It is much misused, and sometimes not innocently.

The statement that women are oppressed is frequently met with the claim that men are oppressed too. We hear that oppressing is oppressive to those who oppress as well as to those they oppress. Some men cite as evidence of their oppression their much-advertised inability to cry. It is tough, we are told, to be masculine. When the stresses and frustrations of being a man are cited as evidence that oppressors are oppressed by their oppressing, the word "oppression" is being stretched to meaninglessness: it is treated as though its scope includes any and all human experience of limitation or suffering, no matter the cause, degree, or consequence. Once such usage has been put over on us, then if ever we deny that any person or group is

This reading first appeared in *The Politics of Reality* (Freedom, Ga.: The Crossing Press), pp. 7–9.

oppressed, we seem to imply that we think they never suffer and have no feelings. We are accused of insensitivity; even of bigotry. For women, such accusation is particularly intimidating, since sensitivity is one of the few virtues that has been assigned to us. If we are found insensitive, we may fear we have no redeeming traits at all and perhaps are not real women. Thus are we silenced before we begin: the name of our situation drained of meaning and our guilt mechanisms tripped.

But this is nonsense. Human beings can be miserable without being oppressed, and it is perfectly consistent to deny that a person or group is oppressed without denying that they have feelings or that they suffer . . .

The root of the word "oppression" is the element "press." *The press of the crowd; pressed into military service; to press a pair of pants; printing press; press the button.* Presses are used to mold things or flatten them or reduce them in bulk, sometimes to reduce them by squeezing out the gasses or liquids in them. Something pressed is something caught between or among forces and barriers which are so related to each other that jointly they restrain, restrict, or prevent the thing's motion or mobility. Mold. Immobilize. Reduce.

The mundane experience of the oppressed provides another clue. One of the most characteristic and ubiquitous features of the world as experienced by oppressed people is the double bind – situations in which options are reduced to a very few and all of them expose one to penalty, censure, or deprivation. For example, it is often a requirement upon oppressed people that we smile and be cheerful. If we comply, we signal our docility and our acquiescence in our situation. We need not, then, be taken note of. We acquiesce in being made invisible, in our occupying no space. We participate in our own erasure. On the other hand, anything but the sunniest countenance exposes us to being perceived as mean, bitter, angry, or dangerous. This means, at the least, that we may be found "difficult" or unpleasant to work with, which is enough to cost one one's livelihood; at worst, being seen as mean, bitter, angry, or dangerous has been known to result in rape, arrest, beating, and murder. One can only choose to risk one's preferred form and rate of annihilation.

Another example: it is common in the United States that women, especially younger women, are in a bind where neither sexual activity nor sexual inactivity is all right. If she is heterosexually active, a woman is open to censure and punishment for being loose, unprincipled, or a whore. The "punishment" comes in the form of criticism, snide and embarrassing remarks, being treated as an easy lay by men, scorn from her more restrained female friends. She may have to lie and hide her behavior from her parents. She must juggle the risks of unwanted pregnancy and dangerous contraceptives.

On the other hand, if she refrains from heterosexual activity, she is fairly constantly harassed by men who try to persuade her into it and pressure her to "relax" and "let her hair down"; she is threatened with labels like "frigid," "uptight," "man-hater," "bitch," and "cocktease." The same parents who would be disapproving of her sexual activity may be worried by her inactivity because it suggests she is not or will not be popular, or is not sexually normal. She may be charged with lesbianism. If a woman is raped, then if she has been heterosexually active she is subject to the presumption that she liked it (since her activity is presumed to show that she likes sex), and if she has not been heterosexually active, she is subject to the presumption that she liked it (since she is supposedly "repressed and frustrated"). Both heterosexual activity and heterosexual non-activity are likely to be taken as proof that you wanted to be raped, and hence, of course, weren't *really* raped at all. You can't win. You are caught in a bind, caught between systematically related pressures.

Women are caught like this, too, by networks of forces and barriers that expose one to penalty, loss, or contempt whether one works outside the home or not, is on welfare or not, bears children or not, raises children or not, marries or not, stays married or not, is heterosexual, lesbian, both, or neither. Economic necessity; confinement to racial and/or sexual job ghettos; sexual harassment; sex discrimination; pressures of competing expectations and judgments about *women, wives,* and *mothers* (in the society at large, in racial and ethnic subcultures and in one's own mind); dependence (full or partial) on husbands, parents, or the state; commitment to political ideas; loyalties to racial or ethnic or other "minority" groups; the demands of self-respect and responsibilities to others. Each of these factors exists in complex tension with every other, penalizing or prohibiting all of the apparently available options. And nipping at one's heels, always, is the endless pack of little things. If one dresses one way, one is subject to the assumption that one is advertising one's sexual availability; if one dresses another way, one appears to "not care about oneself" or to be "unfeminine." If one uses "strong language," one invites categorization as a whore or slut; if one does not, one invites categorization as a "lady" – one too delicately constituted to cope with robust speech or the realities to which it presumably refers.

The experience of oppressed people is that the living of one's life is confined and shaped by forces and barriers which are not accidental or occasional and hence avoidable, but are systematically related to each other in such a way as to catch one between and among them and restrict or penalize motion in any direction. It is the experience of being caged in: all avenues, in every direction, are blocked or booby trapped.

Cages. Consider a birdcage. If you look very closely at just one wire in the cage, you cannot see the other wires. If your conception of what is before you is determined by this myopic focus, you could look at that one wire, up and down the length of it, and be unable to see why a bird would not just fly around the wire any time it wanted to go somewhere. Furthermore, even if, one day at a time, you myopically inspected each wire, you still could not see why a bird would have trouble going past the wires to get anywhere. There is no physical property of any one wire, *nothing* that the closest scrutiny could discover, that will reveal how a bird could be inhibited or harmed by it except in the most accidental way. It is only when you step back, stop looking at the wires one by one, microscopically, and take a macroscopic view of the whole cage, that you can see why the bird does not go anywhere; and then you will see it in a moment. It will require no great subtlety of mental powers. It is perfectly *obvious* that the bird is surrounded by a network of systematically related barriers, no one of which would be the least hindrance to its flight, but which, by their relations to each other, are as confining as the solid walls of a dungeon.

It is now possible to grasp one of the reasons why oppression can be hard to see and recognize: one can study the elements of an oppressive structure with great care and some good will without seeing the structure as a whole, and hence without seeing or being able to understand that one is looking at a cage and that there are people there who are caged, whose motion and mobility are restricted, whose lives are shaped and reduced.

The arresting of vision at a microscopic level yields such common confusion as that about the male door-opening ritual. This ritual, which is remarkably widespread across classes and races, puzzles many people, some of whom do and some of whom do not find it offensive. Look at the scene of the two people approaching a door. The male steps slightly ahead and opens the door. The male holds the door open while the female glides through. Then the male goes through. The door closes after them. "Now how," one innocently asks, "can those crazy womens-libbers say that is oppressive? The guy *removed* a barrier to the lady's smooth and unruffled progress." But each repetition of this ritual has a place in a pattern, in fact in several patterns. One has to shift the level of one's perception in order to see the whole picture.

The door-opening pretends to be a helpful service, but the helpfulness is false. This can be seen by noting that it will be done whether or not it makes any practical sense. Infirm men and men burdened with packages will open doors for able-bodied women who are free of physical burdens. Men will impose themselves awkwardly and jostle everyone in order to get to the door first. The act is not determined by convenience or grace. Furthermore, these very numerous acts of unneeded or even noisome "help" occur in counterpoint to a pattern of men not being helpful in many practical ways in which women might welcome help. What *women* experience is a world in which gallant princes charming commonly make a fuss about being helpful and providing small services when help and services are of little or no use, but in which there are rarely ingenious and adroit princes at hand when substantial assistance is really wanted either in mundane affairs or in situations of threat, assault, or terror. There is no help with the (his) laundry; no help typing a report at 4 a.m.; no help in mediating disputes among relatives or children. There is nothing but advice that women should stay indoors after dark, be chaperoned by a man, or when it comes down to it, "lie back and enjoy it."

The gallant gestures have no practical meaning. Their meaning is symbolic. The door-opening and similar services provided are services which really are needed by people who are for one reason or another incapacitated – unwell, burdened with parcels, etc. So the message is that women are incapable. The detachment of the acts from the concrete realities of what women need and do not need is a vehicle for the message that women's actual needs and interests are unimportant or irrelevant. Finally, these gestures imitate the behavior of servants toward masters and thus mock women, who are in most respects the servants and caretakers of men. The message of the false helpfulness of male gallantry is female dependence, the invisibility or insignificance of women, and contempt for women.

One cannot see the meanings of these rituals if one's focus is riveted upon the individual event in all its particularity, including the particularity of the individual man's present conscious intentions and motives and the individual woman's conscious perception of the event in the moment. It seems sometimes that people take a deliberately myopic view and fill their eyes with things seen microscopically in order not to see macroscopically. At any rate, whether it is deliberate or not, people can and do fail to see the oppression of women because they fail to see macroscopically and hence fail to see the various elements of the situation as systematically related in larger schemes.

As the cageness of the birdcage is a macroscopic phenomenon, the oppressiveness of the situations in which women live our various and different lives is a macroscopic phenomenon. Neither can be *seen* from a microscopic perspective. But when you look macroscopically you can see it – a network of forces and barriers which are systematically related and which conspire to the immobilization, reduction, and molding of women and the lives we live.

Suggested activities

Questions for discussion

1   On the *Ortner* reading:
    (a)   Should Ortner's assumptions about women themselves be considered *essentialist*? Is women's subordination as universal as Ortner alleges? Does the very universality of women's secondary status imply that the commonalities outweigh other differences among women? Why or why not?
    (b)   Does the public/private distinction remain a valid notion with respect to contemporary society? Or have women become so integrated into "public" life that it is no longer appropriate to consider public and private as gender-segregated domains? How would you characterize the "family values" rhetoric of conservative political leaders in relation to the public/private distinction?
    (c)   Should the role of mothers as the primary "acculturators" of children make women blameworthy as perpetuating a sexist culture, as some critics of Chodorow suggest her thesis implies? If not, why not?
    (d)   How well has Ortner's thesis withstood the test of time? Is the linkage between women and nature evident in our contemporary culture? Certainly, symbols of the earth as mother, "Mother Nature," and so on, are still prominent. Many involved in feminist spirituality and *eco-feminism* movements, in particular, have drawn on the connection between women and nature in the cause of ending the exploitation of both. Are there other respects in which the connection between women and nature is either reinforced or undermined by aspects of contemporary American culture?
    (e)   Is Ortner correct that even reordering the whole economic system is unlikely to bring about an end to gender oppression? What kind of cultural and social changes, if any, *would* be adequate to end the subordination of women?
2   On the *Frye* reading:
    (a)   Are women still oppressed in the ways that Frye claims? If so, to the same extent that she depicts? If not, what has changed? To what do you attribute that change?
    (b)   What do you think of Frye's analysis of the "door-opening ritual?" Do you agree with her assessment that it represents a subtle but effective means of perpetuating women's second-class status, or do you think that it is an innocuous gesture that need not be associated with male domination of females?

(c)   Is the birdcage metaphor still an effective illustration of the status of American women? Have we become more aware of the cage as a result of the preceding decades of feminism?

(d)   If you wanted to use the birdcage metaphor to describe the current status of women in culture, what are some of the "invisible wires" that you would include in the construction of the cage? Are they more or less visible than those that Frye points to?

3   What do you think of de Beauvoir's proposal that women can overcome their oppression by transcending their biology, and engaging in the cultural work of production rather than the merely "natural" work of reproduction?

4   Is Chodorow's thesis that women's mothering perpetuates (unequal) gender divisions persuasive? Can it explain women's subordinated social status in cultures where biological mothers are not necessarily the exclusive, or even the primary, child rearers?

5   Is Faludi's "backlash" thesis convincing? Why or why not? How about Wolf's "beauty myth" thesis? Are these two theories about the causes and conditions of women's oppression compatible or mutually exclusive?

6   Which of the explanations for women's (widespread if not universal) subordination described in this chapter do you find most persuasive? Is there another explanation you find more compelling? If so, describe it.

Films and videos

Centuries of Women. Three 3-hour segments. Available from Turner Home Entertainment (tel. 800-430-8585). On women in relation to work, family, sexuality, social justice, and image and culture.

It's Up to Us by Bea Milwe (1986). VHS/58 mins. Distributed by Women Make Movies. Documentary of the 1985 United Nations End of the Decade for Women Conference in Nairobi, Kenya. The issues raised are suggestive for considering the issue of whether women's status in culture should be considered a universal.

Juggling Gender by Tami Gold (1993). VHS/27 mins. Distributed by Women Make Movies. Portrait of Jennifer Miller, a "bearded lady" who works as a performance artist in a circus sideshow. Her lifestyle suggests the impossibility of defining anyone as truly feminine or masculine.

Pumping Iron Two: the Women by Bar Belle Productions (1985). 12 in. videodisc/107 mins. Available from Vestron Video. About female body-builders; useful for exploring the question of what is "feminine" and who decides.

Sex and Gender, Maturing and Aging, produced by Annenberg/CPB (1989). VHS/57 mins. Available from CPB. First program asks whether women and men are psychologically similar or different; examines how sex roles reflect social values.

Other activities

1 Find a current newspaper or magazine article that addresses the status of women in American culture or in another society. Make a photocopy to hand in. Prepare to discuss the issue(s) raised in the article with the rest of the class.

2 For the first day of class, complete a "gender inventory" as follows. Take about 10 minutes to answer the following questions. Be as candid, concise, and descriptive as possible.
   (a) To me, being female means . . .
   (b) To me, being male means . . .
   (c) What I find difficult about being male/female is . . .
   (d) As a male/female, I am proud of . . .
   (e) As a male/female, I feel limited when . . .
   (f) As a female/male, I feel powerful when . . .

Then join with small groups of two or three classmates. Introduce yourselves, and generate lists of some of the positive and negative aspects of being a woman in American culture. Which of the lists is longer? Why? Discuss some of the advantages and disadvantages of being gendered as women and as men in this culture. What other factors – race, class, ethnicity, religion, disability, age, sexual orientation – complicate your analysis?

Bibliography

Altman, Meryl (1996) "Taking thinking seriously," *The Women's Review of Books*, 13(4): 9. Review of recent books on Simone de Beauvoir.

de Beauvoir, Simone (1953) *The Second Sex* (New York: Knopf, trans. and ed. H. M. Parshkey). Classic philosophical discourse about women and their position in society.

Bem, Sandra Lipsitz (1993) *The Lenses of Gender* (New Haven, CT: Yale University Press). On transforming the debate on sexual inequality.

Chodorow, Nancy (1978) *The Reproduction of Mothering: Psychoanalytic Feminism and the Sociology of Gender* (Berkeley, CA: University of California Press).

Cole, Johnnetta B. (ed.) (1986) *All American Women: Lines that Divide, Ties that Bind* (New York: Macmillan).

Conway, Jill, Bourque, Susan and Scott, Joan (eds) (1987) *Learning about Women: Gender, Politics, and Power* (Ann Arbor, MI: University of Michigan Press).

Denmark, Florence, Nielson, Karen and Scholl, Kristina (1993) "United States of America," in Leonore Loeb Adler (ed.), *International Handbook on Gender Roles* (Westport, CT: Greenwood Press).

Dirks, Nicholas, Eley, Geoff, and Ortner, Sherry (eds) (1994) *Culture/Power/History: a Reader in Contemporary Social History* (Princeton, NJ: Princeton University Press).

Faludi, Susan (1991) *Backlash: the Undeclared War against American Women* (New York: Crown Publishers). Examination of the counter-feminist movement in the wake of modern feminism.

Franklin, Sarah, Lury, Celia and Stacey, Jackie (1991) *Off-Center: Feminism and Cultural Studies* (New York: HarperCollins).
Friedan, Betty (1983) *The Feminine Mystique* (New York: W. W. Norton).
Friedan, Betty (1991) *The Second Stage* (New York: Summit Books).
Gilligan, Carol (1982) *In a Different Voice: Psychological Theory and Women's Development* (Cambridge, MA: Harvard University Press).
Harding, Sandra (1986) *The Science Question in Feminism* (Ithaca, NY: Cornell University Press).
Harding, Sandra and Merrill Hintikka (eds) (1983) *Discovering Reality: Feminist Perspectives on Epistemology, Methodology, and the Philosophy of Science* (Dordrecht: Reidel).
Hubbard, Ruth (1988) "Science, facts, and feminism," *Hypatia: a Journal of Feminist Philosophy*, 3: 5–17.
Hutner, Frances (ed.) (1994) *Our Visions and Values: Women Shaping the 21st Century* (Westport, CT: Praeger). A disparate collection of essays on a number of different themes, ranging from women in leadership and religion to work and therapy, adopting the perspectives of feminist scholars looking back on the present from the year 2050. The essays are related by the commonality of women's lives being shaped by patriarchy.
Jamieson, Kathleen Hall (1995) *Beyond the Double Bind: Women's Leadership* (New York: Oxford University Press). Argues that Faludi's backlash thesis is incorrect, and that the real problem is double binds that constrain women on either side. Optimistic that women *can* overcome double binds and continue to make progress.
Kaminer, Wendy (1990) *A Fearful Freedom: Women's Flight from Equality* (Reading, MA: Addison-Wesley). On the subject of backlash.
Kersey, Ethel (1989) *Women Philosophers: a Bio-Critical Source Book* (New York: Greenwood Press). Sections on de Beauvoir and other women philosophers.
Lorber, Judith (1994) *Paradoxes of Gender* (New Haven, CT: Yale University Press). An analysis of gender as a wholly socially constructed institution that structures our relationships in all spheres of life.
Lorber, Judith and Farell, Susan (eds) (1991) *The Social Construction of Gender* (Newbury Park, CA: Sage).
MacCormick, Carol and Strathern, Marilyn (1980) *Nature, Culture, and Gender* (Cambridge: University of Cambridge Press). Includes a number of essays that are both indebted to and challenge Ortner's work on women and culture.
Mann, Judy (1994) *The Difference: Growing up Female in America* (New York: Warner Books). Washington Post writer explores why girls are brought up differently from boys, based on over 200 interviews.
Mehuron, Kate and Percesepe, Gary (eds) (1995) *Free Spirits: Feminist Philosophers on Culture* (Englewood Cliffs, NJ: Prentice-Hall). An anthology of essays organized under the headings "Cultural images," "Community," "Megalopolis," "Technologies of the self," "Ecofeminism," "Sexualities," "Masculinities," and "The politics of hope."
Moi, Toril (1994) *Simone de Beauvoir: the Making of an Intellectual Woman* (Cambridge, MA: Blackwell). A "personal genealogy" of de Beauvoir that includes attention to her published and unpublished autobiographical writings and her fiction, as well as information about her life.
Ortner, Sherry B. (1981) *Sexual Meanings: the Cultural Construction of Gender and Sexuality* (Cambridge: Cambridge University Press).
Ortner, Sherry B. (1996) *Making Gender: the Politics and Erotics of Culture* (Boston: Beacon Press). Collected essays by the pioneering feminist anthropologist.

Renzetti, Clair and Curran, Daniel (1989) *Women, Men, and Society: the Sociology of Gender* (Boston: Allyn and Bacon).

Simons, Margaret (ed.) (1995) *Feminist Interpretations of Simone de Beauvoir* (University Park, PA: Penn State Press). Collection of essays on the feminist philosopher.

Spelman, Elizabeth (1988) *Inessential Woman: Problems of Exclusion in Feminist Thought* (Boston: Beacon Press). Includes a critique of de Beauvoir.

Sydie, R. A. (1987) *Natural Women, Cultured Men: a Feminist Perspective on Sociological Theory* (New York: New York University Press). Focuses on the patriarchal approaches to human nature and to the nature of sex relationships adopted by Durkheim, Weber, Marx, Engels, and Freud.

Taeuber, Cynthia (1996) *Statistical Handbook on Women in America*, 2nd edn (Phoenix, AZ: Oryx Press). Demographics, employment, health, and social characteristics.

Wolf, Naomi (1991) *The Beauty Myth: How Images of Beauty are Used against Women* (New York: W. Morrow).

2
Commonalities and Differences among Women

Introduction

In the Introduction, we saw that there is significant disagreement among feminists about whether women are more similar to or different from each other
than they are to or from men. Research studies indicate that there are more
significant differences *among* women than there are *between* men and women.
That is, sex and gender differences are far *less* significant than differences
based on race, ethnicity, national origin, class, sexual orientation, and so on.
In chapter 1, we saw that American women do share with one another some
experience of being subordinated to men, regardless of their other differences.
However, there are also tremendous differences among women in America
that make it inappropriate to assume that the experience of oppression is the
same for all women. The readings in this chapter address significant areas
of cultural similarities and differences in women's lives. The first reading, by
Johnnetta B. Cole, examines significant areas of commonalities and differences
among American women. The second and third readings, by Audre Lorde and
Sojourner Truth, illustrate some notable ways in which women have spoken
about the fact and experience of women's differences. The fourth and fifth
address some of the assumptions made in American culture about men and
women whose sexual orientation differs from the heterosexual "norm."

Differences among women are especially evident with respect to categories
of race, socioeconomic class, and sexual orientation. Women of color and poor
women experience discrimination and subordination based on these characteristics as well as their gender. However, their experiences cannot be described
simply in terms of being recipients of multiple oppressions in an additive sense
of gender discrimination *plus* racial discrimination *plus* economic discrimination, since these different forms of discrimination cannot be separated from
one another. For example, a poor woman of color experiences discrimination
based on her overall status and characteristics: not, first, because she is a

woman; secondly, because she is a person of color; and, thirdly, because she is poor. Each of these attributes interacts synergistically with the others so that it cannot be separated out. Thus, racism, class prejudice, and homophobia are all factors that need to be considered along with sexism in understanding how a particular woman is oppressed.

In some situations, differences based on the category of race are more significant or important than those based on gender. For example, in 1991, law professor Anita Hill was criticized as a traitor to her race for speaking publicly during Senate confirmation hearings about being sexually harassed by Supreme Court nominee Clarence Thomas, a fellow African-American (see McKay, 1992). In the civil rights and black power movements of the 1960s and 1970s, black women were expected to take supportive, secondary roles, and were refused positions of leadership. At the same time, black women active *in* the struggle for racial equality were discriminated against because of their gender, and reminded of "their place" in positions and roles subordinate to those of men (see Davis, 1981). Even today, black women are expected to put solidarity to their race ahead of resisting sexism and patriarchy.

In addition to discrimination based on race, class, ethnicity, disability, religion, and so on, cultural ideology has contributed to keeping women separate from one another on the grounds of difference. For example, the prescribed social roles for black women and white women have been constructed to be radically opposed: workers versus housewives, strong versus weak, sexual versus asexual. The first wave of the women's movement generally ignored the needs of working-class and black women, illustrated by the lack of consideration of these issues at the Seneca Falls Convention organized by the prominent feminists Elizabeth Cady Stanton and Susan B. Anthony in 1848. No black women were present at the convention. In fact, Stanton is known to have made a number of racist statements. Similarly, the National American Woman's Suffrage Association, a women's group organized to fight for women's suffrage (right to vote) in the early part of the twentieth century, ignored the appeals of black women for a resolution to overturn the Jim Crow laws which replaced slavery in the South with segregation (see Davis, 1981; Hoff-Wilson, 1991).

Early feminist analyses of oppression tended to assume that all women were similar. Elizabeth Spelman's (1991) essay "Simone de Beauvoir and women: just who does she think 'we' is?" describes the roots of these assumptions. In particular, she describes how de Beauvoir's account of women's oppression is accurate only with respect to a small group of women: white, middle class, heterosexual, Western women. As we saw in chapter 1, de Beauvoir observed that, traditionally, few women have resisted their identity as "Other." One important reason for this lack of social solidarity among women as oppressed is that, unlike other oppressed groups, women are divided from one another by racial, ethnic, national, religious, and other boundaries that make collective action difficult. Because they do not share the same social or economic status, it is difficult to communicate. In addition, some women fail to resist male domination, according to de Beauvoir, because they identify with the race and class privileges of the significant males in their lives, and are unwilling to give up these privileges for the benefit of liberation. It is white, middle-class women, according to this analysis, who have the most to lose by challenging gender oppression. De Beauvoir thus understands that the experience of sexism differs according to racial and class status and, reciprocally, that racial and class oppression differ in relation to sexism.

Yet, as Spelman (1991) points out, de Beauvoir "sabotages" her insights about the political consequences of the multiple locations of women by comparing women to other groups, assuming that those groups are comprised only of males. For example, in commenting on slavery in the United States, de Beauvoir says that there was a "great difference" between American blacks and women. The effect of her comparisons is to erase black women (and women in oppressed groups generally). De Beauvoir's references to "women" are plainly only intended to refer to women not subject to racism, classism, and so on, i.e., privileged white women. Yet she does not make explicit her underlying assumption that sexist oppression is easier to see in relation to women not subject to oppression based on race, class, and so on. However, as Spelman (1991) notes, race and class are not irrelevant to the oppression that white middle-class women face, even though they are not themselves directly oppressed on the basis of race and class. In addition, Spelman recognizes that de Beauvoir fails to acknowledge the implications of her own analysis that "women" are constructed differently in different social circumstances, including race and class. As Karen Dugger suggests, false universalization (regarding women's similarities) also sets up white women as the norm against which women of color appear to be deviant (Dugger, 1991: 38).

Feminists are now divided on the extent to which it is appropriate to speak of "women" as an undifferentiated group. The assumption of earlier decades that the similarities among women outweighed the differences was perpetuated by the predominantly white, middle-class women's movement of the 1970s. That situation began to change in the 1980s as black women, such as Toni Cade (editor of the pioneering anthology *The Black Woman*), Audre Lorde, bell hooks, Toni Morrison, Alice Walker, and June Jordan, explained that women of color frequently had radically different experiences from those of white women. Other feminists of color, such as Maxine Hong Kingston and Sonia Sanchez, also challenged the assumption of a "universal" women's experience. Cherrie Moraga and Gloria Anzaldúa's groundbreaking anthology *This Bridge Called my Back: Writings by Radical Women of Color* (1981) illustrates the diversity of women's experiences, especially differences that result from racism, economic discrimination, and homophobia.

The reading by Johnnetta B. Cole, "Commonalities and Differences," systematically explores some of the most significant commonalities and differences among American women. Cole concludes that both aspects are important to describe accurately who American women are. Cole's article is foundational for this volume, as it describes some of the fundamental similarities and differences in American women's experiences in relation to a number of areas that will be explored later in this volume, including work, family life, sexuality, religion, politics, and violence.

In addition to the areas of commonality and difference that Cole points to, consider the following about American women:

- Of 100 women, approximately 84 are white, 13 are black, 3 are of other races and 8 are Hispanic (may be of any race).
- While most families include a mother, 16 percent of white children, 27 percent of Hispanic children, and 51 percent of African-American children live only with their mothers. Of these, the majority of the white and Hispanic mothers are divorced or widowed, while the majority of African-American mothers are never married. In 1988, 56 percent of black women who gave birth were unmarried, compared with 15 percent of white women and 26 percent of Hispanic women. However, while the rate of out-of-wedlock births has been increasing for white women since the 1950s, it has been decreasing for black women since the 1960s.
- While many women have children, the health risks of childbirth are significantly different, with African-American women three times more likely to die in childbirth (approximately 18/1000) than white women. College-educated women have the fewest children and are the most likely to be childless.
- While women on average earn less than men, even at the same level of education, white women have higher average weekly earnings than other women. Unemployment is higher among black women than white women. Women who complete college earn more than double what high school drop-outs earn but considerably less than college-educated men.
- Women who maintain families alone and elderly women who live alone are more likely to be poor than the population as a whole. Half of female-headed households are poor, and they are five times as likely to be poor as families headed by married couples.
- Asian women are the most likely to be college educated. Asian and white women are the most likely to graduate from high school.
- Black women are more likely to be victims of crime (29/1000) than white women (21/1000) or Hispanic women (15/1000) (Taeuber, 1991: 2).

Some of the differences that Cole documents have become even more extreme in the past few years. For example, differences with respect to work are increasing with the downturn in the economy, which has forced more women into low-paying jobs and highlighted the disparity between working-class women and professional, highly educated women in higher-paying careers. Different experiences of family are also growing, as fewer African-American women are marrying and greater numbers of white women are delaying the time before they have children. Not all women *have* children, or even want to. Although most women have responsibility for raising children, how they carry out this responsibility varies widely.

Racist sentiments are increasing the hostility toward women of color, rolling back affirmative action and increasing resentment toward immigrants. Undiscriminating racism often directs this resentment at legal US residents as well as illegal aliens. Asian-American and Latina feminists have noted the difficulties they face in encountering sexism in their own culture as well as sexism and racism in the dominant culture.

Despite this variation, women have been stereotyped in ways that allow us to ignore the reality of significant differences among them. When certain differences among women *are* recognized, such as race, *other* stereotypes may emerge to suggest that all women in that category are alike, such as the stereotype that Asian-American women are docile, submissive, and exotic, or that women on welfare are all black, lazy, and uneducated. These stereotypes have been held by feminists as well. Indeed, even though lesbians have been among the strongest supporters of the women's movement, the second wave of the women's movement has been inattentive to, or even exclusionary of, issues of concern to lesbians.

Many members of mainstream women's movements have also been racist. The problems have begun to be addressed in recent years as lesbians and women of color have spoken out about their exclusion from and/or silencing within mainstream women's movements, and as white, middle-class feminists have made greater efforts to be more sensitive to and inclusive of differences among women, including age, disability, class, and ethnicity, as well as race and sexual orientation. Yet areas of tension remain. Many women, especially lesbians and women of color, have formed their own women's groups that speak more centrally to their concerns and interests.

Cole points to other problems with the assumption of commonality. Her observation that the experience of oppression need not preclude a certain degree of privilege which may be used to oppress others deserves emphasis. Just because European-American women have experienced sexist oppression does not mean that they will not act in racist or homophobic ways toward women of color or lesbians, or that women of color will not act in homophobic ways, or that lesbians will not act in racist ways. Even where there are commonalities in women's experiences, there may be differences in the ways in which commonality is acted out. For example, even though women generally provide emotional caretaking to men, their class differences mean that the consequences of providing such care will have significantly different effects.

The second and third readings of this chapter shift the focus slightly to examine how *women* have expressed their similarities and differences from other women. The reading by Sojourner Truth provides a historical perspective on commonalities and differences among women. Truth was born a slave, named Isabella, in 1795. She became a well-known preacher and anti-slavery advocate after gaining her freedom in 1827. The excerpt from Truth's speech included here is reproduced as it was recorded in Elizabeth Cady Stanton, Susan B. Anthony and Matilda Joslyn Gage's *History of Woman Suffrage*, published in 1889. The speech was made at a women's rights convention in Akron, Ohio in 1851. Gage describes how several persons were opposed to Truth speaking because of her color.

In the past few years, there has been a vast outpouring of published work by women of color and third-world women speaking of their own experiences of commonality and difference. Many of these works are cited in the Bibliography at the end of this chapter. Audre Lorde's 1980 classic essay, "Age, race, class, and sex: women redefining difference," provides a personal perspective on the issue of how differences among women have been ignored under an assumption of commonality. Lorde, a well-known feminist writer and award-winning poet, died of cancer at the age of 60 in 1991. She described herself as a "black lesbian feminist socialist mother of two, including one boy, and a member of an inter-racial couple" (p. 69).

Lorde very graphically describes some of the ways in which black women's lives are far more dangerous, besieged, filled with race hatred and struggle than white women's lives. She also notes some of the differences that divide black women, especially with respect to the issue of lesbianism. Lorde articulates a recurrent theme in the writing of some radical feminists: that the dominant society has defined equality in terms of sameness, making it acceptable to treat those who are different (from the dominant group) as unequal, and making it impossible to speak of those who are different in terms of equality.

Sexuality and sexual orientation are tremendously important considerations in analyzing the status of women in culture. This is not only because sex and sexuality are so basic to being human, but also because Western culture has defined women in large part in terms of sex. Women are too often defined as sex objects, useful for their ability to satisfy male sexual desire, but otherwise lacking in value, as well as lacking in their own agency and subjectivity. Culture also defines the kinds of sexual relationships that are "normal" and "healthy," as well as those that are considered to be "deviant" and culturally unacceptable. For the most part, throughout American history, the normative sexual relationship has been a heterosexual, monogamous one in which the couple is married and has children. Consequently, women's sexuality has been defined in very narrow ways which ignore or reject women who are not interested in pursuing exclusively heterosexual relationships, including women who are lesbian, bisexual, or celibate. Women who do not conform to the normative script for female sexuality are frequently stereotyped and labeled as deviant. Sexuality has also been defined very narrowly, so that women who are disabled, older, overweight, or otherwise "abnormal" are not thought of as sexual at all!

Male-defined attitudes about women's sexuality are reflected in stereotypes that contribute to creating distorted, and sometimes conflicting, expectations of women's sexuality: for example, that women will be heterosexual, both chaste and "willing," virginal yet experienced, compliant but not passive. These images of women are part of the cultural tradition of stereotyping women as either "virgins" or "whores." All women are viewed as falling into one category or the other: either virginally pure and chaste, devoted and selfless mothers, or else sexually available and impassioned temptresses of men. Lesbians are excluded from this dichotomized system of images. They are invisible, since women are presumed to be heterosexual and male-centered, regardless of whether they are sexually active.

Women who do not conform to the normative cultural standards of being "male identified" with respect to their sexual orientation are frequently called lesbians, regardless of the accuracy of the label. Lesbians, as women-loving women, are still vilified and treated with disapproval, if not outright hostility, in mainstream American culture. Popular conceptions of lesbians include many negative stereotypes and labels. Jacquelyn Zita notes that the term "lesbian" has been used to control women by making the label so pejorative that women are scared that it will be used to discriminate against them, whether or not they identify themselves as lesbian. Such labelling, which is also called "lesbian baiting," also teaches that women's erotic desires for other women are wrong (Ferguson et al., 1982: 162).

In earlier decades, and until the women's movement of the 1960s, strong women, especially those who preferred to live independently of men, were sometimes clinically diagnosed as suffering from the "disease" of lesbianism as a way of controlling them. In more recent decades, the attitudes of many experts has shifted from treating homosexuality as a "disease" to viewing it as a sexual orientation. There is still a considerable amount of controversy, however, over whether homosexuality is chosen (i.e., a sexual "preference") or whether it is biologically or genetically determined. This "nature versus nurture" debate is not likely to be resolved in the near future, given the lack of conclusive scientific evidence to support either thesis.

In her classic essay "Compulsory heterosexuality," Adrienne Rich (1986) coined the term "lesbian continuum" to suggest that there are a number of different reasons why a woman may identify herself as lesbian or be drawn to certain practices that have been identified as lesbian. These include personal fulfillment, being in love with a woman, feeling as if one has been a lesbian from birth, and choosing a lesbian lifestyle from a political commitment to certain feminist principles (see Unger and Crawford, 1992: 352–3).

Rich describes how women's oppression is maintained in part through cultural institutions that demand that women's sexuality be oriented toward men and serving male sexual needs. Based on such understandings of male domination, some women have consequently adopted lesbian identity for political

reasons rather than or in addition to reasons of sexual preference. Some lesbians (often called "lesbian separatists") have broken ranks with mainstream
women's movements, and some have attempted to live in woman-centered
communities completely independently of men. Cole points out that lesbian
separatist discussions have mainly taken place among white, middle-class lesbians, since women of color and working-class women who are lesbian have
had different kinds of relationships to their communities.

The political climate has become generally more tolerant of homosexuals.
President Clinton's appointment of Roberta Achtenberg as Assistant Secretary
of Housing and Urban Development in 1992 signalled a historic event as the
first openly homosexual person to be confirmed by the Senate. Famous lesbians, such as country singer k.d. lang, television sit-com star Ellen Degeneris,
and bisexual comedienne Sandra Bernhard, have brought a certain respectability,
even trendiness, to being a lesbian or a woman who associates with them (for
example, Roseanne's much-publicized kiss with Sandra Bernhard on national
television, and Madonna's friendship with her). The "normalizing" of lesbian
lives presented on popular television shows such as *Roseanne* and *Seinfeld*,
and the guest appearances of lesbians on talk shows, such as comic Lea DeLaria's
appearance on *Arsenio Hall* and Ellen Degeneris's on *Late Night with David
Letterman*, has helped to make lesbian identity more mainstream. Hollywood
films have also contributed to this trend, with female "buddy" movies such as
Fried Green Tomatoes, *Boys on the Side*, and *Thelma and Louise*.

None the less, lesbians as well as gay men continue to be discriminated
against. The difficulties that lesbians encounter include the risk of being "gay
bashed," that is, physically or verbally assaulted solely for being homosexual;
loss of family and community relations; loss of employment or inability to find
employment as an openly homosexual person; and increased vulnerability to
losing custody of their children, especially in a custody battle as part of a
divorce (see Pharr, 1995: 2490). In addition, it has been suggested that lesbians in the military have been investigated and discharged at a rate *three
times higher* than that for gay men. These constraints make it very difficult
for lesbians to "come out of the closet" and be open about their homosexuality. Racial and cultural differences also influence the development of sexual
identities, and women's ability to express them freely. Certain cultures and
subcultures, such as Latin "machismo" culture, for example, are less tolerant
of non-heterosexual practices than others.

Many lesbians have not felt comfortable in mainstream women's groups
dominated by heterosexual women, either because they have encountered
homophobia or because their particular interests and concerns have not been
adequately addressed by those groups. For example, in 1970, the women's
group NOW barred open lesbians from membership because of fear that their
presence would damage the movement. Thus, even within the women's movement, lesbians have been discriminated against. They continue to encounter

biased and bigoted attitudes in American society, regardless of the recent trend toward "mainstreaming" lesbian identity in popular culture.

The readings in this chapter all suggest, in one respect or another, that all women are influenced by racism, classism, and homophobia, as well as sexism. Even though some women are members of the dominant group – Caucasian, middle class, and heterosexual – they are none the less part of a culture that is racist, classist, and homophobic. These aspects of culture influence everyone's experience.

Commonalities and Differences (excerpt)
Johnnetta B. Cole

If you see one woman, have you seen them all? Does the heavy weight of patriarchy level all differences among US women? Is it the case, as one woman put it, that "there isn't much difference between having to say 'Yes suh Mr Charlie' and 'Yes dear'?" Does "grandmother" convey the same meaning as "abuela," as "buba," as "gran'ma"? Is difference a part of what we share, or is it, in fact, *all* that we share? As early as 1970, Toni Cade Bambara asked: "How relevant are the truths, the experiences, the findings of white women to black women? Are women after all simply women?" (Bambara, 1970: 9)

Are US women bound by our similarities or divided by our differences? The only viable response is *both*. To address our commonalities without dealing with our differences is to misunderstand and distort that which separates as well as that which binds us as women. Patriarchal oppression is not limited to women of one race or of one particular ethnic group, women in one class, women of one age group or sexual preference, women who live in one part of the country, women of any one religion, or women with certain physical abilities or disabilities. Yet, while oppression of women knows no such limitations, we cannot, therefore, conclude that the oppression of all women is identical.

Among the things which bind women together are the assumptions about the way that women think and behave, the myths – indeed the stereotypes – about what is common to all women. For example, women will be asked nicely in job interviews if they type, while men will not be asked such a

This reading first appeared in *All American Women: Lines that Divide, Ties that Bind*, ed. Johnnetta B. Cole (New York: The Free Press, 1986), pp. 1–6.

question. In response to certain actions, the expression is used: "Ain't that just like a woman?" Or during a heated argument between a man and a woman, as the voice of each rises and emotions run high, the woman makes a particularly good point. In a voice at the pitch of the ongoing argument, the man screams at her: "You don't have to get hysterical!"

In an interesting form of "what goes around comes around," as Malcolm X put it, there is the possibility that US women are bound together by our assumptions, attitudes toward, even stereotypes of the other gender. Folklorist Rayna Green, referring to women of the Southern setting in which she grew up, says this:

> Southern or not, women everywhere talk about sex . . . In general men are more often the victims of women's jokes than not. Tit for tat, we say. Usually the subject for laughter is men's boasts, failures, or inadequacies ("come-uppance for lack of upcommance," as one of my aunts would say). Poking fun at a man's sexual ego, for example, might never be possible in real social situations with the men who have power over their lives, but it is possible in a joke. (Green, 1984: 23–4)

That which US women have in common must always be viewed in relation to the particularities of a group, for even when we narrow our focus to one particular group of women it is possible for differences within that group to challenge the primacy of what is shared in common. For example, what have we said and what have we failed to say when we speak of "Asian-American women"? As Shirley Hune notes (1982), Asian-American women as a group share a number of characteristics. Their participation in the work force is higher than that of women in any other ethnic group. Many Asian-American women live life supporting others, often allowing their lives to be subsumed by the needs of the extended family. And they are subjected to stereotypes by the dominant society: the sexy but "evil dragon lady," the "neuter gender," the "passive/demure" type, and the "exotic/erotic" type.

However, there are many circumstances when these shared experiences are not sufficient to accurately describe the condition of particular Asian-American women. Among Asian-American women there are those who were born in the United States, fourth and fifth generation Asian-American women with first-hand experience of no other land, and there are those who recently arrived in the United States. Asian-American women are diverse in their heritage or country of origin: China, Japan, the Philippines, Korea, India, Vietnam, Cambodia, Thailand, or another country in Asia. If we restrict ourselves to Asian-American women of Chinese descent, are we referring to those women who are from the People's Republic of China or those from Taiwan, those from Hong Kong or those from Vietnam, those from San Francisco's Chinatown or those from Mississippi? Are we subsuming under "Asian-American" those Pacific Island women from Hawaii, Samoa, Guam, and other islands under US control? Although the majority of Asian-American women are working class – contrary to the stereotype of the "ever successful" Asians – there are poor, "middle-class," and even affluent Asian-American women (Hune, 1982: 1–2, 13–14).

It has become very common in the United States today to speak of "Hispanics," putting Puerto Ricans, Chicanos, Dominicans, Cubans, and those from every Spanish-speaking country in the Americas into one category of people, with the women referred to as Latinas or Hispanic women. Certainly there is a language, or the heritage of a language, a general historical experience, and certain cultural traditions and practices which are shared by these women. But a great deal of harm can be done by sweeping away differences in the interest of an imposed homogeneity.

Within one group of Latinas there is, in fact, considerable variation in terms of self-defined ethnic identity, such that some women refer to themselves as Mexican-Americans, others as Chicanas, others as Hispanics, and still others as Americans. Among this group of women are those who express a commitment to the traditional roles of women and others who identify with feminist ideals. Some Chicanas are monolingual – in Spanish or English – and others are bilingual. And there are a host of variations among Chicanas in terms of educational achievements, economic differences, rural or urban living conditions, and whether they trace their ancestry from women who lived in this land well before the United States forcibly took the northern half of Mexico, or more recently arrived across the border that now divides the nations called Mexico and the United States.

Women of the Midwest clearly share a number of experiences which flow from living in the US heartland, but they have come from different places, and they were and are today part of various cultures.

Midwestern women are the Native American women whose ancestors were brought to the plains in the mid-nineteenth century to be settled on reservations, the black women whose fore-bears emigrated by the thousands from the South after Reconstruction. They are the descendants of the waves of Spanish, French, Norwegian, Danish, Swedish, Bohemian, Scottish, Welsh, British, Irish, German, and Russian immigrants who settled the plains, and the few Dutch, Italians, Poles, and Yugoslavs who came with them. (Boucher, 1982: 3)

There is another complexity: when we have identified a commonality among women, cutting across class, racial, ethnic, and other major lines of

difference, the particular ways that commonality is acted out and its consequences in the larger society may be quite diverse. Ostrander (1984: 146)
makes this point in terms of class:

> When women stroke and soothe men, listen to them and accommodate their
> needs, men of every class return to the workplace with renewed energies.
> When women arrange men's social lives and relationships, men of every class
> are spared investing the time and energy required to meet their social needs.
> When women run the households and keep family concerns in check, men of
> every class are freer than women to pursue other activities, including work,
> outside the home. But upper-class women perform these tasks for men at the
> very top of the class structure . . . Supporting their husbands as individuals,
> they support and uphold the very top of the class structure. In this way they
> distinguish themselves from women of other social classes.

Suppose that we can accurately and exclusively identify the characteristics
shared by one particular group of women. For each of the women within
that group, into how many other groups does she want, or is she forced,
to fit? Or can we speak of similarities *only* with respect to a group such as
Puerto Rican women who are 43 years old, were born in San Juan, Puerto
Rico, migrated to New York City when they were five years old, work as
eighth-grade school teachers, attend a Catholic church, are heterosexual,
married, with two male and two female children, and have no physical
disabilities?

Then there is that unpredictable but often present quality of individuality,
the idiosyncrasies of a particular person. Shirley Abbott, describing experiences of growing up in the South, contrasts her mother's attitude and
behavior toward the black woman who was her maid with what was the
usual stance of "Southern white ladies."

> I don't claim that my mother's way of managing her black maid was typical.
> Most white women did not help their laundresses hang the washing on the
> line . . . Compulsive housewifery had some part in it. So did her upbringing
> . . . There was another motive too . . . Had she used Emma in just the right
> way, Mother could have become a lady. But Mother didn't want to be a lady.
> Something in her was against it, and she couldn't explain what frightened her,
> which was why she cried when my father ridiculed her. (Abbott, 1983: 78–9)

Once we have narrowed our focus to one specific group of women
(Armenian-American women, or women over 65, or Arab-American women,
or black women from the Caribbean, or Ashkenazi Jewish women), the
oppression that group of women experiences may take different forms at

different times. Today, there is no black woman in the United States who is the legal slave of a white master: "chosen" for that slave status because of her race, forced to give her labor power without compensation because of the class arrangements of the society, and subjected to the sexual whims of her male master because of her gender. But that does not mean that black women today are no longer oppressed on the basis of race, class, and gender.

There are also groups of women who experience intense gender discrimination today, but in the past had a radically different status in their society. Contrary to the popular image of female oppression as being both universal and as old as human societies, there is incontestable evidence of egalitarian societies in which men and women related in ways that did not involve male dominance and female subjugation. Eleanor Leacock is the best known of the anthropologists who have carried out the kind of detailed historical analysis which provides evidence on gender relations in precolonial North American societies. In discussing the debate on the origins and spread of women's oppression, Leacock points out that women's oppression is a reality today in virtually every society, and while socialist societies have reduced it, they have not eliminated gender inequality. However, it does not follow that women's oppression has always existed and will always exist. What such arguments about universal female subordination do is to project on to the totality of human history the conditions of today's world. Such an argument also "affords an important ideological buttress for those in power" (Leacock, 1979: 10–11).

Studies of precolonial societies indicate considerable variety in terms of gender relations.

> Women retained great autonomy in much of the pre-colonial world, and related to each other and to men through public as well as private procedures as they carried out their economic and social responsibilities and protected their rights. Female and male sodalities of various kinds operated reciprocally within larger kin and community contexts before the principle of male dominance within individual families was taught by missionaries, defined by legal status, and solidified by the economic relations of colonialism. (Leacock, 1979: 10–11)

Even when there is evidence of female oppression among women of diverse backgrounds, it is important to listen to the individual assessment which each woman makes of her own condition, rather than assume that a synonymous experience of female oppression exists among all women. As a case in point, Sharon Burmeister Lord, in describing what it was like to grow up "Appalachian style," speaks of the influence of female role models in shaping the conditions of her development. In Williamson, West Virginia, she grew up knowing women whose occupations were Methodist preacher, elementary school principal, county sheriff, and university professor. Within her own family, her mother works as a secretary, writes poetry and songs, and "swims faster than any boy"; her aunt started her own seed and hardware store; one grandmother is a farmer and the other runs her own boarding house. Summarizing the effect of growing up among such women, Lord says: "When a little girl has had a chance to learn strength, survival tactics, a firm grasp of reality, and an understanding of class oppression from the women around her, it doesn't remove oppression from her life, but it does give her a fighting chance. And that's an advantage!" (Lord, 1979: 25).

Finally, if it is agreed that today, to some extent, all women are oppressed, to what extent can a woman, or a group of women, also act as oppressor? Small as the numbers may be, there are some affluent black women. (In 1979, less than 500 black women had an income of over $75,000 a year. Four thousand black men had such an income, as compared to 548,000 white men who were in that income bracket; *see* Marable, 1983: 101–2.) Is it not possible that among this very small group of black women there are those who, while they experience oppression because of their race, act in oppressive ways toward other women because of their class? Does the experience of this society's heterosexism make a Euro-American lesbian incapable of engaging in racist acts toward women of color? The point is very simply that privilege can and does coexist with oppression (Bulkin et al., 1984: 99) and being a victim of one form of discrimination does not make one immune to victimizing someone else on a different basis.

References

Abbot, S. (1983) *Womenfolks: Growing Up Down South* (New York: Ticknor and Fields).

Bambara, T. C. (ed.) (1970) *The Black Woman: an Anthology* (New York: Signet).

Boucher, S. (1982) *Heartwomen: an Urban Feminist Odyssey Home* (New York: Harper and Row).

Bulkin, E., Pratt, M. E. and Smith, B. (eds) (1984) *Yours in Struggle* (Brooklyn, NY: Long Haul Press).

Green, R. (1984) "Magnolias grow in dirt: the bawdy lore of Southern women," in M. Alexander (ed.), *Speaking for Ourselves*, pp. 20–28 (New York: Pantheon).

Hune, S. (1982) "Asian American women: past and present, myth and reality," unpublished manuscript prepared for Conference on Black Women's Agenda for the Feminist Movement in the 80s, Williams College, Williamstown, Mass., November 12–14, 1982.

Leacock, E. (1979) "Women, development and anthropological facts and fictions," in *Women in Latin America: an Anthology from Latin American Perspectives*, pp. 7–16 (Riverside, CA.: Latin American Perspectives).

Lord, S. B. (1979) "Growin' up – Appalachian, female, and feminist," in S. B. Lord and C. Patton-Crowder (eds), *Appalachian Women: a Learning/Teaching Guide*, pp. 22–5 (Knoxville, TN: University of Tennessee).

Marable, M. (1983) *How Capitalism Underdeveloped Black America* (Boston: South End Press).

Ostrander, S. A. (1984) *Women of the Upper Class* (Philadelphia: Temple University Press).

Age, Race, Class, and Sex: Women Redefining Difference

Audre Lorde

Much of Western European history conditions us to see human differences in simplistic opposition to each other: dominant/subordinate, good/bad, up/down, superior/inferior. In a society where the good is defined in terms of profit rather than in terms of human need, there must always be some group of people who, through systematized oppression, can be made to feel surplus, to occupy the place of the dehumanized inferior. Within this society, that group is made up of black and Third World people, working-class people, older people, and women.

As a 49-year-old black lesbian feminist socialist mother of two, including one boy, and a member of an inter-racial couple, I usually find myself a part of some group defined as other, deviant, inferior, or just plain wrong. Traditionally, in American society, it is the members of oppressed, objectified groups who are expected to stretch out and bridge the gap between the actualities of our lives and the consciousness of our oppressor. For in order to survive, those of us for whom oppression is as American as apple pie have always had to be watchers, to become familiar with the language and manners of the oppressor, even sometimes adopting them for some illusion of protection. Whenever the need for some pretense of communication arises, those who profit from our oppression call upon us to share our knowledge

This reading first appeared in *Sister Outsider* (New York: The Crossing Press, 1984), pp. 401–407.

with them. In other words, it is the responsibility of the oppressed to teach the oppressors their mistakes. I am responsible for educating teachers who dismiss my children's culture in school. Black and Third World people are expected to educate white people as to our humanity. Women are expected to educate men. Lesbians and gay men are expected to educate the heterosexual world. The oppressors maintain their position and evade responsibility for their own actions. There is a constant drain of energy which might be better used in redefining ourselves and devising realistic scenarios for altering the present and constructing the future.

Institutionalized rejection of difference is an absolute necessity in a profit economy which needs outsiders as surplus people. As members of such an economy, we have *all* been programmed to respond to the human differences between us with fear and loathing and to handle that difference in one of three ways: ignore it, and if that is not possible, copy it if we think it is dominant, or destroy it if we think it is subordinate. But we have no patterns for relating across our human differences as equals. As a result, those differences have been misnamed and misused in the service of separation and confusion.

Certainly there are very real differences between us of race, age, and sex. But it is not those differences between us that are separating us. It is rather our refusal to recognize those differences, and to examine the distortions which result from our misnaming them and their effects upon human behavior and expectation.

Racism, the belief in the inherent superiority of one race over all others and thereby the right to dominance. Sexism, the belief in the inherent superiority of one sex over the other and thereby the right to dominance. Ageism. Heterosexism. Elitism. Classism.

It is a lifetime pursuit for each one of us to extract these distortions from our living at the same time as we recognize, reclaim, and define those differences upon which they are imposed. For we have all been raised in a society where those distortions were endemic within our living. Too often, we pour the energy needed for recognizing and exploring difference into pretending those differences are insurmountable barriers, or that they do not exist at all. This results in a voluntary isolation, or false and treacherous connections, Either way, we do not develop tools for using human difference as a springboard for creative change within our lives. We speak not of human difference, but of human deviance.

Somewhere, on the edge of consciousness, there is what I call a *mythical norm*, which each one of us within our hearts knows "that is not me." In America, this norm is usually defined as white, thin, male, young, heterosexual, Christian, and financially secure. It is with this mythical norm that the trappings of power reside within society. Those of us who stand outside that power often identify one way in which we are different, and we assume that to be the primary cause of all oppression, forgetting other distortions around difference, some of which we ourselves may be practicing. By and large, within the women's movement today, white women focus upon their oppression as women and ignore differences of race, sexual preference, class, and age. There is a pretense to a homogeneity of experience covered by the word *sisterhood* that does not, in fact, exist.

Unacknowledged class differences rob women of each other's energy and creative insight. Recently, a women's magazine collective made the decision for one issue to print only prose, saying poetry was a less "rigorous" or "serious" art form. Yet even the form our creativity takes is often a class issue. Of all the art forms, poetry is the most economical. It is the one which is the most secret, which requires the least physical labor, the least material, and the one which can be done between shifts, in the hospital pantry, on the subway, and on scraps of surplus paper. Over the past few years, writing a novel on tight finances, I came to appreciate the enormous differences in the material demands between poetry and prose. As we reclaim our literature, poetry has been the major voice of poor, working-class, and colored women. A room of one's own may be a necessity for writing prose, but so are reams of paper, a typewriter, and plenty of time. The actual requirements to produce the visual arts also help determine, along class lines, whose art is whose. In this day of inflated prices for material, who are our sculptors, our painters, our photographers? Where we speak of broadly based women's culture, we need to be aware of the effect of class and economic differences on the supplies available for producing art

As we move toward creating a society within which we can each flourish, ageism is another distortion of relationship which interferes with our vision. By ignoring the past, we are encouraged to repeat its mistakes. The "generation gap" is an important social tool for any repressive society. If the younger members of a community view the older members as contemptible or suspect or excess, they will never be able to join hands and examine the living memories of the community, nor ask the all-important question, "Why?" This gives rise to a historical amnesia that keeps us working to invent the wheel every time we have to go to the store for bread.

We find ourselves having to repeat and relearn the same old lessons over and over that our mothers did because we do not pass on what we have learned, or because we are unable to listen. For instance, how many times has this all been said before? For another, who would have believed that once again our daughters are allowing their bodies to be hampered and purgatoried by girdles and high heels and hobble skirts?

Ignoring the differences of race between women and the implications of those differences presents the most serious threat to the mobilization of women's joint power.

As white women ignore their built-in privilege of whiteness and define *woman* in terms of their own experience alone, then women of color become "other," the outsider whose experience and tradition is too "alien" to comprehend. An example of this is the signal absence of the experience of women of color as a resource for women's studies courses. The literature of women of color is seldom included in women's literature courses and almost never in other literature courses, nor in women's studies as a whole. All too often, the excuse given is that the literatures of women of color can only be taught by colored women, or that they are too difficult to understand, or that classes cannot "get into" them because they come out of experiences that are "too different." I have heard this argument presented by white women of otherwise quite clear intelligence, women who seem to have no trouble at all teaching and reviewing work that comes out of the vastly different experiences of Shakespeare, Molière, Dostoyevsky, and Aristophanes. Surely there must be some other explanation.

This is a very complex question, but I believe one of the reasons white women have such difficulty reading black women's work is because of their reluctance to see black women as women and different from themselves. To examine black women's literature effectively requires that we be seen as whole people in our actual complexities – as individuals, as women, as human – rather than as one of those problematic but familiar stereotypes provided in this society in place of genuine images of black women. And I believe this holds true for the literature of other women of color who are not black.

The literature of all women of color recreates the textures of our lives, and many white women are heavily invested in ignoring the real differences. For as long as any difference between us means one of us must be inferior, then the recognition of any difference must be fraught with guilt. To allow women of color to step out of stereotypes is too guilt provoking, for it threatens the complacency of those women who view oppression only in terms of sex.

Refusing to recognize difference makes it impossible to see the different problems and pitfalls facing us as women.

Thus, in a patriarchal power system where whiteskin privilege is a major prop, the entrapments used to neutralize black women and white women are not the same. For example, it is easy for black women to be used by the power structure against black men, not because they are men, but because they are black. Therefore, for black women, it is necessary at all times to separate the needs of the oppressor from our own legitimate conflicts within our communities. This same problem does not exist for white women. Black women and men have shared racist oppression and still share it, although in different ways. Out of that shared oppression we have developed joint defenses and joint vulnerabilities to each other that are not duplicated in the white community, with the exception of the relationship between Jewish women and Jewish men.

On the other hand, white women face the pitfall of being seduced into joining the oppressor under the pretense of sharing power. This possibility does not exist in the same way for women of color. The tokenism that is sometimes extended to us is not an invitation to join power; our racial "otherness" is a visible reality that makes that quite clear. For white women there is a wider range of pretended choices and rewards for identifying with patriarchal power and its tools.

Today, with the defeat of the Equal Rights Amendment (ERA), the tightening economy, and increased conservatism, it is easier once again for white women to believe the dangerous fantasy that if you are good enough, pretty enough, sweet enough, quiet enough, teach the children to behave, hate the right people, and marry the right men, then you will be allowed to coexist with patriarchy in relative peace, at least until a man needs your job or the neighborhood rapist happens along. And true, unless one lives and loves in the trenches, it is difficult to remember that the war against dehumanization is ceaseless.

But black women and our children know the fabric of our lives is stitched with violence and with hatred, that there is no rest. We do not deal with it only on the picket lines, or in dark midnight alleys, or in the places where we dare to verbalize our resistance. For us, increasingly, violence weaves through the daily tissues of our living – in the supermarket, in the class-room, in the elevator, in the clinic and the schoolyard, from the plumber, the baker, the saleswoman, the bus driver, the bank teller, the waitress who does not serve us.

Some problems we share as women, some we do not. You fear your children will grow up to join the patriarchy and testify against you; we fear our children will be dragged from a car and shot down in the street, and you will turn your backs upon the reasons they are dying.

The threat of difference has been no less blinding to people of color. Those of us who are black must see that the reality of our lives and our struggle does not make us immune to the errors of ignoring and misnaming difference. Within black communities where racism is a living reality, differ-ences among us often seem dangerous and suspect. The need for unity is often misnamed as a need for homogeneity, and a black feminist vision mistaken for betrayal of our common interests as a people. Because of the continuous battle against racial erasure that black women and black men share, some black women still refuse to recognize that we are also oppressed as women, and that sexual hostility against black women is practiced not only by the white racist society, but implemented within our black communities as well. It is a disease striking the heart of black nationhood, and silence will not make it disappear. Exacerbated by racism and the pressures of powerlessness, violence against black women and children often becomes a standard within our communities, one by which manliness can be measured. But these woman-hating acts are rarely discussed as crimes against black women.

As a group, women of color are the lowest paid wage earners in America. We are the primary targets of abortion and sterilization abuse, here and abroad. In certain parts of Africa, small girls are still being sewed shut between their legs to keep them docile and for men's pleasure. This is known as female circumcision, and it is not a cultural affair as the late Jomo Kenyatta insisted: it is a crime against black women.

Black women's literature is full of the pain of frequent assault, not only by a racist patriarchy, but also by black men. Yet the necessity for and history of shared battle have made us, black women, particularly vulnerable to the false accusation that anti-sexist is anti-black. Meanwhile, woman-hating as a recourse of the powerless is sapping strength from black communities, and our very lives. Rape is on the increase, reported and unreported, and rape is not aggressive sexuality, it is sexualized aggression. As Kalamu ya Salaam, a black male writer points out, "As long as male domination exists, rape will exist. Only women revolting and men made conscious of their responsibility to fight sexism can collectively stop rape."[1]

Differences between ourselves as black women are also being misnamed and used to separate us from one another. As a black lesbian feminist comfortable with the many different ingredients of my identity, and a woman committed to racial and sexual freedom from oppression, I find I am constantly being encouraged to pluck out some one aspect of myself and present this as the meaningful whole, eclipsing or denying the other parts of self. But this is a destructive and fragmenting way to live. My fullest concentration of energy is available to me only when I integrate all the parts of who I am, openly, allowing power from particular sources of my living to flow back and forth freely through all my different selves, without the restrictions of externally imposed definition. Only then can I bring myself and my energies as a whole to the service of those struggles which I embrace as part of my living.

A fear of lesbians, or of being accused of being a lesbian, has led many black women into testifying against themselves. It has led some of us into destructive alliances, and others into despair and isolation. In the white women's communities, heterosexism is sometimes a result of identifying with the white patriarchy, a rejection of that interdependence between women-identified women which allows the self to be, rather than to be used in the service of men. Sometimes it reflects a diehard belief in the protective coloration of heterosexual relationships, sometimes a self-hate which all women have to fight against, taught us from birth.

Although elements of these attitudes exist for all women, there are particular resonances of heterosexism and homophobia among black women. Despite the fact that woman-bonding has a long and honorable history in the African and African-American communities, and despite the knowledge and accomplishments of many strong and creative women-identified black women in the political, social and cultural fields, heterosexual black women often tend to ignore or discount the existence and work of black lesbians. Part of this attitude has come from an understandable terror of black male attack within the close confines of black society, where the punishment for any female self-assertion is still to be accused of being a lesbian and therefore unworthy of the attention or support of the scarce black male. But part of this need to misname and ignore black lesbians comes from a very real fear that openly women-identified black women who are no longer dependent upon men for their self-definition may well reorder our whole concept of social relationships.

Black women who once insisted that lesbianism was a white woman's problem now insist that black lesbians are a threat to black nationhood, are consorting with the enemy, are basically un-black. These accusations, coming from the very women to whom we look for deep and real understanding, have served to keep many black lesbians in hiding, caught between the racism of white women and the homophobia of their sisters. Often, their work has been ignored, trivialized, or misnamed, as with the work of Angelina Grimke, Alice Dunbar-Nelson, Lorraine Hansberry. Yet women-bonded women have always been some part of the power of black communities, from our unmarried aunts to the amazons of Dahomey.

And it is certainly not black lesbians who are assaulting women and raping children and grandmothers on the streets of our communities.

Across this country, as in Boston during the spring of 1979 following the unsolved murders of 12 black women, black lesbians are spearheading movements against violence against black women.

What are the particular details within each of our lives that can be scrutinized and altered to help bring about change? How do we redefine difference for all women? It is not our differences which separate women, but our reluctance to recognize those differences and to deal effectively with the distortions which have resulted from the ignoring and misnaming of those differences.

As a tool of social control, women have been encouraged to recognize only one area of human difference as legitimate, those differences which exist between women and men. And we have learned to deal across those differences with the urgency of all oppressed subordinates. All of us have had to learn to live or work or coexist with men, from our fathers on. We have recognized and negotiated these differences, even when this recognition only continued the old dominant/subordinate mode of human relationship, where the oppressed must recognize the master's difference in order to survive.

But our future survival is predicated upon our ability to relate within equality. As women, we must root out internalized patterns of oppression within ourselves if we are to move beyond the most superficial aspects of social change. Now we must recognize differences among women who are our equals, neither inferior nor superior, and devise ways to use each other's difference to enrich our visions and our joint struggles.

The future of our earth may depend upon the ability of all women to identify and develop new definitions of power and new patterns of relating across difference. The old definitions have not served us, nor the earth that supports us. The old patterns, no matter how cleverly rearranged to imitate progress, still condemn us to cosmetically altered repetitions of the same old exchanges, the same old guilt hatred, recrimination, lamentation, and suspicion.

For we have, built into all of us, old blueprints of expectation and response, old structures of oppression, and these must be altered at the same time as we alter the living conditions which are a result of those structures. For the master's tools will never dismantle the master's house.

As Paulo Freire shows so well in *The Pedagogy of the Oppressed*,[2] the true focus of revolutionary change is never merely the oppressive situations which we seek to escape, but that piece of the oppressor which is planted deep within each of us, and which knows only the oppressor's tactics, the oppressor's relationships.

Change means growth, and growth can be painful. But we sharpen self-definition by exposing the self in work and struggle together with those whom we define as different from ourselves, although sharing the same goals. For black and white, old and young, lesbian and heterosexual women alike, this can mean new paths to our survival.

We have chosen each other
and the edge of each other's battles
the war is the same
if we lose
someday women's blood will congeal
upon a dead planet
if we win
there is no telling
we seek beyond history
for a new and more possible meaning.[3]

Notes

1 From Kalan Salaam, "Rape: a radical analysis, an African-American perspective," *Black Books Bulletin*, 6(4) (1980).
2 Paul Freire, *The Pedagogy of the Oppressed* (New York: Seabury Press, 1970).
3 From "Outlines," unpublished poem.

And A'n't I a Woman?
Sojourner Truth

Sojourner Truth (1795–1883) – born Isabella, a slave, in New York State – became a well-known anti-slavery speaker sometime after gaining her freedom in 1827. This speech, given extemporaneously at a women's rights convention in Akron, Ohio, 1851, was recorded by Frances Gage, feminist activist and one of the authors of the huge compendium of materials of the first wave, *The History of Woman Suffrage* (Stanton et al., 1889). Gage, who was presiding at the meeting, describes the event:

The leaders of the movement trembled on seeing a tall, gaunt black woman in a gray dress and white turban, surmounted with an uncouth sunbonnet, march deliberately into the church, walk with the air of a queen up the aisle, and take her seat upon the pulpit steps. A buzz of disapprobation was heard all over the house, and there fell on the listening ear, "An abolition affair!" "Woman's rights and niggers!" "I told you so!" "Go it, darkey!" . . . Again

This reading first appeared in *Issues in Feminism* by Sheila Ruth (Mountain View, CA: Mayfield, c.1990), pp. 463–4.

and again, timorous and trembling ones came to me and said, with earnestness, "Don't let her speak, Mrs Gage, it will ruin us. Every newspaper in the land will have our cause mixed up with abolition and niggers, and we shall be utterly denounced." My only answer was, "We shall see when the time comes."

The second day the work waxed warm. Methodist, Baptist, Episcopal, Presbyterian, and Universalist minister came in to hear and discuss the resolutions presented. One claimed superior rights and privileges for man, on the ground of "superior intellect"; another, because of the "manhood of Christ; if God had desired the equality of woman, He would have given some token of His will through the birth, life, and death of the Savior." Another gave us a theological view of the "sin of our first mother."

There were very few women in those days who dared to "speak in meeting"; and the august teachers of the people were seemingly getting the better of us, while the boys in the galleries, and the sneerers among the pews, were hugely enjoying the discomfiture as they supposed, of the "strong-minded." Some of the tender-skinned friends were on the point of losing dignity, and the atmosphere betokened a storm. When, slowly from her seat in the corner rose Sojourner Truth, who, till now, had scarcely lifted her head. "Don't let her speak!" gasped half a dozen in my ear. She moved slowly and solemnly to the front, laid her old bonnet at her feet, and turned her great speaking eyes to me. There was a hissing sound of disapprobation above and below. I rose and announced, "Sojourner Truth," and begged the audience to keep silence for a few moments.

The tumult subsided at once, and every eye was fixed on this almost Amazon form, which stood nearly six feet high, head erect, and eyes piercing the upper air like one in a dream. At her first word there was a profound hush. She spoke in deep tones, which, though not loud, reached every ear in the house, and away through the throng at the doors and windows.

One cannot miss that there were those who were staunch for women's rights but yet were racist. It was not until later, much later, that there was much sophisticated analysis linking sexism, racism, and expressions of other kinds.

Truth's speech is reproduced here exactly as Gage recorded it in *History of Woman Suffrage*:

"Wall, chilern, whar dar is so much racket dar must be somethin' out o' kilter. I tink dat 'twixt de niggers of de Souf and de womin at de Norf, all talkin' 'bout rights, de white men will be in a fix pretty soon. But what's all dis here talkin' 'bout?

"Dat man ober dar say dat womin needs to be helped into carriages, and lifted ober ditches, and to hab de best place everywhar. Nobody eber helps me into carriages, or ober mud-puddles, or gibs me any best place!" And raising herself to her full height, and her voice to a pitch like rolling thunder, she asked. "And a'n't I a woman? Look at me! Look at my arm! (and she bared her right arm to the shoulder, showing her tremendous muscular power). I have ploughed, and planted, and gathered into barns, and no man could head me! And a'n't I a woman? I could work as much and eat as much as a man – when I could get it – and bear de lash as well! And a'n't I a woman? I have borne thirteen chilern, and seen 'em mos' all sold off to slavery, and when I cried out with my mother's grief, none but Jesus heard me! And a'n't I a woman?

"Den dey talks 'bout dis ting in de head; what dis dey call it?" ("Intellect," whispered some one near.) "Dat's it, honey. What's dat got to do wid womin's rights or nigger's rights? If my cup won't hold but a pint, and yourn holds a quart, wouldn't ye be mean not to let me have my little half-measure full?" And she pointed her significant finger, and sent a keen glance at the minister who had made the argument. The cheering was long and loud.

"Den dat little man in black dar, he say women can't have as much rights as men, 'cause Christ wan't a woman! Whar did your Christ come from?" Rolling thunder couldn't have stilled that crowd, as did those deep, wonderful tones, as she stood there with outstretched arms and eyes of fire. Raising her voice still louder, she repeated, "Whar did your Christ come from? From God and a woman! Man had nothin' to do wid Him." Oh, what a rebuke that was to that little man.

Turning again to another objector, she took up the defense of Mother Eve. I cannot follow her through it all. It was pointed, and witty, and solemn; eliciting at almost every sentence deafening applause; and she ended by asserting: "If de fust woman God ever made was strong enough to turn de world upside down all alone, dese women togedder (and she glanced her eye over the platform) ought to be able to turn it back, and get it right side up again! And now dey is asking to do it, de men better let 'em." Long-continued cheering greeted this. " 'Bleeged to ye for hearin' on me, and now ole Sojourner han't got nothin' more to say."

Amid roars of applause, she returned to her corner, leaving more than one of us with streaming eyes, and hearts beating with gratitude. She had taken us up in her strong arms and carried us safely over the slough of difficulty turning the whole tide in our favor. I have never in my life seen anything like the magical influence that subdued the mobbish spirit of the day, and turned the sneers and jeers of an excited crowd into notes of respect and admiration. Hundreds rushed up to shake hands with her, and congratulate the glorious old mother, and bid her God-speed on her mission of "testifyin' agin concerning the wickedness of this 'ere people."

Reference

Stanton, Elizabeth Cady, Anthony, Susan B. and Gage, Matilda Joslyn (eds) (1889) *History of Woman Suffrage*, 2nd edn, vol. 1 (Rochester, NY: Charles Mann).

When You Meet a Lesbian:
Hints for the Heterosexual Woman
Indiana University Empowerment Workshop

- Do not run screaming from the room . . . this is rude.
- If you must back away, do so slowly and with discretion.
- Do not assume she is attracted to you.
- Do not assume she is not attracted to you.
- Do not assume you are not attracted to her.
- Do not expect her to be as excited about meeting a heterosexual as you may be about meeting a lesbian . . . she was probably raised by them.
- Do not immediately start talking about your boyfriend or husband in order to make it clear that you are straight . . . she probably already knows.
- Do not tell her that it is sexist to prefer women, that people are people, that she should be able to love everybody. Do not tell her that men are as oppressed by sexism as women and women should help men fight their oppression. These are common fallacies and should be treated as such.
- Do not invite her someplace where there will be men unless you tell her in advance. She may not want to be with them.
- Do not ask her how she got that way . . . Instead, ask yourself how you got that way.
- Do not assume that she is dying to talk about being a lesbian.
- Do not expect her to refrain from talking about being a lesbian.
- Do not trivialize her experience by assuming it is a bedroom issue only. She is a lesbian 24 hours a day.
- Do not assume that because she is a lesbian that she wants to be treated like a man.
- Do not assume that her heart will leap with joy if you touch her arm (condescendingly? flirtatiously? power-testingly?) It makes her angry.
- If you are tempted to tell her that she is sick and is taking the easy way out . . . Think about that . . . Think about that *real* hard.

Heterosexuality Questionnaire
Gay and Lesbian Speakers' Bureau

The following list of questions has been circulating among the gay and lesbian communities for some time. We gratefully acknowledge the anonymous person(s) who created it and present it here as an example of inverting the question.

1 What do you think caused your heterosexuality?
2 When and how did you first decide that you were a heterosexual?
3 Is it possible your heterosexuality is just a phase you might grow out of?
4 Is it possible your heterosexuality stems from a neurotic fear of others of the same sex?
5 If you've never slept with a person of the same sex and enjoyed it, is it possible that all you need is a good gay lover?
6 To whom have you disclosed your heterosexual tendencies? How did they react?
7 Why do you heterosexuals feel compelled to seduce others into your lifestyle?
8 Why do you insist on flaunting your heterosexuality? Can't you just be what you are and keep it quiet?
9 Would you want your children to be heterosexual, knowing the problems they'd face?
10 A disproportionate majority of child molesters are heterosexual. Do you consider it safe to expose your children to heterosexual teachers?
11 Even with all the societal support marriage receives, the divorce rate is spiralling. Why are there so few stable relationships among heterosexuals?
12 Why do heterosexuals place so much emphasis on sex?
13 Considering the menace of overpopulation, how could the human race survive if everyone was heterosexual like you?
14 Could you trust a heterosexual therapist to be objective? Don't you fear s/he might be inclined to influence you in the direction of her/his leaning?
15 How can you become a whole person if you limit yourself to compulsive, exclusive heterosexuality? Shouldn't you at least try to develop your natural, healthy homosexual potential?

16   There seem to be very few happy heterosexuals. Techniques have been developed to help you change if you really want to. Have you considered aversion therapy?

Suggested activities

Questions for discussion

1   As you read the Cole article, think about whether there are other significant commonalities and differences among women that are not included in her discussion. Which commonalities and differences among women are the most significant? Why?
2   Are the differences among women so fundamental that it is not feasible to expect women to work together against oppression, despite their commonalities?
3   What commonalities and differences among women are you aware of in your daily life? What significance do these have for you?
4   Is Cole correct that "it is important to listen to the individual assessment which each woman makes of her own condition, rather than assume that a synonymous experience of female oppression exists among all women"? Does this suggestion adequately account for the possibility of false consciousness, i.e. a women's lack of recognition that she is oppressed? Is it always feasible to make such individualized assessments? How about in the context of establishing public policy that impacts on all women?
5   Can you think of ways that women are simultaneously perpetrators as well as victims of oppression?
6   Do you agree that lesbianism is a form of resistance to patriarchy? Has lesbianism been denied a political existence?
7   Discuss some of the factors that make it difficult for lesbians to "come out of the closet" in our society. Do you think the atmosphere has changed significantly in recent years? What evidence can you give to support your position?

Films and videos

There are a large (and growing) number of films and videos that touch on various aspects of the commonalities and differences among women. The following lists only a sample of what is available.

Adventures in the Gender Trade, produced/directed by Susan Marenco (1992). VHS/40 mins. Available from Filmaker's Library. Explores various manifestations of gender through interviews with trans-sexuals, cross-dressers, drag queens, homosexuals, and academics about gender roles and what defines one's gender.

All of our Lives, produced by Laura Sky and Helene Klodawsky (1985). VHS/ 28 mins. Available from Filmaker's Library. Presents older women as capable, independent, productive people, and shows the effects of economic discrimination on aging women. Includes both historical and contemporary perspectives.

The Disabled Women's Theatre Project, produced and written by Women with Physical Disabilities (1982). VHS/color/60 mins. Distributed by Women Make Movies. A documentary of how a group of disabled women produce theater. Exposes the stereotypes and problems faced by disabled women.

Doctor, Lawyer, Indian Chief, directed by Carole Geddes (1986). VHS/29 mins. National Film Board of Canada. Distributed by Women Make Movies. On the role of women in Native American society.

Double the Trouble, Twice the Fun by Pratibha Parmar (England, 1992). VHS/color/25 mins. Distributed by Women Make Movies. Interviews with disabled lesbians and gays, and an examination of the myth of the non-sexuality of disabled women.

Female Misbehavior by Monika Treut (1992). VHS/82 mins. Distributed by First Run Features, New York, NY. Four short films featuring controversial women on provocative sexual issues (infamous author of *Sexual Personae* Camille Paglia; porn star and performance artist Annie Sprinkle; an S&M practitioner Carol; and a trans-sexual's journey from female to male).

Forbidden Love: the Unashamed Stories of Lesbian Lives by Aerlyn Weissman and Lynne Fernie (Canada, 1992) 16 mm/VHS/color/85 mins. Distributed by Women Make Movies. A documentary of lesbian culture during the "dark ages" of the 1950s and 1960s.

Hair Piece: a Film for Nappy-headed People by Ayoka Chenzira (1985). 16 mm/ VHS/10 mins. Distributed by Women Make Movies. An animated satire on the question of self-image for African-American women living in a society where straight hair is viewed as the only beautiful hair. Portrays the rituals African-American women undergo in order to straighten their hair.

Home is Struggle by Marta Bautis (1991). VHS(subtitled)/color/37 mins. Distributed by Women Make Movies. An examination of Latina immigrants finding and defining their own identity in the United States.

It Starts with a Whisper, written/produced and directed by Shelley Niro and Anna Gronan (1993). VHS/29 mins. Distributed by Women Make Movies. An experimental drama of a young Native American woman who feels she must choose between traditional and contemporary values.

Japanese American Women: a Sense of Place by Rosanna Yamagiwa, Alfaro and Leita Hagemann (1992). VHS/28 mins. Distributed by Women Make Movies. Twelve Japanese-American women shatter the stereotype of Asian women as polite, docile, and exotic by speaking about their experiences as part of the "model minority." Explores the burden of being "different."

Navajo Talking Pictures, produced/directed by Arlene Bowman (1986). $\frac{1}{2}$ in/40 mins. Distributed by Women Make Movies. About a Navajo film-maker's attempt to deal with assimilation.

Older, Stronger, Wiser, produced by National Film Board of Canada (1991). 16 mm/VHS/28 mins. Available from the National Film Board of Canada. Profiles of five African-American women in Canada. Portrays how their perseverance and active involvement in the community preserves their black heritage and fosters a positive identity for black children.

Out in Suburbia by Pam Walton (1988). VHS/28 mins. Available from Filmaker's Library. Interviews lesbians leading very ordinary lives "in suburbia" about coming out, falling in love, relationships, motherhood, work, and living as a lesbian in a dominantly heterosexual culture.

Positive Images: Portraits of Women with Disabilities by Julie Harrison and Marilyn Rousso (1989). VHS/58 mins. Distributed by Women Make Movies. On women with disabilities and the social, economic, and political issues they face, focusing on three strong women.

When She Gets Old, produced/written by Shelley Spencer (1993). VHS/30 mins. Available from Terra Nova Films, Chicago, IL. Examines the economic problems facing many women over the age of 60.

Women Like Us/Women Like That by Suzanne Neild and Rosalind Pearson (2-part video, England, 1990/1991). VHS/color/49 mins. Distributed by Women Make Movies. Interviews with lesbians aged 50+ and their thoughts on the women's movement since the 1920s.

Other activities

Individual exercise

Consider the following differences among women: race, class or socioeconomic status, age, religion, regional location, educational level, occupation, marital status, parental status and family size, disabilities, sexual orientation. Rank order these in terms of most to least significant. Write an essay defending your ordering. What criteria did you use in making your ranking?

Group exercises

1   Brainstorm as many similarities and differences among women in 5 minutes as possible. Are there any characteristics that women in general share that make it appropriate to consider women as more similar to one another than to men? Or at least similar enough to unite women in common political struggle? What differences among women are the most significant in your own lives? Is there any validity to the notion of universal "sisterhood"

among women or is this based on a naïve and outdated assumption of an earlier generation of the women's movement?
2 Brainstorm a list of popular stereotypes of women in relation to sex, race, and class (e.g. "loose," "dykish," "prudish") and discuss the possible reasons for some of these terms. Who imposes these labels, for what purpose, and with what result?
3 Brainstorm a list of popular stereotypes of lesbians, and discuss the discrepancy between these labels and the realities of lesbian lives.
4 Use the video *Out in Suburbia* as the basis for a small group discussion about the factors that make it difficult for lesbians to come out, both those that are mentioned in the video and others students may be able to think of. The video also offers the framework for discussing the commonalities and differences among lesbian women, and how their experiences of oppression compare with those of heterosexual women.

Bibliography

Adleman, Jeanne and Enguidanos, Gloria (eds) (1995) *Racism in the Lives of Women: Testimony, Theory, and Guides to Antiracist Practice* (New York: Haworth Press). Anthology of essays by women on a variety of aspects of dealing with racism, ethnic and racial difference, and multiple oppressions, especially in the contexts of therapy and counseling.
Agnew, Vijay (1995) *Resisting Discrimination: Women from Asia, Africa, and the Caribbean and the Women's Movement in Canada* (Toronto, Ontario: University of Toronto Press). Explores race, class, and gender discrimination in twentieth-century Canada, through the experiences of Asian and black Canadian women, and their critiques of white feminist theories and practices.
Alexander, M. Jacqui, Albrecht, Lisa, Day, Sharon, Segrest, Mab and Alarcon, Norma (eds) (1994) *The Third Wave: Feminist Perspectives on Racism* (New York: Kitchen Table – Women of Color Press). Anthology focusing on racial oppression and strategies for eradicating it from the perspectives of Euro-American women and women of color.
Allen, Jessie and Pifer, Alan (eds) (1993) *Women on the Front Lines: Meeting the Challenge of an Aging America* (Washington, DC: The Urban Institute Press). Describes how aging is gendered: because women typically live longer than men, because women continue to be responsible for caretaking for the elderly, and because sexism shapes policies regarding the elderly.
Allen, Paula Gunn (1986) "Where I come from is like this," in *The Sacred Hoop* (Boston: Beacon Press). On the differences in the experiences of Native American and Anglo-American women.
Anderson, Margaret and Collins, Patricia Hill (eds) (1992) *Race, Class, and Gender: an Anthology* (Belmont, CA: Wadsworth). A useful anthology of readings divided into parts entitled "I. Reconstructing Knowledge: Toward Inclusive Thinking," "II. Conceptualizing Race, Class, and Gender," "III. Rethinking Institutions," and "IV. Social Change and the Politics of Empowerment".
Anzaldúa, Gloria (ed.) (1990) *Making Face, Making Soul/Haciendo Caras: Creative and Critical Perspectives by Feminists of Color* (San Francisco: Aunt Lute Foundation Books).

Collection of essays, stories, and poems by women of color, many of them addressing issues of commonality and difference among women.

Asian Women United of California (1989) *Making Waves: an Anthology of Writings by and about Asian American Women* (Boston: Beacon Press). Collection of primarily previously unpublished works. Contains sections on immigration, war, work, generations, identity, injustice, and activism written since the early 1970s. Includes background history of Asian-American women's experiences in the US.

Cade, Toni (1970) *The Black Woman: an Anthology* (New York: New American Library). A path-breaking collection of writing by and about African-American women.

Califia, Pat (1994) *Public Sex: the Culture of Radical Sex* (Pittsburgh, PA: Cleis Press). By a radical lesbian, advocating feminist acceptance of all forms of sexual expression, including pornography and S&M.

Chow, Esther Ngan-Ling, Wilkinson, Doris and Baca Zinn, Maxine (eds) (1996) *Race, Class, and Gender: Common Bonds, Different Voices* (Thousand Oaks, CA: Sage).

Davis, Angela (1981) *Women, Race, and Class* (New York: Random House). On the history of African-American women in the United States by the renowned former member of the Black Panther movement, political activist, and feminist socialist scholar.

Davis, Nancy, Cole, Ellen and Rothblum, Esther (eds) (1993) *Faces of Women and Aging* (New York: Haworth Press). Includes personal accounts by psychotherapists in their 50s, 60s, and 70s about what it is like to age, based on their own experience as well as that of their patients.

Dubos, Ellen Carol and Ruiz, Vicki (eds) (1990) *Unequal Sisters: a Multicultural Reader in US Women's History* (New York: Routledge).

Dugger, Karen (1991) "Social location and gender-role attitudes: a comparison of black and white women," in Judith Lorber and Susan Farell (eds), *The Social Construction of Gender* (Newbury Park, CA: Sage).

Dunne, Gillian A. (1997) *Lesbian Lifestyles: Women's Work and Politics of Sexuality* (Toronto, Ontario: University of Toronto Press).

Espin, Oliva (1984) "Cultural and historical influences on sexuality in female sexuality," in Carol Vance (ed.), *Pleasure and Danger: Explorations of Female Sexuality* (Boston: Routledge and Kegan Paul).

Ferguson, Ann, Zita, Jacquelyn, N. and Addelson, Kathryn Pine (1982) "On 'Compulsory Heterosexuality and Lesbian Existence': defining the issues," in Nannerl Keohane, Michelle Zimbalist Rosaldo, and Barbara Charlesworth (eds), *Feminist Theory* (Chicago: University of Chicago Press). Essays that reflect upon and critique Rich's "Compulsory Heterosexuality" article.

Frye, Marilyn (1983) "On being white: toward a feminist understanding of race and race supremacy," in *The Politics of Reality* (New York: The Crossing Press).

Geok-Lin Lim, Shirley, Tsutakaw, Mayumi and Donnely, Margarity (eds) (1989) *The Forbidden Stitch: an Asian American Women's Anthology* (Corvallis, OR: Calyx Books). Collection of stories and poems by and about Asian-American women's experience.

Golden, Marita (ed.) (1994) *Wild Women Don't Wear No Blues: Black Women Writers on Love, Men and Sex* (New York: Anchor Books). Includes essays from Bebe Moore Campell, Jewell Gomez, Audre Lorde, Sonia Sanchez, Ntozake Shange, and more.

Green, Rayna (ed.) (1984) *That's What She Said: Contemporary Poetry and Fiction by Native American Women* (Bloomington, IN: Indiana University Press).

Green, Rayna (1992) *Women in American Indian Society* (New York: Chelsea House). Readable and amply illustrated text describing Native American women's lives from the pre-colonialist invasion to speculations about the future for native women.

Greer, Germaine (1992) *Women, Changing, and the Menopause* (New York: Knopf). An account by a prominent second-stage feminist of the cultural status of aging women, especially the invisibility and other difficulties that middle-aged women in Western culture encounter.

Hemmons, Willa Mae (1996) *Women in the New World Order: Social Justice and the African American Female* (Westport, CT: Praeger). Lawyer examines the status of African-American women and the concept of the "new world order" using a socio-legal approach.

Hine, Darlene Clark, Brown, Elsa Barkley and Terborg-Penn, Rosalyn (eds) (1993) *Black Women in America: an Historical Encyclopedia* (Bloomington, IN: Indiana University Press). Accounts of significant American black women in fields as diverse as religion, music, welding, psychiatry, zoology, law, dance, government, medicine, slavery, and motherhood.

Hoff-Wilson, Joan (1991) *Law, Gender, and Injustice: a Legal History of US Women* (New York: New York University Press).

Hull, Gloria, Scott, Patricia Bell and Smith, Barbara (eds) (1982) *All the Women are White, All the Blacks are Men, But Some of Us are Brave: Black Women's Studies* (Old Westbury, NY: Feminist Press). Collection of essays by and about black women.

Jay, Karla (ed.) (1995) *Lesbian Erotics* (New York: New York University Press). Collection of essays on lesbian sexuality.

Kauffman, Linda (ed.) (1993) *American Feminist Thought at Century's End: a Reader* (Cambridge, MA: Blackwell). Part I on "Sexuality and Gender" includes articles by Gayle Rubin, bell hooks, and Tania Modleski on sexuality.

Kaufman, Gershen and Raphael, Lev (1996) *Coming Out of Shame: Transforming Gay and Lesbian Lives* (New York: Doubleday). Discusses the role of shame in shaping the identities of gays and lesbians and presents strategies for overcoming it.

Kesselman, Amy, McNair, Lily and Schniedewind, Nancy (eds) (1995) *Women: Images and Realities: a Multicultural Anthology* (Mountain View, CA: Mayfield). Anthology of readings in women's studies, containing a significant amount of material by women of color.

Lorber, Judith and Farell, Susan (eds) (1991) *The Social Construction of Gender* (Newbury Park, CA: Sage).

Lorde, Audre (1984) "Uses of the erotic," in *Sister Outsider: Essays and Speeches* (Trumansburg, NY: The Crossing Press).

McCormick, Naomi (1994) *Sexual Salvation: Affirming Women's Sexual Rights and Pleasures* (Westport, CT: Praeger). On women's sexuality. Contents include chapters on love and intimacy, lesbian and bisexual identities, women sex-trade workers, sexual victimization and pornography, women-affirming models of sexual fulfillment, and sexual rights and pleasures in the next century.

McKay, Nellie (1992) "Remembering Anita Hill and Clarence Thomas: what really happened when one black woman spoke out," in Toni Morrison (ed.), *Race-ing Justice, En-gendering Power: Essays on Anita Hill, Clarence Thomas, and the Construction of Social Reality* (New York: Pantheon Books).

Martin, Biddy and Mohanty, Chandra Talpade (1986) "Feminist politics: what's home got to do with it?," in Teresa de Lauretis (ed.), *Feminist Studies/Critical Studies* (Bloomington, IN: Indiana University Press). A meditation on the relationship of gender, race, and sexual orientation to home and community, using Minnie Bruce Pratt's autobiographical article (see below) as the point of departure.

Mason-John, Valerie (1995) *Talking Black: Lesbians of African and Asian Descent Speak Out* (New York: Cassell).

Moraga, Cherrie (1990) "La guera," in Gloria Anzaldúa (ed.), *Making Face, Making Soul = Haciendo Caras* (San Francisco: Aunt Lute Foundation Books). A moving autobiographical short story about the hardships faced by a young woman in attempting to cope with the facts of her difference: as a Mexican-American in a racist Anglo society, but as a light-skinned Latina in a dark-skinned family; as a women in a sexist society; as an intellectually gifted young woman in a culture that values females primarily as mothers; and as a lesbian in a homophobic society.

Moraga, Cherrie and Anzaldúa, Gloria (eds) (1981) *This Bridge Called my Back: Writings by Radical Women of Color* (Watertown, MA: Persephone Press). Similar, but earlier, collection of essays, stories, and poems by women of color to *Making Face, Making Soul*.

Pharr, Suzanne (1995) " 'Are you some kind of dyke?' The perils of heterosexism," in Amy Kessleman et al. (eds), *Women: Images and Realities – a Multicultural Anthology* (Mountain View, CA: Mayfield). Informative article about the harm that homophobia and heterosexism causes to lesbians.

Pratt, Minnie Bruce (1984) "Identity: skin blood heart," in Elly Bulkin, Minnie Bruce Pratt and Barbara Smith (eds), *Yours in Struggle: Three Feminist Perspectives on Anti-semitism and Racism* (New York: Long Haul Press). This is a heartfelt autobiographical account of a (self-described) Southern white Christian lesbian mother who has lost custody of her children to her ex-husband, and her attempt to come to terms with the racism, classism, homophobia, and other injustices of her society, and to regain self-respect as a result of being implicated in those injustices.

Raymond, Diane (ed.) (1990) *Sexual Politics and Popular Culture* (Bowling Green, OH: Bowling Green State University Popular Press). Includes sections on desire and sexuality, sexuality and the family, sexuality and images of women, and sexuality and politics.

Rich, Adrienne (1986) "Compulsory heterosexuality and lesbian existence," in *Blood, Bread, and Poetry: Selected Prose, 1979–1985* (New York: W. W. Norton).

Roney, Frances (ed.) (1992) *Our Lives: Lesbian Personal Writings* (Ontario: Second Story Press). Anthology of writing by lesbians of different ages, experiences, cultural, and economic backgrounds on their personal lives.

Rothblum, Esther D. (ed.) (1996) *Classics in Lesbian Studies* (Binghamton, NY: Harrington Park Press).

Rothenberg, Paula, (ed.) (1992) *Race, Class, and Gender in the United States: an Integrated Study*, 2nd edn (New York: St Martin's Press). Collection of readings, organized under the headings: "Defining 'racism' and 'sexism'," "Bias incidents and harassment," "The economics of race, gender, and class in the United States," Many voices, many lives," "How it happened: race and gender issues in US law," "Creating and maintaining hierarchy," and "Revisioning the future."

Smith, Barbara (1982) "Racism and women's studies," in Gloria Hull, Patricia Bell Scott, and Barbara Smith (eds), *All the Women are White, All the Blacks are Men, But Some of Us are Brave: Black Women's Studies* (Old Westbury, NY: Feminist Press). An early voice from a woman of color observing the need for the mainstream women's movement to confront its racism and homophobia.

Smith, Barbara (ed.) (1983) *Home Girls: a Black Feminist Anthology* (New York: Kitchen Table – Women of Color Press). Collection of essays, stories, and poems by black women writers, many of them with lesbian themes.

Smith-Rosenberg, Carroll (1975) "The female world of love and ritual: relations between women in nineteenth-century America," *Signs: Journal of Women in Culture and Society*, 1(1): 1–29 (excerpted in Chapter 9). Describes the intense friendships between women in nineteenth-century America that were arguably "lesbian" in character.

Spelman, Elizabeth (1991) "Simone de Beauvoir and women: just who does she think 'we' is?," in Mary Shanley and Carole Pateman (eds), *Feminist Interpretations and Political Theory* (University Park, PA: Penn State Press).

Taeuber, Cynthia (ed.) (1991) *Statistical Handbook on Women in America* (Phoenix, AZ: Oryx Press). *Lots* of statistics on many different aspects of women's health, marital, childbearing, education, and employment status, and so on, which generally provides breakdowns in accordance with significant differences among women, such as age, race, and ethnicity.

Unger, Rhoda and Crawford, Mary (1992) *Women and Gender: a Feminist Psychology* (New York: McGraw-Hill). Sections on various aspects of female sexuality.

University of Wisconsin System Women's Studies Librarian (1991) *Women, Race, and Ethnicity: a Bibliography* (Madison, WI: University of Wisconsin). Divided by general subjects and by categories of women, including African-American, Latina, Asian-American, Native American, and Caucasian.

Vance, Carole (1984) *Pleasure and Danger: Exploring Female Sexuality* (Boston: Routledge and Kegal Paul). Essays and poems originating in a 1982 conference. Readings explore the tension between sexual danger and sexual pleasure in feminist theory and in women's lives during the past 10 years in Euro-America.

Vicinus, Martha (ed.) (1996) *Lesbian Subjects: a Feminist Studies Reader* (Bloomington, IN: Indiana University Press).

Zinn, Maxine Baca and Dill, Bonnie Thornton (eds) (1994) *Women of Color in US Society* (Philadelphia: Temple University Press). Essays cover the social location of black women and other women of color in education, work, family, prison, urban living, community work, and migration. Part 6, entitled "Rethinking gender," covers images, ideology, and women of color. Challenges the assumption that women can have a sisterhood based on universal commonalities.

3

Cultural Representations of Women

Introduction

We are inundated by representations of women in our daily lives. These representations are produced by the mass media – advertisements, magazines, television, and cinema – as well as emerging in other aspects of culture, such as myths and fairy-tales, fine art and literature, and religion. In chapters 4 and 5, we will be looking more closely at representations of women in popular culture. In this chapter, we will focus on more traditional cultural images and representations of women.

An *image* is a form of expression, a way of seeing, as John Berger (1977: 10) points out in *Ways of Seeing*, an excerpt from which is given as the first reading. As images are usually reproductions or recreations of a sight or appearance, they are detached from their site of origin. The meaning of an image depends on the symbolic associations of the individuals perceiving it. Thus, images are linked to knowledge and beliefs in a complex relationship. Although images of men and women vary across cultures as well as within the same culture over time, in particular contexts they are seen as universal, as providing models for how all men and women should be.

Images of women and men are significant aspects of gender construction: they dictate what women and men should look like and how they should behave. Gender images tend to be *internalized* by males and females and provide the basis for individual identities. John Berger explains that these images accompany women continually, as they are taught from early childhood to see themselves as others see them. Women are usually concerned about their appearance "because how she appears to others, and ultimately how she appears to men, is of crucial importance for what is normally thought of as the success in her life" (Berger, 1977: 46).

In *Women, Art, and Power, and Other Essays*, Linda Nochlin (1988) describes the way in which representations of women in fine art have functioned to reproduce cultural assumptions about women, male difference from women, and male superiority, power and control over women. She explains how fine art has functioned as a form of *ideology*, which masks the actual workings of power in society by representing existing social relations as part of a natural, logical, or eternal order (Nochlin, 1988: 1–2). As John Berger also discusses in *Ways of Seeing*, many paintings in earlier centuries reflect an assumption that men are naturally "entitled" to control and possess women's bodies.

Certain generalizations can be made about the way in which images of women function in different aspects of American culture. As we saw in chapter 1, one generalization is that women are weaker, less intelligent, more connected to nature and biology than men, and thus subordinate and inferior to males. Masculine characteristics, however they have been defined in a particular context, have been viewed as more desirable and valuable than feminine characteristics. It is also possible to make some generalizations about the particular images and stereotypes of women:

- Women are more often represented in terms of their bodies.
- Women are more often evaluated on the basis of physical appearance and attractiveness.
- Women's appearances are scrutinized more closely and held to higher standards.
- Women who are not considered "feminine," especially older women and disabled women, are frequently not represented at all, and are thereby rendered invisible as "real" women.

In addition, images of women in American culture are frequently polarized into extreme opposites. One prominent example is the "Madonna" and the "whore," a prevalent pair of images that have been imposed on women for hundreds of years. Women associated with the Madonna are idealized and sentimentalized as pure, good, modest, at once virginal and maternal (somewhat of a logical contradiction!). In stark contrast, women associated with the whore are disdained and treated with contempt as sexually promiscuous and manipulative temptresses (see Itzin, 1992: 58). Women who fail to fit the Madonna image are labeled as whores or lesbians for refusing to conform to the prescribed parameters of women's sexuality.

A *stereotype* is a culturally determined picture that reflects a prejudiced view of persons based on a single characteristic or set of characteristics. Stereotypes are categories of thought that are used to simplify complex social reality. They influence what we pay attention to and think about what we perceive. The advantages of stereotypes, in making social life more intelligible, and thus manageable, are also shortcomings, since the process of stereotyping *distorts* social reality. Stereotypes replace the complexity of actual lives with simplistic evaluations based on limited information, such as only someone's appearance.

Stereotypes frequently attribute characteristics to individuals based on their identity as a member of a particular group or class, as in "single white female," "gay black male," and so on, and ignore those characteristics that make them a distinctive, unique person. Stereotypes thereby provide the basis for discriminating against individuals on the basis of characteristics that they may or may not share with some group they are a member of.

Members of some groups, like women, the poor, and racial and ethnic minorities, tend to be stereotyped more than others because of their relative lack of social and political power. Stereotypes also help to perpetuate the relative powerlessness of members of certain groups by making it more difficult for them to define themselves. By defining the stereotyped group as outside of or deviant from what is considered normal, stereotypes can be used as forms of social control. In addition, stereotypes are difficult to dislodge, and often persist in the face of contrary evidence. Stereotypes may act as self-fulfilling prophecies by making it difficult for those who are stereotyped to escape from being defined, and thus to define themselves, in terms of the characteristics contained in the stereotype.

Gender stereotypes, in particular, include assumptions about male and female traits, behaviors, roles, and so on, that are widely held, persistent, and based on traditional or conventional understandings. Gender stereotypes are prescriptive as well as descriptive; that is, they instruct males and females about how they *should* look, behave, and feel, as well as how they actually *do* appear, act, feel, and so on.

The acquisition of gender stereotypes typically begins in childhood, by the age of 5. Because there are so few gender-free images to contrast them with, they often appear to be *natural* rather than culturally constructed. Gender stereotypes are often identified with a number of other characteristics that are frequently unrelated to biological sex. They often interact with other stereotypes about persons, especially those based on race, class, ethnicity, religion, and sexual orientation to prescribe what persons in a particular social location are like.

Although representations, images, and stereotypes may not directly *cause* people to act in a particular way, they provide a source of ideas that may influence how people think and therefore how they will act. By defining what the universe of available options is, culture shapes what is thinkable and achievable. Images and stereotypes of women thereby confine real women within certain boundaries by defining them as having certain prescribed characteristics. In addition, representations provide women with images and stereotypes of how to be feminine, and thus succeed at being "real" women. Women internalize the images and stereotypes that culture expects them to conform to.

Catherine Itzin explains that "women are conditioned to conform to the stereotyped images of femininity and womanhood in such a way that they are often unaware that they are misrepresented and mistreated" (Itzin, 1992: 62). The systematic subordination of women is dependent upon individual women's internalization of their oppression by coming to believe that they are less valuable, deserving, intelligent, and worthy of care and respect than others. Images and stereotypes consequently shape our cultural reality as well as influence our self-identity and self-esteem. They also provide models which we internalize, and by which we measure our social acceptability.

In addition to visual representations, language generates stereotyped portrayals of women. Language is the primary means by which a culture is transmitted, both to its members as well as to those of other cultures. As part of this process, language provides a particular kind of image that powerfully shapes our understanding of and attitudes toward gender. Until recently, the English language has been *androcentric* (male-centered) rather than gender neutral and non-sexist.

Among the prominent gendered characteristics of the English language concerning gender is that the feminine is included within the masculine. Unlike many languages, which have separate male and female genders, in English, the masculine is inclusive of both genders and is considered to be gender neutral. Thus, English uses "mankind" to refer to humans generally, whereas "womankind" is restricted to females. The problem with this is that male-gendered language evokes images of males, not of humans generally. Another problem is that the English language is used to portray females negatively – as immature, incompetent, and incapable – but males positively – as competent, capable, and mature. In addition, males are linguistically defined in terms of their sexual prowess (over women), while women are defined as the sexual objects of men's desire.[1]

Certainly, there is no single image or set of images of women in American culture. Rather, there is a whole range of types of images. As with every aspect of our exploration of women in culture, it is important to keep in mind the way that race, socioeconomic status or class, and other significant differences alter the status and experiences of women at different times and social locations. This applies to images and stereotypes of women as well. Because of racism, women of color are often stereotyped as "whores" rather than Madonnas, regardless of whether they are mothers. This has begun to change in recent years as more African-American, Latina, and Asian-American women are employed as public figures, political leaders, television personalities, newscasters, fashion models and actresses, and as more women of color gain recognition for their artistic, scientific, academic, and other accomplishments. For example, books like Darlene Clark Hine's *Black Women in America: an Historical Encyclopedia* (Hine et al., 1993) provides a wealth of positive images of American black women to counterpose to prevailing stereotypes. Yet, for the time being, there remain few images of women of color that can provide role models for young girls.

Negative images and stereotypes of women have changed very little as a result of the women's movement.

Ethnic, racial, and other cultural groups may have images of women that contradict those of the dominant culture. Ideals of femininity have varied in accordance with race, class, and regional considerations. For example, the image of the frail, delicate lady that characterized white, middle- and upper-class women of the nineteenth century was not applied to African-American women, Native American women, or other women of color. Rather, such women have often been defined by conflicting images imposed on them by men of either the dominant culture or their own cultural group. As an example of the former, in an essay entitled "The Pocahontas perplex," Rayna Green (1990), a Native American woman, describes the dominant image of Native American women at the time of first contact with European explorers as willing to betray the men of their tribe in order to assist the white man. This image is promoted in the Disney movie *Pocahontas*. Green also demonstrates that polarized images are present in the contrast between this image of the "good" Indian princess and that of the "bad" squaw, who is maligned for having sex with the white man (Green, 1975: 153). Both images are products of white society. They function to severely limit the ability of Native Americans to represent themselves as Other than the stereotypes of princess or squaw.

Another example of female images being defined by the dominant culture has occurred with portrayals of black women as mothers. The "good woman" is a matriarch: a strong, hard-working and long-suffering woman able to keep her family together even in the absence of a husband or father for her children. The "bad woman" is a welfare mother, lazy, drug-addicted, with too many children. As an example of female stereotyping by males of the same cultural group, Marcia Gillespie describes the prevalent images of black women during the civil rights and black power eras of the 1960s and 1970s, respectively, illustrating how images of women differ both cross-culturally and across time:

> We were castrating bitches if we complained or questioned men's actions or decisions. We were "Good Sisters" if we dutifully followed orders, or mouthed the party line laid down by the brothers. We were "Strong Black Women" if we spoke out against racism but never about sexism, if we shouldered the burden for raising families on our own and placed all blame for the lack of male responsibility on racism. (Gillespie, 1993: 81)

Such stereotypes may create a double bind for women of color, who are torn between the ideal images of their own cultural group and those of the dominant culture. For example, Paula Gunn Allen, a mixed Native American and Caucasian woman, says of herself and the Native American women she knows:

"We vacillate between being dependent and strong, self-reliant and powerless, strongly motivated and hopelessly insecure" (Allen, 1986).

Why are there so many negative images of women? One reason is that throughout much of history, and in most cultures, men have controlled the means of creating representations: the financial prerequisites, the determination of who would be recognized as an artist or writer, and so on. Perhaps if women had been in control of these images, they would differ. This answer, however, fails to address *why* men have wanted to portray women in negative ways. Power and control is one answer, the one that feminist scholars such as Faludi and Wolf would suggest.

In the second reading in this chapter, feminist philosopher Marilyn Friedman discusses the ethics of care and of justice as based on gender stereotypes about, respectively, women and men, that do not correspond to distinct moral practices. Friedman argues for the necessity of moving beyond gender stereotypes that connect "distinct and different moral roles to women and men."

As feminist work has unveiled the power relationships that function in relation to representations of women in art and other media, they have also begun to attend more to women as viewers and consumers of these images of themselves: must women passively accept the prevailing images of themselves or is it possible for them to be "resisting readers" or viewers, refusing to be defined or to define themselves in terms of these prevailing images? Some feminists and social critics, like John Berger, argue that the dominant perspective or way of seeing in our culture is through the *male gaze* or with the perception of the *male spectator*. This means that, because the male perspective is the dominant one in society, women come to view the world as men do, especially themselves and other women.

More recently, some feminists have challenged the assumption of the male gaze (or at least its inevitability), as we will see in the following two chapters. Feminists have been working to unravel the puzzle of how images interact with the reality they represent. More specifically, they have sought ways of empowering women to "revision" their world: to look beyond the images of themselves that are most prevalent in popular culture to conceptualize new and empowering ways for women to be both viewers and viewed.

Note

1   In addition to the way in which language is structured, gender inequalities also exist in the ways that language is used. Studies show that men talk more than women, frequently dominating conversations and often interrupting others, especially women who are attempting to talk. Thus, using language and controlling conversations are another way that men assert power and control over women (see Richardson, 1993).

Ways of Seeing (excerpt)
John Berger

According to usage and conventions which are at last being questioned but have by no means been overcome, the social presence of a woman is different in kind from that of a man. A man's presence is dependent upon the promise of power which he embodies. If the promise is large and credible his presence is striking. If it is small or incredible, he is found to have little presence. The promised power may be moral, physical, temperamental, economic, social, sexual – but its object is always exterior to the man. A man's presence suggests what he is capable of doing to you or for you. His presence may be fabricated, in the sense that he pretends to be capable of what he is not. But the pretense is always toward a power which he exercises on others.

By contrast, a woman's presence expresses her own attitude to herself, and defines what can and cannot be done to her. Her presence is manifest in her gestures, voice, opinions, expressions, clothes, chosen surroundings, taste – indeed, there is nothing she can do which does not contribute to her presence. Presence for a woman is so intrinsic to her person that men tend to think of it as an almost physical emanation, a kind of heat or smell or aura.

To be born a woman has been to be born, within an allotted and confined space, into the keeping of men. The social presence of women has developed as a result of their ingenuity in living under such tutelage within such a limited space. But this has been at the cost of a woman's self being split into two. A woman must continually watch herself. She is almost continually accompanied by her own image of herself. Whilst she is walking across a room or whilst she is weeping at the death of her father, she can scarcely avoid envisaging herself walking or weeping. From earliest childhood she has been taught and persuaded to survey herself continually.

And so she comes to consider the *surveyor* and the *surveyed* within her as the two constituent yet always distinct elements of her identity as a woman.

She has to survey everything she is and everything she does because how she appears to others, and ultimately how she appears to men, is of crucial importance for what is normally thought of as the success of her life. Her own sense of being in herself is supplanted by a sense of being appreciated as herself by another.

This reading first appeared in *Ways of Seeing* by John Berger (New York: Penguin Books, 1977), pp. 45–64.

Men survey women before treating them. Consequently, how a woman appears to a man can determine how she will be treated. To acquire some control over this process, women must contain it and interiorize it. That part of a woman's self which is the surveyor treats the part which is the surveyed so as to demonstrate to others how her whole self would like to be treated. And this exemplary treatment of herself by herself constitutes her presence. Every woman's presence regulates what is and is not "permissible" within her presence. Every one of her actions – whatever its direct purpose or motivation – is also read as an indication of how she would like to be treated. If a woman throws a glass on the floor, this is an example of how she treats her own emotion of anger and so of how she would wish it to be treated by others. If a man does the same, his action is only read as an expression of his anger. If a woman makes a good joke, this is an example of how she treats the joker in herself and accordingly of how she as a joker-woman would like to be treated by others. Only a man can make a good joke for its own sake.

One might simplify this by saying: *men act* and *women appear*. Men look at women. Women watch themselves being looked at. This determines not only most relations between men and women but also the relation of women to themselves. The surveyor of woman in herself is male: the surveyed female. Thus she turns herself into an object – and most particularly an object of vision: a sight.

In one category of European oil painting, women were the principal, ever-recurring subject. That category is the nude. In the nudes of European painting we can discover some of the criteria and conventions by which women have been seen and judged as sights.

The first nudes in the tradition depicted Adam and Eve. It is worth referring to the story as told in Genesis:

> And when the woman saw that the tree was good for food, and that it was a delight to the eyes, and that the tree was to be desired to make one wise, she took of the fruit thereof and did eat; and she gave also unto her husband with her, and he did eat.
> And the eyes of them both were opened, and they knew that they were naked; and they sewed fig-leaves together and made themselves aprons . . .
> And the Lord God called unto the man and said unto him, "Where are thou?" And he said, "I heard thy voice in the garden, and I was afraid, because I was naked; and I hid myself . . ."
> Unto the woman God said, "I will greatly multiply thy sorrow and thy conception; in sorrow thou shalt bring forth children; and thy desire shall be to thy husband and he shall rule over thee."

What is striking about this story? They became aware of being naked because, as a result of eating the apple, each saw the other differently. Nakedness was created in the mind of the beholder.

The second striking fact is that the woman is blamed and is punished by being made subservient to the man. In relation to the woman, the man becomes the agent of God.

In the medieval tradition, the story was often illustrated, scene following scene, as in a strip cartoon. During the Renaissance, the narrative sequence disappeared, and the single moment depicted became the moment of shame. The couple wear fig-leaves or make a modest gesture with their hands. But now their shame is not so much in relation to one another as to the spectator. Later, the shame becomes a kind of display.

When the tradition of painting became more secular, other themes also offered the opportunity of painting nudes. But in them all there remains the implication that the subject (a woman) is aware of being seen by a spectator. She is not naked as she is. She is naked as the spectator sees her.

Often – as with the favorite subject of Susannah and the Elders – this is the actual theme of the picture. We join the Elders to spy on Susannah taking her bath. She looks back at us looking at her. In another version of the subject by Tintoretto, Susannah is looking at herself in a mirror. Thus she joins the spectators of herself.

The mirror was often used as a symbol of the vanity of woman. The moralizing, however, was mostly hypocritical. You painted a naked woman because you enjoyed looking at her, you put a mirror in her hand and you called the painting *Vanity*, thus morally condemning the woman whose nakedness you had depicted for your own pleasure. The real function of the mirror was otherwise. It was to make the woman connive in treating herself as, first and foremost, a sight.

The Judgment of Paris was another theme with the same inwritten idea of a man or men looking at naked women. But a further element is now added: the element of judgment. Paris awards the apple to the woman he finds most beautiful. Thus beauty becomes competitive. (Today the Judgment of Paris has become the beauty contest.) Those who are not judged beautiful are *not beautiful*. Those who are, are given the prize.

The prize is to be owned by a judge – that is to say to be available for him. Charles II commissioned a secret painting from Lely. It is a highly typical image of the tradition. Nominally it might be a Venus and Cupid. In fact, it is a portrait of one of the King's mistresses, Nell Gwynne. It shows her passively looking at the spectator staring at her naked.

This nakedness is not, however, an expression of her own feelings; it is a sign of her submission to the owner's feelings or demands. (The owner of both woman and painting.) The painting, when the King showed it to others, demonstrated this submission and his guests envied him.

It is worth noticing that in other non-European traditions – in Indian art, Persian art, African art, pre-Columbian art – nakedness is never supine in this way. And if, in these traditions, the theme of a work is sexual attraction, it is likely to show active sexual love as between two people, the woman as active as the man, the actions of each absorbing the other.

We can now begin to see the difference between nakedness and nudity in the European tradition. In his book on *The Nude* Kenneth Clark maintains that to be naked is simply to be without clothes, whereas the nude is a form of art. According to him, a nude is not the starting point of a painting, but a way of seeing which the painting achieves. To some degree, this is true – although the way of seeing "a nude" is not necessarily confined to art: there are also nude photographs, nude poses, nude gestures. What is true is that the nude is always conventionalized – and the authority for its conventions derives from a certain tradition of art.

What do these conventions mean? What does a nude signify? It is not sufficient to answer these questions merely in terms of the art form, for it is quite clear that the nude also relates to lived sexuality. To be naked is to be oneself. To be nude is to be seen naked by others and yet not recognized for oneself. A naked body has to be seen as an object in order to become a nude. (The sight of it as an object stimulates the use of it as an object.) Nakedness reveals itself. Nudity is placed on display.

To be naked is to be without disguise. To be on display is to have the surface of one's own skin, the hairs of one's own body, turned into a disguise which, in that situation, can never be discarded. The nude is condemned to never being naked. Nudity is a form of dress.

In the average European oil painting of the nude the principal protagonist is never painted. He is the spectator in front of the picture and he is presumed to be a man. Everything is addressed to him. Everything must appear to be the result of his being there. It is for him that the figures have assumed their nudity. But he, by definition, is a stranger – with his clothes still on.

Consider the *Allegory of Time and Love* by Bronzino. The complicated symbolism which lies behind this painting need not concern us now because it does not affect its sexual appeal – at the first degree. Before it is anything else, this is a painting of sexual provocation.

The painting was sent as a present from the Grand Duke of Florence to the King of France. The boy kneeling on the cushion and kissing the woman is Cupid. She is Venus. But the way her body is arranged has nothing to do with their kissing. Her body is arranged in the way it is to display it to the man looking at the picture. This picture is made to appeal to *his* sexuality. It has nothing to do with her sexuality. (Here, and in the European tradition generally, the convention of not painting the hair on a woman's body helps toward the same end. Hair is associated with sexual power, with passion. The woman's sexual passion needs to be minimized so that the spectator may feel that he has the monopoly of such passion.) Women are there to feed an appetite, not to have any of their own.

Compare the expression of the model for a famous painting by Ingres (*La Grande Odalisque*) with that of a typical model in a girlie magazine. Is not the expression remarkably similar? It is the expression of a woman responding with calculated charm to the man whom she imagines looking at her – although she doesn't know him. She is offering up her femininity as the surveyed.

It is true that sometimes a painting includes a male lover. But the woman's attention is very rarely directed toward him. Often she looks away from him or she looks out of the picture toward the one who considers himself her true lover – the spectator-owner.

There was a special category of private pornographic painting (especially in the eighteenth century) in which couples making love make an appearance. But even in front of these it is clear that the spectator-owner will in fantasy oust the other man, or else identify with him. By contrast, the image of the couple in non-European traditions provokes the notion of many couples making love. "We all have a thousand hands, a thousand feet and will never go alone."

Almost all post-Renaissance European sexual imagery is frontal – either literally or metaphorically – because the sexual protagonist is the spectator-owner looking at it.

The absurdity of this male flattery reached its peak in the public academic art of the nineteenth century. Men of state, of business, discussed under paintings like *Les Oréades* by Bouguereau. When one of them felt he had been outwitted, he looked up for consolation. What he saw reminded him that he was a man.

There are a few exceptional nudes in the European tradition of oil painting to which very little of what has been said above applies. Indeed, they are no longer nudes – they break the norms of the art form; they are paintings of loved women, more or less naked. Among the hundreds of thousands of nudes which make up the tradition there are perhaps a hundred of these exceptions. In each case the painter's personal vision of the particular woman he is painting is so strong that it makes no allowance for the spectator. The painter's vision binds the woman to him so that they become as inseparable as couples in stone. The spectator can witness their relationship – but he can do no more: he is forced to recognize himself as the outsider he is. He cannot deceive himself into believing that she is naked for him. He cannot turn her into a nude. The way the painter has painted her includes her will and her intentions in the very structure of the image, in the very expression of her body and her face.

The typical and the exceptional in the tradition can be defined by the simple naked/nude antinomy, but the problem of painting nakedness is not as simple as it might at first appear.

What is the sexual function of nakedness in reality? Clothes encumber contact and movement. But it would seem that nakedness has a positive visual value in its own right: we want to *see* the other naked: the other delivers to us the sight of themselves and we seize upon it – sometimes quite regardless of whether it is for the first time or the hundredth. What does this sight of the other mean to us, how does it, at that instant of total disclosure, affect our desire?

Their nakedness acts as a confirmation and provokes a very strong sense of relief. She is a woman like any other; or he is a man like any other; we are overwhelmed by the marvellous simplicity of the familiar sexual mechanism. We did not, of course, consciously expect this to be otherwise: unconscious homosexual desires (or unconscious heterosexual desires if the couple concerned are homosexual) may have led each to half expect something different. But the "relief" can be explained without recourse to the unconscious.

We did not expect them to be otherwise, but the urgency and complexity of our feelings bred a sense of uniqueness which the sight of the other, as she is or as he is, now dispels. They are more like the rest of their sex than they are different. In this revelation lies the warm and friendly – as opposed to cold and impersonal – anonymity of nakedness.

One could express this differently: at the moment of nakedness first perceived, an element of banality enters – an element that exists only because we need it.

Up to that instant the other was more or less mysterious. Etiquettes of modesty are not merely puritan or sentimental: it is reasonable to recognize a loss of mystery. And the explanation of this loss of mystery may be largely visual. The focus of perception shifts from eyes, mouth, shoulders, hands – all of which are capable of such subtleties of expression that the personality expressed by them is manifold – it shifts from these to the sexual parts, whose formation suggests an utterly compelling but single process. The other is reduced or elevated – whichever you prefer – to their primary sexual category: male or female. Our relief is the relief of finding an unquestionable reality to whose direct demands our earlier highly complex awareness must now yield.

We need the banality which we find in the first instant of disclosure because it grounds us in reality. But it does more than that. This reality, by promising the familiar, proverbial mechanism of sex, offers, at the same time, the possibility of the shared subjectivity of sex.

The loss of mystery occurs simultaneously with the offering of the means for creating a shared mystery. The sequence is: subjective – objective – subjective to the power of two.

We can now understand the difficulty of creating a static image of sexual nakedness. In lived sexual experience nakedness is a process rather than a state. If one moment of that process is isolated, its image will seem banal and its banality, instead of serving as a bridge between two intense imaginative states, will be chilling. This is one reason why expressive photographs of the naked are even rarer than paintings. The easy solution for the photographer is to turn the figure into a nude which, by generalizing both sight and viewer and making sexuality unspecific, turns desire into fantasy.

Let us examine an exceptional painted image of nakedness. It is a painting by Rubens of his young second wife, Hélène Fourment, whom he married when he himself was relatively old. We see her in the act of turning, her fur about to slip off her shoulders. Clearly, she will not remain as she is for more than a second. In a superficial sense her image is as instantaneous as a photograph's. But, in a more profound sense, the painting "contains" time and its experience. It is easy to imagine that a moment ago, before she pulled the fur round her shoulders, she was entirely naked. The consecutive stages up to and away from the moment of total disclosure have been transcended. She can belong to any or all of them simultaneously.

Her body confronts us, not as an immediate sight, but as experience – the painter's experience. Why? There are superficial anecdotal reasons: her dishevelled hair, the expression of her eyes directed toward him, the tenderness with which the exaggerated susceptibility of her skin has been painted. But the profound reason is a formal one. Her appearance has been literally re-cast by the painter's subjectivity. Beneath the fur that she holds across herself, the upper part of her body and her legs can never meet. There is a displacement sideways of about nine inches: her thighs, in order to join on to her hips, are at least nine inches too far to the left.

Rubens probably did not plan this: the spectator may not consciously notice it. In itself it is unimportant. What matters is what it permits. It permits the body to become impossibly dynamic. Its coherence is no longer within itself but within the experience of the painter. More precisely, it permits the upper and lower halves of the body to rotate separately, and in opposite directions, round the sexual centre which is hidden: the torso turning to the right, the legs to the left. At the same time this hidden sexual centre is connected by means of the dark fur coat to all the surrounding darkness in the picture, so that she is turning both around and within the dark which has been made a metaphor for her sex.

Apart from the necessity of transcending the single instant and of admitting subjectivity, there is, as we have seen, one further element which is essential for any great sexual image of the naked. This is the element of banality which must be undisguised but not chilling. It is this which distinguishes between voyeur and lover. Here such banality is to be found in Rubens's compulsive painting of the fat softness of Hélène Fourment's flesh which continually breaks every ideal convention of form and (to him) continually offers the promise of her extraordinary particularity.

The nude in European oil painting is usually presented as an admirable expression of the European humanist spirit. This spirit was inseparable from individualism. And, without the development of a highly conscious individualism, the exceptions to the tradition (extremely personal images of the naked) would never have been painted. Yet the tradition contained a contradiction which it could not itself resolve. A few individual artists intuitively recognized this and resolved the contradiction in their own terms, but their solutions could never enter the tradition's *cultural* terms.

The contradiction can be stated simply: on the one hand, the individualism of the artist, the thinker, the patron, the owner; on the other hand, the person who is the object of their activities – the woman – treated as a thing or an abstraction.

Dürer believed that the ideal nude ought to be constructed by taking the face of one body, the breasts of another, the legs of a third, the shoulders of a fourth, the hands of a fifth – and so on. The result would glorify Man. But the exercise presumed a remarkable indifference to who any one person really was.

In the art form of the European nude the painters and spectator-owners were usually men and the persons treated as objects, usually women. This unequal relationship is so deeply embedded in our culture that it still structures the consciousness of many women. They do to themselves what men do to them. They survey, like men, their own femininity.

In modern art, the category of the nude has become less important. Artists themselves began to question it. In this, as in many other respects, Manet represented a turning point. If one compares his *Olympia* with Titian's original (*The Venus of Urbino*), one sees a woman, cast in the traditional role, beginning to question that role, somewhat defiantly.

The ideal was broken. But there was little to replace it except the "realism" of the prostitute – who became the quintessential woman of early avant-garde twentieth-century painting (Toulouse-Lautrec, Picasso, Rouault, German Expressionism, etc.). In academic painting, the tradition continued.

Today, the attitudes and values which informed that tradition are expressed through other more widely diffused media – advertising, journalism, television. But the essential way of seeing women, the essential use to which their images are put, has not changed. Women are depicted in a quite different way from men – not because the feminine is different from the masculine – but because the "ideal" spectator is always assumed to be male and the image of the woman is designed to flatter him. If you have any doubt that this is so, make the following experiment. Choose an image of a traditional nude. Transform the woman into a man – either in your mind's eye or by drawing on a reproduction. Then notice the violence which that transformation does. Not to the image, but to the assumptions of a likely viewer.

Beyond Caring:
the De-moralization of Gender
Marilyn Friedman

Carol Gilligan heard a "distinct moral language" in the voices of women who were subjects in her studies of moral reasoning.[1] Though herself a developmental psychologist, Gilligan has put her mark on contemporary feminist moral philosophy by daring to claim the competence of this voice and the worth of its message. Her book, *In a Different Voice*, which one theorist has aptly described as a bestseller,[2] explored the concern with care and relationships which Gilligan discerned in the moral reasoning of women and contrasted it with the orientation toward justice and rights which she found to typify the moral reasoning of men.

According to Gilligan, the standard (or "male") moral voice articulated in moral psychology derives moral judgments about particular cases from abstract, universalized moral rules and principles which are substantively concerned with justice and rights. For justice reasoners: the major moral imperative enjoins respect for the rights of others (p. 100); the concept of duty is limited to reciprocal non-interference (p. 147); the motivating vision

This reading first appeared in *Science, Morality, and Feminist Theory*, eds M. Haner and K. Nielsen, *Canadian Journal of Philosophy*, suppl. vol. 13 (1987), pp. 87–105.

is one of the equal worth of self and other (p. 63); and one important underlying presupposition is a highly individuated conception of persons.

By contrast, the other (or "female") moral voice which Gilligan heard in her studies eschews abstract rules and principles. This moral voice derives moral judgments from the contextual detail of situations grasped as specific and unique (p. 100). The substantive concern for this moral voice is care and responsibility, particularly as these arise in the context of interpersonal relationships (p. 19). Moral judgments, for care reasoners, are tied to feelings of empathy and compassion (p. 69); the major moral imperatives center around caring, not hurting others, and avoiding selfishness (p. 90); and the motivating vision of this ethic is "that everyone will be responded to and included, that no one will be left alone or hurt" (p. 63).

While these two voices are not necessarily contradictory in all respects, they seem, at the very least, to be different in their orientation. Gilligan's writings about the differences have stimulated extensive feminist reconsideration of various ethical themes.[3] In this paper, I use Gilligan's work as a springboard for extending certain of those themes in new directions . . . I will explore a different reason why actual women and men may not show a divergence of reasoning along the care–justice dichotomy, namely, that the notions of care and justice overlap more than Gilligan, among others, has realized. I will suggest, in particular, that morally adequate care involves considerations of justice. Thus, the concerns captured by these two moral categories do not define necessarily distinct moral perspectives, in practice . . . People who treat each other justly can also care about each other. Conversely, personal relationships are arenas in which people have rights to certain forms of treatment, and in which fairness can be reflected in ongoing interpersonal mutuality. It is this latter insight – the relevance of justice to close personal relationships – which I will emphasize here.

Justice, at the most general level, is a matter of giving people their due, of treating them appropriately. Justice is relevant to personal relationships and to care precisely to the extent that considerations of justice itself determine appropriate ways to treat friends or intimates. Justice, as it bears on relationships among friends or family, or on other close personal ties, might not involve duties which are universalizable, in the sense of being owed to all persons simply in virtue of shared moral personhood. But this does not entail the irrelevance of justice among friends or intimates.

Moral thinking has not always dissociated the domain of justice from that of close personal relationships. The earliest Greek code of justice placed friendship at the forefront of conditions for the realization of justice, and construed the rules of justice as being coextensive with the limits of friendship. The reader will recall that one of the first definitions of justice which

Plato sought to contest, in the *Republic*, is that of "helping one's friends and harming one's enemies."[4] Although the ancient Greek model of justice among friends reserved that moral privilege for free-born Greek males, the conception is, nevertheless, instructive for its readiness to link the notion of justice to relationships based on affection and loyalty. This provides an important contrast to modern notions of justice which are often deliberately constructed so as to avoid presumptions of mutual concern on the part of those to whom the conception is to apply.

As is well known, John Rawls, for one, requires that the parties to the original position in which justice is to be negotiated be mutually disinterested.[5] Each party is assumed, first and foremost, to be concerned for the advancement of her own interests, and to care about the interests of others only to the extent that her own interests require it. This postulate of mutual disinterestedness is intended by Rawls to ensure that the principles of justice do not depend on what he calls "strong assumptions," such as "extensive ties of natural sentiment."[6] Rawls is seeking principles of justice which apply to everyone in all their social interrelationships, *whether or not* character-ized by affection and a concern for each other's well-being. While such an account promises to disclose duties of justice owed to all other parties to the social contract, it may fail to uncover *special* duties of justice which arise in close personal relationships the foundation of which is affection or kin-ship, rather than contract. The methodological device of assuming mutual disinterest might blind us to the role of justice among mutually interested and/or intimate parties.

Gilligan herself has suggested that mature reasoning about care incorpor-ates considerations of justice and rights. But Gilligan's conception of what this means is highly limited. It appears to involve simply the recognition "that self and other are equal," a notion which serves to override the problematic tendency of the ethic of care to become *self-sacrificing* care in women's practices. However, important as it may be, this notion hardly does justice to justice.

There are several ways in which justice pertains to close personal relation-ships. The first two ways which I will mention are largely appropriate only among friends, relatives, or intimates who are of comparable development in their realization of moral personhood, for example, who are both mature responsible adults. The third sort of relevance of justice to close relation-ships, which I will discuss shortly, pertains to families, in which adults often interrelate with children – a more challenging domain for the application of justice. But first the easier task.

One sort of role for justice in close relationships among people of com-parable moral personhood may be discerned by considering that a personal relationship is a miniature social system, which provides valued mutual intimacy, support, and concern for those who are involved. The maintenance of a relationship requires effort by the participants. One intimate may bear a much greater burden for sustaining a relationship than the other participant(s) and may derive less support, concern, and so forth than she deserves for her efforts. Justice sets a constraint on such relationships by calling for an appropriate sharing, among the participants, of the benefits and burdens which constitute their relationship.

Marilyn Frye, for example, has discussed what amounts to a pattern of *violation* of this requirement of justice in heterosexual relationships. She has argued that women of all races, social classes, and societies can be defined as a coherent group in terms of a distinctive function which is culturally assigned to them. This function is, in Frye's words, "the service of men and men's interests as men define them."[7] This service work includes personal service (satisfaction of routine bodily needs, such as hunger, and other mundane tasks), sexual and reproductive service, and ego service. Says Frye, "at every race/class level and even across race/class lines men do not serve women as women serve men."[8] Frye is, of course, generalizing over society and culture, and the sweep of her generalization encompasses both ongoing close personal relationships as well as other relationships which are not close or are not carried on beyond specific transactions; for example, that of prostitute to client. By excluding those latter cases for the time being, and applying Frye's analysis to familial and other close ties between women and men, we may discern the sort of one-sided relational exploitation, often masquerading in the guise of love or care, which constitutes this first sort of injustice.

Justice is relevant to close personal relationships among comparable moral persons in a second way as well. The trust and intimacy which characterize special relationships create special vulnerabilities to harm. Commonly recognized harms, such as physical injury and sexual assault, become more feasible; and special relationships, in corrupt, abusive, or degenerate forms, make possible certain uncommon emotional harms not even possible in impersonal relationships. When someone is harmed in a personal relationship, she is owed a rectification of some sort, a righting of the wrong that has been done her. The notion of justice emerges, once again, as a relevant moral notion.

Thus, in a close relationship among persons of comparable moral personhood, care may degenerate into the injustices of exploitation or oppression. Many such problems have been given wide public scrutiny recently as a result of feminist analysis of various aspects of family life and sexual relationships. Woman-battering, acquaintance rape, and sexual harassment are but a few of the many recently publicized injustices of "personal" life. The

notion of distributive or corrective injustice seems almost too mild to cap-
ture these indignities, involving, as they do, violation of bodily integrity and
an assumption of the right to assault and injure. But to call these harms
injustices is certainly not to rule out impassioned moral criticism in other
terms as well.

The two requirements of justice which I have just discussed exemplify the
standard distinction between distributive and corrective justice. They illustrate the role of justice in personal relationships regarded in abstraction from
a social context. Personal relationships may also be regarded in the context
of their various institutional settings, such as marriage and family. Here
justice emerges again as a relevant ideal, its role being to define appropriate
institutions to structure interactions among family members, other household cohabitants, and intimates in general. The family, for example,[9] is a
miniature society, exhibiting all the major facets of large-scale social life:
decision-making affecting the whole unit; executive action; judgments of
guilt and innocence; reward and punishment; allocation of responsibilities
and privileges, of burdens and benefits; and monumental influences on the
life chances of both its maturing and its matured members. Any of these
features *alone* would invoke the relevance of justice; together, they make
the case overwhelming.

Women's historically paradigmatic role of mothering has provided a
multitude of insights which can be reconstructed as insights about the
importance of justice in family relationships, especially those relationships
involving remarkable disparities in maturity, capability, and power.[10] In these
familial relationships, one party grows into moral personhood over time,
gradually acquiring the capacity to be a responsible moral agent. Considerations of justice pertain to the mothering of children in numerous ways. For
one thing, there may be siblings to deal with, whose demands and conflicts
create the context for parental arbitration and the need for a fair allotment
of responsibilities and privileges. Then there are decisions to be made,
involving the well-being of all persons in the family unit, whose immature
members become increasingly capable over time of participating in such
administrative affairs. Of special importance in the practice of raising children are the duties to nurture and to promote growth and maturation.
These duties may be seen as counterparts to the welfare rights viewed by
many as a matter of social justice.[11] Motherhood continually presents its
practitioners with moral problems best seen in terms of a complex framework which integrates justice with care, even though the politico-legal discourse of justice has not shaped its domestic expression.[12]

I have been discussing the relevance of justice to close personal relationships. A few words about my companion thesis – the relevance of care to

the public domain – is also in order.[13] In its more noble manifestation, care in the public realm would show itself, perhaps, in foreign aid, welfare programs, famine or disaster relief, or other social programs designed to relieve suffering and attend to human needs. If untempered by justice in the public domain, care degenerates precipitously. The infamous "boss" of Chicago's old-time Democratic machine, Mayor Richard J. Daley, was legendary for his nepotism and political partisanship; he cared extravagantly for his relatives, friends, and political cronies.[14]

In recounting the moral reasoning of one of her research subjects, Gilligan once wrote that the "justice" perspective fails "to take into account the reality of relationships" (p. 147). What she meant is that the "justice" perspective emphasizes a self's various rights to non-interference by others. Gilligan worried that if this is all that a concern for justice involved, then such a perspective would disregard the moral value of positive interaction, connection, and commitment among persons.

However, Gilligan's interpretation of justice is far too limited. For one thing, it fails to recognize positive rights, such as welfare rights, which may be endorsed from a "justice" perspective. But beyond this minor point, a more important problem is Gilligan's failure to acknowledge the potential for *violence and harm* in human interrelationships and human community.[15] The concept of justice, in general, arises out of relational conditions in which most human beings have the capacity, and many have the inclination, to treat each other badly.

Thus, notions of distributive justice are impelled by the realization that people who together comprise a social system may not share fairly in the benefits and burdens of their social cooperation. Conceptions of rectificatory, or corrective, justice are founded on the concern that when harms are done, action should be taken either to restore those harmed as fully as possible to their previous state, or to prevent further similar harm, or both. And the specific rights which people are variously thought to have are just so many manifestations of our interest in identifying ways in which people deserve protection against harm by others. The complex reality of social life encompasses the human potential for helping, caring for, and nurturing others *as well as* the potential for harming, exploiting, and oppressing others. Thus, Gilligan is wrong to think that the justice perspective completely neglects "the reality of relationships." Rather, it arises from a more complex, and more realistic, estimate of the nature of human interrelationships.

In light of these reflections, it seems wise both to reconsider the seeming dichotomy of care and justice, and to question the moral adequacy of either orientation dissociated from the other. Our aim would be to advance "beyond caring," that is, beyond *mere* caring dissociated from a concern for justice. In addition, we would do well to progress beyond gender stereotypes which assign distinct and different moral roles to women and men. Our ultimate goal should be a non-gendered, non-dichotomized, moral framework in which all moral concerns could be expressed. We might, with intentional irony, call this project, "de-moralizing the genders."

Notes

1 *In a Different Voice* (Cambridge, MA: Harvard University Press, 1982), p. 73. More recently, the following works by Gilligan on related issues have also appeared: "Do the social sciences have an adequate theory of moral development?" in Norma Haan, Robert N. Bellah, Paul Rabinow, and William M. Sullivan (eds), *Social Science as Moral Inquiry* (New York: Columbia University Press, 1983), pp. 33–51; "Reply," *Signs*, 11 (1986), pp. 324–33; and "Remapping the moral domain: new images of the self in relationship," in Thomas C. Heller, Morton Sosna, and David E. Wellbery (eds), *Reconstructing Individualism* (Stanford, CA: Stanford University Press, 1986), pp. 237–52. Throughout this paper, all page references inserted in the text are to *In a Different Voice*.

2 Frigga Haug, "Morals also have two genders," trans. Rodney Livingstone, *New Left Review*, 143 (1984), p. 55.

3 These sources include Owen J. Flanagan, Jr and Jonathan E. Adler, "Impartiality and particularity," *Social Research*, 50 (1983), pp. 576–96; Nel Noddings, *Caring* (Berkeley: University of California Press, 1984); Claudia Card, "Virtues and moral luck," unpublished paper presented at the American Philosophical Association, Western Division Meetings, Chicago, IL, April 1985, and at the Conference on Virtue Theory, University of San Diego, San Diego, CA, February 1986; Marilyn Friedman, *Care and Context in Moral Reasoning*, MOSAIC Monograph no. 1 (Bath, England: University of Bath, 1985), reprinted in Carol Harding (ed), *Moral Dilemmas* (Chicago: Precedent, 1986), pp. 25–42, and in Diana T. Meyers and Eva Feder Kittay (eds), *Women and Moral Theory* (Totowa, NJ: Rowman and Littlefield, 1987), pp. 190–204; all the papers in Meyers and Kittay; Linda K. Kerber, "Some cautionary words for historians," *Signs*, 11 (1986), pp. 304–10; Catherine G. Greeno and Eleanor E. Maccoby, "How different is the 'different voice'?," *Signs*, 11 (1986), pp. 310–16; Zella Luria, "A methodological critique," *Signs*, 11 (1986), pp. 316–21; Carol B. Stack, "The culture of gender: women and men of color," *Signs*, 11 (1986), pp. 321–4; Owen Flanagan and Kathryn Jackson, "Justice, care, and gender: the Kohlberg–Gilligan debate revisited," *Ethics*, 97 (1987), pp. 622–37. An analysis of this issue from an ambiguously feminist standpoint is to be found in John M. Broughton, "Women's rationality and men's virtues," *Social Research*, 50 (1983), pp. 597–642. For a helpful review of some of these issues, cf. Jean Grimshaw, *Philosophy and Feminist Thinking* (Minneapolis: University of Minnesota Press, 1986), esp. chs 7 and 8.

4   Book 1, 322–35. A thorough discussion of the Greek conception of justice in the context of friendship can be found in Horst Hutter, *Politics as Friendship* (Waterloo, ON: Wilfrid Laurier University Press, 1978).
5   J. Rawls, *A Theory of Justice* (Cambridge, MA: Harvard University Press, 1971), p. 13 and elsewhere.
6   Ibid., p. 129.
7   *The Politics of Reality* (Trumansburg, NY: The Crossing Press, 1983), p. 9.
8   Ibid., p. 10.
9   For an important discussion of the relevance of justice to the family, cf. Susan Moller Okin, "Justice and gender," *Philosophy and Public Affairs*, 16 (1987), pp. 42–72.
10 For insightful discussions of the distinctive modes of thought to which mothering gives rise, cf. Sara Ruddick, "Maternal thinking," *Feminist Studies*, 6 (1980) pp. 342–67; and her "Preservative love and military destruction: some reflections on mothering and peace," in Joyce Trebilcot (ed.), *Mothering: Essays in Feminist Theory* (Totowa, NJ: Rowman and Allanheld, 1983), pp. 231–62; also Virginia Held, "The obligations of mothers and fathers," also in Trebilcot (ed.), pp. 7–20.
11 This point was suggested to me by L. W. Sumner.
12 John Broughton also discusses the concern for justice and rights which appears in women's moral reasoning as well as the concern for care and relationships featured in men's moral reasoning; see "Women's rationality and men's virtues," esp. pp. 603–22. For a historical discussion of male theorists who have failed to hear the concern for justice in women's voices, cf. Carole Pateman, "'The disorder of women': women, love, and the sense of justice," *Ethics*, 91 (1980), pp. 20–34.
13 This discussion owes a debt to Francesca M. Cancian's warning that we should not narrow our conception of love to the recognized ways in which women love, which researchers find to center around the expression of feelings and verbal disclosure. Such a conception ignores forms of love which are stereotyped as characteristically male, including instrumental help and the sharing of activities. Cf. "The feminization of love," *Signs*, 11 (1986), pp. 692–709.
14 Cf. Mike Royko, *Boss: Richard J. Daley of Chicago* (New York: New American Library, 1971).
15 Claudia Card has critiqued Gilligan's work for ignoring, in particular, the dismaying harms to which women have historically been subjected in heterosexual relationships, including, but by no means limited to, marriage ("Virtues and moral luck," pp. 15–17).

Suggested activities

Questions for discussion

1   What are some of the most dominant images of women in American popular culture?

2 What are some of the ways in which images of women differ along racial, class, and other lines of social and cultural difference?
3 Are there differences in how women are portrayed in different media; for example, films as opposed to novels, or advertisements as opposed to fine art? If so, what differences do you perceive? Are some of these sources of images of women more harmful than others? In particular, what similarities and differences are there between the way women are represented in advertisements and in pornography?
4 What are some of the contemporary stereotypes of men and women in American culture? How do these compare with those in the readings? Do you think gender stereotypes have changed in the past few decades?
5 Are women represented differently in culture today than they were in earlier eras? If so, how? Is the change, if any, an improvement for women's social status?
6 What happens when *women* define the images of women? *Can* women be the agents of how they are defined when men still dominate the apparatus of representation (the cameras, access to media, and so on)?
7 One arena in which the sexist use of language has become more rather than less pronounced is in rap music. Can you think of other areas in popular culture where the language or images of women are becoming *less* rather than *more* positive?

Films and videos

And Still I Rise by Ngozi Onwurah (England, 1993). 16 mm/VHS/color/30 mins. Distributed by Women Make Movies. Media images and representations of African-American women in the media.
Hair Piece: a Film for Nappy-headed People by Ayoka Chenzira (1985). 16 mm/VHS/color/10 mins. Distributed by Women Make Movies. A satire on the theme of the conflict between the self-image of African-American women and the ideal, flowing, hair type.
Mirror Mirror by Jan Krawitz (1990). 16 mm/VHS/color/17 mins. Distributed by Women Make Movies. A documentary about the relationship between the ideal body image and women's struggles with it.
Perfect Image? by Maureen Blackwood (England, 1988). VHS/color/30 mins. Distributed by Women Make Movies. An examination of stereotypical images of African-American women.
Slaying the Dragon, produced and directed by Deborah Gee, produced by Pacific Productions (1987). VHS/60 mins. Distributed by National Asian American Telecommunications Association/Women Make Movies. About images of Asian-American women.
War on Lesbians by Jane Cottis (1992). VHS/color/32 mins. Distributed by Women Make Movies. A discussion of the lack of positive images for

lesbians in the media, and the barrage of experts and "self-help" programs that are designed to "explain" homosexuality.
Ways of Seeing Part II, by John Berger (1974). $\frac{3}{4}$ inch cassette/25 mins.
Available from Films Incorporated, Wilmette, IL. Describes the relationship between the portrayal of women in popular culture and fine art.
Provides a foundation for discussing similarities and differences between
images of women in eighteenth-century fine art and those in contemporary advertisements.
A Word in Edgewise by Heather MacLeod (1986). VHS/color/26 mins. Distributed by Women Make Movies. Exploration of sexual bias in language and
speech.
(Many of the films listed in chapter 2 would also be relevant here.)

Other activities

1 As a class, brainstorm for about 5–10 minutes, listing as many contemporary images of women in American popular culture as you can think of.
Evaluate these images in terms of whether they are positive or negative for
women, and how they may influence how women perceive themselves,
either as they are or as they "should be."
2 Listen to the lyrics of songs from different kinds of music on the radio (for
example, rock, rap, country, "oldies," hip hop, jazz). Write down references to women, and the terms used to describe them. What sorts of
images of women are evoked by these songs? Do the images differ in
different kinds of music? If so, how do you explain the difference? Do the
lyrics of songs use gender-neutral or male-gendered language?

Bibliography

Allen, Paula Gunn (1986) "Where I come from is like this," in *The Sacred Hoop* (Boston:
    Beacon Press). Allen provides a perspective on images of Native American women based
    on observations of women in her own family and community. According to Allen, promin-
    ent images of Native American women are not significantly different from those of Native
    American males.
Anzaldúa, Gloria (1995) "Cultural tyranny," in Amy Kesselman, Lily McNair, and Nancy
    Schniedewind (eds), *Women: Images and Realities. A Multicultural Anthology* (Mountain
    View, CA: Mayfield). On images of women in Chicano culture.
Bate, Barbara and Bowker, Judy (1997) *Communication and the Sexes*, 2nd edn (Prospect
    Heights, IL: Waveland Press). Comprehensive overview of debates about language, media,
    non-verbal communication, and so on.
Berger, John (1977) *Ways of Seeing* (New York: Penguin).
Bonner, Frances, Goodman, Lizbeth, Allen, Richard et al. (eds) (1992) *Imagining Women:
    Cultural Representations and Gender* (Cambridge: Polity Press). Collection of essays,

mostly from feminist cultural studies, organized under the topics of themes and issues in gender representation, literary representations, visual images, popular television and film, pornography, and humor.

Butterfield, Nancy (1981) "Squaw image stereotyping," in Ohoyo Makachi (ed.), *Words of Today's American Indian Women* (Witchita Falls, TX: Ohoyo). Provides an account of how Native American women have been portrayed in the media, focusing on the "squaw" stereotype.

Cole, Susan G. (1995) *Violence and Pornography* (Toronto, Ontario: Second Story Press).

Foster, Virginia (1971) "The emancipation of pure, white, Southern womanhood," in *New South*, Winter, pp. 46–54. Autobiographical account of the author's images of black and white women, drawn from her extensive network of relations and schoolmates. Provides a vivid illustration of how images of the ideal woman are constructed within a particular social and historical location.

Gaines, Jane and Herzog, Charlotte (eds) (1990) *Fabrications: Costumes and the Female Body* (New York: Routledge). Argues that images of women are "constructions," products of culture that have been manufactured. Just as film gives the viewer the (false) impression that the images of women that it portrays are natural, so does costume, which "delivers gender" as a self-evident and natural attribute of women.

Gillespie, Marcia Ann (1993) "What's good for the race?," *Ms.*, January/February, pp. 80–82.

Green, Rayna (1990) "The Pocahontas perplex: the image of Indian women in American culture," in Ellen Carol DuBois and Vicki L. Ruiz (eds), *Unequal Sisters: a Multicultural Reader in US Women's History* (New York: Routledge).

Hine, Darlene Clark, Brown, Elsa Barkley and Terborg-Penn, Rosalyn (eds) (1993) *Black Women in America: an Historical Encyclopedia* (Bloomington, IN: Indiana University Press).

Itzin, Catherine (ed.) (1992) *Pornography: Women, Violence and Civil Liberties* (Oxford: Oxford University Press).

Lakoff, Robin (1975) *Language and Woman's Place* (New York: Harper Colophon). A groundbreaking, but by now slightly dated, study of sexism in the English language, finding that women are discriminated against both in the ways in which they are taught to use language, as well as in the way in which language treats them, and that both of these tend to subordinate women to roles as sex objects and servants.

Lesser, Wendy (1991) *His Other Half: Men Looking at Women through Art* (Cambridge, MA: Harvard University Press). Examines the images of women in literature, fine art, and Hollywood cinema.

Matlin, Margaret (1987) *The Psychology of Women* (New York: Holt, Rinehart, and Winston). Textbook dealing with general women's issues, including health, sexuality, and crime.

Miles, Margaret (1989) *Carnal Knowing: Female Nakedness and Religious Meaning in the Christian West* (Boston: Beacon Press). (Describes the significance of the visual and artistic representations of female nakedness in Western Christian history from the fourth century to the present.

Morton, Patricia (1991) *Disfigured Images: the Historical Assault on Afro-American Women* (New York: Praeger). Explores the images of African-American women in myths of black womanhood, slave women, twentieth-century women, black studies and women's studies and in images of the black family, and how these fictional, popular media, and scholarly images have shaped a mythical cultural understanding of black women as permanent slave women.

Neuman, Shirley and Stephenson, Glennis (1993) *Re-Imagining Women: Representations of Women in Culture* (Toronto: University of Toronto Press).

Nochlin, Linda (1988) *Women, Art, and Power, and Other Essays* (New York: Harper and Row). Nochlin analyzes the way in which representations of women in fine art have functioned to reproduce cultural assumptions about women, male superiority, and male power over women).

Parker, Rozsika and Pollock, Griselda (1981) *Old Mistresses: Women, Art, and Ideology* (New York: Pantheon Books). Explores women's place in the history of art. Addresses how women have been represented in art as well as why women artists have been ignored in art history.

Richardson, Laurel (1993) "Gender stereotyping in the English language," in L. Richardson and Verta Taylor (eds), *Feminist Frontiers III* (New York: McGraw-Hill).

Thomson, Rosemarie Garland (1997) *Extraordinary Bodies: Figuring Physical Disability in American Culture and Literature* (New York: Columbia University Press). Includes pieces on freak shows and the fiction of Toni Morrison, Audre Lorde, and Harriet Beecher Stowe.

Unger, Rhoda and Crawford, Mary (1992) "Language and women's place," in *Women and Gender: a Feminist Psychology* (New York: McGraw-Hill).

Williams, Patricia (1993) "Essay: from stereotype to archetype," *Ms*, May/June, pp. 70–73. On the contribution of Darlene Clark Hine's *Black Women in America: an Historical Encyclopedia* (included in the bibliography to chapter 2) to changing prevailing stereotypes of black women in America.

Zinn, Maxine Baca and Dill, Bonnie Thornton (eds) (1994) *Women of Color in US Society* (Philadelphia: Temple University Press). Part 6, entitled "Rethinking Gender," covers images, ideology, and women of color. Challenges the assumption that women can have a sisterhood based on universal commonalities.

PART II
Cultural Institutions Defining Women

This second part explores how women have been defined by significant institutions of American culture. We begin with the media and popular culture, first examining how women are defined by the fashion and advertising industries and by "women's" books and magazines (chapter 4), then the film and television industries (chapter 5). In chapter 6, we look at how the beauty industry impacts on women's health and sense of well-being. Chapter 7 explores the institution of motherhood, and how women continue to be defined in culture largely in terms of their roles as child bearers and rearers. The final chapter in this part explores the connections between sex, sexism, sexual harassment, and the sexual abuse of girls and women (chapter 8).

4

Women and Popular Culture I: Advertising, Print Media, and Pornography

Introduction

Images of women and men in popular culture shape our understandings of femininity and masculinity. Whether a woman is considered feminine, in fact, is largely shaped by her appearance. These images tell women how they should look, feel, and act, and how they will be seen by others. In this first of two chapters devoted to exploring images of women in the media and popular culture, we will focus on how women are portrayed in "women's" books and magazines, and in advertising. In chapter 5, we will turn to portrayals of women in film and television. Although these topics have been divided for organizational purposes in this text, there is no sharp division between these different types of media. In fact, they often function in combination with one another. For example, the power of the fashion industry to shape the images and self-images of women has been facilitated by the Hollywood film industry (see Turin, 1983).

Feminist media studies have explored the sexist bias of the media industries, ranging from male-dominated ownership and control of the media to sexist representations of women, as well as how women receive media images as consumers of popular culture, and how women's own media productions differ from men's. These studies have revealed certain similarities in how women are represented in different forms of media. Media images of women include the following:

1 *Relative invisibility* Studies in the early 1980s found that men outnumbered women by two to one in television commercials. Black women were especially invisible. Until a few years ago, the portrayal of professional black women was almost non-existent (see Matlin, 1987: 255).

2 *Relative silence* The voice of authority, especially on the radio and in television commercials, is typically a male voice, not a female one.

3 *Unrepresentative occupations* The percentage of women actually in the workforce is under-represented in media representations. In addition, women are more frequently portrayed in professional roles rather than the low-wage, low-skilled jobs that the majority of women perform.

4 *Housework* Women are portrayed much more frequently than men as responsible for doing the housework.

5 *Families* Women are depicted in relation to their families much more often than men are.

6 *Negative portrayals* Women are frequently represented as ignorant or stupid, passive, and dependent on men.

7 *Body portrayals* As we have already seen, women in American culture are typically defined in terms of their bodies, especially their physically and biologically female sex characteristics that distinguish them from males. The perception of women as sex objects is reinforced in popular culture, especially in advertisements, television and the movies, music videos, and "men's magazines" like *Playboy* and *Penthouse* (as well as more hard-core forms of pornography). Recently, even fashions for pre-adolescent girls have been designed to portray girls as sexually seductive, with bras, seductive neck and hemlines, uncovered midriffs, and so on. Women are more frequently portrayed in terms of their bodies, especially in advertisements, than are men. Women are more often shown as serving a decorative function as an attractive backdrop rather than the central focus of attention. Whereas men's faces are more prominent in magazines and advertisements, women's bodies are more prominent. Men's bodies are more often positioned above those of women, suggesting men's higher status.

Feminist media critics have themselves been subject to criticism, especially by black feminist theorists who argue that white feminist theorists have been inattentive to the ways in which representations and experiences of women involve not only gender, but also race and class, thereby making such generalizations as those above radically incomplete.

Advertisements

Advertising is an all-pervasive aspect of Western capitalist culture, bombarding us from television and radio, from billboards and all manner of printed materials, almost everywhere we go. In addition, advertisers own significant proportions of other media enterprises, including newspapers, mass-circulation magazines and broadcast companies, giving them an influence over the content of these forms of media as well.

Since the early days of the second wave of the women's movement, feminists have pointed out that advertisements serve a political function in reinforcing notions of men as naturally dominant and women as naturally subordinate. In addition, they have observed how images of women are used to sell products by making them appear more desirable. Advertisements have shifted over time from portraying women as primarily interested in housework and child rearing to representations of women as interested primarily in enhancing their female beauty. Naomi Wolf (1991) notes that focusing on women's appearance – as too pretty or not pretty enough – is a way of controlling women because it creates self-doubt about the adequacy of their appearance, and motivates them to attempt to "improve" their looks in order to meet the prevailing standards of beauty and femininity.

Feminist scholar Wendy Chapkis takes this perspective to the global level. She analyzes beauty as a "politics of appearance." Beauty is not limited to the psychologies and aesthetic sensibilities of individual men and women, but is part of a "global culture machine" that joins advertising, the media, and the cosmetics industry in the construction of normative standards of beauty for women all over the world to attempt to achieve (see Chapkis, 1986).

Studies of gender in advertisements conducted by the sociologist Irving Goffman (1979) suggest that portrayals of men and women in ads often do not represent how actual men and women *are*, but rather, how advertisers (and, to a certain extent, through them, the public) *think* they should be. Goffman suggests that (real) men and women take their cues about appropriate masculine and feminine behavior from gendered images in ads, and that they attempt to imitate the characteristics they find. Consequently, Goffman thinks it is possible to gain insight into gender roles by examining images of men and women in advertisements. Among his findings are that advertisements almost never:

- portray a woman as taller than a man except when he is her social inferior;
- show a woman's hands in a powerful grasp;
- depict a man sitting or lying on a bed or the floor, in a lowered or symbolically subordinate position;
- show men averting their eyes to a social inferior (including a woman).

In addition, when the ad portrays an instructional setting, it is almost always a man instructing a woman. More significantly, Goffman illustrates how women are often shown with children, suggesting that they are themselves child-like.

Jean Kilbourne's research, over a decade later, similarly found that gender was a significant factor in advertising. In the first reading, "Beauty and the beast of advertising," Kilbourne describes how powerful the images promoted in advertisements are in influencing social reality and individual identity. She argues that advertising tells us what is "normal." (By this criteria, normal continues to be predominantly white and male by a margin of two to one.) The standard for females is young, beautiful, thin, heterosexual, without disabilities, and a member of a nuclear family. She explains that the problem with gendered advertising is that this is the *only* significant standard of beauty that is widely disseminated in popular culture.

Advertising is also sexist in portraying women primarily as sex objects and housewives. It often portrays women as subservient to men, and as available for men's pleasure and comfort. Kilbourne describes how portrayals of females in advertising trivialize women, contributing to gender stereotyping and to the treatment of female bodies as merchandise, and thereby to creating a climate of tolerance for domestic violence, rape, and the sexual abuse of girls and women. She argues that advertising's approach to sex is pornographic by reducing persons to sex objects and de-emphasizing human contact and individuality.

In the second reading, "Fresh Lipstick," Linda M. Scott challenges the simplistic view that advertisements present only one image of women, contending that, instead, they present multiple, sometimes internally contradictory, images. She challenges the claim of Wolf, Kilbourne, and others that ads portray a single image as the beauty myth that women should conform to. Scott also challenges Wolf's hypothesis that the beauty myth arose in the 1980s as a backlash against feminism.

Women's books and magazines

Women's books and magazines are an important source of images of femininity. They provide models or standards of ideal women by which "real" women measure themselves and, as Naomi Wolf (1991) points out, inevitably find themselves inadequate in relation to. Women's magazines, similar to romance novels, more frequently represent women in traditional roles as housewives and mothers than as independent women with their own lives and careers. Also, like romance novels, many of the fictional stories in women's magazines portray women as helpless victims at the mercy (and pleasure) of male sexual power and domination. Some feminist critics have argued that such portrayals provide unhealthy role models for real women, who attempt to conform to these powerless female characters and expect men to conform to the macho and domineering male characters (see, for example, Radway, 1984).

From the perspective of Anne Snitow (1995), the formulaic plot of romance novels typically involves the romanticization of sexual domination. Janice Radway's (1984) pathbreaking study of women's reception of romance novels showed how one group of white, working-class women found both legitimation of their male partner's dominating behavior as well as the resources to critique certain aspects of male behavior. This understanding of romance novels has been critiqued by more recent theorists of popular culture, however, who contend that the pleasure that women derive from reading romances needs to be given more positive consideration (see, for example, Winship, 1987; Ang, 1988). More recent scholarship suggests that romance novels may either provide a reinforcement of patriarchal values or a means of resistance, or even both.

As noted earlier, magazine advertising promotes the image of women as primarily interested in their appearance. At the same time as they intensify the beauty myth, however, Wolf (1991) notes that women's magazines have done more to popularize feminist ideas than any other medium. For example, they provide one of the few sources where women can find out what other women are thinking about issues of concern to women generally. In a certain way, Wolf argues, the medium of women's magazines brings women together, and thereby creates a kind of club or community for women. In this respect, women's magazines play an important role in reflecting and creating female mass culture.

Portrayals of women in magazines are similar to those on television, but appear to change more rapidly. Women are defined largely in terms of whether or not they are married and what their economic status is. In part, magazine images of women lag behind the reality of women's changing roles because of the control that product advertisers have on the *content* of the articles published. Capitalism thus appears to be largely dominating this aspect of popular culture and, consequently, the gender images and stereotypes that are disseminated in popular culture. These representations, as we have seen, promote an image of female beauty as white, full-busted but slender, able-bodied, and so on. Women of color and other women who are "different" are largely excluded, sending a clear message that they are not beautiful.

Pornography

One type of representation of women that has raised tremendous controversy among feminists (and many others) is pornography. *Pornography* is sexually explicit material. Opinions vary widely regarding what additional qualifiers are necessary to add to the definition, since many argue that material that is *merely* sexually explicit is *erotica*, not *pornography*, and is not harmful or otherwise problematic (Steinem, 1983; Longino, 1991). So called "soft porn" or erotica, like that in *Penthouse* and *Playboy*, typically does not involve portrayals of violence against women, and may, in fact, depict women as well as men as subjects rather than as merely objects of male lust and desire. Feminists such as Diana Russell and Helen Longino have defined erotica as sexually explicit material that is not abusive or sexist (see Longino, 1991).

Some feminists, including Gloria Steinem and Helen Longino, have argued that there is a clear distinction between erotica and pornography such that only the latter, which is clearly degrading and offensive to women, should be censored. For instance, Longino defines pornography as "verbal or pictorial material which represents or describes sexual behavior that is degrading or abusive to one or more of the participants *in such a way as to endorse the degradation*" (Longino, 1991: 87). Other feminists, like the prominent feminist legal scholar Catharine MacKinnon and feminist author and anti-pornography activist Andrea Dworkin, argue that all sexualized images of women are harmful, and should be regulated as reflecting incorrect attitudes toward women. Between these extremes, pornography is usually defined as involving depictions of unequal power relationships, involving some degree of coercion and/or violence, with men in positions of domination and others, especially women, in positions of submission. Pornographic images of women frequently depict women as sex objects with vast and insatiable sexual appetites (nymphomaniacs), and as enjoying sexual violence and participation in degrading acts – being tied up, chained, whipped, beaten, sodomized, urinated upon, and so on – as well as being subjected to brutality, restraint, powerlessness, semi- or unconsciousness, penetration using foreign objects, and having sex with animals.

Alternatively, in some pornography, women are portrayed as passive and submissive victims, totally dependent upon or at the mercy of men. In addition, many pornographic images reduce women to parts of their bodies, such as their breasts or sexual organs. Women or female body parts are often symbolized by animals (such as "pets," "bunnies," and "beavers"). Pornography often involves racist as well as sexist stereotypes. The iconography of pornography has been incorporated in many other forms of popular culture, including advertisements, music videos, Hollywood films, and television programs. Although many of the same techniques are used with both forms of media, including the production of the "male gaze," pornography is also distinctive, both in terms of its production and its consumption.

Pornography is a ten billion dollar a year industry, encompassing photographs, movies and cable TV shows, magazines and books, CD-Rom computer programs, and even telephone sex. The debate over whether pornography should be legally censored raises fascinating questions about the meaning and power of images of women: what influence does pornographic imagery have on how real women are perceived and treated? Does it contribute to or result in the degradation and sexual abuse of women, or does it merely mirror the existing cultural climate? These are difficult questions without clear answers.

The research that has been done to date is inconclusive regarding the influence of pornography on causing or contributing to the sexual abuse of women. It seems evident, however, that the representations of women in much pornographic material – as sexual objects to be bound, beaten, raped, mutilated, and or killed, as passive recipients of aggressive or even violent male sexuality – contribute to a climate in which sexual harassment and sexual abuse of women is acceptable. In addition, some feminists have argued that if "causation" is defined more broadly to include *anything* producing an effect or result, "then pornography can be shown to cause rape: it predisposes some men to want to rape, undermines the individual and social inhibitions of some men against acting out their desire to rape, as well as by undermining the ability of potential victims to avoid or resist rape" (Russell, 1993).

Studies have shown that men who view violent pornography tend to show a decreased sensitivity to women, particularly women portrayed as victims of sexual assault. Men who view pornography may believe that women actually enjoy coerced sex. In one study, researchers found that 57 percent of college men, after being shown violent pornographic images, stated some likelihood of raping a woman if they knew they would not be caught, compared with only 25–30 percent of college men not previously exposed to pornography (Unger and Crawford, 1992: 535–7). None the less, there is no direct evidence of a causal connection between pornography and the sexual coercion of women.

Not surprisingly, feminists have been divided over the issue of whether pornography should be more stringently regulated and restricted, or even prohibited. Currently, US law regulates pornography under *obscenity laws*. These laws generally define what is obscene for "the average person, applying community standards." According to this definition, established by the US Supreme Court, a work is only obscene if it lacks "serious literary, artistic, political, or scientific value." Otherwise, the material is protected under the First Amendment's right of free speech. What would be considered obscene in one community may not be in another. Only pornography that is determined to be obscene under this standard can be legally restricted. Some feminists largely accept this analysis.

In contrast, in "Not a moral issue," MacKinnon argues that obscenity law is inadequate to address the harms of pornography because it deals with issues of morality from a male perspective and because obscenity and pornography are completely different. Whereas obscenity "as such probably does little harm," pornography causes attitudes and behaviors of violence and discrimination that define the treatment and status of half of the population" (MacKinnon, 1987: 147). In her view, pornography is central to the maintenance of male supremacy. MacKinnon argues that pornography "is a form of forced sex, a practice of sexual politics, an institution of gender inequality." It provides the basis of how men view women and, because of male power, "defines who women can be." And this is as wanting to be abused, as subjected to male power and control, as "there to be violated and possessed" (MacKinnon, 1987: 148).

Feminists who take an anti-censorship position often consider pornography to be the presentation of an *idea* and thus subject to protection as speech under the First Amendment's Free Speech clause. Anti-censorship feminists think that banning or more severely regulating pornography would unduly limit the free speech rights of others, including women, and thereby bring about more harm than good. Other feminists opposed to censorship also argue that feminists would not be able to control the use of anti-pornography legislation by conservative religious and political forces to regulate diverse sexualities (see Rodgerson and Wilson, 1991). In part, their view is based on the argument that advocates of censorship, including MacKinnon and Dworkin, have not established that pornography is directly responsible for rape and other acts of sexual violence against women. Those opposing censorship also argue that pornography is less objectionable when the women involved have given their informed consent to participate in its production.

Wendy Kaminer argues that, given the pervasive nature of negative images of women in the mass media and popular culture, legally censoring pornography would not make a dent in the social conditions that contribute to negative portrayals and treatment of women (Kaminer, 1992: 118). In support of Kaminer's thesis, John Berger's analysis of the images of women in fine art in *Ways of Seeing* (see reading on p. 97) shows how the nude was used to represent women's submission to the male owner (of the woman and the painting). Berger's comparison of an oil painting by Ingres with a model in "a girlie magazine" illustrates the remarkable similarity between the two (Berger, 1977: 55). Berger's observations strengthen the argument of anti-censorship feminists that further banning or restricting pornography would not destroy sexist images of women in popular culture.

Some feminists even argue that pornography, as a form of art, should not be censored because it has as much, if not more, potential to liberate as to oppress women. Others argue that pornography can be as pleasurable for women as for men, whether they identify themselves as female or as males exercising power and domination (see, for example, Gibson and Gibson, 1993).

Against this view of pornography as images of women having shifting meanings, which vary in different contexts, opponents of legalized pornography tend to view sexual images of women as having fixed meanings connoting sin or the degradation of women. Religious-based opposition to pornography especially tends to reflect the perspective that sex itself degrades women and that "good" women do not seek and enjoy sex. In this view, the images themselves are viewed as problematic, regardless of how they may be used.

Anti-pornography feminists view porn as contributing to women's subjugation in society generally. For example, Itzin (1992: 67) argues that "through pornography men experience the sexual subordination of women as sex and they experience sexual inequality and sexual violence as sexually exciting and sexually arousing." From this perspective, pornography also sexualizes violence, and thereby contributes to sexual violence against women and children. Through pornography, men come to see women as sex objects who want and deserve to be treated in terms of their sexuality and as inferiors. Although pornography may not, in this view, be solely responsible for women's subordination in society, it is certainly an important part of the problem, one which has been largely overlooked or ignored until recently.

In *Only Words* (1993), MacKinnon argues against the traditional liberal view that uncensored speech is vital to a constitutional democracy, even when that speech is shocking or disgusting. She says that speech acts can contribute to sexual violence. In her view, pornography makes the world a pornographic place through its images of women as existing for, perceived for, and treated as objects of male sexual pleasure. Advocates of censorship, such as MacKinnon and Dworkin, thus argue that pornography is a form of sex discrimination against women. They have said that pornography itself is a form of violence and discrimination against women; a method men use to subordinate women. In this view, genuinely informed consent is impossible when women are economically and/or physically coerced into working as pornography models or prostitutes.

On the basis of such arguments, MacKinnon and Dworkin drafted a proposed amendment to the Minneapolis Human Rights ordinance which defined pornography as a *practice*; that is, as *action* rather than simply speech. As such, they argue that pornography is not protected by the First Amendment, which applies only to *speech*. MacKinnon and Dworkin's proposed Amendment also defined the production, sale, distribution, and exhibition of pornography as a form of discrimination against women and thus a violation of women's civil rights, thereby justifying regulation.

These views on the representations of women in advertising, print media, and pornography demonstrate that there are rival, and even conflicting, understandings about whether these representations are necessarily harmful for women. At a minimum, however, these viewpoints suggest the need for greater awareness of, and attention to, the ways that these forms of popular culture influence our understanding of "what women are" and perhaps, more importantly, what they *should* be.

Beauty and the Beast of Advertising
Jean Kilbourne

"You're a Halston woman from the very beginning," the advertisement proclaims. The model stares provocatively at the viewer, her long blonde

This reading first appeared in *Media and Values: Re-designing Women* (Center for Media Literacy, winter, 1990).

hair waving around her face, her bare chest partially covered by two curved bottles that give the illusion of breasts and a cleavage. The average American is accustomed to blue-eyed blondes seductively touting a variety of products. In this case, however, the blonde is about five years old.

Advertising is an over $100 billion a year industry and affects all of us throughout our lives. We are each exposed to over 2,000 ads a day, constituting perhaps the most powerful educational force in society. The average adult will spend one and a half years of his/her life watching television commercials. But the ads sell a great deal more than products. They sell values, images, and concepts of success and worth, love and sexuality, popularity and normalcy. They tell us who we are and who we should be. Sometimes they sell addictions.

Advertising's foundation and economic lifeblood is the mass media, and the primary purpose of the mass media is to deliver an audience to advertisers, just as the primary purpose of television programs is to deliver an audience for commercials.

Adolescents are particularly vulnerable, however, because they are new and inexperienced consumers and are the prime targets of many advertisements. They are in the process of learning their values and roles and developing their self-concepts. Most teenagers are sensitive to peer pressure and find it difficult to resist or even question the dominant cultural messages perpetuated and reinforced by the media. Mass communication has made possible a kind of nationally distributed peer pressure that erodes private and individual values and standards.

But what does society, and especially teenagers, learn from the advertising messages that proliferate in the mass media? On the most obvious level they learn the stereotypes. Advertising creates a mythical, WASP-oriented world in which no one is ever ugly, overweight, poor, struggling or disabled either physically or mentally (unless you count the housewives who talk to little men in toilet bowls, animated germs in drains or muscle-bound giants clad in white clothing). And it is a world in which people talk only about products.

Housewives or sex objects

The aspect of advertising most in need of analysis and change is the portrayal of women. Scientific studies and the most casual viewing yield the same conclusion: women are shown almost exclusively as housewives or sex objects.

The housewife, pathologically obsessed by cleanliness and lemon-fresh scents, debates cleaning products with herself and worries about her husband's "ring around the collar."

The sex object is a mannequin, a shell. Conventional beauty is her only attribute. She has no lines or wrinkles (which would indicate she had the bad taste and poor judgment to grow older), no scars or blemishes – indeed, she has no pores. She is thin, generally tall and long-legged, and, above all, she is young. All "beautiful" women in advertisements (including minority women), regardless of product or audience, conform to this norm. Women are constantly exhorted to emulate this ideal, to feel ashamed and guilty if they fail, and to feel that their desirability and lovability are contingent upon physical perfection.

Creating artificiality

The image is artificial and can only be achieved artificially (even the "natural look" requires much preparation and expense). Beauty is something that comes from without; more than one million dollars is spent every hour on cosmetics. Desperate to conform to an ideal and impossible standard, many women go to great lengths to manipulate and change their faces and bodies. A woman is conditioned to view her face as a mask and her body as an object, as *things* separate from and more important than her real self, constantly in need of alteration, improvement, and disguise. She is made to feel dissatisfied with and ashamed of herself, whether she tries to achieve "the look" or not. Objectified constantly by others, she learns to objectify herself. (It is interesting to note that one in five college-age women has an eating disorder.)

"When *Glamour* magazine surveyed its readers in 1984, 75 percent felt too heavy and only 15 percent felt just right. Nearly half of those who were actually underweight reported feeling too fat and wanting to diet. Among a sample of college women, 40 percent felt overweight when only 12 percent actually were too heavy," according to Rita Freedman in her book *Beauty Bound.*

There is evidence that this preoccupation with weight begins at ever-earlier ages for women. According to a recent article in *New Age Journal,* "even grade-school girls are succumbing to stick-like standards of beauty enforced by a relentless parade of wasp-waisted fashion models, movie stars and pop idols." A study by a University of California professor showed that nearly 80 percent of fourth-grade girls in the Bay Area are watching their weight.

A recent *Wall Street Journal* survey of students in four Chicago-area schools found that more than half the fourth-grade girls were dieting and three-quarters felt they were overweight. One student said, "We don't expect boys to be that handsome. We take them as they are." Another added, "But boys expect girls to be perfect and beautiful. And skinny."

Dr Steven Levenkron, author of *The Best Little Girl in the World*, the story of an anorexic, says his blood pressure soars every time he opens a magazine and finds an ad for women's fashions. "If I had my way," he said, "every one of them would have to carry a line saying, 'Caution: this model may be hazardous to your health.'"

Women are also dismembered in commercials, their bodies separated into parts in need of change or improvement. If a woman has "acceptable" breasts, then she must also be sure that her legs are worth watching, her hips slim, her feet sexy, and that her buttocks look nude under her clothes ("like I'm not wearin' nothin'"). This image is difficult and costly to achieve and impossible to maintain (unless you buy the product) – no one is flawless and everyone ages. Growing older is the great taboo. Women are encouraged to remain little girls ("because innocence is sexier than you think"), to be passive and dependent, never to mature. The contradictory message – "sensual, but not too far from innocence" – places women in a double bind; somehow we are supposed to be both sexy and virginal, experienced and naïve, seductive and chaste. The disparagement of maturity is, of course, insulting and frustrating to adult women, and the implication that little girls are seductive is dangerous to real children.

Influencing sexual attitudes

Young people also learn a great deal about sexual attitudes from the media and from advertising in particular. Advertising's approach to sex is pornographic: it reduces people to objects and de-emphasizes human contact and individuality. This reduction of sexuality to a dirty joke and of people to objects is the real obscenity of the culture. Although the sexual sell, overt and subliminal, is at a fevered pitch in most commercials, there is at the same time a notable absence of sex as an important and profound human activity.

There have been some changes in the images of women. Indeed, a "new woman" has emerged in commercials in recent years. She is generally presented as superwoman, who manages to do all the work at home and on the job (with the help of a product, of course, not of her husband or children or friends), or as the liberated woman, who owes her independence and self-esteem to the products she uses. These new images do not represent any real progress but rather create a myth of progress, an illusion that reduces complex sociopolitical problems to mundane personal ones.

Advertising images do not cause these problems, but they contribute to them by creating a climate in which the marketing of women's bodies – the sexual sell and dismemberment, distorted body image ideal and children as sex objects – is seen as acceptable.

This is the real tragedy, that many women internalize these stereotypes and learn their "limitations," thus establishing a self-fulfilling prophecy. If one accepts these mythical and degrading images, to some extent one actualizes them. By remaining unaware of the profound seriousness of the ubiquitous influence, the redundant message and the subliminal impact of advertisements, we ignore one of the most powerful "educational" forces in the culture – one that greatly affects our self-images, our ability to relate to each other, and effectively destroys any awareness and action that might help to change that climate.

Fresh Lipstick: Rethinking Images of Women in Advertising
Linda M. Scott

For more than 100 years, American feminist thought has held that the pursuit of a fashionably beautiful appearance is a sign of low self-esteem and a symptom of political oppression. One of the longest-standing gestures of defiance among feminist activists, therefore, has been a refusal to conform to the grooming practices that fashion deemed "beautiful" or "feminine."

Yet feminism's political imperative to reject the pursuit of "beauty" has presented an insuperable obstacle to some women, becoming a barrier that often marks a schism in the movement. "An unadorned face became the honorable new look of feminism in the early 1970s, and no one was happier with the freedom not to wear makeup than I," wrote Susan Brownmiller in *Femininity* (1984), musing on the depth of divisiveness that could be caused by so seemingly trivial an issue. "Yet it could hardly escape my attention that more women supported the Equal Rights Amendment and legal abortion than would walk out of the house without their eye shadow."

"Did I think of them as somewhat pitiable?" Brownmiller asked. "Yes, I did. Did they bitterly resent the righteous pressure put on them to look, in their terms, less attractive? Yes, they did. A more complete breakdown and

This reading first appeared in *Media Studies Journal*, 1993, 7(1–2): 141–55.

confusion of aims, goals and values could not have occurred, and of all the movement rifts I have witnessed, this one remains for me the most poignant and the most difficult to resolve."

The controversy continued into the 1990s. Naomi Wolf's *The Beauty Myth* drew at least as much criticism from some feminists for its "anti-beauty" stance as from the commercial beauty culture it tried to attack.

As the exemplary texts of the beauty industry, image-oriented women's advertisements have been a focal point of many feminist complaints. Criticism of these ads, however, tends to be flawed in several ways. First is the assertion that advertising images present only one standard of beauty at any one time. Second, critics often describe a one-way model of communication, in which a univocal front of advertisers impose their beauty ideal on unwilling victims. Third, the images themselves are said to work in an almost magical fashion, bypassing the faculties of reason to "control" through emotion. Finally, the argument stands on a false dichotomy between the "natural" and the "artificial," which obscures the power issues at stake.

Cultural critic Raymond Williams once remarked that if social control through ideology really worked in this simplistic, top-down fashion, "it would be – and one would be very glad – a much easier thing to overthrow." Let me sketch an alternative approach, in which the multiple, competing images of women presented by advertising are symptomatic of an ongoing historical struggle to define not only "what a beautiful woman looks like," but "what a good feminist looks like." The contestants are not easily cast as "feminists" on the one side and "advertisers" on the other, but include several subgroups and "cross groups," even – astonishing as such a concept may be – "feminists who write image advertising." In this model, advertisements call up competing ideas of beauty for readers to consider and negotiate, rather than simply "holding up" an image that "makes us" try to look a certain way. These images, then, are historical, socially situated artifacts that must be (and are) read in the context of the ongoing discourse and *not* magical icons that control through mere exposure.

Let's begin by looking at a recent advertisement, a Nike ad that ran in many American fashion magazines during 1992. The image is a photograph of Marilyn Monroe, but it is not the simpering starlet, the sex symbol playing to the male gaze. Instead, this is one of those pictures of Marilyn Monroe that experience and convention tell us to read as "the real Marilyn," an innocent destroyed by the beauty myth. So when we look at this ad, we do not topple over in our desire to look like Marilyn Monroe, though she is beautiful and blonde. On the contrary, we know to read this image as a poignant combination of beauty and tragedy. That is, we look at this image critically. In fact, the sense of the ad *depends* on viewing the image critically, as is clear from the copy.

"A woman is often measured by the things she cannot control," the copy begins. We know this feeling of being "measured," so we let the ad talk to us some more. The voice goes on about the way a body curves or doesn't, and how the "inches and ages and numbers . . . don't ever add up to who she is on the inside." This, we know, is the moral of Marilyn. We share this inside/outside paradox with her, whether our bodies curve voluptuously or not. The voice takes on the edge of indignation: "If a woman is to be measured, let her be measured by the things she can control, by who she is and who she is trying to become." We are "with" this voice; it is our own manifesto. The call builds to its climax: "Measurements are only statistics and STATISTICS LIE." We laugh, perhaps ruefully.

From the logo of the well-known maker of athletic shoes displayed unconventionally in the upper right corner, we infer that the voice wants us to buy tennis shoes and start some athletic activity. We are now dealing with another ideal, the one that prefers beauty "from within," the one that advocates exercise rather than creams and lipsticks and the over-obvious eyeliner poor Marilyn is wearing. So the ad itself is discursive, representing an argument between one politics of beauty and another. If we have any historical awareness at all (and we must have *some* in order to get the Marilyn reference in the first place), then we know that the "beauty through health and exercise" position is the one long advocated by feminism.

Perhaps we are pleased that an advertiser is on the "right" side, for once. Or, perhaps we are bothered, as some readers of this ad were, that this voice is advocating a path to beauty that many women are already following to destruction. The fight for "control" here has the intonation of the anorexic, who, in a desperate effort to have control over *something*, works with a vengeance to control her body. In this alternative politics of beauty lies the potential to emerge taut, toned and totally twisted. Now shamelessly curvy Marilyn looks downright healthy, her eyeliner notwithstanding. We have arrived at one of the paradoxes that the beauty controversy produces: the ultimately deceptive idea that one way of being beautiful will be, for all times and all places, more healthy, more natural, and less harmful than all others.

Many traditional beauty practices have indeed been dangerous: tight-lacing corsets, eating arsenic to produce a pale complexion, and using lead-based powders have produced serious health problems in thousands of women. Still, to characterize "feminine" beauty rituals as generally physically harmful is not only untrue but it obscures one of the most powerful reasons that women use beauty products – for the sheer pleasure of experiencing the scented creams, the bright colors, the refreshing tonics. Exhortations to abandon these practices often have the tenor of an unpleasant asceticism.

The quick retort is that psychological harm is done when women feel that they must do these things in order to be beautiful. Women should feel their natural selves are beautiful enough. Unfortunately, the intuitive persuasiveness of this stance masks an assumption that "natural" is an easy thing to define. In all cultures and in all times, human beings decorate and groom themselves. It is not at all uncommon for them to do so in a manner that is harmful or permanent: scarification, mutilation, and tattoos, for example. Given the propensity of human beings everywhere to change their physical appearance, we might ask whether an unadorned human being may be said to be "natural" in any sense at all. What is natural for human beings is artifice.

Self-decoration reflects the sociability of human beings as a species. Humans use artifice to communicate who they are and who they wish to be, and to negotiate their way through the social setting. For this reason, the idea of a totally ungroomed human (unbathed, uncombed, unshaven) presents the picture of a sociopath, a near-beast withdrawn from the social world. Grooming rituals represent an essential element in what it means to be human.

Self-presentation also places a person in the hierarchy: one set of markings for men, another for women; one for the elite, a different one for workers; one for artists, one for hunters. The question of beauty is not really one of nature versus artifice, as it is often cast; the issue is better defined as the way grooming marks an oppressed group and thus perpetuates its oppression. It is also a power struggle over what more appropriate markings would be, as the group works to redefine itself. The texts of the beauty culture are best understood as one ground where these issues are negotiated. This statement is anathema to most feminists, since ads are widely taken as the ideology of a monolithic and paternalistic capitalism. We could explain the Nike ad, after all, by saying it was just another instance of commerce "co-opting" feminist rhetoric.

But just this once, I'm going to ask you to do something that is seldom done: knock down the screen and take a look at the wizard behind it. In this case, we do not find a snarling group of male capitalists, but two young women with counterculture loyalties. Charlotte Moore, an art director, and Janet Champ, a copywriter, work in a team, as is the tradition in advertising. Also according to tradition, they have been segregated as a "girls' team" and been given responsibility for Nike's "women's campaign."

Moore and Champ's first ads for Nike opened with long lists that evoked futility and harmfulness: "Face lifts, body tucks, liposuction, electrolysis, collagen implants, breast lifts, wrinkle creams, face masks, mud baths, chemical peels, wrinkle fills, liquid diets, cellulite reduction, tweezing, plucking, straightening, waxing, waving, herbal heat wraps." Then you turned the page and saw a young woman in athletic gear sprinting up some stairs, and the headline, "The 60-minute makeover from Nike. Just do it." Champ contends their campaign strategy was to attack the other speakers in the beauty discourse, both commercial and editorial. "I mean, every one of them is how to be beautiful and how to get your man and how to be skinny and how to be – you know – cosmetic surgery and everything else," she told an oral-history interviewer from the Smithsonian's Center for Advertising History. "We wanted to show real women, talk to women one on one, and start debunking all these myths that we have to live with every day." The Marilyn ad was another attempt to go after the same myths.

"We'd always been very, very interested in this whole idea of being held up to be the icon of perfection, of beauty, and what happens to a woman when she starts to believe that, what happens to other women when they're forced to try to *be* that," Champ says. "So we started talking about what kind of ad we could do that talked about being a statistic and being accepted as a false image of yourself, and how, once you present that image to the world, you are never accepted for who you really are."

Instead of being motivated by a desire to manipulate or by a feeling of condescension toward their readers, Champ and Moore felt able to communicate their message to other women because they had "been there" themselves. This experience increased Champ's political awareness and renewed a sense of activism she thought she had lost. That a feminist would be reclaimed by writing ads may seem an unlikely turn of events; on the contrary, however, the history of the beauty controversy is full of paradoxical characters, contradictory polemics and the struggle of competing interests in surprising places.

The first feminists to mount a major attack on the commercial beauty culture were mid-nineteenth-century women's activists: Elizabeth Cady Stanton, Susan B. Anthony, Lucretia Mott, Lucy Stone, Antoinette Brown. Their challenge was also a direct response to a competing model of femininity: the "modern" woman. "Moderns" adopted fashion as a means to achieve upward social mobility – they were also called "fashionables." Unlike the feminists themselves, the modern woman was a liminal creature within nineteenth-century class structure, usually a single, working-class immigrant, trying to use her looks to "get ahead," or a daughter of the newly rich commercial class, trying to make an advantageous marriage. These fashionable young women were called "moderns" because their self-presentation was seen as the feminine counterpart to the driving economic ambitions of the modern American male. Though the "Gibson Girl" looks old-fashioned and patrician in today's context, she was seen by her turn-of-the-century contemporaries as the quintessence of the "modern" beauty: athletic, independent, intelligent, and unconventional. She was also "read" as an amalgam of ethnic types, the archetypal beautiful young immigrant.

The nineteenth-century feminists might appear to be very much like the radical, neo-Marxian feminists of today, but they weren't. These were the daughters and wives of prosperous rural families who, riding the wave of evangelism that captured the country during their times, worked as avidly for "moral reform" and temperance as they did for women's rights and abolition. Though many of their political aims were "radical" in a contemporary sense, many were equally conservative, moralistic, and repressive. These women were aggressively anti-sensual, dogmatically condemning pleasurable activities from the theater to dances to carnivals. In *American Beauty*, feminist historian Lois Banner documents their consistently negative attitude toward fashionable working-class women and their pleasurable activities, including their beauty rituals. The historical impact of these attitudes upon the feminism of today is clearly apparent in Banner's own rhetoric – she describes nineteenth-century working women falling victim to "bouts of pleasure" or "outbreaks of sensual expression," as if they had caught a disease. For all the denials from feminist leaders, the anti-sensual attitude still infuses the discourse on this topic, as ongoing controversy over Camille Paglia further attests.

Industrialization brought about many social dislocations. One was the increased freedom that allowed men to marry outside their class. Another was the status deprivation felt by the rural middle class, pressed from either side by rising commercial wealth and the influx of working-class immigrants. Women in these families felt their options narrow as socially mobile "modern" women encroached upon their privileges and their men. Early feminists' anti-beauty, anti-commercial, anti-modern activities must be understood as occurring against this socio-historical backdrop.

Until the end of the nineteenth century, working women still wore very little makeup; the "gentry" wore none. As the twentieth century unfolded, however, wearing cosmetics increased in acceptability, moving up from the working class to the middle class, and, finally, to the upper class. Between 1914 and 1925, cosmetics sales rose from $17 million to $141 million a year. By the time the Jazz Age was in full swing, 90 percent of American women over 18 used powder and 55 percent rouge. A causal factor was the rise in the status of actresses, a subgroup the nineteenth-century feminists had despised. The day Mary Pickford first wore lipstick, the cosmetics world changed forever. The modern young women of the 1920s continued to flout conventions of morality: they wore cosmetics, they flirted, they smoked, they danced, they had sex, they drank, they bobbed their hair and wore their dresses short. They also started participating in sports previously open only to men. So, an "odd" amalgam of behaviors emerged, in which practices considered by the earlier feminists to be morally depraved were combined with assertions of independence and challenges to gender roles.

At this point, we might stop to ask ourselves who the feminists really are in this evolving scenario. Though the women's rights activists can make a nominal claim, the independent working "girl" did much to redefine notions of "moral" and "proper" behavior for women and to reinvent women as independent economic entities. In many ways, these women's daily actions were far more "radical" than the speeches and marches of the activists. We might consider, perhaps, that there are competing notions of feminism at work, including competing ideas of "how a feminist looks." Maybe the real feminist is the one wearing the lipstick.

Current feminist theorizing generally treats modern corporate capitalism as a uniquely white male phenomenon, but cosmetics companies are an exception that produces a curious contradiction. Lois Banner bemoans the dearth of entrepreneurial women in the history of the garment industry, which resulted in female seamstresses going to work for male-dominated factories. In contrast, with the important exceptions of Charles Revson and Richard Hudnut, nearly all the founders of major cosmetics companies in America were women: Elizabeth Arden, Helena Rubinstein, Estée Lauder, Dorothy Gray and others. Banner criticizes these women precisely *because* they were entrepreneurial and commercial. She, like many other feminists writing today, seems unwilling to let *any* commercial enterprise be acceptable to feminism. While such a view may satisfy doctrinaire Marxism, it seems a crude way to deal with a situation that is hardly absolute. The commercial beauty culture has seen upstart challengers, working-class enterprises and avant-garde expressions. A cultural philosophy that cannot distinguish between The Body Shop and Revlon, or between Benetton and Sears, is insufficiently calibrated.

Ignoring or dismissing the women of industry allows critics to claim that cosmetics ads are the patriarchy's directives of "how women should look." Here arises another puzzle, though, because cosmetics advertisements have traditionally been written by women. Historically, advertising has employed more women than other industries, and at higher levels and salaries. But women were usually segregated into their own groups and given a carefully circumscribed list of products to work on, usually the ones men were embarrassed about, including cosmetics if the agency had any.

Models are a third group of women involved in the production of the beauty culture's texts. In the 1900s, artists' models were considered one tiny step up from prostitutes. As mass production of images grew, the beautiful woman who could pose for brush or camera was an increasingly valued player. The anti-beauty faction of feminism still tends to treat models as non-persons, referring to them as "flat images" or "mannikins." This characterization is snobbish, demeaning, inaccurate, and unfair. The relationship between a model and a photographer, artist or designer is not passive, but dialogic and creative, much like that between an actress and a director.

The model's social ascent was indicative of a new ethic of beauty emerging. Arthur Marwick, in his *Beauty in History*, argues that in the "modern" concept of beauty, good looks may be exploited for their own sake to the economic benefit of the bearer, without necessarily being tied to the granting of sexual favors. Beautiful persons, male or female, may use their beauty to please audiences, win contests, advertise products, gain employment in various capacities or, as traditionally, make a good marriage. Physical beauty became another attribute, like intelligence, talent, or wealth, that could be used toward the achievement of material and emotional success. Naomi Wolf's *The Beauty Myth* (1991) discusses the unconscionable discrimination that has resulted from the "Professional Beauty Qualification." However, her assertion that the "beauty myth" arose in the 1980s as part of a backlash against feminism is quite inaccurate and obscures the economic benefits and social mobility offered by this historical shift.

Over the course of this period, advertisements tell much about the ups and downs, the back and forth, of the discourse on beauty. Several notions of "the beautiful" can be seen to compete in any particular period and, over time, the ideals of feminism – athleticism, health, and natural products – make themselves felt in the popular discourse over and over again. Many graphic ideals of beauty followed the Gibson Girl: Maxfield Parrish's girl on a rock, John Held's flappers, the pinups of World War II, and so on. In each, the themes of "modern" versus "traditional," "proper" versus "unconventional," can be discerned, weaving through various strains of the discourse on what it meant to be "modern," "feminine," and even, "feminist." One must interpret these images in context or, as with the Gibson Girl, risk being tricked by contemporary perceptions. Furthermore, understanding one image often requires knowing how it speaks to other images, other ideals, other speakers.

A famous example is the dialogue between Revlon and Cover Girl. Introduced in the early 1950s, Revlon's "Fire and Ice Girl" had several characteristics of the "modern" woman: she dresses as if she were a little "loose" ("Have you ever wanted to wear an ankle bracelet?"), embraces the controversial ("Do you secretly hope the next man you meet will be a psychiatrist?"), is the object of jealousy ("Do you sometimes feel that other women resent you?"), is independent ("Would you streak your hair with platinum without consulting your husband?") and she is frankly interested in sex ("Do you close your eyes when you're kissed?"). Behind the Revlon girl is the fusion of two opposing class standards of beauty: Charles Revson himself referred to her as a "Park Avenue whore." No matter how endearing her lusty unconventionality may be, though, her life's work seems to be presenting the picture of an oversexed "piece of fluff" to men and engaging in a mutually destructive competition with other women. She is the side of Marilyn Monroe we don't like, gripped by the neurosis of narcissism that Simone de Beauvoir was writing about at this time – always playing to the imagined male gaze. She is Betty Friedan's feminine mystique out for the evening.

When Cover Girl cosmetics were introduced in the late 1950s, the new brand was a nuisance upstart and Revlon was a giant. Cover Girl's chemical base was Noxema with a new postwar wonder added, "hexachlorophene," which allowed the ads to make many truthful health claims: using antiseptic, Cover Girl was actually better for your skin than using no makeup at all. In the ad campaign, a beautiful but unknown young woman told how "natural" and "good for you" Cover Girl was, then her face was framed by a famous magazine masthead – and the viewer "discovered" her as that month's "cover girl." After the removal of hexachlorophene from the market (it had started going into nearly everything, and if a little hexachlorophene was a good thing, too much was not), Cover Girl continued to emphasize its "natural, clean" look and began to show the models sailing, swimming, and riding. Thus, the campaign came to have the desirable attributes of a "feminist" approach to makeup: it looked "natural," it was "good for you" and it was associated with a healthy and athletic lifestyle. Cover Girl was tremendously popular among younger women, stepping in line with the growing idealization of athletic women that begins with the Gibson Girl, produces the cult of the cheerleader, and probably reaches its peak in the fitness craze of the 1980s. Cover Girl's arch rival and alter ego was the sexy, night-clubbing Revlon girl, and all the ads were written with that distinction in mind.

Today, Cover Girl is still the biggest seller among women under 40, an honor it owes in no small part to the new aesthetic of beauty espoused by the second wave of feminism. Lynn Giordano was an undergraduate in journalism at the University of Wisconsin during the late 1960s, but by the late 1980s, she was creative director for Cover Girl makeup. Giordano recalls that, with the rise in feminist activity on college campuses, Cover Girl became the makeup you could wear and still hold on to your politics.

"No woman, no matter how radical her politics – this is the real truth, I mean, you'll never get women to admit this, but no matter how left of center they stood, they wanted to look good when they were standing there," she told the Smithsonian's advertising historians. "And they would claim they weren't wearing makeup but you'd sneak some stuff in. And one of the reasons Cover Girl went through the roof was that they were selling a no-makeup look right when it was great to be a no-makeup look."

This is the same moment described by Susan Brownmiller, the ultimate irony: choosing a brand of makeup that will help you look like "a good feminist" when feminism did not allow makeup. It is, again, the complex politics of appearance. Much of the argument against the beauty culture is based on the assumption that the sole purpose for aspiring to beauty is to attract men, despite substantial documentation that cultivating one's appearance has both economic and psychic benefits that may be unrelated to sexual allure. Reducing "beauty" to "sex" ignores other roles played by grooming and fashion, such as the communication of character, the acknowledgment of setting or occasion, the display of rank, the challenge to authority and so forth. In this light, categorically denouncing cosmetics and other beauty tools is an overly simplistic, insensitive response to a complex human practice.

The Cover Girl campaign continued to evolve toward a blonde, blue-eyed ideal of beauty, an athletic, ostensibly "natural" perfection that was airbrushed and retouched into unattainability. By the 1980s, however, other aesthetics began to emerge as challengers: the "Dress for Success" look of new female professionals, the "punk" look of Deborah Harry, Madonna, and Cyndi Lauper, as well as the athletic look epitomized by the aerobics fad. Each of these could make a claim to be more "feminist" than the other. Each had its commercial counterparts in advertising. Each was subject to controversy. Early in the 1980s, for example, feminist students of pop culture buzzed over whether Cyndi Lauper was a better role model for women than Madonna, though both were highly theatrical in their self-presentation. The issue then, as now, was whether Madonna is simply too pretty and too sexy to be a good feminist. We seem to have forgotten (or are now too young to remember) that the same things were once said about Gloria Steinem.

Though feminism has tended to treat beauty as a symbol of oppression, what lurks not far beneath the surface is the reality of beauty as power. In a world in which women have had few legal rights, and even fewer economic ones, beauty has sometimes provided women with some relief and some control over their circumstances. From histories like Lois Banner's *American Beauty* (1983) to contemporary studies like Robin Lakoff and Raquel Scherr's *Face Value: the Politics of Beauty* (1984), we can see that the power of beautiful women is not only over men, but also over other women. "Women cannot join with women in thinking about – much less talking about – looks, without great anguish," Lakoff and Scherr write.

Beauty is extraordinarily difficult for women to talk about with each other, but once they started in interviews with Lakoff and Scherr, the authors felt as if a floodgate had opened. The responses were passionate, poignant, sometimes tearful. Lakoff and Scherr concluded that the intractable position of "official" feminism had made beauty a taboo topic. We are not supposed to care about it, so we don't talk about it (except in so far as the problem can be demonized and externalized). Attempts to rethink the issue are quickly silenced with charges of "anti-feminism" or "backlash." As a consequence, what masquerades for criticism on the topic is often closer to superstition than analysis, more dogma than insight, demagoguery rather than revolution.

References

Banner, Lois (1983) *American Beauty* (New York: Knopf).
Brownmiller, Susan (1984) *Femininity* (New York: Linden Press).
Lakoff, Robin and Scherr, Raquel (1984) *Face Value: the Politics of Beauty* (New York: Routledge).
Marwick, Arthur (1988) *Beauty in History* (London: Thames and Hudson).
Wolf, Naomi (1991) *The Beauty Myth: How Images of Beauty are Used against Women* (New York: W. Morrow).

Suggested activities

Questions for discussion

On advertising

1 Do you find Kilbourne's or Scott's view of images of women in advertising more persuasive? Explain why. Do both approaches have *some* validity? If so, how would you reconcile their seeming differences?
2 Does Scott adequately attend to differences among women?

On pornography

1 Is pornography simply a more extreme form of the sexist portrayals of women in other spheres of culture or does it also differ in kind? If the latter,

is the difference due to the type of sexism involved, the level of violence, the kind of sexual content, or some other feature(s)?

2   How should pornography be dealt with at a formal or governmental level? Consider various alternative remedies or responses: prohibiting only the most violent forms, like child pornography; imposing stricter limits on who is authorized to buy and sell pornography; requiring producers to prove informed consent of all participants; or prohibiting all pornographic materials?

3   In particular, what do you think of allowing civil rights lawsuits to be brought against pornographers rather than censoring or prohibiting the pro- duction of pornography? Should this scheme for regulating pornography be viewed as being in conflict with protecting free speech?

4   Can women give genuine informed consent to participate in the production and consumption of pornography?

5   What is your response to the argument that, as more women become involved in the manufacture of pornography, it will become less sexist, misogynistic, and patriarchal, and more empowering for women by provid- ing them with an outlet for their fantasies about sex and power?

6   What is the difference, if any, between restricting pornography as harmful to women and/or society in general, and requiring a drug company to remove a medication from the market when it is shown to have harmful effects on those who use it, or requiring a toy company to recall toys that risk harm to children's safety?

7   How would you answer the questions raised in the introduction to this chapter: what is the influence of pornographic images on real women? Is pornography harmful to women? Does it contribute to or result in the degradation and sexual abuse of women?

Films and videos

On fashion and advertising

Still Killing Us Softly by Jean Kilbourne and Cambridge Documentary Films (1987). VHS/30 mins. Available from Cambridge Documentary Films. Video of a presentation Jean Kilbourne made at Harvard College, using adver- tisements from magazines, album covers, and billboards to analyze a $100 billion a year industry that promotes sexism, attitudes toward women and girls as sex objects, and fosters a climate that promotes violence against women, eating disorders, sexual harassment, and teenage pregnancy.

On pornography

Not a Love Story, directed by Bonnie Sherr Kline (1983). VHS/69 mins. Avail- able from the National Film Board of Canada. Follows the film's director and a Montreal stripper as they explore the world of peep shows, strip joints, and sex supermarkets.

Patently Offensive: Porn under Siege by Harriet Koskoff (1993). VHS/58 mins. Distributed by Women Make Movies. An examination of the issues surrounding pornography, including footage from the 1986 Meese Commission hearings, and interviews with a spokesperson for the ACLU, a forensic psychiatrist, criminologist, publisher of pornographic magazines, law professors, radical feminist Andrea Dworkin, and representatives of both pro- and anti-pornography women's organizations.

Porn in the USA, produced by Mary Murphy (1992). VHS/48 mins. Distributed by Ambrose Video Publishing, Inc. Segment of 48 hours. Advocates and opponents present their views of the pornography industry in the US.

Pornography: the Double Message, produced by the Canadian Broadcasting Corporation (1985). VHS/28 mins. Distributed by Filmaker's Library. Canadian video about the hard-core pornography industry, the relationship between pornography and violence against women, and how video has made X-rated movies readily accessible. Deals with how viewers of hardcore pornography perceive women and sex, using graphic film clips of violent pornography to demonstrate its current guise.

Rate it X by Lucy Winer and Paula De Koenigsberg (1986). 16 mm/VHS/93 mins. Distributed by Women Make Movies. Looks at sexism in America, as evidenced in pornography, advertising, and less obvious sources that rationalize sexism in commerce, religion, and social values. Sheds light on issues of censorship, advertising, pornography, and violence against women.

Visible Harm, directed by Deborah Perkin, produced by Ann Ross Nuir (1992). VHS/41 mins. Distributed by Landmark Media Inc. Explores the line between erotica and pornography. Has been characterized by one instructor as "less chaotic and frightening than *Not a Love Story*" (above).

Other activities

1 Look at a dozen or so advertisements that include women in them. Analyze how women are portrayed. Which characteristics discussed above did you find present in the advertisements you reviewed? What kinds of roles are women playing, and what is their relationship to others, especially males and children? In what (other) ways are men and women portrayed differently? Analyze how these advertisements compare to what Irving Goffman and Jean Kilbourne said about gendered advertisements more than a decade ago. How accurate are these author's observations today? Can you discern changes in how women are portrayed in contemporary advertisements? If so, how would you characterize these changes, and how would you explain the reasons for them?

2 Compare a number of "men's" and "women's" magazines. What similarities and differences do you find in the types of advertising, the subject
   matter of feature articles, advice columns, and so on? How do the two
   types of magazines compare on the amount of coverage given to diet and
   fitness, cosmetics and personal hygiene, and fashion? What are the images
   of women portrayed in each?
3 Research one (or more) of the feminist activists Scott mentions as the first
   women to challenge commercial beauty culture. What were the prevailing
   standards of beauty that these women opposed? How have these standards changed? Have the prevailing standards of beauty become more rigid
   or more flexible since the nineteenth and early twentieth centuries?
4 Research the prevailing standards of beauty in American culture in some
   period of American history or in another culture, looking at some or all of
   the following: fashion, physical appearance, shape and size, makeup, hair
   styles, accessories, and so on. (Women's magazines are a good source of
   information on this topic.) What do the differences in beauty in different
   times and places and cultures suggest about prevailing standards of beauty
   in our own culture and historical era?
5 In connection with the video *Still Killing Us Softly* (see entry under "Films
   and Videos" above), discuss the merits of Kilbourne's argument, and the
   extent to which the advertising tactics she describes are still in evidence in
   today's ads.
6 Find two advertisements that include images of women used to sell a
   product, one that you think is a positive portrayal and one that you think
   is negative. Turn these in with a 1–2 page typewritten appraisal of the ads
   which considers *why* you think these are negative/positive portrayals, how
   other aspects of the ads (for example, other people, objects, background,
   graphics, text) contribute to the portrayal, and how these ads relate to
   the larger context of advertising and images of women in the media (for
   example, are they representative of the norm, unusual, average?).
7 Conduct a content analysis of one women's magazine for a year period
   (years may be divided among the class in order to provide material from
   different years for comparison and analysis of shifts and trends). Categories
   for analysis include the types of gender roles women occupy, the range
   of women's interests (i.e., do they extend beyond women's "traditional"
   interests in beauty, fashion, health and diet, men, cooking, and domestic
   pursuits), the images of female beauty reflected in the ads, the diversity of
   different types of women represented, and so on.
8 Have a class debate on whether pornography should be legally prohibited. Divide into groups taking the sides of different interest groups
   involved in the contemporary debate, including anti-censorship feminists
   and anti-pornography feminists.

Bibliography

On advertising and print media

Ang, Ien (1988) "Feminist desire and female pleasure: on Janice Radway's *Reading the Romance: Women, Patriarchy, and Popular Literature*," *Camera Obscura*, 16 (special issue: Television and the Female Consumer), pp. 179–89.

Banner, Lois (1983) *American Beauty* (New York: Knopf). A history of women's relationship to beauty in the United States.

Banta, Martha (1987) *Imaging American Women: Idea and Ideals in Cultural History* (New York: Columbia University Press). Examines visual and verbal images of women between 1876 and 1912 and the purposes they were used for.

Betterton, Rosemary (ed.) (1987) *Looking On: Images of Femininity in the Visual Arts and Media* (London: Pandora). Collection of essays organized under sections entitled "Advertising femininity: theoretical perspectives," "Changing stereotypes? Women and Sexuality," "Pornography: the politics of representation," and "New images for old: the iconography of the body".

Chapkis, Wendy (1986) *Beauty Secrets: Women and the Politics of Appearance* (Boston: South End Press). Focuses on the beauty system as central to women's oppression. Contains several autobiographical statements of women's experience in responding to cultural expectations for female beauty.

Ciriello, Sarah (ed.) *Challenging Media Images of Women* (PO Box 902, Framingham, MA 01701). Feminist newsletter devoted to showing biased portrayals of women in the mass media.

Communication Research Associates, Inc., *Media Report to Women* (published bi-monthly). Contact at 10606 Mantz Road, Silver Spring, MD 20993-1228. Describes itself as "the nation's oldest newsletter covering women in the world."

Creedon, Pamela (ed.) (1993) *Women in Mass Communication* (Newbury Park, CA: Sage). Addresses both images and real women working in the mass communications industry.

Dines, Gail and Humez, Jean (eds) (1995) *Gender, Race, and Class in Media: a Text-Reader* (Thousand Oaks, CA: Sage). Collection of essays designed to introduce undergraduates to contemporary media scholarship in a way that builds on their experiences with and interests in media. Most essays take an explicitly critical political perspective.

Dorenkamp, Angela, McClymer, John, Moynihan, Mary and Vadim, Arlene (eds) (1985) *Images of Women in American Popular Culture* (San Diego: Harcourt Brace Jovanovich). A collection of excerpts from a variety of materials: advertisements, newspaper and magazine articles, bestsellers, poems, advice literature, marriage manuals, and political tracts. Includes sections on "Women's nature," "Women's place," "Women as object," "Sweethearts and wives," "Mothers," "Workers," "Sisters," and "Struggles and visions."

Faludi, Susan (1991) "The 'trends' of antifeminism: the media and the backlash," in *Backlash: the Undeclared War against American Women* (New York: Doubleday Press).

Fawcet, Adriene Ward (1993) "Narrowcast in past: women earn revised role in advertising," *Advertising Age*, 64 (41), p. S1(2). Describes the changing images of women over the decades since the early 1900s.

Goffman, Irving (1979) *Gender Advertisements* (Cambridge, MA: Harvard University Press).

Hensen, Joseph, Reed, Evelyn and Waters, Mary-Alice (1986) *Cosmetics, Fashions, and the Exploitation of Women* (New York: Pathfinder Press). Socialist perspectives on the beauty industry as oppressive to women, drawn from *The Militant* magazine.

hooks, bell (1995) "Madonna: phantom mistress or soul sister?," in Gail Dines and Jean Humez (eds), *Gender, Race, and Class in Media: a Text-Reader* (Thousand Oaks, CA: Sage). Shows how gender ideology is racialized by critiquing Madonna for failing to reject conventional ideals of beauty and introduces the concept of the cultural appropriation of blackness in popular media.

Keller, Kathryn (1994) *Mothers and Work in Popular American Magazines* (Westport, CT: Greenwood). Traces changes in the justifications given for gender-based divisions of labor in the home and workplace, and the lack of serious consideration given to the "double bind" of women's dual responsibilities in the domestic spheres and labor market in popular women's magazines from 1950 to 1989.

Labowitz, Leslie and Lacy, Suzanne (1985) "Mass media, popular culture, and fine art," in Richard Hertz (ed.), *Theories of Contemporary Art* (Englewood Cliffs, NJ: Prentice-Hall). Examines the depiction of women as victims of violence in the media and fine art as reinforcing stereotypical understandings of women as powerless. The authors encourage artists to reshape public consciousness by creating images of women as powerful instead.

Lakoff, Robin and Scherr, Raquel (1984) *Face Value: the Politics of Beauty* (New York: Routledge).

Matlin, Margaret (1987) *The Psychology of Women* (New York: Holt, Rinehart, and Winston).

Media Watch, *Action Agenda: Media Action Alliance and Media Watch* (available from Media Watch, PO Box 618, Santa Cruz, CA 95061). Newsletter reporting on the media's portrayal of women.

Radway, Janice (1984) *Reading the Romance: Women, Patriarchy, and Popular Literature* (Chapel Hill, NC: University of North Carolina Press). Study of romance novels. Radway's thesis is that, although women readers of romances may assert their independence in the act of reading, the content of these novels actually undermines their independence by reinforcing stereotypical views of women's proper social roles.

Rapping, Elayne (1994) *Media-tions: Forays into the Culture and Gender Wars* (Boston: South End Press). Series of essays exploring the significance of soap operas, Madonna, and other artifacts of the media's relationship to, and representations of, women.

Snitow, Ann (1995) "Mass market romance: porn for women is different," in Gail Dines and Jean Humez (eds), *Gender, Race, and Class in Media: a Text-Reader* (Thousand Oaks, CA: Sage).

Turin, Maureen (1983) "Fashion shapes: film, the fashion industry, and the image of women," *Socialist Review*, 13, pp. 79–95.

Weir, June (1983) "Door ajar to women of all ages in ads," *Advertising Age*, 64 (41), p. S2(2). On the slow erosion of the advertising definition of beauty, as witnessed by the increasing use of older women in advertisements.

Winship, Janice (1987) *Inside Women's Magazines* (London: Pandora Press). Rejects feminist dismissals of women's magazines as (only) oppressive to women. Provides historical background, portrayals of women at work and leisure, relationships between women, advertising, and trends in women's magazines in the past decade.

Wolf, Naomi (1991) *The Beauty Myth: How Images of Beauty are Used against Women* (New York: W. Morrow).

On pornography

Assiter, Alison and Avedon, Carol (eds) (1993) *Bad Girls and Dirty Pictures: the Challenge to Reclaim Feminism* (London: Pluto Press). Collection of essays which grew out of Feminists against Censorship, organized in 1989 to "provide a voice for many feminists who cannot accept censorship as a useful tool for women." Collection includes anti-censorship feminist scholars, women who work in the sex industry or "pink collar ghetto" of secretarial, office work, nannies and cleaners. Intended to provide a forum for women who object to the anti-sex/anti-pornography campaigns.

Baird, Robert and Rosenbaum, Stuart (eds) (1991) *Pornography: Private Right or Public Menace?* (Buffalo, NY: Prometheus). A collection of articles under the headings of "The commission reports," "Feminist perspectives," "Libertarian perspectives," "Religious perspectives," and "The causal issue." Includes prominent writers in the area, including Susan Brownmiller, Gloria Steinem, Andrea Dworkin, Helen Longino, Ronald Dworkin, and George Will.

Balos, Beverly and Fellows, Mary Louise (eds) (1994) "Pornography," chapter 8 in *Law and Violence against Women: Cases and Materials on Systems of Oppression* (Durham, NC: Carolina Academic Press). A collection of legal cases and scholarly analysis.

Berger, Ronald, Searles, Patricia, and Cottle, Charles (1991) *Feminism and Pornography* (New York: Praeger). A readable and informative "primer" on feminist perspectives about pornography, including background on traditional perspectives, radical and libertarian feminism, liberal, Marxist, socialist and black feminist perspectives, the legal context, and non-legal alternatives.

Burstyn, Varda (ed.) (1985) *Women against Censorship* (Vancouver: Douglas and McIntyre). Mostly Canadian focus, but some materials on US.

Carse, Alisa (1995) "Pornography: an uncivil liberty?," *Hypatia*, 10 (1), pp. 155–82. Argues that, although pornography harms women by contributing to the conditions that undermine their liberty and equality, legal regulation carries with it unwanted consequences that make alternative strategies for combatting pornography preferable.

Cole, Susan (1989) *Pornography and the Sex Crisis* (Toronto, Ontario: Douglas and McIntyre). Feminist anti-censorship *and* anti-pornography perspective on pornography in Canada.

Dworkin, Andrea (1989) *Pornography: Men Possessing Women*, 2nd edn (New York: Perigen Books). An anti-pornography perspective by a prominent feminist writer on pornography and violence against women.

Easton, Susan (1994) *The Problem of Pornography: Regulation and the Right to Free Speech* (London: Routledge).

Gibson, Pamela Church and Gibson, Roma (eds) (1993) *Dirty Looks: Women, Pornography, Power* (London: British Film Institute/Bloomington, IN: Indiana University Press).

Gubar, Susan and Hoff, Joan (1989) *For Adult Users Only: the Dilemma of Violent Pornography* (Bloomington, IN: Indiana University Press). Collection of articles that originated in a faculty seminar at Indiana University.

Kaminer, Wendy (1992) "Feminists against the First Amendment," *The Atlantic Monthly*, November, pp. 111–18. Feminist anti-censorship perspective.

Itzin, Catherine (ed.) (1992) *Pornography: Women, Violence and Civil Liberties* (Oxford: Oxford University Press). A large collection of articles from an anti-pornography perspective, covering the pornography industry, power, racist aspects, portrayals of homosexuals, evidence of harm, and the law, censorship, and civil liberties. Although the collection was published in the United Kingdom, many of the articles relate to the status of pornography in the US.

Lacombe, Dany (1994) *Blue Politics: Pornography and the Law in the Age of Feminism* (Toronto, Ontario: University of Toronto Press). Analyzes the Canadian experience of attempted law reform of pornography in the mid-1980s, which parallels the US experience in significant respects, and focuses on how feminist definitions were employed on both sides of the debate.

Lederer, Laura (ed.) (1980) *Take Back the Night: Women on Pornography* (New York: W. Morrow). Collection of classic essays by prominent feminist authors, including Susan

Brownmiller, Gloria Steinem, Helen Longino, Diana Russell, Charlotte Bunch, Alice Walker, Robin Morgan, Susan Griffin, Andrea Dworkin, Phyllis Chesler, Irene Diamond, Wendy Kaminer, Audre Lorde, and Kathleen Barry. Presents the feminist perspective that "pornography is the ideology of a culture which promotes and condones rape, women-battering, and other crimes of violence against women."

Longino, Helen (1991) "Pornography, oppression, and freedom: a closer look," in Robert Baird and Stuart Rosenblum (eds), *Pornography: Private Right or Public Menace?* (Buffalo, NY: Prometheus). A feminist anti-pornography perspective that directly addresses free speech anti-censorship arguments.

MacKinnon, Catharine (1987) *Feminism Unmodified: Discourses on Life and Law* (Cambridge, MA: Harvard University Press). Part III contains several essays on pornography, including "Linda's Life and Andrea's Work" (about *Deep Throat's* porn star Linda Marciano's abuse and sexual slavery, the legal protection given to the producers of *Deep Throat*, and Andrea Dworkin's work against pornography) and "Not a Moral Issue" (an argument against pornography).

MacKinnon, Catharine (1993) *Only Words* (Cambridge, MA: Harvard University Press). Anti-pornography argument based on the premise that pornography is causally linked to men raping and sexually assaulting women, and violates women's civil rights.

Richardson, Laurel (1993) "Gender stereotyping in the English language," in L. Richardson and Verta Taylor (eds), *Feminist Frontiers III* (New York: McGraw-Hill).

Rodgerson, Gillian and Wilson, Elizabeth (eds) (1991) *Pornography and Feminism: the Case against Censorship* (London: Lawrence and Wishart).

Russell, Diana (1993) "Pornography and rape: a causal model," in Catherine Itzin (ed.), *Pornography: Women, Violence and Civil Liberties* (Oxford: Oxford University Press).

Russell, Diana (ed.) (1993) *Making Violence Sexy: Feminist Views on Pornography* (New York: Teachers College, Columbia University). Collection of essays on pornography and its relationship to violence against women from mostly anti-pornography perspectives.

Segal, Lynne and McIntosh, Mary (eds) (1992) *Sex Exposed: Sexuality and the Pornography Debate* (London: Virago Press). Essays on pornography in both the US and UK. The authors take an anti-censorship perspective based on skepticism about pornography causing violence against women, and the dangers of foreclosing women's search for understanding and expressing the complexity of their sexual lives.

Steinem, Gloria (1980) "Erotica versus pornography: a clear and present difference," in Laura Lederer (ed.), *Take Back the Night: Women on Pornography* (New York: W. Morrow).

Steinem, Gloria (1983) "The real Linda Lovelace," in *Outrageous Acts and Everyday Rebellions* (New York: Holt, Reinhart and Winston). Describes the sexual and physical abuse and exploitation of Linda Marciano, the porn star of *Deep Throat*. Years after the movie was made, Marciano disclosed that she had been coerced into the porn business by her then husband, who threatened to kill her if she refused or tried to leave. Her book *Ordeal* chronicles her difficulties in being believed, and especially in getting reporters to publish her account of her involvement in the porn industry.

Strossen, Nadine (1995) *Defending Pornography: Free Speech, Sex, and the Fight for Women's Rights* (New York: Scribner). Takes an anti-censorship perspective *as* a feminist perspective, contending that the anti-pornography feminists like Dworkin and MacKinnon are undermining women's rights.

Unger, Rhoda and Crawford, Mary (1992) "Pornography," in *Women and Gender: a Feminist Psychology* (New York: McGraw-Hill). Provides a useful overview of the topic, emphasizing the psychological harm pornography may cause to consumers and women.

5
Women and Popular Culture II: Television and Film

Introduction

The media play an incredibly important role in shaping American culture's images of and values about gender. Both television and the movies provide social images of women that shape our definitions of what and who men and women are, often subconsciously. Andrea Press describes the role of fiction television in American culture as one that "comments upon and helps to shape our experience of, and ideas about, the form our private lives should take" (Press, 1991: 49). Press concludes that television contributes to women's oppression in the family, and, for working-class women, both at home and at work.

Portrayals of women in both television and film continue to be primarily male-derived and designed for the enjoyment of a male audience. Even though women have made significant inroads in the field of mass communication, they continue to be a minority in determining the images of women that are produced and disseminated by the mass media. The existence of a majority of women in the mass communications field has not been accompanied by a revaluing of the predominant gender values that privilege male over female. Indeed, the gendered nature of mass communications is seldom addressed (Creedon, 1993: 3–9).

The complex relationship of viewers to film and television has resulted in a number of different approaches and theories about how viewers respond to what they see on the screen. In a path-breaking article on spectatorship in the cinema, entitled "Visual pleasure and narrative cinema" written in 1975 (see Mulvey, 1989), Laura Mulvey showed how viewing films is a gendered activity in which the male director, actor, or viewer makes the male the subject of viewing (the "male gaze"), while placing females in the position of objects. Mulvey argues that visual pleasure in mainstream Hollywood film originates in and reproduces a structure of male looking whereby viewers (both male and female) are asked to identify with the male gaze at an objectified female. In

Mulvey's estimation, this structure parallels and reinforces male domination of women. Mulvey's approach, which is based in psychoanalytic theory, became the basis for much feminist work on popular culture.

In *Viewing Positions: Ways of Seeing Film*, Linda Williams (1995) observes that "by the late 1970s, it had become a kind of orthodoxy of much feminist and ideological film criticism that all dominant cinema was organized for the power and pleasure of a single spectator-subject whose voyeuristic-sadistic gaze became a central figure of visual domination" (Williams, 1995: 3). This paradigm of the male gaze in cinema has been challenged since that time, however, as more work has been done on the diverse ways in which spectators actually relate to films.

According to one school of thought, film and television provide an outlet for our fantasies, enabling us to identify with particular movie and television characters or the stars who portray them, and thereby to escape the mundaneness of our own lives. Maureen Turin (1983) suggests that because most women characters (at least until recent years) have been weak, vulnerable, and self-defeating, women identify with the character's *bodies*, which do project the power to attract desire, and consequently with the fashions that clothe those bodies.

For another school of thought, popular culture is a site of struggle where meanings are shifting and subject to contestation, rather than fixed and unchanging. For example, in *The Female Gaze*, Lorraine Gamman and Margaret Marshment (1988) collected essays that ask how women look at women in popular culture. Moving beyond the thesis of the "male gaze," they inquire about the existence of a "female gaze."

More recent work challenges earlier theories – like Mulvey's and Berger's – that there is only a single way of seeing film, emphasizing that there are a variety of different "viewing positions." More recent film criticism suggests that popular movies may offer multiple "subject positions." Such social locations enable a wide variety of media consumers to derive pleasure from viewing films, regardless of their gender, race, class, sexual orientation, and other differences from the producers of such films. For example, Gamman and Marshment (1988) suggest that the dominant gaze is not necessarily male or heterosexual; that the gaze must shift when there are no women, but only men, to look at. The authors also note that by privileging gender, psychoanalytic criticism tends to ignore other power relations, especially those of race, class, and age. The readings in this chapter focus on representations of women in mainstream American film and television.

Television

Television is a particularly potent conveyor of information about appropriate gender roles. Especially for teenagers, television characters and advertising models provide role models of appropriate gender behavior. Frequently, men are given the dominant roles involving power and authority, and women are portrayed as sex objects who are subordinate to men. Deviating from these expected gendered behaviors may have strong social consequences. Males may be labeled as effeminate or homosexual if they do not adhere to the prescribed "male" behaviors of competitiveness, rough and tumble play, aggressiveness, loudness, and so on, while females may be labeled "tomboys" or "dykes" if they do engage in such behaviors, or fail to adhere to "feminine" behaviors.

Even though over half of television viewers are female, men still comprise approximately two-thirds of the prime-time characters. The majority of narrators and voice-overs on television are male. Women characters are often used as props or background for the dominant male characters, and are less frequently portrayed as people of power or authority (see Unger and Crawford, 1992). Only a minority of female characters are shown in professional roles. Women are less likely than men to work outside the home, and are more frequently classified as homemakers than by occupation.

Standards of physical attractiveness differ significantly for men and women, with women more often physically attractive and thin than men. This is especially the case for African-American women, who are typically thin if they are portraying working women, but heavy set if they are portraying women primarily in the home. Women are four times as likely as male characters to be shown provocatively dressed. Television programs continue to portray women as the helpless victims of male sex and violence: being abused, raped, victimized, wrongly accused and imprisoned. These images and stereotypes spill over into advertising, as we saw in chapter 4.

Portrayals of women on television fail to represent the struggles of real women accurately, such as "the pressures of work and family, finding and paying for child care, balancing home and job responsibilities, and stretching the family budget, which many women experience in their lives" (Press, 1991: 28). Many television images of women distort or misrepresent the reality of American women's lives by, for example, portraying most single mothers as affluent enough not to have to work. Most working women are shown in satisfying professional careers. Working parents are able to balance their work and family responsibilities effortlessly (Steenland, 1995: 76–7). In addition, television offers almost no programs with poor families, and a disproportionately high number of families with a father present. Working-class families are misrepresented as matriarchal (for example, *Rosanne*), whereas, in reality, such families are predominantly patriarchal. Working-class women have very little power in their marriages, since they have few alternatives to domestic roles.

Television has downplayed the significance of systematic discrimination against women by suggesting that women's problems are personal or individualized. Together with portraying the women's movement in a negative light, this may contribute to the low estimation of the term "feminism" among young people today (Press, 1991; see Metzger, 1992). In addition, television shows during the 1980s tended to re-segregate blacks and whites into different shows, narrowly define minorities as black, while omitting most people of color, use sexist humor, and portray violence against women with women as helpless victims.

Observers of how women are portrayed on television have reached conflicting conclusions about whether representations of women have become more positive and/or accurate during the past few decades. For example, in *Backlash*, Susan Faludi (1991) suggests that the portrayal of women on television actually deteriorated during the 1980s. She shows that most roles for independent women were removed, leaving only female characters dependent upon or subservient to men. Television programming of the 1980s reconstructed the hierarchy of female gender, placing suburban homemakers at the top, followed by career women, with single women at the bottom, as if trying to remove women from the workplace and reinscribe them in the home (Faludi, 1991; Press, 1991).

Television portrayals of certain groups of women reveal a discernible lack of progress during the 1980s. For example, portrayals of women of color from racial and ethnic groups other than white or black showed almost no increase, except for a rise in the portrayal of Hispanic women from 0 to 2 percent! Images of working-class women decreased (from over 10 percent to only 2 percent in 1984, then back to 5 percent), replaced by a greater percentage of affluent women (from 20 percent to 56 percent in 1984, then back down to 29 percent). In reality, most women are working class (yearly incomes of $15,000 or less), and only 22 percent are affluent (earn more than $50,000) (Steenland, 1995).

However, there are other indications that the 1980s was a decade of improvement in the portrayal of women on television. The presence of more working mothers, non-traditional families, older women, stronger black women characters, female "buddy" shows, working-class heroines, and authentic female police, along with the "mainstreaming" of women's issues, can all be interpreted as positive improvements (Steenland, 1995: 80).

In the reading "Solace in Soapland," Elayne Rapping provides a defense of soap operas as fantasies for women. She argues that they introduce progressive ideas such as inter-racial romance and homosexuality gradually so that they can be accepted by the viewing public. Contrary to Jean Kilbourne (in chapter 4), Rapping suggests that female viewers influence the television shows' sponsors, rather than the reverse: that women have been influenced by feminism and expect to see feminist themes in the television they watch.

Film

Representations of women in Hollywood movies have been similar in many respects to those on television. Portrayals of strong women are rare in Hollywood

films. Beautiful and/or intelligent women are frequently depicted as dangerous. Since few women are screenwriters, producers, or directors, there are
a disproportionate number of "action" films filled with sex, sexism, and violence. In these films, women are mute, present only as sex objects, or absent
completely.

Mainstream Hollywood films continue to be racist as well as sexist (Turin,
1983: 90). As dismal as the portrayal of women in Hollywood films has generally been, it has been even more abysmal with respect to women of color
(Hadley Freydberg, 1979: 4). When women of color have been portrayed at
all, which has been rarely, they have usually been cast in roles revolving around
sex, especially as "prostitutes, concubines, whores, and bitches," according to
the title of Elizabeth Hadley Freydberg's article.

Faludi (1991) concludes that the backlash also operated with respect to
Hollywood movies, revealing itself in portrayals of women as competing with
one another; as unhappy due to personal depression or to their freedom rather
than to unequal treatment or disadvantaging social circumstances; and as "good"
in roles as mothers, and "bad" in roles as independent women. Faludi suggests
that the few strong women characters in the movies of the 1980s are *mothers*,
in contrast to films of the 1970s, which offered a number of strong women
characters.

Many films of the 1980s portray men as taking the lead, raising the children,
saving the woman, winning the legal case, and so on. As the reading "No Way
to Treat a Lawyer" by Terry Kay Diggs shows, the disparities between Hollywood's portrayals of male and female lawyers change negatively in several
significant respects when the character is female.

In sum, the assessment of how women are portrayed in American films
and television, two of the dominant industries shaping cultural gender ideals,
is a negative one. As long as women are represented by such powerful media
as subordinate sex objects, secondary in significance and value to their male
counterparts, the status of "real" women will be negatively affected.

Solace in Soapland
Elayne Rapping

So what do you do when things get really bad? When your checkbook
won't balance, your relationship is on the rocks, your job may be phased

This reading first appeared in *Media-tions: Forays into the Culture and Gender Wars* (Boston:
South End Press, 1994), pp. 183–191.

out, your kids are threatening to run away, or worse, to never move out, and the headlines are giving you nightmares and indigestion? Most of our traditional escapes from such moments have been discredited. Drugs, alcohol, chocolate, shopping, sex – you name it, it's forbidden these days at the risk of jail, death, or, at best, a Twelve-Step Program.

Never mind. There is hope – daytime soap operas, where the air is pure, the money flows into your bank account automatically, and most people have a profound capacity for intimacy, compassion, and emotional growth – or are quick studies.

Soap operas are among the most popular and lucrative of all popular culture forms. Women of all ages, and an increasing number of men and children, for that matter, watch them religiously, staying loyal to a favorite show for years and passing on their particular rituals to later generations like family cookie recipes. The growing number of fan magazines like *Soap Opera Digest*, the increasing number of prime-time award shows for the genre, and the growing fad of college students – male and female alike – watching favorite shows together are clear signs of that. But, while you're likely to overhear private discussions of favorite soaps in office cafeterias, school corridors, and dentists' waiting rooms, most soap fans, in less "safe" environments, are likely to deny their guilty pleasure and even to join in the mockery and denigration that is the standard "official" attitude toward soaps.

Never mind, soap lovers, it's time to come out of the closet. Repeat after me: "it is not a sign of dementia, stupidity, or intellectual laziness to like soap operas." In fact, there are very good reasons for preferring the company of soap characters to one's usual daily routine, especially for women. As fantasies go, the ones presented by soaps are extremely seductive. They offer a lot of things that most of us need and desire but don't get much of in reality. The men on soaps, for one thing, are infinitely supportive and available, living for the women in their lives and never forgetting to buy flowers, gifts, and plan surprise parties for their loves. The women on soaps, even single working women, have beautifully furnished homes, professionally coiffed hair, and the most stylish, expensive wardrobes you've ever drooled over in *Vogue*. Good friends and functional families are pretty much a given for anyone who wants them. Which, in Soapland, is everyone, even the villains, who always have at least one or two understanding supporters who believe in their ability to reform.

And – contrary to popular opinion – soaps are more intelligent and progressive in their treatment of personal and social issues than most of what passes for "serious" fiction, film, and prime-time television. Amidst the current furor over date rape, for example, it is interesting to note that this topic has almost never been treated (as a problem as opposed to an accepted style of courting) in movies or on prime time. But, in the past several years, at least two soaps have treated the issue from a decidedly feminist perspective, at great length and in some psychological and social detail. In both cases, the victim was a lover of the rapist, a woman whose past (as is inevitable on soaps, the most sexually graphic shows on the air) was certainly checkered. In both cases the jury, realistically, acquitted the man. And, in both cases, he saw the light (in one case after witnessing a gang rape and realizing, at last the horror of his deed), confessed, and set about working with other sexual violators in treatment programs!

As long as relationships make the world go round and money and power are trivial afterthoughts, feminism can, conceivably, triumph. And if that's absurd, so be it. Realism offers cold comfort these days.

I could go on almost endlessly with similar examples of feminist story lines and influences. Media scholar George Gerbner has documented that the single greatest source of medical information in America is soap operas, which religiously present information and advice about things like breast cancer, venereal disease, drug and alcohol abuse, and other medical problems. A few years ago, when the AIDS crisis broke, one soap actually had professionals from treatment programs appear as characters on the show and run a town meeting to inform people and correct misinformation.

Soaps are also particularly good at helping people deal with tough issues in their daily lives that arise from changing mores, often brought about by the demands and successes of the women's movement. What a half-hour sitcom will, at best, cautiously mention and moralize about superficially, a soap will often treat for months on end, involving perhaps 30 different characters in endless discussions and raising many different points of view, representing the many angles that tough issues engender.

When black and white characters fall in love, for example, it is likely that everyone in town will discuss and argue about it and that popular characters will start off as downright bigots and gradually, through persuasion by friends as well as the dramatic examples set by the loving couple themselves, come to change their views. And because audiences so identify with and respect their favorite characters on these shows – after all, they've "known" them for years and visit them daily – the characters who represent unpopular but progressive ideas gradually gain audience sympathy and support, as first one and then another of the town Fathers and Mothers and Elected Officials come to their senses.

The most remarkable example of this process happened several years ago, on *All my Children*, when a regular character, a young woman with many scars from the heterosexual relationship wars (a given on soaps), got a crush on the woman who was treating her daughter for emotional problems. The therapist, an "out and proud" lesbian, was a model of dignity and integrity and, gradually, as everyone watched and talked, and talked and watched, the parents of the young woman went from horror to acceptance. After all, on soaps, it's love that matters and "good" characters eventually recognize healthy love when they see it.

Of course, nothing came of this relationship. We aren't in feminist heaven, after all. But this was no small thing, none the less. And I bet you are hearing about it here for the first time. That's because, as I said, people don't usually take soaps seriously enough to write about them or talk about them in highbrow discussions of "the horrors of mass culture."

But this doesn't mean these shows don't affect public opinion. They certainly do. I have no doubt at all that the initial reaction of outrage on the part of so many women at the accusations of sexual harassment against Clarence Thomas – and the way in which this reaction took the Senate Judiciary Committee by surprise – had a lot to do with the fact that women were emotionally primed to take this issue very seriously. Unlike the aging white men in Congress, who follow *The New York Times* and *The MacNeil–Lehrer News Hour* but wouldn't deign to watch *Days of our Lives*, they had been participating, vicariously, in all sorts of dramatic presentations over the years in which feminist assumptions and values are increasingly taken for granted as "common sense." Soap fans know a male chauvinist pig when they see one.

There are a couple of reasons why soaps treat women's issues more seriously than more "highbrow" art forms. Most obviously, soaps cater to a largely female audience targeted by the sponsors – the guys who pay the bills – as the major consumers of household products like cake mix, aspirin, and yes, soap. And women – as the guys who do the marketing research for sponsors and networks are paid to know – have, in the decades since feminism hit the cultural scene, come to think about things very differently from their pre-1960s foremothers. Issues like rape, domestic violence, sexual harassment, incest – the list goes on – are taken very seriously by female audiences these days, because of feminism, and sponsors know and respect that.

Of course, these issues also show up on prime time and in movies and novels, but not as emphatically – trust me. And that's because, for better or worse, soaps are a female ghetto that those in power (read men) don't take seriously or worry about too much. You won't hear Ted Koppel leading lofty discussions of the date rape incidents on *Santa Barbara* or *All my Children* (both of which took place years ago). But women all over America discussed these cases passionately.

But it's not just as audiences that women with feminist ideas influence soaps. Another effect of feminism has been to push women increasingly into professional work previously done by men. Television, a medium with less status than film or print journalism, and less rigid "old boy network" exclusiveness, has proven more fertile ground for women in creative fields. (The number of women film directors and hard news correspondents, for example, can be counted easily.) Television has been easier for women to get into than other media. But even in the looser television world, prime time is infinitely more male-dominated than daytime, for obvious reasons. The best place for ambitious, creative women to begin as writers, directors, and actresses, then, is daytime TV, especially soaps and talk shows. And so, we have an interesting situation: a daytime ghetto peopled and watched by women while the big guys – they still don't get it – tear their hair out over the significance of Murphy Brown's pregnancy. (Women on soaps have been bearing and raising children alone forever.)

Okay, you're thinking, if soaps are so hot, how come when I check them out they seem so incredibly stupid? You've asked the right question. The answer is, because they are. And here's where the question of realism comes in. As a culture, we have come to equate quality with "true-to-lifeness." We buy our kids books with titles like *Uncle Jim Gets AIDS*, which explain, simply and antiseptically, how such tragedies occur, and we steer them away from "upsetting" fantasies like *Hansel and Gretel* in which two kids, abandoned by their horrible parents, successfully battle a wicked witch and stick her in an oven.

And we proudly assert that shows such as *L. A. Law* and *Thirtysomething* are "the only TV I watch" because – like *Uncle Jim Gets AIDS* – they are simplistic but "realistic." Daytime soaps, like *Hansel and Gretel*, are incredibly unrealistic. They are also – in both cases – melodramatic, violent, intense, extreme in their portrayals of both good and evil, danger and pleasure. And that is their great appeal and their great virtue. (Who ever accused Shakespeare of being unrealistic, Wagner of being melodramatic or emotionally extreme?)

I raise the issue of children's drama because the analogy to women's drama is important. The appeal of *Hansel and Gretel* is that it allows children to fantasize about being so powerful that they can survive abusive, negligent parents, and, if things get too scary, even kill them. Soaps have the same appeal. They create fantasy worlds in which women are all powerful, in which men and male institutions, like banks, corporations, the FBI and CIA, are shadowy structures in the background of life, while the really important people and institutions are women and women's arenas – houses (especially kitchens and bedrooms), boutiques, restaurants, health clubs. Of course, everyone works on soaps, but workplaces, like everything else, are totally dominated by traditionally female values, values that women, in sexist societies, are socialized to maintain but that – except in the fantasy worlds of soaps – are in fact given little real importance or power.

It is this total lack of social realism that allows soaps to present the most progressive feminist storylines on television while at once – and here's where they are totally contradictory and wacky – presenting a vision of political and economic life that is downright feudal in its reactionary nature. You can't have everything. The trade-off for presenting a kind of women's uto-pia in which traditional female values run the show is that all larger issues – inequality, poverty, foreign policy, and militarism, whatever – are ignored or sugar-coated to fit the most asinine Reaganesque "City on a Hill" scen-ario the Great Communicator ever dreamed up. But, then, "realistically" it couldn't be any other way, could it? Only by ignoring the realities of the marketplace and global conflicts – the male concerns that really run the show – could we possibly envision a world in which traditional feminine values – caring, sharing, communication, intimacy, neighborliness, and so on – could be seen as socially determinate.

And so we have a female fairy world where dreams come true and every-one lives in castles, or at least visits regularly. Everyone on soaps lives in a small town that is pretty much run by two corporate patriarchs who employ everyone in the town and whose extended families of relatives and loyal employees intermarry and reproduce endlessly. That's why you have all those long explanatory sentences about who's been married and divorced and in bed with whom. If you miss a week or two the musical beds are likely to have been rescrambled any number of times, leaving assorted off-spring in danger of unwittingly committing incest or betraying family loy-alties at every turn.

People on soap operas are not concerned with race or class difference. Such things just don't matter in Emotion Land. Like the Smurfs and Care Bears, soap characters judge people strictly on moral grounds: are they good or bad? Moreover, when a bad character becomes popular (this often happens), she or he is likely to undergo a rapid character transformation. Suddenly, a lying, scheming would-be murderer becomes a caring, self-sacrificing pillar of virtue. At which point, he or she is given a job as vice president of one of the town multinationals and soon runs for mayor. It happens a lot.

Doctors, lawyers, and cops are the only other people in these towns. Oh, except for the people who run the local meeting places – restaurants and clubs, boutiques, hair salons, and, recently, health clubs. People on soap operas eat out a lot. They also shop and visit a lot. And they are notorious for using any old excuse to throw a masked ball or gala dinner dance at which everyone gets to wear elaborate gowns and coiffures and someone ends up dead in the swimming pool while everyone else was sneaking off to the bushes to commit adultery or plan and scheme someone else's downfall.

Weddings and holidays are equally popular and elaborate. No one who watches soap operas need fear the holiday season. Christmas, Thanksgiving, even Valentine's Day will be filled with warmth, companionship, and a suitable moral message from one of the Good Fathers even for those who are home alone. That's one of the big appeals of the genre. It does not desert you when times get tough. You or anyone in the cast, for that matter. People who go through crises and tragedies – which are the narrative mainstays of soaps – do not suffer alone. They are visited, cajoled out of their misery, befriended by former enemies, and ultimately – even when their misfortune is of their own doing – reintegrated into the community, reformed, and, in short order, remarried or at least in love.

This sense of community and warmth prevailing, even in the worst of times, is obviously one of the major draws of daytime soaps. We live in an age when more and more of us simply have no sense of community, no family gatherings that are not themselves causes of trauma, and no support systems during times of need, and in which – worse yet – our troubles are multiplying. In and out of the home, on the streets, in the political arena, at work, things are scary. Pine Valley, on the other hand, is never scary in that generalized, free-floating way. Evil is contained in the persons of specific evil people and it is invariably thwarted either through the banishment of the bad guy or his or her (at least temporary) reformation.

In this insane world, anything, obviously, is possible, as long as it concerns personal, emotional life. And since feminist issues for the most part do concern emotional and sexual matters, it is easy to see that they can be incorporated into the soap world and negotiated in ways that promote happiness and justice. As long as we stay in the world of economic and political fantasy, gender justice can, conceivably, exist. If love, rather than money and missiles, made the world go round, after all, women would be in pretty good shape.

And so it goes in the strange world of American media and politics. Life is a trade-off and what's touted as "good for you" – like socially realistic prime-time drama and "pro-social" kiddie fare – is generally pretty thin stuff, stuff so marginally progressive, so cautious and grudging in its lip service to the real needs and desires of children and other weaker folk, like women, that it is insulting. (For every "positive" message about women's rights I've seen on *L. A. Law*, I've suffered through a dozen smirky little sexual "jokes" and inanities, offered as "liberated" but really meant to assuage the prurient tastes of male audiences and producers. Remember the transvestite lawyer? The secret sexual device that made the less-than-classically attractive Stuart an instant lady killer?)

But, if you're willing to swallow your college-girl (or -boy) highbrow values and go where MacNeil and Lehrer have never trod; if you're willing to suspend your disbelief and jump into the swamp of outrageously unreal-istic and corny daytime drama, your "inner child" will thank you and so will the other kids in the house. After all, it was Nancy Drew and Wonder Woman, not June Cleaver, who inspired us to dream of a better world for women, back in the 1940s and 1950s. And I'm willing to bet you Clarence Thomas's porn collection that little girls today are collecting more danger-ous attitudes from the amazingly tough and powerful women on *Guiding Light* than Steven Bochco and Norman Lear have dreamed up in their entire collective lifetimes.

No Way to Treat a Lawyer
Terry Kay Diggs

The American trial film is one of Hollywood's most popular and enduring genres. More than a dozen have been released in the past decade alone. Trial films typically feature prestigious directors (Sidney Lumet in *The Ver-dict*, 1982), comfortable budgets ($20 million for *Presumed Innocent*, 1991), and box-office stars (Robert Redford and Debra Winger in *Legal Eagles*, 1986).

These films also share a predictable paradigm. In the conventional court-room drama, the hero is a male lawyer who has deviated from the natural order, usually by taking a case that itself mirrors social ills. But he resolves the case, restoring balance both to himself and society. Justice is done.

Eight of the last major trial films featured a pronounced twist in the generic formula: the starring lawyer was a woman. But when women law-yers become protagonists, Hollywood changes the rules of the genre, in at least four basic ways.

This reading first appeared in *California Lawyer*, December 1992.

Breaching the natural order

When the male lawyer deviates from accepted practices, it may be in any one of a hundred ways. He may be disreputable, like Anthony Franciosa in *The Story on Page One* (1959), or drunk, like Spencer Tracy in *The People against O'Hara* (1951) or disabled, like Charles Laughton in *Witness for the Prosecution* (1957). He takes a case that signifies a rift in the social order: an innocent man is accused (*True Believer*, 1989), a crime is unpunished (*They Won't Forget*, 1937), an injustice is uncompensated (*The Chaser*, 1938).

Women attorneys are also represented as at odds with the natural order, but their stigma has only one source. They have failed at their natural roles – as daughter, mother, and mate. And Hollywood knows what caused them to fail: their careers.

The woman lawyer of Hollywood can be a bad cook (*The Accused*, 1988), an indifferent housekeeper (*Class Action*, 1991) or an annoying eccentric (*Legal Eagles*, 1986). But her ultimate failure is as mate and mother. The career woman's manlessness, typically the result of divorce, arises from the woman's having become – well, the kind of person career women become. The prospective husband in *Physical Evidence* (1988) abandons bombshell Theresa Russell with the remarkable observation that trial work has rendered her "manly."

The female attorney fails at being a mother (*Jagged Edge*, 1985) or she is a failure because she is *not* a mother (*Suspect*, 1987). Mary Elizabeth Mastrantonio's wistful frolic with tots in toy cars becomes *Class Action*'s (1991) not-so-veiled commentary on the litigator's empty career defending auto-makers.

Attractive, loving "exes" (*Music Box*, 1989) or gorgeous, available leading men (*Legal Eagles*, 1986) hint that domestic bliss awaits only the protagonist coming to her senses. And surrendering one's problems to a man is clearly a happier ending than coping with life as a professional. Attorney Barbara Hershey emerges from the climactic scene of *Defenseless* (1991) to find that both her car and her life are stalled. The film concludes with a pointed metaphor: Hershey moves over and surrenders the driver's seat to male lead Sam Shepard.

Restoring law and order

In the courtroom drama of Hollywood, the male hero is the Ultimate Lawyer, restoring order before the final credits roll. Typically, an innocent client has been accused. The lawyer risks his life to reveal the truth (Edward G. Robinson in *Illegal*, 1955). He finds hidden witnesses, as Gig Young does in *Hunt the Man Down* (1951), or he traps adverse parties with sharp cross-examination, Henry Fonda's forte in *Young Mr Lincoln* (1939). This convention is so strong that the male attorney may triumph despite his own glaring ineptitude (Jeff Chandler in *The Tattered Dress*, 1957; Richard Chamberlain in *Twilight of Honor*, 1963; Paul Newman in *The Verdict*, 1982).

On the other hand, women lawyers do not find the truth, they obfuscate it; they do not restore order, they destroy it. Women's trial skills free Nazi war criminals (*Music Box*), psychopaths (*Jagged Edge*, 1985) and lunatics (*Defenseless*, 1991).

Typically, when the male hero restores order, he is in court. Many courtroom dramas – *State's Attorney* (1932), *The Trial* (1955), *The Young Savages* (1961) and scores of others – feature compelling in-court finales. Even when the hero's Moment of Truth occurs outside the courtroom proper, he is clearly acting as a lawyer. Warren William frees a client by setting an out-of-court trap in *The Case of the Curious Bride* (1935). The male attorney may reveal a truth that destroys his client (*The Paradine Case*, 1948). But when he does, he is in court. He is a lawyer.

Hollywood's female lawyers are not in court when justice is restored, and they do not act as lawyers. At the film's climax, the protagonist has resumed one of her natural roles – mother, wife, daughter – and she has gone home to do it. When Glenn Close reinstates justice in *Jagged Edge* – as she does by killing Jeff Bridges – she is at home, in bed, in the same physical position as Bridge's wife, seen in the film's horrific opening sequence. Jessica Lange makes it possible for male prosecutor Frederic Forrest to do justice in *Music Box* by sending him a package of photos revealing her father to be a former Nazi. When Lange mails the package, she is at home, a mother protecting her son from his grandfather.

The films featuring female litigators may also culminate in clever schemes enacted out of court. But the scheme is not concocted by the woman, it is the brainchild of her male lead. And, not surprisingly, his bright idea puts her back in the domestic sphere. Attorney Barbara Hershey goes along with Sam Shepard's scheme in *Defenseless* and winds up in the kitchen when the truth is revealed. Mary Elizabeth Mastrantonio acts out Gene Hackman's scenario in *Class Action*, but she is excluded from the in-chambers confrontation that resolves the film. Her status? "If you so much as look in my daughter's direction," Hackman, the protective father, snarls at his opponent, "they won't be able to identify you at Dental Records."

Breaking the code

Hollywood's male attorney, like the male protagonist of any other genre film, lives by his code, one loosely based on the ABA's Canons of Ethics. He may violate the code, but his actions bring about one of two results. He is punished for the violation – typically by dying, or by coming close to dying (*The Mouthpiece*, 1932; *The People against O'Hara*, 1951). Or, the male attorney's breach calls into question the very society upon which the code is based (. . . *And Justice for All*, 1979; *Criminal Law*, 1988). Ultimately, the code separates the boys from the girls.

Hollywood's women lawyers have violated the code early and often. In the 1947 favorite, *Adam's Rib*, Katherine Hepburn enthusiastically volunteers to defend the assault case she knows her husband, District Attorney Spencer Tracy, is prosecuting. Since then, women lawyers have visited judges in private (*Jagged Edge*, 1985). They have romanced jurors in public (*Suspect*, 1987). They have revealed evidence they were obliged to withhold (*Music Box*). When these women lawyers violate the code, they aren't punished for it. By allowing her to spurn the code without recourse, the trial film does not liberate its female attorney. Rather, the film marks her as deviant, a lawyer outside the code. When women play, these trial films say, they do not play by the rules. This reasoning is history's oldest justification for ostracism based upon gender.

In three films, *Music Box*, *Jagged Edge*, and *Class Action*, female litigators break the code of silence. They go public with the malfeasance of a male superior, but no film ever shows any ensuing professional repercussions. The women lawyers speak out, then return to the family. Having once come forward, the female attorneys are never again seen as lawyers.

"Counselor," Larry Fishburne greets Mastrantonio at the close of *Class Action*. "I can still call you that, can't I?" Mastrantonio's affirmation is tentative, her guilty smile leaving the matter in doubt.

Sending a deliberate message

Film signals are invariably mixed, and no rule of interpretation is without its exceptions. After all, female litigator Kelly McGillis is in court for the conclusion of *The Accused* (1988), and *Music Box*'s Lange is apparently a fine cook. But, when it comes to women attorneys, Hollywood has a definite point of view.

In *Presumed Innocent* (1991), director Alan J. Pakula uses camerawork to show the subjugation of powerful female prosecutor Carolyn Polhemus (Greta Scacchi). When Rusty Sabich, Polhemus's supervisor (Harrison Ford), has sex with her atop her office desk, Pakula's camera places the viewer inside Sabich's head, seeing and savoring the sexual conquest along with him. The visual image – Polhemus seen from the male perspective, supine in sex – cuts to crime scene photographs of her, once again seen from the male perspective, this time supine in death.

The executives who marketed *Presumed Innocent* chose this scene for ads hawking the film. The implication of the ad campaign was obvious: the sexual domination of a woman lawyer in the workplace is not only acceptable, it's attractive. Desk-sex sells.

In *Class Action* (1991), film-makers chose a script that denounced the women's movement. When Mastrantonio challenges her father's superiority in a high-stakes law-suit, her mother literally drops dead on the courthouse steps. Mastrantonio ultimately relinquishes control of the case *against* her dad *to* her dad. "You were my scapegoat," Mastrantonio tells him. "If anything ever went wrong, I blamed you . . . Now I look at things as they are, and I realize I need a new approach." Mastrantonio's new vision requires her to jettison her career and return to the sanctuary of her father's arms.

The team that produced *Jagged Edge* (1985) used dialogue to allocate power. When Glenn Close condemns her former boss, Peter Coyote, for sending an innocent man to prison, Coyote fingers his cigar and sneers, "He had a rap sheet as long as my dick." Close is initially speechless but finally sputters, "I'll nail you." But she has already lost the war of words. The problem was not gag writing, but gender. In 1989, the producers of *Jagged Edge* recycled Coyote's line verbatim in their *Physical Evidence*. To, "He had a rap sheet as long as my dick," comes a pointed zinger: "Oh, he'd never been arrested, huh?" Tellingly, Burt Reynolds – not the film's female attorney, Theresa Russell – gets to deliver the punch.

Hollywood has used the trial film to send a message to women lawyers, but Hollywood's message has been a lie. For every screen lawyer who packs up to go home, a hundred real women gear up to go to court. For every screen lawyer who is blinded by emotion, a hundred real women are guided by responsibility.

"You need to get yourself a lawyer, Mrs Talbot," Jessica Lange's opponent Frederic Forrest says in *Music Box*. "A real lawyer this time." That advice goes double for film-makers. Hollywood needs to get itself some women lawyers – some real women lawyers. They are not in short supply.

Suggested activities

Questions for discussion

1 Have images of women on television improved or deteriorated over the past several years? What criteria is your assessment based on?

2 Can you think of particular female characters on television or film that you think provide healthy role models for women? Do your classmates agree? If not, why not? What problems can you point to in prominent female characters in films or on television?

3 What kinds of roles or portrayals of women in film and television should be more prominent? Which should be less so?

4 What do you think of Rapping's thesis that soap operas provide a forum for the introduction of feminist issues? Are soap operas as progressive as Rapping claims? (You may want to discuss these questions in connection with the suggested activity on viewing soap operas, described below).

5 Is Rapping correct that soap operas *must* ignore pressing social issues like poverty and global conflict in order to present a utopia where traditional feminist values like caring and sharing are determinative? Why must soaps be unrealistic in order to grapple with feminist concerns?

6 Do you agree with Rapping that soap operas are generally more progressive in presenting feminist values than other television shows?

7 Do television and Hollywood films emphasize the commonalities or differences among women? To what extent are women who are not white, glamorous, young, thin, able-bodied, healthy, or heterosexual portrayed?

8 Do you agree with Faludi's thesis regarding the backlash on television and in Hollywood movies? Has the situation changed in either medium since the 1980s?

9 Do television and films tend to portray women as weak and unsuited to compete with men? What female film characters would you point to as examples or counter-examples?

10 How do mainstream images of women in other professional roles compare with Diggs's analysis of film portrayals of female lawyers? Are the women occupying these roles competent at their jobs? Are they overshadowed or outwitted by males? Do they succeed in the end or are they thwarted by men?

Films and videos

Dreamworlds: Desire/Sex/Power in Rock Video, written, edited, and narrated by Sut Jally (1991). VHS/55 mins. Available from University of Massachusetts,

Department of Communication, Centre for the Study of Communication, Amherst, MA 01002. About the portrayal of women in rock videos, which Jally contends create a "dreamworld" for the fantasies of young men, in which women are usually depicted as highly sexed, aggressive pursuers of men or passive victims of male sexual aggression, victims of rape, physical assault, sexual coercion, and so on.

Slaying the Dragon by Deborah Gee (1988). VHS/60 mins. Produced by Asian Women United, and distributed by Women Make Movies. A comprehensive look at media stereotypes of Asian and Asian-American women since the silent era. Shows how the stereotypes of exoticism and submissiveness have affected the perception of Asian-American women.

Women who Made the Movies by Gwendolyn Foster and Wheeler Dixon (1992). BW/color/55 mins. Distributed by Women Make Movies. Portrait of seminal women film-makers like Ruth Ann Baldwin, Leni Riefenstahl, and Cleo Madison. Examines their impact on the history of cinema.

Other activities

1   See *Dreamworlds* in connection with critique by Laurie Meeker (1993, see Bibliography). Meeker suggests bringing rock video clips to class to discuss and critique in relation to Jally's film.

2   Bring in video clips of portrayals of women from Hollywood films and/or television. These might be limited to a particular time period or genre (for example, soap operas or comedies or science fiction). Analyze the portrayals of women and how they compare to the lives of "real" women. How do you explain the disparities that you find?

3   Bring the movie page from the newspaper to class. Consider the portrayals of women in each of the films listed that you have seen, read about, or heard discussed by others who have seen it. What kinds of generalizations, if any, can you reach about how women are portrayed in Hollywood films? What kinds of differences among women can you observe? For example, are women of color portrayed as often or in similar ways to the depictions of white women? If not, what kinds of differences do you observe? How about roles for older women? Women with disabilities? Indigent women? Lesbians? Single mothers? Working mothers? What kinds of occupations are women portrayed as working in? Do they include non-traditional roles for women?

4   As a class exercise, generate a list of movies on the board, including them under the heading "feminist" or "non-feminist," leaving films over which there is significant disagreement in the middle. Which list is longer? Discuss the reasons you put particular films in one category or the other. Are there any generalizations you can draw?

5   Test the validity of Rapping's claims about soap operas by conducting your own "research." Watch a few episodes of a few different soap operas.

Record the names of the shows you watched, and your observations about the number of female characters, how they are portrayed, what roles they have, their marital/relationship status, whether they are mothers, whether they are employed outside the home (and, if so, in what capacity), how they relate to the men in their lives, how they relate to other women, and what impression they give the viewer about the status and characteristics of women in American culture. What are the major themes or issues addressed by each program? Would you characterize these as "feminist?" Why or why not? Prepare a 1–2 minute summary of your findings for the class, focusing on whether your brief examination confirms or conflicts with Rapping's claims.

6   Observe several hours of television in one week, at different times of the day and evening. What are the differences in the way that women are portrayed in the programs you watch? Do you observe a difference between daytime and evening television? If so, in what respects? Do some programs appear to be targeted more at women than at men? If so, what sort of considerations lead you to this conclusion? What are your conclusions about the portrayals of women in television?

Bibliography

General

Creedon, Pamela J. (1993) *Women in Mass Communication*, 2nd edn (Newbury Park, CA: Sage). Contains sections on revisioning gender values in mass communication, perspectives on the status of women in the mass communications industries, and perspectives on the mass communication classroom.

Dines, Gail and Humez, Jean (eds) (1995) *Gender, Race, and Class in Media: a Text-Reader* (Thousand Oaks, CA: Sage). Collection of essays designed to introduce undergraduates to contemporary media scholarship in a way that builds on their experiences with and interests in media. Most essays take an explicitly critical political perspective.

Douglas, Susan (1994) *Where the Girls Are: Growing up Female with the Mass Media* (New York: Random House). Disagrees with Faludi's view of the mass media, contending that the media promote contradictory images of women as *both* compliant airheads and rebellious thinkers.

Gamman, Lorraine and Marshment, Margaret (eds) (1988) *The Female Gaze: Women as Viewers of Popular Culture* (London: The Women's Press).

hooks, bell (1990) *Yearning: Race, Gender, and Cultural Politics* (Boston: South End Press). A collection of essays by a prominent African-American feminist theorist and social critic. Among the more pertinent essays are "Stylish nihilism: race, sex, and class at the movies," and "Seductive sexualities: representing blackness in poetry and on screen".

Kaplan, E. Anne (1992) *Motherhood and Representation: the Mother in Popular Culture and Melodrama* (London: Routledge). Analyzes the representation of mothers in psychoanalytic theory, literature, and Hollywood films from the 1920s through the 1980s.

Rapping, Elayne (1994) *Media-tions: Forays into the Culture and Gender Wars* (Boston: South End Press). Series of essays by a media critic, who explores the significance of soap operas, Madonna, and other artifacts of the media's relationship to women.

On television

Brown, Mary Ellen (ed.) (1990) *Television and Women's Culture: the Politics of the Popular* (London: Sage). Poststructuralist and feminist perspectives on television criticism. Examines how gendered audiences relate to and use television in their lives. Essays cover the topics of integrating TV and work, women watching *Dallas*, girl audiences watching Madonna and Cyndi Lauper, music video programs, *Cagney and Lacey*, quiz and game shows, sports, *Dynasty*, and class audiences and soap operas.

Brown, Mary Ellen (1994) *Soap Operas and Women's Talk: the Pleasure of Resistance* (Thousand Oaks, CA: Sage). Study of how women use soaps and gossip networks surrounding them as a form of "resistive pleasure." Brown's thesis is based on the idea that some soaps problematize women's actions and choices, thereby providing "real" women with a way of resisting patriarchal cultural norms. She claims that women's talk can do the same.

D'Acci, Julie (1994) *Defining Women: Television and the Case of Cagney and Lacey* (Chapel Hill: University of North Carolina Press). Deals with the cultural construction of gender and the place of US television in that process. Investigates the "struggle over meanings" of women and femininity, the role of TV producers and advertisers in disseminating these meanings, the ways in which TV viewers and the press respond with counter-meanings, and how all of these meanings compete. Asks how these meanings help to shape real human females along particular lines, and focuses on *Cagney and Lacey* as a clear illustration of this process.

Dow, Bonnie J. (1970) *Prime-time Feminism: Television, Media Culture, and the Women's Movement since 1970* (Philadelphia, PA: University of Pennsylvania Press). An examination of popular entertainment as a shaper of modern culture.

Faludi, Susan (1991) "Teen angels and unwed witches: the backlash on TV," in *Backlash: the Undeclared War against American Women* (New York: Doubleday Press).

Heide, Margaret (1995) *Television Culture and Women's Lives: Thirtysomething and the Contradictions of Gender* (Philadelphia: University of Pennsylvania Press). Argues that the television show *Thirtysomething* is an exemplar of television creating a culture which audiences draw on to think about their own lives. Based on interviews with the show's viewers.

Hill, George, Raglin, Lorraine and Johnson, Chas Floyd (1989) *Black Women in Television* (Hamden, CT: Garland). Covers the years 1939–1989. Highlights the black actresses, singers, directors, writers, and producers who have overcome the challenges of being black in Hollywood and have become successful. Includes a bibliography and lists of entertainment award winners and nominees.

Joyrich, Lynne (1996) *Re-viewing Reception: Television, Gender, and Postmodern Culture* (Bloomington, IN: Indiana University Press). Focuses on US television of the 1980s.

Meeker, Laurie (1993) "Whose fantasy? Sut Jally's *Dreamworld*," *Visual Anthropology Review*, 9 (1). Criticizes Jally's examination of the images of women in rock videos for tending to blame women for their sexist representations and for lacking a critique of patriarchal ideology.

Metzger, Gretchen (1992) "TV is a blonde, blonde world," *American Demographics*, 14, p. 51.

Nochimson, Martha (1992) *No End to Her: Soap Opera and the Female Subject* (Berkeley, CA: University of California Press). Argues that soap operas are an art form, which addresses women and their experiences, and respects female values, with more authenticity than almost any other genre.

Press, Andrea (1991) *Women Watching Television: Gender, Class, and Generation in the American TV Experience* (Philadelphia, PA: University of Pennsylvania Press). Study of women's responses to television which takes class and age differences into account, concluding that these factors affect how televised portrayals of women are received.

Rapping, Elayne (1992) *The Movie of the Week: Private Stories, Public Events* (Minneapolis, MN: University of Minnesota Press). On made-for-TV films as a female genre, reflecting a female gaze rather than a male one, and addressing female concerns.

Steenland, Sally (1995) "Ten Years in Prime Time: an Analysis of the Image of Women on Entertainment Television from 1979 to 1988," in Amy Kesselman, Lily McNair, and Nancy Schniedewind (eds), *Women: Images and Realities. A Multicultural Anthology* (Mountain View, CA: Mayfield).

Unger, Rhoda and Crawford, Mary (1992) *Women and Gender: a Feminist Psychology* (New York: McGraw-Hill).

On film

Cook, Pam and Dodd, Philip (eds) (1993) *Women and Film: a Sight and Sound Reader* (Philadelphia: Temple University Press). Collection from the British Film Institute Journal *Sight and Sound*. Essays are organized under the headings "Icons" (on Hollywood movie stars), "Women against the grain" (on women's resistance), "Deconstructing masculinity," "Queer alternatives," and "Women direct."

Faludi, Susan (1991) "Fatal and fetal visions: the backlash in the movies," in *Backlash: the Undeclared War against American Women* (New York: Doubleday Press).

Hadley Freydberg, Elizabeth (1979) "Prostitutes, concubines, whores and bitches: black and Hispanic women in contemporary American film," in Audrey McCluskey (ed.), *Women of Color: Perspectives on Feminism and Identity* (Bloomington, IN: Women's Studies Program). Discusses how the predominant portrayal of women of color in Hollywood films reflects negative stereotypes.

Haskell, Molly (1997) *Holding my Own in No Man's Land: Women and Men and Film and Feminism* (New York: Oxford University Press). Film criticism.

hooks, bell (1992) *Black Looks: Race and Representation* (Boston: South End Press). Collection of hooks's essays, several of which address issues of how women and African-Americans are represented in film.

Mulvey, Laura (1989) "Visual pleasure and narrative cinema," in *Visual and Other Pleasures* (Bloomington, IN: Indiana University Press).

Turin, Maureen (1983) "Fashion shapes: film, the fashion industry, and the image of women," *Socialist Review*, 13, pp. 79–95.

Williams, Linda (1995) *Viewing Positions: Ways of Seeing Film* (New Brunswick, NJ: Rutgers University Press). A set of sophisticated analyses of spectatorship in movies, going beyond Laura Mulvey's foundational work in the field.

6

Fashion, Beauty, and Women's Health

Introduction

In Western culture, subordinate groups are frequently defined by their bodies. This includes individuals who are labeled "Other," including women, people of color, homosexuals, and the disabled. As previous chapters have shown, the "beauty myth," prompted by the fashion, advertising, television and film industries in particular, and the mass media in general, all contribute to the view that women *are* their bodies. Naomi Wolf has provided an in-depth description of this phenomenon in her book *The Beauty Myth* (1991), an excerpt from which forms our first reading. Wolf notes that the images of beauty that women in American culture encounter are not objective facts, but are products of a politics that is culturally and historically variable, and that keeps male dominance in force. She describes the myth as a modern phenomenon that replaced the older myth of domesticity, that is, that women belonged in the home as wives and mothers, not in the public sphere of paid employment, politics, or other worldly affairs.

The beauty myth arose when the development of technologies in the early nineteenth century made the reproduction of images on a grand scale possible. Interestingly, the development of such techniques as photography coincided with the industrial revolution, which disrupted traditional patterns of a gendered division of labor within the family. The rise of the beauty myth thus acted to counteract the new freedoms, literacy, and leisure time that the industrial revolution afforded to middle-class women. It arose again in the 1960s when the cult of domesticity was no longer effective in keeping middle-class women happy being housewives and mothers in the suburbs, as the tremendous influence of Betty Friedan's *The Feminine Mystique* demonstrated.

The beauty myth is not simply a cultural fable, however; it has real-world consequences. Women are so often viewed as being fundamentally ornamental and decorative that many attempt to measure their own value and self-worth in terms of their appearance. The seemingly ubiquitous emphasis of American culture on women's physical appearance has led many women to pursue "beauty at any cost." Although American culture condemns the physically painful practices of other cultures considered to make women more attractive or desirable, such as foot-binding in China or female circumcision in some Islamic cultures, many American women seek to improve their physical appearance by any means necessary, even if it means cosmetic surgery, engaging in anorexic and/ or bulimic forms of behavior, or going on rigid and austere diet and exercise programs.

The beauty myth keeps women dependent upon outside approval for their sense of self-worth. Both the causes of the myth and its effects are economic. Its effectiveness is demonstrated, as Wolf points out, by the diet industry making $33 billion a year, the cosmetics industry $20 billion, the cosmetic surgery industry $300 million, and the pornography industry $7 billion (1991 figures). Just as these industries thrive because of women's anxieties about their physical appearance, they also serve to reinforce the beauty myth, and the importance, even necessity, for women to attempt to achieve the standards of beauty promoted by the myth. This, in turn, promotes the profits of the beauty industry, and devalues working women's sense of self-worth so that they feel they are in fact worth less than men in the job market.

Since mainstream American culture requires women to be physically attractive, girls are socialized to comply with prevailing norms of beauty, and find being beautiful essential (but never adequate) to their self-esteem. Even beautiful women do not feel good about themselves, since social norms of female inferiority have been so ingrained in most women that their physical beauty is not enough to provide them with self-esteem. American culture thereby makes it more difficult for women than men to have positive body images. Poor body image contributes to eating disorders as well as psychological problems like stress, shame, and guilt. There are class and race dimensions to the beauty system as well. Beauty standards set up hierarchies among women that privilege fair-skinned women over women of color and other non-Anglo-looking women. White women are given the message that they are special because of their looks. This privilege provides them with an incentive to maintain the beauty system, which excludes non-white women (see Davis, 1995: 52).

The readings in this chapter examine how the beauty myth contributes to health problems women risk as a result of attempting to conform to its ideal standards for physical appearance. In particular, we will look at the relationship of the beauty myth to fashion, and health-risking body modifications. Fashion helps to shape culture as well as reflecting it. Fashion defines female bodies by its messages about what is feminine. Just as film gives the viewer the (false) impression that the images of women it portrays are natural, so does fashion, which portrays gender as a self-evident and natural attribute of women. Over time, fashion has changed the definition of what is feminine. Fashion also reflects culture. Culture uses fashion to shape women's bodies and desires. As Kim Chernin says, fashion "is a mirror in which we can read the responses of conventional culture to what is occurring at the deepest levels of cultural change" (p. 209).

To some extent, fashion is a product of class, ethnicity, and subculture as well as of the dominant white middle and upper middle-class culture. Thus, there is no single definition of what is fashionable. Rather, there are a number of different notions of fashion circulating in culture at any one time. What is fashionable for a particular woman is partly dependent upon context: her age, race, social class, regional location, occupation, ethnic background, and so on.

Many feminists have rejected fashion as reinforcing the sexual objectification of women and reinforcing the image of women as property. They have viewed fashion as uncomfortable and confining for women. Much female fashion has involved the physical constriction and/or restriction of women's bodies: items that have dictated fashionableness in different eras – such as corsets, girdles, bras, high heels, and mini-skirts – have all involved a significant restriction of women's comfort and ease of movement. In general, the more "feminine" fashions are, the more confining and restricting they are for women's bodies, forcing women to walk using small steps, sit with their knees together or their legs crossed, or be unable to bend over or stretch or move freely without unacceptably revealing certain parts of their bodies.

At the same time, however, women are expected to reveal more of their bodies than men are. This kind of expected disclosure generally places women at a disadvantage with respect to power and control in relation to men. Fashion is also viewed as oppressive in that it is always implicated in a capitalist economy which functions to induce us to constantly buy new clothing, make up, and accessories. In this way, the fashion industry attempts to deny women's subjectivity and turn them into consumers whose desires can be controlled (Turin, 1983: 95).

More generally, the fashion and advertising industries inundate women with messages that they are not adequate as they are, undressed, unadorned, unaltered by makeup and toiletries, but need to modify themselves in order to be acceptable to the outside world. This pressure is particularly intense for women of color, who are unable to achieve cultural ideals of beauty no matter how hard they try, even if they straighten or dye their hair in an effort to look more like "white" women. (The repeated cosmetic surgeries and skin-lightening treatments that Michael Jackson has undergone illustrate the depths to which white standards of beauty may be internalized by people of color, and the extremes to which some may go in order to achieve these standards.)

While early feminist theory viewed fashion as simply an aspect of women's oppression, feminist theory informed by film theory has shifted from a blanket condemnation of culture for its sexism and patriarchy to an examination of how women both receive pleasure from, and resist, aspects of fashion for their own purposes. Postmodern theorists, in particular, have argued that fashion is an important dimension of culture that functions as an important vehicle for self-expression. In popular culture, a woman *is* what she wears. Because women are typically judged on the basis of their appearance, how they dress conveys messages about their character and status (Craik, 1994: 46). Fashion represents the body in culture; that is, it makes the body culturally acceptable by providing it with a way of appearing that will be considered attractive (or at least acceptable).

Thus, fashion enables us to shape our identities by giving us control over the way in which we present ourselves to the outside world, and in this sense may be viewed as liberating. Many women use clothing – of particular styles, colors, cuts, and sizes, as well as hairstyles, makeup, jewelry and other accessories – to express themselves, to publicly disclose something about their personalities. In turn, prevailing fashions provide a limited number of models or templates to choose from and still remain within the parameters of acceptability. Those who ignore or deliberately refuse to conform to the prevailing cultural norms for fashion and stylishness risk being viewed as deviant, "uncool," "unhip," "dweebish," "nerdy," and so on. Thus, one way that culture limits the range of acceptable expressions of identity is by prescribing what is fashionable in any particular time and place.

Douglas Kellner's essay "Madonna, fashion, and identity" (an excerpt from which is given as the second reading) is one of a large number of scholarly studies of the "Madonna phenomenon." Kellner argues that Madonna's image and its reception in popular culture illustrates how identity, fashion, and sexuality are culturally constructed. Kellner argues that Madonna has both challenged and simultaneously reinforced prevailing cultural norms that make image, looks, and fashion the locus of identity. In other words, for Kellner, while Madonna has confronted, opposed, transgressed, and flaunted convention, she has none the less based her own identity on the same foundations that traditionally have defined women's identities: how they appear to others.

In *Beauty Secrets* (1986), Wendy Chapkis argues that women are taught that by controlling their bodies, they can control their lives. This frequently leads women to engage in behaviors that carry health risks, such as eating disorders and cosmetic surgery. Chapkis is confident that such oppressive messages can be unlearned; that women can overcome the beauty system by refusing to accept its prescriptions and by developing alternative strategies for attaining happiness and self-worth. Kathy Davis (1995) points to some problems with Chapkis's analysis, and the strand of radical feminism that it is part of. One problem is that Chapkis's type of approach cannot explain why women who themselves *understand* the beauty system as oppressive to women and as maintaining male power nevertheless buy into it, and eagerly seek its offered (even if illusive) rewards. According to Davis, treating women who participate in unhealthy beauty practices as "cultural dopes" is short-sighted for several reasons. First, it perpetuates dualistic understandings of mind and body as polar opposites, and fails to understand women as *embodied* subjects for whom cosmetic surgery or a diet is a transformation of the self, not only of "a body." Secondly, it rests on a faulty conception of agency that precludes understanding unhealthy beauty practices as a choice that women can make actively and knowledgeably. Thirdly, it ignores the moral contradictions in the reasons women give for their decisions, and the internally split or divided character of their justifications. If we accept that women in American culture are defined largely in terms of and by their bodies, it is understandable that women engage in potentially harmful beauty practices like cosmetic surgery, since their very identities, not only their physical appearances, are at stake.

In recent years, the thin, muscular male body has also provided the standard for women's bodies. The beauty myth tells real-life women that they are overweight, chubby, chunky, obese, heavy, and too fat in relation to this standard. While men as well as women are both subject to the messages that being heavy is socially unacceptable, the failure to conform to the standards promoting these messages is more devastating for women, who are defined by Western culture much more in terms of their appearance than are men. The social obsession with thinness makes it extremely difficult for women to be socially accepted or to have power if they are heavy.

This message that social acceptability is dependent on thinness is transmitted with frightening success. For example, 75 percent of respondents to a *Glamour* magazine survey in 1984 indicated that they were overweight, whereas only 15 percent thought they were just right. Other studies have shown that large numbers of women who are of normal, or even less than normal, weight according to life-insurance tables, consider themselves to be overweight (Siebecker, 1995: 107).

In addition to the tremendous amount of time, money, and energy that many women invest in diet and exercise programs in an endless effort to lose weight, the culturally created obsession leads many women to jeopardize their health and self-worth. The disparity between the standards for appearance established by the beauty myth, and the inability of most real women to conform to these standards, no matter how hard they try, contributes to low self-esteem. For the effort to be thin is seldom successful. Only 5 percent of women will ever have the figures of fashion models, and only 2 percent of them naturally. For most women, such gaunt appearances are an unattainable – and unhealthy – way of being.

Research studies have found that 98 percent of people who are able to lose weight on diets gain it all back (and 90 percent of them gain additional pounds as well) within a short time after ending the diet. "Yo-yo dieting," which involves repeated dieting and weight gain, often results in permanent weight *gain*. Human bodies have a biologically built-in "set-point" or weight which the body works to attain, counteracting the efforts of diet or exercise to achieve a thinner appearance or lighter weight. What a person weighs is frequently determined by their physiology, not their willpower.

Despite these physiological facts, eating disorders are on the rise in the US. Conservative estimates are that one in five college women suffers from some sort of eating disorder. These involve three distinct types of behaviors. *Anorexia nervosa* is probably the most extreme and dangerous form of health risk. Anorexics refuse to eat. They generally have a distorted body image, which makes them appear to be much heavier than they actually are. *Bulimia* involves repeated "binging" (excessive eating), immediately followed by purging through vomiting or enemas. *Compulsive eating* involves eating to excess, frequently in response to tension, stress, pressure, depression, and other forms of anxiety. All three disorders are extreme, afflicting a small percentage of all women. However, the symptoms of a lesser form of each of these eating behaviors are common among American women.

In the reading "Obsession: the tyranny of slenderness," Kim Chernin describes how the beauty myth, and the national obsession with weight and fitness, especially for women, is translated into eating disorders. Just as Wolf points out that the beauty myth is culturally constructed rather than an objective reality, Chernin explains that women's obsession with their weight and hatred of their bodies is similarly a product of our particular historical and cultural location, rather than revealing any truth or natural fact about the way women are or must relate to their bodies. We have already seen how standards of beauty are culturally variable and shift over time. The same is true for standards of physical size and shape. In the eighteenth century, the cultural standard of beauty was that of a much heavier woman than today's ideal. Even Marilyn Monroe, Hollywood icon of the 1960s, was much plumper and more voluptuous than current beauty ideals accept.

Chernin's view of the beauty myth differs somewhat from Wolf's. Whereas Wolf suggests that the beauty myth influences all women in American culture to some extent, regardless of whether they consider themselves to be feminists, in Chernin's opinion, the cultural obsession with thinness as the standard of beauty is embraced only by women who fear women's power, and thus shy away from the feminist movement. Eating disorders cannot be attributed only to the beauty myth, however. In *A Hunger So Wide and So Deep: American Women Speak*, Becky Thompson (1994) theorizes that women turn to food – and thus develop eating disorders – as a response to the "atrocities" deriving from racism, sexism, homophobia, classism, physical and sexual abuse, and other life stresses. Her interviews with African-American, Latina, and lesbian women about the effects of racism, sexism, and sexual abuse on women's eating patterns shows that eating disorders are not only a problem of white, middle-class women.

None the less, not all American women today are (as) susceptible to prevailing cultural standards of female thinness. Studies conducted among high-school girls have suggested that black adolescents are much more comfortable with their bodies than their white counterparts. However, even if women are happy with being larger – or weighing more – than the standards established by the beauty myth, they will still experience discrimination and ostracism from the larger society.

In addition to eating disorders, cosmetic surgery is another method women use in their pursuit of beauty, even though it may risk their health. In *Reshaping the Female Body* (1995), Kathy Davis addresses the reasons why women undergo cosmetic surgery, what experiences prompt them to have their bodies altered, and how they explain their decisions and view them in light of the outcome. As already noted, Davis's study found that women seek cosmetic surgery, first and foremost, not because they are dupes of the beauty system, but because they want a "normal" appearance. Intervention enables them to achieve a better and more accepting relationship to their bodies.

Davis analyzes how women's bodies become defined as appropriate objects for this type of medical intervention and why women are so eager and willing to have their bodies altered. She explains that an intelligent woman can reach the rational conclusion that cosmetic surgery might be the best possible course of action for herself. For example, since breasts are linked in Western culture with femininity and sexual desirability, many women who undergo breast augmentation view it as a way to become more feminine. At the same time, Davis recognizes the problematic cultural context that makes cosmetic surgery an attractive alternative for otherwise healthy women (Davis, 1995: 5).

The beauty myth has an especially pernicious influence on the self-perception and esteem of disabled women. The handicaps of these women are only accentuated by cultural standards of beauty which they have even less hope of achieving than able-bodied women. The beauty myth tells women that not only must they be beautiful, but also that they must be free from weakness, dependency, pain, and loss. Disabled women are stereotyped to be weak and completely dependent upon others, asexual, and uninteresting. Not surprisingly, this can be debilitating to the self-esteem of disabled women, who must contend with *two* sets of myths about who they are.

There are other issues of women's health that should be noted, although there is no space to discuss them at length in this volume. Not all health-care problems experienced by women today are the result of the beauty myth. The provision of health care is often inflected by gender bias, as well as racist and economic discrimination. Women are generally disadvantaged in relation to health care, receiving fewer resources, and less specialized treatment and medical research devoted to illnesses specific to or disproportionately affecting women. This has resulted from male domination of the medical profession and from past assumptions that male bodies set the norm or standard for treatment and medical care for both men and women. Until recently, most research studies included only male subjects, even though there are significant differences between male and female physiology.

Indigent women and women of color receive especially inadequate health care. For example, black women, many of whom are poor, are still often denied health care, either because of their inability to pay for health insurance or because of blatant discrimination by health-care administrators. In addition, they are more likely to contract certain illnesses and diseases, and to die from them, than are white women. Thus, race and class are significant factors influencing the type and quality of health care that women receive. These groups include many of the growing number of women with AIDS, who are largely ignored and invisible. Proposals in recent years for revisioning the health-care system in the US to significantly cut-back or eliminate Medicare and Medicaid would disproportionately influence women, who comprise a majority of the elderly and the indigent.

Another area of women's health we will not be able to examine in depth concerns the impact of new reproductive technologies on the cultural meanings of women's bodies, and how women are treated in relation to their bodies. The "medicalization of women's bodies" refers to the increasing use of medical technologies to regulate women's health and reproductive capacity, especially during pregnancy and childbirth. Technological advances in prenatal screening raises vexed questions for feminists about the acceptability of using techniques such as ultrasound, which enable doctors and parents to know, at an early stage of pregnancy, whether fetal abnormalities exist.

Reproductive technologies have reshaped women's relationship to motherhood, a topic we will explore further in chapter 7. Contraception and abortion make it possible for women to avoid becoming mothers. Techniques like *in vitro* fertilization, sperm and egg donation, and fertility drugs make it possible for many women to become mothers who would not be able to do so otherwise. Fetal monitoring equipment makes it possible for women to know if a fetus they are carrying is severely defective or the "wrong" sex (almost always female) and perhaps to have an abortion. Such technology has also led to a further erasure of women, as their bodies become merely the vessels or wombs through which an unborn child develops.

More problematically, such techniques can detect, in addition, the *sex* of the fetus, and have been increasingly used as the basis for what is called *sex selective abortions*. This practice almost always involves aborting *female* fetuses, especially in highly patriarchal countries like India and China, where males are far more highly valued than females. It is estimated that 100 million women are missing globally because of this practice in combination with the infanticide of female babies. Sex selective abortion has increasingly become a cause for concern in countries such as the US, Canada, and Great Britain, where immigrants from countries where sex selective abortion is acceptable have attempted to use the practice.

The readings in this chapter suggest that women's health is affected not only by cultural norms and practices regarding gender and medical treatment and research, but also by prevailing cultural norms and practices surrounding beauty and fashion.

The Beauty Myth (excerpt)
Naomi Wolf

At last, after a long silence, women took to the streets. In the two decades of radical action that followed the rebirth of feminism in the early 1970s, Western women gained legal and reproductive rights, pursued higher education, entered the trades and the professions, and overturned ancient and revered beliefs about their social role. A generation on, do women feel free?

The affluent, educated, liberated women of the First World, who can enjoy freedoms unavailable to any women ever before, do not feel as free as they want to. And they can no longer restrict to the subconscious their sense that this lack of freedom has something to do with – with apparently frivolous issues, things that really should not matter. Many are ashamed to admit that such trivial concerns – to do with physical appearance, bodies, faces, hair, clothes – matter so much. But in spite of shame, guilt, and denial, more and more women are wondering if it isn't that they are entirely neurotic and alone but rather that something important is indeed at stake that has to do with the relationship between female liberation and female beauty.

The more legal and material hindrances women have broken through, the more strictly and heavily and cruelly images of female beauty have come to weigh upon us. Many women sense that women's collective progress has stalled; compared with the heady momentum of earlier days, there is a

This reading first appeared in *The Beauty Myth: How Images of Beauty are Used against Women* (New York: W. Morrow, 1991), pp. 9–19.

dispiriting climate of confusion, division, cynicism, and above all, exhaustion. After years of much struggle and little recognition, many older women feel burned out; after years of taking its light for granted, many younger women show little interest in touching new fire to the torch.

During the past decade, women breached the power structure; meanwhile, eating disorders rose exponentially and cosmetic surgery became the fastest-growing medical specialty. During the past five years, consumer spending doubled, pornography became the main media category, ahead of legitimate films and records combined, and 33,000 American women told researchers that they would rather lose 10–15 lb than achieve any other goal. More women have more money and power and scope and legal recognition than we have ever had before; but in terms of how we feel about ourselves *physically*, we may actually be worse off than our unliberated grandmothers. Recent research consistently shows that inside the majority of the West's controlled, attractive, successful working women, there is a secret "underlife" poisoning our freedom; infused with notions of beauty, it is a dark vein of self-hatred, physical obsessions, terror of aging, and dread of lost control.

It is no accident that so many potentially powerful women feel this way. We are in the midst of a violent backlash against feminism that uses images of female beauty as a political weapon against women's advancement: the beauty myth. It is the modern version of a social reflex that has been in force since the industrial revolution. As women released themselves from the feminine mystique of domesticity, the beauty myth took over its lost ground, expanding as it waned to carry on its work of social control.

The contemporary backlash is so violent because the ideology of beauty is the last one remaining of the old feminine ideologies that still has the power to control those women whom second-wave feminism would have otherwise made relatively uncontrollable. It has grown stronger to take over the work of social coercion that myths about motherhood, domesticity, chastity, and passivity no longer can manage. It is seeking right now to undo psychologically and covertly all the good things that feminism did for women materially and overtly.

This counterforce is operating to checkmate the inheritance of feminism on every level in the lives of Western women. Feminism gave us laws against job discrimination based on gender; immediately case law evolved in Britain and the United States that institutionalized job discrimination based on women's appearances. Patriarchal religion declined; new religious dogma, using some of the mind-altering techniques of older cults and sects, arose around age and weight to functionally supplant traditional ritual. Feminists, inspired by Friedan, broke the stranglehold on the women's popular press of advertisers for household products, who were promoting the feminine mystique; at once, the diet and skin-care industries became the new cultural censors of women's intellectual space, and because of their pressure, the gaunt, youthful model supplanted the happy housewife as the arbiter of successful womanhood. The sexual revolution promoted the discovery of female sexuality; "beauty pornography" – which for the first time in women's history artificially links a commodified "beauty" directly and explicitly to sexuality – invaded the mainstream to undermine women's new and vulnerable sense of sexual self-worth. Reproductive rights gave Western women control over our own bodies; the weight of fashion models plummeted to 23 percent below that of ordinary women, eating disorders rose exponentially, and a mass neurosis was promoted that used food and weight to strip women of that sense of control. Women insisted on politicizing health; new technologies of invasive, potentially deadly "cosmetic" surgeries developed apace to re-exert old forms of medical control of women.

Every generation since about 1830 has had to fight its version of the beauty myth. "It is very little to me," said the suffragist Lucy Stone in 1855, "to have the right to vote, to own property, etcetera, if I may not keep my body, and its uses, in my absolute right." Eighty years later, after women had won the vote, and the first wave of the organized women's movement had subsided, Virginia Woolf wrote that it would still be decades before women could tell the truth about their bodies. In 1962, Betty Friedan quoted a young woman trapped in the feminine mystique: "Lately, I look in the mirror, and I'm so afraid I'm going to look like my mother." Eight years after that, heralding the cataclysmic second wave of feminism, Germaine Greer described "the stereotype": "To her belongs all that is beautiful, even the very word beauty itself . . . she is a doll . . . I'm sick of the masquerade." In spite of the great revolution of the second wave, we are not exempt. Now we can look out over ruined barricades: a revolution has come upon us and changed everything in its path, enough time has passed since then for babies to have grown into women, but there still remains a final right not fully claimed.

The beauty myth tells a story: the quality called "beauty" objectively and universally exists. Women must want to embody it and men must want to possess women who embody it. This embodiment is an imperative for women and not for men, which situation is necessary and natural because it is biological, sexual, and evolutionary: strong men battle for beautiful women, and beautiful women are more reproductively successful. Women's beauty must correlate to their fertility, and since this system is based on sexual selection, it is inevitable and changeless.

None of this is true. "Beauty" is a currency system like the gold standard. Like any economy, it is determined by politics, and in the modern age in the West it is the last, best belief system that keeps male dominance intact. In assigning value to women in a vertical hierarchy according to a culturally imposed physical standard, it is an expression of power relations in which women must unnaturally compete for resources that men have appropriated for themselves.

"Beauty" is not universal or changeless, though the West pretends that all ideals of female beauty stem from one Platonic Ideal Woman: the Maori admire a fat vulva, and the Padung, droopy breasts. Nor is "beauty" a function of evolution: its ideals change at a pace far more rapid than that of the evolution of species, and Charles Darwin was himself unconvinced by his own explanation that "beauty" resulted from a "sexual selection" that deviated from the rule of natural selection; for women to compete with women through "beauty" is a reversal of the way in which natural selection affects all other mammals. Anthropology has overturned the notion that females must be "beautiful" to be selected to mate. Evelyn Reed, Elaine Morgan, and others have dismissed sociobiological assertions of innate male polygamy and female monogamy. Female higher primates are the sexual initiators; not only do they seek out and enjoy sex with many partners, but "every nonpregnant female takes her turn at being the most desirable of all her troop. And that cycle keeps turning as long as she lives." The inflamed pink sexual organs of primates are often cited by male sociobiologists as analogous to human arrangements relating to female "beauty," when in fact that is a universal, non-hierarchical female primate characteristic.

Nor has the beauty myth always been this way. Though the pairing of the older rich men with young "beautiful" women is taken to be somehow inevitable, in the matriarchal goddess religions that dominated the Mediterranean from about 25,000 BCE to about 700 BCE, the situation was reversed: "In every culture, the Goddess has many lovers. . . . The clear pattern is of an older woman with a beautiful but expendable youth – Ishtar and Tammuz, Venus and Adonis, Cybele and Attis, Isis and Osiris . . . their only function the service of the divine 'womb.'"

Nor is it something only women do and only men watch: among the Nigerian Wodaabes, the women hold economic power and the tribe is obsessed with male beauty; Wodaabe men spend hours together in elaborate makeup sessions, and compete – provocatively painted and dressed, with swaying hips and seductive expressions – in beauty contests judged by women. There is no legitimate historical or biological justification for the beauty myth; what it is doing to women today is a result of nothing more exalted than the need of today's power structure, economy, and culture to mount a counter-offensive against women.

If the beauty myth is not based on evolution, sex, gender, aesthetics, or God, on what is it based? It claims to be about intimacy and sex and life, a celebration of women. It is actually composed of emotional distance, politics, finance, and sexual repression. The beauty myth is not about women at all. It is about men's institutions and institutional power.

The qualities that a given period calls "beautiful" in women are merely symbols of the female behavior that that period considers desirable: *The beauty myth is always actually prescribing behavior and not appearance.* Competition between women has been made part of the myth so that women will be divided from one another. Youth and (until recently) virginity have been "beautiful" in women since they stand for experiential and sexual ignorance. Aging in women is "unbeautiful" since women grow more powerful with time, and since the links between generations of women must always be newly broken: older women fear young ones, young women fear old, and the beauty myth truncates for all the female lifespan. Most urgently, women's identity must be premised upon our "beauty" so that we will remain vulnerable to outside approval, carrying the vital sensitive organ of self-esteem exposed to the air.

Though there has, of course, been a beauty myth in some form for as long as there has been patriarchy, the beauty myth in its modern form is a fairly recent invention. The myth flourishes when material constraints on women are dangerously loosened. Before the industrial revolution, the average woman could not have had the same feelings about "beauty" that modern women do who experience the myth as continual comparison to a mass-disseminated physical ideal. Before the development of technologies of mass production – daguerreotypes, photographs – an ordinary woman was exposed to few such images outside the Church. Since the family was a productive unit and women's work complemented men's, the value of women who were not aristocrats or prostitutes lay in their work skills, economic shrewdness, physical strength, and fertility. Physical attraction, obviously, played its part; but "beauty" as we understand it was not, for ordinary women, a serious issue in the marriage marketplace. The beauty myth in its modern form gained ground after the upheavals of industrialization, as the work unit of the family was destroyed, and urbanization and the emerging factory system demanded what social engineers of the time termed the "separate sphere" of domesticity, which supported the new labor category of the "breadwinner" who left home for the workplace during the day. The middle class expanded, the standards of living and of literacy rose, the size of families shrank; a new class of literate, idle women developed, on whose submission to enforced domesticity the evolving system of industrial capitalism depended. Most of our assumptions about the way women have always thought about "beauty" date from no earlier than the 1830s, when the cult of domesticity was first consolidated and the beauty index invented.

For the first time new technologies could reproduce – in fashion plates, daguerreotypes, tintypes, and rotogravures – images of how women should look. In the 1840s the first nude photographs of prostitutes were taken; advertisements using images of "beautiful" women first appeared in mid-century. Copies of classical artworks, postcards of society beauties and royal mistresses, Currier and Ives prints, and porcelain figurines flooded the separate sphere to which middle-class women were confined.

Since the industrial revolution, middle-class Western women have been controlled by ideals and stereotypes as much as by material constraints. This situation, unique to this group, means that analyses that trace "cultural conspiracies" are uniquely plausible in relation to them. The rise of the beauty myth was just one of several emerging social fictions that masqueraded as natural components of the feminine sphere, the better to enclose those women inside it. Other such fictions arose contemporaneously: a version of childhood that required continual material supervision; a concept of female biology that required middle-class women to act out the roles of hysterics and hypochondriacs; a conviction that respectable women were sexually anesthetic; and a definition of women's work that occupied them with repetitive, time-consuming, and painstaking tasks such as needlepoint and lacemaking. All such Victorian inventions as these served a double function – that is, though they were encouraged as a means to expend female energy and intelligence in harmless ways, women often used them to express genuine creativity and passion.

But in spite of middle-class women's creativity with fashion and embroidery and child rearing, and, a century later, with the role of the suburban housewife that devolved from these social fictions, the fictions' main purpose was served. During a century and a half of unprecedented feminist agitation, they effectively counteracted middle-class women's dangerous new leisure, literacy, and relative freedom from material constraints.

Though these time- and mind-consuming fictions about women's natural role adapted themselves to resurface in the post-war feminine mystique, when the second wave of the women's movement took apart what women's magazines had portrayed as the "romance," "science," and "adventure" of homemaking and suburban family life, they temporarily failed. The cloying domestic fiction of "togetherness" lost its meaning and middle-class women walked out of their front doors in masses.

So the fictions simply transformed themselves once more. Since the women's movement had successfully taken apart most other necessary fictions of femininity, all the work of social control once spread out over the whole network of these fictions had to be reassigned to the only strand left intact, which action consequently strengthened it a hundredfold. This reimposed on to liberated women's faces and bodies all the limitations, taboos, and punishments of the repressive laws, religious injunctions and reproductive enslavement that no longer carried sufficient force. Inexhaustible but ephemeral beauty work took over from inexhaustible but ephemeral housework. As the economy, law, religion, sexual mores, education, and culture were forcibly opened up to include women more fairly, a private reality colonized female consciousness. By using ideas about "beauty," it reconstructed an alternative female world with its own laws, economy, religion, sexuality, education, and culture, each element as repressive as any that had gone before.

Since middle-class Western women can best be weakened psychologically now that we are stronger materially, the beauty myth, as it has resurfaced in the past generation, has had to draw on more technological sophistication and reactionary fervor than ever before. The modern arsenal of the myth is a dissemination of millions of images of the current ideal; although this barrage is generally seen as a collective sexual fantasy, there is in fact little that is sexual about it. It is summoned out of political fear on the part of male-dominated institutions threatened by women's freedom, and it exploits female guilt and apprehension about our own liberation – latent fears that we might be going too far. This frantic aggregation of imagery is a collective reactionary hallucination willed into being by both men and women stunned and disoriented by the rapidity with which gender relations have been transformed: a bulwark of reassurance against the flood of change. The mass depiction of the modern woman as a "beauty" is a contradiction. Where modern women are growing, moving, and expressing their individuality, as the myth has it, "beauty" is by definition inert, timeless, and generic. That this hallucination is necessary and deliberate is evident in the way "beauty" so directly contradicts women's real situation.

And the unconscious hallucination grows ever more influential and pervasive because of what is now conscious market manipulation: powerful industries – the $33-billion-a-year diet industry, the $20-billion cosmetics industry, the $300-million cosmetic surgery industry, and the $7-billion pornography industry – have arisen from the capital made out of unconscious anxieties, and are in turn able, through their influence on mass culture, to use, stimulate, and reinforce the hallucination in a rising economic spiral.

This is not a conspiracy theory; it doesn't have to be. Societies tell themselves necessary fictions in the same way that individuals and families do. Henrik Ibsen called them "vital lies," and psychologist Daniel Goleman describes them working the same way on the social level that they do within families: "The collusion is maintained by directing attention away from the fearsome fact, or by repackaging its meaning in an acceptable format." The costs of these social blind spots, he writes, are destructive communal illusions.

Possibilities for women have become so open-ended that they threaten to destabilize the institutions on which a male-dominated culture has depended, and a collective panic reaction on the part of both sexes has forced a demand for counter-images.

The resulting hallucination materializes, for women, as something all too real. No longer just an idea, it becomes three-dimensional, incorporating within itself how women live and how they do not live: it becomes the Iron Maiden. The original Iron Maiden was a medieval German instrument of torture, a body-shaped casket painted with the limbs and features of a lovely, smiling young woman. The unlucky victim was slowly enclosed inside her; the lid fell shut to immobilize the victim, who died either of starvation or, less cruelly, of the metal spikes embedded in her interior. The modern hallucination in which women are trapped or trap themselves is similarly rigid, cruel, and euphemistically painted. Contemporary culture directs attention to imagery of the Iron Maiden, while censoring real women's faces and bodies.

Why does the social order feel the need to defend itself by evading the fact of real women, our faces and voices and bodies, and reducing the meaning of women to these formulaic and endlessly reproduced "beautiful" images? Though unconscious personal anxieties can be a powerful force in the creation of a vital lie, economic necessity practically guarantees it. An economy that depends on slavery needs to promote images of slaves that "justify" the institution of slavery. Western economies are absolutely dependent now on the continued underpayment of women. An ideology that makes women feel "worth less" was urgently needed to counteract the way feminism had begun to make us feel worth more. This does not require a conspiracy; merely an atmosphere. The contemporary economy depends right now on the representation of women within the beauty myth. Economist John Kenneth Galbraith offers an economic explanation for "the persistence of the view of homemaking as a 'higher calling'": the concept of women as naturally trapped within the feminine mystique, he feels, "has been forced on us by popular sociology, by magazines, and by fiction to disguise the fact that woman in her role of consumer has been essential to the development of our industrial society. . . . Behavior that is essential for economic reasons is transformed into a social virtue." As soon as a woman's primary social value could no longer be defined as the attainment of virtuous domesticity, the beauty myth redefined it as the attainment of virtuous beauty. It did so to substitute both a new consumer imperative and a new justification for economic unfairness in the workplace where the old ones had lost their hold over newly liberated women.

Another hallucination arose to accompany that of the Iron Maiden: the caricature of the Ugly Feminist was resurrected to dog the steps of the

women's movement. The caricature is unoriginal; it was coined to ridi-
cule the feminists of the nineteenth century. Lucy Stone herself, whom
supporters saw as "a prototype of womanly grace . . . fresh and fair as the
morning," was derided by detractors with "the usual report" about Victorian feminists: "a big masculine woman, wearing boots, smoking a cigar,
swearing like a trooper." As Betty Friedan put it presciently in 1960, even
before the savage revamping of that old caricature: "The unpleasant image
of feminists today resembles less the feminists themselves than the image
fostered by the interests who so bitterly opposed the vote for women in
state after state." Thirty years on, her conclusion is more true than ever.
That resurrected caricature, which sought to punish women for their public
acts by going after their private sense of self, became the paradigm for new
limits placed on aspiring women everywhere. After the success of the women's
movement's second wave, the beauty myth was perfected to checkmate
power at every level in individual women's lives. The modern neuroses of
life in the female body spread to woman after woman at epidemic rates. The
myth is undermining – slowly, imperceptibly, without our being aware of
the real forces of erosion – the ground women have gained through long,
hard, honorable struggle.

The beauty myth of the present is more insidious than any mystique of
femininity yet. A century ago, Nora slammed the door of the doll's house;
a generation ago, women turned their backs on the consumer heaven of the
isolated multi-applianced home; but where women are trapped today, there
is no door to slam. The contemporary ravages of the beauty backlash are
destroying women physically and depleting us psychologically. If we are to
free ourselves from the dead weight that has once again been made out of
femaleness, it is not ballots or lobbyists or placards that women will need
first; it is a new way to see.

Madonna, Fashion, and Identity (excerpt)
Douglas Kellner

For the past decade, Madonna has been a highly influential fashion and pop
culture icon and the center of a storm of controversy. She is the bestselling
and most discussed female singer in popular music, one of the great stars

This reading first appeared in *On Fashion*, eds Shari Benstock and Suzanne Ferris (New
Brunswick, NJ: Rutgers University Press, 1994), pp. 159–82.

of music video, a hard-working movie actress, and, most of all, a superstar of pop culture. "Madonna" has become a site of contestation and controversy, adored and abhorred by audiences, critics, and academics alike. Most of the polemics, however, are contentious and fail to grasp the many sides of the Madonna phenomenon. While some celebrate her as a subversive cultural revolutionary, others attack her politically as an anti-feminist cultural conservative, or as irredeemably trashy and vulgar. Against such one-sided interpretations, however, I shall argue that Madonna is a genuine site of contradiction that must be articulated and appraised to adequately interpret her images and works, and their effects.

My argument is that Madonna's image and reception highlight the social constructedness of identity, fashion, and sexuality. By exploding boundaries established by dominant gender, sexual, and fashion codes, she encourages experimentation, change, and production of one's individual identity. Yet by privileging the creation of image, looks, and fashion in the production of identity, Madonna reinforces the norms of the consumer society that offers the possibilities of a new commodity "self" through consumption and the products of the fashion industry. I argue that grasping this contradiction is the key to Madonna's effects, and interrogate the conditions under which the multiplicity of discourses on Madonna, and contradictory readings and evaluations, are produced. Madonna pushes the most sensitive buttons of sexuality, gender, race, and class, offering challenging and provocative images and texts, as well as ones that reinforce dominant conventions. Madonna is her contradictions, and I shall take pleasure in the following pages in immersing myself in the Madonna phenomenon to explore her highly volatile and charged artifacts.

Fashion and identity

Ultimately, Madonna is interesting for cultural theory because her work, popularity, and influence reveal important features of the nature and function of fashion and identity in the contemporary world. Fashion offers models and material for constructing identity. Traditional societies had fixed social roles and fixed sumptuary codes, so that clothes and one's appearance instantly denoted one's social class, profession, and status. Identity in traditional societies was usually fixed by birth, and the available repertoire of roles was tightly constricted to traditional social functions. Gender roles were especially rigid, while work and status were tightly circumscribed by established social codes and an obdurate system of status ascription.

Modern societies eliminated rigid codes of dress and cosmetics, and, beginning around 1700, changing fashions of apparel and appearance began proliferating.[1] Although a capitalist market dictated that only certain classes could afford the most expensive attire, which signified social privilege and power, in the aftermath of the French Revolution fashion was democratized so that anyone who could afford certain clothes and makeup could wear and display what they wished. Previously, sumptuary laws forbade members of certain classes from dressing and appearing like the ruling elites.

Modernity also offered new possibilities for constructing personal identities. Modern societies made it possible for individuals to produce – within certain limits – their own identities and experience identity crises. Already in the eighteenth century, the philosopher David Hume formulated the problem of personal identity, of what constituted one's true selfhood, even suggesting that there was no substantial or transcendental self. The issue became an obsession with Rousseau, Kierkegaard, and many other Europeans, who experienced rapid change, the breakdown of traditional societies, and the emergence of modernity.[2]

In modernity, fashion is an important constituent of one's identity, helping to determine how one is perceived and accepted.[3] Fashion offers choices of clothes, style, and image through which one can produce an individual identity. In a sense, fashion is a constituent feature of modernity, interpreted as an era of history marked by perpetual innovation, by the destruction of the old and the creation of the new. Fashion itself is predicated on producing ever new tastes, artifacts, artifices, and practices. Fashion perpetuates a restless, modern personality, always seeking what is new and admired, while avoiding what is old and passé. Fashion and modernity go hand in hand to produce modern personalities who seek their identities in constantly new and trendy clothes, looks, attitudes, and behavior, and who are fearful of being out of date or unfashionable.

Of course, fashion in modern societies was limited by gender codes, economic realities, and the force of social conformity, which continued to dictate what one could or could not wear, and what one could or could not be. Documentary footage from the 1950s in artifacts such as the 1982 ABC documentary *Heroes of Rock* showed parents, teachers, and other arbiters of good taste attempting to dictate proper and improper fashion, thus policing the codes of fashion and identity. Crossing gender codes in fashion was for centuries a good way to mark oneself as a social outcast or even to land in jail or a mental institution.

The 1960s exhibited a massive attempt to overthrow the cultural codes of the past, and fashion became an important element of the construction of new identities, along with sex, drugs, and rock 'n' roll, phenomena also involved in the changing fashions of the day. In the 1960s, anti-fashion in clothes and attire became fashionable, and the subversion and overthrowing of cultural codes became a norm.

During this period, pop culture became a particularly potent source of cultural fashions, providing models for appearance, behavior, and style. The long-haired and unconventionally dressed rock stars of the 1960s and the 1970s influenced changes in styles of hair, dress, and behavior, while their sometimes rebellious attitudes sanctioned social revolt. More conservative television programming, films, and pop music provided mainstream models for youth. During the past two decades, cultural conservatives have been reacting strongly against 1960s radicalism, and fashion and youth culture have become battlefields between traditionalists and conservatives and cultural radicals, attempting to overturn traditional gender roles, fashion codes, values and behavior.

High school in particular is a period in which young people construct their identities, attempting to "become someone."[4] High school has been a terrain of contradiction for the past several decades. While some parents and teachers attempt to instill traditional values and ideas, youth culture is often in opposition to conservative culture. Although the 1980s were a predominantly conservative period, with the election of Ronald Reagan and a "right turn" in US culture, the images from popular music figures sometimes cut across the conservative grain.[5] Michael Jackson, Prince, Boy George, and other rock groups undermined traditional gender divisions and promoted polymorphic sexuality. Cyndi Lauper reveled in offbeat kookiness, and Pee Wee Herman engaged in silly and infantile behavior to the delight of his young (and older) audiences. Throwing off decades of cool sophistication, maturity, respectability, and taste, Pee Wee made it OK to be silly and weird, or at least different.

Enter Madonna

It was during this period that Madonna first came to prominence. Her early music videos and concert performances transgressed traditional fashion boundaries, and she engaged in overt sexual behavior and titillation, subverting the boundaries of "proper" female behavior. Thus, from the beginning, Madonna was one of the most outrageous female icons among the repertoire of circulating images sanctioned by the culture industries. Although there were no doubt many farther-out and more subversive figures than Madonna, their images and messages did not circulate through mainstream culture and thus did not have the efficacy of the popular. The early Madonna sanctioned rebellion, nonconformity, individuality, and experimentation with fashion and lifestyles. Madonna's constant change of fashion, image, and identity promoted experimentation and the creation of one's own style and identity. Her sometimes dramatic shifts in identity suggested that identity was a construct, that it was something that one produced and could be modified at will. The way Madonna deployed fashion in the construction of her identity made it clear that one's appearance and image helps produce what one is, or least how one is perceived.

Thus, Madonna problematized identity and revealed its constructedness and alterability. Madonna was successively a dancer, musician, model, singer, music video star, movie and stage actress, "America's most successful businesswoman," and a pop superstar who excelled in marketing her image and selling her goods. Consciously crafting her own image, she moved from boy toy, material girl, and ambitious blonde to artiste of music videos, films, and concerts. Her music shifted from disco and bubble-gum rock to personal statements and melodic torch singing, then, with the aid of her music videos, to pop modernism. Madonna's hair changed from dirty blonde to platinum blonde, to black, brunette, redhead, and multifarious variations thereof. Her body changed from soft and sensuous to glamorous and svelte to hard and muscular sex machine to futuristic technobody. Her clothes and fashion changed from flashy trash to haute couture to far-out technocouture to lesbian S&M fashion to postmodern pastiche of all and every fashion style. New clothes and a new identity for all occasions and epochs. As it turns out, Madonna's fashion moves generally caught shifts in cultural style and taste and thus achieved the status of the popular, becoming important cultural icons and influences.

While there are certain continuities in Madonna's development that I shall be concerned to explicate, there are also at least three distinct periods that can be (roughly) equated to shifts in her music production, her deployment of fashion and sexuality, and her image. . . .

Madonna I: the boy toy

In 1983, Madonna released her first album, *Madonna*, and two of the songs ("Lucky Star" and "Holiday") became hits. Her early music and songs are rather conventional popular dance music aimed at a teenage market. But Madonna was an especially flashy performer and began to attract notice at this point with music videos of her top hits, which were featured on MTV, a relatively new channel that was to play a key role in her career. The music video *Lucky Star* features her as an especially voluptuous sex object, energetic dancer, and innovative fashion trendsetter. The video opens with a black-and-white sequence: Madonna is wearing black sunglasses, which she slowly pulls down, revealing sultry eyes intensely focusing on the camera (and viewer). The sunglasses, of course, were symbols of the punk generation out of which Madonna emerged and would later become a symbol of the cyberpunk movement as well (as Bruce Sterling claims in the introduction to his anthology *Mirrorshades*). Their deployment suggested that Madonna would reveal something of herself in the video, but that she knew her performance was an act and that she would maintain her control and subjectivity. The final sequence returns to black and white and shows Madonna pulling the shades over her eyes as the screen fades to black.

At the end of the brief opening sequence, the screen dissolves to white, and a color sequence shows Madonna dressed totally in black. As the music slowly begins, she writhes in an erotic pose, the camera cuts to a freeze frame of her face, she winks, and the video cuts to Madonna dancing and cavorting with two dancers. Eschewing the narrative frame of most music videos of the day, Madonna presents instead a collage of images of her body. The video shows her energetically dancing, alone or with the two dancers, striking erotic poses, and showing off her body and clothes. Madonna is dressed in a tight and short black skirt with a black leotard underneath. She wears a loose black blouse that lightly covers a black veiled lace body shirt underneath. One sees around her waist the famous "unchastity belt" – later marketed by her Boy Toy line of fashion – with a large buckle and chains around the waist. Madonna has a large black bow in her hair and a large star ear-ring, with smaller crucifix ear-rings. Completing the outfit are black bobby socks and short black boots.

Madonna's fashion at this stage constituted a subversion of conventional codes and justified wearing any combination of clothes and ornaments that one wished. Of course, Madonna herself became a model of teen fashion and the infamous Madonna "wannabes" slavishly imitated every aspect of her early "flashy trash" clothing and ornamentation. She linked fashion to exhibitionism and aggressive sexuality, connecting fashion revolt with sexual rebellion. Thus, Madonna legitimated unconventional fashion and sexual behavior, endearing her to an audience that felt empowered by Madonna's flouting of traditional standards and codes.

Her other early rock video-hit, *Borderline*, depicts motifs and strategies that would make Madonna a lucky star. The video narrative images weave two sequences together to illustrate the love song. In color sequences, Madonna sings, flirts, and seduces a Hispanic youth, while in a black-and-white sequence an Anglo photographer snaps pictures of her and courts her.

In one black-and-white sequence, she sprays graffiti over lifeless classical sculptures, a modernist gesture of the sort that would later typify Madonna's music videos. The lyrics once again promise a utopia of sexual ecstasy ("You keep on pushing my love over the borderline"), and the music has upbeat dancing rhythms that enable Madonna to exhibit her energy and talent as a dancer. In this video, Madonna wears several different outfits, and her hair ranges from dirty and messy blonde in the Hispanic color sequences to beautifully fashioned glamorous blonde in the black-and-white sequences.

Offering herself to males of various colors, Madonna broke down racial barriers to sexuality. This was also a clever marketing strategy, inviting white, Hispanic, and black youth to fantasize that they too can have or be Madonna. In her first music videos Madonna is already deploying fashion, sexuality, and the construction of image to present herself both as an alluring sex object and as a transgressor of established borderlines. On one hand, the video validates inter-racial sex and provides all-too-rare images of Hispanic barrio culture. Yet the two contrasting narrative sequences convey the message that, although you might have a good time hanging out with Hispanics, it is the white photographer who will provide the ticket to wealth and success. But she ends up with the Hispanic youth, and the narrative valorizes multiple relationships, for the Madonna character continues to see both guys during the narrative sequences, projecting the fantasy image that one can have it all, crossing borderlines from one culture to another, appropriating the pleasures of both cultures and multiple relationships.

The video also puts on display the contrasting fashion codes between upper-class culture and Hispanic culture, identifying Anglo culture with high fashion, high art, and luxury. By contrast, Hispanic culture is equated with blue jeans, pool halls, and less-expensive and stylish clothes and ornamentation. A later Madonna video, *La Isla Bonita*, however, utilizes fantasy images of Hispanic fashion as an icon of beauty and romanticism. Such "multiculturalism" and her culturally transgressive moves (such as explicit sexuality and inter-racial sexuality) turned out to be highly successful marketing moves that endeared her to large and varied youth audiences.

Madonna became a major pop culture figure with the beginning of her concert tours in 1985, and she began consciously marketing her own image and a wide range of fashion accoutrements, which she sold under the Boy Toy label. *People* reported: "At concerts her per capita sales of T-shirts and memorabilia are among the highest in rock history. 'She sells more than Springsteen, the Rolling Stones or Duran Duran,' says Dell Furano, the concession merchandiser for her tour. At her San Francisco date, $20 T-shirts sold at the rate of one every six seconds." She began marketing "Madonna-wear," which she described as "sportswear for sexpots." The line included "a $25 lace tank top, a $30 sweatshirt, $20 pants and a medium-priced ($30) tube skirt that can be rolled down for public navel maneuvers."[6]

Although an upscale version of Madonna-wear was also marketed, as were Madonna makeup kits, her image also encouraged thrift-shop downscale fashion for the Madonna look: underwear worn outside skirts, loose T-shirts, cheap bracelets, ear-rings, chains, and crucifixes also provided appropriate decoration. Indeed, the Madonna look became known as "flash-trash," so that almost any teenage girl could afford to look like Madonna and share her attitudes and styles. Madonna fashion made it possible for teenage girls to produce their own identity, to make their own fashion statements, and to reject standard fashion codes.

During the Virgin tour, Madonna wore a brightly colored jacket and tight micro-miniskirt, a sparkly lingerie harness, black lace stockings that stopped at the knee, and an array of ornaments, including crucifixes, a peace medallion, and bracelets. Prancing around in spiked boots, her belly button exposed, Madonna would take off the jacket to reveal a lacy purple shirt and black bra, accenting a lush and accessible sexuality. For the hit song "Like a Virgin," Madonna appeared in a white wedding dress and screamed, "Do you want to marry me?" to which the girls and boys both answered, "Yesss!" Thrusting her hip as she sang, "You make me feel like a virgin," she unfolded a belly roll as she intoned, "touched for the very first time." This highly sexual rendition of the song mocks virginity, but also makes fun of sexuality by ironizing its codes and gestures. Her play with sexual codes reveals sexuality to be a construct, fabricated in part by the images and codes of popular culture, rather than a "natural" phenomenon.

Madonna's deployment of fashion and sexuality during this early phase is more complex than it appears at first glance. Although it is easy to dismiss the early Madonna's posturing as that of a shameless sex object, boy toy, and material girl who reinforces traditional gender roles, a closer reading of her music videos produces another picture. For instance, her music video *Material Girl* (1984) seems at first glance to be an anthem of Reaganism, glorifying shallow materialism and celebrating greed and manipulation ("The boy with the cold hard cash/Is always Mr Right . . . cause I'm just a Material Girl"). On this reading, the song is a replay of Marilyn Monroe's "Diamonds are a Girl's Best Friend" and is advocating the same calculating and shallow materialist attitudes.

Although Madonna has assumed a Monroe-like look in this video and does deploy some of the fashion and poses of Monroe's 1950s hymn to bourgeois materialism, a closer look at the music video provides some different perspectives. In one reading, which Madonna herself advanced, the video shows the "material girl" rejecting her wealthy suitors in favor of a

poor working boy. When confronted with the critique that she was celebrating crass greed, Madonna responded, "Look at my video that goes with
the song. The guy who gets me in the end is the sensitive guy with no
money."[7] On this account, Madonna turns down the guys courting her in
the music and dance sequences for the poor but sincere boy shown in the
"realism" sequences.

A closer reading raises questions, however, as to whether the "poor boy"
in the video, played by Keith Carradine, is really "poor" and whether
Madonna doesn't actually get a very rich and successful guy in the video.
The narrative images reveal the Carradine character to be a studio mogul
who cleverly poses as a sincere poor boy who wins Madonna's heart. Thus,
in *Material Girl* Madonna is all things to all people and has it every way:
for conservatives of the Reagan years, she is a celebrant of material values,
the material girl, who takes the guilt away from sex, greed, and materialism.
For this audience, she is Marilyn Monroe reincarnated, the superpop superstar, the super ideal male fantasy sex object and female fantasy icon. For
romantic idealist youth, however, she is the good girl seeking love who
chooses true love over material temptations. Yet in the music video narrative, she gets both love and a successful guy.

Moreover, the video *Material Girl* problematizes identity and decouples
the link between expensive clothes, wealth, and position. Carradine wears
a brown work shirt and pants, and this is perfectly acceptable, the video
suggests, indicating that fashion and identity are up to the individual, not
to societal codes. Madonna's images and music videos thus legitimate individual choice in appropriating fashion and producing one's image. Yet the
most attractive images in the musical production numbers do celebrate high
and expensive fashion, diamonds, and other costly ornaments as keys to a
successful image and identity. And it could be that the powerful images of
wealth and high fashion, reinforced by the musical lyrics, do endorse bourgeois materialism over romance and individual choice.

A high level of ambiguity, irony, and humor permeates Madonna's work
and image. Her use of fashion is humorous and ironic, as are many of her
videos and concert acts. The items marketed in her Boy Toy and Slutco
lines are often humorous, as are the very titles of the lines themselves.
Indeed, the much maligned term "Boy Toy" itself is ironic and allows
multiple readings. On one level, Madonna is a toy for boys, but on another
level boys are toys for her, the Boy Toys are there for her toying around
and the unchastity belt comes off at her whim and desire. Indeed, *Material
Girl* shows the guys as Madonna's toys, and her dance numbers with men
during the Virgin tour concerts shows them as her underlings, accessories
that she toys with and totally dominates.

Crucially, the early Madonna projects in her videos and music an all-too-rare cultural image of a free woman, making her own choices and determining her life. The early Madonna image of a free spirit floating through life on her own terms is perfectly captured in her role as Susan in Susan Seidelman's *Desperately Seeking Susan* (1985). The message here, consistent with Madonna's other early work, is that one can fundamentally change one's identity by changing one's fashion, appearance, and image. Madonna herself would dramatically exemplify this philosophy in her two succeeding stages, in which she radically altered her image and identity.

Madonna II: who's that girl?

Madonna had arrived. In 1985, her records had sold 16 million singles and albums. She had number-one pop hits, "Like a Virgin" and "Crazy for You," and by the time she was 26, Madonna had produced seven Top Twenty singles in 17 months. (It took Barbra Streisand 17 years to have that many.) Madonna made a successful film debut in *Desperately Seeking Susan*, and her Virgin tour established her as one of the hottest figures in pop music. She was featured on the cover of *Time* magazine and was profiled in *People, Newsweek, Rolling Stone*, and other popular magazines. Her first album, *Madonna*, eventually sold over three million copies, and her *Like a Virgin* album racked up 4.5 million copies in domestic sales, with 2.5 million more worldwide by 1985. Moreover, Madonna *knew* she was a superstar and plotted her moves accordingly.

Needless to say, Madonna deployed fashion and sexuality to produce the image that would mark her mid- to late 1980s stage, characterized by continued megasuccess as a record producer with best-selling albums and music videos, another successful concert tour ("Who's that Girl?"), a much discussed and eventually failed marriage with movie actor Sean Penn, and two movies that flopped with critics and audiences (*Shanghai Surprise* and *Who's that Girl?*). . . .

During this period, Madonna adopted more traditional fashion and attitudes and tried to appear more respectful of traditional gender roles. Trying to make her doomed marriage with Sean Penn work, Madonna appeared in romantic love songs videos (for example, *True Blue*) singing of the joys of devotion, commitment, and true love. Madonna decided to shed the trampy sex kitten look and boy-toy image for a more conventional feminine appearance. As *Forbes* put it, "She began singing in a deeper, more serious voice, and in a video from her third album wore honey-blonde hair and a demure flowered dress. In July 1987 she got herself on the cover of *Cosmopolitan* as a glamorous blonde, and in May 1988 she graced the cover of *Harper's Bazaar* as a prim brunette. Her *True Blue* album of that period sold nearly 17 million copies, and she sold more albums among the over-20 crowd than ever."[8] . . .

Madonna III: blonde ambition

After the breakup of her marriage in 1989, Madonna continued to explore the boundaries of the permissible in the representations of sexuality and gender, entering upon the stage of her work where she would systematically challenge conventional representations of sexuality. During the 1990s, Madonna produced a series of complex modernist music videos that expanded the boundaries of the art form and even led MTV to ban one of her productions, *Justify my Love*, in 1990 and to play *Erotica* only rarely in 1992. Madonna had obviously developed from young sex object on the move to mature woman, prepared to control her own destiny.

During her most recent period, marked by a series of highly controversial rock videos, the Blonde Ambition tour and the 1991 film of the tour (*Madonna: Truth or Dare*), the 1992 album *Erotica* and book *Sex*, Madonna has been recognized as a top pop superstar and even "America's shrewdest businesswoman." In the 1990s, her use of fashion was even more eclectic, drawing on some of her earlier images, which she frequently quoted and sometimes parodied. Madonna also became political during this period, making statements on behalf of AIDS victims, the homeless, saving the rainforests, and women's rights; in 1990 she even made a "get out and vote" video, threatening to spank those who refused to vote.[9] In 1992, she supported Bill Clinton for President. . . .

In the 1990s, Madonna has employed fashion and image to attempt to produce an identity as an artist. Her rock videos became increasingly complex, or attempted to expand the boundaries of the permissible in terms of male and female gender roles, overt sexuality, parody of religion, and modernist ambiguity. Fashionwise, she sometimes returned to the sexy and flamboyant attire of her early stage, but mixed it with haute couture, futuristic technofashion, S&M chic, and a postmodern pastiche of various fashion styles, subverting oppositions between high and low fashion, much as postmodern art explodes established modernist cultural hierarchies between high and low culture. Yet, arguably, Madonna deployed the typically modernist strategy of shock in her outlandish use of fashion, sexuality, and religious imagery, especially in her rock videos, which are highly complex cultural texts that allow a multiplicity of readings.[10]

Throughout the Blonde Ambition tour, Madonna played out this decon-structive drama, frequently wearing men's clothes, grabbing her crotch, and declaring she was the boss, thus occupying male positions. She also had her male dancers wear fake breasts, women's clothes, and submit to her power and control. The message was that "male" and "female" were social con-structs that could be deconstructed and that women could occupy male positions, roles, and behavior and vice versa. Yet, as I shall argue in the conclusion of this paper, Madonna does not subvert relations of domina-tion or offer alternative images. Like conservative deconstruction, Madonna puts on display binary oppositions that constitute our culture and society, demonstrates their artificiality, and questions the prioritizing of one of the oppositions over the other, without putting anything new in its place. Thus, she tends to place women, primarily herself, in positions of power and authority, which are aggressively exercised over males.

To deconstruct traditional gender oppositions and relations of power and domination, Madonna uses irony, humor, and parody to push the sens-itive buttons of "masculine" and "feminine" and to provoke reaction to the overthrowing of traditional images and stereotypes and their exchange and mixture in the genders of the future, which would presumably be multiple rather than binary. There was indeed always a strong mixture of irony and satire in Madonna's work from the beginning, and her concert perform-ances became increasingly campy, as was the dramatization of her life on the road in *Truth and Dare*.[11] Her performance of "Material Girl" in the Blonde Ambition tour, for instance, is pure camp, with Madonna and two female singers sitting on a raised platform in hair curlers and bathrobes, singing the song with false accents, out of tune and in high-pitched voices. The image puts on display the labor and ridiculous activities that women go through to make themselves "beautiful" and mocks the ideal of the "material girl" (of course, on another level, Madonna herself is the extreme example of almost superhuman labor and expense to make herself "beautiful," a con-tradiction that pervades her work and that I shall return to). . . .

Conclusion

The Madonna phenomenon suggests that in a postmodern image culture identity is constructed through image and fashion, involving one's look, pose, and attitude. For Madonna, postmodern identity-construction is change, constantly redeveloping one's look and striking outrageous and constantly different poses. Fashion and identity for Madonna are inseparable from her aesthetic practices, from her cultivation of her image in her music videos, films, TV appearances, concerts, and other cultural interventions. A genuinely complex and challenging phenomenon like Madonna, however, puts in question and tests one's aesthetic categories and commitments. . . .

Although some have attacked Madonna as being anti-feminist and a disgrace to women, others have lauded her as the true feminist for our times and as a role model for young women. Camille Paglia, for instance, has celebrated Madonna as "a true feminist," and a role model of the strong, independent and successful woman, who successfully affirms her own power and sexuality and defies conventional stereotypes.[12] I, too, have stressed the extent to which Madonna reverses relations of power and domination and provides strong affirmative images of women. But one could argue that Madonna merely transposes relations of domination, reversing the roles of men and women, rather than dissolving relations of domination. In her concert performances, her dancers are mere appendages whom she dominates and controls, overtly enacting rituals of domination on the stage. In the HBO Blonde Ambition tour video of 1990, for example, she constantly places herself in positions of power and control over the male (and female) dancers. In simulated sex scenes in the tour, Madonna was usually on top and in her infamous masturbation/simulated orgasm scene in *Like a Virgin*, the male dancers first fondle Madonna and then disappear as she writhes in an exaggerated orgasm. . . .

Someone who cultivates an aesthetic of shock and excess, as does Madonna, is certain to offend and to become a target of criticism. Madonna, however, thrives on criticism, which, along with her deployment of fashion and sexuality, helps her produce an identity as rule-breaker and transgressor. Her breaking of rules has progressive elements in that it goes against ruling gender, sex, fashion, and racial hierarchies, and her message that identity is something that everyone can and must construct for themselves is also appealing. Yet by constructing identity largely in terms of fashion and image, Madonna plays into precisely the imperatives of the fashion and consumer industries that offer a "new you" and a solution to all of your problems by the purchase of products and services.[13] By emphasizing image, she plays into the dynamics of the contemporary image culture that reduces art, politics, and the theatrics of everyday life to the play of image, downplaying the role of communication, commitment, solidarity, and concern for others in the constitution of one's identity and personality.

Madonna is thus emblematic of the narcissistic 1980s, a period not yet over, in which the cultivation of the individual self and the obsessive pursuit of one's own interests was enshrined as cultural mythology. The imperative "go for it!" echoes through the 1980s, and Madonna went for it and got it. Yet in becoming the most recognizable woman entertainer of her era (and perhaps of all time), Madonna produced works that have multiple and contradictory effects and that in many ways helped subvert dominant conservative ideologies. Yet her work has become increasingly complex, and it is precisely this complexity, as well as her continued popularity, that has made Madonna a highly controversial object of academic analysis in recent years. Madonna allows many, even contradictory, readings which are grounded in her polysemic and modernist texts and her contradictory cultural effects. At dull gatherings, mention Madonna and you can be sure that there will be violent arguments, with some people attacking and others passionately defending her. Whether one loves or hates her, Madonna is a constant provocation who reveals the primacy of fashion and image in contemporary culture and in the social constructedness of identity.

Notes

1 Elizabeth Wilson, *Adorned in Dreams* (London: Virago, 1985).
2 Following Marshall Berman, I am interpreting modernity as an epoch of rapid change, innovation, and negation of the old and creation of the new, a process bound up with industrial capitalism, the French Revolution, urbanization, and social and cultural differentiation. "Modernism," from this perspective, denotes a series of artistic practices that attempt to produce innovation in the arts in form, style, and content, which begin with Baudelaire in the mid-nineteenth century and continue through Madonna. See Marshall Berman, *All that is Solid Melts into Air* (New York: Simon and Schuster, 1982).
3 See Wilson, *Adorned in Dreams.*
4 Philip Wexler, *Becoming Somebody* (London and Washington, DC: Falmer Press, 1982).
5 See Douglas Kellner and Michael Ryan, *Camera Politica: the Politics and Ideology of Contemporary Hollywood Film* (Bloomington IN: Indiana University Press, 1988), and Douglas Kellner, *Television and the Crisis of Democracy: Contributions toward a Critical Theory of Television* (Boulder, CO: Westview Press, 1990).
6 *People*, May 13, 1985.
7 *People*, March 13, 1985.
8 *Forbes*, October 1, 1990.
9 Madonna started giving AIDS benefits in the late 1980s and her album *Like a Prayer* contained AIDS/HIV information and safe-sex advice. In the 1990s, however, she became more overtly political for a variety of causes and began referring to herself as a "revolutionary."
10 If one conceives "postmodern art" to be a fragmented display of disconnected elements in a flat, superficial play of surface without any depth or meaning, as Fredric Jameson, *Postmodernism: or, the Cultural Logic of Late Capitalism* (Durham, NC: Duke University Press, 1991) and others would have it, Madonna is emphatically not "postmodern." Rather, both her more realist videos and

modernist videos convey meanings and messages, but in the more modernist music videos, like *Express Yourself,* the meanings are often elusive and difficult to grasp. The modernist strategy of adopting shock techniques has been a constant in Madonna's work, and although she deploys camp, irony, and humor, her subject matter and themes are often quite serious. So, in a sense, Madonna is more modernist than postmodernist, although her work also embodies post-modern themes and aesthetic strategies.

11 On camp, see Susan Sontag, who defines it as an "unmistakably modern" (note: not "postmodern") sensibility, characterized by love of the unnatural, artifice, exaggeration, irony, involving play with cultural forms and images, involving a high level of theatricality and travesty – an excellent characterization of Madonna's aesthetic strategies. See *Against Interpretation* (New York: Dell Books, 1969), p. 277ff.

12 Camille Paglia, *New York Times,* December 14, 1990, B1. Paglia's labeling of Madonna as "true feminist" underscores the dogmatism and essentialism that characterizes her work. For Paglia, there is a "real feminism" and Madonna is it – as opposed to a multiplicity of models of feminism. Moreover, it is Paglia who denotes what "real feminism" is, enabling her to savage sundry versions of "false feminism." Likewise, she theorizes the essentially and genuinely "feminine" and "masculine," binary opposites which she believes provide a metaphysical foundation for culture.

13 *Entertainment* magazine, in a special issue on fashion (September 4, 1992), estimates that it could cost $377,012 to cultivate the Madonna look if one adds up the expenses from a year's collection of clothes, jewelry, makeup, and services. The early Madonna, by contrast, legitimated mix-and-match fashion in which anything goes. Madonna's transformation of her fashion strategies and body images thus reflects increased immersion in consumer culture and a growing commodification of her image.

Obsession: the Tyranny of Slenderness
Kim Chernin

The flesh and the devil

We know that every woman wants to be thin. Our images of womanhood are almost synonymous with thinness.

Susie Orbach

This reading first appeared in *The Obsession: Reflections on the Tyranny of Slenderness* (New York: Harper and Row, 1981).

I must now be able to look at my ideal, this ideal of being thin, of being without a body, and to realize:"it is a fiction."

Ellen West

When the body is hiding the complex, it then becomes our most immediate access to the problem.

Marian Woodman

The locker room of the tennis club. Several exercise benches, two old-fashioned hair-dryers, a mechanical bicycle, a treadmill, a reducing machine, a mirror, and a scale.

A tall woman enters, removes her towel; she throws it across a bench, faces herself squarely in the mirror, climbs on the scale, looks down.

A silence.

"I knew it," she mutters, turning to me. "I knew it."

And I think, before I answer, just how much I admire her, for this courage beyond my own, this daring to weigh herself daily in this way. And I sympathize. I know what she must be feeling. Not quite candidly, I say:"Up or down?" I am hoping to suggest that there might be people and cultures where gaining weight might not be considered a disaster. Places where women, stepping on scales, might be horrified to notice that they had reduced themselves. A mythical, almost unimaginable land.

"Two pounds," she says, ignoring my hint. "Two pounds." And then she turns, grabs the towel and swings out at her image in the mirror, smashing it violently, the towel spattering water over the glass, "Fat pig," she shouts at her image in the glass. "You fat, fat pig. . . ."

Later, I go to talk with this woman. Her name is Rachel and she becomes, as my work progresses, one of the choral voices that shape its vision.

Two girls come into the exercise room. They are perhaps 10 or 11 years old, at that elongated stage when the skeletal structure seems to be winning its war against flesh. And these two are particularly skinny. They sit beneath the hair-dryers for a moment, kicking their legs on the faded green uphol-stery; they run a few steps on the eternal treadmill; they wrap the rubber belt of the reducing machine around themselves and jiggle for a moment before it falls off. And then they go to the scale.

The taller one steps up, glances at herself in the mirror, looks down at the scale. She sighs, shaking her head. I see at once that this girl is imitating someone. The sigh, the headshake are theatrical, beyond her years. And so, too, is the little drama enacting itself in front of me. The other girl leans forward, eager to see for herself the troubling message imprinted upon the scale. But the older girl throws her hand over the secret. It is not to be revealed. And now the younger one, accepting this, steps up to confront the ultimate judgment. "Oh God," she says, this growing girl. "Oh God," with only a shade of imitation in her voice:"Would you believe it? I've gained five pounds."

These girls, too, become a part of my work. They enter, they perform their little scene again and again; it extends beyond them and in it I am finally able to behold something that would have remained hidden – for it does not express itself directly, although we feel its pressure almost every day of our lives. Something, unnamed as yet, struggling against our emergence into femininity. This is my first glimpse of it, out there. And the vision ripens.

I return to the sauna. Two women I have seen regularly at the club are sitting on the bench above me. One of them is very beautiful, the sort of woman Renoir would have admired. The other, who is probably in her late sixties, looks, in the twilight of this sweltering room, very much an adolescent. I have noticed her before, with her tan face, her white hair, her fashionable clothes, her slender hips and jaunty walk. But the effect has not been soothing. A woman of advancing age who looks like a boy.

"I've heard about that illness, anorexia nervosa," the plump one is saying, "and I keep looking around for someone who has it. I want to go sit next to her. I think to myself, maybe I'll catch it. . . ."

"Well," the other woman says to her, "I've felt the same way myself. One of my cousins used to throw food under the table when no one was looking. Finally, she got so thin they had to take her to the hospital . . . I always admired her."

What am I to understand from these stories? The woman in the locker room who swings out at her image in the mirror, the little girls who are afraid of the coming of adolescence to their bodies, the woman who admires the slenderness of the anorexic girl. Is it possible to miss the dislike these women feel for their bodies?

And yet, an instant's reflection tells us that this dislike for the body is not a biological fact of our condition as women – we do not come upon it by nature, we are not born to it, it does not arise for us because of anything predetermined in our sex. We know that once we loved the body, delighting in it the way children will, reaching out to touch our toes and count over our fingers, repeating the game endlessly as we come to knowledge of this body in which we will live out our lives. No part of the body exempt from our curiosity, nothing yet forbidden, we know an equal fascination with the feces we eliminate from ourselves, as with the ear we discover one day and the knees that have become bruised and scraped with falling and that warm, moist place between the legs from which feelings of indescribable bliss arise.

From that state to the condition of the woman in the locker room is a journey from innocence to despair, from the infant's naïve pleasure in the body, to the woman's anguished confrontation with herself. In this journey we can read our struggle with natural existence – the loss of the body as a source of pleasure. But the most striking thing about this alienation from the body is the fact that we take it for granted. Few of us ask to be redeemed from this struggle against the flesh by overcoming our antagonism toward the body. We do not rush about looking for someone who can tell us how to enjoy the fact that our appetite is large, or how we might delight in the curves and fullness of our own natural shape. We hope instead to be able to reduce the body, to limit the urges and desires it feels, to remove the body from nature. Indeed, the suffering we experience through our obsession with the body arises precisely from the hopeless and impossible nature of this goal. . . .

The boutique

It is now fashionable to be thin, but if it were fashionable to be fat, women would force-feed themselves like geese, just as girls in primitive societies used to stuff themselves because the fattest girl was the most beautiful. If the eighteen-inch waist should ever become fashionable again, women would suffer the tortures of tight lacing, convinced that though one dislocated one's kidneys, crushed one's liver, and turned green, beauty was worth it all.

Una Stannard

Well then, why can't we manage to be proud of our large bodies? Why can't we altogether grasp the fact that there might be something of a positive nature in the very fact of fleshy existence? What, we say? Woman's abundance, her fullness of body, her pot-belly and her fat ass and her big thighs regarded as beauty? Somehow it remains very hard for us to imagine women fashioning an ideal image for ourselves that required us to be grand and voluptuous. We can't quite conceive what it would be like to take back to ourselves the right to decide how our bodies should look, choosing an aesthetic according to health and nature, wishing our bodies to bear witness to our celebration of appetite, natural existence, and women's power.

And yet we do know that there were times, not so long ago, when women did not feel about their bodies the way we do. Then, a woman considered it a disaster if she stepped on the scale and found that she had lost weight. There once actually were women who had no respect for the anxieties of their physicians, who went ahead and caused their doctors to feel despair. These women would not lose weight because they did not wish to, and they did not wish to because their bodies seemed more beautiful to them when they were fat.

A physician in that day actually complained that it was fashion and aesthetic that interfered with prescribed weight-reducing programs.

> One must mention here that aesthetic errors of a worldly nature to which all women submit, may make them want to stay obese for reasons of fashionable appearance. It is beyond a doubt that in order to have an impressive decollete each woman feels herself duty bound to be fat around the neck, over the clavicle and in her breasts. Now it happens that fat accumulates with greatest difficulty in these places and one can be sure, even without examining such a woman, that the abdomen and the hips, and the lower members are hopelessly fat. As to the treatment, one cannot obtain weight reduction of the abdomen without the woman sacrificing in her spirits the upper part of her body. To her it is a true sacrifice because she gives up what the world considers beautiful.[1]

That was in 1911. And the little parable tells us one thing quite clearly. If the standard of beauty that prevailed in Paris in 1911 were still in fashion in America of 1980, none of us would go home tonight after a large meal, and take laxatives, and run the risk of ruining our digestion, upsetting our electrolyte imbalance, and disturbing the natural condition of the flora of our intestine. If we were admired for having fat around the neck, as women were in 1911, and were permitted to have large abdomens and well-padded hips, tens of thousands of women would not kneel down next to the toilet tonight and put our fingers down our throat, and vomit.

From this simple fact we come to appreciate, all over again, the way an aesthetic ideal affects our lives with an extreme coercive power. Fashion lets us know what our culture expects us to be, or to become, or to struggle to become, in order to be acceptable to it, thereby exercising a devastating power over our lives on a daily basis. The image of women that appears in the advertisements of a daily newspaper has the power to damage a woman's health, destroy her sense of well-being, break her pride in herself, and subvert her ability to accept herself as a woman.

Thus, it is possible to study fashion the way one can study a work of art, so that it reflects significantly upon the issues and conflicts of its own day. The nude body of a woman, as we have seen, carries a tale that proves interesting beyond the boundaries of aesthetic speculation. Similarly, fashion, in the image it creates of woman, expresses itself on a variety of issues its makers would never imagine so deeply concerned them. By studying the face, the expression, the body, the gesture of the recurring images in our culture, we begin to read our culture's attitudes toward power in a woman, her sensual freedom, her right to joyfulness, subjectivity, and expressiveness through her body, her right to age, to grow mature in her body, to acquire authority, to bear this authority in the angle of her jaw, the settling back of her shoulders, the tilt of her head. If the pages of *Vogue* presented us with pictures of large women, their bodies muscular like those of athletes, their heads held high like those of a person of prestige and influence; if the pages of the daily newspaper showed women wearing clothes that emphasized the beauty of a powerful back, the strength of a large hip, hands and feet that were able to work and to accomplish, necks that were capable of carrying life's burden, or a softness, a fullness, and abundance that seemed, like a ripening fruit, to stand for the abundance and fullness of life itself, there would not be six million women in the US today who had joined Weight Watchers to change the size of their bodies; eight thousand of us next week would not be moving through the doors of the diet salon, and the word bulmarexia might never have had to be created, in 1974, to describe our unique cultural disorder – a disease that includes simultaneously the symptoms of insatiable appetite (bulimia) and (anorexia) the rejection of food.[2]

But it is also true that the fashions we are speaking about have changed several times since 1911. We know that, during the 1920s, women were binding their breasts and bobbing their hair and hoping to look like boys; and we remember that in 1960 Marilyn Monroe, when she made the film *Some Like It Hot*, was still permitted to be as large as a woman in a drawing by Modersohn-Becker. We who fell in love with her then and yearned as growing girls to look like her, seeing this film now, and the size of the woman who was our heroine, must marvel at what has happened to our very perception of beauty. For Monroe, if she were alive now, and still as grand and voluptuous as she was then, would today no doubt be considered fat. . . .

But this zaftig body of Monroe, when it appears on a woman of our time, becomes a source of profound despair; it is measured, frowned upon, afflicted with starvation, hidden away, and taken finally into surgery, where for $2,500 the buttocks are reduced, and where for another $3,000 the thighs are made smaller, and where for yet more thousands of dollars the roundness of the belly is made flat. . . .

And so we make our way into the street life of our culture, hoping now to look again, with a new quality of perception, at the most commonplace expression of the conflicts and dilemmas that inspire literature and art, philosophy and psychological perceptions. But we are now not surprised to find that the conflict over the flesh is reflected here too, in this stamping ground of the anorexic heroine, whose picture is repeated on every page of the fashion magazine, and whose form is sculpted in the stylish mannequins of the store windows, and whose representative greets us, with a false smile, a secret disparagement, as we enter a clothing store, for it is clear that we enter without being able to conform – we will need a size nine or ten or maybe eleven; we will not do justice to the new, slender line, the tapering curve at the hip, the girdle-like constriction of the jeans. How often we have been filled with panic, catching a glimpse of ourselves, in all our unredeemed femininity, looking back with a frantic expression from the mirrors that reflect everything we are supposed to be – those girls who have succeeded where we have failed, those long-limbed mannequins who have become our omnipresent reminder, our reproach. . . .

. . . The signs on the rack are bold and explicit – they wish to make it clear that here, in the showplace of our culture, some significant transformation has occurred. SIZE THREE? But what has happened to the sevens or the nines? The place is thick with ones and twos and there, shamefacedly in the far corner, is a rack of fives. They don't have size nine, the girl tells us, although we have not asked. "But don't you know," we want to say to her, "that there are over twenty-five million women in this country who wear size sixteen and over? That, if you want to know, is more than 30 percent of the women in this land.[3] And what of all the rest of us, uncounted, who are unable to adapt ourselves to these styles suited for adolescents? And what, if you come to that, do you make of the fact that the large-size clothes are called, in the vernacular of the garment industry, 'women's sizes,' and just what, if you follow me, does that reveal about these gaunt garments hanging here? For surely, you see that they were not intended for a woman?"

Why now?

A woman should never give the impression that she is so capable, so self-sufficient, that she doesn't need him at all. Men are enchanted by minor, even amusing frailties.

This quality of vulnerability, of needing a man, is something that the mature woman should study very carefully. Because it's that quality that she loses most easily. Years of dealing with home and family, of making decisions, of coping, can turn the woman of forty-plus into a brusque, cold-eyed, and somewhat frightening figure.

Gloria Heidi

Is it a conspiracy, unknown even to those who participate in it? A whole culture busily spinning out images and warnings intended to keep women from developing their bodies, their appetites, and their powers?

Maybe, when we see another calorie counter on the stand, or read of another miracle diet in a women's magazine, or pick up another container of low-calorie cottage cheese, we must begin to understand these trivial items symbolically and realize that what we are purchasing is the covert advice not to grow too large and too powerful for our culture.

Maybe, indeed, this whole question of the body's reduction is analogous to the binding of women's feet in pre-revolutionary China?[4]

"My mother buys me a girdle when I am fifteen years old," says Louise Bernikow, "because she doesn't like the jiggle ... Tighter. I hold myself tighter, as my mother has taught me to do ... Is the impulse to cripple a girl peculiar to China between the eleventh and twentieth centuries? The lotus foot was the size of a doll's and the woman could not walk without support. Her foot was four inches long and two inches wide. A doll. A girl-child. Crippled, indolent, and bound."[5]

There is a relationship between the standards set for women's beauty and the desire to limit their development. In the name of a beautiful foot, the women of China were deprived of autonomy and made incapable of work. A part of the body was forced to remain in a childish condition. They did not walk, they hobbled. In the name of beauty they were crippled.

What happens to women today in the name of beauty?

> I'd never wear a girdle, she said,
> just medieval throwbacks
> to whale baleen brassieres 'n'
> laced-up waist confiner corsets.
> We burned 'em in the sixties,
> girdles, she said walking
> into Bloomingdales, grabbing
> a pair of cigarette-legged
> tight denim jeans off the rack.
> Hoisting them up to her hips,
> how do ya get 'em on, she said,
> have surgery, take steam baths,
> slimnastic classes 'n' Dr Nazi's
> diet clinic fatshots for a month?
> These aren't jeans for going
> to lunch in, she said trying
> to do the snap, these
> aren't even jeans

for eating an hour
before ya put 'em on, just
for standin' up in without
your hands in the pockets,
there's not even room
in here for my underpants.
One hour later she returns
to the store for a new zipper,
front snap, and the side seams
re-stitched. These're jeans
for washing in cold water only
then wearin' round the house
til they dry on yr shape,
put 'em in a clothes dryer,
she said, and you'll get
all pinch bruised
round the crotch 'n'
your stomach covered
with red streak marks
cross the front.
We burned 'em in the sixties,
girdles, she said.[6]

We must not imagine that it is only the fashion industry that is upset about the large size of our bodies. Fashion creates and it reflects. Creates, as we have seen, an image few women in this culture are able to realize for themselves. Creates longing – and we all know this longing to win the approval of our culture even at cost to our health, our identity as women, our experience of pleasure in our bodies. But fashion also reflects hidden cultural intentions, as it did in China with the binding of women's feet. As it does in our own day, with pants so tight they serve as an adequate replacement for the girdles that used to bind us. Fashion, for all its appearance of superficiality, is a mirror in which we can read the responses of conventional culture to what is occurring, at the deepest levels of cultural change, among its people.

For instance, if the problem of body and mind is as old in this culture as I have suggested, why is anorexia a new disease and bulmarexia a condition first named during the 1970s? Why, for that matter, is Christine Olman a model now and not 20 years ago when Marilyn Monroe inspired our admiration?

These questions may help us to understand that something has happened in our culture during the past 20 years that has made us particularly uneasy about the abundance of our flesh. Something, unnamed as yet, which fashion expresses as a shift from the voluptuous to the ascetic.

I wish to place before us a cluster of related facts that constitutes an important cultural synchronicity.

FACT: During the 1960s Marilyn Monroe stood for the ideal in feminine beauty. Now Christine Olman represents that ideal.

FACT: During the 1960s anorexia nervosa began to be a widespread social disease among women.

FACT: During the late 1960s and early 1970s bulmarexia began to be observed as a condition among women.

FACT: During the 1960s Weight Watchers opened its doors. In 1965 Diet Workshop appeared, in 1960s Over-Eaters Anonymous, in 1966 Why Weight, in 1968 Weight Losers Institute, in 1969 Lean Line.

FACT: During the 1960s the feminist movement began to emerge, asserting a woman's right to authority, development, dignity, liberation and, above all, power.

What am I driving at here? I am suggesting that the changing awareness among women of our position in this society has divided itself into two divergent movements, one of which is a movement toward feminine power, the other a retreat from it, supported by the fashion and diet industries, which share a fear of women's power.

In this light it is significant that one of the first feminist activities in our time was an organized protest against the Miss America Contest and the idea of feminine beauty promulgated by the dominant culture through this pageant, in which women strut and display their bodies, as men sit passively, judging them. It is interesting, further, that as a significant portion of the female population in the past two decades began to go to consciousness-raising groups and to question the role and subservience of women in this society, other women hastened to groups where the large size of their bodies was deplored. The same era gave birth to these two contradictory movements among women.

Yet we sense that there is an underlying similarity of motive in both movements. In both, women are driven to gather together and make confessions and find sisterly support for the new resolutions they are taking. In both, women have created new forms of social organization, apart from the established institutions of the dominant culture.

There is, however, also a fundamental divergence here. The groups that arise among feminists are dedicated to the enlargement of women. Confessions made in these groups reveal anger over rape and the shame women have been taught to feel about their bodies; there is interest in the longing to develop the self, concern for the boredom and limitations of motherhood, acknowledgment of the need for sisterly support in the resolution to return to work, go back to school, become more of oneself, grow larger. But in the other groups, confessions are voiced about indulgence in the pleasures of eating, and resolutions are made to control the amount of food consumed, and sisterly support is given for a renewed warfare against the appetite and the body.

Listen to the spontaneous metaphor that finds its way into the discussions of these two groups. In the feminist group it is *largeness* in a woman that is sought, the *power* and *abundance* of the feminine, the assertion of a woman's right to be taken seriously, to *acquire weight*, to *widen* her *frame* of reference, to be *expansive*, *enlarge* her views, *acquire gravity*, *fill out*, and *gain* a sense of self-esteem. It is always a question of *widening*, *enlarging*, *developing*, and *growing*. But in the weight-watching groups the women are trying to *reduce* themselves; and the metaphoric consistency of this is significant: they are trying to make themselves *smaller*, to *narrow* themselves, to become *lightweight*, to lose *gravity*, to be-*little* themselves. Here, emphasis is placed upon *shrinking* and *diminution*, *confinement*, and *contraction*, a *loss* of pounds, a *losing* of flesh, a *falling* of weight, a *lessening*.

These metaphoric consistencies reveal a struggle that goes beyond concern for the body. Thus, in the feminist groups the emphasis is significantly upon liberation – upon release of power, the unfettering of long-suppressed ability, the freeing of one's potential, a woman shaking off restraints and delivering herself from limitations. But in the appetite-control groups the emphasis is upon restraint and prohibition, the keeping of watch over appetites and urges, the confining of impulses, the control of the hungers of the self.

When all other personal motives for losing weight are stripped away – the desire to be popular, to be loved, to be successful, to be acceptable, to be in control, to be admired, to admire one's self – what unites the women who seek to reduce their weight is the fact that they look for an answer to their life's problems in the control of their bodies and appetites. A woman who walks through the doors of a weight-watching organization and enters the women's reduction movement has allowed her culture to persuade her that significant relief from her personal and cultural dilemma is to be found in the reduction of her body. Thus, her decision, although she may not be aware of it, enters the domain of the body politic and becomes symbolically a political act.

It is essential to interpret anorexia nervosa, that other significant movement among women during the past decades, so that it, too, can be understood as part of women's struggle for liberation during the past decades. Indeed, Hilde Bruch calls it a new disease because in the past 15 or 20 years it has occurred at a "rapidly increasing rate." From 1960 on, she writes, "reports on larger patient groups have been published in countries as far apart as Russia and Australia, Sweden and Italy, England and the United States."[7]

The fact that these are highly developed industrial countries, and that anorexia occurs primarily among girls of the upper-middle class, should remind us that anorexia is a symbolic illness. Where hunger is imposed by external circumstances, the act of starvation remains literal, a tragic biological event that does not serve metaphoric or symbolic purposes. It is only in a country where one is able to choose hunger that elective starvation may come to express cultural conflict or even social protest. . . .

In America of the 1970s and 1980s, no woman can possibly remain unaware of the fact that significant numbers of her sisters are asserting their rights to autonomy, to power, to the development of their full emotional and creative capacities. This movement of women into their enlargement is likely to affect her in a number of ways. She may grow depressed with the life she is living and rebel against it. She may refuse to recognize that her life depresses her and fail to develop a meaningful analysis of her condition as a woman. Or she may feel the force of these contradictory tendencies and enact her entire response to them through her body.

Let us imagine then that a woman comes to awareness of her condition one day in 1969. She is, let us say, 45 years old, she wears old, dreary clothes, and she is seriously depressed. She is a woman who has tried to diet and failed and who has exhausted her tolerance for weight-watching groups. For her the anorexic solution is simply not a possibility. And so she decides to join a women's consciousness-raising group. There, she tells the other women that her husband has just left her after 25 years. She tells how she is stuck in a job with a poverty wage in an insurance company, how she feels a thousand years old. She blames herself, she says, and the fatness in her body, for everything that has gone wrong with her life. But now, because she is encouraged to talk and because no one here believes her rounded belly is the cause of these complex failures, she speaks about a dream she had once as a young girl when she wished to become a writer. She tells how absurd this old dream seems now and how she is afraid. But because the women listen to her fears and encourage her to speak further, she goes home and she begins to dream that she might want to dream of becoming a writer.

Let us also imagine that another similar woman comes to a group intended to help women change their lives. But here, in fact, we do not have to provide the script, for the story of a middle-aged woman named Faye has been written for us by Gloria Heidi, in her unintentionally revealing book:

She was about forty-five years old when she enrolled in my class – a gray, doughy woman in a dreary maroon, half-size dress – a woman who had obviously come to me as a last resort. "Look, my husband Harry has just walked out after twenty-five years. I'm stuck in a poverty-wage, nowhere job at the insurance company. I feel a thousand years old – and look sixty. But I'm determined to be a new me . . . and I want to start by losing this excess weight. After all, now that I've lost Harry" – her eyes filled with tears – "what else have I got to lose?"[8]

In this group, where the woman comes with a complex social and personal situation, her terrible despair is attributed to the fact that she is fat. She is therefore encouraged to lose weight; a chart is kept of the weight she loses. When the magical transformation finally takes place we are told that the horror of her personal and social position has miraculously altered. A moral is drawn. We are assured that we, too, if only we will lose weight, can be "filled with energy, go aggressively after a better job and with a new figure, a revitalized personality, and an exciting new social life, [like] formerly dowdy and half-sized Faye, [soon] be sitting on top of the world."

The hidden message in this story is profoundly disturbing. Implicitly, we are asked to believe that if every woman lost 25 or 30 pounds she would be able to overcome the misogyny in our land; her social problems would be solved, the business world would suddenly fling wide its gates and welcome her into its privileges. Isn't it incredible? We, as women, need only lose weight and all of us will find jobs equal in authority and status and salary to those of men? The need for the Equal Rights Amendment will vanish? Unemployment figures will dissolve and the very structure of our society will be transformed?

There is a profound untruth here and a subversion of the radical discontent women feel. In a class of this sort, women are directed to turn their dissatisfaction and depression toward their own bodies. They are encouraged to look at their large size as the cause of the failure they sustain in their lives. Consider what it means to persuade a woman who is depressed and sorrowful and disheartened by her entire life, that if only she succeeds in reducing herself, in becoming even less than she already is, she will be acceptable to this culture which cannot tolerate her if she is any larger or more developed than an adolescent girl. The radical protest she might utter, if she correctly understood the source of her despair and depression, has been directed toward herself and away from her culture and society. Now, she will not seek to change her culture so that it might accept her body; instead, she will spend the rest of her life in anguished failure at the effort to change her body so that it will be acceptable to her culture.[9]

We should not be misled by the fact that we feel more at home in our culture when we lose weight. It may indeed happen that a woman becomes more attractive to men, finds it easier to get a job, experiences less discrimination, receives fewer gibes from strangers, and endures far less humiliation in her own family. Culture rewards those who comply with its standards. But we have to wonder what cost the woman is paying when she sacrifices her body in this way for the approval of her culture. . . .

It is only when we cease to trivialize our bodies and our feelings about our bodies that we begin to appreciate how powerful a tool against the development of women is daily exercised by this conventional orientation, which assures us that our sufferings and our depressions are caused by the recalcitrant behavior of our bodies – by their insistence upon feeding themselves, by their unsuppressible urges and wantings and desires, which make us fat.

For what happens when the woman gains back the weight? (Ninety-eight percent of women who have lost weight gain it back.)

What happens when she gains back even more than she lost? (Ninety percent of women gain back more weight than they ever lost.)

What indeed happens to her job and her lover and her new social power and her status in her family and her freedom from the hostility that our culture directs against women who live out their lives in large bodies? . . .

. . . For we can imagine that a culture based upon the suppression of women will be inclined, precisely in that era when a significant number of women are rediscovering the imagery and meaning of the Amazon, to turn away from whatever is powerful in women. The images in fashion magazines, on billboards, in store windows reflect this turning away from female power, but so also does the masculine retreat from grown women as erotic images. This retreat runs a parallel course to the women's reduction movement and expresses an identical fear of female power. Thus we come upon one final cultural synchronicity. In the era of women's liberation, which is also the era of fat farms and the body's emaciation, popular culture begins to produce movies in which photographers, grown men, become entranced with the Pretty Baby who lives in a whorehouse. In this same era of women's development some 264 periodicals appear on the marketplace with child pornography.[10] In 1975, Houston police uncover "a warehouse filled with child pornography . . . 15,000 color slides of children, 1,000 magazines, and thousands of reels of film."[11] During this time of the assertion of woman's power we have films like *Taxi Driver*, "in which a twelve-year-old prostitute happily gratifies any male whim in order to please her loathsome pimp. Jodie Foster, who played the adolescent prostitute, was so well received in the role that she soon starred in *The Little Girl who Lives Down the Lane*, in which she performed as a thirteen-year-old bundle of budding sexuality."[12] In the film *Manhattan* the most popular comedian of his day, a man 40 or so, afflicted with an old-fashioned European melancholy and an entirely modern haplessness in the face of existence, turns for comfort and redemption to a 17-year-old girl when his wife, a grown woman, leaves him and becomes a lesbian. There is Chester the Molester who seduces little girls and boys as humor in the pages of *Hustler* magazines. And there is the adolescent girl who wrote the following letter to the author of *Kiss Daddy Goodnight*, a book of horror tales of the incest inflicted upon little girls by their fathers. "So if a girl wants my advice now I would say it is OK to do it with Dad until you are about thirteen or fourteen but after that he will lose interest in you and abuse you sexually by letting other people do it up you so it is best to stop at that age, and if I did, then I would still like Dad and not be mad at him like I am."[13]

Naturally, I cannot prove that the masculine preference for little girls is on the increase in our time because grown women are asserting their right to power. The preference itself is not as easy to document as the fact that the women in the fashion magazines are made to look like adolescent children or that the sizes in the clothing stores are growing smaller or that millions of women are attending diet organizations and seeking to reduce themselves while tens of thousands of others cause themselves to vomit every night. I am asking only that we begin to think about these simultaneous events in our cultural life; that we ponder the words of a fifth grade teacher in a city school: "Sexual abuse . . . incest . . . you don't know," she says, "you don't know . . . the kids in my class, the littlest girls . . . the uncles, the brothers, the fathers. It's epidemic and they all cover it up."[14]

Taken together, these words and the books and films and cartoons and letters we have been considering suggest a tendency in which men prefer to encounter little girls instead of grown women. Upon reflection, there is even something highly predictable about this. "Certainly," says Grace Paley, "any culture that prefers women to be childlike and dependent will, with a certain terrible logic, use its children as though they were grown women."[15]

Thus, what we are seeing in this tyranny of slenderness is more than a cultural warfare between body and mind, more even than a bitter struggle against the life-cycle and the free expression of our kinship with nature. In this age of feminist assertion men are drawn to women of childish body and mind because there is something less disturbing about the vulnerability and helplessness of a small child – and something truly disturbing about the body and mind of a mature woman.

Notes

1   Hilde Bruch, *Eating Disorders: Obesity, Anorexia Nervosa, and the Person Within* (New York: Basic Books, 1973).
2   Maria Brenner, "Bulmarexia," *Savvy*, June 6, 1980.
3   Morey Stanyan on Carole Shaw, *San Francisco Examiner and Chronicle*, January 20, 1980.
4   Alice Walker, in a conversation about women and their bodies, suggested this analogy to me.
5   Louise Bernikow, *Among Women* (New York: Harmony Books, 1980).
6   Jana Harris, *Manhattan as a Second Language* (New York: Harper and Row, 1982).
7   Hilde Bruch, *The Golden Cage: the Enigma of Anorexia Nervosa* (Cambridge, Mass.: Harvard University Press, 1978).
8   Gloria Heidi, *Winning the Age Game* (Garden City, NY: Doubleday, 1976).
9   Adapted from a very similar utterance by Louise Wolfe, "The politics of body size," Pacifica Tape Library.
10 Florence Rush, "Child pornography," in L. Lederer (ed.), *Take Back the Night*, pp. 71–81 (New York: W. Morrow).
11 Ibid.
12 Ibid.
13 Louise Armstrong, *Kiss Daddy Goodnight: a Speak-out on Incest* (New York: Hawthorn Books, 1978).
14 Grace Paley, "Review of *The Best Kept Secret* by Florence Rush," *Ms.*, January 1981.
15 Ibid.

Suggested activities

Questions for discussion

1   According to Wolf, why is the "beauty myth" a myth? Do you agree with her? Why or why not?

2   Assuming you find some plausibility in the concept of the beauty myth, do you agree with Wolf's analogy to the Iron Maiden? Why or why not? What aspects of American culture reinforce rigid ideals of beauty for women?

3   Do you agree with Chernin that American culture's obsession with weight reduction is analogous to the historical Chinese practice of foot-binding for women? Why or why not?

4   What connections can you make between advertising and eating disorders?

5   How do you explain the rise of eating disorders, especially among young women, in recent years?

6 Do you agree with Kathy Davis's claim that American culture largely defines women in terms of their bodies? If so, are there ways to change this definition?

7 What changes would you recommend in the way that women's health care is provided, especially to black women and other women of color?

8 Is fashion a confining or oppressive way of controlling women or a liberating means for self-expression? Both? Or neither? What specific observations is your answer based on?

9 What role does fashion have in your own life or those of your friends? What gender differences have you observed about the significance of fashion?

10 Can women simply ignore the messages about gender and femininity that are transmitted in popular culture through ads, magazines, and fashion?

11 Would you characterize Madonna as a feminist? Why or why not? What does the "Madonna phenomenon" tell us about the role of fashion in shaping gender identity?

Films and videos

The Body Beautiful by Ngozi Onwurah (1991). 1 mm/VHS/color/23 mins. Available from Women Make Movies. Deals with body issues in terms of beauty, race, and health, centered on a white mother undergoing a mastectomy and her black daughter embarking on a modeling career. Examines the sexual and racial tensions women face.

Breast Cancer: Speaking Out by KCTS/TV (1992). VHS/30 mins. Distributed by KCTS/TV, Seattle, WA. Shows women freeing themselves from the constraint of being well-behaved patients, and fighting for federal funds for more breast-cancer research.

Bulimia and Road to Recovery by Sandra Smith (1988). VHS/color/27 mins. Distributed by Women Make Movies. Smith, as a bulimia survivor, raises awareness of the disease among young women.

The Famine Within by Katherine Gilday, produced by Kendor Productions Ltd (1990). VHS/58 mins. Available from Direct Cinema Ltd. Focuses on the North American obsession with body size and shape in advertising and modeling and the eating disorders it encourages.

Fighting for our Lives: Women Confronting AIDS produced by the Center for Women Policy Studies (1990). VHS/color/29 mins. Distributed by Women Make Movies. Documentary on the struggle for AIDS education and prevention in minority communities.

Her Giveaway: a Spiritual Journey with AIDS by Mona Smith (1988). VHS/color/21 mins. Distributed by Women Make Movies. Documentary of Carole Lafavor, an American Indian, lesbian, and person with AIDS.

I'm You, You're Me by Catherine Saalfield (1993). VHS/color/26 mins. Distributed by Women Make Movies. An examination of HIV-positive women who are released from prison to an independent life.

I Need your Full Cooperation by Kathy High (1989). VHS/color/28 mins. Distributed by Women Make Movies. Documentary examining the relationship between women and the medical community. Uses experimental film techniques, and includes interview with Barbara Ehrenreich.

(In)Visible Women by Marina Alvarez and Ellen Spiro (1991). VHS/color/26 mins. Distributed by Women Make Movies. Subtitled documentary about the responses of three Latina women living with AIDS.

Mirror, Mirror by Jan Krawitz (1990). VHS/17 mins. Distributed by Women Make Movies. This award-winning film explores the relationship between a woman's body image and the quest for an idealized female form. Interviews 13 diverse women about their relationship to their bodies.

Never Too Thin by Willie Werby and Wendy Werby (1992). VHS/57 mins. Distributed by Landmark Media, Falls Church, VA. Explores the attitudes of women and men toward women's bodies, the negative self-image that many women have, its causes, and the beauty industry that exploits it.

Warning: the Media May be Hazardous to your Health. An evening with Ann Simonton produced and directed by Jenai Lane (1990). VHS/36 mins. Distributed by Media Watch. On the eating disorders and other problems that fashion models and other women confront. Narrated by Ann Simonton, a former model who has become an activist against sexist advertising.

A Woman's Body (1989). VHS/58 mins. Examines the physiological and sociological health problems that contemporary women have, and their growing demands for more control over their own bodies. Focuses on particular areas of concern, including unnecessary hysterectomies, breast cancer, PMS, eating disorders, infertility, and the menopause.

A Woman's Health by Katie Jennings, produced by KCTS/Seattle (1994). Available from the PBS Adult Learning Satellite Service. Documentary of seven women involved in fighting health battles typical to women: heart disease, smoking, breast cancer, osteoporosis, domestic violence, and depression.

Other activities

See one of Madonna's films or videos or listen to an audiotape of her music. Discuss how accurately Kellner has described the "Madonna phenomenon," and what Madonna's phenomenal success can tell us about the relationship between gender, fashion, and identity.

Bibliography

Ash, Juliet and Wilson, Elizabeth (eds) (1992) *Chic Thrills: a Fashion Reader* (Berkeley, CA: University of Berkeley). Collection of essays on a variety of periods/styles of fashion, from cultural studies and postmodern perspectives.

Avery, Billye (1990) "The evolution of the National Black Women's Health Project," in Evelyn C. White (ed.), *The Black Women's Health Book: Speaking for Ourselves* (Seattle, WA: Seal Press). By the founder of the project, an organization committed to the health and well-being of black women.

Bair, Barbara and Cayleff, Susan (eds) (1993) *Wings of Gauze: Women of Color and the Experience of Health and Illness* (Detroit, MI: Wayne State University Press). Collection of essays by social science and humanities scholars, health professionals, and community activists documents the multifaceted factors that shape women of color's experiences of illness and health. Covers traditional systems of health and medicine among people of color, the relationship of health to socioeconomic factors, and the ways in which government and institutional health organizations have responded to issues of rape, domestic violence, reproductive rights, substance abuse, and sexually transmitted disease among women of color.

Banner, Lois (1983) *American Beauty* (New York: Knopf). Explores the relationship that women have had to images of beauty throughout US history.

Benstock, Shari and Ferris, Suzanne (eds) (1994) *On Fashion* (New Brunswick, NJ: Rutgers University Press). This collection of essays examines a variety of aspects of beauty and fashion in popular culture, including Barbie, Twiggie, fashion magazines, fashion designers and photographers, and Madonna. Considers the question of what fashion is, the relation of fashion to repression, expression, revolution, and its relationship to the body.

Berman, Nina (1993) "Disappearing acts," *Ms.* (March/April), pp. 38–40. Interviews with women who are in treatment for self-starvation.

Bordo, Susan (1993) *Unbearable Weight: Feminism, Western Culture, and the Body* (Berkeley, CA: University of California Press). On how women's bodies are a source of their oppression in Western culture. Analyzes the messages about the body produced in US culture from the perspective of postmodern feminist philosophy.

Boston Women's Health Collective (1992) *The New Our Bodies, Ourselves* (New York: Simon and Schuster). On women's health and hygiene, diseases, and psychology.

Brown, Catrina and Jasper, Karin (1992) *Consuming Passions: Feminist Approaches to Weight Preoccupation and Eating Disorders* (Ontario: Second Story Press).

Brumberg, Joan (1988) *Fasting Girls: the Emergence of Anorexia Nervosa as a Modern Disease* (Cambridge, MA: Harvard University Press). Describes American society as "obesophobic."

Callahan, Karen (ed.) (1994) *Ideals of Feminine Beauty: Philosophical, Social, and Cultural Dimensions* (Westport, CT: Greenwood Press). Focuses on beauty ideals and the relationship between beauty and patriarchy.

Chapkis, Wendy (1986) *Beauty Secrets: Women and the Politics of Appearance* (Boston: South End Press). Focuses on the beauty system as central to women's oppression. Analyzes beauty as a "politics of appearance." Includes fascinating interviews with women on their difference from the culturally dominant standards of beauty because of their disabilities or facial hair or breastlessness or obesity or other "difference."

Chernin, Kim (1981) *The Obsession: Reflections on the Tyranny of Slenderness* (New York: Harper and Row).

Chernin, Kim (1985) *The Hungry Self: Women, Eating, and Identity* (New York: Times Books).

Collins, Catherine Fisher (ed.) (1996) *African-American Women's Health and Social Issues* (Westport, CT: Auburn House). Essays dealing with topics of concern to African-American women such as AIDS, lupus, and alcohol abuse.

Corea, Gena (1992) *The Invisible Epidemic: the Story of Women and AIDS* (New York: HarperCollins).

Craik, Jennifer (1994) *The Face of Fashion: Culture Studies in Fashion* (London: Routledge). Explores the relationships between high and everyday fashion. Chapter 4, "Fashioning women: techniques of femininity," and Chapter 5 "Fashion models: female bodies and icons of femininity," are especially pertinent.

Daly, Mary (1978) *Gynecology* (Boston: Beacon Press). Section on foot-binding and genital mutilation.

Davis, Angela (1992) "Sick and tired of being sick and tired," *Women of Power*, 18 (Fall), pp. 28–9.

Davis, Fred (1992) *Fashion, Culture, and Identity* (Chicago: University of Chicago Press). Explores how clothing choices are shaped by social and cultural forces beyond "individual taste," reflecting tensions over gender roles, social status, and the expression of sexuality.

Davis, Kathy (1995) *Reshaping the Female Body: the Dilemma of Cosmetic Surgery* (New York: Routledge).

Ehrenreich, Barbara (1992) "Stamping out a dread scourge," *Time*, February 17, pp. 88. A humorous look at the "disease" of small breastedness which makes breast implants so desirable for some women.

Fallon, Patricia, Katzman, Melanie, and Wooley, Susan (eds) (1994) *Feminist Perspectives on Eating Disorders* (New York: Guilford Press). Collection of essays covering historical background, treatment issues, fashion, images of women, appearance, power, sexual abuse, obesity, hospitalization, adolescents, multiculturalism, politics, advertising, education, and research.

Faludi, Susan (1991) "Beauty and the backlash" and "Dressing the dolls: fashion and the backlash," in *Backlash: the Undeclared War against American Women* (New York: Doubleday Press).

Fisher, Sue and Davis, Kathy (eds) (1993) *Negotiating at the Margins: the Gendered Discourses of Power and Resistance* (Camden, NJ: Rutgers State University Press). Anthology of essays on gender and power. The first section, entitled "Negotiating the body and its adornments," addresses the relationship between beauty, fashion, and gender identity.

Freedman, Rita (1985) *Beauty Bound: Why We Pursue the Myth in the Mirror* (New York: The Free Press/Lexington Books). Analysis of women's oppression through physical appearance and its consequences.

Friedan, Betty (1997) *The Feminine Mystique* (New York: W. W. Norton).

Halperin, Sara (1995) *Look at my Ugly Face: Myths and Musings on Beauty and Other Perilous Obsessions with Women's Appearance* (New York: Viking). About the roles of beauty and ugliness, their connection with an obsession about appearance that haunts women's lives, and ways to work creatively with them.

Herndl, Diane Price (1993) *Invalid Women: Figuring Feminine Illness in American Fiction and Culture* (Chapel Hill, NC: University of North Carolina Press). Looks at representations of women's invalidism in literature, advertising, and film during the period 1840–1940 from the perspectives of feminist and medical history and literary postmodernism.

Hollander, Anne (1978) *Seeing through Clothes* (New York: Viking Press). Looks at how clothing in works of art have been connected with clothes in real life, as providing a form of identity, during two and a half thousand years of Western history.

Hollander, Anne (1994) *Sex and Suits* (New York: Knopf). Addresses clothing as a form of artistic expression. Speculates about the reasons for the enduring popularity of men's suits in terms of their meaning in relation to sex, power, and imagination.

hooks, bell (1993) *Sisters of the Yam: Black Women and Self-Recovery* (Boston: South End Press). Self-help book for black women: hooks advises that black women need to tell their stories of emotional and psychological problems in order to show how their lives are constantly demeaned by institutionalized oppression; how self-hatred and low self-esteem are reflections of a political system that devalues black people.

Johnson, Ruth (ed.) (1995) *African American Voices: African American Health Educators Speak Out* (New York: National League for Nursing). Anthology of essays on the health ailments, distinctively or disproportionately suffered by African-Americans, as well as the reasons for their higher morbidity and mortality rates.

King, Ynestra (1993) "The other body: reflections on difference disability, and identity politics," *Ms.*, March/April, pp. 72–5.

Koblinsky, Marge, Timyan Judith, and Gay, Jill (1993) *The Health of Women: a Global Perspective* (Boulder, CO: Westview Press). Chapters cover poverty, nutrition, family planning, abortion, violence, mental health, quality of and access to care.

Lakoff, Robin and Scherr, Robin (1984) *Face Value: the Politics of Beauty* (London: Routledge and Kegan Paul).

Layton, Lynne (1994) "Who's that Girl? A Case Study of Madonna," in Carol Franz and Abigail Stewart (eds), *Women Creating Lives: Identities, Resilience, and Resistance* (Boulder, CO: Westview Press). Analysis of Madonna's public and private identities.

Leland, John (1992) "The new voyeurism: Madonna and the selling of sex," *Newsweek*, November 2, pp. 94–103. On Madonna's book *Sex*.

Munter, Carol and Hirschmann, Jane (1995) *When Women Stop Hating their Bodies: Freeing Yourself from Food and Weight Obsession* (New York: Ballantine Books). On compulsive eating, the psychology of weight loss, and treatment.

Overall, Christine (1993) *Human Reproduction: Principles, Practices, Policies* (Toronto: Oxford University Press). Series of essays on various aspects of reproductive technologies from a feminist perspective.

Rooks, Noliwe M. (1996) *Hair Raising: Beauty, Culture, and African American Women* (New Brunswick, NJ: Rutgers University Press). Exploration of beauty culture in African-American communities, 1800s to the present.

Rubenstein, Ruth (1995) *Dress Codes: Meanings and Messages in American Culture* (Boulder, CO: Westview Press). Addresses both contemporary fashion and nineteenth-century theories of clothing; dressing the public self; clothing as a conveyor of images of power, authority, gender and sexual seductiveness, wealth and beauty, and leisure. Also discusses the notion of beauty as the perfection of physical form, the youth ideal, and the health ideal, and clothing as an expression of social protest and self-definition.

Rudd, Andrea and Taylor, Darien (1992) *Positive Women: Voices of Women Living with Aids* (Ontario: Second Story Press). Contributors from five countries talk about living with AIDS.

Schneider, Beth and Stoller, Nancy (eds) (1995) *Women Resisting AIDS: Feminist Strategies of Empowerment* (Philadelphia: Temple University Press). Nineteen essays by sociologists, anthropologists, public health professionals, nurses, activists, and a law professor.

Schoenfielder, Lisa and Wieser, Barb (eds) (1987) *Shadows on a Tightrope: Writings by Women on Fat Oppression* (San Francisco: Aunt Lute Foundation Books). Collection of articles, personal studies, and poems by fat women about their lives and our fat-hating society.

Shwichtenberg, Cathy (ed.) (1993) *The Madonna Connection: Representational Politics, Subcultural Identities, and Cultural Theory* (Boulder, CO: Westview Press). Part 3 is entitled "Gender trouble: Madonna poses the feminist question."

Siebecker, July (1995) "Women's oppression and the obsession with thinness," in Amy Kesselman, Lily McNair, and Nancy Schniedewind (eds), *Women: Images and Realities. A Multicultural Anthology* (Mountain View, CA: Mayfield). Describes the social ostracism and damage to women's self-esteem and self-worth that accompanies being designated as overweight.

Thompson, Becky (ed.) (1994) *A Hunger So Wide and So Deep: American Women Speak* (Minneapolis: University of Minnesota Press).

Turin, Maureen (1983) "Fashion shapes: film, the fashion industry, and the image of women," *Socialist Review*, 13, pp. 79–95.

Winkler, Mary and Cole, Letha (eds) (1994) *The Good Body: Asceticism in Contemporary Culture* (New Haven, CT: Yale University Press). A number of experts from various disciplines analyze the reasons for the recent interest in control of the body, ranging from the epidemic of eating disorders to the obsession with diet and exercise, fitness and health, and cosmetic surgery.

Wolf, Naomi (1991) "Religion," in *The Beauty Myth: How Images of Beauty are Used against Women* (New York: W. Morrow). On the "beauty rites" that women undergo in consuming beauty products, and engaging in weight loss and fitness programs.

7
Motherhood and Families

Introduction

Women's relationship to motherhood and families is a vast topic. As has been noted elsewhere in this volume, women have been historically defined in terms of the role of mother. Even when women have not been biological mothers, they have been expected to act as "social mothers," selflessly nurturing and caring for others. Indeed, motherhood has sometimes been considered to be women's highest achievement. Motherhood has generally been considered a natural aspect of women's lives. Women who did not become mothers, whether by choice or inability to conceive, have been viewed as abnormal, deviant, less than "true women." Religious ideologies, in particular, reinforce the view of women as mothers.

These images, stereotypes, and identities of women *as* mothers have persisted stubbornly, even though not all women can, or choose to, mother. All women are unable to bear children during some stage of their lives, and some women are unable to bear children at all. Other women either choose not to become mothers or, having decided to carry a pregnancy to term, choose not to take on the role of mothering their offspring, but instead give their child to others to raise. Statistics show that most women do become mothers, however. Approximately 88 percent do so by the age of 45. In recent years, women have had more choice about whether or not to become mothers.

The definition and role of motherhood in American culture has been transformed by socioeconomic and technological changes in recent decades. The availability of contraception and abortion has made it possible for women to avoid unwanted pregnancies, and to plan the timing and spacing of their children, a degree of control that women in earlier generations did not have. Some older women and women with reproductive difficulties (or partners with such difficulties), who only a decade ago would have been unable to become mothers, are now able to do so with the assistance of reproductive technologies, such as *in vitro* fertilization, artificial insemination, and the use of so-called "surrogate" mothers. Some women are becoming mothers only for the purpose of birthing a child for others, sometimes under a so-called "surrogacy contract." More lesbian mothers and single women are deliberately choosing to become mothers without husbands or male partners. These changes are challenging basic understandings of what motherhood means.

In this chapter, we will explore several aspects of women's relationship to the institutions of motherhood and the family. In the first half of the chapter, we will look at some recent feminist views about traditional mothering and motherhood, including the relationship of motherhood to issues of race and class. The second half addresses the alternatives to traditional motherhood. It includes an essay by Shirley Glubka about a woman who gave up her son because she determined that she was not suited to motherhood, as well as an essay by Susan Sherwin about abortion from the perspective of feminist ethics.

In general, feminists view motherhood as an *institution* as well as a primary *relationship* between mothers and their children. As an institution, motherhood has been defined as women's primary role in life, one in which they selflessly devote their lives to the nurture and rearing of their offspring. Women's social roles as mothers was used historically as an argument that women were unsuited for other roles. In recent decades, those assumptions about women have broken down. None the less, vestiges remain.

Popular culture and the mass media have had a significant role in shaping public attitudes about mothers and mothering. They help to perpetuate the identification of women with motherhood, children, and families by representing women in these roles more frequently than in others. In *Backlash*, Susan Faludi documents how Hollywood movies during the 1980s supported a return to traditional roles for women as wives and mothers. They did this not only by portraying such roles in a more favorable light, but also by depicting single and independent women as unhappy, neurotic, unfulfilled, and even, as in *Fatal Attraction*, as dangerous to the traditional family. Thus, at the same time that women are stereotyped as mothers, the significance and value of motherhood continues to be devalued in popular culture.

Other aspects of popular culture have also devalued or maligned mothers and motherhood. For example, much literature of this century written by men portrays mothers negatively, as devouring, destructive, and sexually seductive. In recent decades, there has been a spate of books and films by and about *women* that are highly critical of their mothers, as the Bibliography at the end of the chapter shows.

Not all images of mothers in popular culture have been negative, however. For example, television situation comedy star Roseanne has been tremendously popular in portraying a working-class, working mom. The character Murphy Brown's decision to become a single mother contributed to making single parenthood a national issue, and illustrated how much popular support exists among Americans for women who choose single parenthood. Mainstream television programs like *Grace under Fire* illustrate the difficulties that single mothers encounter in their daily lives.

Women's roles as traditional mothers

The subject of women's relationship to motherhood becomes especially unwieldy when we consider that motherhood usually brings with it women's relationship to a family, and all of the issues that this entails. More and more families are becoming headed by single mothers, both because more women are having children out of wedlock and without a permanent partner, as well as because of increasingly high rates of divorce. Female-headed households are often unable to maintain a decent standard of living because many single mothers have difficulty finding adequate day care to allow them to work, jobs that pay more than a minimum wage or have the potential of leading to satisfying careers, or access to the education or job training needed to secure decent jobs.

As in other areas of women's lives, the experience of motherhood and family is shaped by race and class differences. Patricia Hill Collins explores some of these differences in the first reading "Shifting the center: race, class, and feminist theorizing about motherhood." She illustrates how these differences challenge prevailing feminist assumptions about families as being in the "private" sphere of domesticity as opposed to the "public" sphere of wage labor, and about families being assured of material and physical well-being. More and more families are becoming "public" in being supported by, and thus subject to, the regulation of public welfare. This is especially the case for families of single parents, who are disproportionately women of color and women lacking educational or job training. Being on welfare means being subject to continual invasive regulation, surveillance, and intrusion by the state into the "privacy" of the family.

The issues in this area have become broader and more complex as well. In American culture, the general assumption remains that women will have children, whether in marriage or out of wedlock. And as Shari L. Thurer observes, in the reading excerpted from her book *The Myths of Motherhood*, even though most mothers with young children now work, expectations about housework, household management, and cooking being the women's responsibility have not changed to keep up with these changes in lifestyle. The consequence is that many women who mother labor under a "double bind": they are blamed for having a career in addition to their role as mother and also blamed when they do not. Thurer describes how the myth of "the good mother" as someone who is a full-time, stay-at-home-with-the-kids parent serves to reinforce the problems actual mothers have in finding adequate support with child care when they need or want to go outside the home to work.

Over one million teenage women become pregnant annually (Wattleton, 1989). Some of these pregnancies end in abortion or miscarriage, but over half of them result in teenage girls becoming mothers before they have finished high school. The mass media contributes to the problem by disseminating distorted notions of sex and the consequences of sexual activity. This gives the US the dubious distinction of having the highest rate of adolescent pregnancy, birth, and abortion rates among affluent countries. Studies suggest that teen-agers are more likely to bear children when they do not foresee prospects for decent employment or educational advancement.

Many women of color are especially divided on reproductive rights (Cole, 1986; Davis, 1986). Based on the widespread sterilization of Native American and other women of color in the 1970s, many women of color are rightly skeptical of campaigns for limiting pregnancy and childbirth as strategies of genocide against their racial or ethnic group. Women from certain religious groups have also been opposed to mainstream feminist reproductive rights agendas favoring birth control and abortion rights on the basis of beliefs that favor pro-life (anti-abortion) or pro-natalist (favoring child bearing) approaches.

The decision to remain childless has become a recent topic of feminist writing (Mattes, 1994; Morell, 1994; Bartlett, 1995). Even in the late twentieth century, it continues to be difficult for many women to challenge social expectations by remaining childless. Mothers and the work entailed in mothering are devalued by society; none the less, women who defy still-prevalent social expectations that they will become mothers are still viewed negatively in much popular culture. The choice to forgo child bearing has been opposed, in particular, by certain religious institutions, the Roman Catholic church prominent among them, especially when doing so involves the use of certain forms of birth control, especially abortion.

For decades, feminists have noted that women's economic contribution to the economy in reproducing the labor force was ignored even by such monumental thinkers as Karl Marx. Women's status as mothers continues to decline as their large-scale entry into the labor market has created the presumption that women will engage in paid labor regardless of whether they are now, or intend to become, mothers. At the same time, mothers who do work, increasingly out of economic necessity rather than choice, have been vilified for leaving their children in day care – with strangers – rather than caring for them at home.

The economic difficulties of mothers are increasing rapidly. Studies have revealed that divorce frequently results in a lowering of the wife's standard of living, while raising that of the husband. This is partly the consequence of the husband being more often the primary breadwinner of the family, who has a superior wage-earning capability as the result of a better educational background, job training, and/or more years in the labor force. The wife more often has taken time off for the children, or had part-time or supplemental rather than full-time employment. The unwillingness of many fathers to pay child support also exacerbates this "feminization of poverty."

Many fathers may be unwilling to support their children financially, especially following a divorce or separation, due to the influence of cultural messages that children "belong" to or with their mothers. Until recently, the legal presumption in divorce cases involving young children that the mother would be the custodial parent was encapsulated in the "tender years" doctrine. More recently, courts apply a "best interests of the child" standard to determine custody. In most cases involving small children, custody is still awarded to the mother. However, more and more judges are willing to at least consider awarding custody to the father on the basis of his superior economic status and consequent ability to "provide for" the children. The result is that more and more single mothers are in poverty, a situation that reforms in federal welfare can only worsen.

In recent decades, feminists have come to challenge the identification of women with motherhood, emphasizing that not all women are – or will ever be – mothers. None the less, as with most issues, feminists vary widely in their views about women's relationship to motherhood. Some feminists, especially radical feminists from the early years of the second wave of the women's movement, argued that maternity was central to women's oppression because it kept them tied to the home and economically dependent on men (for example, Firestone, 1970; Rich, 1976).

More recent feminist writing has generally viewed mothering and motherhood as more positive for women. Some feminists have raised women's role as mothers from the private or domestic sphere to the public one, pointing out how women's role as mothers has been central (or could be central) to cultural and social change. For example, Sarah Ruddick (1989) has argued that women's role as mothers gives them a distinctive moral sensibility that could alter the nature of conflict resolution. Yet, as Ellen Ross has observed, "mothers' actual voices and vantage-points continue to be scarce in public policy debates on the immense range of issues where it is they who ought to be viewed as the relevant experts, from welfare and health-care reform to adoption and surrogacy law" (Ross, 1995b: 6). Frequently overworked and underpaid, women's labor as mothers is devalued, when it is viewed as work at all.

As discussed in chapter 1, in *The Reproduction of Mothering,* Nancy Chodorow (1978) forwarded the thesis that gender inequality is perpetuated in society because it is women who mother. She suggests that dual parenting would facilitate the breakdown of gender inequality. Although Chodorow's work has been criticized, especially as blaming women for gender inequality

and for making universalizing assumptions based on white, middle-class culture, her theory continues to have significant influence on feminist theorizing
about motherhood.

Alternatives to traditional motherhood

Many women, especially in contemporary America, are choosing alternatives to
traditional roles as wives and mothers. Some are living alone, without husbands
or other male "partners." Some are choosing to live in alternative sorts of
families, such as those built on lesbian, bisexual, or non-exclusive heterosexual
relationships. Many women are using birth control and abortion in order to
avoid pregnancy and motherhood.

Although no longer as popular, during the late 1960s and 1970s many
people experimented with communal lifestyles in which several people, not
only the biological parents, were responsible for child care and rearing. Many
women find themselves in non-traditional family relationships by necessity rather
than choice, such as teenage mothers living at home with one or both parents,
elderly women living with one of their children's families or in other extended
family networks, and single mothers who are heads of household, especially
those living on welfare.

The new possibilities available to women to become mothers or to avoid
motherhood have increased women's options with respect to families, but have
also made issues relating to motherhood and families more complicated. As
noted in chapter 6, reproductive technologies have reshaped traditional notions
about women and the relationship of women's bodies to motherhood by making
pregnancy and childbirth less "natural" and more technologically assisted. Such
technologies have made it possible for women to avoid motherhood – through
contraception and abortion – in ways that were not possible in earlier generations. In addition, they have made it possible for many women previously
unable to have children to become mothers through techniques such as *in vitro*
fertilization, artificial insemination, and surrogacy. Such techniques have made
it possible for infertile and homosexual couples to have families with children
who are (at least in part) biologically related to them.

It is unclear whether the development of reproductive technologies enabling
more women to become mothers is actually an improvement in women's lives.
Some feminists argue that rather than increasing women's choices, the existence of these technologies actually increases the pressures on women to conform to cultural expectations to become mothers. As technologies make it
possible for more women to become mothers, previously infertile women,
older women, women with infertile partners, and lesbians may be increasingly
viewed as "breeders," reinforcing the cultural stereotypes that equate women
with motherhood as their primary role in life.

Similarly, some are suspicious that the increasing use of *surrogate* mothers to gestate a fetus for a non-related couple actually represents a regression in the status of women. From this perspective, the use of surrogates actually enhances the socioeconomic disparities between women who become surrogates (generally women who need the money) and the more affluent men (and their wives) whose children they contract to bear. In this view, women become surrogates – primarily, at least – out of economic necessity. This puts them at an economic disadvantage in setting the terms of the agreement under which they become contractually bound to become mothers. This disparity in bargaining power, it is argued, contributes to a perpetuation of women's inequality rather than providing them with greater autonomy and control over their bodies and reproductive lives.

From another perspective, however, surrogacy enhances women's options, both those of the surrogate as well as those of the legal mother. Lori Andrews's research suggests that many women who become surrogates do so not because they have been economically coerced into it, but because they love children, and feel empathy for childless couples (Andrews, 1992). None the less, surrogacy contracts raise vexed questions about whether the practice constitutes baby selling, whether it should be regulated by family law or contract law, and whether surrogacy contracts should be legally recognized and enforced at all.

Alternatives to motherhood

Many women face an unwanted pregnancy at some time in their lives, even if they use contraception responsibly, are married and/or already have other children. What alternatives are available for these women? Adoption and abortion are the two most common. Adoption is problematic for a number of reasons. It is not always available, especially for women of color whose babies are not as sought after by adopting couples as white babies. In addition, some women are unable to cope with the thought of having a child that will be raised by others.

The difficulties with adoption sometimes leave abortion as the only realistic alternative for women with an unwanted pregnancy. Abortion is also becoming more problematic as an alternative, however. Abortion was legally recognized as a constitutionally protected right in 1973 by the Supreme Court in its landmark case of *Roe* v. *Wade*. The Court in *Roe* specifically ruled that a pregnant woman has a constitutionally protected right of privacy during the first trimester (three months), in consultation with her physician, to decide to terminate her pregnancy. During the second trimester, the state can permissibly regulate the conditions of the abortion procedure, but only to protect the health of the pregnant woman. During the third trimester – approximately the point of viability – the state can permissibly limit, even ban, abortions.

Since 1973, the Court has ruled that certain restrictions on the woman's right to choose are legally permissible. For example, it has ruled that the federal Hyde Amendment, allowing states to decline to fund abortions for indigent women, did not violate women's constitutionally protected right to choose. It has also upheld parental consent statutes restricting the ability of pregnant women who are minors to have an abortion. In 1992, it ruled in *Casey v. Planned Parenthood* that states can regulate abortion *throughout* pregnancy as long as they do not place an "undue burden" on women's right to choose.

Although abortion continues to be a *legally* available choice for most women, it is not a realistically available choice for many women. This is especially true for poor women (who are disproportionately women of color), who cannot afford to pay for an abortion. The politically conservative climate of the 1990s, coupled with heavy lobbying of legislatures by religious and other pro-life groups, has made abortion practically unavailable to many women in the US. In addition to the lack of public funding, the levels of protest and opposition by pro-life groups has resulted in many doctors and hospitals discontinuing abortion services. Although legalization of RU486, the "morning after pill," may significantly reduce the necessity for abortion, the abortion controversy is not likely to end soon.

Women are deeply divided about the issue of the morality and legality of abortion, often even within themselves. In a study of women abortion activists conducted in 1984, feminist sociologist Kristin Luker found that women pro-choice activists held fundamentally different worldviews and identities than women pro-life activists (Luker, 1984). From most feminist perspectives, the appropriate question regarding regulation by the state is not the moral status of the fetus, but *who* should decide. It is important to keep in mind that there is an important distinction between the legal *right* to have an abortion and the moral *appropriateness* of an abortion in a particular circumstance: *pro-choice* does not mean *pro-abortion*. Having a pro-choice position does not entail being in favor of abortion; it simply means that the decision should be left to the pregnant woman to decide, not to the state or some other entity or individual.

Susan Sherwin's reading provides an explicit feminist argument in support of women's right to choose abortion, centered on the importance of women's right to control their reproductive lives, especially in the context of a sexist and patriarchal society. She discusses the circumstances that frequently make pregnancy the result of less than voluntary sexual activity, and forcefully makes the case that women should not be legally required to carry an unwanted pregnancy to term.

However, according this power over life and death to individual women has sparked the concern of even some feminists, especially in certain contexts. One of these is sex-selective abortion, a practice that is far more widely used in developing countries such as India and China, states which restrict the number of children that families are legally entitled to have in order to limit population growth. In the context of strongly patriarchal cultures which value males far more highly than females, and reward mothers for bearing sons, not daughters, social pressures frequently result in abortions of female fetuses. As the practice of sex-selective abortions becomes more widespread, and as women from cultures where this practice is condoned immigrate to North America, feminists have become increasingly concerned about its legal and moral dimensions. For feminists committed to a strongly pro-choice position – which imposes no constraints on the woman except those of her own conscience – it is difficult to condemn a woman's decision to have an abortion on the basis of the sex of the fetus.

As you will find, the readings in this chapter illustrate how complex is women's relationship to motherhood in contemporary American culture, and how many issues relating to women and motherhood are unlikely to be easily resolved.

Shifting the Center: Race, Class, and Feminist Theorizing about Motherhood (excerpt)
Patricia Hill Collins

I dread to see my children grow, I know not their fate. Where the white boy has every opportunity and protection, mine will have few opportunities and no protection. It does not matter how good or wise my children may be, they are colored.
An anonymous African-American mother in 1904,
reported in Lerner, 1972, p. 158

For Native American, African-American, Hispanic, and Asian-American women, motherhood cannot be analyzed in isolation from its context. Motherhood occurs in specific historical contexts framed by interlocking structures of race, class, and gender, contexts where the sons of white mothers have "every opportunity and protection," and the "colored" daughters and sons of racial ethnic mothers "know not their fate." Racial domination and economic exploitation profoundly shape the mothering context not only for racial ethnic women in the United States but for all women.[1]

This reading first appeared in *Representations of Motherhood*, eds Donna Bassin, Margaret Honey, and Meryle Mahrer Kaplan (New Haven, CT: Yale University Press, 1994), pp. 56–74.

Despite the significance of race and class, feminist theorizing routinely minimizes their importance. In this sense, feminist theorizing about motherhood has not been immune to the decontextualization in Western social thought overall. Although many dimensions of motherhood's context are ignored, the exclusion of race and/or class from feminist theorizing generally and from feminist theorizing about motherhood specifically merits special attention (Spelman, 1988).

Much feminist theorizing about motherhood assumes that male domination in the political economy and the household is the driving force in family life and that understanding the struggle for individual autonomy in the face of such domination is central to understanding motherhood (Eisenstein, 1983). Several guiding principles frame such analyses. First, such theories posit a dichotomous split between the public sphere of economic and political discourse and the private sphere of family and household responsibilities. This juxtaposition of a public political economy to a private, non-economic, and apolitical domestic household allows work and family to be seen as separate institutions. Secondly, reserving the public sphere for men as a "male" domain leaves the private domestic sphere as a "female" domain. Gender roles become tied to the dichotomous constructions of these two basic societal institutions – men work and women take care of families. Thirdly, the public/private dichotomy separating the family/household from the paid labor market shapes sex-segregated gender roles within the private sphere of the family. The archetypal white middle-class nuclear family divides family life into two oppositional spheres – the "male" sphere of economic providing and the "female" sphere of affective nurturing, mainly mothering. This normative family household ideally consists of a working father who earns enough to allow his spouse and dependent children to forgo participation in the paid labor force. Owing in large part to their superior earning power, men as workers and fathers exert power over women in the labor market and in families. Finally, the struggle for individual autonomy in the face of a controlling, oppressive "public" society or the father as patriarch constitutes the main human enterprise.[2] Successful adult males achieve this autonomy. Women, children, and less-successful males – namely, those who are working class or from racial ethnic groups – are seen as dependent persons, as less autonomous, and therefore as fitting objects for élite male domination. Within the nuclear family, this struggle for autonomy takes the form of increasing opposition to the mother, the individual responsible for socializing children by these guiding principles (Chodorow, 1978; Flax, 1978).

Placing the experiences of women of color in the center of feminist theorizing about motherhood demonstrates how emphasizing the issue of father as patriarch in a decontextualized nuclear family distorts the experiences of women in alternative family structures with quite different political economies. While male domination certainly has been an important theme for racial ethnic women in the United States, gender inequality has long worked in tandem with racial domination and economic exploitation. Since work and family have rarely functioned as dichotomous spheres for women of color, examining racial ethnic women's experiences reveals how these two spheres actually are interwoven (Glenn, 1985; Dill, 1988; Collins, 1990).

For women of color, the subjective experience of mothering/motherhood is inextricably linked to the sociocultural concerns of racial ethnic communities – one does not exist without the other. Whether under conditions of the labor exploitation of African-American women during slavery and the ensuing tenant farm system, the political conquest of Native American women during European acquisition of land, or exclusionary immigration policies applied to Asian-Americans and Latinos, women of color have performed motherwork that challenges social constructions of work and family as separate spheres, of male and female gender roles as similarly dichotomized, and of the search for autonomy as the guiding human quest. "Women's reproductive labor – that is, feeding, clothing, and psychologically supporting the male wage earner and nurturing and socializing the next generation – is seen as work on behalf of the family as a whole rather than as work benefiting men in particular," observes Asian-American sociologist Evelyn Nakano Glenn (1986: 192). The locus of conflict lies outside the household, as women and their families engage in collective effort to create and maintain family life in the face of forces that undermine family integrity. But this "reproductive labor" or "motherwork" goes beyond ensuring the survival of members of one's family. This type of motherwork recognizes that individual survival, empowerment, and identity require group survival, empowerment, and identity.

In describing her relationship with her grandmother, Marilou Awiakta, a Native American poet and feminist theorist, captures the essence of motherwork: "Putting my arms around the Grandmother, I lay my head on her shoulder. Through touch we exchange sorrow, despair that anything really changes." Awiakta senses the power of the Grandmother and of the motherwork that mothers and grandmothers do. "But from the presence of her arms I also feel the stern, beautiful power that flows from all the Grandmothers, as it flows from our mountains themselves. It says, 'Dry your tears. Get up. Do for yourselves or do without. Work for the day to come' " (1988: 127).

Awiakta's passage places women and motherwork squarely in the center of what are typically seen as disjunctures, the place between human and nature, between private and public, between oppression and liberation. I use the term *motherwork* to soften the dichotomies in feminist theorizing about motherhood that posit rigid distinctions between private and public, family and work, the individual and the collective, identity as individual autonomy and identity growing from the collective self-determination of one's group. Racial ethnic women's mothering and work experiences occur at the boundaries demarking these dualities. "Work for the day to come" is motherwork, whether it is on behalf of one's own biological children, children of one's racial ethnic community, or children who are yet unborn. Moreover, the space that this motherwork occupies promises to shift our thinking about motherhood itself.

Shifting the center: women of color and motherwork

What themes might emerge if issues of race and class generally, and understanding racial ethnic women's motherwork specifically, became central to feminist theorizing about motherhood? Centering feminist theorizing on the concerns of white middle-class women leads to two problematic assumptions. The first is that a relative degree of economic security exists for mothers and their children. A second is that all women enjoy the racial privilege that allows them to see themselves primarily as individuals in search of personal autonomy instead of members of racial ethnic groups struggling for power. These assumptions allow feminist theorists to concentrate on themes such as the connections among mothering, aggression, and death, the effects of maternal isolation on mother–child relationships within nuclear family households, maternal sexuality, relations among family members, all-powerful mothers as conduits for gender oppression, and the possibilities of an idealized motherhood freed from patriarchy (Chodorow and Contratto, 1982; Eisenstein, 1983).

   Although these issues merit investigation, centering feminist theorizing about motherhood in the ideas and experiences of African-American, Native American, Hispanic, and Asian-American women might yield markedly different themes (Andersen, 1988; Brown, 1989). This stance is to be distinguished from adding racial ethnic women's experiences to pre-existing feminist theories without considering how these experiences challenge those theories (Spelman, 1988). Involving much more than consulting existing social-science sources, placing the ideas and experiences of women of color in the center of analysis requires invoking a different epistemology concerning what type of knowledge is valid. We must distinguish between what has been said about subordinated groups in the dominant discourse, and what such groups might say about themselves if given the opportunity. Personal narratives, autobiographical statements, poetry, fiction, and other personalized statements have all been used by women of color to express self-defined standpoints on mothering and motherhood. Such knowledge reflects the authentic standpoint of subordinated groups. Placing these sources in the center and supplementing them with statistics, historical material, and other knowledge produced to justify the interests of ruling élites should create new themes and angles of vision (Smith, 1990).[3]

Specifying the contours of racial ethnic women's motherwork promises to point the way toward richer feminist theorizing about motherhood. Issues of survival, power, and identity – these three themes form the bedrock of women of color's motherwork. The importance of working for the physical survival of children and community, the dialectical nature of power and powerlessness in structuring mothering patterns, and the significance of self-definition in constructing individual and collective racial identity comprise three core themes characterizing the experiences of Native American, African-American, Hispanic, and Asian-American women. Examining survival, power, and identity reveals how racial ethnic women in the United States encounter and fashion motherwork. But it also suggests how feminist theorizing about motherhood might be shifted if different voices became central in feminist discourse.

Motherwork and physical survival

> When we are not physically starving we have the luxury to realize psychic and emotional starvation. (Moraga, 1979: 29)

Physical survival is assumed for children who are white and middle class. Thus, examining their psychic and emotional well-being and that of their mothers appears rational. The children of women of color, many of whom are "physically starving," have no such assurances. Racial ethnic children's lives have long been held in low regard. African-American children face an infant mortality rate twice that for white infants. Approximately one-third of Hispanic children and one-half of African-American children who survive infancy live in poverty. Racial ethnic children often live in harsh urban environments where drugs, crime, industrial pollutants, and violence threaten their survival. Children in rural environments often fare no better. Winona LaDuke reports that Native Americans on reservations frequently must use contaminated water. On the Pine Ridge Sioux Reservation in 1979, for example, 38 percent of all pregnancies resulted in miscarriages before the fifth month or in excessive hemorrhaging. Approximately 65 percent of the children who were born suffered breathing problems caused by under-developed lungs and jaundice (LaDuke, 1988: 63).

Struggles to foster the survival of Native American, Latino, Asian-American, and African-American families and communities by ensuring the survival of children are a fundamental dimension of racial ethnic women's motherwork. African-American women's fiction contains numerous stories of mothers fighting for the physical survival both of their own biological children and of those of the larger African-American community.[4] "Don't care how much death it is in the land, I got to make preparations for my baby to live!" proclaims Mariah Upshur, the African-American heroine of Sara Wright's novel *This Child's Gonna Live* (1986: 143). The harsh climates that confront racial ethnic children require that their mothers, like Mariah Upshur, "make preparations for [their babies] to live" as a central feature of their motherwork.

Yet, like all deep cultural themes, the theme of motherwork for physical survival contains contradictory elements. On the one hand, racial ethnic women's motherwork for individuals and the community has been essential for their survival. On the other hand, this work often extracts a high cost for large numbers of women, such as loss of individual autonomy or the submersion of individual growth for the benefit of the group. Although this dimension of motherwork is essential, the question of whether women are doing more than their fair share of such work for community development merits consideration.

Histories of family-based labor have shaped racial ethnic women's mother-work for survival and the types of mothering relationships that ensue. African-American, Asian-American, Native American, and Hispanic women have all worked and contributed to family economic well-being (Glenn, 1985; Dill, 1988). Much of these women's experiences with motherwork stems from the work they performed as children. The commodification of children of color – from the enslavement of African children who were legally owned as property to the subsequent treatment of children as units of labor in agricultural work, family businesses, and industry – has been a major theme shaping motherhood for women of color. Beginning in slavery and continuing into the post-World War II period, African-American children were put to work at young ages in the fields of Southern agriculture. Sara Brooks began full-time work in the fields at the age of 11 and remembers, "We never was lazy cause we used to really work. We used to work like mens. Oh, fight sometime, fuss sometime, but worked on" (Collins, 1990: 54). Black and Latino children in contemporary migrant farm families make similar contributions to their family's economy. "I musta been almost eight when

I started following the crops," remembers Jessie de la Cruz, a Mexican-American mother with six grown children. "Every winter, up north. I was on the end of the row of prunes, taking care of my younger brother and sister. They would help me fill up the cans and put 'em in a box while the rest of the family was picking the whole row" (de la Cruz, 1980: 168). Asian-American children spent long hours working in family businesses, child labor practices that have earned Asian-Americans the dubious distinction of being "model minorities." More recently, the family-based labor of undocumented racial ethnic immigrants, often mother–child units doing piecework for the garment industry, recalls the sweatshop conditions confronting turn-of-the-century European immigrants. . . .

Motherwork and power

How can I write down how I felt when I was a little child and my grandmother used to cry with us 'cause she didn't have enough food to give us? Because my brother was going barefooted and he was cryin' because he wasn't used to going without shoes? How can I describe that? I can't describe when my little girl died because I didn't have money for a doctor. And never had any teaching on caring for sick babies. Living out in labor camps. How can I describe that? (de la Cruz, 1980: 177)

Jessie de la Cruz, a Mexican-American woman who grew up as a migrant farm worker, experienced firsthand the struggle for empowerment facing racial ethnic women whose daily motherwork centers on issues of survival. A dialectical relation exists between efforts of racial orders to mold the institution of motherhood to serve the interests of élites, in this case, racial élites, and efforts on the part of subordinated groups to retain power over motherhood so that it serves the legitimate needs of their communities (Collins, 1990). African-American, Asian-American, Hispanic, and Native American women have long been preoccupied with patterns of maternal power and powerlessness because their mothering experiences have been profoundly affected by this dialectical process. But instead of emphasizing maternal power in dealing either with father as patriarch (Chodorow, 1978; Rich, 1986) or with male dominance (Ferguson, 1989), women of color are concerned with their power and powerlessness within an array of social institutions that frame their lives.

Racial ethnic women's struggles for maternal empowerment have revolved around three main themes. The struggle for control over their own bodies in order to preserve choice over whether to become mothers at all is one fundamental theme. The ambiguous politics of caring for unplanned children has long shaped African-American women's motherwork. For example, the widespread institutionalized rape of African-American women by white men both during slavery and in the segregated South created countless bi-racial children who had to be absorbed into African-American families and communities (Davis, 1981). The range of skin colors and hair textures in contemporary African-American communities bears mute testament to the powerlessness of African-American women in controlling this dimension of motherhood. . . .

A second dimension of racial ethnic women's struggles for maternal empowerment concerns getting to keep the children that are wanted, whether they were planned or not. For racial ethnic mothers like Jessie de la Cruz whose "little girl died" because she "didn't have money for a doctor," maternal separation from one's children becomes a much more salient issue than maternal isolation with one's children within an allegedly private nuclear family. Physical or psychological separation of mothers and children designed to disempower racial ethnic individuals forms the basis of a systematic effort to disempower their communities. . . .

A third dimension of racial ethnic women's struggles for empowerment concerns the pervasive efforts by the dominant group to control their children's minds. In her short story "A Long Memory," Beth Brant juxtaposes the loss felt in 1890 by a Native American mother whose son and daughter were forcibly removed by white officials to the loss that Brant felt in 1978 when a hearing took away her custody of her daughter. "Why do they want our babies?" queries the turn-of-the-century mother. "They want our power. They take our children to remove the inside of them. Our power" (Brant, 1988: 105). This mother recognizes that the future of the Native American way of life lies in retaining the power to define that worldview through educating the children. By forbidding children to speak their native languages and in other ways encouraging them to assimilate into Anglo culture, external agencies challenge the power of mothers to raise their children as they see fit.

Schools controlled by the dominant group comprise one important location where this dimension of the struggle for maternal empowerment occurs. In contrast to white middle-class children, whose educational experiences affirm their mothers' middle-class values, culture, and authority, African-American, Latino, Asian-American, and Native American children typically receive an education that derogates their mothers' perspective. For example, the struggles over bilingual education in Latino communities are about much more than retaining Spanish as a second language. Speaking the language of one's childhood is a way of retaining the entire culture and honoring the mother teaching that culture (Moraga, 1979; Anzaldúa, 1987). . . .

In confronting each of these three dimensions of their struggles for empowerment, racial ethnic women are not powerless in the face of racial and class oppression. Being grounded in a strong, dynamic, indigenous culture can be central in racial ethnic women's social constructions of motherhood. Depending on their access to traditional culture, women of color invoke alternative sources of power.[5] "Equality *per se* may have a different meaning for Indian women and Indian people," suggests Kate Shanley. "That difference begins with personal and tribal sovereignty – the right to be legally recognized as people empowered to determine our own destinies" (1988: 214). Personal sovereignty involves the struggle to promote the survival of a social structure whose organizational principles represent notions of family and motherhood different from those of the mainstream. "The nuclear family has little relevance to Indian women," observes Shanley. "In fact, in many ways, mainstream feminists now are striving to redefine family and community in a way that Indian women have long known" (1988: 214).

African-American mothers can draw upon an Afrocentric tradition where motherhood of varying types, whether bloodmother, othermother, or community othermother, can be invoked as a symbol of power. Many African-American women receive respect and recognition within their local communities for innovative and practical approaches to mothering, not only their own biological children but also the children in their extended family networks and in the community overall. Black women's involvement in fostering African-American community development forms the basis of this community-based power. In local African-American communities, community othermothers can become identified as powerful figures through furthering the community's well-being (Collins, 1990).

Despite policies of dominant institutions that place racial ethnic mothers in positions where they appear less powerful to their children, mothers and children empower themselves by understanding each other's position and relying on each other's strengths. In many cases, children, especially daughters, bond with their mothers instead of railing against them as symbols of patriarchal power. . . .

Motherwork and identity

Please help me find out who I am. My mother was Indian, but we were taken from her and put in foster homes. They were white and didn't want to tell us about our mother. I have a name and maybe a place of birth. Do you think you can help me? (Brant, 1988: 9)

Like this excerpt from a letter to an editor, the theme of loss of racial ethnic identity and the struggle to maintain a sense of self and community pervade the remaining stories, poetry, and narratives in Beth Brant's volume, *A Gathering of Spirit.* Carol Lee Sanchez offers another view of the impact of the loss of self. "Radicals look at reservation Indians and get very upset about their poverty conditions," observes Sanchez. "But poverty to us is not the same thing as poverty is to you. Our poverty is that we can't be who we are. We can't hunt or fish or grow our food because our basic resources and the right to use them in traditional ways are denied us" (Brant, 1988: 165). Racial ethnic women's motherwork reflects the tensions inherent in trying to foster a meaningful racial identity in children within a society that denigrates people of color. The racial privilege enjoyed by white middle-class women makes unnecessary this complicated dimension of the mothering tradition of women of color. Although white children can be prepared to fight racial oppression, their survival does not depend on gaining these skills. Their racial identity is validated by their schools, the media, and other social institutions. White children are socialized into their rightful place in systems of racial privilege. Racial ethnic women have no such guarantees for their children. Their children must first be taught to survive in systems that would oppress them. Moreover, this survival must not come at the expense of self-esteem. Thus, a dialectical relation exists between systems of racial oppression designed to strip subordinated groups of a sense of personal identity and a sense of collective peoplehood, and the cultures of resistance to that oppression extant in various racial ethnic groups. For women of color, motherwork for identity occurs at this critical juncture (Collins, 1990). . . .

Concluding remarks

Survival, power, and identity shape motherhood for all women. But these themes remain muted when the mothering experiences of women of color are marginalized in feminist theorizing about motherhood. The theories reflect a lack of attention to the connection between ideas and the contexts in which they emerge. Although such decontextualization aims to generate universal theories of human behavior, in actuality the theories routinely distort or omit huge categories of human experience.

Placing racial ethnic women's motherwork in the center of analysis recontextualizes motherhood. Whereas the significance of race and class in shaping the context in which motherhood occurs is virtually invisible when white middle-class women's experiences are the theoretical norm, the effects of race and class stand out in stark relief when women of color are accorded theoretical primacy. Highlighting racial ethnic mothers' struggles concerning their children's right to exist focuses attention on the importance of survival. Exploring the dialectical nature of racial ethnic women's empowerment in structures of racial domination and economic exploitation demonstrates the need to broaden the definition of maternal power. Emphasizing how the quest for self-definition is mediated by membership in different racial and social class groups reveals how the issue of identity is crucial to all motherwork.

Existing feminist theories of motherhood have emerged in specific intellectual and political contexts. By assuming that social theory will be applicable regardless of social context, feminist scholars fail to realize that they themselves are rooted in specific locations, and that the contexts in which they are located provide the thought-models of how they interpret the world. Their theories may appear to be universal and objective, but they actually are only partial perspectives reflecting the white middle-class context in which their creators live. Large segments of experience, those of women who are not white and middle class, have been excluded (Spelman, 1988). Feminist theories of motherhood thus cannot be seen as *theories* of motherhood generalizable to all women. The resulting patterns of partiality inherent in existing theories – for example, the emphasis placed on all-powerful mothers as conduits for gender oppression – reflect feminist theorists' positions in structures of power. Such theorists are themselves participants in a system of privilege that rewards them for not seeing race and class privilege as important. Their theories can ignore the workings of class and race as systems of privilege because their creators often benefit from that privilege, taking it as a given and not as something to be contested.

Theorizing about motherhood will not be helped, however, by supplanting one group's theory with that of another – for example, by claiming that women of color's experiences are more valid than those of white middle-class women. Just as varying placement in systems of privilege, whether race, class, sexuality, or age, generates divergent experiences with motherhood, examining motherhood and mother-as-subject from multiple perspectives should uncover rich textures of difference. Shifting the center to accommodate this diversity promises to recontextualize motherhood and point us toward feminist theorizing that embraces difference as an essential part of commonality.

Notes

1   In this paper, I use the terms *racial ethnic women* and *women of color* interchangeably. Grounded in the experiences of groups who have been the targets of racism, the term *racial ethnic* implies more solidarity with men involved in struggles against racism. In contrast, the term *women of color* emerges from a feminist background where racial ethnic women committed to feminist struggle aimed to distinguish their history and issues from those of middle-class white women. Neither term captures the complexity of African-American, Native American, Asian-American, and Hispanic women's experiences.

2   The thesis of the atomized individual that underlies Western psychology is rooted in a much larger Western construction concerning the relation of the individual to the community (Hartsock, 1983). Theories of motherhood based on the assumption of the atomized human proceed to use this definition of the individual as the unit of analysis and then construct theory from this base. From this grow assumptions that the major process to examine is that between freely choosing rational individuals engaging in bargains (Hartsock, 1983).

3   The narrative tradition in the writings of women of color addresses this effort to recover the history of mothers. Works from African-American women's autobiographical tradition such as Ann Moody's *Coming of Age in Mississippi*, Maya Angelou's *I Know Why the Caged Bird Sings*, Linda Brent's *Incidents in the Life of a Slave Girl*, and Marita Golden's *The Heart of a Woman* contain the authentic voices of African-American women centered on experiences of motherhood. Works from African-American women's fiction include *This Child's Gonna Live*, Alice Walker's *Meridian*, and Toni Morrison's *Sula* and *Beloved*. Asian-American women's fiction, such as Amy Tan's *The Joy Luck Club* and Maxine Hong Kingston's *Woman Warrior*, and autobiographies, such as Jean Wakatsuki Houston's *Farewell to Manzanar*, offer a parallel source of authentic voice. Connie Young Yu (1989) entitles her article on the history of Asian-American women "The world of our grandmothers" and recreates Asian-American history with her grandmother as a central figure. Cherrie Moraga (1979) writes a letter to her mother as a way of coming to terms with the contradictions in her racial identity as a Chicana. In *Borderlands/La Frontera*, Gloria Anzaldúa (1987) weaves autobiography, poetry, and philosophy together in her exploration of women and mothering.

4   Notable examples include Lutie Johnson's unsuccessful attempt to rescue her son from the harmful effects of an urban environment in Ann Petry's *The Street*, and Meridian's work on behalf of the children of a small Southern town after she chooses to relinquish her own child, in Alice Walker's *Meridian*.

5   Noticeably absent from feminist theories of motherhood is a comprehensive theory of power and an account of how power relations shape any theories actually developed. Firmly rooted in an exchange-based marketplace with its accompanying assumptions of rational economic decision-making and white male control of the marketplace, this model of community stresses the rights of individuals,

including feminist theorists, to make decisions in their own interest, regardless of the impact on larger society. Composed of a collection of unequal individuals who compete for greater shares of money as the medium of exchange, this model of community legitimates relations of domination either by denying they exist or by treating them as inevitable but unimportant (Hartsock, 1983).

References

Andersen, M. (1988) "Moving our minds: studying women of color and reconstructing sociology," *Teaching Sociology*, 16(2): 123–32.

Anzaldúa, G. (1987) *Borderlands/La Frontera: the New Mestiza* (San Francisco: Spinsters).

Awiakta, M. (1988) "Amazons in Appalachia," in B. Brant (ed.), *A Gathering of Spirit*, pp. 125–30 (Ithaca, NY: Firebrand).

Brant, B. (ed.) (1988) *A Gathering of Spirit: a Collection by North American Indian Women* (Ithaca, NY: Firebrand).

Brown, E. B. (1989) "African-American women's quilting: a framework for conceptualizing and teaching African-American women's history," *Signs*, 14(4): 921–9.

Chodorow, N. (1978) *The Reproduction of Mothering* (Berkeley: University of California Press).

Chodorow, N. and Contratto, S. (1982) "The fantasy of the perfect mother," in B. Thorne and M. Yalom (eds), *Rethinking the family: Some feminist questions*, pp. 54–75 (New York: Longman).

Collins, P. H. (1990) *Black Feminist Thought: Knowledge, Consciousness and the Politics of Empowerment* (New York: Routledge).

de la Cruz, J. (1980) "Interview," in S. Terkel (ed.), *American Dreams: Lost and Found* (New York: Ballantine).

Davis, A. Y. (1981) *Women, Race, and Class* (New York: Random House).

Dill, B. T. (1988) "Our mothers' grief: racial ethnic women and the maintenance of families," *Journal of Family History*, 13(4): 415–31.

Eisenstein, H. (1983) *Contemporary Feminist Thought* (Boston: G. K. Hall).

Ferguson, A. (1989) *Blood at the Root: Motherhood, Sexuality, and Male Dominance* (New York: Unwin Hyman/Routledge).

Flax, J. (1978) "The conflict between nurturance and autonomy in mother–daughter relationships and within feminism," *Feminist Studies*, 4(2): 171–89.

Glenn, E. N. (1985) "Racial ethnic women's labor: the intersection of race, gender and class oppression," *Review of Radical Political Economics*, 17(3): 86–108.

Glenn, E. N. (1986) *Issei, Nisei, War Bride: Three Generations of Japanese American Women in Domestic Service* (Philadelphia: Temple University Press).

Hartsock, N. (1983) *Money, Sex and Power* (Boston: Northeastern University Press).

LaDuke, W. (1988) "They always come back," in B. Brant (ed.), *A Gathering of Spirit*, pp. 62–7 (Ithaca, NY: Firebrand).

Lerner, G. (ed.) (1972) *Black Women in White America: a Documentary History* (New York: Vintage).

Moraga, C. (1979) "La guera," in C. Moraga and G. Anzaldúa (eds), *This Bridge Called my Back: Writings by Radical Women of Color*, pp. 27–34 (Watertown, MA: Persephone Press).

Rich, A. (1986) *Of Woman Born: Motherhood as Institution and Experience* (New York: Norton).

Shanley, K. (1988) "Thoughts on Indian feminism," in B. Brant (ed.), *A Gathering of Spirit*, pp. 213–15 (Ithaca, NY: Firebrand).

Smith, D. E. (1990) *The Conceptual Practices of Power: a Feminist Sociology of Knowledge* (Boston: Northeastern University Press).

Spelman, E. V. (1988) *Inessential Woman: Problems of Exclusion in Feminist Thought* (Boston: Beacon Press).

Wright, S. (1986) *This Child's Gonna Live* (Old Westbury, NY: Feminist Press).

Yu, C. Y. (1989) "The world of our grandmothers," in Asian Women United of California (eds), *Making Waves: an Anthology of Writings by and about Asian American Women*, pp. 33–41 (Boston: Beacon Press).

Fall from Grace: Twentieth-century Mom (excerpt)

Shari L. Thurer

Reinventing the myth: 1980–1990s

After decades of sensory deprivation with regard to their palates, Americans in the late twentieth century developed a taste for gourmet food. Cuisinarts proliferated in upscale kitchens, along with a myriad of other gadgets for food preparation. Americans had rediscovered the craft tradition in cooking. Nature and all things natural were back in business. That was the good news. It was also the bad news. For along with their elevated palates came elevated expectations for women, who were still doing 84 percent of the housework, despite media depictions of participant husbands (Snitow, 1992). Ironically, while our mothers may have preferred to cook from scratch but were obliged to pry open a can of Campbell's soup, heat, and serve, in order to appear up to date, modern mothers would be considered slack for

This reading first appeared in *The Myths of Motherhood: How Culture Reinvents the Good Mother* (New York: Houghton Mifflin, 1994), pp. 286–301.

serving up canned food, if not downright malevolent for foisting chemical additives on their unsuspecting families. Standards for domestic excellence have *increased* since the appearance of labor-saving devices, and the aggregate time we spend on housework has remained much the same as that of our grandmothers, but, unlike our grandmothers, almost 70 percent of today's educated mothers with young children are in the labor force, most of them full time. At the moment, mothers are trapped in a cultural time warp. They have changed, but mainstream expectations have not (Cowan, 1983: 199; Chira, 1992: 1, 30).

Thirty years after Friedan, many women are on the edge of a huge generational divide, and they are experiencing vertigo. We are the first cohort of women, who, whether by choice or necessity, work outside the home. We are the first generation of women among whom many dare to be ambitious. But there is no getting around the fact that ambition is not a maternal trait. Motherhood and ambition are still largely seen as opposing forces. More strongly expressed, a lack of ambition – or a professed lack of ambition, a sacrificial willingness to set personal ambition aside – is still the virtuous proof of good mothering. For many women, perhaps most, motherhood versus personal ambition represents the heart of the feminine dilemma.

Part of the problem is that we still do not know what to make of nurturance. When nurturance is given out of love, inclination, or a sense of responsibility, the assumption persists that whatever form it takes – dropping one's work to minister to a sick child, baking a tray of chocolate chip cookies – the behavior expresses a woman's biological nature. But when nurturing acts are performed by men, they are interpreted as extraordinary. When nurturance is provided by housekeepers, child-care workers, or kindergarten teachers, its value in the marketplace is low (Brownmiller, 1984: 221, 222, 230; Walsh, 1993). So, in performing nurturance, in becoming stay-at-home mothers (should we have the luxury of that option), we fear that we are turning into our own mothers, complete with their low status, self-sacrifices, and frustrations. And it feels politically incorrect to talk about how much many women want to stay home, at least part time, when they finally do have children.

But if we are ambitious, or even if we work outside our homes out of necessity, we are afraid of what our distraction will do to our children. Publishing, advertising, psychology, and the child-rearing establishment still conspire to convince women that their careers are at home. Today's steady rise of divorce and a recessionary economy (mandating a dual paycheck for a middle-class lifestyle) collide with our failure to get flexible work hours, maternity and paternity leaves, federal financial support and uniform standards for day care, reliable help from men, and, finally, a rational child-care ideology that is sensitive to both children *and* mothers. So where does this leave us? Either childless or very mixed up. . . .

New heights of mother-bashing by the media were reached in the 1980s and early 1990s, matching in reverse the ludicrousness of the syrupy odes to mothers in the Victorian period. Various unsympathetic, tell-all biographies, of which *Mommie Dearest* by Joan Crawford's daughter is the most famous, became commonplace. Bette Davis's daughter, B. D. Hyman, also composed one (*My Mother's Keeper*), as did Cheryl Crane, daughter of Lana Turner. The genre was not limited to disgruntled daughters. Writing about his mother, Rebecca West, in 1984, Anthony West was determined to show that "she was minded to do me what hurt she could, and she remained set in that determination as long as there was breath in the body to sustain her malice" (West, 1984). In the first half of 1993 alone, we heard grievances from a long list of bitter offspring, including the choreographer-dancer Twyla Tharp and the daughters of Marlene Dietrich, and the feminist Alva Myrdal. Rarely are the mothers around to defend themselves. But "first daughter" Patti Davis did not wait for Nancy Reagan's demise to impugn her in a thinly veiled novel, an exquisite irony, in light of the Reagans' pro-family stance. . . .

Parent blaming takes on a special color in women's books and magazines, where the mother–daughter relationship, in particular, is portrayed as perpetually adversarial. Just a glance at some titles conveys the gist: "How to get over your Mother," or *Mothers and Daughters: Loving and Letting Go*, or *Mother Love, Mother Hate: Breaking Dependent Love Patterns in Family Relationships*. This literature suggests that mothers, because of their own emptiness, cling to their daughters. But while mothers try to fuse, daughters try to disengage. If you believe these books, mothers and daughters are locked in eternal combat (Walters, 1992: 190). Interestingly, some of the better novelists of the decade also conveyed this conflict. Maxine Hong Kingston's Chinese mother, Jamaica Kincaid's black Caribbean mother, and Louise Erdrich's Native American mother all tried to hold back their daughters, to bind them to their old ways and to themselves. Though the novels are compelling and highly nuanced works, they are written from a daughter's perspective. One's sympathy is directed toward the child, not the mother.

Meanwhile, mothers were getting a mixed press, at best, in the movies, even as parenthood and children were being extolled. The films *Kramer v. Kramer* (1981), *Three Men and a Baby* (1988), and *Raising Arizona* (1987) all valorized fathers, though there are no data showing that large numbers of fathers are, in fact, fulfilled by making child care the center of their lives.

And toxic movie mothers kept on coming. In 1980, Mary Tyler Moore, the controlling, uptight mom in *Ordinary People*, caused much misery as she unfairly blamed her lovable surviving son for the death of his brother, her favorite. In the 1990s' Hollywood saga *Postcards from the Edge*, a former movie queen virtually causes her daughter's drug overdose, presumably by stubbornly refusing to surrender the spotlight to her and fade quietly away. The archetype monster mother in *Like Water for Chocolate*, the 1993 contribution to the genre, is mythic in her near-destruction of her Cinderella-like daughter.

Furthermore, mothers are now being usurped in the public consciousness by their fetuses. Whether this is a conspiracy perpetrated by the New Right, which may want to portray the fetus as human so as to portray women who have abortions as murderers, is questionable. Nevertheless, there has been a new centrality given to the embryo in everyday culture: witness the 1990 comedy *Look Who's Talking*; the famous Lennart Nilsson photos of life in the womb in *Life* (most recently in August 1990); the use of ultrasound wherein a mother can see her fetus on a TV monitor. To doctors, the fetus is now an "unborn patient," and a mother a mere "fetal container," the empty place in the sonogram. Suits for "fetal abuse" are on the rise. All these representations portray the fetus as an entity in its own right, subtly shifting attention and sympathy away from mother. Some feminists worry that mothers are being marginalized in favor of their embryos in a regressive step back to the nineteenth-century view of women, defining their lives solely by their reproductive capacity.

The burgeoning interest in the fetus was probably enhanced by the explosion of new reproductive technologies in the 1980s – artificial insemination, *in vitro* fertilization, embryo transfer, and surrogate mothering – all of which raised troubling questions. Do egg and sperm donors have the right to know their children? May a surrogate mother change her mind about releasing for adoption the child she bears? Does biological maternity constitute motherhood? Thanks to new technologies, parents can detect fetal anomalies early on and choose to abort a defective baby, or even one of a less-preferred gender. Indeed, female fetuses are being disproportionately aborted at this very moment, a practice reminiscent of the female infanticide of ancient Greece. The ratio of newborn children in China, for example, has reached 118.5 males for every 100 females. According to a recent *New York Times* article, as the ultrasound machine became more popular in China, and authorities began a tough crackdown on unauthorized pregnancies, the ratio became increasingly unbalanced in favor of boys. Last year, more than 12 percent of all female fetuses were aborted or otherwise unaccounted for

(Kaplan, 1992: 202–9). Does this imply that mother love is operative only when a child is unblemished or the gender of choice? The fragmenting of the female sexual and reproductive body, through implantation or surrogacy, or through the removal of eggs, is a breaking-up of that object – Mom – which has been made to symbolize so much of the social order for so long. All this has triggered deep cultural anxiety. . . .

On the night in 1992 when Murphy Brown became an unwed mother, she gave birth to more than a baby. Thirty-four million Americans tuned in and CBS posted a 35 percent share of the audience. Despite Vice President Quayle's debunking, the show did not stir up significant grassroots protest nor lose any of its advertisers. By any standard, Murphy Brown – she who would have been stoned in Babylonia, or burned at the stake in early modern Europe – was a hit at the box office (Whitehead, 1993: 55). Brown had proudly and joyously borne an illegitimate baby, and the public obviously shared her maternal bliss. Her defiant act liberated women from the tyranny of mainstream domestic expectations, expectations that had long ceased to reflect reality, given the number of single mothers in this country. Of course, if Brown had been on welfare she would have been regarded as a "parasite," and if this were her second baby, she would have been seen as a "breeder," that is, unless she had been left by a man, in which case she would be a victim (Goodman, 1993). Nevertheless, Brown's insouciant motherhood has signaled a sea change in the unconscious sexism that once pervaded everyday life. She has forged new ways for women to mother.

We are living in a moment when women's identities are expanding. How else can we interpret the fact that women are marrying later, using contraceptives and abortion, having fewer children, and entering the labor force in ever greater percentages (Snitow, 1992)? Despite a concerted effort to amplify a conservative backlash in public sentiment, the New Right coalition was unable to reverse the social and cultural transformations that had already taken place: women's new roles in the workplace; freer sexuality (despite AIDS); the mobilization of a powerful pro-choice movement; the election of a president with a "liberated" wife; and the appointment of a mother with feminist sympathies to the Supreme Court (Skolnick, 1991: 223). . . .

At long last mothers have been allowed a voice in literature and, unlike their counterparts a decade earlier, they have an audience. We are beginning to see a new kind of mother in novels – the mentor, the one who guides her children to independent adulthood. She is no angel, however. She makes mistakes; she is not wholly fulfilled by her experience; she is ambivalent about her children. In sum, she is real. We can find her in Mary

Gordon's *Men and Angels* and Gail Godwin's *A Mother and Two Daughters*. And she is all over the novels of the 1993 Nobel Prize winner Toni Morrison. In *Beloved*, for example, the black mother Sethe murders her child. Yet Morrison has the reader understand that the murder is an act not of barbarism, but of mother love – Sethe is protecting her daughter from slavery. Morrison avoids a simplistic maternal characterization. She pays careful attention to the maternal perspective. She does not blame Sethe, but applauds her endurance. Sethe is a latter-day Neolithic goddess. She is no one's bad mother.

Thirty thousand years after her birth, mother is leaving the realm of mythology and is joining the human race or, more accurately, rejoining it after the patriarchal takeover. It's about time.

For thousands of years, because of her awesome ability to spew forth a child, mother has been feared and revered. She has been the subject of taboos and witch hunts, mandatory pregnancy and confinement in a separate sphere. She has endured appalling insults and perpetual marginalization. She has also been the subject of glorious painting, chivalry, and idealization. Through it all, she has rarely been consulted. She is an object, not a subject.

As the primary caretaker of children during most of history, she has been variously obliged to nurse and not to nurse; to facilitate free expression and to suppress it; to cuddle and to avoid contact. During the Middle Ages, she might have overlaid her child in bed; in the eighteenth century, she might have exiled the infant to a wet nurse in the country; in the late twentieth century, she is probably cognitively stimulating *ad infinitum*. But by and large, when supported by her social milieu, she seems to have loved her babies.

Over the centuries, despite wild variations in child care, the incidence of mental illness among children, as best we can determine, seems to have been fairly constant. Whether children were empathized with or were the subject of Watson's behaviorism, whether they were sternly disciplined or spoiled, they managed to thrive. Apparently ordinary mothering does not cause psychological problems.

All this casts serious doubt on the validity of our current image of ideal mother. Perhaps she needn't be all-empathic, after all. Perhaps she can be personally ambitious without damaging her child. Perhaps she does not have unlimited power in the shaping of her offspring. Good mothering, history reminds us, is a cultural invention – something that is man-made, not a lawful force of nature.

As such, it is subject to human intervention. When mothers are able to see through the mythology, they may see that their "failures" stem not necessarily from personal defects, but from the way society is structured. They may stop blaming themselves. When mothers understand the biases inherent in our current conception of good mothering, they may learn to select among the rules and begin to create their own philosophy of child rearing, one that works for them and their children.

By unmasking the myths of motherhood, we can enlarge the possibility for taking control – through education, public policy, psychotherapy, even moral preachment – to achieve the climate we desire. In such a family climate, there would be personal sacrifice for a common good, but it would not be mother doing all of the sacrificing. It would be shared sacrifice. Such a family would not promote the self-fulfillment of any *one* member at the expense of another. At the societal level, child rearing would not be dismissed as an individual mother's problem, but one in which nurturance and the well-being of *all* children are a transcendent public priority. This society would accept changes in family structure as inevitable (and not necessarily bad) and would devise for them new forms of public and private support. I hope for a society that will tolerate and encourage a diversity of mothering styles and cohabiting groups. I hope for a society in which both women and men have the power of the world and the nurturant experience. I hope for a society that will, finally, listen to Mrs Portnoy's complaint. As a mother, she has something to say.

References

Brownmiller, Susan (1984) *Femininity* (New York: Linden Press).

Chira, Susan (1992) "New realities fight old images of mother," *New York Times*, October, 4, s. I, p. 30.

Cowan, Ruth Schwartz (1983) *More Work for Mother: the Ironies of Household Technology from the Open Hearth to the Microwave* (New York: Basic Books).

Goodman, Ellen (1993) "The changing form – and often conflicting views – of the family," *Boston Globe*, August 19, p. 19.

Kaplan, E. Anne (1992) *Motherhood and Representation: the Mother in Popular Culture and Melodrama* (New York: Routledge).

Skolnick, Arlene (1991) *Embattled Paradise* (New York: Basic Books).

Snitow, Ann (1992) "Feminism and motherhood: an American reading," *Feminist Review*, 40: 32–51.

Walsh, Joan (1993) "Up front: the mother mystique," *Vogue*, August, pp. 96–102.

Walters, Suzanna Danuta (1992) *Lives Together/Worlds Apart: Mothers and Daughters in Popular Culture* (Berkeley, CA: University of California Press).

West, Anthony (1984) "Mother to son," *New York Review of Books*, 31(1): 9–11.

Whitehead, Barbara (1993) "Dan Quayle was right," *The Atlantic*, 10(3): 47–84.

Out of the Stream: an Essay on Unconventional Motherhood

Shirley Glubka

As I started this paper for the sixth or seventh time, I wondered how far back I would have to go to understand my unusual relationship to motherhood. Beyond my own life, I knew – to my mother and my grandmothers and aunts and great-aunts and generations of women behind them. I thought about those generations and was struck by a vision: I saw a swollen stream of women, all taking on the role of mother without the least sign of rebellion. I saw myself leaping out of this stream and landing hard, alone and disoriented, flopping like the proverbial fish out of water. Quite a sad scene.

Then I remembered reality. In my family there were plenty of good Catholic mothers with the mandatory five to seven children trailing them through aisles of grocery stores. But there were also others: the one who never married, never had children, and cleaned houses for a living; the one who did marry, never had children, and worked in the college cafeteria; the one who had children and, when the last one came along, suggested to her husband that this child might be better raised by someone else, someone who was not tired of starting over with baby after baby. The husband would not hear of such a thing and the woman stayed in the stream of conventional mothers – but not without rebellion. Those others stand in my personal history as surely as those women who seem to have taken on the role of mother without a qualm.

How peculiar, then, that I should have such a strong and immediate image that all the women before me were mothers, compliant in their role. On the other hand, how understandable that I should be assaulted by such an image. I, who left the conventional role of mother years ago, have no more protection from the myths surrounding motherhood than any other woman. In fact, I might be more vulnerable than most. Like the outcast, I sometimes imagine that all other women belong to an inner circle of mothers, a circle full of warmth and goodness, the locus of satisfying and productive activity.

I severed whatever connection I might have had to that imagined inner circle 10 years ago when my son Kevin was 3 years old and I was 30. At

This reading first appeared in *Feminist Studies*, 1983, 9(2): 223–34.

that time, Kevin and I were separated, by my choice. Kevin acquired a new mother in the form of Gretchen Ulrich, who was a teacher in his day-care center.

If I believed in such things, I would regard Gretchen as one of the more enduring and beneficent apparitions of my life. She appeared as if by magic in my living room one day (actually, we were having an unscheduled parent–teacher conference) and by the end of several hours of conversation, we had come to an agreement. She would try being Kevin's mother and I would try something that was not quite not being his mother. He would live with her, I would live alone, and occasionally he and I would visit with each other. We determined a trial period which was to last one month, but we knew quite well by the end of our conversation that the arrangement would be permanent.

I had begun my experience with motherhood in a conventional enough way: inside the institution of marriage, a little haphazardly (through a failure of birth control that did not unduly distress either my husband or me – we had planned to have children eventually, why not now?) and, all in all, quite happily. When Kevin was eight months old, I left my husband, taking Kevin with me. For all practical purposes, that was the end of our involvement with my ex-husband. I had become a single mother.

I had also become a feminist, a critic of the status quo on many fronts, committed to finding sensible, humane, non-sexist ways to live. I tried communal living in what seemed to be an ideal situation – with other women from my consciousness-raising group, other children, and a few politically aware, thoroughly sincere, men. We based our experiment on feminist principles. All work, including child care, was divided equally among us. The experiment was a success – for a year. The reasons for the disintegration of any living situation are, to say the least, hard to catch hold of. I could say we had personality conflicts; I could say it was extremely difficult to maintain a way of living that was unsupported by society at large. Both the purely personal and the social/political explanations would be true and, even taken together, they are not all of the truth. For whatever complex combination of reasons, our collective household split apart.

I continued to seek and find ways to break the isolation of single motherhood. I found excellent day care, neighbors with preschoolers who wanted to exchange babysitting, friends both female and male who volunteered days, evenings, nights, and even whole weekends of their time caring for Kevin. Compared with most single mothers, I was superbly supported; yet I felt constantly burdened. It was becoming clear that I did not like the role of mother. Specifically, I did not like the kind of work involved in being a mother.

Having written this, I stop to think. And the voices come – among them one that sounds suspiciously like my own: "You didn't like the work? You left your child because you didn't *like* the *work?*" And the images come of irresponsible mothers abandoning their children for no reason: lazy, flighty, selfish, or just plain *bad* women – loose women in garish green silky dresses with long slits up the leg, tossing their babies into garbage cans and going out for a good time . . . When my fantasy reaches this height of stereotyped ridiculousness it becomes easier to deal with. No mother separates from her child lightly. Yes, I left the mother role because in a radical way I did not like the job of being a mother; and because I believed that Kevin would be better off if he were raised by someone who wanted to do that kind of work; and because, by some miracle, that person appeared in my life.

It would be a simplification to say that I liked nothing about the mother role. That role is complex – and one of its complexities is that it changes radically again and again as time passes. I rather liked the work of mothering during Kevin's infancy – all the holding, the nursing, washing him, even changing his diapers was fine with me. I was good at it, I was playing out a lifelong fantasy, and he was an "easy baby." When I went to women's liberation meetings, I held him in my lap. If he cried, I nursed him. When he fell asleep I put him down on the carpet beside me and went on participating in the meeting. I could write when he was a baby, too. He would play quietly and I would type. When I took a break I would go and cuddle him – then return to typing. Easy, I thought.

By the time he was a year-and-a-half old it wasn't easy any more. He didn't stay put. He was developing into a person who would not be cuddled and ignored. He would *not* be ignored – and I didn't want to pay attention. Much of the work of mothering a small child (especially if you have only one) consists in being present for another, being ready to respond to emergencies, being ready to appreciate accomplishments, being there for long periods of time with nothing, really, to do – except watch and wait. During these times (which, if they were not in our living room, seem always to have been in some park or other) I would try to read or write, try to keep my mind active, try to keep my sense of myself. But I never managed the trick of being with myself and being ready to respond to Kevin at the same time. I vacillated between two approaches. For a while I would try shutting him out, focusing on my reading or writing or thinking; and I would feel abruptly invaded by any small demand he made. Then I would try the opposite tack and hold myself in a state of dull readiness, trying to forget my own mind, my own need to be with myself, trying to be ready for whatever he needed without anger, without that painful sense of violation.

Neither worked well, of course. I was trying to do work for which I was not suited.

Not everyone responds this way to the demands of mothering a small child. There are women who amaze me with their skills. Like jugglers (I have always been in awe of jugglers) they seem able to keep track of many simultaneous movements. They can balance their own lively consciousness with the activities and needs of their children – without losing themselves in the complicated, ever-changing pattern. On good days they even make beauty and fun out of the juggle. I have often wondered, at least half-seriously, if my simple inability to pay attention to two things at once might lie at the core of my problems with mothering.

I don't know if my difficulties with the mother role were made more or less painful by the fact that I found Kevin to be the most attractive child I had ever met. I liked him very much. He was bright and beautiful. I liked being related to him, was proud to be his mother. My affection for him was powerful, tender, and could well up in tears easily and often. It was not Kevin I disliked; it was the work of being his mother day by day.

Many aspects of that work were difficult for me. I was overwhelmed, for example, to find myself responsible for the physical existence of a little person who could suddenly move about under his own power. How could I know when he might step in front of a moving car, climb high and fall to his death, swallow poison? I could not lose the feeling that Kevin was at every moment vulnerable to a multitude of dangers. It was as if I were on guard duty, constantly vigilant, never fully relaxed.

Many mothers feel that when their infants become toddlers the job of being mother becomes easier and more rewarding – especially after the development of language and the completion of toilet training. In contrast, I felt the job expand into a complexity that I could hardly handle. Suddenly, for example, I was to pass on values to a malleable young soul. "Pass on" was, in my case, quite a euphemism. My own ethical stance and value system were still in the process of being reconstructed after the blitz of the late sixties. I felt absolutely inadequate to the task of building a strong structure for a preschool child. I struggled painfully with every situation that called for a decision about values: should I teach him non-violence or the art of self-defense? Should I encourage him to question my commands or respect my need to have things done in certain ways? Should I demand that he maintain order in his room or allow him a measure of chaos? Every decision seemed to matter immensely – and to present unresolvable difficulties. I knew too much to opt simply for a highly structured universe on the one hand, or an existence that would trust to benign natural spontaneity on the other. And I was too confused to create a complex, workable blend of both.

The fact that I was now spending hour upon hour with a person who was verbal but not very good at being verbal was also difficult for me. I am the sort of person who can concentrate easily in the presence of jackhammers and roaring highway traffic, but let the most routine whispered conversation start up and I become totally distracted. When Kevin talked, whether to me or to one of his beloved stuffed animals, my whole mind swerved in his direction. But I was not good at child-level conversation and not particularly appreciative of the verbal gems of a 3-year-old. I was, in fact, bored. I have often envied friends who take an easy delight in the speech of the very young. Not only do they enjoy the spontaneous comments of children; they also have mysterious ways of eliciting the most peculiar and interesting responses from them. Gretchen is one of these people and in the past 10 years she has shared with me many instances of Kevin's verbal brilliance. Oddly enough, I have often taken special pleasure in hearing Gretchen tell me what Kevin has said. It is as if her appreciation of his words has provided a setting in which I can enjoy them.

Gretchen and I have always seemed to fit together like two radically different pieces adjacent in the same puzzle. I did a very good job of mothering during Kevin's infancy and then entered the painful period that taught me I did not want to go with the mother role. When I looked ahead I saw the grade school years as a severe challenge and if I imagined Kevin's adolescence I shuddered. Gretchen, on the other hand, got queasy at the thought of diapers and had no desire to be a mother to a small helpless non-verbal specimen of humanity; she liked a child she could talk to and she even, to my amazement, liked the fact that the child would become a teenager; she wanted to be a mother through that whole long growing process. More specifically, she wanted to be Kevin's mother. And so we made the change.

There is a stubborn, clear-headed part of me that has never doubted the rightness of my decision. With that part I know that Kevin, Gretchen, and I all have more satisfying lives because I made that decision. With that part I have organized groups for women who, like me, have left the mother role. With that part I fight the demons of the night.

There are two of these demons, both expert tormentors. One springs from reality; the other from myth. They are given to impersonating each other, like clever twins. I have spent many hours trying to pin down their identities, and I get a little better at it as time goes on. The first demon is decidedly unpleasant, but necessary. It is the caretaker of all the genuine pain that comes from giving up a child. That pain rises and subsides through the months and years. It feels demon-controlled because it comes without warning, without apparent cause, and most often in the middle of the night.

In the beginning, soon after Kevin and I separated, this demon of genuine pain was quite distinct, not readily confused with the second tormentor. I remember one night especially well. It was as if all the pain had gathered to a single point in time and I must experience it in a sort of purity. I felt as if Kevin and I had been surgically separated. The pain felt physical, deep, radical – and I knew it would lessen with time. That I had *chosen* the separation and believed it was going to be good for both Kevin and me must have determined the kind of pain I felt – pain that could be so accurately described by the image of surgery. When I think of the thousands of women who have been forcibly separated from their children – because they were black and slaves and sold in separate lots, because they were lesbians and considered by that fact unfit, because they made their living by prostitution and were therefore put in prison, or for whatever reason – when I think of those women I imagine a pain that is not the clean and chosen pain of surgery but instead the ragged, uncontrollable pain of flesh torn at random which heals slowly into an ugly scar and which hurts terribly even though new flesh has formed.

The second demon is not only unpleasant, but also unnecessary. It is the demon of myth and illusion and it is part of what is now being called the institution of motherhood.[1] The foundation stone of that institution and the constant message of its demon is this: *children are meant to be raised by their natural (that is, biological) mothers.*

I grew up in the all-white, working-class world of the small town Midwest and went to Catholic schools in the forties and fifties. I did not routinely encounter challenges to this basic tenet of the institution of motherhood. On the contrary, I absorbed the precept into my being. I imagined I would someday be Mother Supreme. With infinite patience, good humor, and wisdom, I would faithfully raise not one child, but 12. Having read *Cheaper by the Dozen* and *Jo's Boys*, I had decided to fill my life with wonderful, wacky children. I planned to have a few of my own, but the majority would be homeless waifs, "abandoned" by their mothers who were too poor or too ill to take care of them. With me a child would have a secure home.

That sort of self-image does not dissolve easily. In some very old part of my soul I still believe that I am a superior mother. I also still believe, with that same anachronistic part of my soul, that all children are best raised by their natural mothers. I have learned that neither of these beliefs is true, but in weak moments I forget what I have learned and thus open the door to the demon of myth and illusion. Like the demon of genuine pain, this creature comes most often at night. I know he has come when I find myself lying awake and nursing the terrible feeling that I have deprived my child of the most blessed of relationships; that my child is denied the special depth of bonding that could only come between him and me; that if I had stayed with him, he and I would have a full, clear, honest, tension-free relationship. I can remain in the grip of this demon for hours, colluding with society against myself.

But at some point I break free. I remember reality. I did not like the mother role. As long as I continued in it, I was doing something that aroused in me boredom, anxiety, depression, anger, and at times a fear that I would lose my sanity; it aroused in me also a deep fear that I would do violence to my child; at its best it turned me into a highly responsible, joyless, rather rigid person. Out of such things, great relationships are not made. I am not the best person to raise my child; only a powerful myth can make me think that I am.

The demon of myth and illusion has a strong grip which is not broken entirely by the act of remembering my own experience. I have also been faced with the task of sorting through distortions in my vision of Kevin's experience. The demon would paint the child as abandoned, damaged, a tragic figure. In my effort to correct this portrait I have sometimes drawn my own false picture: the child who moved easily from one mother to the next, happily relieved and blessedly unhurt. Somewhere between the demon and my own wishful thinking the truth hides. My memory, when it clears, tells me that Kevin's experience was as complex as mine, a mixture of pain and benefit.

I will never know all that Kevin felt during the time of transition, but two scenes come to my mind and I suspect that each is a hint and an essence, a clue to the nature of his first days and nights in Gretchen's house. One scene is painful, the other quietly delightful.

About a week after the separation I visited Kevin in his new house – our first visit. What I remember is saying goodbye. Gretchen held him, standing on the edge of the porch. I told him I was leaving and hugged him while she still held him. He got his arms around me like a vice, would not let go, and sobbed out all the loss, powerlessness, frustration, and pain that he felt. After a while we pried him loose from me and I turned and went down the porch steps crying and drove home crying. Gretchen called me a couple of hours later to say that he had gotten calm before too long and had had a quiet, happy game before bedtime.

The second scene that comes to mind was at the beginning of one of those early visits. Kevin and Gretchen were in their living room and had not heard me coming. For several minutes, which is a very long time, I did the thing that anyone in my position would dearly want to do: I spied on them. I was the mouse in the corner. I had the privilege of seeing my child and his new mother in a spontaneous moment. Classical music was playing on the stereo, one of those pieces of music that is subtle and engaging and moves like water in rough country with swift clarity and little falls and still places following on each other over and over. Gretchen sat with Kevin on her lap and their hands pantomimed what I later found out were two alligators who talked and kissed and then fiercely ate each other up; which caused much laughing in Kevin and the familiar lump in my throat.

So he must have felt pain and he must have felt joy, too, in having a mother now who was as overflowing with energy for being his mother as I had been drained of it. It must have been confusing for quite a while to want to be with me and to be having such a good time with Gretchen. He got attached to her quickly. He began to express pride in the fact that he had two mothers – this made him special. But he was torn; he liked living with Gretchen and at the same time he wanted to live with me. Sometime during the first year he came up with the perfect solution for his dilemma: he proposed that we should all live together, he, Gretchen, and I. An intelligent idea, certainly; just the thing from his point of view. Needless to say, being only four, he did not have the power to transform his idea into reality.

Mixed with the pain, relief, fun, and confusion Kevin felt during those early days of the transition was at least one more set of feelings: frustration, impatience, irritation, anger. Anger was not a new thing in Kevin's life. His anger and mine had mixed and grown together for some time before our separation. Several months before Gretchen appeared and changed our lives, Kevin found a way to express that building rageful energy: he took a new name. He called himself Fire. With great seriousness he instructed everyone he met to call him Fire, his name was no longer Kevin. A month or so after our separation, he issued new instructions: we were all to stop calling him Fire; his name was Kevin.

Kevin's stay in the angry realm of Fire was relatively brief, I think. The fact that he was separated not only from me, but also from my anger, must have had something to do with that. But the separation could not, by itself, have dissolved his rage. In fact, it must have generated new anger. Gretchen's obvious abundant good feeling about Kevin and about her new job as mother did much to help him toward resolution of his feelings. In addition, he had invaluable assistance from the staff at his new day-care center (to which he was moved when Gretchen became his mother and decided she should not also be his teacher). Presented not only with his unusual name, but also with more tangible evidence of his anger (biting, kicking, and so forth), they reacted with intelligence and creativity – and patience. They taught him how to be angry without being destructive. The central character in this lesson on anger was Fred. Fred was life-sized, stuffed, and beat-up-looking – with good reason, since the point of his existence was to be an object of punching, biting, kicking, verbal assault, and any other manner of attack a creative preschooler might invent. Kevin, I am told, learned to use Fred as no other child in the center ever had.

The fact that Kevin was encouraged to express his rage must have something to do with its disappearance. As far as I can tell, he is not now a particularly angry person; and he does not seem to have any resentment (at least at this point in his life) about having been required to leave me and adopt a new mother.

I can say this with some confidence because one recent spring (Kevin was 11) I found the precise mixture of relaxation, courage, and support from other people in my life that allowed me, finally, to ask The Question. The setting was an A & W Restaurant situated on a busy road along with K-Mart, G. I. Joe's, and quite a number of auto dealers. Kevin and I were having hamburgers and root beer. In the middle of my hamburger, I asked him, "So, Kevin, what do you think about the fact that I am your real mom and we don't live together?"

He was quite ready with his answer and considerably calmer than I was. He had a theory: he supposed that I had not been able to afford having a child and so had given him to Gretchen. (Other children in Kevin's situation have expressed similar theories. It seems that children who do not live with their parents are likely to come up with an explanation of their situation that absolves both them and their parents of responsibility for the separation. In Kevin's case it was lack of money; in another child's it was immigration laws that required the parent to leave. In neither case did the external force actually have anything to do with the separation.) I told Kevin that money had not been a problem and talked a little about the real reason for my decision. Then I held my breath.

His response was calm and thoughtful. He said it was a good thing I had given him to Gretchen; he was sure the job of being a mother would have gotten harder and harder for me, and Gretchen was a good mom. He added, clearly not ready to abandon a well-thought-out theory, that he supposed I would have had financial problems if I had kept him.

Before that day in the A & W, I had a recurring fantasy that Kevin would, sometime in his thirties, go to a psychotherapist and, hour by expensive hour, unearth his anger at me for "giving him away." Perhaps he will do just that, I cannot know. But the fantasy does not come to me now. I have asked the crucial question, which is really many questions: is it all right? do you hate me? were you damaged? And I have received the gift of a calm answer from a child who seems to believe his life is just fine.

Still the demons come. Worry, guilt, romantic notions of what-might-have-been, a deep sense of loss – all mix together in the middle of the night.

In the daytime, out in the world, I am bothered by another tangle of difficulties: I feel vulnerable to the judgments of others, isolated, different; I am afraid and I hide the fact that I am a mother; I cultivate a habit of cautious speech; I deny an aspect of my being. Any gay person will recognize this syndrome. It is called living in the closet.

I have lived partly in and partly out of the closet ever since I gave up my child. I told my family and close friends as soon as I made the decision, but for the first five years I did not talk about it with anyone who had left the mother role. I assumed there were hardly any of us. I did know of one woman, a friend of friends, but I avoided meeting her. Then I decided to do some intensive dealing with this huge fact in my life. I wrote my master's thesis on the experience of giving up my child. I organized a couple of groups for women who had left the mother role – groups that were a sort of coming out for me, complete with highs and lows, moments of clarity and confusion, and a sense that my life was changing. And I am still closeted. There are many people from whom I have hidden the fact of my motherhood: bosses, co-workers, neighbors, the families of my friends, any casual acquaintance. I feel the power of the institution of motherhood too clearly to take the revelation of my status lightly.

On the other hand, as the existence of this paper demonstrates, I feel compelled to tell the world about the experience of giving up my child. This is cathartic for me. Every time I wrestle anew with my mothering experience and get it pinned down for a while to a (somewhat) solid floor of words, I feel both relief and a fresh sense of control. I get my reward. But this is the most difficult writing I ever tackle, and I do not do it for pleasure. I do it because it needs doing and has been so little done.[2] In these days when the threat of a "Family Protection Act" hangs over us like some sharp and dangerous appendage to the institution of motherhood, it seems more important than ever to speak about alternative ways of raising our children. We must make it clear that many women cannot or will not be forced into the mold of happy motherhood; and this includes many women who already have children. Mothers – and fathers, too – who need to give up their children must be able to do so with dignity, without stigma, not only for their own sake, but also (and perhaps especially) for the sake of the children.

If ever I were to lose my conviction about this (and I could, in one of those sloppy, sentimental nights when a soft glow surrounds the image of the Mother Supreme), the morning news would quite likely help me remember reality. In the past month my local radio station has reported the murders of two young children – one by the father while the mother looked on, one by the mother. These murders are hardly unusual. I happen to have the statistics from 1966. In that year, 496 children were murdered by their parents in the United States. I am convinced that if it were an acceptable option to decide not to continue in the parenting role, at least some of these children would still be alive. Some battered children, too, would escape the bruises, the broken bones, the burns. Other children, less obviously abused, would find themselves released from the subtle prison of their parents' tension, anger, and unhappiness. They would find themselves being raised by someone who wanted to do the job. And that, I believe, would make all the difference.

Notes

1   The institution of motherhood is, by my definition, a system of customs, laws, ideals, and images that (a) determines how the *work* of mothering is generally defined, organized, and performed in a society; (b) powerfully influences the form and quality of the mother–child *relationship* in that society. For an excellent description of the working of this institution, see Adrienne Rich's *Of Woman Born: Motherhood as Experience and Institution* (New York: W. W. Norton, 1976).
2   For more writing by women who have given up their children, see the following: Louise Billotte, "Mothers don't have to lie," *Mother Jones*, May (1976), pp. 22–5; *The Living of Charlotte Perkins Gilman: an Autobiography* (n.p., Katharine Beecher Stetson Chamberlain, 1935; reprint, New York: Harper & Row, 1963); Martha Jane Cannary Hickok, *Calamity Jane's Letters to her Daughter* (n.p., Dr Nolie Mumie, n.d., limited edn; n.p., Don C. Foote and Stella A Foote, n.d., limited edn; reprint, San Lorenzo, CA: Shameless Hussy Press, 1976); Patricia Preston, "Parenting in absentia," *Branching Out* (May/June 1977), pp. 8–10; Judy Sullivan, *Mama Doesn't Live Here Anymore* (New York: Pyramid Books, 1974); Lucia Valeska, "If all else fails, I'm still a mother" *Quest*, 1 (Winter 1975), pp. 52–63.

Abortion through a Feminist Ethics Lens (excerpt)
Susan Sherwin

Abortion has long been a central issue in the arena of applied ethics, but, the distinctive analysis of feminist ethics is generally overlooked in most

This reading first appeared in *Dialogue*, 1991, 30: 327–42.

philosophical discussions. Authors and readers commonly presume a familiarity with the feminist position and equate it with liberal defenses of women's right to choose abortion, but, in fact, feminist ethics yields a different analysis of the moral questions surrounding abortion than that usually offered by the more familiar liberal defenders of abortion rights. Most feminists can agree with some of the conclusions that arise from certain non-feminist arguments on abortion, but they often disagree about the way the issues are formulated and the sorts of reasons that are invoked in the mainstream literature.

Among the many differences found between feminist and non-feminist arguments about abortion is the fact that most non-feminist discussions of abortion consider the questions of the moral or legal permissibility of abortion in isolation from other questions, ignoring (and thereby obscuring) relevant connections to other social practices that oppress women. They are generally grounded in masculinist conceptions of freedom (for example, privacy, individual choice, individuals' property rights in their own bodies) that do not meet the needs, interests, and intuitions of many of the women concerned. In contrast, feminists seek to couch their arguments in moral concepts that support their general campaign of overcoming injustice in all its dimensions, including those inherent in moral theory itself.[1] There is even disagreement about how best to understand the moral question at issue: non-feminist arguments focus exclusively on the morality and/or legality of performing abortions, whereas feminists insist that other questions, including ones about accessibility and delivery of abortion services must also be addressed.

Although feminists welcome the support of non-feminists in pursuing policies that will grant women control over abortion decisions, they generally envision very different sorts of policies for this purpose than those considered by non-feminist sympathizers . . . Here, I propose one conception of the shape such an analysis should take.

The most obvious difference between feminist and non-feminist approaches to abortion can be seen in the relative attention each gives to the interests and experiences of women in its analysis. Feminists consider it self-evident that the pregnant woman is a subject of principal concern in abortion decisions. In most non-feminist accounts, however, not only is she not perceived as central, she is rendered virtually invisible. Non-feminist theorists, whether they support or oppose women's right to choose abortion, focus almost all their attention on the moral status of the developing embryo or the fetus.

In pursuing a distinctively feminist ethics, it is appropriate to begin with a look at the role of abortion in women's lives. Clearly, the need for abortion can be very intense; women have pursued abortions under appalling and dangerous conditions, across widely diverse cultures and historical periods. No one denies that if abortion is not made legal, safe, and accessible, women will seek out illegal and life-threatening abortions to terminate pregnancies they cannot accept. Anti-abortion activists seem willing to accept this price, but feminists judge the inevitable loss of women's lives associated with restrictive abortion policies to be a matter of fundamental concern.

Although anti-abortion campaigners imagine that women often make frivolous and irresponsible decisions about abortion, feminists recognize that women have abortions for a wide variety of reasons . . .

Whatever the reason, most feminists believe that a pregnant woman is in the best position to judge whether abortion is the appropriate response to her circumstances. Since she is usually the only one able to weigh all the relevant factors, most feminists reject attempts to offer any general abstract rules for determining when abortion is morally justified. Women's personal deliberations about abortion include contextually defined considerations reflecting her commitment to the needs and interests of everyone concerned – including herself, the fetus she carries, other members of her household, and so on. Because there is no single formula available for balancing these complex factors through all possible cases, it is vital that feminists insist on protecting each woman's right to come to her own conclusions. Abortion decisions are, by their very nature, dependent on specific features of each woman's experience; theoretically dispassionate philosophers and other moralists should not expect to set the agenda for these considerations in any universal way. Women must be acknowledged as full moral agents with the responsibility for making moral decisions about their own pregnancies.[2] Although I think that it is possible for a woman to make a mistake in her moral judgment on this matter (i.e. it is possible that a woman may come to believe that she was wrong about her decision to continue or terminate a pregnancy), the intimate nature of this sort of decision makes it unlikely that anyone else is in a position to arrive at a more reliable conclusion; it is, therefore, improper to grant others the authority to interfere in women's decisions to seek abortions.

Feminist analysis regards the effects of unwanted pregnancies on the lives of women individually and collectively as a central element in the moral evaluation of abortion. Even without patriarchy, bearing a child would be a very important event in a woman's life. It involves significant physical, emotional, social, and (usually) economic changes for her. The ability to exert control over the incidence, timing, and frequency of child bearing is often tied to her ability to control most other things she values. Since we live in a patriarchal society, it is especially important to ensure that women have the authority to control their own reproduction.[3] Despite the diversity of opinion among feminists on most other matters, virtually all feminists seem to agree that women must gain full control over their own reproductive lives if they are to free themselves from male dominance.[4] Many perceive the commitment of the political right wing to opposing abortion as part of a general strategy to reassert patriarchal control over women in the face of significant feminist influence (Petchesky, 1980: 112).

Women's freedom to choose abortion is also linked with their ability to control their own sexuality. Women's subordinate status often prevents them from refusing men sexual access to their bodies. If women cannot end the unwanted pregnancies that result from male sexual dominance, their sexual vulnerability to particular men can increase, because caring for an(other) infant involves greater financial needs and reduced economic opportunities for women.[5] As a result, pregnancy often forces women to become dependent on men. Since a woman's dependence on a man is assumed to entail that she will remain sexually loyal to him, restriction of abortion serves to channel women's sexuality and further perpetuates the cycle of oppression.

In contrast to most non-feminist accounts, feminist analyses of abortion direct attention to the question of how women get pregnant. Those who reject abortion seem to believe that women can avoid unwanted pregnancies by avoiding sexual intercourse. Such views show little appreciation for the power of sexual politics in a culture that oppresses women. Existing patterns of sexual dominance mean that women often have little control over their sexual lives. They may be subject to rape by strangers, or by their husbands, boyfriends, colleagues, employers, customers, fathers, brothers, uncles, and dates. Often, the sexual coercion is not even recognized as such by the participants, but is the price of continued "good will" – popularity, economic survival, peace, or simple acceptance. Few women have not found themselves in circumstances where they do not feel free to refuse a man's demands for intercourse, either because he is holding a gun to her head or because he threatens to be emotionally hurt if she refuses (or both). Women are socialized to be compliant and accommodating, sensitive to the feelings of others, and frightened of physical power; men are socialized to take advantage of every opportunity to engage in sexual intercourse and to use sex to express dominance and power. Under such circumstances, it is difficult to argue that women could simply "choose" to avoid heterosexual activity if they wish to avoid pregnancy. Catherine MacKinnon (1989: 192) neatly sums it up: "the logic by which women are supposed to consent to sex [is]: preclude the alternatives, then call the remaining option 'her choice.'" . . .

From a feminist perspective, a central moral feature of pregnancy is that it takes place in *women's bodies* and has profound effects on *women's* lives. Gender-neutral accounts of pregnancy are not available; pregnancy is explicitly a condition associated with the female body.[6] Because the need for abortion is experienced only by women, policies about abortion affect women uniquely. Thus, it is important to consider how proposed policies on abortion fit into general patterns of oppression for women. Unlike non-feminist accounts, feminist ethics demands that the effects on the oppression of women be a principal consideration when evaluating abortion policies. . . .

A feminist view of the fetus

Because the public debate has been set up as a competition between the rights of women and those of fetuses, feminists have often felt pushed to reject claims of fetal value in order to protect women's claims. Yet, as Addelson (1987: 107) has argued, viewing abortion in this way "tears [it] out of the context of women's lives." There are other accounts of fetal value that are more plausible and less oppressive to women.

On a feminist account, fetal development is examined in the context in which it occurs, within women's bodies rather than in the imagined isolation implicit in many theoretical accounts. Fetuses develop in specific pregnancies which occur in the lives of particular women. They are not individuals housed in generic female wombs, nor are they full persons at risk only because they are small and subject to the whims of women. Their very existence is relational, developing as they do within particular women's bodies, and their principal relationship is to the women who carry them.

On this view, fetuses are morally significant, but their status is relational rather than absolute. Unlike other human beings, fetuses do not have any independent existence; their existence is uniquely tied to the support of a specific other. Most non-feminist commentators have ignored the relational dimension of fetal development and have presumed that the moral status of fetuses could be resolved solely in terms of abstract metaphysical criteria of personhood. They imagine that there is some set of properties (such as genetic heritage, moral agency, self-consciousness, language use, or self-determination) which will entitle all who possess them to be granted the moral status of persons (Tooley, 1972; Warren, 1973). They seek some particular feature by which we can neatly divide the world into the dichotomy of moral persons (who are to be valued and protected) and others (who are not entitled to the same group privileges); it follows that it is a merely empirical question whether or not fetuses possess the relevant properties.

But this vision misinterprets what is involved in personhood and what it is that is especially valued about persons. Personhood is a social category, not an isolated state. Persons are members of a community; they develop as concrete, discrete, and specific individuals. To be a morally significant category, personhood must involve personality as well as biological integrity.[7] It is not sufficient to consider persons simply as Kantian atoms of rationality; persons are all embodied, conscious beings with particular social histories. Annette Baier (1985) has developed a concept of persons as "second persons," which helps explain the sort of social dimension that seems fundamental to any moral notion of personhood:

> A person, perhaps, is best seen as one who was long enough dependent upon other persons to acquire the essential arts of personhood. Persons essentially are *second* persons, who grow up with other persons . . . The fact that a person has a life *history*, and that a people collectively have a history depends upon the humbler fact that each person has a childhood in which a cultural heritage is transmitted, ready for adolescent rejection and adult discriminating selection and contribution. Persons come after and before other persons. (Baier, 1985: 84–5)

Persons, in other words, are members of a social community which shapes and values them, and personhood is a relational concept that must be defined in terms of interactions and relationships with others.

A fetus is a unique sort of being in that it cannot form relationships freely with others, nor can others readily form relationships with it. A fetus has a primary and particularly intimate relationship with the woman in whose womb it develops; any other relationship it may have is indirect, and must be mediated through the pregnant woman. The relationship that exists between a woman and her fetus is clearly asymmetrical, since she is the only party to the relationship who is capable of making a decision about whether the interaction should continue and since the fetus is wholly dependent on the woman who sustains it while she is quite capable of surviving without it.

However much some might prefer it to be otherwise, no one else can do anything to support or harm a fetus without doing something to the woman who nurtures it. Because of this inexorable biological reality, she bears a unique responsibility and privilege in determining her fetus's place in the social scheme of things. Clearly, many pregnancies occur to women who place very high value on the lives of the particular fetuses they carry, and choose to see their pregnancies through to term despite the possible risks and costs involved; hence, it would be wrong of anyone to force such a woman to terminate her pregnancy under these circumstances. Other women, or some of these same women at other times, value other things more highly (for example, their freedom, their health, or previous responsibilities which conflict with those generated by the pregnancies), and choose not to continue their pregnancies. The value that women ascribe to individual fetuses varies dramatically from case to case, and may well change over the course of any particular pregnancy. There is no absolute value that attaches to fetuses apart from their relational status determined in the context of their particular development . . .

Feminist politics and abortion

Feminist ethics directs us to look at abortion in the context of other issues of power and not to limit discussion to the standard questions about its moral and legal acceptability. Because coerced pregnancy has repercussions for women's oppressed status generally, it is important to ensure that abortion not only be made legal but that adequate services be made accessible to all women who seek them. This means that within Canada, where medically approved abortion is technically recognized as legal (at least for the moment), we must protest the fact that it is not made available to many of the women who have the greatest need for abortions: vast geographical areas offer no abortion services at all, but unless the women of those regions can afford to travel to urban clinics, they have no meaningful right to abortion. Because women depend on access to abortion in their pursuit of social equality, it is a matter of moral as well as political responsibility that provincial health plans should cover the cost of transport and service in the abortion facilities women choose. Ethical study of abortion involves understanding and critiquing the economic, age, and social barriers that currently restrict access to medically acceptable abortion services.[8]

Moreover, it is also important that abortion services be provided in an atmosphere that fosters women's health and well-being; hence, the care offered should be in a context that is supportive of the choices women make. Abortions should be seen as part of women's overall reproductive health and could be included within centers that deal with all matters of reproductive health in an open, patient-centered manner where effective counseling is offered for a wide range of reproductive decisions.[9] Providers need to recognize that abortion is a legitimate option so that services will be delivered with respect and concern for the physical, psychological, and emotional effects on a patient. All too frequently, hospital-based abortions are provided by practitioners who are uneasy about their role and treat the women involved with hostility and resentment. Increasingly, many anti-abortion activists have personalized their attacks and focused their attention on harassing the women who enter and leave abortion clinics. Surely requiring a woman to pass a gauntlet of hostile protestors on her way to and from an abortion is not conducive to effective health care. Ethical exploration of abortion raises questions about how women are treated when they seek abortions;[10] achieving legal permission for women to dispose of their fetuses if they are determined enough to manage the struggle should not be accepted as the sole moral consideration . . .

Feminists support abortion on demand because they know that women must have control over their reproduction. For the same reason, they actively oppose forced abortion and coerced sterilization, practices that are sometimes inflicted on the most powerless women, especially those in the Third World. Feminist ethics demands that access to voluntary, safe, effective birth control be part of any abortion discussion, so that women have access to other means of avoiding pregnancy.[11]

Feminist analysis addresses the context as well as the practice of abortion decisions. Thus, feminists also object to the conditions that lead women to abort wanted fetuses because there are not adequate financial and social supports available to care for a child. Because feminist accounts value fetuses that are wanted by the women who carry them, they oppose practices that force women to abort because of poverty or intimidation. Yet, the sorts of social changes necessary if we are to free women from having abortions out of economic necessity are vast; they include changes not only in legal and health-care policy, but also in housing, child care, employment, and so on (Petchesky, 1980: 112). None the less, feminist ethics defines reproductive freedom as the condition under which women are able to make truly voluntary choices about their reproductive lives, and these many dimensions are implicit in the ideal.

Clearly, feminists are not "pro-abortion," for they are concerned to ensure the safety of each pregnancy to the greatest degree possible: wanted fetuses should not be harmed or lost. Therefore, adequate pre- and postnatal care and nutrition are also important elements of any feminist position on reproductive freedom. Where anti-abortionists direct their energies to trying to prevent women from obtaining abortions, feminists seek to protect the health of wanted fetuses. They recognize that far more could be done to protect and care for fetuses if the state directed its resources at supporting women who continue their pregnancies, rather than draining away resources in order to police women who find that they must interrupt their pregnancies. Caring for the women who carry fetuses is not only a more legitimate policy than is regulating them; it is probably also more effective in ensuring the health and well-being of more fetuses.

Feminist ethics also explores how abortion policies fit within the politics of sexual domination. Most feminists are sensitive to the fact that many men support women's right to abortion out of the belief that women will be more willing sexual partners if they believe that they can readily terminate an unwanted pregnancy. Some men coerce their partners into obtaining abortions the women may not want.[12] Feminists understand that many women oppose abortion for this very reason, being unwilling to support a practice that increases women's sexual vulnerability (Luker, 1984: 209–15). Thus, it is important that feminists develop a coherent analysis of reproductive freedom that includes sexual freedom (as women choose to define it). That requires an analysis of sexual freedom that includes women's right to refuse sex; such a right can only be assured if women have equal power to men and are not subject to domination by virtue of their sex.[13]

In sum, then, feminist ethics demands that moral discussions of abortion be more broadly defined than they have been in most philosophical discussions. Only by reflecting on the meaning of ethical pronouncements on actual women's lives and the connections between judgments on abortion and the conditions of domination and subordination can we come to an adequate understanding of the moral status of abortion in our society. As Rosalind Petchesky (1989: 113) argues, feminist discussion of abortion "must be moved beyond the framework of a 'woman's right to choose' and connected to a much broader revolutionary movement that addresses all of the conditions of women's liberation."

Acknowledgments

Earlier versions of this paper were read to the Department of Philosophy, Dalhousie University and to the Canadian Society for Women in Philosophy in Kingston. I am very grateful for the comments received from colleagues in both forums; particular thanks go to Lorraine Code, David Braybrooke, Richmond Campbell, Sandra Taylor, Terry Tomkow, and Kadri Vihvelin for their patience and advice.

Notes

1 For some idea of the ways in which traditional moral theory oppresses women, see Morgan (1987) and Hoagland (1988).
2 Critics continue to want to structure the debate around the *possibility* of women making frivolous abortion decisions and hence want feminists to agree to setting boundaries on acceptable grounds for choosing abortion. Feminists ought to resist this injunction, though. There is no practical way of drawing a line

fairly in the abstract; cases that may appear "frivolous" at a distance, often turn
out to be substantive when the details are revealed, i.e. frivolity is in the eyes
of the beholder. There is no evidence to suggest that women actually make the
sorts of choices worried critics hypothesize about: e.g., a woman eight months'
pregnant who chooses to abort because she wants to take a trip or gets in "a
tiff" with her partner. These sorts of fantasies, on which demands to distinguish
between legitimate and illegitimate personal reasons for choosing abortion chiefly
rest, reflect an offensive conception of women as irresponsible; they ought not
to be perpetuated. Women, seeking moral guidance in their own deliberations
about choosing abortion, do not find such hypothetical discussions of much use.

3   In her monumental historical analysis of the early roots of Western patriarchy,
    Gerda Lerner (1986) determined that patriarchy began in the period from
    3100 to 600 BC when men appropriated women's sexual and reproductive
    capacity; the earliest state entrenched patriarchy by institutionalizing the sexual
    and procreative subordination of women to men.

4   There are some women who claim to be feminists against choice in abortion.
    See, for instance, Callahan (1987) and Maloney (1994), though few spell out
    their full feminist program. For reasons I develop in this paper, I do not think
    this is a consistent position.

5   There is a lot the state could do to ameliorate this condition. If it provided
    women with adequate financial support, removed the inequities in the labour
    market, and provided affordable and reliable child care, pregnancy need not so
    often lead to a woman's dependence on a particular man. The fact that it does
    not do so is evidence of the state's complicity in maintaining women's subor-
    dinate position with respect to men.

6   See Zillah Eisenstein (1988) for a comprehensive theory of the role of the
    pregnant body as the central element in the cultural subordination of women.

7   This apt phrasing is taken from Petchesky (1980: 342).

8   Some feminists suggest we seek recognition of the legitimacy of non-medical
    abortion services. This would reduce costs and increase access dramatically,
    with no apparent increase in risk, provided that services were offered by trained,
    responsible practitioners concerned with the well-being of their clients. It would
    also allow the possibility of increasing women's control over abortion. See, for
    example, McDonnell (1984), ch. 8.

9   For a useful model of such a center, see Van Wagner and Lee (1989).

10 See CARAL/Halifax (1990) for women's stories about their experiences with
    hospitals and free-standing abortion clinics.

11 Therefore, the Soviet model, where women have access to multiple abortions
    but where there is no other birth control available, must also be opposed.

12 See CARAL/Halifax (1990: 20–21) for examples of this sort of abuse.

13 It also requires that discussions of reproductive and sexual freedom not be
    confined to "the language of control and sexuality characteristic of a techno-
    logy of sex" (Diamond and Quinby, 1988: 197), for such language is alienating
    and constrains women's experiences of their own sexuality.

References

Addelson, Kathryn Pyne (1987) "Moral passages," in Eva Feder Kittay and Diana T. Meyers (eds), *Women and Moral Theory* (Totowa, NJ: Rowman and Littlefield).

Baier, Annette (1985) *Postures of the Mind: Essays on Mind and Morals* (Minneapolis: University of Minnesota Press).

Callahan, Sidney (1987) "A pro-life feminist makes her case," *Utne Reader* (March/April), pp. 104–14.

CARAL/Halifax (1990) *Telling our Stories: Abortion Stories from Nova Scotia* (Halifax: Canadian Abortion Rights Action League).

Diamond, Irene, and Quinby, Lee (1988) "American feminism and the language of control," in Irene Diamond and Lee Quinby (eds), *Feminism and Foucault: Reflections on Resistance* (Boston: Northeastern University Press).

Eisenstein, Zillah R. (1988) *The Female Body and the Law* (Berkeley, CA: University of California Press).

Hoagland, Sara Lucia (1988) *Lesbian Ethics: Toward New Value* (Palo Alto, CA: Institute of Lesbian Studies).

Lerner, Gerda (1986) *The Creation of Patriarchy* (New York: Oxford University Press).

Luker, Kristin (1984) *Abortion and the Politics of Motherhood* (Berkeley, CA: University of California Press).

MacKinnon, Catherine (1989) *Toward a Feminist Theory of the State* (Cambridge, MA: Harvard University Press).

McDonnell. Kathleen (1984) *Not an Easy Choice: a Feminist Re-examines Abortion* (Toronto: The Women's Press).

Maloney, Anne (1994) "Women and children first?," in Alison M. Jaggar (ed.), *Living with Contradictions: Controversies in Feminist Social Ethics* (Boulder, CO: Westview Press).

Morgan, Kathryn Pauly (1987) "Women and moral madness," in Marsha Hatten and Kai Nielsen (eds), *Science, Morality and Feminist Theory. Canadian Journal of Philosophy*, supplementary volume 13: 201–26.

Petchesky, Rosalind Pollack (1980) "Reproductive freedom: beyond 'a woman's right to choose'," in Catharine R. Stimpson and Ethel Spector Person (eds), *Women: Sex and Sexuality* (Chicago: University of Chicago Press).

Tooley, Michael (1972) "Abortion and infanticide," *Philosophy and Public Affairs*, 2, 1 (Fall): 37–65.

Van Wagner, Vicki, and Lee, Bob (1989) "Principles into practice: an activist vision of feminist reproductive health care,' in Christine Overall (ed.), *The Future of Human Reproduction* (Toronto: The Women's Press).

Warren, Mary Anne (1973) "On the moral and legal status of abortion," *The Monist*, 57: 43–61.

Warren, Mary Anne (1989) "The moral significance of birth," *Hypatia*, 4, 2 (Summer): 46–65.

Suggested activities

Questions for discussion

1 What are some of the most significant obstacles to women having control over the decision of whether or not to become mothers?
2 Is motherhood necessarily an oppressive institution? Discuss the reasons for your answer.
3 What are some of the commonalities and differences among women who mother? Among mothers and non-mothers?
4 Several factors we have examined suggest that the status of both women and families would improve dramatically if men were more involved with their families and with raising their children. What social changes would encourage men to become so involved?
5 According to Patricia Hill Collins, what is "motherwork?" How does it expose the limitations of feminist theorizing that assumes mothers are all white and middle class? Why are issues of survival, power, and identity central to the motherwork of women of color?
6 Do you agree with Thurer that motherhood and ambition are still largely viewed in opposition to one another? Do you think the two are compatible?
7 What is the "superwoman syndrome" as Thurer describes it? Is there a way that women can avoid getting caught in this double bind?
8 What do you think of Shirley Glubka's decision to give up her son rather than continuing to mother him? Should she be praised or criticized for her decision?
9 Should the practice of sex-selective abortion be legal in the US? Why or why not? If you think that other abortions should be legal, but not those performed for the reason of sex selection, how do you justify the disparity?
10 Can persons opposed to abortion be feminist? Why or why not?
11 Is there room for compromise between the pro-life and pro-choice positions on abortion, or is this an issue without possibility of amicable resolution?
12 One dimension of the abortion issue that Sherwin does not discuss in any detail is the impact of race and class differences on attitudes toward abortion. Given the other material we have read, what do you think some of these differences are?
13 According to Sherwin, what makes feminist arguments regarding abortion different from non-feminist ones? Do you find her position persuasive?
14 On balance, are the new reproductive technologies positive or negative developments in terms of the status of women? Does the existence of these technologies make motherhood more of a free choice or more of an expectation that *all* women become mothers?

15 In particular, is surrogate motherhood a positive institution for women? Are women who become surrogates necessarily exploited? Should the practice of surrogate motherhood be legal? Why or why not?

16 Should motherhood be defined primarily in terms of biological parenthood or in terms of mothering roles? What considerations are important to your view?

17 What are some of the most significant factors that contribute to teenage women having sex, getting pregnant, and becoming mothers? What role do media images of women and sex play?

18 Why does the US have the highest rate of teenage pregnancy among industrialized countries? What alternatives might provide young women with the ability either to resist becoming sexual while still adolescents or to prevent becoming pregnant if they are sexually active?

Films and videos

Access Denied, produced by Repro Vision, associated with WHAM, the Women's Health Action Mobilization (1991). VHS/color/28 mins. Distributed by Women Make Movies. Analyses the backlash against the abortion rights movement and civil rights.

Back Alley Detroit by Daniel Friedman and Sharon Grimberg (1992). VHS/47 mins. Available through Filmaker's Library. Historical documentary about illegal abortions as they were experienced by all kinds of women, and the physicians, clergy, and women's health activists who defied abortion prohibitions.

Black Mother, Black Daughter, produced by Shelagh MacKenzie and the National Film Board of Canada (1989). VHS/29 mins. Available from the National Film Board of Canada. About the history and life experiences of black women in Nova Scotia.

Casting the First Stone, produced and directed by Julie Gustafson (1991). VHS/ 58 mins. Available from First Run Icarus Films. About the pro-choice and pro-life activists involved in the abortion debate in a small town in Pennsylvania. Illustrates some of the differences in worldview and identity of pro-choice and pro-life activists.

Margaret Sanger: a Public Nuisance, directed by Terese Svoboda and Steve Bull (1992). VHS/color/28 mins. Distributed by Women Make Movies. A history of Sanger's use of the media to advance the cause of birth control.

Mommy Track, produced by ABC Nightline with Ted Koppel (1989). VHS/22 mins. Examines the controversy over whether professional and executive women should be placed on a slower advancement or "mommy" track when they have children, how businesses are adapting to the needs of working mothers, and how experts from women's groups and businesses address the issue.

Motherless: a Legacy of Loss from Illegal Abortions by Barbara Attie et al. (1992). VHS/30 mins. Available from Filmaker's Library. Explores the effects of fatalities from illegal abortions on surviving children. Chronicles the history of abortion in America.

Mother's Day: New Reproductive Technology by Jane Walmsley Productions. VHS/52 mins. Available from Filmaker's Library. Looks at the new reproductive technologies from the perspectives of satisfied donors and recipients.

On Becoming a Woman by Cheryl Chisholm (1987). 16 mm/VHS/color/90 mins. Distributed by Women Make Movies. Deals with health issues affecting African-American women, including teenage pregnancy and birth control. Produced before AIDS became a major health issue for women.

On the Eighth Day by Gwynne Basen (1992). VHS/2 videos, each 50 mins. Produced by the National Film Board of Canada. Available from Women Make Movies. Two-part film ("Making Babies" and "Making Perfect Babies") on the new reproductive technologies and the troubling questions about how they may impact on women's lives.

Single Mothers: Living on the Edge, produced by Insight Video (1989). VHS/29 mins. Available from Insight Video. Examines the pressures and obstacles faced by single women raising families, most of whom are living below the poverty line. Introduces a single white mother, a teenage black mother, and a Spanish-speaking Hispanic mother, each of whom tells her own story of trying to support her family.

Underexposed: the Temple of the Fetus by Kathy High (1992). VHS/72 mins. Available from Women Make Movies. Both drama and documentary on the business of high-tech baby-making. Tracks the history of the treatment of women's sexual and reproductive systems as "diseased," and the social and political context in which contemporary reproductive technologies exploit women's bodies.

What's the Common Ground on Abortion?, produced by William Shanley (1989). VHS/29 mins. Distributed by WNYC Productions. Places the current controversy on abortion in historical perspective, including changing conceptions of when life begins. Leading figures in the controversy debate their opposing viewpoints in a search for understanding.

When Abortion was Illegal, produced by KTEH-TV (1992). VHS/16 mm/28 mins. Distributed by Bullfrog Films, PO Box 149, Oley, PA 19547. Tells the story of the ordeals women underwent before abortion was legalized. Interviews women who had illegal abortions, their friends and family members, and doctors and health-care workers who attempted to save women after botched abortions.

With a Vengeance by Lori Hiris (1989). VHS/16 mm/40 mins. Available from Women Make Movies. History of the struggle for reproductive freedom since the 1960s in the context of the wider history of the women's movement. Archival footage and interviews with early abortion rights activists.

Women: the New Poor by Bea Milwe (1990). VHS/28 mins. Distributed by Women Make Movies. On divorced women and single mothers who lack skills and opportunities for economic self-sufficiency. Illustrates commonalities among poor women of different backgrounds and their attempts to defy the statistics of poverty.

Women of Substance by Rory Kennedy and Robin Smith (1994). 16 mm/VHS/color/55 mins. Distributed by Women Make Movies. An exploration of how women deal with overcoming addiction during pregnancy.

Other activities

1 Brainstorm a list of the ways in which women are stereotyped as mothers. Does the list reflect more positive or negative evaluations? How do stereotypes of women of color and women from different ethnic groups differ from those of Caucasian women?

2 Organize a skit, mock television talk show, or panel discussion on some aspect of the abortion debate for the class, presenting a number of different perspectives. Prepare for questions from the rest of the class on difficult aspects of the issue.

3 Write an essay describing the changing roles of mothers in the different generations within your own family: how has your own mother's life been different from those of your grandmothers? If you become a mother, how do you expect that your life will be different still? Do you think one of these types of mothering is preferable for women rather than the others? If so, why?

4 Read a novel about mothers and write a book review and a brief, five-minute presentation for the class about how this book represents women as mothers and their status and role in American culture.

5 In small groups or as a class, brainstorm a list of Hollywood films that portray women as mothers. Assess whether these women are positive role models, and the reasons for your views.

Bibliography

On mothers, mothering, and families

Adams, Alice (1995) "Maternal bonds: recent literature on mothering," *Signs: Journal of Women in Culture and Society*, 20(1): 414–27.

Alecson, Deborah (1995) *Lost Lullaby* (Berkeley, CA: University of California Press). Autobiographical account of a woman whose child is born severely damaged.

Alexander, Shoshona (1994) *In Praise of Single Parents: Mothers and Fathers Embracing the Challenge* (Boston: Houghton Mifflin).

Ames, Lynda J., with Ellsworth, Jeanne (1997) *Women Reformed, Women Empowered: Poor Mothers and the Endangered Promise of Head Start* (Philadelphia: Temple University Press).

Andrews, Lori (1992) "Surrogacy wars," *California Lawyer* (October), pp. 43–9.

Bartolet, Elizabeth (1993) *Family Bonds: Adoption and the Politics of Parenting* (Boston: Houghton Mifflin).

Bassin, Donna, Honey, Margaret and Kaplan, Meryle Mahrer (eds) (1995) *Representations of Motherhood* (New Haven, CT: Yale University Press). A collection of essays, many from psychoanalytic perspectives, on the importance of motherhood in women's development, the conflicting views about motherhood within feminism, mothers' ambivalent feelings about their children, the influence of reproductive technologies on the meaning of motherhood, and the specific experiences of non-white, non-middle-class mothers.

Bell-Scott, Patricia, et al. (eds) (1991) *Double Stitch: Black Women Write about Mothers and Daughters* (New York: HarperCollins). Collection of essays, short stories, poems, and studies on relationships between black mothers and daughters, and the commonality among black mothers that comes from having to raise their children in a racist and sexist society.

Blakely, Mary Kay (1994) *American Mom: Motherhood, Politics, and Humble Pie* (Chapel Hill, NC: Algonquin Books. On becoming an "outlaw mom" as a result of experiences with single parenting.

Burke, Phyllis (1993) *Family Values: Two Moms and their Son* (New York: Random House). Based on the author's own family experiences with lesbian parenting.

Burstein, Janet Handler (1996) *Writing Mothers, Writing Daughters: Tracing the Maternal in Stories by American Jewish Women* (Urbana, IL: University of Illinois Press). Discusses writers including Anzia Yezierska, Adrienne Rich, Erica Jong, and Vivian Gornick.

Chodorow, Nancy (1978) *The Reproduction of Mothering: Psychoanalytic Feminism and the Sociology of Gender* (Berkeley, CA: University of California Press).

Cohen, Cynthia B. (ed.) (1996) *New Ways of Making Babies: the Case of Egg Donation* (Bloomington, IN: Indiana University Press). Philosophical and ethical examination of the ramifications of modern fertility technology.

Cole, Johnnetta B. (ed.) (1986) *All American Women: Lines that Divide, Ties that Bind* (New York: Macmillan).

Collins, Patricia Hill (1991) "The meaning of motherhood in black culture," in Patricia Bell-Scott, et al. (eds), *Double Stitch: Black Women Write about Mothers and Daughters* (New York: HarperCollins). Much reprinted essay by a nationally recognized African-American feminist scholar and educator. Explores whether there is a distinctive Afrocentric ideology of motherhood; if so, what are its enduring themes, and what effect might it have on relationships between black mothers and daughters.

Daniels, Cynthia (1993) *At Women's Expense: State Power and the Politics of Fetal Rights* (Cambridge, MA: Harvard University Press). Argues that reproductive technologies are being used to control women through intervening in their pregnancies and regulating their pregnant bodies. "Fetal rights" are being used to treat pregnant women's bodies as public property and are jeopardizing women's fundamental rights of self-determination.

Davis, Angela (1986) "Racism, birth control, and reproductive rights," in Johnnetta Cole (ed.), *All American Women: Lines that Divide, Ties that Bind* (New York: The Free Press).

Dickerson, Bette (1995) *African American Single Mothers: Understanding their Lives and Families* (Thousand Oaks, CA: Sage).

Dill, Bonnie Thornton, *Our Mother's Grief: Racial Ethnic Women and the Maintenance of Families* (Memphis, TN: Center for Research on Women, Memphis State University). Explores how racial ethnic women's work in maintaining the family in the nineteenth century became a source of cultural resistance.

Dixon, Penelope (1984) *Mothers and Mothering: an Index to American Women* (Phoenix, AZ: Oryx Press).

Dolgin, Janet L. (1997) *Defining the Family: Law, Technology, and Reproduction in an Uneasy Age* (New York: New York University Press).

Dowd, Nancy E. (1997) *In Defense of Single-Parent Families* (New York: New York University Press). An examination of the controversy of single parenting, including single parenting as the result of choice and divorce.

Duden, Barbara (1993) *Disembodying Women: Perspectives on Pregnancy and the Unborn* (Cambridge, MA: Harvard University Press). Organized as a series of brief vignettes designed to illustrate that contemporary understandings about the fetus are a recent social construction.

Faludi, Susan (1991) *Backlash: the Undeclared War against American Women* (New York: Crown Publishers).

Farquhar, Dion (1996) *The Other Machine: Discourse and Reproductive Technologies* (New York: Routledge). Philosophical exploration of the potential of technology to change ideas of gender, parenthood and kinship.

Fineman, Martha Albertson (1991) *The Illusion of Equality: the Rhetoric and Reality of Divorce Reform* (Chicago: University of Chicago Press). Criticizes divorce reform efforts based on an equality model.

Fineman, Martha Albertson (1992) "The concept of the natural family and the limits of American family law," *International Review of Comparative Public Policy*, 4: 15–33. Argues that unmarried mothers in America are viewed as deviant merely because they are single women, not identified with a male. Describes the differences between the "public" or welfare family and the "private" or "natural" family, and the differences in legal regulation and state supervision and intervention that accompany them.

Fineman, Martha Albertson (1995) *The Neutered Mother, the Sexual Family, and Other Twentieth Century Tragedies* (New York: Routledge). A radical feminist proposal to eliminate the legal status of families and replace it with legal recognition of the mother/child dyad as a more appropriate unit of caretaking and caregiving in contemporary society.

Firestone, Shulamith (1970) *The Dialectic of Sex: the Case for Feminist Revolution* (New York: Bantam Books).

Fox, Bonnie (ed.) (1993) *Family Patterns, Gender Relations* (Ontario: Oxford University Press). Collection of essays examining the family throughout history, exploring the elements of the family, different opportunities for men and women within families, having and raising children, and problems in family life today.

Friday, Nancy (1987) *My Mother/Myself: the Daughter's Search for Identity* (New York: Dell).

Glenn, Evelyn Nakano, Chang, Grace, and Forcey, Linda Rennie (eds) (1994) *Mothering: Ideology, Experience, and Agency* (New York: Routledge). Essays take a social constructionist approach, challenging universalizing assumptions about mothering.

Gordon, Linda (1994) *Pitied but not Entitled: Single Mothers and the History of Welfare* (New York: The Free Press). Demonstrates that the worst problems with the current welfare system are at least partly the consequence of the activities of élite women activists during the New Deal era of the 1890s through the 1930s.

Harris, Kathleen Mullan (1997) *Teen Mothers and Revolving Welfare Door* (Philadelphia: Temple University Press). Exploration of the welfare system for working mothers and their careers.

Hays, Sharon (1996) *The Cultural Contradictions of Motherhood* (New Haven, CT: Yale University Press). Sociologist examines the contradictions between ideas about being a nurturing mother and being a successful career woman.

Hoffnung, Michelle (1989) "Motherhood: contemporary conflict for women," in Jo Freeman (ed.), *Women: a Feminist Perspective*, 4th edn (Mountain View, CA: Mayfield). Describes the negative impact of the ideology of motherhood on the ability of "real" mothers to live independently of those constraints, and the need to revalue motherhood to make it a more socially respected and valued activity.

Holmes, Helen Bequaert (1992) *Issues in Reproductive Technology: an Anthology* (New York: Garland). Collection of essays covering contraceptive choice, Norplant, contraceptive vaccines, male contraception, condoms, cervical caps, teenage pregnancy, abortion, cryopreservation of human embryos, IVF, and surrogacy.

Jackson, Marnie (1992) *The Mother Zone: Love, Sex, and Laundry in the Modern Family* (New York: Holt). About the author's own experiences with motherhood and family, and how motherhood is either ignored or sentimentalized, but not given access to money and power.

Kaplan, E. Anne (1992) *Motherhood and Representation: the Mother in Popular Culture and Melodrama* (London: Routledge). Analyzes the representation of mothers in psychoanalytic theory, literature, and Hollywood films from the 1920s through the 1980s. Shows how reproductive technologies, science, and consumerism are creating contesting and even contradictory discourses on the mother.

Kaplan, Meryle (1992) *Mother's Images of Motherhood: Case Studies of Twelve Mothers* (London: Routledge). Study of upper middle-class American mothers of toddlers, and the meaning they make of motherhood, by a developmental psychologist.

Lawson, Annette and Rhode, Deborah (eds) (1993) *The Politics of Pregnancy: Adolescent Sexuality and Public Policy* (New Haven, CT: Yale University Press). Fifteen essays exploring many aspects of the relationship between adolescent sexuality and public policy.

Leslie, Marsha (ed.) (1994) *The Single Mother's Companion: Essays and Stories by Women* (Seattle: The Seal Press).

Lewin, Ellen (1993) *Lesbian Mothers: Accounts of Gender in American Culture* (Ithaca, NY: Cornell University Press).

Lieberman, Jan, *Giving away Simone: a Memoir* (New York: Times Books). Autobiographical account by the daughter of a family in which three successive generations of women gave their child up for adoption.

Mattes, Jane (1994) *Single Mothers by Choice: a Guidebook for Single Women who are Considering or have Chosen Motherhood* (New York: Random House). Covers the decision-making process, alternatives for conception, adoption, pregnancy, birth and postpartum, preparing for "the Daddy" questions, special developmental issues, legal and moral aspects, and social life.

Mayerson, Charlotte (1996) *Goin' to the Chapel: Dreams of Love, Realities of Marriage* (New York: Basic Books). Conclusions from interviews with women from across the US comparing their married lives to their early dreams of the future.

Minow, Martha (ed.) (1993) *Family Matters: Readings on Family Lives and the Law* (New York: New Press). Collection of essays on a wide range of topics relating to family life, from "What is a family?" to "Violence in families."

Morell, Carolyn (1994) *Unwomanly Conduct: the Challenges of Intentional Childlessness* (New York: Routledge).

Moskowitz, Faye (ed.) (1994) *Her Face in the Mirror: Jewish Women on Mothers and Daughters* (Boston: Beacon Press). Collection of poetry and prose, fiction and non-fiction, most of it positively describing relationships between Jewish mothers and daughters.

Musick, Judith (1994) *Young, Poor, and Pregnant: the Psychology of Teenage Motherhood* (New Haven, CT: Yale University Press). An expert on adolescent pregnancy focuses on the social and economic roots of adolescent pregnancy, as well as the psychology of adolescent women who get pregnant. A thoughtful analysis of the pressures on poor adolescent females to become sexually active, pregnant, and mothers.

Nelson, Hilde Lindemann (1997) *Feminism and Families* (New York: Routledge). A volume of essays covering the social context of the meaning of "family" in US society.

Oakley, Ann (1980) *Becoming a Mother* (New York: Schocken Books). Study by a feminist sociologist of women having their first babies and adjusting to being mothers.

Oakley, Ann (1992) *Social Support and Motherhood: the Natural History of a Research Project* (Cambridge, MA: Blackwell).

Overall, Christine (1993) *Human Reproduction: Principles, Practices, Policies* (Toronto: Oxford University Press). Series of essays on various aspects of reproductive technologies from a feminist perspective.

Phoenix, Ann (1991) "Mothers under twenty: outsider and insider views," in Ann Phoenix, Anne Woollet and Eva Lloyd (eds), *Motherhood: Meanings, Practices, and Ideologies* (London, Sage). Other essays in the volume address commonalities and differences in motherhood for women.

Polakow, Valerie (1993) *Lives on the Edge: Single Mothers and their Children in the Other America* (Chicago, University of Chicago Press). Explores the differences in meanings of motherhood to the poor and affluent and the prevailing images of childhood, myths of motherhood and the family, and the place of private wealth and public responsibility.

Raymond, Janice (1993) *Women as Wombs: Reproductive Technologies and the Battle over Women's Freedom* (New York: HarperCollins). Takes a very negative perspective on the impact of reproductive technologies on the status of women as "publicly sanctioned violence against women defended in the name of women's right to choose." Concludes that *in vitro* fertilization, egg donation, sex predetermination, fetal reduction, fetal tissue research and transplantation, injectable and implantable contraceptive techniques, and surrogate motherhood all violate women's bodily integrity and should be abolished.

Reddy, Maureen, Roth, Martha, and Sheldon, Amy (eds) (1994) *Mother Journeys: Feminist Write about Mothering* (Minneapolis: Spinsters). Collection of essays, stories, poems, graphics, and autobiographical accounts that describe the daily details of mothering work.

Rich, Adrienne (1976) *Of Woman Born: Motherhood as Experience and Institution* (New York: Bantam). Prominent early second-wave feminist argues that the *institution* of motherhood works to ensure that women remain under male control, and has historically "ghettoized" and degraded female potential.

Richardson, Diane (1993) *Women, Motherhood, and Childrearing* (New York: St Martins Press). Looks at the relationship between women's identity and the capacity for motherhood. Examines the changing social conditions in which women become mothers (or not). Considers the impact of the new reproductive technologies, and feminism's response to motherhood.

Roberts, Tara (ed.) (1997) *Am I the Last Virgin? Ten African American Reflections on Sex and Love* (New York: Simon and Schuster).

Ross, Ellen (1989) *Recreating Motherhood: Ideology and Technology in a Patriarchal Society* (New York: W. W. Norton). Accessible and engaging description of motherhood and the impact of reproductive technologies.

Ross, Ellen (1995a) "New thoughts on 'the oldest vocation': mothers and motherhood in recent feminist scholarship," *Signs: Journal of Women in Culture and Society*, 20(1): 397–413.

Ross, Ellen (1995b) "The secret life of mothers," in *The Women's Review of Books*, 12(6): 6–7.

Ruddick, Sarah (1989) *Maternal Thinking: towards a Politics of Peace* (Boston: Beacon Press). Proposes that mothering work offers a distinctive way of thinking that can provide the framework for an alternative to war and armed violence.
Schwartz, Adria (1995) "Taking the nature out of mother," in Donna Basim, Margaret Honey and Meryle Mahrer Kaplan (eds), *Representations of Motherhood* (New Haven, CT: Yale University Press). Analyzes the impact of new reproductive technologies on conceptions of motherhood.
Simonds, Wendy and Rothman, Barbara Katz (1992) *Centuries of Solace: Expressions of Maternal Grief in Popular Literature* (Philadelphia: Temple University Press). Two sociologists explore the silence surrounding maternal grief over losing children, and attribute break in silence to women's increasing power in society and consequential greater public attention.
Slater, Suzanne (1994) *The Lesbian Family Life Cycle* (New York: The Free Press). By a psychologist about the wide spectrum of lesbian families.
Trebilcot, Joyce (ed.) (1983) *Mothering: Essays in Feminist Theory* (Totowa, NJ: Rowman and Allanheld). Influential anthology of essays by a number of prominent feminist theorists, organized under the headings "Who is to look after children?," "Mothering and the explanation of patriarchy," "Concepts of mothering," and "Pronatalism and resistance."
Van Gelder, Lindsey (1991) "A lesbian family revisited," *Ms.* (March/April), pp. 44–7. Interviews with members of a lesbian family.
Walker, Alice (1985) "In search of our mother's gardens," in Susan Gubar and Sandra Gilbert (eds), *The Norton Anthology of Literature by Women* (New York: W.W. Norton).
Walters, Suzanna Danuta (1992) *Lives Together/Worlds Apart: Mothers and Daughters in Popular Culture* (Berkeley, CA: University of California Press). Illustrates how the Hollywood culture industry from the 1930s through the 1980s operated to reinforce the view that it was necessary for daughters to become separate and independent from their mothers.
Wattleton, J. (1989) "Teenage pregnancy: the case for national action," *The Nation*.
Zinn, Maxine Baca (1991) "Families, feminism, and race in America," in Judith Lorber and Susan Farrell (eds), *The Social Construction of Gender* (Newbury Park, CA: Sage).

On alternatives to motherhood

Bartlett, Jane (1995) *Will You be Mother? Women who Choose to Say No* (New York: New York University Press). Explores the social pressures to have children, maternal instinct, the experience of being a mother, contraceptive choices and abortion, "child-free" women and their relationships, work and leisure styles, and infertility, based on interviews with over 50 women who *chose* not to have children.
Carmody, Denise Lardner (1986) *The Double Cross: Ordination, Abortion, and Catholic Feminism* (New York: Crossroad). A feminist pro-life perspective.
Colker, Ruth (1992) *Abortion and Dialogue: Pro-Choice, Pro-Life, and American Law* (Bloomington, IN: Indiana University Press). Feminist perspective on abortion, proposing that feminist lawyers adopt a more equality-based approach to abortion litigation.
Fried, Marlene Gerber (ed.) (1990) *From Abortion to Reproductive Freedom: Transforming a Movement* (Boston: South End Press). Collection of essays on various aspects of the abortion rights movement from scholars and practitioners.
Ginsburg, Faye (1989) *Contested Lives: the Abortion Debate in an American Community* (Berkeley, CA: University of California Press). An anthropological study of pro-life and pro-choice activists, in Fargo, North Dakota.

Glendon, Mary Ann (1987) *Abortion and Divorce in Western Law: American Failures, European Challenges* (Cambridge: Harvard University Press). Comparison of abortion rights in the US and a number of Western European nations, recommending that the US adopt a more European approach to abortion policy.

Gordon, Linda (1990) *Woman's Body, Woman's Right: a Social History of Birth Control in America*, rev. edn (New York: Penguin). Historical background on the struggle for women's reproductive rights.

Harrison, Beverly (1983) *Our Right to Choose: toward a New Ethic of Abortion* (Boston: Beacon Press). Essays on abortion by a pro-choice feminist Protestant minister and theologian.

Luker, Kristin (1984) *Abortion and the Politics of Motherhood* (Berkeley, CA: University of California Press).

McDonagh, Eileen L. (1996) *Breaking the Abortion Deadlock: from Choice to Consent* (New York: Oxford University Press).

Mills, Sarah (1989) "Abortion under siege," *Ms.* (July/August). An autobiographical account of a young woman's experience with pro-life protesters at an abortion clinic to undergo a medically necessary abortion.

Moskowitz, Ellen H. and Jennings, Bruce (eds) (1996) *Coerced Contraception? Moral and Policy Challenges of Long-acting Birth Control* (Washington, DC: Georgetown University Press). Essays by doctors, sociologists, and specialists in biomedical ethics.

Petchesky, Rosalind (1990) *Abortion and Woman's Choice: the State, Sexuality, and Reproductive Freedom* (Boston: Northeastern University Press). An excellent resource on the historical, legal, and ethical dimensions of abortion from a feminist perspective.

Reagan, Leslie J. (1997) *When Abortion was a Crime: Women, Medicine, and Law in the United States, 1867–1973* (Berkeley, CA: University of California Press). An analysis of the interaction between women seeking abortions, the medical community, and state agencies.

Tone, Andrea (ed.) (1997) *Controlling Reproduction: an American History* (Wilmington, DE: Scholarly Resources). Essays by historians; includes documents by Margaret Sanger, the AMA, Theodore Roosevelt.

Weddington, Sarah (1992) *A Question of Choice* (New York: Putnam). Autobiography of the attorney for "Jane Roe" in the Supreme Court *Roe* v. *Wade* case relates the events that led up to the Court's decision and provides an in-depth history of the ongoing abortion debate.

8

Sex, Sexism, Sexual Harassment, and Sexual Abuse

Introduction

In this chapter, we turn to one of the most difficult topics involving women in American culture: that of the sexualization of women and girls and the consequent sexual harassment and sexual abuse perpetrated against them. The four terms that frame the title of this chapter form a natural progression: because of sex (differences), sexism regards females as sex objects and as inferior to males. This inequality is frequently expressed through the medium of sexual harassment and, in more extreme forms, in the sexual abuse of women and girls. Women encounter sexism, sexual harassment, and abuse in all spheres of American culture, but especially at work and in school. Consequently, the focus of the following discussion will be on these two gender-defining institutions.

Sexism and sexual harassment of women in the fields of work and education are evident in popular culture as well as real life. Television shows and Hollywood films have included more women in working contexts and professional roles in recent years. The myth of the "stay-at-home mom" and the "breadwinner dad" have begun to break down in popular culture, although these myths outlive the reality of working women's lives. In its portrayal of sexual harassment, however, Hollywood turned reality on its head. Although most sexual harassment is committed by males against females, Hollywood prefers to portray the reverse. For example, in the movie *Disclosure*, the woman character played by Demi Moore is the sexual harasser of her male employee, played by Michael Douglas. This film underscores feminist critiques of Hollywood as producing "male fantasies" about the current status of gender relations.

Sex and sexism

The sexual revolution of the 1960s did not eliminate the double standards that allow (perhaps even compel) men to be openly and unabashedly sexual, while holding women to more restrictive standards. Women are required to keep their expressions of sexuality subtle and indirect in order to avoid being labeled "loose" or "promiscuous." At the same time, women who resist being defined as sex objects are ridiculed as "prudish" or "out of date." These cultural constructions of female sexuality (along with the fear or experience of sexual assault and rape) make it very difficult for some women to experience their sexuality as a positive and liberating aspect of their lives. In a classic article entitled "Uses of the erotic" (1978), Audre Lorde argues that sexuality can be used by women as a means to their own *power* and fulfillment, rather than their continued subservience to, and domination by, men. Her article illustrates the joy and pleasure that women can experience in relation to their sexuality, and how sexuality can be a source of liberation and not only constraint.

The sexual double standard for women is particularly difficult for younger women, especially adolescents. Some young men use "scoring" sex with women, along with other "sports," as a way of competing with other males. Adolescent females, especially those who are poor, of color, and living in urban areas, are often put under tremendous peer pressure to "give in" and become sexually active with males. A survey conducted by the Centers for Disease Control and Prevention in 1990 indicated that seven of every 10 high-school seniors and 54 percent of ninth through twelfth graders have had sexual relations at least once. Yet only one-third of sexually active youth uses contraceptives on any regular basis. One consequence of this sexual activity has been a 25 percent increase in the number of HIV and AIDS cases, and three million cases of sexually transmitted disease among teenagers.

The potential consequences of sexual activity – pregnancy and childbirth – profoundly alter women's lives, sometimes in negative ways. Having children is rewarding and fulfilling for many women, but for others it may severely limit their opportunities to find reasonable work or a career or other kinds of fulfillment. Although women are no longer compelled to have children because effective forms of birth control are unavailable or illegal, limited access to contraception severely curtails the opportunities of many women *not* to become mothers.

Research shows that teachers, most of them women, contribute to the lower achievement of girls. They encourage boys more in the classroom, call on them more often than girls, are twice as likely to have extended conversations with them, and tolerate more interruptions and unruly behavior from them (Bell, 1995; Sadker and Sadker, 1995). Boys are more likely to be given detailed instructions on how to perform tasks, whereas teachers are more likely simply to perform tasks *for* girls. In addition, girls are criticized more for inappropriate behavior, yet are given less specific and more generalized criticism in feedback on performance.

A report issued by the American Association of University Women (AAUW) in 1992 suggested that sexist bias in the classroom may be the worst form of discrimination girls encounter in their education. Girls are taught from their earliest years in school to accept gender discrimination and sexual intimidation. Although most girls begin school with the same aspirations, expectations, and enthusiasm as boys, by the end of high school most of this has disappeared. The result is that fewer girls than boys achieve their potential. In addition, females still receive fewer resources than males from educational institutions. The disparity has been most prominent with respect to funding for sports programs. Law-suits brought by female athletes in recent years against high schools and colleges for discriminatory treatment have made some progress in obtaining more access to sports funding for girls and women. However, many schools are still reluctant to reallocate funds away from male sports teams, which generally have a well-established reputation and consequently are able to generate revenue for their institutions (Lederman, 1993a, b).

Another significant area of sexism in education is the traditional exclusion of the *study of women* from the educational curriculum. Until the second wave of the women's movement, women's contributions to knowledge were barely recognized, with the rare exception for an "exceptional" woman like Marie Curie or Rachel Carson. Most biographers considered women's lives too insignificant to warrant writing about; women writers were rarely published, and when they were, seldom made it on to required reading lists of "great books."

Much has changed as a result of feminist efforts to reinscribe women into history. Women's studies programs now exist at over 600 institutions of higher education in the US, and many more offer courses on issues relating to women. None the less, women still have not received the credit they deserve in the educational arena. Perhaps part of this is because gender bias continues to operate in hiring and promotion in educational institutions, as in almost all other places of employment. Although a larger percentage of kindergarten and elementary school teachers are women than men, these numbers plummet in university and graduate schools. The numbers also reveal predictable, gender-stratified patterns. For example, the numbers of fully tenured women professors in the biological and life sciences and in mathematics are a tiny percentage of the total numbers of faculty in these departments, whereas the percentages are proportionately higher in the "softer" social sciences and the humanities.

Affirmative action for women has made a significant difference for white women, and a somewhat lesser one for African-American and other women of color. Affirmative action policies will probably continue to benefit women in education, even after other sectors of social life revert to gender-biased practices under the rationale of ending "reverse discrimination."

As in education, many women were denied access to paid labor throughout earlier decades of American history, sometimes by social convention and sometimes by legal restrictions. The assumption was that women's primary and proper roles were as housewives and stay-at-home mothers, not as paid laborers. The days when it was taken for granted that mothers did not work outside the home are long over. Many mothers are the only breadwinner in the family, especially in single-parent families. Statistics suggest that 80 percent of divorced mothers are working. Many times, even in two-parent households, however, the family depends on income from both parents. Even when women are fortunate enough to have obtained both adequate child care (if they have children) and an interesting profession, the battle is not always over. The efforts of O. J. Simpson prosecutor Marcia Clark's ex-husband to obtain temporary primary custody of their two kids – because Marcia wasn't home enough to be an appropriate parent – illustrates the ongoing struggle working mothers confront.

Clark's dilemma is not an isolated case. In several custody battles in recent years, courts have awarded physical custody to the father because of the mother's effort to improve her earning capacity through furthering her education or job training. In 1994, Jennifer Ireland lost custody of her 4-year-old daughter to her ex-boyfriend because she decided to return to college, and put her daughter in day care.

Sex-linked social roles have been fundamental historically in shaping gender: males are culturally conditioned to play active social and economic roles, have outside jobs and careers, and participate in government and public life. In contrast, females have been socialized to become primarily wives and mothers: the primary caretakers, not only of their children, but also of their husbands and aging parents. According to dominant cultural norms, the acceptability of women working (which basically referred to white, middle-class women) was restricted to situations of necessity.

These cultural expectations have changed in the past few decades. As more women work outside the home, stereotypical expectations about gendered social roles are breaking down. More and more women are seeking professional careers, work in traditionally male occupations, including those of public office. Employment opportunities for women in traditionally male-only occupations, such as politics, the sciences, business, construction and road maintenance, are slowly growing. Some men are taking on traditionally female tasks, such as child rearing and domestic duties, nursing, social work, and elementary education.

Women have made significant inroads into the world of work since the Second World War, when employers needed women to replace men who had gone off to war. This statement requires clarification in two important respects, however. First, it refers to *paid* work, since women have always been engaged in the unpaid labor of housework and child care. Secondly, it refers more directly to Euro-American than to African-American women, since the latter have always worked for wages in order to help support their families – out of financial necessity rather than the luxury of choice.

Until the second wave of the women's movement, however, there were few protections for women seeking to join men in the workforce: employers could refuse to hire women simply on the basis of gender; they could pay women less than men; and they could fire them for any reason, including pregnancy. Blatant employment discrimination has been illegal since the 1960s, when Congress passed Title VII of the Civil Rights Act of 1964. This legislation prohibits employers from discriminating on the basis of race and sex in hiring and firing, and in the terms of compensation. The Equal Pay Act of 1963 prohibits the paying of men and women different amounts for the same work.

However, a significant gendered wage gap remains. Women only earn around 70 cents to every dollar men earn. Black women fare even more poorly, earning only around 86 percent of white women's salaries. Part of the reason that women earn less than men is that most women work in traditional female occupations like secretarial, nursing, and teaching (and, more recently, entry level jobs in the fast food industry), occupations that traditionally pay less than men's jobs. Since the so-called "women's" occupations are typically less well paid than men's, this "pink-collar ghetto" contributes to women earning less than men. Male professions continue to have support staff who are predominantly female. Over 60 percent of women in the workforce are in such low-paying jobs.

Even for women in professions, gender discrimination operates to relegate many women into so-called "women's professions" like nursing, social work, elementary and secondary school teaching, and library work. Segregation even operates within professions. So, for example, many women physicians are in pediatrics, women lawyers are in probate, and women professors are in the humanities rather than the sciences. Further, professional women often encounter what has been called the "glass ceiling." This refers to the invisible, but impenetrable, barrier that prevents women from achieving the highest levels of their profession or occupation.

Women still comprise only a tiny percentage of top management at Fortune 500 companies (approximately 3 percent in 1995). There are a number of reasons for women's inability to break into the upper levels of management in companies. One is traditional discrimination against women, the lingering effect of "the Old Boys' network," which perpetuates the dominance of white male élites. Those in power often continue to hire "their own" rather than members of a different racial, ethnic, or gender group. Along with this goes women's traditional exclusion from the informal, but important, social organizations to which the Old Boys belong, such as country clubs and other private all-male institutions. Another is the prejudice against motherhood already discussed.

A "glass ceiling" also operates to discriminate against women with children. Stereotypes about new mothers being less committed to their work motivate some employers to attempt to terminate their employment or fail to promote them. Even if not explicit, this prejudice operates indirectly through government and employers' unwillingness to provide flexible work schedules or adequate child care. Employer or government-subsidized day care would go a long way toward enabling working mothers to improve their wage-earning capacity and career opportunities. And the proposed solution to the wage gap is to recognize that working mothers need to have more flexible schedules, more part-time and shared employment and a generally longer timeframe for accomplishment than either males or women without children. This idea of the "mommy track" is very controversial. Since "the mommy track" involves discriminating among employees on the basis of gender, there is some opposition to such schemes for working mothers. In addition to the problems that parents have in finding adequate child care, child-care workers, who are mostly women, are also exploited. They are one of the least well-paid groups of workers in the country. Those who are in the United States without legal documentation are especially vulnerable to exploitation and abuse. The child-care dilemma presents problems for all those involved.

By and large, traditional divisions of social roles by gender remain intact. Women in traditionally male occupations are still viewed as unusual, or even deviant. Most young adults in America continue to view men's occupations as more important than women's, and believe that when a conflict between work and family develops the woman should leave her job to take care of the family. Female adolescents in the US experience significant anxiety over potential conflicts between family and work, whereas males do not (see Denmark et al., 1993: 460). These attitudes mirror the reality that most men are not taking on a commensurate share of domestic responsibilities as women have entered the world of paid employment. Women continue to spend much more time in child care and household responsibilities than men do. This leaves most working wives and mothers with a "double shift" of having to perform most domestic duties in addition to a full day of performing paid work. Employers have contributed to this problem by failing to assist in coordinating work and family roles to make the division of paid and domestic labor more equitable.

As socialists and socialist feminists observed early on in the second wave of the women's movement, women's unpaid labor is indispensable to the functioning of society. And because women's labor is valued less than men's, women end up doing a disproportionate share of unpaid labor. This double burden keeps many working women from traditional male jobs that would pay more. Despite more and more women working in the paid labor force, many women are not engaged in work for wages. Some of these women are unemployed and unable to work. Some are single mothers on welfare who do not receive the social services that would enable them to work. A few are wealthy enough (or married to men who are) not to work. And some are new mothers on maternity leave.

When women become pregnant, employers are no longer legally allowed to fire them, as they once were. Instead, some employers are attempting to eliminate new moms by changing their schedules several weeks after they return from pregnancy leave in order to make it difficult for them to meet their family responsibilities, or transferring them to a dead-end position or failing to promote them to a once-promised higher position. Another strategy some employers have used to exclude women from higher-paying positions within their companies has been to implement "fetal protection policies." These typically bar females of child-bearing age from working in jobs that involve the risk of exposure to certain hazardous chemicals. Ostensibly designed to protect the health of women and any fetal life they may carry now or in the future, these policies frequently operate to exclude women from occupations involving significantly higher wages. Such policies have frequently been implemented without analogous measures being taken to insure that *males* of child-bearing age are similarly protected from the risk of exposure that could cause birth defects in *their* offspring. The double standard convinced the Supreme Court in the case of *U.A.W.* v. *Johnson Controls* in 1991 that a fetal protection policy violated women's rights to equal protection.

As in other areas of culture we have considered, women's experiences with sexism at work also vary in accordance with race and class differences, among others. Women of color are even more discriminated against in the workplace than white women. Immigrant women are generally able to obtain only the most minimal kinds of jobs as maids, house cleaners, and nannies. Women of color are often employed by more privileged working women, demonstrating the vast disparity that racial, ethnic, and class differences create among women in relation to work.

One final area of employment in which women encounter sexism and sexual harassment in high percentages is the sex industry in which women work as prostitutes, actresses in porn films or as models for pornographic magazines, photographs, and CD-Roms, as well as strippers, topless dancers in nightclubs, and as telephone sex-callers. Women working in such occupations have traditionally been condemned in mainstream culture. Yet their existence has always been tolerated, even promoted, by some quarters as a "necessity" for the excesses of male sexual desire. Prostitution, in particular, has been regarded with ambivalence. On the one hand, the services of prostitutes are welcomed, as the "Hollywood Madame" Heidi Fleiss's widely publicized arrest and trial, revealing her "blackbook" of famous male clients, suggests. At the same time, prostitution has traditionally been, and continues to be, illegal. Generally, it is the women performing the sex work, *not* the men who use their services, who are subject to arrest, detention, and fines. The denigrated and marginalized status of prostitutes in American culture graphically illustrates how patriarchal power is used to simultaneously exploit and condemn women.

However, feminists are divided over the issue of whether women working in the sex industry are universally exploited. In one view, women who work in the pornography industry are the helpless victims of a sexist and patriarchal society that exploits women for its own benefit. For some feminists, sex work is necessarily degrading and oppressive to women. They point out, for example, that many women working as pornography models or prostitutes were sexually abused as children (Itzin, 1992: 66).

In addition, many women working in the sex industry are economically and/or sexually and physically, abused. Linda Marciano, porn star of *Deep Throat*, discussed in Chapter 3, provides one example of such exploitation. In some countries, like Thailand, parents sell their daughters into prostitution because it is economically advantageous for them to do so. Opponents of women's involvement in sex work view it as a necessarily unequal practice defined by the intersection of capitalism and patriarchy, as involving an inherently unequal power relationship in which politically and economically privileged males sexually exploit relatively powerless and non-privileged females (see Overall, 1992). In this view, then, sex work is necessarily exploitative of women, and should be legally prohibited and morally condemned.

Another, more libertarian, perspective, places emphasis on the fact that *most* women have agency to freely *choose* whether or not to participate in sex work. Proponents of this view argue that working in the sex industry is *less* exploitative of women than many other jobs: it frequently pays higher wages, and allows women more control over the hours and conditions under which they work. Further, in this view, it is paternalistic and sexist to prevent women from using their bodies sexually to make money, especially when this is often the only avenue open to them to achieve a decent standard of living.

Sexual harassment

Even though sexual harassment has only been acknowledged as a significant problem in recent decades, it is one of the most serious obstacles confronting women in social institutions. It has been estimated that from 42 to 90 percent of women will be sexually harassed during their working lives (Hill, 1992). Women are vulnerable to being harassed at all levels of institutions, regardless of whether they are entry-level workers or executive officers, entering students or tenured professors.

Before laws and policies were enacted to redress sexual harassment, many women suffered in silence, unable to publicly discuss harassment without fear of being blamed for provoking it or, even worse, without risk of being fired or ostracized as a "whistle-blower." Women of color and working-class women led the fight against sexual harassment (Brownmiller and Alexander, 1992). The Senate hearings on Clarence Thomas's (ultimately successful) nomination for the Supreme Court in 1991, at which law professor Anita Hill testified that Thomas had sexually harassed her while he was her supervisor at the EEOC, did more than any other single event to bring the problem of sexual harassment to public consciousness, and to galvanize women to protest against sexual harassment in their own workplaces.

Sexual harassment involves the use of control by males to demean females. It generally involves unequal power relationships in which a male with authority or some other kind of power over a woman exploits that inequality to gain sexual favors. Sometimes the woman's job is at stake; sometimes it is a matter of a promotion, or a grade or recommendation. Regardless of the context, however, sexual harassment is now illegal. Laws prohibiting sexual harassment cover unwelcome or unwanted touching, advances, and/or sexually provocative comments, usually within formal institutions such as schools and workplaces. It generally involves an ongoing pattern or practice of conduct, rather than a single incident or isolated episode.

In the employment context, under guidelines issued by the EEOC pursuant to Title VII of the Civil Rights Act (which prohibits discrimination based on race and gender), sexual harassment encompasses three kinds of conduct: unwelcome sexual advances, requests for sexual favors, and verbal or physical conduct of a sexual nature. In a 1986 case, the Supreme Court ruled that sexual harassment is a form of gender discrimination under Title VII. *Quid pro quo* is sexual harassment that requires submission to sex as a term or condition of employment (for example, getting or keeping a job) or when submission to or rejection of such conduct is used as the basis for employment decisions. A *hostile work environment* occurs when the harassment has the purpose or effect of substantially interfering with an individual's work performance or creates an intimidating, hostile, or offensive working environment.

Congress vested the EEOC with formal authority to investigate claims of workplace sexual harassment under Title VII. Some employers have also established internal processes to investigate complaints, and attempt to resolve them so that more formal proceedings do not have to be instituted. Many employers have instituted sensitivity training programs about sexual harassment to help clarify the lines of appropriate and inappropriate behavior by all employees. None the less, a lack of clear boundaries in the law leaves much room for ambiguity.

In the educational arena, sexual harassment is defined by Title IX as the use of authority to emphasize the sexuality or sexual identity of students. However, women are not just harassed by teachers and others in positions of authority within educational institutions. Frequently, they are also harassed by their male classmates. The behavior of high school and college-aged males competing with one another for the highest number of sexual "scores" with women is a stark example of the sexual harassment of females by their peers. One study indicated that 90 percent of college-aged men would sexually harass if given an opportunity where they knew they would not be caught.

The impact of sexual harassment on the victim can be traumatic. Harassment may rattle a woman's self-esteem and adequacy, making her wonder whether she measures up to men's competence. It sometimes provokes feelings of guilt in women who believe they are responsible for provoking the harassment. It often causes the victims anxiety and tension and makes work an unpleasant environment. Harassment may even cause serious psychological or physical health problems for its victims.

Sexual harassment is a particularly vexed offense because its existence is dependent in part on the *subjective* response of the person to whom the conduct is directed. What is *unwanted* and *offensive* varies with the individual. However, the law requires consistency and generalizable rules. Most courts determine whether sexual harassment occurred in accordance with whether a *reasonable person* would be offended by the particular conduct in question. On the assumption that women in general respond to sexual advances differently from men, some courts have adopted a "reasonable woman" standard rather than a "reasonable person" standard to assess whether the conduct in question was offensive.

The existence of laws making sexual harassment formally illegal does not mean that the problem has been resolved, however. There have been a number of problems in attempting to change practices in male-dominated schools and workplaces that have always viewed sexual harassment as acceptable. Many women continue to be afraid to speak out when they have been sexually harassed, fearing that they will not be believed, or that they will be fired, or that their co-workers will refuse to support them or even turn against them. Some women continue to take a "victim-blaming" attitude, believing that they were responsible for provoking the harassing conduct. Even where there are remedies formally available, many employers do not take them seriously.

Even agencies within the federal government, the military in particular, have engaged in foot-dragging rather than responding in a timely manner to allegations of sexual harassment. The Tailhook scandal, involving severe sexual harassment of females by male naval personnel during a naval convention, is an obvious illustration of obstreperous behavior by employees. In order to obtain redress, women have to be prepared for protracted legal battles. Anita Hill has argued that laws are not enough to address sexual harassment: it is also necessary to change attitudes.

Sexual harassment and abuse of women are also serious problems in religious institutions. The problems may be even *more severe* within religious institutions than in many others because the (usually) male religious or spiritual leader carries the mantle of *spiritual* knowledge and behavior in addition to the usual disparity of power and authority that exists between perpetrator and victim. The expectation that spiritual leaders will behave ethically encourages others to have faith and trust in them, and consequently serves to enhance their power and authority. It also increases their opportunities to betray that trust.

Sexual abuse by male spiritual leaders is a problem that transcends doctrinal and affiliational lines; it has been found in all religious traditions and denominations. (Males have not been spared this kind of sexual abuse; in recent years, a number of men abused as boys, especially by Catholic priests, have brought charges against their perpetrators, sometimes decades after the incidents were alleged to have occurred). Victims usually have had a very difficult time in speaking out about the abuse. Frequently, their stories are not believed – after all, who *could* believe that a trusted spiritual adviser would be capable of exploiting his position to obtain sexual favors?

Even when the victim is believed, the religious institution involved has often been reluctant to take responsibility and sanction the perpetrator appropriately (Bonavoglia, 1992; Sheler, 1992). In several cases, the religious organization has attempted to cover up the incident, paying the victim to keep her silence, denying the incident completely, or transferring the perpetrator to a different parish or congregation far from the scene of the alleged abuse (Bonavoglia, 1992). These difficulties are ongoing problems that women associated with religious institutions must confront.

The reading by Miranda Van Gelder is a humorous look at sexual harassment in high school. Van Gelder's experiences with a high-school teacher's inappropriate remarks and suggestions are repeated in high schools, colleges, universities, and graduate schools throughout the country. The problem has recently received a good deal of attention in the context of colleges and universities establishing or revising policies regarding student/teacher relationships, especially at Oberlin College. On one side of the issue, more libertarian proponents argue that it is paternalistic and unduly restrictive of rights to free association to restrict students (more frequently female) and professors (usually male) from developing consensual intimate relationships. At least by college age, it is argued, students have the maturity of judgment and discretion to make appropriate decisions concerning who they get romantically and/or sexually involved with.

On the other side of the issue, those concerned about the inequalities of gender and authority that are frequently involved in student/teacher relationships argue that the disparity in power between the parties precludes the possibility of a truly consensual relationship. The teacher will almost always have more authority, because of his (usually) institutional position, gender, and age, which places the student in a vulnerable position, regardless of how mature the student is, or how mutual the relationship appears to be.

Sexual abuse and violence against women

The National Crime Victimization Survey published in 1994 shows that *more than two and a half million American women experience violence each year,* and about one-third of them are injured as a result. Women are as likely to experience violence by a spouse or partner as by a stranger: almost two-thirds of victims of violence know their attacker. Women who were the most vulnerable to becoming the victims of crime were black, Hispanic, young, never married, with lower family incomes and education levels, and from urban areas (Bachman, 1994).

Violence functions as a form of social control. Violence against women is built into the very fabric of American culture. As we have seen in previous chapters, women are stereotyped (and expected) to be weak, emotional, passive and submissive, while men are stereotyped (and expected) to be strong, emotionless, powerful, dominating, and controlling. These stereotypes align women with pacifism and men with the use of force. They contribute to a climate in which violence against women is accepted as ordinary, not exceptional and outrageous. In addition, women are frequently portrayed as victims of physical and sexual assault in the mass media. As we saw earlier, many of Hollywood's most popular images are filled with violence against women, as well as heavy metal and rap music, television police shows and "action" films. In addition, popular culture frequently links sex and violence, furthering the identification of women with violence, as in advertising, soap operas and romance novels, as well as hard-core pornography.

In this section, we will focus on three of the most prevalent forms of such violence and abuse: rape and other forms of sexual assault, domestic violence (also called "spousal abuse" and "wife abuse") and childhood sexual abuse. All three of these forms of abuse of women have gained significant public attention only in the past two decades. Before that, there was an atmosphere of silence that inhibited women from speaking out and retaliating against their abusers. The law largely ignored violence against women, especially that involving family members, on the rationale (explicit or implicit) that since it was taking place in the "domestic" sphere, it was protected by rights of privacy beyond the reach of state regulation.

The women's movement has largely been responsible for publicizing these forms of sexual and physical abuse of women, and for questioning the boundaries between public and private that rationalized the failure of government to intervene to protect victims. In addition, it should be given most credit for lobbying effectively for new and modified legislation to punish the perpetrators and provide some measure of protection for the victims.

One of the most significant advances for the status of women has been success in breaking the silence surrounding physical and sexual abuse. The ability to speak out has enabled women to hear that these forms of abuse *are not their fault* and that they are not alone. Although legal measures have made a significant difference in addressing violence against women, they have not yet had the impact on society and culture required to fully address the problems. In part, this is because eliminating the abuse of women requires changing cultural attitudes that condone and tolerate such abuse, attitudes that are deeply ingrained in Western cultural practices.

Violence against women does not only result in crimes being committed *against* women; it also contributes to crimes committed *by* women. The Bureau of Justice statistics on women in prison for 1991 reports that "before entering prison a large percentage of the women had experienced physical or sexual abuse." More than four out of 10 women stated that they were abused at least once before being admitted to prison. About 34 percent reported being physically abused, and 34 percent reported sexual abuse. About 32 percent said the abuse had occurred before the age of 18 (Snell, 1991: 1, 5). These statistics illustrate how violence breeds violence, and that women are capable of inflicting violence as well as being its recipients.

Rape and sexual abuse

The federal government defines rape as "forced sexual intercourse" which "includes both psychological coercion as well as physical force" (Bachman, 1994: 14). In *Rape and Representation* (Higgins and Silver, 1991), a collection of essays on how rape is depicted in literary works, the editors explain that rape and rapability are central to the very construction of gender identity. Catharine MacKinnon has often made this point in her writing as well: that women are defined as being rapable. While many would find these formulations extreme, the possibility of being raped is certainly *one* of the defining characteristics of being a woman in our culture. It is widely accepted in American culture that it is far less safe for a woman than a man to walk alone late at night because of the far greater risk that she will be raped.

Some men (especially gay men) are raped or battered, but the vast majority of rapes are committed by men against women. In fact, statistics suggest that half of the women in America will confront a potential rapist at some point in their lives. One half of these women will successfully ward off the potential attacker; the other half will be raped or sexually assaulted.

Among the most conservative of studies, the National Victim Center estimates that one in eight women will be raped. Data collected by the National Crime Victimization Survey from 1987 to 1991 show that almost 133,000 women are victims of rape or attempted rape each year. More than half (56 percent) of these crimes were committed by someone known to the victim. Although most literature and publicity is about perpetrators unknown to the victims (*stranger rapes*), in actuality, a far greater number of rapes are committed by persons known to the victim, either slightly (*acquaintance* or *date rape*), or intimately, involving spouses or partners (*marital rape*). Although date rape is the most common form of sexual assault, the law helps to perpetuate a distorted focus on stranger rapes. In a number of states, for example, marital rape is still not illegal.

First of all, the large majority of rapes are never even reported. A number of factors contribute to the unwillingness of victims to step forward. Many feel ashamed – as if they are somehow responsible for the rape. Others fear the stigma for their friends and family if they admit that they were sexually assaulted. Many victims (justifiably) do not want to deal with the police and the rest of the criminal justice system, which is necessary in order to prosecute the rape. Their reluctance is well founded, since many rape victims still report that police treat them with callous disregard or disbelief, or trivialize their experience. Acquaintance and marital rapes are more difficult for the law to deal with, in part because they are more difficult to prove since the possibility of consent is greater than in stranger rape.

Understanding violence against women is made more complex by differences among women. For example, the myth that black men were a constant threat to the sexual purity of white women was used in earlier decades of the twentieth century as a pretense for lynching black men. The myth has made some black women reluctant to endorse the anti-rape campaigns of the mainstream women's movement, even though a higher percentage of women of color are victims of sexual violence than white women.

The reading by Carol Bohmer and Andrea Parrot addresses the issue of sexual assault in the specific context of college campuses. They discuss some of the psychological factors on both sides that contribute to the sexual assault of college women by college men. Many law reforms have taken place in recent years that are designed to make it easier for victims to come forward and report their rapes without becoming victims of the criminal justice system that was supposedly there to assist them, and to improve the procedures for the prosecution and conviction of rapists. For example, in 1992, Congress passed the Campus Sexual Assault Victim's Bill of Rights. This bill is designed to ensure that campus authorities treat sexual assault victims with respect, clearly explain their legal rights and options, and fully cooperate with victims in the exercise of these rights. These rights include according the victim the same representation and right for others to be present in campus proceedings as the accused is given. In addition, the Student Right-to-Know and Campus Security Act requires that institutions of higher education report the number of on-campus crimes, and publish safety-related policies and procedures.

Despite such changes in the formal legal system to prevent "she asked for it" justifications, women frequently continue to be blamed for rapes, either directly or indirectly. In recent high-profile rape cases, such as those involving William Kennedy Smith and Mike Tyson, the victim's credibility was impugned, while the long-term impact on their perpetrators appears to be insignificant.

Domestic violence

The issue of domestic violence received unprecedented coverage in popular culture as a result of the O. J. Simpson trial. Although the jury acquitted the famous football star and media celebrity of brutally murdering his estranged wife Nicole Brown and her friend Ronald Goldman, the media attention given to Simpson's repeated incidents of physical abuse of his wife during their marriage made domestic violence a household topic for the first time in American history.

Domestic violence or battering is defined as "a crime of power and control committed mainly by men against women, a crime in which the perpetrator does not consult the victim's wishes and from which he will not let her escape" (Jones, 1994: 126). In a small percentage of cases, women are physically abusive to their husbands and male partners. However, statistics suggest that women are *eleven times* more often victims than they are perpetrators of physical abuse.

Lesbian abuse also comprises a small percentage of physically abusive relationships, although it is far less than the often-publicized "one-third" figure of married relationships that involve the physical abuse of wives. Spousal or wife abuse appears to be one of the "universals" of women's experience around the globe. In 1989, the United Nations Centre for Social Development and Humanitarian Affairs recognized: "In all countries and cultures, women have frequently been the victims of abuse by their intimates. They have been battered, sexually abused and psychologically injured by persons with whom they should share the closest trust. This maltreatment has gone largely unpunished, unremarked, and has even been tacitly, if not explicitly condoned" (United Nations, 1989: 11; see also Adler, 1993: x).

Domestic violence is a serious problem in American culture as well. In 1992, the Surgeon General of the US named the physical abuse of women by their husbands or partners as the leading cause of injuries to women aged 15 to 44. In the same year, the American Medical Association declared domestic violence to be an "epidemic." Here are a few statistics. Domestic violence is the leading cause of injury to women in the US. Estimates of the numbers of women who have been physically assaulted by their husbands or lovers are at least four million a year, and potentially as high as *one-half*. It is estimated that a man beats a woman in the US every 9 seconds. About 1400 women are killed by their husbands, ex-husbands, and boyfriends each year, averaging one death every six hours. In Massachusetts, a woman is killed by her husband or boyfriend every nine days (Jones, 1994: 7). More than half of the women assaulted are injured, and at least 25 percent of these seek medical treatment. Between 10 and 33 percent of the injured women who visit hospital emergency rooms, and as many as 25 percent seeking prenatal care, have been abused by their husband or partner. In general, pregnant women are between one-in-six and one-in-four times more susceptible to being abused. One in five women who visits an emergency room does so because of "ongoing abuse."

Battering has other consequences besides physical harm to the women involved. Battering accounts for half of all cases of alcoholism in women. It accounts for half of all rapes of women over the age of 30. Battering is a cause of one-quarter of suicide attempts by all women, and one-half of suicide attempts by black women (Jones, 1994: 145). It also contributes to psychological problems of the victims as well as the children who witness the abuse.

In an earlier era, experts said that battered wives had "asked for it." Although that is no longer true, many people in Western culture are still willing to turn a blind eye to domestic violence, using the sphere of privacy surrounding the home and family as an excuse not to inquire further into suspected cases of abuse. Many still believe that battered women are somehow "different" from other women. Some researchers, for example, claim that women who are less educated, unemployed, young, and poor are more vulnerable to being abused than other women.

While studies show that pregnant women are more susceptible to being abused, in general women who are abused are no different from other women. Battery transcends class, race, educational, religious, age, and all other categories of distinction. Similarly, the men who are abusers do not fall into any particular category or type. However, those who lack higher education or good jobs are somewhat more likely to be abusive, and those who grew up in homes where abuse was present are *much* more likely to be abusive themselves.

More women are fighting back – and ending up in jail. The statistics on women in prison cited earlier also show that "women in prison for homicide were almost twice as likely to have killed an intimate (husband, ex-husband, or boyfriend) as a relative like a parent or sibling" (Snell, 1991: 3). In the past decade, feminist attorneys have also turned their attention to the issue of battered women who kill. Part of the law reform efforts in relation to domestic violence have involved changing the legal standard under which it is considered to be reasonable for a battered woman to kill her abuser. They have attempted to reform the law so that courts will allow battered women accused of killing their husbands the opportunity to show that their sentence should be mitigated. These attorneys argue that battered women who operate under *battered women's syndrome*, defined as a debilitated condition brought about through years of being abused, should have lesser convictions. They argue that what is reasonable for a woman who has been subjected to years of violence and physical and psychological abuse is different from what is reasonable for a person who has not been subject to such abuse.

The reading by Martha R. Mahoney describes how the law views battered women. She shows how cultural assumptions about battered women and domestic violence influence how women are treated by the law, how this in turn influences cultural assumptions, and how both ignore or distort the realities of women's lives. Mahoney draws on the stories and poems of survivors of domestic abuse to refute popular cultural conceptions of battered women. By treating domestic violence as exceptional, both culture and the law promote the impression that it is a rare occurrence, rather than the everyday one that statistics reveal.

Viewing violence as exceptional also discourages others from being able to identify with its victims, or to see the connections to domestic violence in their own lives or the lives of those they know. In addition, as Ann Jones observes in her book *Next Time She'll Be Dead: Battering and How to Stop It*, the unwillingness to identify with battered women is in part a self-protective move that denies that a similar fate could confront us (Jones, 1994: 195). According to Jones, "today most people recognize that women have a right – even a responsibility – to leave abusive men, but we don't yet recognize our responsibility as a society to help: our duty as a society to protect the right of every woman to be free from bodily harm" (Jones, 1994: 201). Mahoney urges that meaningful change will require focusing on the issues of power and control that underlie domestic violence.

Mahoney's article is part of a growing body of literature on battered women that recognizes how society continues to blame battered women for their abuse, even though it has shifted its message from telling a woman that she should stay with the batterer to insisting that she leave. This sets up a double bind for women because society frequently fails to provide the necessary social services that would make it both *safe* and feasible for battered women to leave. Jones explains that some battered women may not want their husbands arrested, since they are unable to contribute financially to the family if they are in jail. Courts, however, are unable to understand such complexity of desires, which cannot be translated into simple black and white, good guy versus bad guy scenarios (Jones, 1994: 25).

There are more serious inadequacies with the criminal justice system as it relates to domestic violence as well. For example, the males who dominate the justice system tend to identify with the male batterers' point of view more easily than with that of the women. This bias is reflected in statistics indicating that abusive men who kill their partners serve prison terms averaging two to six years, whereas women who kill their partners, usually in self-defense, serve an average of 15 years! In addition, the different branches of the justice system blame the victim, as well as one another, rather than adopting procedures that would improve the system for battered women (Jones, 1994: 145).

These problems with the way in which the criminal justice system operates means that even where there are adequate laws on the books to protect women against domestic violence, those who administer the laws are often ill equipped to deliver justice. In addition, the lack of adequate resources also contributes to the perpetuation of the problem of domestic violence. Women need a safe place to go when they are abused, and the existing system of shelters is inadequate to meet the demand. Cutbacks in welfare spending by federal and state government limit the financial ability of many women to leave their abusers, as well as the ability of battered women's shelters, and other organizations serving victims of domestic violence, to continue to serve their clients. These stark realities are perhaps the most graphic illustrations of women's oppression in American culture.

Child sexual abuse

Most of the victims of childhood sexual abuse, including incest, are girls. Most perpetrators are males, either grown men or boys. Like rape and domestic violence, then, the sexual abuse of children also involves issues of gendered power and control. And, like the other issues addressed in this chapter, Western culture has ignored and suppressed the problem of the sexual abuse of children until the past couple of decades. Where the subject was not ignored totally, there was a tendency to blame the victim. Popular culture still reinforces this tendency, as illustrated in images of pre-pubescent and adolescent girls coming on to grown men in movies such as *Pretty Baby* (starring Brooke Shields as a child prostitute) and Nabokov's popular novel *Lolita* (about a pubescent girl successfully seducing a grown man). More recently, the press played up the similarities to *Lolita* in the case involving Amy Fisher's shooting of Mary Jo Buttafuco (allegedly at the direction of her boyfriend and Mary Jo's husband Joey Buttafuco) by naming Fisher "the Long Island Lolita." Such images reinforce the tendency of culture to attribute blame for sexual contact between adult males and non-adult females to the latter.

Since the silence surrounding childhood sexual abuse has been lifted (at least to some extent) in the past two decades, thousands of women who had previously been silenced have come forward to tell how they were abused, and often to name their abusers. This has included such well-known personalities as Oprah Winfrey and Roseanne. The issue has also been the subject of significant media coverage, including talk shows as well as journalistic accounts in both television and print media. Although this proliferation of coverage carries a danger of trivializing childhood sexual abuse, it also signifies that necessary attention is finally being given to addressing the problem.

The legal system has responded as well, albeit slowly. In 1974, Congress passed the Child Abuse Prevention and Treatment Act. To qualify for funding, states needed to require mandatory reporting of suspected or documented child abuse by personnel in agencies that deal with children, such as teachers, nurses, and doctors. (None the less, only about two-thirds of the children at risk receive the necessary resources.)

In recent years, many states have made it easier for victims to bring charges against their abusers, even years after the fact. Because sexual abuse is so traumatic, memories of the experience are often repressed for years, only to emerge in adulthood once some trigger, such as sexual activity, causes deeply buried memories to surface to consciousness. In recognition of the possibility of suppressed memories, several states have made it possible for victims to bring charges against their abusers many years after the original events.

More recently, there has been a movement oriented toward discrediting the stories of childhood sexual abuse. Frequently, the tool used to discredit the defendant's testimony is so-called *false memory syndrome*. According to proponents of this theory, most allegations of child sexual abuse are fabricated, though not necessarily deliberately (at least by the victim). Certainly, some alleged victims, under the sway of the power of suggestion by therapists and others, have made false allegations of sexual abuse. But, in many cases, the abuse is real, and false memory syndrome is suggested by the defense only as a ploy to discredit the witnesses' stories.

Insufficient attention has been paid to the particular harms that incest and childhood sexual abuse cause to black girls and women. Only a small fragment of the literature on this topic is addressed specifically to black women's experience, or to how the legacy of slavery, racism, sexism, and classism combined are used by men to deter black women from speaking out on this form of violence against them. Racism compounds the sexist tendency to ignore this crime. As Evelyn Barbee (1994: 30) notes, "Black women's marginalization in white societies magnifies the isolation and pain that are the legacies of incest and child sexual abuse."

The reading by Ellen Bass explores some of the factors that contribute to child sexual abuse, why many children do not resist, and how society helps to perpetuate such abuse by devaluing women and girls, especially through the cultural institutions of religion, mass media, and jokes about sex.

High School Lowdown
Miranda J. Van Gelder

A swaggering, slovenly, self-centered scumbag who we'll call Mr Lecherman was one of my history teachers. He was an annoying jerk any way you looked at him, always being astounded by his own pearls of wisdom, basking in the belief that he was God's gift to teaching, mentioning his

This reading first appeared in *Ms.*, March–April 1992, pp. 94–5.

girlfriend at relevant moments when we were discussing, say, the French Revolution. But I could handle all that. What made me want to puke in his lap was one particular habit – he called all the girls in my class "Beautiful," "Adorable," "Gorgeous."

I finally confronted him after class one day and asked if it was really too much to drop all the honey-cookie-pieface-lambchop stuff, adding that I considered it sexist and demeaning. Mr Lecherman's eyes nearly popped out of his head. When I pointed out that none of the guys in my class were "Hot Harold" or "Studmuffin Stan," he whined, "But I'm not interested in guys!" (And *I'm* not interested in 50-year-old history teachers.)

O.K., it's quiz time. The above scenario took place in: (a) the Stone Age, (b) the Dark Ages, (c) 1955, (d) 1990.

If you chose answer (d) you're absolutely right. If you answered (a), (b), or (c), you're close enough. Anyway, the next day, Mr Lecherman announced to the kids in my class that I thought he was "a sexist" because he didn't think guys were pretty. AARRGGHH!

All this time later (I'm 18 and a senior now), I still have fantasies about bashing Mr Lecherman's head in with a copy of *Sisterhood is Powerful*. I've always considered myself a pacifist, but the guys I'm up against could switch even the most diligent Quaker into Rambo mode. One teacher drooled all over my friend, "I'll give you a [grade] 96 if you give me a 69."

What makes these comments even more shocking is that they're not being made in a dopey cheerleading/rah-rah type school in one of those scary places where some folks are convinced that if the ERA were ratified women and men would have to share bathrooms. No – I have the pleasure of dealing with Who's Who of Certified Satyrs at a high school in New York City. This particular school is a prestigious bastion of learning that pats itself on the back every few weeks for having another one of its alumni win the Nobel Peace prize or something; this is high school that champions itself for having a student body made up of every possible racial/religious/socioeconomic background you could possibly dream up; this is a school most people consider one of the few good urban public high schools in the country. Yet sexism is a serious problem here.

If you're not convinced, how about the time:

- A student was constructing a sine curve at the blackboard and her teacher snickered, "Hey, everyone, doesn't Barbie have nice curves?"
- A history teacher announced that if the girls had a lower combined average on the history exam than the boys, they had to bake cakes for the guys, whereas in the reverse, the boys would have to buy something of the Sara Lee variety.

- The same history teacher informed one male student that the only way he could get out of doing an assignment was to convince a specific young woman in the class to stand up and denounce women's liberation.
- Another teacher apparently thought it was appropriate to say to a young woman wearing a skirt, "Why don't you lift that up for me?"
- An English teacher stated, "Only boys and intelligent girls will enjoy this book."
- Another cool guy asked, "You don't have the homework ready? Oh, that's right – you girls do dishes every night." (To which a friend of mine quipped, "No, I was watching Monday Night Football.")

Not to mention countless other honeybunch/come sit on my lap/pats on the shoulder that were a little too friendly/good old acceptable sexist comments disguised as "all in good fun!" or "Hey, I was only kidding; can't you take a joke?" Ha.

I've always resented the fact that whenever I assert myself as a feminist some moron thinks my ambitions in life entail breaking the kneecaps of any guy who tries to open a door for me. I'm not a raving activist; I am hardly out to kill anyone who calls me a "girl" instead of a "young woman" (I'd just hurt him a little). But there are certain struggles I always figured had been overcome long ago, and this high school is proof that I was living in fantasy land. Now, I'd like to make it *absolutely clear* that I don't think every teacher at this high school is a deranged psycho rapist. I have met some excellent, entirely professional teachers, including one English instructor who very coolly blamed Macbeth, not his wife, for his shady actions. And my biology teacher is living evidence of the adeptness of females in the sciences.

But too often I've felt like a second-rate student, expected to cater to every grungy Mr Wonderstud whose class I happened to be in, and be a vapid, chipper, Doris-Day-goes-to-high-school bimbo. My middle years were a catastrophe. Was I overreacting? Were my teachers really as gross as they seemed? My grades plummeted. I developed a surly attitude and decided that school sucked.

Fortunately, there are other female students who are equally repulsed (and even a small number of O.K. guys who support us) but, sadly, the majority aren't. One young woman in my history class came to Mr Lecherman's defense and claimed that he was complimenting us. Oooookay, sister: (a) Do you always feel flattered when men who are old enough to be your grandfather call you "gorgeous"? (b) Can you tell me what being "adorable" has to do with the Battle of Hastings? (c) Do you really want to be considered beautiful by a man whose idea of snazzy taste consists of brown polyblend slacks and a tie that resembles a Lava lamp?

Another girl told me, "People tell me to forget it – that it's just high school and that I shouldn't feel bothered. But what about later on? Will people say, 'Oh, it's just the office, don't get so upset'?" Or just the Supreme Court?

One strategy I use is to point out that the same comments aimed at any "minority" group wouldn't be tolerated. Miserably, this doesn't work, since some of these slobs don't see *that* as wrong *either*. A science teacher once got the class to predict that a particular liquid in an experiment was going to turn yellow by asking us to guess the "favorite color" of Tonya, Kate, and Marvin – all of whom just happened to be Asian-Americans. My history teacher would explain the defeat of the Spanish Armada in an offensive Speedy Gonzalez-type accent and always accompanied Asian history with kung fu gestures and shouts of "HaaaayAH!" Not to mention the substitute teacher who made bathroom passes out to "faggots" and "butch dykes" – for "laughs."

I wish I could say that the students at my school are outraged, but the truth is too many don't notice (scary), or do notice but choose not to say anything (scarier). Guys have told me I'm lucky to be a girl in my school (don't ask me what drugs they're on) because all this attention means male teachers like us more and give us higher grades. O.K., I'll admit it's happened, but give me the professional over the pervert any day and I'll prove myself on my own merit – thank you very much.

I've always envisioned machismo maniacs dying from testosterone globs clogging their brains. But it hasn't happened yet, and the comments continue.

"We've come a long way, baby"? Have we even reached the starting point, Hot Stuff?

Scope of the Problem
Carol Bohmer and Andrea Parrot

Most people, including those who have experienced it, have trouble understanding sexual assault. This is especially true if the victim and assailant are acquainted, are friends, or are dating. Many of the common questions about sexual assault on a college campus will be addressed in this chapter.

This reading first appeared in *Sexual Assault on Campus: the Problem and the Solution* (New York: Lexington Books, 1993).

Who are the victims of campus sexual assault?

The case that follows includes many of the elements common to cases of sexual assault on campus. In this case the victim did report the sexual assault to the campus authorities, but she was manipulated into not pursuing legal or judicial authorities.

> Ellen, a first-year student, went to several parties the first Saturday of the fall semester. She had a lot to drink over the course of the evening. She was then taken by one of the men she had met at one of the parties to his residence hall, where there was a toga party under way. They both dressed in sheets and drank more alcohol at the residence hall party. Ellen passed out, and when she gained consciousness, she discovered his penis in her mouth.

Ellen was a typical victim of campus sexual assault in that she was female, a freshman in college, and had been drinking alcohol. Victims of rape may be men or women of any age; however, they are usually females between the ages of 15 and 24. Most of them are of college age, an age when they are dating most frequently (Koss et al., 1987). Most sexual assaults occur between acquaintances, frequently on dates. The sexual assault victims we will be discussing in this paper are most often college women between 17 and 21. It is possible for men to be raped by male assailants – or, more rarely, by female assailants – but because the vast majority of acquaintance rapes involve male assailants and female victims, this paper will primarily focus on this type of sexual assault.

The two most important determining factors regarding whether a date rape will occur are the number of men a woman dates (Burkhart and Stanton, 1985), and the degree of intoxication of those men (Polonko et al., 1986). The first factor is based on probability of exposure, in part because it is impossible to tell a date rapist by the way he looks, and in part because women are socialized to ignore cues that may indicate that some men are a threat. For example, if a man calls a woman a derogatory name (such as "bitch") or continues to tease her when she asks him to stop, he is harassing her and is likely to exploit her. If he harasses, exploits, and/or objectifies her in a non-sexual situation, he is likely to do so in a sexual situation as well. Most women are socialized to put up with harassment, however, because saying something assertive is considered contrary to proper feminine behavior. The more times a woman experiences harassing kinds of behavior, the more they become part of her social environment, and the more she learns to "grin and bear it."

Some sexual assault victims have such low self-esteem that they feel that they are worthless without a relationship, and that it is better to be associated with any man than no man at all. This attitude is also enforced in American culture. The victim may say, "As soon as he gets to know the real me, he will fall in love with me, and will stop doing that. He will change for me." Or she may say, "I know he did something to me that I didn't like, but that is all I deserve." The victim may have watched her father harass or assault her mother, making her believe that this is the way adult sexual relationships are supposed to be. She may even have been sexually assaulted as a child; forced sexual experiences may be the only kind of sexual relationships she knows. Some victims may not want to believe that someone they love could do anything as terrible as rape them, so these victims may define the sexual assault as their own fault rather than believe that their boyfriends are rapists. For example, a victim may say, "I got him so excited that he couldn't stop himself."

With regard to the second factor, the more intoxicated a man is, the greater the likelihood that he will ignore a woman's protests or be unable to interpret her words and actions as she intended them. This is especially true if she does not want to have sex but he does, which is a common pattern in acquaintance sexual assaults.

> While visiting from another institution, John got drunk at a fraternity party and raped a woman at the party. His friends, who were fraternity brothers, helped to get her drunk and then encouraged the assault by cheering him on. After the party the woman filed a complaint with the college administration, but because the alleged rapist was not a student at the college, the administration was not able to do anything to him.

Studies have not consistently indicated any female personality traits that make a woman more likely to become a date or acquaintance rape victim. Our research indicates that the typical scenario of sexual assault on college campus includes the woman's drinking at a party (especially a fraternity party) and playing drinking games, a situation where she has been given a drink in which the alcohol has been disguised as punch. First-year college students are most likely to become the victims of sexual assault while in college (Koss et al., 1987). Sexual assault, however, can and does also happen in other circumstances.

Sexual assault victims sometimes have sex again with their assailant. In many cases in which the victim has sex with the assailant again, the latter was the boyfriend of the victim. The victim may believe that, although he did force her to have sex, he will treat her better and not rape her once he really gets to know what a wonderful person she is (and, presumably, falls in love with her). Only after repeated sexual assaults over time does she realize that he will not change, and so she ends the relationship.

Neil Gilbert, a professor of social work at Stanford University, believes that if a woman does not know that what has happened to her is rape, then it is not rape (Collison, 1992). This type of attitude is probably pervasive among the administrations of some colleges. Gilbert cites FBI statistics, which consist disproportionately of reports of stranger rape, to prove that the 20–25 percent estimate of sexual assaults on female college students is inflated. The FBI estimates that fewer than one in ten stranger rapes are actually reported to them, however, and data from national studies suggest that fewer than one in a hundred acquaintance rapes are reported to the police (Burkhart, 1983; Parrot, 1992). Because most rapes and sexual assaults that occur in college are between acquaintances, they are not likely to be reported to the police or even the college administration. This is especially true if administrators have made it clear to victims that they don't believe sexual assault happens on their campus.

Who are the assailants?

Approximately 5–8 percent of college men know that raping acquaintances is wrong, but choose to do it because they know the odds of their being caught and convicted are very low (Koss et al., 1987; Koss, 1992; Hannan and Burkhart, 1994). There is a larger group of men who rape acquaintances but do not believe it is rape. They often believe they are acting in the way men are "supposed to act" – that "no" really means "maybe," and "maybe" really means "yes." Once a case becomes public, several other women often come forth who are willing to testify that the assailant sexually assaulted them as well, even though the other women had not pressed charges themselves. This was the case in the William Kennedy Smith trial, although the three women who also claimed to have been raped by him were not permitted to testify.

Some studies have compared the incidence of sexual assault among various groups of men. One study indicated that 35 percent of fraternity men reported having forced someone to have sexual intercourse. This figure was significantly higher than for members of student government (9 percent) or men not affiliated with other organizations (11 percent) (Garrett-Gooding and Senter, 1987). Based on an FBI survey, basketball and football players from NCAA colleges were reported to the police for committing sexual assault 38 percent more often than the average for males on college campuses (Hoffman, 1986).

The men who are most likely to rape in college are fraternity pledges (Bird, 1991; Koss, 1991). It is unclear whether this is because either forced sexual intercourse or sexual intercourse under any circumstances is a condition of pledging, or because the pledges are trying to act in a way that they believe the brothers will admire. The process of pledging a fraternity often desensitizes men to behaviors that objectify women, and it also creates a "groupthink" mentality (Sanday, 1990). As a result, once men become pledges, or fraternity members, some of them may commit a sexual assault to be "one of the brothers." All of these factors, plus the heavy alcohol consumption that occurs in fraternities, contribute to the likelihood that a sexual assault will occur on campus. Not all fraternity pledges who abuse alcohol, however, actually commit sexual assault. Conversely, women should not automatically feel safe with a man who is not in a fraternity and who is a teetotaler.

> Tom sexually assaulted Carol, the girlfriend of one of his fraternity brothers. Carol passed out from drinking too much at a fraternity party, and Tom had sex with her while she was unconscious in her boyfriend's bedroom. When she started moaning her boyfriend's name during the rape, Tom panicked and went to get the boyfriend, encouraging him to have sex with her so that if she regained consciousness, she would see him instead of Tom. Friends of Carol saw Tom leave the room and then reappear with her boyfriend, who he pushed into the room. Tom, however, had inadvertently left his tie in the bed, which was seen as evidence that he had been there with Carol. Tom was subsequently convicted of sexual assault by the campus judicial board.

The likelihood to commit a sexual assault also increases if men choose to live in all-male living units when co-educational units are also available. In fact, men who elect to live in all-male residences often do so in order to be able to behave in a violent or antisocial way, such as punching walls or getting drunk and vomiting in the hallways. There is significantly more damage done in all-male living units than on male floors of co-educational residences for this reason (Walters et al., 1981).

Another group at risk for committing rape in college are athletes competing in such aggressive team sports as football, lacrosse, and hockey. Athletes are most likely to sexually assault after a game, when they are out either celebrating a win or drowning their sorrows after a loss. Drinking parties are frequently part of the post-game ritual, with female fans helping the athletes celebrate or commiserating with them. The likelihood of a sexual assault is greatest at this point if a female "groupie" appears to be "throwing herself" at an athlete with the intent of being seen with him or because she wants to be his friend. The athlete may be unable to distinguish between her desire for friendship and his perception that she is throwing herself at him because she wants sex. Further, he may believe that this is what he deserves as a result of his "star" status. There have been many celebrated cases of high school, college, and professional athletes who were successfully charged with rape or sexual assault by college and civil authorities.

Assailants are not limited to fraternity members and athletes, however, and the vast majority of fraternity men and athletes do not rape. The rate is higher among these two groups because of their position of privilege on campus, and because of their involvement with alcohol. The characteristics that are most important in determining if a man will become an acquaintance rapist are macho attitudes, antisocial behavior, and abuse of alcohol (either on a regular basis, or through binge experiences) (Malamuth and Dean, 1991; Rapaport and Posey, 1991). Athletes and fraternity men may exhibit some or all of these traits.

> Bill, a fraternity pledge, was a virgin at the time he was pledging. He was told by the brothers that they did not accept virgins into their house, and so he would have to do something about his virginity status. When he protested that he did not have a girlfriend, he was told that he should bring a girl to their fraternity formal, and the brothers would do the rest. He invited a very naïve first-year student, Lori, to the party. Once there, she was given punch spiked with grain alcohol. When Lori blacked out, Bill took her to the bedroom of one of the brothers, put a condom on, and forced her to have sex over her feeble protests. She was also a virgin at the time, and she became pregnant because the condom broke during the rape.

Different types of campus sexual assault and rape

Each different type of sexual assault has specific characteristics and problems associated with it. Campus sexual assaults vary by the status of the victim (student, faculty, staff, visitor, and so on), the status of the assailant, the number of assailants involved, and the degree of acquaintanceship between those involved. Rape or sexual assault on college campuses may be committed by an acquaintance or a stranger; most typically, the assailant is someone the victim knows. For the purposes of this book we have defined *campus sexual assault* as assault cases in which at least one of the people involved is associated with the institution.

Sexual assault of a member of the college community by a stranger from outside the campus community

We probably hear about this type of sexual assault more often than any other. Women are much more likely to report a sexual assault in which they are seen as having little or no culpability. Therefore, victims are more likely to report a sexual assault to the police or campus authorities if they do not know the assailant, do not share the same friends, and consequently do not receive any pressure from friends or acquaintances to keep quiet so the assailant's life will not be "ruined." Stranger rape usually occurs more in urban than rural areas because of higher crime rates in urban areas.

On the night of January 2, 1989, a female employee of the University of Southern California was attacked near the school's credit union building by an unknown man who dragged her into some bushes, where she was beaten, stabbed, robbed, and raped. The attack lasted 40 minutes, during which time no one came to the woman's aid. She was rescued by two passersby, who scared off the assailant and then helped her to walk to the security office about a block away. It turned out that only one security officer was in the field at the time of the attack. Six months before the attack, there was a report that identified the building as a security risk, but no one had ever followed up on the report's recommendations, which included increasing the lighting and cutting back the bushes.

A young woman at Clarkson University was assaulted while walking home through an isolated area behind the field house. A fire watchman who was inside the field house reported it to another fire watchman who was on patrol on another part of campus. The watchman in the car came to the building to investigate. He came upon two people having what he believed to be consensual sex. He called the other fire watchman and they were unsure of how to respond. When they went to check the scene again, they found the woman alone, bloody, and unconscious. They then called the village police, who responded and apprehended the man after he had raped and beaten the woman. She later died in the hospital. Clarkson College was sued and settled out of court. The college has subsequently hired a director of campus safety with a law enforcement background and has dramatically upgraded the training for its campus safety personnel (Cooper, 1992).

Sexual assault by a stranger (other than a student) from within the campus community is more likely in large campus communities than on smaller campuses, where most people tend to know each other. These rapes may be between students and faculty, administrators, or college staff members or visitors to the campus community.

Rape by a student unknown to the victim

This type of sexual assault is also more common in larger schools, and may happen in circumstances such as after the assailant notices the victim in a bar or at a large party. It may also occur if a woman has a "bad" reputation, passes out at a party after drinking alcohol, and is used sexually by male students who are strangers to the victim. In some instances, the victim is in a presumably safe place but is attacked by a stranger who has gained access based on false pretenses (for example, posing as a student or pizza delivery person). It is typical in gang rape that at least some of the assailants are strangers to the victim.

> In 1986, Lehigh freshman Jeannie Clery was raped, sodomized, and murdered while sleeping in her bed at 6.00 a.m. That night another student, who had been drinking and who did not know her, entered her residence hall through three automatically locking doors that were propped open, entered her room, and sexually assaulted and strangled her. Her parents sued the university for failing to provide a safe environment for their daughter and for violation of "foreseeable action." They settled for an undisclosed sum, and in addition, they committed Lehigh to extensive improvements in dormitory security.

Acquaintance rape and sexual assault

"Acquaintance rape" and "date rape" are not legal categories; the term *rape* usually applies to any forced intercourse, regardless of the degree of acquaintance. We are using the terms *acquaintance rape* and *date rape* for clarity of understanding in a sociological rather than a legal sense.

> Amy, a senior in high school, was visiting her sister, Jill (a first-year student), for the weekend at a small liberal arts college. They went to a lacrosse game, and Jill had a party in her room afterward. One of the lacrosse players, Adam, attended the party after the game, and Amy spent over an hour with him there. Amy and Adam both got drunk and went into an adjoining room during the party for about an hour. When they emerged, he went home, and Amy told Jill that Adam had raped her. Amy and Jill reported the event to the authorities, and Adam was suspended. Adam sued the college on the grounds that the campus policy explicitly stated that the college community would protect its students, but it said nothing about protecting visitors. (Parrot and Bechhofer, 1991)

Acquaintance sexual assaults are by far the most common type of rape both on and off the campus; however, they are rarely reported to authorities.

Date rape (the most common type on college campuses) and acquaintance rape are estimated to happen to one-fifth of college women, whereas one-quarter of college women will experience either attempted or completed forced sex (Koss et al., 1987). These sexual assaults happen most often during the woman's first year, although a victim may also experience further episodes later on. Sexual assaults often happen to victims in the first week of college, before they know the social "rules." At colleges where first-year students live on campus and then must move off campus during their sophomore year, however, the incidence increases when students no longer have the protection of the structured college living environment (Parrot and Lynk, 1983; Parrot, 1985).

Gang rape and sexual assault

Although gang rape occurs on college campuses, it is not unique to them. It usually occurs in all-male living units where alcohol and peer pressure are abundant. Fraternity gang rape is especially difficult to prove because an accused's fraternity brothers are usually unwilling to provide evidence to the local or campus police. In fact, of the documented cases of alleged gang rape by college students from 1980 to 1990, 55 percent were committed by fraternity members, 40 percent were committed by members of team sports (football, basketball, and lacrosse), and only 5 percent were committed by men who were not affiliated with formal organizations (O'Sullivan, 1991). Other studies also show that a majority of gang rapes committed on college campuses occur in fraternity houses (Tierney, 1984).

Many of the people who are involved in gang rape are "followers" rather than initiators (Groth and Birnbaum, 1979). One of five Kentucky State University defendants charged with sodomizing a fellow student told police that at first he left the woman alone when he found her partially undressed in his room, because she was unwilling to have sex with him. When he later returned and found his friends assaulting her, he joined them (O'Sullivan, 1991).

Tanja was raped in her dormitory in September of her first year of college at the University of California at Berkeley. An unsupervised party had been held in the dorm during which alcohol was consumed, despite the agreement between students and the university that there would be no drinking in the dorms. After the party, Tanja went to the room of an acquaintance, Donald, to borrow a cassette tape. There she met Donald's twin brother Ronald, who forced her down the interior stairs of the building to a dark landing where a light bulb had been shattered. He forced Tanja to have intercourse and oral sex with him. Ronald then took Tanja to a room occupied by John and

Christian, where Donald soon joined them. Donald suggested that they all go to his room, where he encouraged the other three men to have oral sex with Tanja against her wishes. When she protested forcefully, Donald told the others to leave, but told her that if she didn't stop yelling, he would beat her. Donald then forced Tanja to have intercourse with him, while the other three friends watched, laughing. Tanja was finally permitted to leave. All four men were members of the university football team.

Like other acquaintance rape victims, the victim in a gang rape may be drunk or passed out at the time and therefore may have no memory of the rape; if she does remember it, her memory may be incomplete. She may have voluntarily gone to the location of the rape and may have consented to have sex with one of the men, but not with all of them. If she has a reputation for sleeping around, she may fear that she will not be believed if she reports the event to the police or the campus authorities. In fact, regardless of her reputation, when a woman is being gang raped, the last men are likely to feel more justified in forcing her because they feel that she deserves it for being so "loose." Gang rape may occur when women who are believed to be "easy" are imported from off campus for this purpose (Sanday, 1990).

In the event of a fraternity gang rape, powerful alumni and current brothers may put pressure on the institution to squelch the case. Information is often covered up in these cases to protect the assailant or to prevent the charter of the fraternity from being revoked. Members of the group that raped the victim, as well as the rapists themselves, may also harass her or put pressure on her not to report the assault, or to drop the charges. For all of these reasons, charges are rarely filed in gang rape cases, whether they occur on or off campus. If they are filed and the case goes to trial, the result is often an acquittal. In such cases, it is usually the word of the victim against that of the assailants, and the assailants' stories usually agree with each other. In addition, the assailants are often "nice boys" from "good families," in contrast with the victim's frequently "bad" reputation. In such cases it is difficult to convince the entire jury beyond a reasonable doubt that she was not a willing participant.

Peggy Sanday (1990) suggests that gang rape is often the means by which homophobic men who want to share a sexual experience with other men are able to do so through a woman. Sanday believes that these men want to have sex with each other, but will not do so because of the societal taboo against homosexual behavior. Therefore they select a woman whom they do not know and have sex with her in the presence of their male friends as a means of sharing a sexual experience in a "socially acceptable" heterosexual way. This process is unspoken, and perhaps unconscious, because these men would never admit wanting to have sex with another man. They are also misogynistic if they are able to abuse a woman in this manner to fulfill their own desires.

Judge Lois Forer (1991) believes that gang rape is becoming less acceptable off campus, but is viewed much less negatively on campus. In gang rape, as in acquaintance rape, if we hear of only a small number of cases being reported to the police or campus judicial authorities, it probably means that many more are actually taking place. We very rarely hear, for example, about gang rapes being reported to the authorities in which the victim has a "bad" sexual reputation (as many of them do).

St John's University case study

The rape trial involving members of the St John's University lacrosse team was a highly celebrated case that involved alcohol, athletes, and a groupthink mentality. It will be presented here as a case study because it illustrates the very points we are making about campus sexual assault. The St John's case includes many of the common elements present in the response to a campus sexual assault when the victim reports to the authorities.

> The three men on trial from St John's University (Andrew Draghi, Walter Gabrinowitz, and Matthew Grandinetti) were accused of making a woman perform oral sex on them, using force at some moments and at other times taking advantage of her helplessness from liquor that the victim says a fourth student (Michael Calandrillo) pressured her to drink. Not all of the men were tried together, because some of the defendants agreed to provide testimony against the other assailants.
>
> The woman testified that she was told by Michael that he would drive her home from an evening college meeting, but that he needed to stop by at his nearby house for gas money. She agreed to that arrangement. According to the prosecutor, however, when they entered the house she was the victim of sexual advances by Michael and was forced to drink cups of vodka and orange soda, a mixture that caused her to fade in and out of consciousness. When she awoke periodically, she found Michael's housemates (and former teammates) shoving their penises, in turn, into her mouth. The woman asserted that she tried to ward off her attackers verbally but that she was too weak. A Queens, New York, jury in 1991 rejected her allegations, and the three defendants were acquitted. (Parrot, 1993)

The facts in the St John's case illustrate many of the issues that often contribute to not-guilty verdicts. The victim waited many months before she reported the incident, and there was another significant time period between the report and the trial. When she provided accounts of the alleged crime to her minister, detectives, and lawyers, there were subtle differences in her story, such as exactly how much liquor she drank (from one to three cups). As in most acquaintance rape cases, the major legal issue here was not whether the event in fact took place, but whether the woman consented. The victim said she did not consent; the jury did not believe her.

It is important to understand that a verdict of not guilty does not necessarily mean that the assailant is innocent. It simply means that there was not sufficient evidence to convince all the jurors, beyond a reasonable doubt, that he committed the crime of which he was accused. Although this is, of course, true for all crimes, the acquittal rate in rape trials is higher than for other serious felonies. Jurors often do not believe that the defendant committed the crime because he was a credible witness, or because the victim was a poor witness; because there was not enough corroborating evidence; or because they could not understand why such a nice, upstanding (often married) pillar of the community would have to resort to raping a woman of questionable character in order to have sex.

This last line of reasoning assumes that men rape for sex. Although sexual organs are used in rape, that does not make it sex. As Linda Sanford, author of *Women and Self Esteem*, says, "If I hit you over the head with a rolling pin, you wouldn't call it cooking, would you?" In the same way, if a penis is used to commit violence, it does not make the act sex.

Stranger rapists often plan rape, whereas acquaintance or date rapists often plan sex. In acquaintance rape it is only when the assailant's plan for a perfect evening (ending with sex) goes wrong that he resorts to violence to get what he wants and may think he is owed. But even though the motivation may be different in stranger and acquaintance rape, the consequence is the same for the victim.

In many cases of acquaintance rape, the man may truly *not* believe that what he did was rape, or even that he did anything wrong. He may believe that a woman does not really mean no when she says it, and that all she needed was a little push, and she will be happy about the outcome. This scenario is played out in the media time after time, from *Gone with the Wind* to the soap opera *General Hospital*, the television series *Moonlighting*, and the movie *Baby Boom*. Just because an alleged assailant believes he is innocent, however, does not mean that he is within the law. The law does not define the crime of rape in terms of what the defendant thought, but rather uses a more objective standard.

Newspaper accounts of the trial of the members of the St John's lacrosse team suggested that this trial represented a miscarriage of justice, and that the legal system of the old South had returned because the victim was black, the defendants were white, and the defendants were found not guilty. Many feminists agreed that the verdict will have a chilling effect on the willingness of sexual assault victims to press charges.

Although the defendants were acquitted, St John's University nevertheless expelled the three men. The university waited until after the trial, however, to pass judgment on the men through the campus judicial process. The university's president found that each of the students was guilty of "conduct adversely affecting his suitability as a member of the academic community of St John's," noting that the court verdict acquitting the three of sodomy and criminal charges involved "different standards" from those related to the code of behavior that governs students' actions toward one another and toward teachers.

Many St John's University students felt that this was a harsh verdict for a Catholic university and that better punishment would have been some type of forgiveness and rehabilitation, such as psychotherapy. Catholic colleges seem to respond more harshly, in general, than most other colleges in the judicial handling of sexual assault cases on their campuses. Sexual assault is considered immoral and is not usually tolerated there, even if other segments of society do tolerate or even condone those behaviors.

Although the St John's case was typical in many ways, it differs from the norm because it actually went to trial. The victims of sexual assault rarely report either to the police or to the campus judicial system. Approximately 90 percent of sexual assault cases involving people who know each other are never reported to the police. Some victims prefer to report the rape to the campus judicial authorities; however, the majority of victims of acquaintance sexual assault do not tell anyone about it (Biden, 1991). . . .

What happens when victims report to campus or criminal authorities

Even when victims do report to the police, they are frequently disbelieved or blamed. This phenomenon was seen in the William Kennedy Smith case, in which the victim did report being raped. Although this case was not a campus sexual assault, the issues are similar. Because it was so highly publicized, we will use it as an example for purposes of illustration. Patricia Bowman's character was called into question; she was criticized for being in a bar drinking, for going to his home voluntarily, and for using poor judgment. The same things happen when campus sexual assault victims report to the campus authorities. But in the campus system, because rules of evidence are more flexible than in the criminal courts, victims are also often asked inappropriate questions about their sexual behavior (for example, "Do you have oral sex with all the men you date? Do you like it?").

In most acquaintance sexual assault cases, the victim is usually blamed by her peers and her support system. Martha Burt (1991) found that a majority of Americans think that at least half of all rape reports are false and that they are invented by women to retaliate against men who have wronged them. Many people believe that the charge of acquaintance rape or gang rape occurs because a woman feels guilty after a sexual encounter with a man and cries "rape" in order to ease her conscience. The fact is that only 2 percent of rape reports prove to be intentionally reported falsely to the police (Brownmiller, 1975).

Many victims find it cathartic and healing to tell their stories in court and to play a role in their assailant's punishment. But a plea bargain is often negotiated for a lesser charge, and the victim feels cheated when the assailant pleads guilty to a much less serious crime than that which he committed against her.

> Mary, a graduate student, was raped by another student in her apartment and reported the assault to the police. (Because the rape was not on college property, it was not within the jurisdiction of that particular college.) The district attorney accepted the case and was preparing it for trial. In order to obtain information from the alleged assailant about another crime, however, the district attorney offered the assailant a plea bargain, and the latter received a light sentence. Mary was very angry and disappointed at having been denied the right to "have her day in court" or to see the man sentenced to what she considered an appropriate penalty. At least in her case, however, the assailant was sentenced for some offense and as a result will have a criminal record.

The low reporting and conviction rates are generally characteristic of what are called *simple rapes*: those with no violence, a single attacker, and no other crime committed at the time (Estrich, 1987). Acquaintance rapes are usually simple rapes. The report and criminal conviction rates are much higher in the case of aggravated rapes, but those are far less likely than simple rapes to take place, especially on a college campus. Therefore, more assailants may be punished if acquaintance rape cases are heard by the college judicial board or officer, because the campus system can operate under different rules of evidence. Campus judicial processes are able to find more defendants guilty of sexual assault violations, all other things being equal, than the criminal courts, provided that the system is well designed and administered. The most serious penalty that may be administered in the campus system, however, is expulsion from the institution, which is not comparable to the loss of liberty that may follow a guilty verdict in the criminal justice system.

In many cases of sexual assault reported to the criminal justice system, the case is not accepted by the district attorney or indicted by the grand jury, which may make the victim feel powerless or very angry, especially if she wants to see her assailant behind bars. Victims who report their assaults to the campus criminal judicial system often also experience anger, frustration, and disappointment. For example, victims may be told that their case is not eligible for action by the campus judicial system because it occurred outside of the jurisdiction of the system. Other cases may fail because the victim is not taken seriously by law enforcement officials or campus officials, or because of long delays, among other reasons.

If the case is handled within a campus system, the result may be an acquittal. Although on some campuses, the cases of campus sexual assault that are brought to the judicial body for hearing almost always result in a guilty verdict, this is not universally the case. The outcome depends, in large part, on the thoroughness of the investigation and the mind-set of the administrator(s) hearing the case. The way the campus code is written may also make a guilty verdict very difficult. Alternatively, there may not be enough evidence to convict the defendant, even when the rules of evidence are more flexible.

Even if the defendant is found guilty, he may receive an extremely light sentence (for example, 30 hours of community service). Additionally, the victim often has to face harassment by other students on campus who believe that she was not really raped, that it was her fault, that she is ruining the assailant's life, or that it was not "that big a deal." She may also be harassed by the assailant or his friends, especially if the former is a member of a fraternity that stands to be sanctioned if he is found guilty. Fear of this kind of harassment is more likely if the victim is on a small campus, where students tend to know almost everyone and everything that occurs on campus. All of these factors may contribute to reluctance on the part of women to report campus sexual assault. . . .

Public attitudes about acquaintance rape

The role of public opinion in general, and the influence of highly publicized cases of sexual assault in particular, help to shape the way campus sexual assault is viewed. This book is about the problem of campus sexual assault in general, and those cases resulting in civil suits are but one small segment of the cases that occur. Case studies that did not occur on a college campus, involving the campus judicial process, or result in civil litigation are also included here if they are celebrated and have played a major role in developing societal attitudes about acquaintance rape. Examples of such cases include the William Kennedy Smith and Mike Tyson rape trials and the confirmation hearings for Clarence Thomas's appointment to the Supreme Court. Each of these events took place within a 12-month period early in the 1990s and were instrumental in shaping public opinion about "real rape" and attitudes blaming the victim.

We have learned a great deal about how the American public views rape, sexual assault, and sexual harassment involving acquaintances from cases that have received wide publicity. The victim is held to a higher standard than is the assailant; her testimony must be perfectly consistent and impeccable. She is blamed for her behavior if she has been drinking, and for not being able to stop him. His drinking behavior, on the other hand, excuses his sexual needs. ("He couldn't stop himself"; "He got carried away.")

Most people in our culture are socialized to believe rape myths. Rape myths allow us to believe that a "real rape" is one in which a victim is raped by a stranger who jumps out of the bushes with a weapon, and in which she fought back, was beaten and bruised, reported the event to the police, and had medical evidence collected immediately. In a "real rape," the victim has never had sex with the assailant before, is preferably a virgin, was not intoxicated, was not wearing seductive clothing, and has a good reputation. If a rape occurred under these circumstances, most people would agree that the woman was indeed raped. Unfortunately, acquaintance sexual assaults contain few, if any, of these elements. In many acquaintance rape situations the victim had been drinking, did voluntarily go with the man to his apartment or room, was not threatened with a weapon, did not fight back, did not report the event to the police immediately, did not have medical evidence collected, and may have even had sex with the assailant voluntarily before.

In many of the highly publicized cases of 1990 and 1991, the verdict was simply based on the man's word against the woman's. It is a matter of whom we believe and why. Societal messages have suggested that men must always be ready and willing to have sex, that a woman who says "no" never means it, and that sex is a man's right if he spent money on the date (Muehlenhard et al., 1985). Some men also feel that a woman is asking for sex if she gets drunk, goes to a man's apartment, or asks him over to hers. These ideas are in stark contrast to the legal definitions of rape and sexual assault in the United States. Most states have laws that define rape as a situation in which sexual intercourse is forced on one person by another against the victim's will and without the victim's consent, or if the victim submits out of fear for his or her safety or life. In theory, the victim does not have to say "no" more than once, and does not have to explain why he or she wants the offender to stop. Many people, however, do not believe that an event was rape if the woman is not bruised and hysterical, and if the offender was not a stranger (Burt, 1980, Johnson, 1985). Legally, these factors do not have to be present for a sexual assault to have occurred.

In some cases, members of society believe that the victim should have known better, such as in the Mike Tyson case. Even though Tyson was convicted of rape and sexual assault, the behavior of his victim, Desiree Washington, was still questioned, and victim-blaming statements were abundant. Many of the following comments were made by people who disbelieved the victim. Why did she go up to his hotel room unescorted? She must have known of his reputation. He was reported as having sexually harassed beauty pageant contestants earlier that day, and she surely must have seen that. In reality, most women have a hard time believing that men they know would hurt them if they have never hurt them before. If attacked, women often have a difficult time defending themselves against most men. In the case of the former heavyweight boxing champion of the world, she could never have fought her way out if he behaved inappropriately.

Tyson's reputation as a man who had previously been involved in sexual violence was very different from that of William Kennedy Smith, who was a physician and a member of a very influential family. Desiree Washington's background (as a pillar of the community, an upstanding member of her church, and a member of the National Honor Society) was very different from that of Smith's accuser, Patti Bowman. Bowman had obviously had sex before (because she was a mother) and was drinking in a bar where she met Smith. Undoubtedly, racial factors were also a likely contributor to Tyson's conviction, in contrast to the acquittal in the William Kennedy Smith trial.

The public often assumes that victims will make false accusations for some kind of personal gain. Anita Hill was accused of making up charges against Clarence Thomas because she was either a woman scorned, emotionally imbalanced, looking for a movie or book contract and a way to become famous, or a pathological liar. Patricia Bowman, the woman who accused William Kennedy Smith of rape, was portrayed as a "wild girl" with a "taste for glitz" by the media. Sexual assault and rape victims are often charged by public opinion with trying to ruin a man's life; when a public figure is charged, the victim is viewed as being out for fame and fortune as well.

College students are aware of news events of this nature, and one can assume that they are influenced by them. Potential rapists may believe that they can rape with impunity as long as they choose the right kind of victim.

Victims are likely to have learned the lesson that there are many factors, unrelated to the sexual assault, that will have bearing on whether their cases will be treated seriously. If victims do decide to report the assault, they must know that their chances of a conviction are not good, and that their chances of being further harassed and blamed are high. Current and highly publicized cases will undoubtedly have an important impact on the number of sexual assaults committed and the number of cases reported to authorities, both on and off the campus.

References

Biden, J. (1991) *Violence against Women: the Increase in Rape in 1990* (Washington, DC: Committee on the Judiciary, United States Senate).

Bird, L. (1991) "Psycho-social and environmental predictors of sexually assaultive attitudes and behaviors among American college men," PhD dissertation at the University of Arizona.

Brownmiller, S. (1975) *Against Our Will: Men, Women and Rape* (New York: Simon and Schuster).

Burkhart, B. (1983) "Acquaintance rape statistics and prevention," paper presented at the Acquaintance Rape and Prevention on Campus Conference in Louisville, KY.

Burkhart, B. R. and Stanton, A. L. (1985) "Sexual aggression in acquaintance relationships," in G. Russel (ed.), *Violence in Intimate Relationships* (New York: Spectrum Press).

Burt, M. (1980) "Cultural myths and supports for rape," *Journal of Personality and Social Psychology*, 38: 217–30.

Burt, M. (1991) "Rape myths and acquaintance rape," in A. Parrot and L. Bechhofer (eds), *Acquaintance Rape: the Hidden Crime*, pp. 26–40 (New York: John Wiley and Sons).

Collison, M. (1992) "A Berkeley scholar clashes with feminists over validity of their research on date rape," *Chronicle of Higher Education*, February 26.

Cooper, Dean (1992) Personal communication from the dean of students, Clarkson College, October 15.

Estrich, S. (1987) *Real Rape: How the Legal System Victimizes Women who Say No* (Cambridge, MA: Harvard University Press).

Forer, Lois (1991) Personal communication, March 18.

Garrett-Gooding, J. and Senter, R. (1987) "Attitudes and acts of sexual aggression on a university campus," *Sociological Inquiry*, 59: 348–71.

Groth, N. and Birnbaum, H. J. (1979) *Men who Rape* (New York: Plenum Press).

Hannan, K. E. and Burkhart, B. (1994) "The typography of violence in college men: frequency, and comorbidity of sexual and physical aggression," *Journal of College Student Psychotherapy*.

Hoffman, R. (1986) "Rape and the college athlete: part one," *Philadelphia Daily News*, March 17, p. 104.

Johnson, K. M. (1985) *If You are Raped* (Holmes Beach, FL: Learning Publications).

Koss, M. (1991) Keynote address presented at the First International Conference on Sexual Assault on Campus, Orlando, FL.

Koss, M. (1992) "Alcohol, athletics, and the fraternity rape connection," paper presented at the Second International Conference on Sexual Assault on Campus, Orlando, FL.

Koss, M. P., Gidicz, C. A., and Wisniewski, N. (1987) "The scope of rape: incidence and prevalence of sexual aggression and victimization in a national sample of higher education students," *Journal of Consulting and Clinical Psychology*, 55(2): 162–70.

Malamuth, N. and Dean, C. (1991) "Attraction to sexual aggression," in A. Parrot and L. Bechhofer (eds), *Acquaintance Rape: the Hidden Crime* (New York: John Wiley & Sons).

Muehlenhard, C. L., Friedman, D. E., and Thomas, C. M. (1985) "Is date rape justifiable? The effects of dating activity, who initiated, who paid, and man's attitudes toward women," *Psychology of Women Quarterly*, 9(3): 297–310.

O'Sullivan, C. (1991) "Acquaintance gang rape on campus," in A. Parrot and L. Bechhofer (eds), *Acquaintance Rape: the Hidden Crime*, pp. 140–56 (New York: John Wiley and Sons).

Parrot, A. (1985) "Comparison of acquaintance rape patterns among college students in a large co-ed university and a small women's college," paper presented at the Annual Meeting of the Society for the Scientific Study of Sex, San Diego, CA.

Parrot, A. (1992) "A comparison of male and female sexual assault victimization experiences involving alcohol," paper presented at the Annual Meeting of the Society for the Scientific Study of Sex, San Diego, CA.

Parrot, A. (1993) *Coping with Date Rape and Acquaintance Rape*, 2nd edn. (New York: Rosen).

Parrot, A. and Bechhofer, L. (eds) (1991) *Acquaintance Rape: the Hidden Crime* (New York: John Wiley & Sons).

Parrot, A. and Lynk, R. (1983) "Acquaintance rape in a college population," paper presented at the Eastern Regional Meeting of the Society for the Scientific Study of Sex, Philadelphia, PA.

Polonko, K., Parcell, S., and Teachman, J. (1986) "A methodological note on sexual aggression," paper presented at the National Convention of the Society for the Scientific Study of Sex, St Louis, MO.

Rapaport, R. R. and Posey, D. (1991) "Sexually coercive college males," in A. Parrot and L. Bechhofer (eds), *Acquaintance Rape: the Hidden Crime* (New York: John Wiley & Sons).

Sanday, P. (1990) *Fraternity Gang Rape* (New York: New York University Press).

Tierney, B. (1984) "Gang rape on college campuses," *Response to Violence in the Family and Sexual Assault*, 7(2): 1–2.

Walters, J., McKellar, A., Lyston M., and Karme, L. (1981) "What are the pros and cons of coed dorms?" *Medical Aspects of Human Sexuality*, 15(8): 48–56.

Legal Images of Battered Women (excerpt)
Martha R. Mahoney

> . . . /I found an
> announcement/not the woman's
> bloated body in the river/floating
> not the child bleeding in the
> 59th street corridor/not the baby
> broken on the floor/
> "there is some concern
> that alleged battered women
> might start to murder their
> husbands and lovers with no
> immediate cause"[1]

I am writing about women's lives. Our lives, like everyone's, are lived within particular cultures that both reflect legal structures and affect legal interpretation. Focusing on domestic violence, this paper describes an inter-relationship between women's lives, culture, and law. This relationship is not linear (moving from women's lives to law, or from law to life) but interactive: cultural assumptions about domestic violence affect substantive law and methods of litigation in ways that in turn affect society's percep-tions of women; both law and societal perceptions affect women's under-standing of our own lives, relationships, and options; our lives are part of the culture that affects legal interpretation and within which further legal moves are made. Serious harm to women results from the ways in which law and culture distort our experience.

The courtroom is the theater in which the dramas of battered women have been brought to public attention. Trials like that of Francine Hughes, whose story became the book and movie *The Burning Bed*,[2] create a cultural and legal spotlight that has in some ways benefited women by increasing public knowledge of the existence of domestic violence. However, the press has emphasized sensational cases that have a high level of terrorism against women and a grotesque quality of abuse.[3] These cases come to define a cultural image of domestic violence, and the women in these cases define an image of battered women.

This reading first appeared in *Michigan Law Review*, 1991, 90(1): 2–19 (a few of the more technical footnotes have been edited).

These images disguise the commonality of violence against women. Up to one-half of all American women – and approximately two-thirds of women who are separated or divorced – report having experienced physical assault in their relationships.[4] However, litigation and judicial decision-making in cases of severe violence reflect implicit or explicit assumptions that domestic violence is rare or exceptional.

For actors in the courtroom drama, the fiction that such violence is exceptional allows denial of the ways in which domestic violence has touched their own lives. Perhaps most damagingly, the fiction of exceptionality also increases the capacity of women to deny that the stories told in the publicized courtroom dramas have anything to do with our own lives. Therefore, it limits the help we may seek when we encounter trouble, the charges we are willing to file, our votes as jurors when charges have been filed by or against others, and our consciousness of the meaning of the struggles and dangers of our own experience.

Although domestic violence is important in many areas of legal doctrine, including family law and torts, the criminal justice system places the greatest pressures on cultural images of battered women. The self-defense cases in which women kill their batterers are small in number compared to the overall universe of domestic violence, yet they are highly emotionally charged as well as highly publicized. In many states, the right to expert testimony on behalf of these defendants has been won through much dedicated feminist litigation.[5] The justification for admitting expert testimony is determined in large part by cultural perceptions of women and of battering; therefore, many points made by experts respond to just these cultural perceptions.[6] Yet the expert testimony on battered woman syndrome and learned helplessness can interact with and perpetuate existing oppressive stereotypes of battered women.[7]

Academic expertise on women has thus become crucial to the legal explanation of women's actions and the legal construction of women's experience. Psychological analysis, in particular, has responded to the sharp demand for explanation of women's actions in the self-defense cases.[8] Yet the sociological and psychological literature still reflect some of the oppressive cultural heritage that has shaped legal doctrines.[9] Even when expertise is developed by feminists who explain that women act rationally under circumstances of oppression, courts and the press often interpret feminist expert testimony through the lens of cultural stereotypes, retelling a simpler vision of women as victims too helpless or dysfunctional to pursue a reasonable course of action.[10] These retold stories affect other areas of law, such as custody cases, which share the problems of professional evaluation of women and the incorporation of cultural stereotypes.[11] The portrait of battered women as pathologically weak – the court's version of what feminists have told them – therefore holds particular dangers for battered women with children.

Legal pressures thus distort perceptions of violence in ways that create real problems for women. Many of us cannot recognize our experience in the cultural picture that develops under the influence of legal processes. The consequence is that we understand ourselves less, our society less, and our oppression less, as our capacity to identify with battered women diminishes ("I'm not like *that*"). Before the feminist activism of the early 1970s brought battering to public attention, society generally denied that domestic violence existed. Now, culturally, we know what it is, and we are sure it is not us.

Recent feminist work on battering points to the struggle for power and control – the *batterer's quest for control* of the woman – as the heart of the battering process. Case law and the popular consciousness that grows from it have submerged the question of control by psychologizing the recipient of the violence[12] or by equating women's experience of violence with men's experience.[13] We urgently need to develop legal and social explanations of women's experience that illuminate the issue of violence as part of the issue of power, rather than perpetuating or exacerbating the images that now conceal questions of domination and control.

As one example of a strategic effort to change both law and culture, this paper proposes that we seek to redefine in both law and popular culture the issue of women's separating from violent relationships.[14] The question "why didn't she leave?" shapes both social and legal inquiry on battering; much of the legal reliance on academic expertise on battered women has developed in order to address this question. At the moment of separation or attempted separation – for many women, the first encounter with the authority of law[15] – the batterer's quest for control often becomes most acutely violent and potentially lethal.[16] Ironically, although the proliferation of shelters and the elaboration of statutory structures facilitating the grant of protective orders[17] vividly demonstrate both socially and legally the dangers attendant on separation, a woman's "failure" to permanently separate from a violent relationship is still widely held to be mysterious and in need of explanation, an indicator of *her* pathology rather than her batterer's. We have had neither cultural names nor legal doctrines specifically tailored to the particular assault on a woman's body and volition that seeks to block her from leaving, retaliate for her departure, or forcibly end the separation. I propose that we name this attack "separation assault."

Separation assault is the common though invisible thread that unites the equal protection suits on enforcement of temporary restraining orders, the cases with dead women that appear in many doctrinal categories, and the cases with dead men – the self-defense cases. As with other assaults on women that were not cognizable until the feminist movement named and explained them,[18] separation assault must be identified before women can recognize our own experience and before we can develop legal rules to deal with this particular sort of violence. Naming one particular aspect of the violence then illuminates the rest: for example, the very concept of "acquaintance rape" moves consciousness away from the stereotype of rape (assault by a stranger)[19] and toward a focus on the woman's volition (violation of her will, "consent"). Similarly, by emphasizing the urgent control moves that seek to prevent the woman from ending the relationship, the concept of separation assault raises questions that inevitably focus additional attention on the ongoing struggle for power and control in the relationship.

Because of the interactive relationships between law and culture in this area, law reform requires such an approach to simultaneously reshape cultural understanding. Separation assault is particularly easy to grasp because it responds to prevailing cultural and legal inquiry ("why didn't she leave") with a twist emphasizing the batterer's violent quest for control. However, meaningful change requires rethinking the entire relationship of law and culture in the field of domestic violence and developing many approaches to revealing power and control. Otherwise, since separation assault is so resonant with existing cultural stereotypes, it may be understood as justifying or excusing the woman's failure to leave rather than challenging and reshaping legal and social attitudes that now place this burden on the woman.

To illustrate the contrast between women's lives and legal and cultural stereotypes, and to accomplish a translation between women's lives and law, this paper offers narratives and poems from the lives of survivors of domestic violence, and a few from the stories of non-survivors, as part of its analysis and argument.[20] Seven women's stories have come to me through their own accounts.[21] Five of these have at some time identified themselves as battered women.[22] Three of these women were Stanford Law School students or graduates; another was an undergraduate student at Stanford. One was an acquaintance in a support group. One is black, the rest are white. All but two were mothers when the violence occurred. Though our class backgrounds vary, only one was a highly educated professional before the battering incidents described, but several have acquired academic degrees since the marriages ended. The other women's voices in this paper are drawn from identified published sources.

One of these stories is my own. I do not feel like a "battered woman."[23] Really, I want to say that I am not since the phrase conjures up an image that fails to describe either my marriage or my sense of myself. It is a difficult claim to make for several reasons: the gap between my self-perceived competence and strength and my own image of battered women, the inevitable attendant loss of my own denial of painful experience, and the certainty that the listener cannot hear such a claim without filtering it through a variety of derogatory stereotypes.[24] However, the definitions of battered women have broad contours, at least some of which encompass my experience and the experiences of the other strong, capable women whose stories are included here. In fact, women often emphasize that they do not fit their own stereotypes of the battered woman:

> The first thing I would tell you is that very little happened. I am not one of those women who stayed and stayed to be beaten. It is very important to me not to be mistaken for one of them, I wouldn't take it. Besides, I never wanted to be the one who tells you what it was really like.

The rejection of stereotypes, the fear of being identified with these stereotypes, is expressed by lesbian women as well as heterosexual women:

> First I want you to know that I am an assertive and powerful woman. I do not fit my stereotype of a battered woman. I am telling you this because I *never* thought it could happen to me. Most lesbians I know who have been battered impress me with their presence and strength. None of them fit my stereotype. Do not think that what happened to me could not happen to you.[25]

Although there is relatively little published material on lesbian battering, this literature can shed light on the ways in which we conceptualize the battering process. Although lesbian battering is similar to heterosexual battering, the analysis of lesbian battering is unique in two ways that are significant for this paper: it has been generated entirely by feminist activists, and it has developed in isolation from the legal system. Therefore, it provides one clue to the question, "[W]hat would this . . . landscape look like if women had constructed it for ourselves?"[26] . . .

Violence and the ordinary lives of women

The prevalence of violence and the phenomenon of denial

> Most people I have known who have been abused in marriage have come out – once burned, twice shy. But that doesn't mean fire's not hot. But people treat marriage and relationships and love, in our society, as if fire's not hot.

Statistics show that domestic violence is extremely widespread in American society. Exact figures on its incidence are difficult to come by. Some studies have counted incidents of violence by or against either spouse regardless of context and found a nearly equal incidence of violence by men and women.[27] Other studies show that women are far more frequently victimized than men,[28] and that women's violence is almost always in self-defense and generally less severe than their partner's.[29] The most conservative figures estimate that women are physically abused in 12 percent of all marriages,[30] and some scholars estimate that as many as 50 percent[31] or more[32] of all women will be battering victims at some point in their lives. Accurate estimates are difficult,[33] in part because of the likelihood of underreporting.[34] However, using any of these estimates, marriages that include violence against the woman represent a relatively widespread phenomenon in our society.[35]

Although these statistics are widely reproduced, there is little social or legal recognition that domestic violence has touched the lives of many people in this society and must be known to many people. Judicial opinions, for example, treat domestic violence as aberrant and unusual: "a unique and almost mysterious area of human response and behavior,"[36] "beyond the ken of the average lay [person]."[37] This radical discrepancy between the "mysterious" character of domestic violence and repeatedly gathered statistics reflects massive denial throughout society and the legal system.

Denial is a defense mechanism well recognized in psychology that protects people from consciously knowing things they cannot bear to reckon with at the time. A powerful if undiscussed force affecting the evolution of the law and litigation on battered women, denial exists at both the societal and individual levels. Societal denial amounts to an ideology that protects the institution of marriage by perpetuating the focus on individual violent actors, concealing both the commonality of violence in marriage and the ways in which state and society participate in the subordination of women. "Societal" denial – albeit within a smaller, more consciously self-defined society – also slowed recognition of lesbian battering. . . .

The ideology that protects the institution of marriage and the state's participation in subordinating women is consistent with the findings of James Ptacek's study of batterers.[38] Ptacek found that both batterers and the criminal justice system tended to blame women for their abuse and deny or trivialize the violence involved.[39] These excuses and justifications are ideological in nature: "At the individual level, they obscure the batterer's self-interest in acting violently; *at the societal level, they mask the male domination underlying violence against women.* Clinical and criminal justice responses to battering are revealed as ideological in the light of their collusion with batterers' rationalizations."[40] This ideology pervades the courtroom as well as other areas of the criminal justice system. . . .

Social workers and psychologists play an important role in this process. Our legal system – like the rest of society – has to a large extent entrusted these professionals with the definition of what is normal and functional. Despite the statistics on the epidemic incidence of domestic violence, there is almost no legal or social science scholarship that describes an author's experience of violence[41] or even indicates that the author has had any such experience.[42] It is unlikely that a disinterested body of social scientists is doing all this research. However, scholars may be reluctant to indicate their own experience because they fear intellectual marginalization[43] or familial repercussions. Scholarly fears of marginalization probably reflect some acceptance of stereotypes of battered women; certainly, they reflect caution about the power and danger of stereotyping by others.

This silence among professionals and scholars is one intersection between individual denial and an ideology of societal denial. This is where one of the lenses through which we see the world is constructed: if scholars are silent for "personal" reasons, their "professional" silence then perpetuates the social stereotypes that construct battered women as different, exceptional, "other." Ultimately, the denial of personal experience of domestic violence in social science literature and forensic testimony permits continued societal blindness to the implications of the statistics these same experts gather and employ.[44]

Individual denial protects the images of self and marriage held by individual women and men, as well as being the mechanism through which much societal denial operates. This is true elsewhere as it is in the courtroom: people need to know that their own marriages are sound, therefore it is important to know that they (or their wives) do not "stay" in the relationship; they "are" in the relationship. Their own relationships define what is normal and appropriate; it is appropriate for their own relationships to continue. The battered woman *must* be different. Therefore, the question "why did she stay?" commonly finds answers that attempt to explain difference: "because she had children" or "because she was frightened" or "because she became pathologically helpless" – not, significantly, because I/you/we "stayed" too.

Do we "stay," or are we simply married? Writing this article forced me to grapple with my own image of battered women, my "credentials" in claiming this identity, and my experience of marriage. As I worked, I found similar conceptions of self and marriage in several of the women who spoke with me. These women described their marriages as "bad" or "unhappy"

and then went on to recount attacks that were almost murderous – threats
with guns and knives, partial strangling, deliberately running into a woman
with a car:

> I tried to nurse John [her colicky baby], but Ed screamed that I was trying
> to poison him. I said, "OK, I'll get you a bottle." I had to kneel down by
> the microwave, and Ed pushed me over, so that I fell over. So I put the bottle
> in the micro and stood up, and finished microwaving the bottle, put the
> nipple on, and gave it to Ed . . . Ed began screaming almost incoherently, and
> grabbed John, and started to storm back out to the car with him.
>
> At this point I got worried. The first time [earlier that night, when her
> husband first stormed out and drove around with the baby] I thought he was
> angry because I had yelled, and I felt guilty . . . it didn't seem that aberrant.
> But screaming about poison when I tried to nurse him, knocking me over . . .
> it just seemed like there was something wrong. I said, "You're welcome to
> leave, but you can't take John. I don't think you're all there."
>
> He pushed past. I stood in front of the car. He drove into me. I tried to
> go over the hood of the car, hit the pavement quite hard, and blacked out
> for a minute. When I came to, he had turned the car around, he was like a
> foot from me, and he was saying "get up, or I'll drive over you."
>
> [Her husband had "scared himself . . . realized he had gone too far" and
> gave her the baby to nurse. They finally fell asleep.] Next morning, Ed had
> gone to work. I couldn't move, I couldn't move my legs. I remember think-
> ing, I'm going to die. [The baby] is going to wake up next to a corpse . . .
> When I look back, there was so much rage in that thought [at the colicky
> baby as well as the husband] . . . I had a very hard time functioning. I was
> able to make it to the bathroom, but the tunnel vision seemed worse.

Women often discussed the relationship at length before they mentioned
any violence. Finally, I began to understand that the violence against these
women seemed shocking to me – and the violence against me seemed
shocking to them – precisely because we heard each others' reports of violence isolated from the context of the marriages. For ourselves, on the other
hand, the daily reality of the marriages – none of which included daily or
even weekly violent episodes – defined most of our memories and retro-
spective sense of the relationship: these were "bad" marriages, not ordeals
of physical torture. We resisted defining the entire experience of marriage
by the episodes of violence that had marked the relationship's lowest points.
Our understanding of marriage, love, and commitment in our own lives –
as well as our stereotypes of battered women – shaped our discussion.

This question of the line between "normal" marriage and violent marriage is a common one. One activist social worker recounts that when she
speaks on domestic violence in any forum, someone *always* asks why women

"stay." She says, "When should she have left? At what point? Maybe the time she watched while he smashed up the furniture?" A silence, a shock of recognition, falls over the audience. It is, relatively speaking, *normal* for a woman to watch a man smash up the furniture. Many of the women in the room have seen something like it – and called it "marriage," and not "staying."[45]

Denial conditions women's perceptions of our own relationships and need for assistance. An extreme example is a woman who founded a shelter for battered women; although her husband was beating her during this period, she never identified with the women she sought to help:

> I just thought that the incidents of violence that I – in order to be a battered woman you had to be really battered. I mean OK, I had a couple of bad incidents, but mostly it was pretty minor, in inverted commas, "violence." I didn't see myself in that category, as a battered woman at all.[46]

Similarly, women may fail to perceive armed attacks that do not result in injury as physical abuse – or indeed fail to so perceive anything other than an archetypal brutal beating:

> I don't know what I'd have done if I had to live with what [I assume] you did. My marriage wasn't physically abusive, but there was emotional abuse. My husband had a pistol . . . he did pull his gun on me . . .

This may happen even when the woman calls for help:

> When I finally called the Battered Women's Center for help, I was just look-ing for advice – my husband had threatened to move back in without my consent while I was recovering from a Cesarian section . . . He said "you can't stop me" . . . I told the counselor that I was just looking for a referral, as I didn't qualify for their help because my marriage had not been violent, although I had left after he attacked me with a loaded shotgun. There was a tiny pause, and then she said gently: "We classify that as extreme violence."

Other aspects of women's denial of oppression within ordinary marriage also affect our perception of battered women. Battered women interviewed by social workers often say they felt a responsibility to support their chil-dren's relationship with their father because "he's really good with the children."[47] This is not dissimilar to statements by women in non-violent relationships – or relationships they do not perceive as violent. Women often admit when pressed that they are actually describing a father who is loving with a child when he chooses to interact with it, even if that interaction happens seldom, yet insist on the value of his presence in the children's lives. However, this is a parallel that makes many women uncomfortable: how could a batterer be like their husband? Similarly, although sexual abuse is often a part of domestic violence, many battered women who did not experience sexual abuse describe sex as having been "the only good thing about the marriage."[48] Women who are in relationships of unequal power that are not violent must also find sexual pleasure under conditions of inequality, yet they may not wish to recognize the similarity in experience.

The literature on battering notes, clinically and sometimes with condescending undertones, that women tend to "perceive" the onset of violence as atypical.[49] Of course, the *onset* of violence *is* atypical, and therefore our perceptions are in many ways appropriate.[50] Yet we may ignore danger signals and early attacks because we believe that the "battered-ness" is a characteristic of the woman – a characteristic we do not have – rather than a characteristic of her partner or a symptom of a dynamic in the relationship. Denial creates and reinforces the perceptions (a) that battered women are weak; (b) that we are not weak; and (c) that therefore we are safe.

Finally, individual denial leads women to minimize the pain and oppressiveness of our experiences while we continue to live with them. This is also a familiar dynamic in women's relationships; yet if violence is what we are minimizing, we face great costs and dangers.

> That session in the hospital when I had been married one month, and the nurse came and sat on the bed and said she had heard I didn't care if I went home for Christmas . . . The truth was, I couldn't face what I was going home to. I instinctively knew it was very bad to lie about this but I couldn't bear to tell the truth. It was too humiliating. I didn't tell her anything. To my friends, I said I fell down. I did not intend to cover for him but for myself . . . for the confusion and humiliation . . . for finding myself in this unbelievable position.

This woman's images of battered women and herself make her position "unbelievable." Her response, based on these images, is to disguise her experience. She allows her husband to avoid the censure of family and friends in order to protect *herself* from their opinions, setting up the possibility of more such lies in the future because the image itself has not been confronted, and making it likely that she will minimize her own pain in order to maintain silence.[51]

The cumulative effect of this denial has been very destructive for women. We have difficulty recognizing ourselves and our experience on the continuum of violence and power in which we actually live. To the extent that we cannot recognize ourselves, we are hindered in formulating an affirmative vision in which our integrity is protected. Although much of this paper emphasizes legal aspects of the related forces of law, society, and academia at work in the field of battered women, I believe that the ways in which women are divided from each other – and deprived of the capacity to understand our own experience in relation to other women – are ultimately most important.

Notes

1 Ntozake Shange, "With no immediate cause," in Mary McAnally (ed.), *Family Violence: Poems on the Pathology*, pp. 66, 67 (1982).

2 Faith McNulty, *The Burning Bed* (1980).

3 See Julie Blackman, "Emerging images of severely battered women and the criminal justice system," *Behavioral Science and Law*, 8 (1990), p. 121. Women who kill their batterers are likely to have experienced extremely severe violence during the course of their marriages (see Angela Browne, *When Battered Women Kill*, 1987).

4 For discussion of the estimates of the incidence of domestic violence in the United States, see below and notes 28–36.

5 See, e.g., *State* v. *Kelly: Amicus Briefs*, 9 *Women's Rights Law Reporter*, 245 (1986).

6 See, e.g., *State* v. *Kelly*, 478 A.2d 364, 378 (N.J. 1984) ("[Expert testimony] is aimed at an area where the purported common knowledge of the jury may be very much mistaken . . . an area where expert knowledge would enable the jurors to disregard their prior conclusions as being common myths rather than common knowledge.") A telling example of the relationship between the *need* for expert testimony and the *points* made by experts is the issue of women's "failure" to leave violent relationships. Many cases review the jury's common-sense belief that women can and will leave violent relationships freely. The experts explain the women's incapacity and failure as a function of many factors, especially the psychology of abused women and traditionalism about the family. See, e.g., *People* v. *Torres*, 488 N.Y.S.2d 358, 361–62 (Sup. Ct 1985); *State* v. *Kelly*, 478 A.2d 364, 370–73.

7 See Elizabeth M. Schneider, "Describing and changing: women's self-defense work and the problem of expert testimony on battering", 9 *Women's Rights Law Reporter*, 195 (1986); Lenore Walker, "A response to Elizabeth M. Schneider's 'Describing and Changing'", 9 *Women's Rights Law Reporter*, 223–25 (1986).

8 For example, see three recent books on this subject: Julie Blackman, *Intimate Violence* (1989); Cynthia Gillespie, *Justifiable Homicide* (1989); Lenore Walker, *Terrifying Love* (1989).

9 Compare Emerson Dobash and Russell Dobash, *Violence Against Wives*, pp. 193–9 (New York: Free Press, 1979) (describing traditional psychological approaches)

Cultural Institutions Defining Women

and Edward Gondolf and Ellen Fisher, *Battered Women as Survivors: an Alternative to Treating Learned Helplessness*, pp. 13–15 (1988) (describing psychological views of women as masochistic) with Dobash and Dobash, pp. 211–26 (criticizing the legal system).

10 Schneider, "Describing and changing," p. 198.

11 In contested custody decisions, for example, women are also at risk that either too little strength or too much strength may be held against them. See generally Phyllis Chesler, *Mothers on Trial: the Battle for Children and Custody* (1986). Therefore, the portrait of battered women as pathologically weak – the courts' version of what feminists have told them – may disserve battered mothers seeking custody. Myra Sun and Elizabeth Thomas, "Custody litigation on behalf of battered women," 21 *Clearinghouse Review*, 563, 570 (1987); Laura Crites and Donna Coker, "What therapists see that judges may miss," *Judges Journal*, Spring 1988, pp. 8, 13 (1988).

12 See Gondolf and Fisher, *Battered Women as Survivors*, pp. 1–3 (describing "psychologizing" of domestic violence).

13 See Phyllis Crocker, "The meaning of equality for battered women who kill in self-defense," 8 *Harvard Women's Law Journal*, 121 (1985); see also Gillespie, *Justifiable Homicide*, pp. 115–17 (discussing women's and men's differing experiences of violence in layperson's terms).

14 Redefining separation must include rethinking many assumptions – that it is the woman's job to separate from a battering relationship, that separation is the appropriate choice for all women when violence first occurs within a relationship, that appropriate separation is an immediate and final break rather than the process of repeated temporary separations made by many women – as well as identifying the violent assault on women's attempts to separate.

15 These encounters may take many forms, including the attempt to have a violent partner arrested, the filing of a temporary restraining order or legal separation, or the rush to find legal counsel because the partner has threatened to take custody of the children.

16 See Desmond Ellis, "Post-separation woman abuse: the contribution of lawyers as 'barracudas,' 'advocates,' and 'counsellors,' " 10 *International Journal of Law and Psychiatry*, 403, 408 (1987). Many authors note the dangers of this period. See, e.g., Gillespie, *Justifiable Homicide*, pp. 150–52; Ann Jones, *Women who Kill*, pp. 298–9 (1980).

17 Gondolf and Fisher, *Battered Women as Survivors*, p. 1.

18 Examples are "date rape" and sexual harassment. In her book *Sexual Harassment of Working Women*, Catharine MacKinnon defined sexual harassment in terms of power and inequality ("sexual harassment . . . refers to the unwanted imposition of sexual requirements in the context of a relationship of unequal power") and argued that sexual harassment was sex discrimination. Catharine MacKinnon, *Sexual Harassment of Working Women* 1, 4 (1979). Within a decade, this argument had transformed both sex discrimination law and cultural understanding of sexual harassment.

19 Susan Estrich, *Real Rape*, pp. 3–4 (Cambridge, MA: Harvard University Press, 1987).
20 Particularly thoughtful input has come from Kim Hanson and Donna Coker. This citation form is deliberately chosen and consistent with the method of the paper. Each citation credits the woman with an original thought or contribution that has not appeared in a form suitable for conventional citation as this paper goes to press. There are three reasons for my choice of citation form. The first is honesty: when other women who have not yet published scholarly work have offered me so much of their best thought – and it has become so deeply part of my own best thought – I must either falsely claim their ideas as my own or credit them as they spoke. The second reason is methodological: much of feminist theory, and much of the strength women draw upon for survival, grows out of conversations with each other. This is, for example, the fundamental method of consciousness-raising. See, e.g., Ronnie Lichtman, "Consciousness raising – 1970," in Gerda Lerner (ed.), *The Female Experience* (1977), p. 456. For a discussion of consciousness-raising and its role in feminist method, see, e.g., Christine A. Littleton, "Feminist jurisprudence: the difference method makes," 41 *Stanford Law Review*, 751 (1989), reviewing Catharine MacKinnon, *Feminism Unmodified* (1987). The third reason for citing women's conversations is political: women may not have published their thoughts because of constraints on their time and effort imposed by uniquely womanly responsibilities. This paper had its roots in conversations between Kim Hanson and myself, neighbors in family student housing, when I was a first-year and she a third-year law student at Stanford. Our children played together, and we talked around them over the back fence, encountering each other while hanging laundry, while carrying groceries in from the car. This work is in part the product of that shared work and thought. Since then, Kim has litigated for a major law firm, started her own firm, become known as a battered women's advocate, and remarried. She has had two more babies since we first met. I hope some day she writes her own papers. Until then, I acknowledge her thought in my work as a way of acknowledging her *work* as part of my own.
21 These are women who talked with me or sought me out for help over the past several years. One was my nextdoor neighbor at Stanford; another sought me out during my second year of law school, six months after I gave a talk for incoming women students about emotional reactions to the materials in casebooks. When I relate these women's stories, I do not include specific citations.
22 Most did not generally use the term when describing themselves.
23 This term labels the woman instead of the process or the man. I would prefer some term that lets us discuss stereotyping without hopelessly dooming the discourse from the start. However, I think it is important to overcome our fear of the stigma and stereotype that come with the term "battered woman," so I accept it for this paper.
24 I fear derogatory stereotypes of myself and of my ex-husband and of that marriage. See Liz Kelly, "How women define their experiences of violence,"

in Kersti Yllo and Michele Bograd (eds), *Feminist Perspectives on Wife Abuse*, pp. 114, 116 (1988) (meaning of terms like "rape" and "battering" often taken for granted).

25 Arlene Istar, "The healing comes slowly," in Kerry Lobel (ed.), *Naming the Violence: Speaking Out About Lesbian Battering*, pp. 163, 164 (1986).

26 Christine A. Littleton, "Women's experience and the problem of transition: perspectives on male battering of women," 1989 *University of Chicago Legal Forum*, 23: 30 (1989) (paraphrasing Heather R. Wishik, "To question everything: the inquiries of feminist jurisprudence," 1 *Berkeley Women's Law Journal*, 64, 75 (1985) "In an ideal world, what would this woman's life situation look like, and what relationship, if any, would the law have to this future life situation?").

27 Murray A. Straus et al., *Behind Closed Doors: Violence in the American Family* (1980).

28 In New Jersey, wives or girlfriends were victims in 85 percent of all reported domestic violent offenses. Gail A. Goolkasian, "Confronting domestic violence: a guide for criminal justice agencies," in *US Department of Justice Report* (1986).

29 Daniel G. Saunders, "Wife abuse, husband abuse, or mutual combat? A feminist perspective on the empirical findings," in *Feminist Perspectives on Wife Abuse*, pp. 90, 103–8.

30 Straus et al., *Behind Closed Doors*.

31 Lenore Walker, *The Battered Woman*, p. 19 (1979). The 50 percent estimate is weighed and accepted by Christine A. Littleton "Women's experience and the problem of transition", p. 28, n. 19. For the reasons articulated by Littleton, and from the stories told to me by women, the 50 percent figure seems reasonable to me as well.

32 Jennifer B. Fleming, *Stopping Wife Abuse*, p. 155 (1979), quoted in "Achieving equal justice for victims of domestic violence," in Advisory Committee on Gender Bias in the Courts, California Judicial Council, *Achieving Equal Justice for Women and Men in the Courts*, pt. 6, p. 3 (draft March 23, 1990) (estimating 60 percent of married women experience domestic violence sometime during their marriages); Robin Morgan (ed.), *Sisterhood is Global*, p. 703 (50–70 percent of women experience battering during marriage).

33 The incidence of domestic violence is hard to determine, in part because it takes place within the home, and in part because the many studies in the field present statistical information that is not directly comparable with that in other studies. Some focus on the number of women who are victims of spouse abuse: estimates of women physically abused by husbands or boyfriends in the United States range from 1.5 million (Browne, *When Battered Women Kill*, p. 5) to 3–4 million (Mary Pat Brygger, "Domestic violence: the dark side of divorce," *Family Advocate*, Summer 1990, p. 48). Straus, Gelles, and Steinmetz studied violence against spouses of either gender and found that more than 1.7 million Americans at some time faced a spouse wielding a knife or gun (Straus et al., *Behind Closed Doors*, p. 34).

34 Browne, *When Battered Women Kill*, pp. 4–5 (citing studies by Straus, Gelles, and Steinmetz and the Louis Harris organization). Self-reports may undercount

significantly. See generally Diana E. Russell, *Rape in Marriage*, pp. 96–101 (Bloomington, IN: Indiana University Press) (reviewing statistical techniques and results of several surveys on domestic violence).

35 Stating violence is normal does not mean it is normative or culturally accepted, as it once was. See Dobash and Dobash, *Violence against Wives*, pp. 48–74, for a discussion of violence that was historically part of control of women within marriage. Violence against women was an early focus of feminist protest and efforts at reform. By the mid-nineteenth century, contrary to some popular stereotypes, wifebeating was already considered "a disreputable, seamy practice"; it was illegal in most states by the 1870s. Linda Gordon, *Heroes of their Own Lives: the Politics and History of Family Violence*, p. 255 (1988). Although today domestic violence is indeed "disreputable," that does not mean that it has disappeared in fact – only that the commonality of its occurrence in normal marriage is widely denied.

36 See, e.g., *Sinns* v. *State*, 283, S.E.2d 479, 481 (Ga. 1981) (explaining *Smith* v. *State*, 277 S.E.2d 678 (Ga. 1980)).

37 See, e.g., *Ibn-Tamas* v. *United States*, 407 A.2d 626, 634 (D.C. 1983).

38 See generally James Ptacek, "Why do men batter their wives?," in Kersti Yllo and Michele Bograd (eds), *Feminist Perspectives on Wife Abuse*. A New York judge told the state's Task Force on Women in the Courts that, when a woman gives up an attempt to separate, judges either smile (thinking they have brought the couple back together) or snicker. The snickering response is based on their perception "that the woman who accepts this violent behavior and reconciles with the man[,] even if she reconciles in a split but doesn't pursue the case, isn't worthy of our respect because she does not respect herself" (New York Task Force on Women in the Courts, "Report of the New York Task Force on Women in the Courts," 15 *Fordham Urban Law Journal*, 11: 36–7 (1986–7).

39 Ptacek, "Why do men batter their wives?," pp. 141–9 (batterers), 154–5 (criminal justice system).

40 Ibid., p. 155 (emphasis added).

41 The exceptions here are Robin West, who discusses her own experience of battering in Robin L. West, "The difference in women's hedonic lives: a phenomenological critique of feminist legal theory," 3 *Wisconsin Women's Law Journal*, 81: 98–9 (1987); and Terry Davidson, who discusses being the child of a wife-beater, in *Conjugal Crime: Understanding and Changing the Wife-beating Pattern* pp. 14–15, 131–54 (1978).

42 But see Jan E. Stets's preface to her excellent study, *Domestic Violence and Control*, p. v (1988) (research on domestic violence brought understanding of violence she had witnessed and experienced while growing up).

43 See, e.g., West, "The difference in women's hedonic lives," p. 99 (describes grappling with this anxiety but goes on to discuss her own experience).

44 Conversation with Kim Hanson (1989): "As long as you don't speak out, you're part of the conspiracy of silence."

45 Conversation with Donna Coker (1989), discussing four years of activist feminist social work with battered women in Honolulu.

46 Kelly, "How women define their experiences of violence," pp. 114, 123–4.

47 Conversation with Donna Coker (1989).

48 Ibid. See also Lenore Walker's discussion of her difficulty understanding the reports of sexual pleasure among the battered women she interviewed (Walker, *The Battered Women*, pp. 108–12).

49 Browne, *When Battered Women Kill*, p. 85.

50 The initial violent episode is not treated as though it signals the beginning of a violent relationship. It is treated as an isolated, exceptional event, which is what one would expect it to be treated as. Only in retrospect does the woman begin to examine the first violent act more broadly, seeking signs that "she should have noticed . . ." The evidence is that there has never been any violence before, that the husband rejects this behavior in principle . . . There is no reason to expect the violence to be repeated (Dobash and Dobash, *Violence against Wives*, pp. 95–6).

51 Battered women tend to minimize the history of assault against them and the pain they have suffered. See Julie Blackman, "Potential uses for expert testimony: ideas toward the representation of battered women who kill," 9 *Women's Rights Law Reporter* 227: 228–9 (1986).

In the Truth Itself, There is Healing (excerpt)

Ellen Bass

Years ago, in my writing workshop, a woman wrote of her experience: a small child, asleep in her bed, her father's whispers, his hands between her legs, the pain, confusion, fear, blurred in sleep. In waking, his penis in her mouth, forced against her throat, the gagging, the vomit, the repetition through childhood, into adolescence – a cycle of rape, shame, and unshared, unshareable torment. This woman read her words aloud. Slowly and with great effort, with perseverance, with willingness to face the pain, the rage, the disgust – with courage, with tears, with integrity, with hunger for survival and for a meaningful, nurturing life, she spoke the words, she mourned her past, she celebrated her survival, her strength.

Another woman, farther back, a slight wisp of a girl-woman, woman-child, not yet twenty. She wanted to write – her words on scraps of paper, half-sheets, envelopes. She brought them to me tucked between pages of a

This reading first appeared in *I Never Told Anyone: Writings by Women Survivors of Child Sexual Abuse*, eds Ellen Bass and Louise Thornton (New York: Harper & Row, 1983), pp. 23–42.

notebook, stuffed into her purse. Apologizing, she fumbled through papers, searched for the page, and finally, showed me her writing. Her meanings were hidden: she used words to veil, to obscure. She wanted to write her story, but the task was unfathomable. She could not face what had happened to her – her guilt, her fury, her memory of helplessness, isolation. But she did not give up. She wrote. She began typing fragments; she used full sheets of paper; she constructed whole paragraphs. She sought her mother and talked with her. She was slow and relentless. She married, bore a daughter, cut funny cardboard shapes to make her a mobile, and nursed her in the pre-dawn lightening of the sky. And between cooking, working, driving, cleaning, feeding the baby, loving, and sleeping, she wrote. She stayed up late to write; she wrote while the baby napped. She told her story. She published it in a college literary journal – and won a prize. This woman is Maggie Hoyal and her story, "These Are the Things I Remember," is included here.

These women – and more – women whose courage gives me courage, whose lives are a testament to the strength and beauty of women – our rugged tenacity; our unwillingness, in the midst of widespread, smothering violence and a history of atrocities, to give up, give in, die – these women inspired me to collect these stories. In the process of writing, of saying what has not been said, of giving voice to the unnameable, we claim our experience. We are brave. We are no longer victims. We show what we have endured. We look at this reality in order to destroy it.

The abuse is extensive

The sexual abuse of children spans all races, economic classes, and ethnic groups. Even babies are its victims – hospitals treat 3-month-old infants for venereal disease of the throat. Sexually abused children are no more precocious, pretty, or sexually curious than other children. They do not ask for it. They do not want it. Like rape of women, the rape and molestation of children are most basically acts of violation, power, and domination.

Parents United, a self-help support group for people who have been involved with child molestation, estimates that one out of four girls and one out of seven boys will be sexually abused. Other studies find the ratio of girls to be higher, closer to ten girls for each boy. The sex of the molester, however, is consistent from study to study. At least 97 percent of child molesters and rapists are men; 75 percent are family members, men well known to the child.[1] These are statistics. Because the majority of abuses are not reported, exact figures are impossible to obtain. The true numbers may be greater. But even these show clearly that the sexual abuse of children is common; that the abusers are men – not exceptional, but average; that the victims are mostly girls – not exceptional, but ordinary. This is violence by men against children, and, although there can be individual explanations, individual resolution, and though there is always individual pain, individual wounding, scarring, the issue is not an individual issue but a societal one. We live in a society where men are encouraged to do violence to women and children, subtly and overtly.

Professionals advocate the sexual use of children

Many of our institutions seek to eradicate all sense of guilt, all standards of decency, all respect for another's bodily integrity. When Freud was confronted with frequent accounts of sexual assault by fathers against daughters in his psychiatric practice, he felt he had discovered a major cause of hysteria. But as the enormity of this indictment against fathers became apparent to him, and as he "inferred from the existence of some hysterical features in his brother and several sisters that even his father had been thus incriminated," he revised his opinion and decided that women had fantasized these rapes.[2]

Today psychologists, psychiatrists, anthropologists, and researchers no longer deny the reality of sex between adults and children. Instead, a growing number rename it, calling it a "sexual encounter," "sexual experience," or "sexual relationship," and give their approval. . . .

These kinds of attitudes can distort the authentic needs of the abused child and ignore the anguish documented here. There can be no equality of power, understanding, or freedom in sex between adults and children. Children are dependent upon adults: first, for their survival; then for affection, attention, and an understanding of what the world in which they live is all about.

Though there may be no physical force involved, every time a child is sexually used by a man, there is coercion. A child submits to sex with a man for many reasons: she is afraid to hurt the man's feelings; she wants and needs affection and this is the only form in which it's being offered; she is afraid that if she resists, the man will hurt her or someone else; she is afraid that if she resists, the man will say she started it and get her in trouble; she is taken by surprise and has no idea what to do; the man tells her it's okay, the man says he's teaching her, the man says everybody does it; she has been taught to obey adults; she thinks she has no choice.

Children trust the adults in their lives, even when the adults are untrustworthy, because they have no choice. When that trust is betrayed, they learn that the world is not dependable. By actions as well as by words, adults teach children what to fear, what to trust, what is good, bad, shameful, safe, possible. Children either accept our definitions or, if their experience is radically different (as it is for children who are molested), they are thrown into conflict, confusion, insecurity, and anguish.

When a man sexually uses a child, he is giving that child a strong message about her world: he is telling her that she is important because of her sexuality, that men want sex from girls, and that relationships are insufficient without sex. He is telling her that she can use her sexuality as a way to get the attention and affection she genuinely needs, that sex is a tool. When he tells her not to tell, she learns that there is something about sex that is shameful and bad; and that she, because she is a part of it, is shameful and bad; and that he, because he is a part of it, is shameful and bad. She learns that the world is full of sex and is shameful and bad and not to be trusted, that even those entrusted with her care will betray her; that she will betray herself.

Although sometimes a child is able to say no, most children are not able to say no even when they desperately want to. Fortunately, programs are being developed to teach children how to refuse sexual advances, unwanted touching, and other invasions of their persons,[3] but even though these programs are immensely valuable, there is no way to equalize the basic inequality of power, understanding, or freedom between a child and an adult. . . .

The history: ownership and desecration

People are becoming alarmed, and rightly so, about the extent of child abuse in general and child sexual abuse specifically. The taboo against speaking about this abuse is being torn open. But, as Florence Rush states in her article "Child pornography," "We do not have a history of taboos against the sexual use of children."[4] It is important to understand that the phenomenon of violence against women and children and the condoning of this violence is not simply a contemporary perversion but part of an ancient and pervasive worldwide tradition.

In biblical times, sex was sanctioned between men and young girls.[5] Under talmudic law, the sexual use of girls over the age of 3 was permissible, provided the girl's father consented and appropriate moneys were transferred. Sexual intercourse was an acceptable means of establishing betrothal, and the use of both women and girls was regulated by a detailed set of laws reflecting the property status of females. Women and girls were owned, rented, bought, and sold as sexual commodities. As long as these transactions were conducted with proper payment to the males, rabbis and law-makers approved.

The sexual use of girls under the age of 3 was not regulated legally, as these children were considered too young to be legal virgins, and were therefore without monetary value. Sex with girls under the age of 3 was not subject to any restrictions. As in hunting, it was open season. Boys under the age of 9 were also fair game. Though sex between adult men was severely punished, men could – and did – use young boys at will.

The advent of Christianity did not change things substantially. Canon law held that sexual intercourse established possession, and popes through the centuries upheld rape as an indissoluble means of contracting a marriage. However, Christian law raised the age for legally valid sex from 3 to 7, making sexual intercourse with girls over 7 binding and sexual intercourse with girls under 7 of no consequence to the authorities. In the thirteenth century, the concept of statutory rape was introduced. Its enforcement was not impressive, however, as the clergy itself infamously exploited girls sexually – in the confessional and in the convent schools.

In India, for centuries, marriages have been arranged between men, often old men, and young girls. By the age of 10 or 12, sometimes much younger, the girl-child is forced to submit to intercourse. She is subjected to the physical pain and sometimes permanent injury that repeated intercourse wreaks on a child. The child does not wish for her husband's death, however, since she may be killed when he dies. For centuries, the widow-child was forced to burn herself upon her husband's funeral pyre. This practice, *suttee*, though legally banned for over a century and no longer common, is still in existence.[6]

For a thousand years, girl children in China were compelled to undergo the excruciating pain of foot-binding. This torturous process reduced the feet to three- or four-inch stumps – feet the size of a baby's – which became infected and putrefied, sometimes to the extent that toes dropped off. Tiny feet were crucial to marriage, and marriage was crucial to economic survival. Men found the tiny, child-like, mutilated feet sexually attractive. This process began at the age of 5 or 6 or 7.[7]

In many African countries today and on other continents in the past, girl children have been subjected to the atrocities of genital mutilation, excision, and infibulation. These processes include cutting away the clitoris, inner labia, and parts of the outer labia, then closing the vulva again, leaving an opening for urine. No anesthetic, no antiseptic – the knife may be broken glass, the closing may be thorns, or sometimes the vulva is scraped and the child's legs tied together for weeks until the wound adheres. Often she becomes infected; sometimes she dies. When she marries, she is cut again for intercourse; for childbirth again. The cutting and resewing continue. This process begins as early as several weeks after birth or as late as adolescence. Organizations such as UNICEF and the United Nations Children's Commission have been unwilling to speak out against such tortures because, they say, they do not wish to interfere with native customs.[8]

In every war, along with the glorified killing of men by men, the women and children are also raped, tortured, and killed. This is cross-cultural: Cossacks raped Jewish children, Pakistanis raped Bengali children, Americans raped Vietnamese children, Germans raped French children.[9]

In Europe, between the late 1400s and late 1800s, an estimated nine million people were murdered as witches, most of them women and girls. With the full support of the Christian church, they were gang-raped, tortured with horrendous instruments, forced to confess to sexual crimes, maimed, and burned alive. Commonly, women and girls as young as 5 were accused of copulation with the devil. Sometimes the girls were so abused they believed it *was* the devil who tormented them. In a manner of speaking, it was.[10]

In America today, juvenile prisons incarcerate children who have committed no crime but whose parents want them off their hands: 70 percent of these are girls. Often they will be raped by sheriff, coroner, or attendants.[11]

The sexual abuse of girls spans centuries and continents. It is perpetrated by men, either directly, as in rape, or through women as pawns. In China, for example, foot-binding was administered by women. However, it was not they who originated the idea. Men created the horror of foot-binding; men found it erotic that women should be maimed, suffering, and homebound. Women complied because a bound foot was the only way to insure a daughter's marriage and thus economic and literal survival. The same is true of genital mutilation. The same is true when a mother will not let herself see that her daughter is being molested by her husband. Sometimes she is afraid of the loss of economic support, sometimes she is afraid of further physical violence to herself or her children. Sometimes she is afraid of something much more vague, but just as real – confronting the momentum of an old and deeply embodied attitude that allows men the privilege of ownership and desecration.

We are in danger

In this volume, we say no to that desecration. We look clearly at what sexual abuse and rape have meant in these women's lives. We do not avert our eyes to avoid the pain. Statistics, for all the horror they imply, can be so vast that we shield ourselves from the individual lives they represent. We wanted to make the statistics real, to present the pain of the individual. At times the enormity overwhelmed us. It is not easy to open oneself to the knowledge that millions of children are raped. Our defenses rush to protect us from experiencing that pain. But we cannot close ourselves off and hope for the best. We are in danger. Our daughters are in danger. Even our sons are in danger. Behind each statistic, there is a child. She may be you. She may be your daughter. She may be your sister. She may be your friend. You cannot protect her until we can protect all children.

Advertisements, media, pornography

Advertisements, the media, and pornography encourage acceptance of the sexual use of children. By blurring the distinction between woman and girl-child, these omnipresent images sometimes leave the message that children, as well as women, can be – and should be – sexually consumed. Women are photographed in seductive poses dressed in ankle socks, holding lollipops and teddy bears. Adolescent and pre-adolescent girls are photographed soft-focus in and out of lacy, ribboned lingerie.

David Hamilton is one of the best-known photographers of this kind. The preface to his book, *David Hamilton's Private Collection*, introduces his photographs of young girls in various stages of undress as "moments when innocence and eroticism mingle." In one photograph a young girl lies on her stomach, her illuminated buttocks exposed. The caption reads: "To what caresses, pleasures, and mischiefs do you thus offer your perfect and obedient body?"[12]

In one month, December 1981, I bought four widely distributed men's magazines: *Playboy, Oui, Gallery*, and *Hustler*. Each had at least one reference to sex with children, either explicit or an innuendo. *Gallery* announced a nude photography contest with a photo of a woman dressed only in socks and roller skates, her hair in pigtails, holding a child's school composition book in mittened hands. In *Oui*, a letter to the editor asked, "Would it be possible to have your models wear white ankle socks and saddle shoes?" In the same issue, as part of a "Celebrity Sex Lives" quiz, readers were invited to guess who said "I have never been able to understand how a father could tenderly love his charming daughter without having slept with her at least once." *Playboy* printed a cartoon in which a little girl on Santa's knee asks for ben-wa balls, body lotion, and a talking vibrator and then says, "Mm, your knee feels nice! I just adore older men." *Hustler* advertised "Little Magazines and Movies," offering men the chance to look at children being sexually exploited by adults. Other times *Hustler* cartoons have featured "Chester the Molester," joking about child molestation.

In movies, young girls are portrayed as sexual commodities. Jodie Foster in *Taxi Driver* and Brooke Shields in *Pretty Baby* both play the parts of happy 12-year-old prostitutes.[13]

The same day I bought the magazines, the *Oakland Tribune* reported that Brooke Shields was in court seeking to block future commercial use of nude photographs made of her when she was 10 years old.[14] Under that article was another about a 17-year-old runaway who had been sexually abused by adult male friends of his family at the age of 7. By the age of 15 he was a drug-dependent male prostitute. The newspapers have been reporting similar tragedies often over the past few years. The *Minneapolis Star* reported that children are recruited for prostitution in large numbers, that poor tenants in Minneapolis accept money from pimps who use their apartments as "catches" where children are broken in before being shipped to New York or Chicago.[15]

The *Los Angeles Times* estimated that "one and a half million children under sixteen are used annually in commercial sex (prostitution or pornography)."[16] In 1977, *Time* magazine reported that the child pornography industry had become a billion-dollar-a-year business.[17] By now the actual figures can only be worse. In San Francisco, at a child's eye level, newspaper vending machines feature tabloids of prostitution and pornography. The cover of the issue I picked up portrayed a young woman's body with a child-like face and long hair in pigtails. The face could have been that of a 12-year-old. Inside, along with much advertisement for adult sex, there were also ads for movies and magazines that sexually exploit children, such as *Nasty Playmate*, *Lollipop Pet*, and *Wanna See my P.P.* The price: "$2.00 per tiny tot."

The record industry uses sex and violence against children for profit. The British cover of *Virgin Killers* by the group Scorpion shows a little girl with broken glass projecting from her vagina.[18] Though that album cover is now banned in the United States, the group continues to distribute other albums here with covers consistently degrading to women.

On the cover of Rachel Sweet's album *Protect the Innocent*, a woman dressed in a black leather jacket and black gloves wraps her hands around the mouth and nose of a child, leaving only the child's eyes exposed.

The portrayal of women and girls on record albums ranges from explicitly violent to insipidly degrading. One cover shows woman-girl as cake: the white iced cake, complete with eyes, mouth, arms, and legs, swinging on a garden swing, one piece sliced from between her legs, exposing the chocolate inside. A man watches from the corner behind her.

Hartman's Heart Breakers, a 1930s reprint of hillbilly songs sung by Betty Lou, shows a drawing of an old man fiddler leering at a woman-girl with huge breasts, a bow in her hair, and panties showing under a short, little-girl skirt. She leans into him with the caption, "Give it to me, Daddy." On the back it says, "Prepare your ears for an apparent 11-year-old elucidating the pleasure of mattresses, springs, How to Diddle and Shake That Thing. Betty Lou's voice lies somewhere between those of Shirley Temple, Baby Rose Marie, and a Tennessee Williams wanton." Quoting from the songs, the blurb ends with, "Daddy, O Daddy, don't be so mean! Reach up on the shelf and get the Vaseline."

Even television advertisements convey the message that little girls are sexually available. One ad for a major mattress company showed a little girl curled up on the mattress. The caption, in large black letters, read: "Try something new." And in an ad for a department store, a little girl tries on frilly dresses for her daddy, posing coyly, with the narration, "For the man in her life."

Jokes about child sexual abuse abound. A couple of years ago, a major cosmetics company introduced a new shade of nail polish called "Statutory Grape." Only after widespread feminist protest did they drop the name.

Linda Lee Curns, author of "Sittin' Pidgins," a story about a child who outwits a molester, wrote that she was repeatedly told, "A Tennessee virgin is a girl who can outrun her brothers."[19] One man who had molested his stepdaughter and is now involved with Parents United told us he'd heard many times growing up, "Old enough to bleed, old enough to slaughter." He also told another so-called joke: "A guy comes home and says, 'Pa, I'm in love. I found a virgin and I want to marry her.' The old man says, 'A virgin? How old is she?' 'She's twelve.' 'Good grief! Doesn't she have any brothers?' 'Yes, she's got six brothers.' 'Well, I'm sorry but you can't marry her.' 'Why not?' 'If she's not good enough for her own kin, she's not good enough for us.' "

Several years ago I was at a Hallowe'en party. One man walked in dressed in a raincoat. Upon opening the coat, he revealed a long salami sticking out of his fly. Almost everyone there thought it was funny – or pretended to. They were unaware that joking about men exposing their genitals is a way of condoning that behavior and ignoring the real damage done to children.

Though child molestation is ostensibly condemned, it is in actuality sanctioned by our institutions, by movies, magazines, advertising, even art and literature.[20] All of these confuse adult women with children; vulnerability with sexual invitation; masculinity with aggression; yes with no; women with their genitals; and both women and children with property, owned by men. Men are taught to equate power and violence with a sense of well-being. Many seek this sense of well-being so desperately, so recklessly, that they are willing to look for it even in the bodies of children. Their concern for the child is too weak to check them, their desire for domination too strong.

Notes

1 For sources on the scope of child sexual abuse, see Sandra Butler, *Conspiracy of Silence: the Trauma of Incest* (New York: Bantam, 1978). Susan Brownmiller, *Against our Will: Men, Women and Rape* (New York: Bantam, 1975), and Florence Rush, *The Best Kept Secret: Sexual Abuse of Children* (Englewood Cliffs, NJ: Prentice-Hall, 1980). All of these cite a variety of studies to which you can refer for more complete statistics.

2 Ernest Jones, *The Life and Work of Sigmund Freud* (New York: Basic Books, 1961), p. 211, quoted by Rush in *The Best Kept Secret*, p. 91. See Rush's entire chapter, "A Freudian Cover Up."

3 For example, the Child Assault Prevention Project of Women against Rape, Columbus, Ohio, has developed an excellent program that they present in elementary schools for teachers, parents, and children. Their pioneering work in teaching children ways to become "safe, strong, and free" is a hopeful model that could – and should – be extended across the country. A number of publications include guidelines for parents and other adults to help children protect themselves. Parents United groups in many cities also speak in schools, teaching children that they have a right to protect themselves from sexual abuse and offering help.

4 Florence Rush, "Child pornography," in Laura Lederer (ed.), *Take Back the Night: Women on Pornography* (New York: W. Morrow, 1980), p. 71.

5 Rush, *The Best Kept Secret*, pp. 16–47. Rush documents abuse through biblical, talmudic, and Christian eras. Her research is detailed and stunning, providing historical validation for these terrible realities. I am indebted to her for the following information and invite those of you who want to know more to read *The Best Kept Secret* and to investigate Rush's sources. For her chapter on the Bible and the Talmud, she cites, among others, *The Babylonian Talmud*, ed. Seder Nezikin; Moses Maimonides, *The Book of Women; The Mishna*, ed. Eugene J. Lipinan; David M. Feldman; *Marital Relations, Birth Control, and Abortion in Jewish Law*; Louis M. Epstein, *Sex Laws and Customs in Judaism*; and the Old Testament itself. For the Christians, she cites, among others, Henry Charles Lea, *History of Sacerdotal Celibacy in the Christian Church*; C. C. Coulton, *Medieval Panorama*; John C. O'Dea, *The Matrimonial Impediment of Nonage*; H. A. Aytinhae, *Marriage Legislation in the New Code of Canon Law*; V. H. H.

Green, *Medieval Civilization in Western Europe*; and John Fulton, *Laws of Marriage*.

6 This information is from Mary Daly, *Gyn/Ecology* (Boston: Beacon Press, 1978), pp. 113–33.

7 This information is from Daly, *Gyn/Ecology*, pp. 134–52, and Andrea Dworkin, *Woman Hating* (New York: E. P. Dutton, 1974), pp. 95–117. (In *Woman Hating*, Andrea Dworkin has a small section on incest in which she advocates the destruction of the incest taboo as being "essential to the development of cooperative human community based on the free-flow of natural androgynous eroticism." Because I know her as a pioneer in the exposure of violence toward women and children, I wrote to her asking whether she would send me a clarifying statement or disclaimer to include in this reference. She replied, "I hope some day I will be able to figure out how what we call 'the incest taboo' functions to, in fact, sanction especially father–daughter rape . . . The problem is the nature of sexuality in this male supremacist system, so that all the love, sensuality, and curiosity of children ends up being cynically used against them, in sex as in so many other areas. So I do not advocate incest; and I do speak out against it, naming it the sexual abuse of children. It has become one of my priority concerns.")

8 Daly, *Gyn/Ecology*, pp. 153–77.

9 This information is from Brownmiller, *Against our Will*, pp. 23–130.

10 This information is from Barbara Ehrenreich and Deirdre English, *Witches, Midwives, and Nurses: a History of Women Healers* (Old Westbury, NY: The Feminist Press, 1973); Daly, *Gyn/Ecology*, pp. 178–222; Dworkin, *Woman Hating*, pp. 118–50; Rush, *The Best Kept Secret*, pp. 37–43.

11 Vera Goodman, "Juvenile detention for girls a horror," *New Directions for Women*, 8 (3) (Summer, 1979), pp. 7–8.

12 *David Hamilton's Private Collection* (New York: Morrow Quill, 1980).

13 Rush discusses these movies in "Child pornography," pp. 74–5.

14 *Oakland Tribune*, November 6, 1981, p. A-3. (In a statement representative of the conflicting messages this society gives girls and women, the judge said both that Brooke Shields's mother shouldn't have allowed the pictures to be taken and that there was nothing wrong with the pictures. He ruled against blocking future commercial use.)

15 *Minneapolis Star*, March 19, 1981, p. 8-A.

16 Statistics from John Hurst, "Children – a big profit item from the smut producers," *Los Angeles Times*, May 26, 1977, quoted in Rush, "Child pornography," p. 77.

17 *Time*, April 1977.

18 Copies of this album were destroyed by members of the Preying Mantis Women's Brigade of Santa Cruz, California, a group dedicated to ending violence against women and children.

19 Linda Lee Curns's story is one of the many excellent submissions we were not able to include due to space limitations.

20 See Rush, *The Best Kept Secret*, for more examples.

Suggested activities

Questions for discussion

On work

1 Is there any legitimate justification for the wage gap between men's and women's earnings? Why do you think it persists?
2 Debate the merits and limitations of affirmative action policies. Regardless of your overall views about affirmative action, do you think that affirmative action policies should be the same for women as for racial minorities? If not, why not? What sort of differences between the two groups might justify different treatment? What is the status of women of color in relation to your proposed answer?
3 Are women obtaining more job and career opportunities in the 1990s than earlier? Or is the picture mixed? What particular considerations support your views?
4 Should quotas be used to ensure a certain proportion of women in the workforce? Should the answer depend on the particular kind of work involved, and its history of allowing or prohibiting women from participation?

On sex work

1 Can women who participate in sex work be feminist? What assumptions do you make about women, sex, and sex work in answering this question?
2 Should prostitution be legalized? Should women working in the sex industry be legally protected against exploitation and physical and sexual abuse? Why or why not? How do feminist answers to these questions differ, if at all, from non-feminist ones?
3 Discuss some of the factors that contribute to women working in the sex industry. How would these factors have to be different, if at all, for your views about women's involvement in sex work to change? For example, would your views be different if all women who wanted them had access to jobs outside the sex industry with reasonable salaries and working conditions?
4 Do women actually "choose" to become prostitutes? What assumptions and evidence are your conclusions based on? What influence does the statistic that approximately 80 percent of female prostitutes have been sexually abused have on your answer?

On education

1 Reflect on your own experiences in elementary, junior high and high school. Were boys and girls treated differently? In what respects? If there were

differences, which sex was treated more favorably? What sorts of messages were boys and girls given regarding future education? For example, were girls encouraged to take advanced classes in math and science, or directed into other areas? How about the guidance that boys received?

2   What should schools be doing to reduce the disparity in the quality of education that girls and boys receive?

3   What do you think of proposals to enhance the educational opportunities for girls by establishing more single-sex schools where girls need not compete with boys for the teacher's time and attention, as they now have to?

On sexual harassment

1   How would you define sexual harassment? Have you ever been sexually harassed within your definition? How does your definition compare with that of the EEOC? Do you think sexual harassment should be a legally recognized offense? How about the version of sexual harassment known as "hostile environment"?

2   Why do you think sexual harassment has been such a problem in schools and workplaces? What measures, if any, do you think are necessary to eliminate it as a problem?

3   Should students and teachers be able to date? If so, what kind of restrictions, if any, would you recommend? Can regulations ensure that such relationships are consensual? What reasons justify your position? Should the appropriateness of student/teacher relationships depend on the ages of the parties involved? The gender of the particular teacher and student involved? Whether the student is in high school, college or graduate school? Whether the student is currently taking classes from the teacher or could potentially have the teacher as an instructor in the future?

4   What impact did the race and gender of the parties involved have on the Hill/Thomas hearings? Consider the factors relevant to Anita Hill's decision to testify against Clarence Thomas. What might *you* have done if you were Anita Hill? Why?

5   Should the principles governing sexual harassment in the workplace be applied in schools? Should boys be held to the same standards of behavior as men? If not, who should be held responsible for sexual harassment in schools, the parents or school officials?

6   What factors may make it even more difficult for women abused by spiritual leaders to come forward than where abuse is by others?

On sexual abuse and violence against women

1   What are some of the factors that contribute to domestic violence? What are some of the cultural assumptions and stereotypes that have prevented

an effective legal response to the problem of domestic violence? Do you think the incidence of violence against women would be reduced if more women were employed in roles involving the use of force, such as the military and police?

2 Do you think enough is being done by law-makers and others to prevent and deter the physical and sexual abuse of women? If not, what more needs to be done? Are you optimistic or pessimistic that such steps will be taken?

3 Is enough done to prevent and deter rape? Why or why not? If not, what further steps should be taken – at your college or university, home town, state? How about on a national or even international level?

4 According to the survivors' stories that Mahoney relates in her article, what are some of the reasons that women stay in physically abusive relationships? How do these reasons compare with those that are most dominant in the media and public opinion?

5 Was the publicity about domestic violence in the O.J. Simpson case helpful in educating the public about the extent of the problem? Why or why not?

6 Can the law adequately protect women from violence in a free society? If not, what other changes in society and culture are necessary? Even apart from these changes, what additional law-reform efforts, if any, might further protect women from violence?

7 What responsibility, if any, does the mass media have for violence against women? Does it have a social responsibility to curb its portrayals of violence? Or only if evidence conclusively shows a connection between the *images* it projects and the *reality* of the abuse of women?

Films and videos

The Accused starring Jodie Foster as a victim of gang rape who reluctantly decides to prosecute. Based on real-life events of a gang rape that took place in a working-class bar in New Bedford, Massachusetts. Contains graphic scenes of the rape. Excerpts of this film are also in the "Dreamworlds" video (see below).

Dating Rites: Gang Rape on Campus, produced by Alison Stone, Stonescape Productions (1992). VHS/28 mins. Available from Filmaker's Library. Documentary about gang rape and acquaintance rape on college campuses. Includes interviews with a gang-rape survivor and a convicted rapist as well as rape crisis counselors, psychologists, and sociologists.

Dreamworlds: Desire/Sex/Power in Rock Video, written, edited, and narrated by Sut Jally (1991). VHS/55 mins. Available from Foundation for Media Education, Amherst, MA. About the portrayals of women in rock videos, which Jally contends create a "dreamworld" for the fantasies of young men, in which women are usually depicted as highly sexed, aggressive pursuers of men or passive victims of male sexual aggression, victims of rape, physical assault, sexual coercion, and so on.

Every Woman's Fear, Parts 1 and 2, from the Without Consent series (1992). $\frac{1}{2}$ inch VHS. Part 1 is 60 mins; Part 2 is 26 mins. Uses re-enactments and commentary from rape and sexual assault victims and perpetrators to portray rape and its immediate aftermath. Considers different kinds of rape. Contains graphic language. Part 2 discusses the aftermath of rape, including reactions of others related to the victim or the criminal justice system.

Honoring our Voices by Judi Jeffrey (Canada, 1992). VHS/color/33 mins. Distributed by Women Make Movies. Interviews with six Native American women trying to overcome domestic violence and abuse with the aid of native healing strategies.

Just Because of who We Are by Heramedia Collective (1986). VHS/28 mins. Available from Women Make Movies. Documentary focused on the neglected issue of violence against lesbians. Interviews a range of women, including writers Cherrie Moraga and Barbara Smith.

Mommy Track, produced by ABC Nightline with Ted Koppel (1989). VHS/22 mins. Examines the controversy over whether professional and executive women should be placed on a slower advancement or "mommy track" when they have children, how businesses are adapting to the needs of working mothers, and how experts from women's groups and businesses address the issue.

No Means No by Ann-Sargent Wooster (1993). VHS/color/13 mins. Distributed by Women Make Movies. Discussion piece that raises issues with regard to date rape.

Rape by Any Name by Angelique LaCouer and Wade Hanks (1990). VHS/60 mins. Available from Women Make Movies. On acquaintance rape, featuring candid interviews with rape survivors, counselors and male and female college students.

Rape Stories, by Margie Strosser (1989). VHS/color/BW/25 mins. Distributed by Women Make Movies. Story of Strosser's rape experience and her recounting of the memory as a way of coping.

Rape Victim: No Longer Anonymous (1990). VHS/30 mins. Available from Films for the Humanities. Interviews two women who were raped by strangers, using the Phil Donohue Show as a setting for the interviews. Covers the feelings of the survivors and how they decided to fight back using the legal system.

Rate it X by Luce Winer and Paula De Koenigsberg (1986). 16 mm/VHS/color/ 93 mins. Documentary on the portrayal of women's images in popular culture and its consequences on sexism in America.

Rule of Thumb: Order of Protection by Jill Petzall (1989). VHS/22 mins. Available from Women Make Movies. Explores domestic violence through the perspectives of five women who have left abusive relationships. Supplemented with testimonies from a woman judge, a police officer and a former abuser.

Sandra's Garden: Women and Incest by Bonnie Dickie (Canada, 1991). VHS/color/34 mins. Distributed by Women Make Movies. The story of Sandra, a lesbian and an incest survivor, who speaks out to overcome the fear and shame of her experience.

Secret Sounds Screaming: the Sexual Abuse of Children by Ayoka Chenzira (1986). VHS/color/30 mins. Distributed by Women Make Movies. Exploration of the dynamics that link victims, abusers, parents, and social workers who handle children's cases. Includes a multicultural approach.

Seven Lucky Charms by Lisa Mann (1992). 16 mm/VHS/16 mins. Available from Women Make Movies. Documentary weaves animated imagery together with statistical information on violence against women in order to help the viewer understand the reality of battered women, especially those who kill their batterers in self-defense.

Sex, Power, and the Workplace, written/produced by Robert Dean (1992). VHS/60 mins. Available through KCET Video. 20/20 video on sexual harassment to empower women.

Sexual Harassment: How Far is Too Far?, ABC News 20/20 (1987). VHS/17 mins. Report on sexual harassment in the workplace. Interviews two women who filed sexual harassment suits against their supervisors.

So Like You (1990). VHS/28 mins. Available from MTI Film and Video. Reviews an incident of sexual harassment from the point of view of both the man and the woman, revealing how the same events are interpreted differently.

Stories from the Riverside: Women Jailed for Killing their Abusers, produced by Susanne Mason (1993). VHS/30 mins. Available from Filmaker's Library. Documentary visits Gatesville Penitentiary in Texas, where three female inmates convicted of murder describe the domestic violence that led to their killing their abusers, challenging attitudes toward victims who act in violent self-defense.

They Never Call it Rape, produced by Abigail L. Rockmore (1990). VHS/21 mins. Available from ABC News. On gang rape on college campuses. Interviews students, school officials, rape experts and victims, showing the double standards that end up re-victimizing the survivor, and universities' protection of perpetrators.

Two Million Women: Domestic Violence (1987). VHS/29 mins. Available from MTI Film and Video. Examines domestic violence against women and explores the emotionally complex and cyclical patterns of abuse. Presents interviews and case studies of three victims of abuse, as well as interviews with perpetrators. Also presents the issue of battering in dating relationships.

Union Maids, produced/directed by James Klein, Julia Reichert, and Miles Magulescu (1976). 16 mm/VHS/48 mins. Available from New Day Films. Oral history of women organizing labor unions in the 1930s.

Violence in the Home: Living in Fear, produced by AIMS Media (1989). VHS/ 30 mins. Available from AIMS Media. Explains the cycle of domestic violence, its causes, consequences, and the effects of intervention and treatment. Uses dramatizations, showing the arrest of the abuser, and the personal and legal consequences. Interviews victims, perpetrators, health professionals, and shelter personnel.

Voices Heard Sisters Unseen by Grace Poore (1995). VHS/color/75 mins. Distributed by Women Make Movies. Interviews, poetry, and music combine to create a feminist criticism of the justice system with regard to domestic violence. Includes study guide.

Waiting Tables, produced by Linda Chapman, Pam LeBlanc, and Freddi Stevens Jacobi (1986). VHS/20 mins. Available through Filmaker's Library. Light-hearted social commentary on waitressing as part of the "pink-collar" work that is done predominantly by women. Includes a Lily Tomlin routine and Gloria Steinem's experiences as a Playboy Bunny.

Waking Up to Rape, by Meri Weingarten (1985). VHS/35 mins. Available from Women Make Movies. Examines the personal trauma of rape, its long-term psychological effects, and the problem of racism in the criminal justice system. Three rape survivors (black, Chicana, and white) describe their experiences with rape and its aftermath.

War Zone by Maggie Hadleigh-West, Film Fatale (1993). VHS/13 mins. Available from Carousel Film & Video. The film-maker is seen filming men in the act of harassing her on the city streets. Documents her experience with this damaging behavior and her attempts to define it.

We're Here Now (1983). VHS/30 mins. Available from Filmaker's Library. Portrays a group therapy session of female prostitutes in varying stages of changing their lives, showing the relationship between former abuse, drug use, low self-esteem, family, history, and the choice of prostitution as a way of life.

Who Cares for the Children?, hosted by Rhea Perlman; produced by Dave Davis for KCTS/TV (1988). VHS/55 mins. Available through Filmaker's Library. Examines the current child-care crisis through the eyes of parents, providers, children, and experts. Shows model programs of effective child care.

Why God, Why Me?, produced by Varied Productions (1988). VHS/27 mins. Available from Varied Directions, Camden, ME. Award-winning program about childhood sexual abuse dramatizing the life-story of victims. Several women recall their childhood sexual encounters with adults.

Why Women Stay by Jacqueline Shortell-McSweeney and Debra Zimmerman (1980). VHS/BW/30 mins. Distributed by Women Make Movies. A documentary that explores the complex issues that often persuade women to stay in an abusive relationship. Examines battered women's attitudes and the lack of shelters for battered women.

With Babies and Banners, produced by Women's Labor History Film Project (1978). VHS/16mm/45 mins. Available from New Day Films. Story of the women at the center of the Great General Motors Sit-Down Strike of 1937, told by nine of the women who participated.

Women of Steel by Mon Valley Media (1984). VHS/28 mins. Available from Filmaker's Library. Award-winning historical documentary on women's short-lived gains from entering the steel mills in the 1970s that is relevant to understanding women's economic situation in the 1990s.

You are the Game: Sexual Harassment on Campus, produced/directed by Chris Lamar, written by Constance Dyer and Chris Lamar (1985). VHS/60 mins. Available from Indiana University Radio and Television Services. Dramatizes the situations of two women college students who experienced different forms of sexual harassment. Follow-up panel provides insight into the broader issues of why sexual harassment occurs, how it affects the educational climate, and what can be done about it.

You Don't Have to Take It (1994). VHS/17 mins. Focuses on the concept of sexual harassment in schools among young adults. Defines the term and explains what the victim can do to stop it. Uses interviews with school administrators and faculty, a law professor, a social worker and several students, as well as dramatizations and voice-over.

Other activities

1 Research the policy, if any, at your educational institution regarding student/teacher dating, and evaluate its adequacy. Does it treat the student as a responsible adult or a helpless victim? Does it recognize the potential for abuse of power? Does it impose blanket rules or allow for differences in particular cases? What procedures does it establish, if any, for evaluating and reviewing cases that violate its provisions?

2 Review televised footage of the Hill/Thomas hearings. Consider the likely reaction of various groups to Hill's testimony, Thomas's defense, and to the Senate questioners based on race and gender differences. Do these reactions differ on the basis of racial and gender differences? If so, how do you explain these differences?

3 For a group project, arrange to conduct brief interviews with women who work in a variety of different occupations and professions. Develop a questionnaire designed to obtain information about gender discrimination and sexual harassment, and the impact of affirmative action policies. What commonalities and differences are there among these women's experiences?

Do you think their particular experiences are representative of other women working in that field? Why or why not? Can you conclude that some occupations and professions are more "women-friendly" than others? If so, are these traditionally female jobs?

4   As an alternative to activity (3) above, invite women from a variety of professions and occupations to speak to your class. Ask them to address the questions raised in activity (3). Again, consider the similarities and differences among these women's experiences. What insights do these women provide about the obstacles and advantages of being a woman working in a particular field?

5   Coordinate with a small group of classmates to interview staff from community-based agencies that provide services for women survivors of rape or domestic violence or sexual abuse. Report your findings to the class.

6   As an alternative to activity (5) above, invite staff, volunteers, and/or willing survivors from these agencies to speak to your class. Many local therapists, prosecutors, child advocacy workers, and judges have had extensive experience in dealing with these topics that they are willing to share. If you invite a speaker, be sure to plan a number of questions to ask them in advance.

7   As a large group activity, brainstorm the social and cultural changes that would be necessary to end violence against women. Is progress being made in this regard? How might progress be improved?

Bibliography

Although there is some overlap among these categories, the references have been categorized in accordance with the primary topic addressed.

On education

Barbieri, Maureen (1995) *Sounds from the Heart: Learning to Listen to Girls* (Portsmouth, NY: Heinemann). Teacher describes seventh grade girls' lives and expectations.

Bell, Lee Ann (1995) "Something's wrong here and it's not me: challenging the dilemmas that block girls' success," in Amy Kesselman, Lily McNair, and Nancy Schniedewind (eds), *Women: Images and Realities. A Multicultural Anthology* (Mountain View, CA: Mayfield).

Carroll, Constance (1982) "Three's a crowd: the dilemma of the black woman in higher education," in Gloria Hull, Patricia Bell Scott and Barbara Smith (eds), *All the Women are White* (Westbury, NY: The Feminist Press).

Orenstein, Peggy (1994) *SchoolGirls* (New York: Doubleday). Using *How Schools Shortchange Girls* as background, describes research she conducted on discrimination against girls in two middle-schools.

Sadker, Myra and Sadker, David (1994) *Failing at Fairness: How America's Schools Cheat Girls* (New York: Charles Scribner).

Sadker, Myra and Sadker, David (1995) "Sexism in the schoolroom of the '80s," in Amy Kesselman, Lily McNair, and Nancy Schniedewind (eds), *Women: Images and Realities. A Multicultural Anthology* (Mountain View, CA: Mayfield).

Stone, Lynda (1994) *The Education Feminist Reader: Developments in a Field of Study* (London: Routledge). Collection of classic essays by prominent feminist theorists in education. Essays are organized under the headings of "Self and identity," "Education and schooling," "Knowledge, curriculum and instructional arrangement," "Teaching and pedagogy," and "Diversity and multiculturalism."

On employment

Cole, Johnnetta (ed.) (1986) *All American Women: Lines that Divide, Ties that Bind* (New York: Macmillan). Several interesting essays on women's relationship to work.

Denmark, Florence, Nielson, Karen and Scholl, Kristina (1993) "United States of America," in Leonore Loeb Adler (ed.), *International Handbook on Gender Roles* (Westport, CT: Greenwood Press).

Faludi, Susan (1991) "The wages of the backlash: the toll on working women," in *Backlash: the Undeclared War against American Women* (New York: Crown Publishers).

Hutner, Frances (1994) *Our Vision and Values: Women Shaping the 21st Century* (New York: Praeger). Chapters on women's lives at home and at work, and women in management.

Lunneborg, Patricia (1990) *Women Changing Work* (Westport, CT: Greenwood Press). On gender differences in work, based on interviews with women employees.

Malveaux, Julianne (1990) "Gender difference and beyond: an economic perspective on diversity and commonality among women," in Deborah Rhode (ed.), *Theoretical Perspectives on Sexual Difference* (New Haven, CT: Yale University Press). Essay on the influence that race has on women's experiences in the economy.

Malveaux, Julianne (1991) "No peace in sisterly space," *The Black Scholar*, 22(1–2): 68–71. Describes who supported and who criticized Anita Hill for her testimony against Clarence Thomas.

Marano, Cynthia (1995) "Running harder to catch up: women, work and the future," in Amy Kesselman, Lily McNair, and Nancy Schniedewind (eds), *Women: Images and Realities. A Multicultural Anthology* (Mountain View, CA: Mayfield).

Romero, Mary (1992) *Maid in the USA* (New York: Routledge). Describes the relationships between the women who work as housekeepers and those who employ them in the United States, and how they are influenced by race, ethnicity, and class differences.

Yoder, Janice (1989) "Women at West Point: lessons for token women in male-dominated occupations," in Jo Freeman (ed.), *Women: a Feminist Perspective* (Mountain View, CA: Mayfield). On the consequences of gender integration in the US military academy at West Point.

On sexual harassment

Association of American University Women (1993) "Hostile hallways: the AAUW survey on sexual harassment in America's schools" (AAUW Educational Foundation, 1111 16th Street, NW, Washington, DC 20036-4873).

Borgida, Eugene and Fiske, Susan (eds) (1995) Special issue on *Gender Stereotyping, Sexual Harassment, and the Law, Journal of Social Issues*, 51(1). Prominent social scientists examine how stereotyping contributes to sexual harassment.

Brownmiller, Susan and Alexander, Dolores (1992) "From Carmita Wood to Anita Hill," *Ms.* (January/February), pp. 70–71. Overview of the history of women's fight against sexual harassment, which has been led by women of color and working-class women.

Conte, Alba (1994) *Sexual Harassment in the Workplace: Law and Practice*, 2nd edn (New York: Wiley). Law-oriented analysis and discussion.

Hill, Anita (1992) "The nature of the beast," *Ms.* (January/February), pp. 32–3.

Ihle, Elizabeth (1992) *Black Women in Higher Education: an Anthology of Essays, Studies, and Documents* (New York: Garland). Documentary collection of both early and contemporary sources organized into sections on black women at Oberlin, Virginia State University, North Carolina A & T, Brandeis, and at white institutions during the 1940s, each preceded by explanatory notes. Includes an introductory essay, a selected bibliography, and an index of authors.

Lederman, Douglas (1993a) "Colgate U. becomes a battleground over equity in college athletics," *Chronicle of Higher Education* (February 17), pp. A27–8.

Lederman, Douglas (1993b) "Women turn to the courts in fight for more sports opportunities," *Chronicle of Higher Education* (February 17), pp. A27–8.

McKay, Nellie (1992) "Remembering Anita Hill and Clarence Thomas: what really happened when one black woman spoke out," in Toni Morrison (ed.), *Race-ing Justice, En-gendering Power: Essays on Anita Hill, Clarence Thomas, and the Construction of Social Reality* (New York: Pantheon Books).

Morris, Celia (1994) *Bearing Witness: Sexual Harassment and Beyond – Everywoman's Story* (Boston: Little, Brown). Inspired by Anita Hill's treatment, and based on interviews with women victims, which "teach us that male violence against women is endemic, that it cripples us all profoundly, and that we can do something about it."

Morrison, Toni (ed.) (1992) *Race-ing Justice, En-Gendering Power: Essays on Anita Hill, Clarence Thomas, and the Construction of Social Reality* (New York: Pantheon Books). A collection of essays on the Hill/Thomas hearings, several from a feminist or womanist perspective.

Rutter, Peter (1996) *Sex, Power and Boundaries: Understanding and Preventing Sexual Harassment* (New York: Bantam Books).

Sandler, Bernice R. and Shoop, Robert J. (1997) *Sexual Harassment on Campus: a Guide for Administrators, Faculty and Students* (Boston: Allyn and Bacon).

Stan, Adel (ed.) (1995) *Debating Sexual Correctness: Pornography, Sexual Harassment, Date Rape, and the Politics of Sexual Equality* (New York: Delta).

Sumrall, Amber and Taylor, Dena (eds) (1992) *Sexual Harassment: Women Speak Out* (Freedom, CA: Crossing Press). Anthology of essays on women's experiences of sexual harassment.

On sexual abuse and violence against women

Adler, Leonore Loeb (1993) *International Handbook on Gender Roles* (Westport, CT: Greenwood Press, 1993).

Armstrong, Louise (1994) *Rocking the Cradle of Sexual Politics: What Happened When Women Said Incest* (Reading, MA: Addison-Wesley). Explores how the incest movement has been depoliticized and "clinicalized," and thereby removed from the public policy agenda as an issue in need of social change.

Bachman, Ronet (1994) *Violence against Women: a National Crime Victimization Survey Report* (Washington, DC: US Department of Justice).

Barbee, Evelyn (1994) "A legacy of silence," *The Women's Review of Books*, 12(2): 30–31. Gives a mixed review of Melba Wilson's *Crossing the Boundary* (see below), finding it uneven, but filling a need for writing on the issue of incest and childhood sexual abuse of black girls and women.

Bass, Ellen and Davis, Laura (1994) *The Courage to Heal: a Guide for Women Survivors of Child Sexual Abuse*, 3rd edn (New York: Perennial Library). A self-help guide, organized under the headings "Taking stock," "The healing process," "Changing patterns," "For supporters of survivors," "Courageous women," "Honoring the truth: a response to the backlash," and "Resource guide."

Bass, Ellen and Thornton, Louise (eds) (1983) *I Never Told Anyone: Writings by Women Survivors of Child Sexual Abuse* (New York: Harper & Row). Includes, as its introduction, the reading by Ellen Bass included in this chapter, as well as a number of stories by survivors of childhood sexual abuse.

Bergen, Raquel Kennedy (1996) *Wife Rape: Understanding the Response of Survivors and Service Providers* (Newbury Park, CA: Sage). Part of the "Sage Series on Violence against Women"; stories of 40 women and a resource guide.

Bohmer, Carol and Parrot, Andrea (1993) *Sexual Assault on Campus: the Problem and the Solution* (New York: Lexington Books). An extremely informative and practical guide to the problem in the college context. Traces the institutional response to sexual assault from the incident through the university, criminal justice, and legislative processes. Appendix includes a "Summary of recommendations to create a campus free of acquaintance rape."

Bonavoglia, Angela (1992) "The sacred secret," *Ms.*, November/December, pp. 40–45.

Browne, Angela (1987) *When Battered Women Kill* (New York: Free Press). Covers the childhood roots of violence, courtship and early marriage, typical violence, psychological differences between men and women in ways of relating, factors contributing to women killing their abusers, and the legal system's response to battered women.

Buchwald, Emilie, Fletcher, Pamela, and Roth, Martha (eds) (1993) *Transforming a Rape Culture* (Minneapolis, MN: Milkweed Editions). Collection of over 30 essays, mostly offering constructive and non-polarizing proposals for changing a society that currently fosters sexual violence. Essays cover neglect of the problem by religious institutions and the entertainment industry. Includes current statistics, a list of sexual violence resources and a reading list.

Bumiller, Kristin (1991) "Fallen angels: the representation of violence against women in legal culture," in Martha Albertson Fineman and Nancy Sweet Thomadsen (eds), *At the Boundaries of Law* (New York: Routledge).

Buzawa, Eve and Buzawa, Carl (eds) (1992) *Domestic Violence: the Changing Criminal Justice Response* (Westport, CT: Auburn House). Collection of essays on how law enforcement and criminal justice have addressed domestic violence.

Cardarelli, Albert P. (ed.) (1997) *Violence between Intimate Partners: Patterns, Causes, and Effects* (Needham Heights, MA: Allyn and Bacon). An examination of the causes and social constructions of violence between domestic partners.

Carosella, Cynthia (ed.) (1995) *Who's Afraid of the Dark? A Forum of Truth, Support, and Assurance for Those Affected by Rape* (New York: HarperCollins). Collection of heart-wrenching stories by 28 women rape survivors about the long-term effects of rape, and the stigma and isolation that result from being a rape victim.

Cuklanz, Lisa M. (1996) *Rape on Trial: How the Mass Media Construct Legal Reform and Social Change* (Philadelphia: University of Pennsylvania Press).

Dobash, Emerson and Dobash, Russell (1979) *Violence against Wives: a Case against the Patriarchy* (New York: The Free Press).

Epstein, Joel and Langenbahn, Stacie (1994) *The Criminal Justice and Community Response to Rape* (Washington, DC: US Department of Justice). Report describing recent key reforms designed to protect victims and facilitate prosecution and conviction of offenders.

Estrich, Susan (1987) *Real Rape* (Cambridge, MA: Harvard University Press). Begins with her own experience of being raped, and continues by describing the inadequacies of police response, and the continuing legal bias against women victims.

Fairstein, Linda (1993) *Sexual Violence: our War against Rape* (New York: W. Morrow). By the head of the Sex Crimes Prosecution Unit in the office of the New York County District Attorney. Story of her career and establishment of the Sex Crimes Prosecution Unit.

Fineman, Martha Albertson and Mykitiuk, Roxanne (eds) (1994) *The Public Nature of Private Violence* (New York: Routledge). Collection of essays organized under the headings "Images of violence," "Feminist theory and legal norms," "International and comparative perspectives on domestic violence," and "Policy postscript."

French, Marilyn (1992) *The War against Women* (New York: Summit Books). The title of this classic second-wave feminist work refers to male efforts to defeat feminism in areas such as the "glass ceiling," fundamentalism, and abortion regulations. French takes the position that patriarchy began and spread as a war against women. Part I addresses systematic wars against women, such as the sexual division of labor, economic disadvantage of women which leads to political discrimination, and religious control over women's bodies and dress. Part III addresses women hatred in culture, language and art. Part IV covers assaults on women's bodies such as rape, domestic violence, incest, and how they have been tolerated by courts and the police.

Henderson, Lynne (1992) "Rape and responsibility," *Law and Philosophy*, 11: 127–78. Explores the continuing resistance to taking rape seriously in American culture, suggesting that it is related to the myth of heterosexuality, in which men "cannot help themselves" and women are responsible for both their own and men's sexual activity.

Higgins, Lynn and Silver, Brenda (eds) (1991) *Rape and Representation* (New York: Columbia University Press). Essays on the way that rapes are portrayed in literature, recognizing that *who* gets to tell the story defines the reality of what *is*, thus that rape looks very different when the author is male than female.

Hughes, Jean O'Gorman (1987) "Friends raping friends: could it happen to you?," in *Information on Rape: What is it and What Can I Do about It?* (Washington, DC: Project on the Status and Education of Women, Association of American Colleges). Educational booklet of practical advice and help on rape, oriented specifically to women in college and university.

Itzin, Catherine (ed.) (1992) *Pornography: Women, Violence and Civil Liberties* (Oxford: Oxford University Press). Collection of articles from an anti-pornography perspective.

Jones, Ann (1994) *Next Time She'll be Dead: Battering and How to Stop It* (Boston: Beacon Press).

Koss, Mary (1994) *No Safe Haven: Male Violence against Women at Home, at Work, and in the Community* (Washington, DC: American Psychological Association). Discusses domestic violence against women, as well as rape and sexual harassment.

Ledray, Linda, C. (1988) *Recovering from Rape* (New York: Holt). Subtitled "Practical advice on overcoming the trauma and coping with police, hospitals, and court – for survivors of sexual assault and for their families, lovers, and friends."

Liebman, Janet Jacobs (1994) *Victimized Daughters: Incest and the Development of the Female Self* (New York: Routledge). Research seeking a framework for understanding the relationship between incest and the construction of the female self through in-depth interviews with 50 incest survivors.

McKenzie, V. Michael (1995) *Domestic Violence in America* (Lawrenceville, VA: Brunswick). Psychologist examines causes, effects, state laws, and current programs.

MacKinnon, Catharine (1987) "Linda's life and Andrea's work," in *Feminism Unmodified: Discourses on Life and Law* (Cambridge, MA: Harvard University Press). On the relationship between pornography and violence against women.

Martin, Del (1976) *Battered Wives* (San Francisco: Glide Publications). A classic study that describes domestic violence in the context of efforts by men in patriarchal societies to keep women subordinate. Proposes that ending domestic violence requires eradicating unequal power relationships, which in turn requires restructuring the traditional family.

Murphy-Milano, Susan (1996) *Defending our Lives: Getting Away from Domestic Violence and Staying Safe* (New York: Anchor Books).

National Victims Resource Center, *Domestic Violence Reading List* (tel.: 1-800-627-6872). Contains a number of publications on violence against women, with addresses and other information on availability.

Radford, J. and Russell, Diana (eds) (1992) *Femicide: the Politics of Women Killing* (New York: Twayne Publishers). Collection of 40 contributors documenting the killing of women across the globe, analyzing the roles that social values and institutions play in perpetuating it, and proposing strategies for combatting it.

Renzetti, Claire (ed.), *Violence against Women: an International and Interdisciplinary Journal*. A new journal "dedicated to the dissemination of original research and scholarship on all aspects of violence against women."

Rosen, Leora N. and Etlin, Michelle (1996) *The Hostage Child: Sex Abuse Allegation in Custody Disputes* (Bloomington, IN: Indiana University Press). Anthropologist and activist critique of how the legal system deals with incest and child custody.

Russell, Diana (1986) *The Secret Trauma: Incest in the Lives of Girls and Women* (New York: Basic Books). On incest, including case studies and stories of survivors.

Russell, Diana (1990) *Rape in Marriage*, rev. edn (Bloomington, IN: Indiana University Press). Study of physical and sexual abuse of women by their spouses. Includes an international perspective on the problem.

Russell, Diana (ed.) (1993) *Making Violence Sexy: Feminist Views on Pornography* (New York: Teachers College, Columbia University). Collection of essays on pornography and its relationship to violence against women.

Sanday, Peggy Reeves (1990) *Fraternity Gang Rape: Sex, Brotherhood, and Privilege on Campus* (New York: New York University Press). An investigation of the topic by an anthropologist.

Sanday, Peggy Reeves (1996) *A Woman Scorned: Acquaintance Rape on Trial* (New York: Doubleday). Anthropologist looks at sexual stereotypes in US culture.

Schecter, Susan (1992) *Women and Male Violence: the Visions and Struggles of the Battered Women's Movement* (Boston: South End Press). On the movement for battered women. Part II also analyzes violence against women in the family, assessing existing services, internal conflicts and organizing for the 1980s.

Sheler, Jeffrey (1992) "The unpardonable sin," *US News and World Report*, November 16, pp. 94–6. On the Church's slow move in responding to sexual misconduct by the clergy.

Snell, Tracy (1991) *Bureau of Justice Statistics Special Report: Women in Prison* (Washington, DC: US Department of Justice).

Stark, Evan, and Flitcraft, Anne (1996) *Women at Risk: Domestic Violence and Women's Health* (Thousand Oaks, CA: Sage). Theory, practical consequences, and intervention strategies.

Swisher, Karen and Wekesser, Carol (eds) (1994) *Violence against Women* (San Diego, CA: Greenhaven Press). Collection of essays taking contrasting viewpoints on a number of issues relating to violence against women.

Thompson, Stephen (1987) *No More Fear* (Dubuque, IA: Kendall Hunt). Practical strategies for avoiding rape and for self-defense.

Thorne-Finch, Ron (1992) *Ending the Silence: the Origins and Treatment of Male Violence against Women* (Toronto: University of Toronto Press). On abusive men, abused women, and sex role in North America.

United Nations Centre for Social Development and Humanitarian Affairs (1989) *Violence against Women in the Family* (New York: United Nations). Shows the global dimensions of violence against women.

Vanderbilt, Heidi (1992) "Incest: a four-part chilling report," *Lears*, 4(12): 49–77. Examines the children, the offenders, the courts, and recovery.

Whately, Mark A. (1993) "For better or worse: the case of marital rape," *Violence and Victims*, 8(1): 29–39. A literature review of the material on marital rape. Finds a disproportionate amount of literature on stranger rape as compared with marital rape, suggesting that marital rape is taken less seriously as a crime by the law as well as by scholars.

Wilson, Melba (1994) *Crossing the Boundary: Black Women Survive Incest* (Seattle, WA: The Seal Press). First half of the book describes the "why" of black incest and childhood sexual abuse. Second half attempts to explain black women's varied responses, develop a black feminist understanding, and describe a specific treatment approach for survivors.

Zawitz, Marianne (1994) *Bureau of Justice Statistics Selected Findings: Domestic Violence – Violence between Intimates* (Washington, DC: US Department of Justice).

PART III

Opportunities for Women in Culture

In the third and final part of this book, we turn from our examination of how women have been defined by culture to look at how women have been *defining* culture themselves. Chapter 9 looks both at women as producers of culture – artists, writers, performers, and so on – as well as the issue of whether there is a distinctive women's culture. The final chapter, chapter 10, looks at the future prospects of women in American culture, first looking at feminist politics, then turning to the backlash against feminism, and concluding with some possibilities for new directions for women in the future.

9
Women Creating Culture

Introduction

Women have historically been ignored as creators of culture. This is true generally, as well as with respect to culture defined specifically in relation to art and literature. In this chapter, we will look specifically at the contributions women have made to American culture. In addition, we will consider whether women have a separate culture apart from mainstream or male-dominated culture.

The products of women's artistic expression have largely been ignored or devalued in American culture. In a now-classic feminist essay entitled "Why have there been no great women artists?" art historian Linda Nochlin debunks the myth that women have not had the talent to become recognized artists. She describes how, instead, women's artistic talents have been ignored, disparaged, and even suppressed (Nochlin, 1988). The story is similar with respect to women authors. Most biographers have not considered women's lives to be important or significant enough to write about. Consequently, many women's contributions to culture have gone unrecognized. Some of them have been irretrievably lost to history.

Women's contributions to culture

In one obvious sense, women have contributed to shaping American culture. Simply by comprising over half of the American population, it stands to reason that they have had a hand in creating culture. In another sense, however, the artistic expressions and other artifacts and products that are traditionally considered to be exemplars of American culture – music, fine art, photography, cinema, literature, even science and technology – are dominated by works of men. How should the relative absence of women from cultural creativity be explained? Early second-wave feminists recognized that those with the power to define culture and select what work would be recognized as culturally valuable have been males, and they have exercised an obvious bias against the cultural work produced by women. Thus, the cause of women's absence from culture is *not* women's lack of talent and creativity, but, rather, the operation of gender bias against their work having cultural merit. So-called "lesser" forms of art and culture that *have* been the province of women – many textile-based crafts such as quilt-making and basketry, for example – have been devalued as merely "folk art" rather than "fine art" by the male arbiters of culture.

In addition, women have frequently not been able to acquire the resources necessary to become primary producers of American culture. Artists need time, space, equipment, materials, and privacy in order to work effectively. These are resources that most women historically have not had available, both because they were not viewed as having the talent to be artistic producers and because their primary responsibilities in the domestic sphere limited their ability to pursue art. Alice Walker's (1974) classic essay "In search of our mother's gardens" traces the obstacles that African-American women, like the author Phyllis Wheatley, have faced in becoming writers, even to the extent of being denied the opportunity to learn to write. Walker also addresses women's often unrecognized and unacknowledged artistic expressions.

Feminist scholars in the past two decades have drawn attention to the exclusion of women from male-dominated culture. Feminist criticism of the established canons of literature and art have revealed the male bias in these genres of cultural expression. In particular, feminist critics have observed male bias in evaluations of what constitutes "quality" art and literature, and how these standards have operated to exclude or devalue work by women artists and writers, as well as by people of color. British author Virginia Woolf (1882–1941) wrote *A Room of One's Own* (1929) in which she describes how an imaginary sister of William Shakespeare, endowed with equivalent talent, would have been ignored, suppressed, and ridiculed, and would have died without her abilities being recognized, simply because she was a woman.

There are now a number of published and nationally recognized African-American women poets and writers, with Alice Walker, Toni Morrison, Bebe Moore Campell, Jewell Gomez, Audre Lorde, Sonia Sanchez, Ntozake Shange, Jamaica Kincaid, and June Jordan prominent among them. However, prior to the 1970s, when Alice Walker's *The Color Purple* was published, Lorraine Hansberry (a playwright best known for *A Raisin in the Sun*) was the only African-American woman writer to receive national acclaim. The positive, courageous, and forward thinking spirit of African-American women writers has encompassed a concern with the oppression of African-Americans in society generally, and of women of color in particular.

In addition to literature, women have made analogous strides in the creation of works of art. Feminist struggles to make the art world pay serious attention to women began in the 1970s. These efforts were obstructed during the 1980s backlash that Faludi describes. In the 1990s, women artists have again become visible. They have used art to express opposition to sexism and the abuse of women (Nemser, 1992). A group called "Guerrilla Girls" in New York City has waged a campaign using posters to publicize the denigration of women's work in the art world (Gillespie, 1993). They plastered New York City with posters with slogans stating, for example, that less than 10 percent of the art displayed in most city museums is by women, "less than 5 percent of the artists in the Modern Art Sections [of the Met. Museum] are women, but 85 percent of the nudes are female." The Guerrilla Girls have met with some success in persuading galleries and museums to show more female artists.

In other ways, too numerous to discuss in any depth here, women have finally gained recognition as artists in other areas as well. Books on women artists, photographers, writers, painters, sculptors, choreographers and dancers, film directors, and other artists, have proliferated in the past several years. The publication of this material indicates that women's contributions to American culture are finally being given the recognition they deserve. In particular, a tradition of "women's music" has evolved over the past 25 years. Female musicians, writing music for women and *about* women – such as Holly Near and k.d. lang – have gained national recognition and recording contracts. Several organizations across the country host "women's music festivals." These events draw together hundreds of women from different socioeconomic, racial and ethnic backgrounds and sexual orientation, sometimes for several days, to enjoy music by women performers, buy and sell women-manufactured arts and crafts, attend workshops on women's issues, listen to women comediennes, poets, performance artists, and see women-produced and directed films.

One final area in which women have had a significant role in contributing to culture is in the sphere of religion. Religion has been shaped by, and in turn has shaped, cultural understandings of women. Historically, and to a significant extent still today, religion has reinforced normative views of women's appropriate roles as (exclusively) those of wives and mothers, condemned homosexuality and sexual activity outside wedlock, abortion and birth control, and generally accorded women a subordinate social role. In addition, traditional religions have perpetuated a strict division of sex roles, limiting women to roles as wives and mothers, and discouraging women from developing their own intellects and abilities in non-domestic realms. Feminists have questioned the authority of religious institutions to define the normative status and roles of women.

As in the other cultural and social institutions we have examined thus far, women have had a secondary status in all of the world's major religious traditions. Since the United States is a multicultural nation, it includes peoples with religious faiths from around the world. In addition, a number of religious traditions are distinctly American in origin. Some of the best-known religions were founded or established in America by women, including Quakers (Anne Hutchinson), the Shakers ("Mother" Ann Lee), Christian Science (Mary Baker Eddy), and Seventh Day Adventism (Ellen Darmon White).

Yet almost all of these religions – including the culturally dominant Christian and Jewish faiths – have traditionally relegated women to a secondary role. The dominant symbols of God and the divine are expressed in male-gendered language. Feminist scholars have observed how the maleness of God marginalizes or excludes the value and importance of femaleness, and thus of women, while promoting the value and importance of men, thereby reinforcing patterns of male domination and female subordination in the larger society. For example, radical feminist Mary Daly has argued that the logic of the biblical religions is that since "God is male, males are God"! The nineteenth-century feminist reformer Elizabeth Cady Stanton addressed this problem by publishing a *Woman's Bible* which eliminated the male-gendered references.

Neither Christianity nor Judaism has a major female figure of the stature of either Moses or Jesus. There are a number of women in the Bible, but they more often play supporting and secondary roles to men than being described as significant in their own right. The most prominent female figure in the Hebrew Bible is Eve, and she is responsible for having brought about the exclusion of Adam and Eve from the Garden of Eden, and bringing sin into the world! A similar lack of prominent women is evident in the Qu'ran, the Holy Book of Islam.

Early Christian theologians blamed women's pain in childbirth on the "sins" of their foremother Eve! This story is itself symbolic of the way in which many traditional religions have blamed women for the ills of the world. The craze against witches and witchcraft in the fifteenth through eighteenth centuries was largely an organized effort of Christian church authorities directed against women, especially those who failed to conform to prevailing cultural standards for female behavior (subservience and silence).

Feminist scholars and theologians, including Starhawk, the author of one of the readings in this chapter, have criticized the dominance of male symbols in Christianity and Judaism, contending that they send a message that human males are more important than females. This symbolism, in turn, reinforces the authority of males to control women. Feminist theologian Carol Christ argues that sexist and patriarchal symbols of God are harmful to women and need to be replaced – in her view, by symbols of the Goddess (Christ, 1986).

In addition to male-gendered language and symbols, women have been excluded from positions of leadership in most religious organizations. In Orthodox Judaism, for example, women are segregated in a special part of the temple. Similarly, in Islam, women are either excluded from the Mosque completely or segregated to a women's section. Even in Catholicism today, women are precluded from becoming priests (on the grounds that Jesus and all of the original disciples were male). Such exclusion has meant that women usually have not been permitted to participate in the formulation of religious codes of ethics – including those that relate to issues of particular significance to women, such as abortion – theology, liturgy, or other aspects of religious doctrine and activity.

It is not possible to generalize too much about the status of women in religion today because the variations among various religious groups, even within Christianity and Judaism, are far too great. More liberal religious traditions have admitted women to positions of leadership, eliminated male-gendered language from their liturgy and services, included the participation of more women in the establishment of official church policy, and even changed their traditional views on issues of significant concern to women, such as abortion, sexual harassment, women's employment outside the home, and violence against women. Other religious organizations have retained sexist and patriarchal traditions, even in the face of opposition and efforts for change. Perhaps the most visible example is the refusal of the Roman Catholic Church to change official church policies toward birth control, abortion, divorce, or the ordination of women, despite the contrary views of many Catholics.

None the less, some women have found meaning and spiritual nourishment even within traditional patriarchal and sexist religions. Some strategies that women remaining within traditional religions have used are: emphasizing aspects of the religion other than the male-gendered symbols; finding a liberating strand in the tradition that includes women's liberation from sexist oppression; stressing the lives of the Saints as positive role models; and emphasizing the female symbols that do exist, such as Esther in the Hebrew Bible, and Mary, mother of Jesus, in the New Testament.

Religion also has an impact on women who are *not* directly associated with a religious tradition. This has been evident in recent years in efforts by religious institutions to influence the law and public policy to promote "family values." These include several areas of particular concern for women's rights, including abortion, access to birth control (especially for minors), mothers working outside the home, sexual activity out of wedlock (including that leading to teenage pregnancy), homosexuality, censorship of school books, movies, television shows, and rock music.

Paralleling the rise in New Age spiritualities has been a decline in membership within many mainstream Christian and Jewish religious organizations. Dissatisfaction with the sexism and patriarchy of traditional religions has motivated some women to leave their traditional places of worship, and join or create alternative women-centered spiritual groups. There has been a growing interest in "Wicca," witchcraft, and other alternative New Age spiritualities and Eastern religious traditions in recent years, especially among women seeking female-centered or affirming spiritualities. *In the Lap of the Goddess*, by Cynthia Eller (1993), describes the feminist spirituality movement as including a reverence for nature, the use of magic and ritual, a commitment to the empowerment of women, acceptance of "sacred history," and the use of gender as a central category of analysis.

"Witchcraft as Goddess Religion," the third reading in this chapter, provides one example of an alternative female-centered spirituality. The author, Starhawk, a self-proclaimed "witch," describes the attractiveness of a spiritual tradition – for both men and women – that is centered around the Goddess rather than a male God. Women of color, including Zora Neal Hurston, Audre Lorde, Toni Cade Bambara, Ntozake Shange, Toni Morrison, and Alice Walker, have also been involved in recovering or discovering, and writing about, alternative women-affirming spiritual traditions within their own heritage.

Some critics of witchcraft and goddess-centered spiritualities contend that these are not authentic or genuine religions with a historical past, but, rather, are fabricated to serve the self-interests of women unwilling to struggle for change within their original religious tradition. Despite the views of critics, the development of women-centered spiritualities has also enabled women to reject religious institutions they believe do not respect them or their particular needs and interests, without needing to abandon religion altogether. It has enabled women to retain their identity as *both* feminist *and* religious, rather than being forced to choose between one or the other.

Women from the different subcultures that comprise multicultural society in America are often at the center of efforts to preserve and maintain their traditional cultures: teaching their children their native languages, songs, and customs, working in native arts and crafts, and teaching these techniques to others, and so on. Women's preservation of their native culture is illustrated, for example, in the films about Native American women included in the Film and Video listing at the end of the chapter. These kinds of activities by women raise the question of whether they are also part of a distinctive "women's culture," the topic of the following section.

Woman's culture

Since women historically were largely excluded from the public domain, they have been required to rely on private forms of expression (in diaries and letters, for example) rather than public ones. Many feminists have argued that the circumstances of cultural oppression and discrimination against women have contributed to the development of a separate women's culture. In popular culture, this notion of "women's culture" encompasses practices by women *for* women, such as writers of romance novels, creators of women-oriented arts and crafts, entertainment – even gossip. Other feminists look to the existence of women's organized opposition to male-dominated culture as evidence of a separate women's culture. Lesbian separatism, for example, falls into this category. This idea of women's culture is sometimes coupled with the normative claim that, since women have been relegated to a separate sphere, they *should* cultivate a distinctive culture which excludes males.

Other feminist scholars have criticized the concept of woman's culture, both the notion that such a separate women's culture objectively *does* exist, as well as that it *should* exist. The problem with the latter claim, they argue, is that it assumes that the commonalities among women are more important than the differences, and that the commonalities of gender *should* be treated as more important than differences based on considerations such as race, ethnicity, religion, or class.

The readings in this chapter present two very different perspectives on women's culture, comparing Carroll Smith-Rosenberg's classic essay on female friendships in the nineteenth century with a look at the contemporary "Grrls" movement among young women. Although they examine very different time periods and activities, the two articles suggest that there is some merit in the notion of a separate women's culture apart from mainstream or male-dominated culture.

Smith-Rosenberg's essay was path-breaking for women's history when it appeared in 1975. It has provided the foundation for a significant amount of feminist scholarship, some supportive, and some critical, of the essay's thesis that women (specifically white, middle-class women living in the eastern states) in the nineteenth century had far closer female friendships than women do today. Some of these relationships, Smith-Rosenberg contends, might be considered lesbian by today's standards, given the intensity of emotions and intimacy that many women had for one another. Much of Smith-Rosenberg's explanation for why this phenomenon existed in the nineteenth century but not today rests on the ideology of "separate spheres" that we have already encountered in earlier chapters. According to this ideology, males existed in the public world of commerce and government, while women were largely relegated to the private domestic sphere of home and family. Since cultural conventions forced gender segregation, women came naturally to depend upon one another for emotional, as well as material, support and companionship.

By contrast, Farai Chideya's "Revolution, girl style," explores the self-designated "Riot Grrls," a loosely affiliated group of adolescent and young women who are simultaneously parodying and rejecting conventional sex-role stereotypes. Their "in your face" rejection of male standards of femininity, sexuality, and so on has empowered many young women to want to live on their own terms, not those dictated by male-derived and dominated conventions about proper codes of behavior (especially sexual ones) for girls and women. The sharply contesting views of women's relationship to culture presented in these two readings will provide an interesting basis for deciding whether there is or ought to be a separate women's culture.

The Female World of Love and Ritual: Relations between Women in Nineteenth-century America (excerpt)
Carroll Smith-Rosenberg

The female friendship of the nineteenth century, the long-lived, intimate, loving friendship between two women, is an excellent example of the type of historical phenomena which most historians know something about, which few have thought much about, and which virtually no one has written about.[1] It is one aspect of the female experience which consciously or unconsciously we have chosen to ignore. Yet an abundance of manuscript evidence suggests that eighteenth- and nineteenth-century women routinely formed emotional ties with other women. Such deeply felt, same-sex friendships were casually accepted in American society. Indeed, from at least the late eighteenth through the mid-nineteenth century, a female world of varied and yet highly structured relationships appears to have been an essential aspect of American society. These relationships ranged from the supportive love of sisters, through the enthusiasms of adolescent girls, to sensual avowals of love by mature women. It was a world in which men made but a shadowy appearance.[2]

Defining and analyzing same-sex relationships involves the historian in deeply problematical questions of method and interpretation. This is especially true since historians, influenced by Freud's libidinal theory, have discussed these relationships almost exclusively within the context of individual psychosexual developments or, to be more explicit, psychopathology.[3] Seeing same-sex relationships in terms of a dichotomy between normal and abnormal, they have sought the origins of such apparent deviance in childhood or adolescent trauma and detected the symptoms of "latent" homosexuality in the lives of both those who later became "overtly" homosexual and those who did not. Yet theories concerning the nature and origins of same-sex relationships are frequently contradictory or based on questionable or arbitrary data. In recent years such hypotheses have been subjected to

This reading first appeared in *Signs: Journal of Women in Culture and Society*, 1975, 1(1): 1–29. The author's extensive source notes have been edited (substantive notes remain). For detailed information on the sources of the letters and diaries on which this reading is based, please refer to the original paper.

criticism from both within and without the psychological professions. Historians who seek to work within a psychological framework, therefore, are faced with two hard questions: do sound psychodynamic theories concerning the nature and origins of same-sex relationships exist? If so, does the historical datum exist which would permit the use of such dynamic models?

I would like to suggest an alternative approach to female friendships – one which would view them within a cultural and social setting rather than from an exclusively individual psychosexual perspective. Only by thus altering our approach will we be in the position to evaluate the appropriateness of particular dynamic interpretations. Intimate friendships between men and men and women and women existed in a larger world of social relations and social values. To interpret such friendships more fully they must be related to the structure of the American family and to the nature of sex-role divisions and of male–female relations both within the family and in society generally. The female friendship must not be seen in isolation; it must be analyzed as one aspect of women's overall relations with one another. The ties between mothers and daughters, sisters, female cousins, and friends at all stages of the female life-cycle constitute the most suggestive framework for the historian to begin an analysis of intimacy and affection between women. Such an analysis would not only emphasize general cultural patterns rather than the internal dynamics of a particular family or childhood; it would shift the focus of the study from a concern with deviance to that of defining configurations of legitimate behavioral norms and options.[4]

This analysis will be based upon the correspondence and diaries of women and men in 35 families between the 1760s and the 1880s. These families, though limited in number, represented a broad range of the American middle class, from hard-pressed pioneer families and orphaned girls to daughters of the intellectual and social élite. It includes families from most geographic regions, rural and urban, and a spectrum of Protestant denominations ranging from Mormon to orthodox Quaker. Although scarcely a comprehensive sample of America's increasingly heterogeneous population, it does, I believe, reflect accurately the literate middle class to which the historian working with letters and diaries is necessarily bound. It has involved an analysis of many thousands of letters written to women friends, kin, husbands, brothers, and children at every period of life from adolescence to old age. Some collections encompass virtually entire lifespans; one contains over 100,000 letters as well as diaries and account books. It is my contention that an analysis of women's private letters and diaries which were never intended to be published permits the historian to explore a very private world of emotional realities central both to women's lives and to the middle-class family in nineteenth-century America.[5]

The question of female friendships is peculiarly elusive; we know so little or perhaps have forgotten so much. An intriguing and almost alien form of human relationship, they flourished in a different social structure and amidst different sexual norms. Before attempting to reconstruct their social setting, therefore, it might be best first to describe two not atypical friendships. These two friendships, intense, loving, and openly avowed, began during the women's adolescence and, despite subsequent marriages and geographic separation, continued throughout their lives. For nearly half a century these women played a central emotional role in each other's lives, writing time and again of their love and of the pain of separation. Paradoxically to twentieth-century minds, their love appears to have been both sensual and platonic.

Sarah Butler Wister first met Jeannie Field Musgrove while vacationing with her family at Stockbridge, Massachusetts, in the summer of 1849.[6] Jeannie was then 16, Sarah 14. During two subsequent years spent together in boarding school, they formed a deep and intimate friendship. Sarah began to keep a bouquet of flowers before Jeannie's portrait and wrote complaining of the intensity and anguish of her affection. Both young women assumed *nom de plumes*, Jeannie a female name, Sarah a male one; they would use these secret names into old age. They frequently commented on the nature of their affection: "If the day should come," Sarah wrote Jeannie in the spring of 1861, "when you failed me either through your fault or my own, I would forswear all human friendship, thenceforth." A few months later Jeannie commented: "Gratitude is a word I should never use toward you. It is perhaps a misfortune of such intimacy and love that it makes one regard all kindness as a matter of course, as one has always found it, as natural as the embrace in meeting."

Sarah's marriage altered neither the frequency of their correspondence nor their desire to be together. In 1864, when 29, married, and a mother, Sarah wrote to Jeannie: "I shall be entirely alone [this coming week]. I can give you no idea how desperately I shall want you . . ." After one such visit Jeannie, then a spinster in New York, echoed Sarah's longing: "Dear darling Sarah! How I love you & how happy I have been! You are the joy of my life . . . I cannot tell you how much happiness you gave me, nor how constantly it is all in my thoughts . . . My darling how I long for the time when I shall see you. . . ." After another visit Jeannie wrote: "I want you to tell me in your next letter, to assure me, that I am your dearest . . . I do not doubt you, & I am not jealous but I long to hear you say it once more & it seems already a long time since your voice fell on my ear. So just fill a quarter page with caresses & expressions of endearment. Your silly Angelina." Jeannie ended one letter: "Goodbye my dearest, dearest lover – ever your own Angelina." And another, "I will go to bed . . . [though] I could write all night – A thousand kisses – I love you with my whole soul – your Angelina."

When Jeannie finally married in 1870 at the age of 37, Sarah underwent a period of extreme anxiety. Two days before Jeannie's marriage, Sarah, then in London, wrote desperately: "Dearest darling – How incessantly have I thought of you these eight days – all today – the entire uncertainty, the distance, the long silence – are all new features in my separation from you, grievous to be borne . . . Oh Jeannie, I have thought & thought & yearned over you these two days. Are you married I wonder? My dearest love to you wherever and *who*ever you are." Like many other women in this collection of 35 families, marriage brought Sarah and Jeannie physical separation; it did not cause emotional distance. Although at first they may have wondered how marriage would affect their relationship, their affection remained unabated throughout their lives, underscored by their loneliness and their desire to be together.

During the same years that Jeannie and Sarah wrote of their love and need for each other, two slightly younger women began a similar odyssey of love, dependence and – ultimately – physical, though not emotional, separation. Molly and Helena met in 1868 while both attended the Cooper Institute School of Design for Women in New York City. For several years these young women studied and explored the city together, visited each other's families, and formed part of a social network of other artistic young women. Gradually, over the years, their initial friendship deepened into a close intimate bond which continued throughout their lives. The tone in the letters which Molly wrote to Helena changed over these years from "My dear Helena," and signed "your attached friend," to "My dearest Helena," "My Dearest," "My Beloved," and signed "Thine always" or "thine Molly."[7]

The letters they wrote to each other during these first five years permit us to reconstruct something of their relationship together. As Molly wrote in one early letter:

> I have not said to you in so many or so few words that I was happy with you during those few so incredibly short weeks but surely you do not need words to tell you what you must know. Those two or three days so dark without, so bright with firelight and contentment within I shall always remember as proof that, for a time, at least – I fancy for quite a long time – we might be sufficient for each other. We know that we can amuse each other for many idle hours together and now we know that we can also work together. And that means much, don't you think so?

She ended: "I shall return in a few days. Imagine yourself kissed many times by one who loved you so dearly."

The intensity and even physical nature of Molly's love was echoed in many of the letters she wrote during the next few years, as, for instance in this short thank-you note for a small present: "Imagine yourself kissed a dozen times my darling. Perhaps it is well for you that we are far apart. You might find my thanks so expressed rather overpowering. I have that delightful feeling that it doesn't matter much what I say or how I say it, since we shall meet so soon and forget in that moment that we were ever separated . . . I shall see you soon and be content."

At the end of the fifth year, however, several crises occurred. The relationship, at least in its intense form, ended, though Molly and Helena continued an intimate and complex relationship for the next half-century. The exact nature of these crises is not completely clear, but it seems to have involved Molly's decision not to live with Helena, as they had originally planned, but to remain at home because of parental insistence. Molly was now in her late twenties. Helena responded with anger and Molly became frantic at the thought that Helena would break off their relationship. Though she wrote distraught letters and made despairing attempts to see Helena, the relationship never regained its former ardor – possibly because Molly had a male suitor. Within six months Helena had decided to marry a man who was, coincidentally, Molly's friend and publisher. Two years later Molly herself finally married. The letters toward the end of this period discuss the transition both women made to having male lovers – Molly spending much time reassuring Helena, who seemed depressed about the end of their relationship and with her forthcoming marriage.

It is clearly difficult from a distance of 100 years and from a post-Freudian cultural perspective to decipher the complexities of Molly and Helena's relationship. Certainly Molly and Helena were lovers – emotionally if not physically. The emotional intensity and pathos of their love becomes apparent in several letters Molly wrote Helena during their crisis:

> I wanted so to put my arms round my girl of all the girls in the world and tell her . . . I love her as wives do love their husbands, as *friends* who have taken each other for life – and believe in her as I believe in my God . . . If I didn't love you do you suppose I'd care about anything or have ridiculous notions and panics and behave like an old fool who ought to know better. I'm going to hang on to your skirts . . . You can't get away from [my] love.

Or as she wrote after Helena's decision to marry: "You know dear Helena, I really was in love with you. It was a passion such as I had never known until I saw you. I don't think it was the noblest way to love you." The theme of intense female love was one Molly again expressed in a letter she wrote to the man Helena was to marry: "Do you know sir, that until you came along I believe that she loved me almost as girls love their lovers. *I know I loved her so.* Don't you wonder that I can stand the sight of you." This was in a letter congratulating them on their forthcoming marriage.[8]

The essential question is not whether these women had genital contact and can therefore be defined as heterosexual or homosexual. The twentieth-century tendency to view human love and sexuality within a dichotomized universe of deviance and normality, genitality and platonic love, is alien to the emotions and attitudes of the nineteenth century and fundamentally distorts the nature of these women's emotional interaction. These letters are significant because they force us to place such female love in a particular historical context. There is every indication that these four women, their husbands and families – all eminently respectable and socially conservative – considered such love both socially acceptable and fully compatible with heterosexual marriage. Emotionally and cognitively, their heterosocial and their homosocial worlds were complementary.

One could argue, on the other hand, that these letters were but an example of the romantic rhetoric with which the nineteenth century surrounded the concept of friendship. Yet they possess an emotional intensity and a sensual and physical explicitness that is difficult to dismiss. Jeannie longed to hold Sarah in her arms; Molly mourned her physical isolation from Helena. Molly's love and devotion to Helena, the emotions that bound Jeannie and Sarah together, while perhaps a phenomenon of nineteenth-century society, were not the less real for their Victorian origins. A survey of the correspondence and diaries of eighteenth- and nineteenth-century women indicates that Molly, Jeannie, and Sarah represented one very real behavioral and emotional option socially available to nineteenth-century women.

This is not to argue that individual needs, personalities, and family dynamics did not have a significant role in determining the nature of particular relationships. But the scholar must ask if it is historically possible and, if possible, important to study the intensely individual aspects of psychosexual dynamics. Is it not the historian's first task to explore the social structure and the worldview which made intense and sometimes sensual female love both a possible and an acceptable emotional option? From such a social perspective a new and quite different series of questions suggests itself. What emotional function did such female love serve? What was its place within the hetero- and homosocial worlds which women jointly inhabited? Did a spectrum of love-object choices exist in the nineteenth century across which some individuals, at least, were capable of moving? Without attempting to answer these questions it will be difficult to understand either nineteenth-century sexuality or the nineteenth-century family.

Several factors in American society between the mid-eighteenth and the mid-nineteenth centuries may well have permitted women to form a variety of close emotional relationships with other women. American society was characterized in large part by rigid gender-role differentiation within the family and within society as a whole, leading to the emotional segregation of women and men. The roles of daughter and mother shaded imperceptibly and ineluctably into each other, while the biological realities of frequent pregnancies, childbirth, nursing, and menopause bound women together in physical and emotional intimacy. It was within just such a social framework, I would argue, that a specifically female world did indeed develop, a world built around a generic and unself-conscious pattern of single-sex or homosocial networks. These supportive networks were institutionalized in social conventions or rituals which accompanied virtually every important event in a woman's life, from birth to death. Such female relationships were frequently supported and paralleled by severe social restrictions on intimacy between young men and women. Within such a world of emotional richness and complexity, devotion to and love of other women became a plausible and socially accepted form of human interaction.

An abundance of printed and manuscript sources exists to support such a hypothesis. Etiquette books, advice books on child rearing, religious sermons, guides to young men and young women, medical texts, and school curricula all suggest that late eighteenth- and most nineteenth-century Americans assumed the existence of a world composed of distinctly male and female spheres, spheres determined by the immutable laws of God and nature.[9] The unpublished letters and diaries of Americans during this same period concur, detailing the existence of sexually segregated worlds inhabited by human beings with different values, expectations, and personalities. Contacts between men and women frequently partook of a formality and stiffness quite alien to twentieth-century America and which today we tend to define as "Victorian." Women, however, did not form an isolated and oppressed subcategory in male society. Their letters and diaries indicate that women's sphere had an essential integrity and dignity that grew out of women's shared experiences and mutual affection and that, despite the profound changes which affected American social structure and institutions between the 1760s and the 1870s, retained a constancy and predictability. The ways in which women thought of and interacted with each other remained unchanged. Continuity, not discontinuity, characterized this female world. Molly Hallock's and Jeannie Field's words, emotions, and experiences have direct parallels in the 1760s and the 1790s.[10] There are indications in contemporary sociological and psychological literature that female closeness and support networks have continued into the twentieth century – not only among ethnic and working-class groups but even among the middle class.[11]

Most eighteenth- and nineteenth-century women lived within a world bounded by home, church, and the institution of visiting – that endless trooping of women to each other's homes for social purposes. It was a world inhabited by children and by other women.[12] Women helped each other with domestic chores and in times of sickness, sorrow, or trouble. Entire days, even weeks, might be spent almost exclusively with other women. Urban and town women could devote virtually every day to visits, teas, or shopping trips with other women. Rural women developed a pattern of more extended visits that lasted weeks and sometimes months, at times even dislodging husbands from their beds and bedrooms so that dear friends might spend every hour of every day together. When husbands traveled, wives routinely moved in with other women, invited women friends to teas and suppers, sat together sharing and comparing the letters they had received from other close women friends. Secrets were exchanged and cherished, and the husband's return at times viewed with some ambivalence.

Summer vacations were frequently organized to permit old friends to meet at water spas or share a country home. In 1848, for example, a young matron wrote cheerfully to her husband about the delightful time she was having with five close women friends whom she had invited to spend the summer with her; he remained at home alone to face the heat of Philadelphia and a cholera epidemic. Some 90 years earlier, two young Quaker girls commented upon the vacation their aunt had taken alone with another woman; their remarks were openly envious and tell us something of the emotional quality of these friendships: "I hear Aunt is gone with the Friend and wont be back for two weeks, fine times indeed I think the old friends had, taking their pleasure about the country . . . and have the advantage of that fine woman's conversation and instruction, while we poor young girls must spend all spring at home . . . What a disappointment that we are not together. . . ."

Friends did not form isolated dyads but were normally part of highly integrated networks. Knowing each other, perhaps related to each other, they played a central role in holding communities and kin systems together. Especially when families became geographically mobile women's long visits to each other and their frequent letters filled with discussions of marriages and births, illness and deaths, descriptions of growing children, and reminiscences of times and people past provided an important sense of continuity in a rapidly changing society. Central to this female world was an inner core of kin. The ties between sisters, first cousins, aunts, and nieces provided the underlying structure upon which groups of friends and their network of female relatives clustered. Although most of the women within this sample would appear to be living within isolated nuclear families, the emotional ties between non-residential kin were deep and binding and provided one of the fundamental existential realities of women's lives.[13] . . .

Women frequently spent their days within the social confines of such extended families. Sisters-in-law visited each other and, in some families, seemed to spend more time with each other than with their husbands. First cousins cared for each other's babies – for weeks or even months in times of sickness or childbirth. Sisters helped each other with housework, shopped and sewed for each other. Geographic separation was borne with difficulty. A sister's absence for even a week or two could cause loneliness and depression and would be bridged by frequent letters. Sibling rivalry was hardly unknown, but with separation or illness the theme of deep affection and dependency re-emerged.[14]

Sisterly bonds continued across a lifetime. In her old age, a rural Quaker matron, Martha Jefferis, wrote to her daughter Anne concerning her own half-sister, Phoebe: "In sister Phoebe I have a real friend – she studies my comfort and waits on me like a child . . . She is exceedingly kind and this to all other homes (set aside yours) I would prefer – it is next to being with a daughter." Phoebe's own letters confirmed Martha's evaluation of her feelings. "Thou knowest my dear sister," Phoebe wrote, "there is no one . . . that exactly feels [for] thee as I do, for I think without boasting I can truly say that my desire is for thee."[15]

Such women, whether friends or relatives, assumed an emotional centrality in each other's lives. In their diaries and letters they wrote of the joy and contentment they felt in each other's company, their sense of isolation and despair when apart. The regularity of their correspondence underlines the sincerity of their words. Women named their daughters after one another and sought to integrate dear friends into their lives after marriage. As one young bride wrote to an old friend shortly after her marriage: "I want to see you and talk with you and feel that we are united by the same bonds of sympathy and congeniality as ever." After years of friendship one aging woman wrote of another: "Time cannot destroy the fascination of her manner . . . her voice is music to the ear. . . ." Women made elaborate presents for each other, ranging from the Quakers' frugal pies and breads to painted velvet bags and phantom bouquets. When a friend died, their grief was deeply felt. Martha Jefferis was unable to write to her daughter for three weeks because of the sorrow she felt at the death of a dear friend. Such distress was not unusual. A generation earlier a young Massachusetts farm woman filled pages of her diary with her grief at the death of her "dearest friend" and transcribed the letters of condolence other women sent her. She marked the anniversary of Rachel's death each year in her diary, contrasting her faithfulness with that of Rachel's husband, who had soon remarried.

These female friendships served a number of emotional functions. Within this secure and empathetic world women could share sorrows, anxieties, and joys, confident that other women had experienced similar emotions. . . .

This was, as well, a female world in which hostility and criticism of other women were discouraged, and thus a milieu in which women could develop a sense of inner security and self-esteem. As one young woman wrote to her mother's longtime friend: "I cannot sufficiently thank you for the kind unvaried affection & indulgence you have ever shown and expressed both by words and actions for me. . . . Happy would it be did all the world view me as you do, through the medium of kindness and forbearance." They valued each other. Women, who had little status or power in the larger world of male concerns, possessed status and power in the lives and worlds of other women.

An intimate mother–daughter relationship lay at the heart of this female world. The diaries and letters of both mothers and daughters attest to their closeness and mutual emotional dependency. Daughters routinely discussed their mother's health and activities with their own friends, expressed anxiety in cases of their mother's ill health and concern for her cares.[16] Expressions of hostility which we would today consider routine on the part of both mothers and daughters seem to have been uncommon indeed. On the contrary, this sample of families indicates that the normal relationship between mother and daughter was one of sympathy and understanding.[17] Only sickness or great geographic distance was allowed to cause extended separation. When marriage did result in such separation, both viewed the distance between them with distress.[18] . . .

Central to these mother–daughter relations is what might be described as an apprenticeship system. In those families where the daughter followed the mother into a life of traditional domesticity, mothers and other older women carefully trained daughters in the arts of housewifery and motherhood. Such training undoubtedly occurred throughout a girl's childhood but became more systematized, almost ritualistic, in the years following the end of her formal education and before her marriage. At this time a girl either returned home from boarding school or no longer divided her time between home and school. Rather, she devoted her energies on two tasks: mastering new domestic skills and participating in the visiting and social activities necessary to finding a husband. Under the careful supervision of their mothers and of older female relatives, such late-adolescent girls temporarily took over the household management from their mothers, tended their young nieces and nephews, and helped in childbirth, nursing, and weaning. Such experiences tied the generations together in shared skills and emotional interaction.[19]

Daughters were born into a female world. The mother's life expectations and sympathetic network of friends and relations were among the first realities in the life of the developing child. As long as the mother's domestic role remained relatively stable and few viable alternatives competed with it, daughters tended to accept their mothers' world and to turn automatically to other women for support and intimacy. It was within this closed and intimate female world that the young girl grew toward womanhood.

One could speculate at length concerning the absence of that mother–daughter hostility today considered almost inevitable to an adolescent's struggle for autonomy and self-identity. It is possible that taboos against female aggression and hostility were sufficiently strong to repress even that between mothers and their adolescent daughters. Yet these letters seem so alive and the interest of daughters in their mothers' affairs so vital and genuine that it is difficult to interpret their closeness exclusively in terms of repression and denial. The functional bonds that held mothers and daughters together in a world that permitted few alternatives to domesticity might well have created a source of mutuality and trust absent in societies where greater options were available for daughters than for mothers. Furthermore, the extended female network – a daughter's close ties with her own older sisters, cousins, and aunts – may well have permitted a diffusion and a relaxation of mother–daughter identification and so have aided a daughter in her struggle for identity and autonomy. None of these explanations are mutually exclusive; all may well have interacted to produce the degree of empathy evident in those letters and diaries.

At some point in adolescence, the young girl began to move outside the matrix of her mother's support group to develop a network of her own. Among the middle class, at least, this transition toward what was at the same time both a limited autonomy and a repetition of her mother's life seemed to have most frequently coincided with a girl's going to school. Indeed, education appears to have played a crucial role in the lives of most of the families in this study. Attending school for a few months, for a year, or longer was common even among daughters of relatively poor families, while middle-class girls routinely spent at least a year in boarding school.[20] These school years ordinarily marked a girl's first separation from home. They served to wean the daughter from her home, to train her in the essential social graces, and, ultimately, to help introduce her into the marriage market. It was not infrequently a trying emotional experience for both mother and daughter.[21]

In this process of leaving one home and adjusting to another, the mother's friends and relatives played a key transitional role. Such older women routinely accepted the role of foster mother, they supervised the young girl's deportment, monitored her health, and introduced her to their own network of female friends and kin.[22] Not infrequently women, friends from their own school years, arranged to send their daughters to the same school so that the girls might form bonds paralleling those their mothers had made. . . .

Even more important to this process of maturation than their mothers' friends were the female friends young women made at school. Young girls helped each other overcome homesickness and endure the crises of adolescence. They gossiped about beaux, incorporated each other into their own kinship systems, and attended and gave teas and balls together. Older girls in boarding school "adopted" younger ones, who called them "Mother." Dear friends might indeed continue this pattern of adoption and mothering throughout their lives; one woman might routinely assume the nurturing role of pseudomother, the other the dependency role of daughter. The pseudomother performed for the other woman all the services which we normally associate with mothers; she went to absurd lengths to purchase items her "daughter" could have obtained from other sources, gave advice and functioned as an idealized figure in her "daughter's" imagination. Helena played such a role for Molly, as did Sarah for Jeannie. Elizabeth Bordley Gibson bought almost all Eleanor Parke Custis Lewis's necessities – from shoes and corset covers to bedding and harp strings – and sent them from Philadelphia to Virginia, a procedure that sometimes took months. Eleanor frequently asked Elizabeth to take back her purchases, have them redone, and argue with shopkeepers about prices. These were favors automatically asked and complied with. Anne Jefferis Sheppard made the analogy very explicitly in a letter to her own mother written shortly after Anne's marriage, when she was feeling depressed about their separation: "Mary Paulen is truly kind, almost acts the part of a mother and tries to aid and *comfort me*, and also to *lighten my new cares*." . . .

Girls routinely slept together, kissed and hugged each other. Indeed, while waltzing with young men scandalized the otherwise flighty and highly fashionable Harriet Manigault, she considered waltzing with other young women not only acceptable but pleasant.

Marriage followed adolescence. With increasing frequency in the nineteenth century, marriage involved a girl's traumatic removal from her mother and her mother's network. It involved, as well, adjustment to a husband, who, because he was male, came to marriage with both a different worldview and vastly different experiences. Not surprisingly, marriage was an event surrounded with supportive, almost ritualistic practices. (Weddings are one of the last female rituals remaining in twentieth-century America.) Young women routinely spent the months preceding their marriage almost exclusively with other women – at neighborhood sewing bees and quilting parties or in a round of visits to geographically distant friends and relatives. Ostensibly they went to receive assistance in the practical preparations for their new home – sewing and quilting a trousseau and linen – but, of equal importance, they appear to have gained emotional support and reassurance. . . .

Sisters, cousins, and friends frequently accompanied newlyweds on their wedding night and wedding trip, which often involved additional family visiting. Such extensive visits presumably served to wean the daughter from her family of origin. As such they often contained a note of ambivalence. . . . Perhaps they also functioned to reassure the young woman herself, and her friends and kin, that though marriage might alter it would not destroy old bonds of intimacy and familiarity.[23]

Married life, too, was structured about a host of female rituals. Childbirth, especially the birth of the first child, became virtually a *rite de passage*, with a lengthy seclusion of the woman before and after delivery, severe restrictions on her activities, and finally a dramatic re-emergence. This seclusion was supervised by mothers, sisters, and loving friends. Nursing and weaning involved the advice and assistance of female friends and relatives. So did miscarriage. Death, like birth, was structured around elaborate unisexed rituals. . . . Virtually every collection of letters and diaries in my sample contained evidence of women turning to each other for comfort when facing the frequent and unavoidable deaths of the eighteenth and nineteenth centuries. . . . Among rural Pennsylvania Quakers, death and mourning rituals assumed an even more extreme same-sex form, with men or women largely barred from the deathbeds of the other sex. Women relatives and friends slept with the dying woman, nursed her, and prepared her body for burial.[24]

Eighteenth- and nineteenth-century women thus lived in emotional proximity to each other. Friendships and intimacies followed the biological ebb and flow of women's lives. Marriage and pregnancy, childbirth and weaning, sickness and death involved physical and psychic trauma which comfort and sympathy made easier to bear. Intense bonds of love and intimacy bound together those women who, offering each other aid and sympathy, shared such stressful moments.

These bonds were often physical as well as emotional. An undeniably romantic and even sensual note frequently marked female relationships. This theme, significant throughout the stages of a woman's life, surfaced first during adolescence. As one teenager from a struggling pioneer family in the Ohio Valley wrote in her diary in 1808: "I laid with my dear R[ebecca] and a glorious good talk we had until about 4[A.M.] – O how hard I do *love* her." Only a few years later Bostonian Eunice Callender carved her initials and Sarah Ripley's into a favorite tree, along with a pledge of eternal love, and then waited breathlessly for Sarah to discover and respond to her declaration of affection. The response appears to have been affirmative. A half-century later urbane and sophisticated Katherine Wharton commented upon meeting an old school chum: "She was a great pet of mine at school & I thought as I watched her light figure how often I had held her in my arms – how dear she had once been to me." Katie maintained a long intimate friendship with another girl. When a young man began to court this friend seriously, Katie commented in her diary that she had never realized "how deeply I loved Eng and how fully." She wrote over and over again in that entry: "Indeed I love her!" and only with great reluctance left the city that summer since it meant also leaving Eng with Eng's new suitor. . . .

How then can we ultimately interpret these long-lived intimate female relationships and integrate them into our understanding of Victorian sexuality? Their ambivalent and romantic rhetoric presents us with an ultimate puzzle: the relationship along the spectrum of human emotions between love, sensuality, and sexuality. . . .

It is possible to speculate that in the twentieth century a number of cultural taboos evolved to cut short the homosocial ties of girlhood and to impel the emerging women of 13 or 14 toward heterosexual relationships. In contrast, nineteenth-century American society did not taboo close female relationships but rather recognized them as a socially viable form of human contact – and, as such, acceptable throughout a woman's life. Indeed, it was not these homosocial ties that were inhibited but rather heterosexual leanings. While closeness, freedom of emotional expression, and uninhibited physical contact characterized women's relationships with each other, the opposite was frequently true of male–female relationships. One could thus argue that within such a world of female support, intimacy, and ritual it was only to be expected that adult women would turn trustingly and lovingly to each other. It was a behavior they had observed and learned since childhood. A different type of emotional landscape existed in the nineteenth century, one in which Molly and Helena's love became a natural development.

Of perhaps equal significance are the implications we can garner from this framework for the understanding of heterosexual marriages in the nineteenth century. If men and women grew up as they did in relatively homogeneous and segregated sexual groups, then marriage represented a major problem in adjustment. From this perspective we could interpret much of the emotional stiffness and distance that we associate with Victorian marriage as a structural consequence of contemporary sex-role differentiation and gender-role socialization. With marriage both women and men had to adjust to life with a person who was, in essence, a member of an alien group.

I have thus far substituted a cultural or psychosocial for a psychosexual interpretation of women's emotional bonding. But there are psychosexual implications in this model which I think it only fair to make more explicit. Despite Sigmund Freud's insistence on the bisexuality of us all and the recent American Psychiatric Association decision on homosexuality, many psychiatrists today tend explicitly or implicitly to view homosexuality as a totally alien or pathological behavior – as totally unlike heterosexuality. I suspect that in essence they may have adopted an explanatory model similar to the one used in discussing schizophrenia. As psychiatrists can speak of schizophrenia and of a borderline schizophrenic personality as both ultimately and fundamentally different from a normal or neurotic personality, so they also think of both homosexuality and latent homosexuality as states totally different from heterosexuality. With this rapidly dichotomous model of assumption, "latent homosexuality" becomes the indication of a disease in progress – seeds of a pathology which belie the reality of an individual's heterosexuality.

Yet at the same time we are well aware that cultural values can affect choices in the gender of a person's sexual partner. We, for instance, do not necessarily consider homosexual object choice among men in prison, on shipboard, or in boarding schools a necessary indication of pathology. I would urge that we expand this relativistic model and hypothesize that a number of cultures might well tolerate or even encourage diversity in sexual and non-sexual relations. Based on my research into this nineteenth-century world of female intimacy, I would further suggest that rather than seeing a gulf between the normal and the abnormal we view sexual and emotional impulses as part of a continuum or spectrum of affect gradations strongly effected by cultural norms and arrangements, a continuum influenced in part by observed and thus learned behavior. At one end of the continuum lies committed heterosexuality, at the other uncompromising homosexuality; between a wide latitude of emotions and sexual feelings. Certain cultures and environments permit individuals a great deal of freedom in moving across this spectrum. I would like to suggest that the nineteenth century was such a cultural environment. That is, the supposedly repressive and destructive Victorian sexual ethos may have been more flexible and responsive to the needs of particular individuals than those of the twentieth century.

Acknowledgments

Research for this paper was supported in part by a grant from the Grant Foundation, New York, and by National Institutes of Health trainee grant 5 FO3 HD48800-03. I would like to thank several scholars for their assistance and criticism in preparing this paper: Erving Goffman, Roy Schafer, Charles E. Rosenberg, Cynthia Secor, Anthony Wallace. July Breault, who has just completed a biography of an important and introspective nineteenth-century feminist, Emily Howland, served as a research assistant for this paper, and her knowledge of nineteenth-century family structure and religious history proved invaluable.

Notes

1   The most notable exception to this rule is William R. Taylor and Christopher Lasch. "Two 'kindred spirits': sorority and family in New England, 1839–1846," *New England Quarterly*, 36 (1963), pp. 25–41. Taylor has made a valuable contribution to the history of women and the history of the family with his concept of "sororial" relations. I do not, however, accept the Taylor–Lasch thesis that female friendships developed in the mid-nineteenth century because of geographic mobility and the break-up of the colonial family. I have found these friendships as frequently in the eighteenth century as in the nineteenth and would hypothesize that the geographic mobility of the mid-nineteenth century eroded them as it did so many other traditional social institutions. Helen Vendler (review of *Notable American Women, 1607–1950*, ed. Edward James and Janet James, *New York Times*, November 5, 1972, sec.7) points out the significance of these friendships.

2   I do not wish to deny the importance of women's relations with particular men. Obviously, women were close to brothers, husbands, fathers, and sons. However, there is evidence that despite such closeness, relationships between men and women differed in both emotional texture and frequency from those between women. Women's relations with each other, although they played a central role in the American family and American society, have been so seldom examined either by general social historians or by historians of the family that I wish in this paper simply to examine their nature and analyze their implications for our understanding of social relations and social structure. I have discussed some aspects of male–female relationships in two articles: "Puberty to menopause: the cycle of femininity in nineteenth-century America," *Feminist Studies* 1 (1973), pp. 58–72, and, with Charles Rosenberg, "The female animal: medical and biological views of women in 19th century America," *Journal of American History* 59 (1973), pp. 331–56.

3   See Freud's classic paper on homosexuality, "Three essays on the theory of sexuality," in *The Standard Edition of the Complete Psychological Works of Sigmund*

Freud, trans. James Strachey (London: Hogarth Press, 1953), 7, pp. 135–72. The essays originally appeared in 1905. Prof. Roy Shafer, Department of Psychiatry, Yale University, has pointed out that Freud's view of sexual behavior was strongly influenced by nineteenth-century evolutionary thought. Within Freud's schema, genital heterosexuality marked the height of human development (Shafer, "Problems in Freud's psychology of women," *Journal of the American Psychoanalytic Association* 22 [1974], pp. 459–85).

4 For a novel and most important exposition of one theory of behavioral norms and options and its application to the study of human sexuality, see Charles Rosenberg, "Sexuality, class and role," *American Quarterly* 25 (1973), pp. 131–53.

5 See, e.g., the letters of Peggy Emlen to Sally Logan, 1768–72, Wells Morris Collection, Box 1, Historical Society of Pennsylvania; and the Eleanor Parke Custis Lewis letters, Historical Society of Pennsylvania, Philadelphia.

6 Sarah Butler Wister was the daughter of Fanny Kemble and Pierce Butler. In 1859 she married a Philadelphia physician, Owen Wister. The novelist Owen Wister is her son. Jeannie Field Musgrove was the half-orphaned daughter of constitutional lawyer and New York Republican politician David Dudley Field. Their correspondence (1855–98) is in the Sarah Butler Wister Papers, Wister Family Papers, Historical Society of Pennsylvania.

7 This is the 1868–1920 correspondence between Mary Hallock Foote and Helena, a New York friend (the Mary Hallock Foote Papers are in the Manuscript Division, Stanford University). Wallace E. Stegner has written a fictionalized biography of Mary Hallock Foote, *Angle of Repose* (Garden City, NY: Doubleday, 1971). See, as well, her autobiography: Mary Hallock Foote, *A Victorian Gentlewoman in the Far West: the Reminiscences of Mary Hallock Foote*, ed. Rodman W. Paul (San Marino, CA: Huntington Library, 1972). In many ways these letters are typical of those women wrote to other women. Women frequently began letters to each other with salutations such as "Dearest," "My Most Beloved," "You Darling Girl," and signed them "tenderly" or "to my dear dear sweet friend, good-bye." Without the least self-consciousness, one woman in her frequent letters to a female friend referred to her husband as "my other love." She was by no means unique. . . . The basis and nature of such friendships can be seen in the comments of Sarah Alden Ripley to her sister-in-law and long-time friend, Sophia Bradford: "Hearing that you are not well reminds me of what it would be to lose your loving society. We have kept step together through a long piece of road in the weary journey of life. We have loved the same beings and wept together over their graves" O. J. Wister and Agnes Irwin (eds). *Worthy Women of our First Century* (Philadelphia: Lippincott, 1877) p. 195.

8 Molly's and Helena's relationship continued for the rest of their lives. Molly's letters are filled with tender and intimate references, as when she wrote, 20 years later and from 2,000 miles away: "It isn't because you are good that I love you – but for the essence of you which is like perfume" (n.d. [1890s?]).

9 I am in the midst of a larger study of adult gender roles and gender-role socialization in America, 1785–1895. For a discussion of social attitudes toward appropriate male and female roles, see Barbara Welter, "The cult of true womanhood, 1820–1860," *American Quarterly* 18 (1966), pp. 151–74; Ann Firor Scott, *The Southern Lady: from Pedestal to Politics, 1830–1930* (Chicago: University of Chicago Press, 1970), chs 1–2; Smith-Rosenberg and Rosenberg, "The female animal."

10 See, e.g., the letters of Peggy Emlen to Sally Logan, 1768–72, Wells Morris Collection, Box 1, Historical Society of Pennsylvania; and the Eleanor Parke Custis Lewis Letters, Historical Society of Pennsylvania.

11 See esp. Elizabeth Botts, *Family and Social Network* (London: Tavistock, 1957); Michael Young and Peter Willmott, *Family and Kinship in East London*, rev. edn (Baltimore: Penguin, 1964).

12 This pattern seemed to cross class barriers. A letter that an Irish domestic wrote in the 1830s contains 17 separate references to women and only seven to men, most of whom were relatives and two of whom were infant brothers living with her mother and mentioned in relation to her mother (Ann McGrann, Philadelphia, to Sophie M. DuPont, Philadelphia, July 3, 1834, Sophie Madeleine DuPont Letters, Eleutherian Mills Foundation).

13 Place of residence is not the only variable significant in characterizing family structure. Strong emotional ties and frequent visiting and correspondence can unite families that do not live under one roof. Demographic studies based on household structure alone fail to reflect such emotional and even economic ties between families.

14 Sophie DuPont filled her letters to her younger brother Henry (with whom she had been assigned to correspond while he was at boarding school) with accounts of family visiting. . . . Mary Hallock Foote vacationed with her sister, her sister's children, her aunt, and a female cousin in the summer of 1874; cousins frequently visited the Hallock farm in Milton, NY. In later years Molly and her sister Bessie set up a joint household in Boise, Idaho. . . . Jeannie Field, after initially disliking her sister-in-law, Laura, became very close to her, calling her "my little sister" and at times spending virtually every day with her.

15 A number of other women remained close to sisters and sisters-in-law across a long lifetime (see Wister and Irwin, *Worthy Women*, p. 195).

16 This pattern appears to have crossed class lines. When a former Sunday school student of Sophie DuPont's (and the daughter of a worker in her father's factory) wrote to Sophie, she discussed her mother's health and activities quite naturally.

17 The Jefferis family papers are filled with empathetic letters between Martha and her daughters, Anne and Edith. . . . A representative letter is this of March 9, 1837, from Edith to Martha: "My heart can fully respond to the language of my own precious Mother, that absence has not diminished our affection for each other, but has, if possible, strengthened the bonds that have united us together & I have had to remark how we had been permitted to mingle in sweet fellowship and have been strengthened to bear one another's burdens. . . ."

18   Sarah Alden Ripley wrote weekly to her daughter, Sophy Ripley Fisher, after the latter's marriage. . . . Eleanor Parke Custis Lewis's long correspondence with Elizabeth Bordley Gibson contains evidence of her anxiety at leaving her foster mother's home at various times during her adolescence and at her marriage, and her own longing for her daughters, both of whom had married and moved to Louisiana. . . . Anne Jefferis Sheppard experienced a great deal of anxiety on moving two days' journey from her mother at the time of her marriage. This loneliness and sense of isolation persisted through her marriage until, finally a widow, she returned to live with her mother. . . . Daughters evidently frequently slept with their mothers into adulthood. . . . Daughters also frequently asked mothers to live with them and professed delight when they did so. See, e.g., Sarah Alden Ripley's comments to George Simmons, October 6, 1844, in Wister and Irwin *Worthy Women*, p. 185: "It is no longer 'Mother and Charles came out one day and returned the next,' for mother is one of us: she has entered the penetratice, been initiated into the mystery of the household gods . . . Her divertissement is to mend the stockings . . . whiten sheets and napkins . . . and take a stroll at evening with me to talk of our children, to compare our experiences, what we have learned and what we have suffered, and, last of all, to complete with pears and melons the cheerful circle about the solar lamp. . . ." We did find a few exceptions to this mother–daughter felicity. Sarah Foulke Emlen was at first very hostile to her stepmother, but they later developed a warm supportive relationship.

19   Eleanor Parke Custis Lewis's correspondence with Elizabeth Bordley Gibson describes such an apprenticeship system over two generations – that of her childhood and that of her daughters. Indeed, Eleanor Lewis's own apprenticeship was quite formal. She was deliberately separated from her foster mother in order to spend a winter of domesticity with her married sisters and her remarried mother. It was clearly felt that her foster mother's (Martha Washington) home at the nation's capital was not an appropriate place to develop domestic talents.

20   Education was not limited to the daughters of the well to do. Sarah Foulke Emlen, the daughter of an Ohio Valley frontier farmer, for instance, attended day school for several years during the early 1800s. Sarah Ripley Stearns, the daughter of a shopkeeper in Greenfield, MA, attended a boarding school for but three months, yet the experience seemed very important to her. Mrs S. S. Dalton, a Mormon woman from Utah, attended a series of poor country schools and greatly valued her opportunity, though she also expressed a great deal of guilt for the sacrifices her mother made to make her education possible.

21   In a letter to Elizabeth Bordley Gibson, March 28, 1847, Eleanor Parke Custis Lewis from Virginia discussed the anxiety her daughter felt when her granddaughters left home to go to boarding school. Eleuthera DuPont was very homesick when away at school in Philadelphia in the early 1820s.

22   Elizabeth Bordley Gibson, a Philadelphia matron, played such a role for the daughters and nieces of her lifelong friend, Eleanor Parke Custis Lewis, a

Virginia planter's wife. . . . The wife of Thomas Gurney Smith played a similar role for Sophie and Eleuthera DuPont.

23 Eleanor Parke Custis Lewis and her daughter Parke experienced similar sorrow and anxiety when Parke married and moved to Cincinnati. Helena DeKay visited Mary Hallock the month before her marriage; Mary Hallock was an attendant at the wedding; Helena again visited Molly about three weeks after her marriage; and then Molly went with Helena and spent a week with Helena and Richard in their new apartment.

24 This is not to argue that men and women did not mourn together. Yet in many families women aided and comforted women and men, men. The same-sex death ritual was one emotional option available to nineteenth-century Americans.

Revolution, Girl Style
Farai Chideya, with Melissa Rossi and Dogen Hannah

Jessica Hopper was on her way to photography class at her Minneapolis high school last month when she saw it: splashed across her locker was a crude obscenity scrawled in purple magic marker. An effusive 16-year-old with long brown hair, Hopper loves taking pictures more than anything but punk-rock music. When she saw the scrawl, she thought she knew who did it: one of two guys who she says regularly called her names like "feminazi." Just a few days earlier, she had found herself alone in the school darkroom with one of them – a boy, she says, "who touches girls." According to Hopper, he came up and placed both his hands on her shoulders. She told him to stop. "He went," – she fakes a low, suggestive moan – " '*Oooh*.' And I said, 'I mean it'." So he started doing the same thing to another girl nearby. "And I said, 'Don't touch me *or* my friends!' "

All girls get harassed. Most learn during adolescence to ignore it, hoping it will end. But Hopper had an outlet for her frustration. She's a Riot Grrrl – part of a support network of activist "girls" from 14 to 25 who are loosely linked together by a few punk bands, weekly discussion groups, pen-pal friendships and more than 50 homemade fanzines. Hopper started her own fanzine last year, which she photocopies for friends and pen-pals. She calls it *Hit It or Quit It*, and every few months she pours herself into her very feminist, very gushy essays, like the recent one that began coyly, "I used to say that I hated men," only to follow with the knockout punch: "I guess I actually did."

This reading first appeared in *Newsweek*, November 23, 1992.

The Riot Grrrls are a new feminist voice for the video-age generation, inflamed not so much by economic issues as by social ones – incest, child abuse, abortion, eating disorders, harassment. Patching together wildly mixed ideas from Madonna, *Sassy* magazine and feminist critics like Susan Faludi and Naomi Wolf, they've set out to make the world safe for their kind of girlhood: sexy, assertive and loud. The Riot Grrrl credo runs: "We are mad at a society that tells us that Girl=Dumb, Girl=Bad, Girl=Weak . . . [We] can and will change the world for real." They may be the first generation of feminists to identify their anger so early and to use it.

The Riot Grrrls follow in the very '90s footsteps of groups like Queer Nation or the rap act Niggers with Attitude, who apply a kind of linguistic ju-jitsu against their enemies. Instead of downplaying the negative stereotypes used against them, they exaggerate them – starting with the very notion of "girls." At last summer's Riot Grrrl convention in Washington, DC, which drew scores of the faithful to Dupont Circle to talk teen feminism and listen to punk rock, Grrrls marked their bodies with blunt five-inch-high letters reading RAPE or SLUT – an MTV-era way of saying, "That's what you think of me; confront your own bigotry." Courtney Love of the Los Angeles band Hole – who's not a Riot Grrrl but, as Hopper says, "the patron saint of Riot Grrrls" – wears vintage little-girl dresses that barely make it past her hips – all the better to sing songs about rape and exploitation. "I prefer being a minority because it makes me feel special," says Love. As Riot Grrrl wanna-be Camille Paglia says, "It's like Madonna – she dresses like a whore, but she always knows what she wants. These girls are dressed to kill but ready to fight."

Riot Grrrls run the gamut from 14-year-olds who trade fanzines to keep up with their favorite bands to the truly – and sanctimoniously – committed. "We don't have a doctrine," says Molly Neuman, 21, who plays drums in the Olympia, Wash., band Bratmobile. "There's no specific leader, no 10-point program." The nearest thing they have to a founder is Kathleen Hanna, 23, of the band Bikini Kill. A former stripper who sings and writes about being a victim of rape and child abuse, Hanna represents the extreme edge of the Grrrls' rage. But Jessica Hopper is more typical. She's young, white, urban and middle class. She's also a child of divorce: she cherishes her stepfather (or "dad") and father ("biological dad"), who are friends. Every week, she attends Riot Grrrl meetings, where like minds talk about everything from tuning guitar strings to coming out of the closet. And, like most teenage girls, she's a bundle of contradictions. She uses *Hit It or Quit It* to gush about some "incredibleee cute bass player," but she started a pro-choice group when she was 12. Riot Grrrl embraces this contradiction as the secret strength of girls, calling it a "revolutionary soul force." Riot Girl is feminism with a loud happy face dotting the "i."

For people accustomed to more august models of feminism, the Riot Grrrls might seem a bit of a stretch. But like the women's movement of the '70s, Riot Grrrl is a response to its own times. "We're definitely in a time of gender war," says Naomi Wolf, author of *The Beauty Myth*, a best-selling feminist critique. "Teenage girls are either more aware and angry and impatient than older women, or they're even more frightened." At a time when sex is both stigmatized and potentially lethal, the Grrrls are exuberantly pro-sex. In blocky, adolescent handwriting, Hopper writes, SEX ISN'T DIRTY . . . AND IT ISN'T 'BAD' UNLESS SOMEONE IS FORCING IT ON YOU. The fanzine *Hungry Girl* is even more explicit: "SLUT. Yeah, I'm a slut. My body belongs to me. I sleep with who I want . . . I'm not your property."

For all its deadly seriousness, this movement isn't just about anger, it's about fun. Nurtured in the punk-rock clubs of Olympia, the trend gets much of its energy and style from music. It's about sex and rock and roll, but not drugs. As part of their cause of self-preservation, the Grrrls are anti-drug, breaking out in homilies so plain and nerdy they'd seem stilted at a school assembly. "Pure foods and a clean lifestyle – the best high," Hopper cheerfully writes in *Hit It*.

As a formal entity, Riot Grrrl numbers just a few hundred souls, but its influence spreads much wider. *Sassy* magazine, which now claims a readership of 3 million, runs a constant exchange between Riot Grrrl and mainstream culture. "We took [the use of] 'girls' from them," says Editor-in-Chief Jane Pratt. For the December issue, the magazine turned itself over to some of its readers, with interesting results: boldly ideological, but with a mushy warm spot for cute skater boys – sort of like a Riot Grrrl fanzine with a budget. "I think things that are cool have political overtones – bands, magazines like *Sassy*," says Samantha Shapiro, a 16-year-old senior from New York who guest-edited the issue. "People compliment me on my combat boots. That something so angry is fashionable for women shows things have changed." Shapiro is your typical super-woman-in-training: she volunteers for AIDS and homeless organizations, interns with an assembly-woman, and wrote a *New York Times* op-ed piece last week praising Chelsea Clinton's every-girlness. She likes Bikini Kill, she says, because "they're being as sexy and as womanly as they can be . . . They're about accepting and appreciating differences – enhancing them."

Shapiro isn't a Riot Grrrl, but she's braced for the same issues they are, and with the same mixture of idealism and disillusionment. "I'm never going to be in the sit-home-and-wait-for-my-husband category," she says, then adds, self-deprecatingly, "Like, I kind of want to be president."

There's no telling whether this enthusiasm or the Riot Grrrls' catchy passion for "Revolution, Girl Style" will evaporate when it hits the adult real world. Most of the Grrrls are still in the shelters of home or college

– a far cry from what they'll face in the competitive job market or as they start to form their own families. But Wolf, for one, is "absolutely optimistic." After all, the older members of this young generation helped vote in the Clinton administration, while teens like Shapiro cheered them on. Says Seattle fanzine publisher Alice Wheeler, a mature 31, "Now that she's moved to DC, I'm hoping Chelsea will become a Riot Grrrl too."

Witchcraft as Goddess Religion
Starhawk

Witchcraft has always been a religion of poetry, not theology. The myths, legends, and teachings are recognized as metaphors for "That-Which-Cannot-Be-Told," the absolute reality our limited minds can never completely know. The mysteries of the absolute can never be explained – only felt or intuited. Symbols and ritual acts are used to trigger altered states of awareness, in which insights that go beyond words are revealed. When we speak of "the secrets that cannot be told," we do not mean merely that rules prevent us from speaking freely. We mean that the inner knowledge literally *cannot* be expressed in words. It can only be conveyed by experience, and no one can legislate what insight another person may draw from any given experience. For example, after participating in a certain ritual, a woman said, "As we were chanting, I felt that we blended together and became one voice; I sensed the oneness of everybody." Another woman said, "I became aware of how different the chant sounded for each of us, of how unique each person is." A man said simply, "I felt loved." To a Witch, all of these statements are equally true and valid. They are no more contradictory than the statements, "Your eyes are as bright as stars" and "Your eyes are as blue as the sea."

The primary symbol for "That-Which-Cannot-Be-Told" is the Goddess. The Goddess has infinite aspects and thousands of names – She is the reality behind many metaphors. She *is* reality, the manifest deity, omnipresent in all of life, in each of us. The Goddess is not separate from the world – She *is* the world, and all things in it: moon, sun, earth, star, stone, seed, flowing river, wind, wave, leaf and branch, bud and blossom, fang and claw, woman and man. In Witchcraft, flesh and spirit are one.

This reading first appeared in *The Spiral Dance* (New York: Harper and Row, 1979).

As we have seen, Goddess religion is unimaginably old, but contemporary Witchcraft could just as accurately be called the New Religion. The Craft, today, is undergoing more than a revival, it is experiencing a renaissance, a re-creation. Women are spurring this renewal, and actively reawakening the Goddess, the image of "the legitimacy and beneficence of female power."[1]

Since the decline of the Goddess religions, women have lacked religious models and spiritual systems that speak to female needs and experience. Male images of divinity characterize both Western and Eastern religions. Regardless of how abstract the underlying concept of God may be, the symbols, avatars, preachers, prophets, gurus, and Buddhas are overwhelmingly male. Women are not encouraged to explore their own strengths and realizations; they are taught to submit to male authority, to identify masculine perceptions as their spiritual ideals, to deny their bodies and sexuality, to fit their insights into a male mold.

Mary Daly, author of *Beyond God the Father*, points out that the model of the universe in which a male god rules the cosmos from outside serves to legitimize male control of social institutions. "The symbol of the Father God, spawned in the human imagination and sustained as plausible by patriarchy, has, in turn, rendered service to this type of society by making its mechanisms for the oppression of women appear right and fitting."[2] The unconscious model continues to shape the perceptions even of those who have consciously rejected religious teachings. The details of one dogma are rejected, but the underlying structure of belief is imbibed at so deep a level it is rarely questioned. Instead, a new dogma, a parallel structure, replaces the old. For example, many people have rejected the "revealed truth" of Christianity without ever questioning the underlying concept that truth is a set of beliefs revealed through the agency of a "Great Man," possessed of powers or intelligence beyond the ordinary human scope. Christ, as the "Great Man," may be replaced by Buddha, Freud, Marx, Jung, Werner Erhard, or the Maharaj Ji in their theology, but truth is always seen as coming from someone else, as only knowable secondhand. As feminist scholar Carol P. Christ points out, "Symbol systems cannot simply be rejected, they must be replaced. Where there is no replacement, the mind will revert to familiar structures at times of crisis, bafflement, or defeat."[3]

The symbolism of the Goddess is not a parallel structure to the symbolism of God the Father. The Goddess does not rule the world; She *is* the world. Manifest in each of us, She can be known internally by every individual, in all Her magnificent diversity. She does not legitimize the rule of either sex by the other and lends no authority to rulers of temporal hierarchies. In Witchcraft, each of us must reveal our own truth. Deity is seen in our own forms, whether female or male, because the Goddess has Her male aspect. Sexuality is a sacrament. Religion is a matter of relinking, with the divine within and with Her outer manifestations in all of the human and natural world.

The symbol of the Goddess is *poemagogic*, a term coined by Anton Ehrenzweig to "describe its special function of inducing and symbolizing the ego's creativity."[4] It has a dreamlike, "slippery" quality. One aspect slips into another. She is constantly changing form and changing face. Her images do not define or pin down a set of attributes; they spark inspiration, creation, fertility of mind and spirit: "One thing becomes another,/In the Mother . . . In the Mother . . ." (ritual chant for the winter solstice).

The importance of the Goddess symbol for women cannot be overstressed. The image of the Goddess inspires women to see ourselves as divine, our bodies as sacred, the changing phases of our lives as holy, our aggression as healthy, our anger as purifying, and our power to nurture and create, but also to limit and destroy when necessary, as the very force that sustains all life. Through the Goddess, we can discover our strength, enlighten our minds, own our bodies, and celebrate our emotions. We can move beyond narrow, constricting roles and become whole.

The Goddess is also important for men. The oppression of men in Father God-ruled patriarchy is perhaps less obvious but no less tragic than that of women. Men are encouraged to identify with a model no human being can successfully emulate: to be mini-rulers of narrow universes. They are internally split, into a "spiritual" self that is supposed to conquer their baser animal and emotional natures. They are at war with themselves: in the West, to "conquer" sin; in the East, to "conquer" desire or ego. Few escape from these wars undamaged. Men lose touch with their feelings and their bodies, becoming the "successful male zombies" described by Herb Goldberg in *The Hazards of Being Male*:

> Oppressed by the cultural pressures that have denied him his feelings, by the mythology of the woman and the distorted and self-destructive way he sees and relates to her, by the urgency for him to "act like a man," which blocks his ability to respond to his inner promptings both emotionally and physiologically, and by a generalized self-hate that causes him to feel comfortable only when he is functioning well in harness, not when he lives for joy and personal growth.[5]

Because women give birth to males, nurture them at the breast, and in our culture are primarily responsible for their care as children, "every male brought up in a traditional home develops an intense early identification with his mother and, therefore, carries within him a strong feminine imprint."[6]

The symbol of the Goddess allows men to experience and integrate the feminine side of their nature, which is often felt to be the deepest and most sensitive aspect of self. The Goddess does not exclude the male; She contains him, as a pregnant woman contains a male child. Her own male aspect embodies both the solar light of the intellect and wild, untamed animal energy.

Our relationship to the earth and the other species that share it has also been conditioned by our religious models. The image of God as outside nature has given us a rationale for our own destruction of the natural order, and justified our plunder of the earth's resources. We have attempted to "conquer" nature as we have tried to conquer sin. Only as the results of pollution and ecological destruction become severe enough to threaten even urban humanity's adaptability have we come to recognize the importance of ecological balance and the interdependence of all life. The model of the Goddess, who is immanent in nature, fosters respect for the sacredness of all living things. Witchcraft can be seen as a religion of ecology. Its goal is harmony with nature, so that life may not just survive, but thrive.

The rise of Goddess religion makes some politically oriented feminists uneasy. They fear it will sidetrack energy away from direct action to bring about social change. But in areas as deeply rooted as the relations between the sexes, true social change can only come about when the myths and symbols of our culture are themselves changed. The symbol of the Goddess conveys the spiritual power both to challenge systems of oppression and to create new, life-oriented cultures.

Modern Witchcraft is a rich kaleidoscope of traditions and orientations. Covens, the small, closely knit groups that form the congregations of Witchcraft, are autonomous; there is no central authority that determines liturgy or rites. Some covens follow practices that have been handed down in an unbroken line since before the Burning Times. Others derive their rituals from leaders of modern revivals of the Craft – the two whose followers are most widespread are Gerald Gardner and Alex Sanders, both British. Feminist covens are probably the fastest-growing arm of the Craft. Many are Dianic, a sect of Witchcraft that gives far more prominence to the female principle than the male. Other covens are openly eclectic, creating their own traditions from many sources. My own covens are based on the Faery Tradition, which goes back to the Little People of Stone Age Britain, but we believe in creating our own rituals, which reflect our needs and insights of today. In Witchcraft, a chant is not necessarily better because it is older. The Goddess is continually revealing Herself, and each of us is potentially capable of writing our own liturgy.

In spite of diversity, there are ethics and values that are common to all traditions of Witchcraft. They are based on the concept of the Goddess as immanent in the world and in all forms of life, including human beings.

Theologians familiar with Judeo-Christian concepts sometimes have trouble understanding how a religion such as Witchcraft can develop a system of ethics and a concept of justice. If there is no split between spirit and nature, no concept of sin, no covenant or commandments against which one can sin, how can people be ethical? By what standards can they judge their actions, when the external judge is removed from his place as ruler of the cosmos? And if the Goddess is immanent in the world, why work for change or strive toward an ideal? Why not bask in the perfection of divinity?

Love for life in all its forms is the basic ethic of Witchcraft. Witches are bound to honor and respect all living things, and to serve the life-force. While the Craft recognizes that life feeds on life and that we must kill in order to survive, life is never taken needlessly, never squandered or wasted. Serving the life-force means working to preserve the diversity of natural life, to prevent the poisoning of the environment and the destruction of species.

The world is the manifestation of the Goddess, but nothing in that concept need foster passivity. Many Eastern religions encourage quietism not because they believe the divine is truly immanent, but because they believe She/He is not. For them, the world is Maya, Illusion, masking the perfection of the Divine Reality. What happens in such a world is not really important; it is only a shadow play obscuring the Infinite Light. In Witchcraft, however, what happens in the world is vitally important. The Goddess is immanent, but She needs human help to realize Her fullest beauty. The harmonious balance of plant/animal/human/divine awareness is not automatic; it must constantly be renewed, and this is the true function of Craft rituals. Inner work, spiritual work, is most effective when it proceeds hand in hand with outer work. Meditation on the balance of nature might be considered a spiritual act in Witchcraft, but not as much as would cleaning up garbage left at a campsite or marching to protest an unsafe nuclear plant.

Witches do not see justice as administered by some external authority, based on a written code or set of rules imposed from without. Instead, justice is an inner sense that each act brings about consequences that must be faced responsibly. The Craft does not foster guilt, the stern, admonishing, self-hating inner voice that cripples action. Instead, it demands responsibility. "What you send, returns three times over" is the saying – an amplified version of "Do unto others as you would have them do unto you." For example, a Witch does not steal, not because of an admonition in a sacred book, but because the threefold harm far outweighs any small material gain. Stealing diminishes the thief's self-respect and sense of honor; it is an admission that one is incapable of providing honestly for one's own needs and desires. Stealing creates a climate of suspicion and fear, in which even thieves have to live. And, because we are all linked in the same social fabric, those who steal also pay higher prices for groceries, insurance, taxes. Witchcraft strongly imparts the view that all things are interdependent and interrelated and, therefore, mutually responsible. An act that harms anyone harms us all.

Honor is a guiding principle in the Craft. This is not a "macho" need to take offense at imagined slights against one's virility – it is an inner sense of pride and self-respect. The Goddess is honored in oneself, and in others. Women, who embody the Goddess, are respected, not placed on pedestals or etherealized, but valued for all their human qualities. The self, one's individuality and unique way of being in the world, is highly valued. The Goddess, like nature, loves diversity. Oneness is attained not through losing the self, but through realizing it fully. "Honor the Goddess in yourself, celebrate your self, and you will see that Self is everywhere."

In Witchcraft, "All acts of love and pleasure are My rituals." Sexuality, as a direct expression of the life-force, is seen as numinous and sacred. It can be expressed freely, so long as the guiding principle is love. Marriage is a deep commitment, a magical, spiritual, and psychic bond. But it is only one possibility out of many for loving, sexual expression.

Misuse of sexuality, however, is heinous. Rape, for example, is an intolerable crime because it dishonors the life-force by turning sexuality to the expression of violence and hostility instead of love. A woman has the sacred right to control her own body, as does a man. No one has the right to force or coerce another.

Life is valued in Witchcraft, and it is approached with an attitude of joy and wonder, as well as a sense of humor. Life is seen as the gift of the Goddess. If suffering exists, it is not our task to reconcile ourselves to it, but to work for change.

Magic, the art of sensing and shaping the subtle, unseen forces that flow through the world, of awakening deeper levels of consciousness beyond the rational, is an element common to all traditions of Witchcraft. Craft rituals are magical rites: they stimulate an awareness of the hidden side of reality, and awaken long-forgotten powers of the human mind.

The magical element in Witchcraft is disconcerting to many people. I would like to speak to the fear I have heard expressed that Witchcraft and occultism are in some way a revival of Nazism. There does seem to be evidence that Hitler and other Nazis were occultists – that is, they may have practiced some of the same techniques as others who seek to expand the horizons of the mind. Magic, like chemistry, is a set of techniques that can be put to the service of any philosophy. The rise of the Third Reich played on the civilized Germans' disillusionment with rationalism and tapped a deep longing to recover modes of experience Western culture had too long ignored. It is as if we had been trained, since infancy, never to use our left arms: the muscles have partly atrophied, but they cry out to be used. But Hitler perverted this longing and twisted it into cruelty and horror. The Nazis were not Goddess worshippers; they denigrated women, relegating them to the position of breeding animals whose role was to produce more Aryan warriors. They were the perfect patriarchy, the ultimate warrior cult – not servants of the life-force. Witchcraft has no ideal of a "superman" to be created at the expense of inferior races. In the Craft, all people are already seen as manifest gods, and differences in color, race, and customs are welcomed as signs of the myriad beauty of the Goddess. To equate Witches with Nazis because neither are Judeo-Christians and both share magical elements is like saying that swans are really scorpions because neither are horses and both have tails.

Mother-Goddess is reawakening, and we can begin to recover our primal birthright, the sheer, intoxicating joy of being alive. We can open new eyes and see that there is nothing to be saved *from*, no struggle of life *against* the universe, no God outside the world to be feared and obeyed; only the Goddess, the Mother, the turning spiral that whirls us in and out of existence, whose winking eye is the pulse of being – birth, death, rebirth – whose laughter bubbles and courses through all things and who is found only through love: love of trees, of stones, of sky and clouds, of scented blossoms and thundering waves; of all that runs and flies and swims and crawls on her face; through love of ourselves; life-dissolving world-creating orgasmic love of each other; each of us unique and natural as a snowflake, each of us our own star, her Child, her lover, her beloved, her Self.

Notes

1   Carol P. Christ, "Why women need the Goddess," in Carol P. Christ and Judith Plaskow (eds), *Womanspirit Rising: a Feminist Reader in Religion* (San Francisco: Harper and Row, 1979), p. 278.
2   Mary Daly, *Beyond God the Father* (Boston: Beacon Press, 1973), p. 13.
3   Christ, "Why women need the Goddess," p. 275.
4   Anton Ehrenzweig, *The Hidden Order of Art* (London: Paladin, 1967), p. 190.
5   Herb Goldberg, *The Hazards of Being Male* (New York: Signet, 1977), p. 4.
6   Ibid., p. 39.

Suggested activities

Questions for discussion

1 Are women's contributions to culture adequately recognized today? What evidence can you give for your views?

2 Are women's art and writing distinctive? If so, in what respects? Is this distinctiveness related to Carol Gilligan's notion of women having a "different voice" that is more concerned with caring and relationships than with individual rights and justice?

3 What are the obstacles, if any, that women artists face today?

4 Is there a separate women's culture? What evidence can you point to support your view? Should a separate women's culture be fostered? For example, should men be allowed into women's or feminist organizations? Or only men who are sympathetic to or consider themselves to be feminists? How about transgendered males? *Should* there be a separate woman's culture?

5 How has American culture and society changed since the "female world" that Smith-Rosenberg writes about? Do you think these changes have also altered the kinds of relationships that women have with one another?

6 How do the "Riot Grrls" compare with the nineteenth-century women described by Smith-Rosenberg? Which, if either, do you think is more representative of the concept of "women's culture"?

7 Is the status of women in contemporary religion still an issue that requires feminist attention or have the major problems been resolved?

8 What do you think of women's alternative spiritualities like Wicca? Should they be viewed as authentic religious traditions or as a misguided attempt to find an alternative to traditional (patriarchal) religious traditions?

Films and videos

The Artist was a Woman by Suzanne Bauman and Mary Bell (1980). VHS/58 mins. Distributed by Filmaker's Library. Documentary uncovering the works of some gifted women artists, and exploring why their talent was overlooked, including Rosa Boheur, Mary Cassatt, and Georgia O'Keeffe. Narrated by Jane Alexander, and commentary by Germaine Greer.

The Color Purple, produced by Steven Spielberg (1993; originally released as a motion picture in 1985). Warner Brothers Pictures. 3 videodiscs/154 mins. Based on the novel by Alice Walker. Tells the story of an uneducated woman living in the rural American South who was raped by her father, deprived of the children she bore him and forced to marry a brutal man she calls "Mister," and whose life is transformed by the friendship of two remarkable women.

Conjure Women by Demetria Royals and produced by Louise Diamond (1995). 16 mm/VHS/color/BW/85 mins. Distributed by Women Make Movies. Performance-based documentary of four African-American female artists. Includes performances of singers and dancers.

The Desert is no Lady by Shelley Williams in collaboration with Susan Palmer (1995). VHS/51 mins. Available from Women Make Movies. Looks at the Southwest through the eyes of leading contemporary women artists and writers from Pueblo, Navajo, Mexican-American, and Anglo backgrounds.

Faith Even to the Fire, produced by Sylvia Morales and Jean Victor (1993). VHS/58 mins. Available from Filmaker's Library. Documentary depicting contemporary US nuns in "action," living out a mission of social justice – fighting racism, sexism, and economic injustice – even when it conflicts with the established church.

Guerrillas in our Midst by Amy Harrison (1993). VHS/35 mins. On the Guerrilla Girls, an anonymous group of "art terrorists" who have succeeded in making gender and race part of the agenda of the art world.

High Heels and Ground Glass: Pioneering Women Photographers, produced by Deborah Irmas and Barbara Kasten (1992). VHS/29 mins. Distributed by Filmaker's Library. Portrays the lives and work of five outstanding women photographers, all born around the turn of the century: Gisels Freund, Louise Dahl-Wolfe, Maurine Loomis, Lisette Model (teacher to another famous woman photographer, Diana Arbus), and Eiko Yamazawa.

Identifiable Qualities: a Film on Toni Morrison by Sindamani Bridglal (1989). Corentyne Productions. Available from Women Make Movies. Interviews the Pulitzer Prize-winning black novelist about the events of the 1960s which led to her first novel, the use of personal experience as sources of her strong black female characters, and on placing black writers into the mainstream.

Sisters in the Struggle, directed by Dionne Brand, produced by Ginny Stikeman. National Film Board of Canada (1991). VHS/50 mins. Explores the diversity, vision, and impetus of the contemporary black woman's movement in Canada.

Song Journey by Arleen Bowman and Jeanine Moret (1994). VHS/57 mins. Available from Women Make Movies. Follows Arleen Bowman on the pow-wow circuit in the hope of reviving her connection to traditional native culture, and her discovery of Native American women musicians who are both preserving native culture as well as rebelling against the male monopoly of the "inner circle."

They are their own Gifts by Lucille Rhodes and Margaret Murphy (1989). VHS/55 mins. Available from Women Make Movies. Uses documentary photographs and interviews to present the lives and contributions of poet Muriel Rukeyser, portrait artist Alice Neel, and choreographer Anna Sokolow.

Visions of the Spirit: a Portrait of Alice Walker by Elena Featherston (1989). 16 mm/VHS/color/58 mins. Distributed by Women Make Movies. Portrait of the Pulitzer-Prize winning author. Filmed on location in her home town and on the set of *The Color Purple*.

Women who Made the Movies by Gwendolyn Foster and Wheeler Dixon (1992). VHS/BW/color/55 mins. Distributed by Women Make Movies. Portrait of seminal women film-makers like Ruth Ann Baldwin, Leni Riefenstahl, and Cleo Madison. Examines their impact on the history of cinema.

Women, Ritual, and Religion, (rev. edn, 1983). VHS/60 mins. Examines contemporary currents in feminist theology, including liberation theology, Wicca, and the prophetic tradition, featuring Elizabeth Schussler Fiorenza, Z. Budapest, Madonna Kolbenschlag, and Carol Christ.

. . . And Women Wove It in a Basket . . . by Bushra Azzouz, Marlene Farnum, and Nettie Kuneki (1989). VHS/70 mins. Available from Women Make Movies. Demonstrates a Native Klickitat woman's basket-weaving as a way of reclaiming Native American values and culture.

Other activities

1 Write a biographical essay on a woman who has made a significant contribution to American culture. She may or may not have been publicly recognized, but should be someone whose contributions you do not think have been given the recognition they deserve. There are a number of bibliographies of women that may assist you in locating a subject. In preparing this assignment, you need not do an exhaustive search of everything that has been written about your subject. However, you *should* have a clear understanding of your subject's basic life chronology, her location within the area of culture she contributed to, her significant contributions, how these contributions have been regarded by her contemporaries or others, and why you believe these contributions warrant broader attention. In considering the social location of your subject in relation to American culture, keep in mind the time period in which she lived or lives, her race, ethnicity, socioeconomic class, sexual orientation, whether she had children, married or remained single, had a supportive work environment, and so on. Consider how these characteristics influenced your subject's ability to operate: did they facilitate or obstruct her creativity, access to resources, and ability to achieve recognition?

2 Visit an art museum. Look at the holdings by women artists. Approximately what percentage of the holdings are by women artists? What kinds of differences, if any, do you see between the work of male and female artists, for example, in themes or subjects, style of drawing, color schemes,

size of canvas? Is it possible to generalize about such differences? Why or why not?

3   Listen to the radio or watch music videos on television. Approximately what percentage of the songs are written or sung by women? What differences, if any, are there between male and female musicians and performers, for example, in themes or subjects, emotional tone, mode of expression, type of music, band, instruments played? Is it possible to generalize about such differences? Why or why not?

4   Read a number of short stories by male and female writers. What differences, if any, do you discern between them, for example, in themes or subjects, genre or style of writing, background setting, plot and character development, underlying moral or message? Is it possible to generalize about such differences? Why or why not?

5   Watch films made by woman producers, directors, and writers. Are there ways women's films differ from films made by men? If so, how would you characterize these differences? Is it possible to make generalizations about them? Why or why not?

Bibliography

On women as creators of culture

Acker, Ally (1992) "Arts: women behind the camera," *Ms.* (March/April), pp. 63–7. On contemporary women film-makers trying to break into the Hollywood establishment.

Antrobus, Helen (1993) "Revolution girl-style now," *Utne Reader* (March/April), pp. 17–18. On the Guerrilla Girls.

Apostolos-Cappadona, Dian, and Ebersole, Lucinda (eds) (1995) *Women, Creativity, and the Arts: Critical and Autobiographical Perspectives* (New York: Continuum). Essays by Monique Wittig, Michele Wallace, Georgia O'Keefe, and others.

Armitage, Shelley (1995) *Women's Work: Essays in Cultural Studies* (West Cornwall, CT: Locus Hill Press). Essays on women and art, photography, literature, humor, popular culture, and autobiography.

Austin, Bryn (1993) "Arts: the irreverent (under) world of 'zines," *Ms.* (January/February), p. 68. On the "burgeoning underworld of renegade publications called 'zines," many of which are published by young feminists like the Riot Grrls.

Bataille, Gretchen (ed.) (1993) *Native American Women: a Biographical Dictionary* (New York: Garland Press).

Betterton, Rosemary (1996) *Intimate Distance: Women, Artists and the Body* (New York: Routledge). Critical essays exploring women artists' treatment of the changing relationships among women, the body and its representation in art.

Cahill, Susan (ed.) (1994) *Writing Women's Lives: an Anthology of Autobiographical Narratives by Twentieth-century American Women Writers* (New York: HarperPerennial). Especially moving is the excerpt from Nancy Mairs' book *Carnal Acts*, written by a professor of English literature afflicted with multiple sclerosis.

Chadwick, Whitney (1990) *Women, Art and Society* (New York: Thames and Hudson).

Christian, Barbara (1985) *Black Feminist Criticism: Perspectives on Black Women Writers* (New York: Pergamon Press).

Cooper, Sarah (ed.) (1996) *Girls! Girls! Girls! Essays on Women and Music* (New York: New York University Press). Includes rap, salsa, classical, contemporary Asian, indie-pop and jazz music.

Francke, Lizzie (1994) *Script Girls: Women Screenwriters in Hollywood* (Bloomington, IN: Indiana University Press). Shows how women screenwriters have both helped to shape, as well as sometimes subvert, the dominant Hollywood patterns of representing gender.

Fraser, Kennedy (1996) *Ornament and Silence: Essays on Women's Lives* (New York: Knopf). Interpretations of Virginia Woolf, Edith Wharton, Amelie Matisse, and others by a former fashion critic.

Gillespie, Marcia Ann (1993) "Guerrilla girls: from broadsides to broadsheets," *Ms.* (March/April), p. 69.

Gomez, Edward (1990) "Quarreling over quality," *Time* (Fall), pp. 61–2. On feminist criticism of art history.

Gubar, Susan and Gilbert, Sandra (1979a) *Madwoman in the Attic: the Woman Writer and the Nineteenth Century Literary Imagination* (New Haven, CT: Yale University Press). Psychological aspects, history, and criticism of nineteenth-century women authors.

Gubar, Susan and Gilbert, Sandra (1979b) *Shakespeare's Sisters: Feminist Essays on Women Poets* (Bloomington, IN: Indiana University Press).

Gubar, Susan and Gilbert, Sandra (eds) (1985) *Norton Anthology of Literature by Women* (New York: W. W. Norton).

Gubar, Susan and Gilbert, Sandra (1988) *No Man's Land: the Place of the Woman Writer in the Twentieth Century* (New Haven, CT: Yale University Press).

Guerrilla Girls (1995) *Confessions of the Guerilla Girls* (New York: HarperPerennial). Contains an essay by Whitney Chadwick.

Hedges, Elaine and Wendt, Ingrid (eds) (1980) *In her own Image: Women Working in the Arts* (Old Westbury, CT.: Feminist Press). Collection of the artistic works of Western women artists, writers, sculptors, musicians, needleworkers, dancers, graphic artists, photographers, and painters.

Heilbron, Carolyn (1978) *Writing a Woman's Life* (New York: W. W. Norton). On writing biographies of women.

Isaak, Jo Anna (1996) *Feminism and Contemporary Art: the Revolutionary Power of Women's Laughter* (New York: Routledge).

Koppelman, Susan (1994) *Two Friends and other Nineteenth-century Lesbian Stories by American Women Writers* (New York: Meridian).

Leland, John (1994) "Our bodies, our sales," *Newsweek*, January 31, pp. 56–7. On "girl groups" like Salt 'n' Pepa and En Vogue, and whether female music artists can still be feminists.

Lewin, Ellen (ed.) (1996) *Inventing Lesbian Cultures in America* (Boston: Beacon Press). Essays explore how women use the idea of being lesbian in their creation of identity and community.

Lippard, Lucy (1995) *The Pink Glass Swan: Selected Feminist Essays on Art* (New York: New Press).

Nemser, Cindy (1992) "Arts: to defy, reveal – and heal," *Ms.*, November/December, pp. 64–7. On contemporary art by women.

Neuls-Bates, Carol (1996) *Women in Music: an Anthology of Source Readings from the Middle Ages to the Present*, rev. edn (Boston, MA: Northeastern University Press). An anthology of source readings in Western art music.

Nochlin, Linda (1988) *Women, Art, and Power and other Essays* (New York: Harper and Row). Collection of essays exploring depictions of women by male artists, women artists, and the issue of why so few women artists have been recognized.

Norris, Gloria Norris (ed.) (1996) *The Seasons of Women: an Anthology* (New York: W. W. Norton). Stories, memoirs, and essays by contemporary American women writers.

O'Brien, Lucy (1995) *She Bop: the Definitive History of Women in Rock, Pop, and Soul – from Billie Holliday, Ella Fitzgerald, and Dusty Springfield to Patti Smith, Madonna, and Courtney Love* (New York: Penguin).

Orenstein, Gloria Feman (1990) "Artists as healers: envisioning life-giving culture," in Irene Diamond and Gloria Orenstein (eds), *Reweaving the World: the Emergence of Ecofeminism* (San Francisco: Sierra Club Books).

Parker, Rozsika and Pollock, Griselda (1981) *Old Mistresses: Women, Art, and Ideology* (New York: Pantheon Books). Explores women's place in the history of art. Addresses how women have been represented in art as well as why women artists have been ignored in art history).

Parker, Rozsika and Pollock, Griselda (eds) (1987) *Framing Feminism: Art and the Women's Movement, 1970–85* (London: Pandora).

Rebolledo, Tey Diana and Rivero, Eliana (eds) (1993) *Infinite Divisions: an Anthology of Chicana Literature* (Tucson, AZ: University of Arizona Press). Collection of Chicana writing by 50 authors who live "on the border" between Spanish and English language cultures, grouped according to major themes in the literature, including family, social and geographical space, childhood constructions of self, and writing.

Reynolds, Margaret (1994) *The Penguin Book of Lesbian Short Stories* (New York: Penguin).

Rosenblum, Naomi (1994) *A History of Women Photographers* (New York: Abbeville Press). Covers 240 women photographers, three-fifths of whom are from the United States.

Salem, Dorothy (1993) *African American Women: a Biographical Dictionary* (New York: Garland Press).

Tierney, Helen (1990) *Women's Studies Encyclopedia, Volume II: Literature, Arts, and Learning* (Westport, CT: Greenwood Press). Coverage of these topics from a woman's perspective.

Todd, Janet (1988) *Feminist Literary History* (New York: Routledge). Charts the history of feminist literary criticism.

Uno, Roberta (1993) *Unbroken Thread: an Anthology of Plays by Asian American Women* (Amherst: University of Massachusetts Press).

Van Hook, Betty (1996) *Angels of Art: Women and Art in American Society, 1876–1914* (University Park, PA: Pennsylvania State University Press). An examination of the hypothesis that images of women in the Gilded Age reflect the attitudes and social constructions of femininity of the period.

Walker, Alice (1985) "In search of our mothers' gardens," in Susan Gubar and Sandra Gilbert (eds), *The Norton Anthology of Literature by Women* (New York: W. W. Norton).

Witzling, Mara (ed.) (1994) *Voicing Today's Visions: Writings by Contemporary Women Artists* (New York: Rizzoli). Interviews with 14 artists.

Woolf, Virginia (1929) *A Room of One's Own* (New York: Harcourt, Brace).

On women in religion

Adler, Margot (1986) *Drawing Down the Moon: Witches, Druids, Goddess-Worshippers, and other Pagans in America Today* (Boston, MA: Beacon Press).

Biale, Rachel (1984) *Women and Jewish Law: an Exploration of Women's Issues in Halakhic Sources* (New York: Schocken Books).

Billington, Sandra and Green, Miranda (eds) (1996) *The Concept of the Goddess* (New York: Routledge). Interdisciplinary essays exploring the nature of goddesses from a variety of traditions and cultures, for example, Celtic, Roman, Norse.

Bonavoglia, Angela (1992) "The sacred secret," *Ms.* (November/December), pp. 40–45.

Boucher, Sandy (1993) *Turning the Wheel: American Women in Creating the New Buddhism* (Boston: Beacon Press).

Christ, Carol (1986) "Why women need the Goddess: phenomenological, psychological, and political reflections," in Johnnetta Cole (ed.), *All American Women: Lines that Divide, Ties that Bind* (New York: Macmillan).

Eller, Cynthia (1993) *In the Lap of the Goddess: the Feminist Spirituality Movement in America* (New York: Crossroads). On the diversity of beliefs and practices in "spiritual feminism."

Ferraro, Barbara and Hussey, Patricia (1990) *No Turning Back: Two Nuns' Battle with the Vatican over Women's Right to Choose* (New York: Poseidon Press).

Gross, Rita (1992) *Buddhism after Patriarchy* (New York: State University of New York Press). On the relationship of Western women to Buddhism.

Gross, Rita (1996) *Feminism and Religion: an Introduction* (Boston: Beacon Press).

Hampson, Daphne (1990) *Theology and Feminism* (Cambridge, MA: Blackwell). Proposes that feminism offers new ways to conceive of God and reformulate theology in a world in which Christianity is no longer tenable.

Holm, Jean and Bowker, John (eds) (1994) *Women in Religion* (New York: St Martins Press). Collection of essays on women in relation to the major world religions. Looks at religious attitudes to women in relation to marriage, family, and the home; the role women play in religious institutions; and the significance of cultural influences on attitudes to women in religion.

King, Ursala (ed.) (1994) *Religion and Gender* (Cambridge, MA: Blackwell).

Klein, Anne (1994) *Meeting the Great Bliss Queen: Feminism, Buddhism, and the Art of the Self* (Boston: Beacon Press). On Western women's relationship to Buddhism.

McCloud, Beverly (1991) "African-American muslim women," in Yvonne Yazbeck Haddad (ed.), *The Muslims of America* (New York: Oxford University Press).

Miles, Margaret (1989) *Carnal Knowing: Female Nakedness and Religious Meaning in the Christian West* (Boston: Beacon Press).

Muir, Elizabeth Gillan and Whitely, Marilyn Fardig (eds) (1995) *Changing Roles of Women within the Christian Church in Canada* (Ontario: University of Toronto Press). Anthology tracing the history of Canadian women in the Roman Catholic, Anglican, and Protestant traditions from the early days through the 1960s.

O'Failain, Julia and Lauro, Martines (eds) (1973) *Not in God's Image: Women in History from the Greeks to the Victorians* (New York: Harper Colophon Books, 1973).

Paul, Diana (1982) "Buddhist attitudes toward women's bodies," *Buddhist Christian Studies*, 2: 63–71.

Peach, Lucinda (1993–4) "From spiritual descriptions to legal prescriptions: religious imagery of women as 'fetal containers' in the law," *Journal of Law and Religion*, 10(1): 73–93.

Reilly, Patricia Lynn (1995) *A God who Looks Like Me: Discovering a Woman-centered Spirituality* (New York: Ballantine Books).

Ruether, Rosemary Radford (1983) *Sexism and God-Talk: toward a Feminist Theology* (Boston: Beacon Press).

Ruether, Rosemary Radford and Keller, Rosemary Skinner (eds) (1995) *In our own Voices: Four Centuries of American Women's Religious Writing* (New York: HarperCollins).

Smith, Karen Sue (1990) "Catholic women: two decades of change," in Mary Segers (ed.), *Church Polity and American Politics: Issues in Contemporary Catholicism* (New York: Garland).

Spring Wind Editorial Staff (1986) *Women and Buddhism: a Special Issue of Spring Wind – Buddhist Cultural Forum*, 6(1–3): 166–72.

Umansky, Ellen (1985) "Feminism and the reevaluation of women's roles within American Jewish life," in Yvonne Yasbeck Haddad and Ellison Banks-Findley (eds), *Women, Religion, and Social Change* (Albany, NY: State University of New York Press).

Weaver, Mary Jo (1985) *New Catholic Women: a Contemporary Challenge to Traditional Religious Authority* (San Francisco: Harper and Row).

Williams, Delores (1993) *Sisters in the Wilderness: the Challenge of Womanist God-Talk* (Marymount, NY: Orbis Books). Challenge to racist, sexist, and homophobic dimensions of Christianity, focusing on black women's lives.

10

Feminism and the Future

Introduction

In this final chapter we will assess the current status of feminism in the US, recent challenges to its credibility and continued existence, and its prospects for the future. In the past several years, feminism has come under increasingly vocal attack in popular culture, which Susan Faludi (1991) persuasively documents in *Backlash: the Undeclared War against American Women*. The diversity of feminist organizations, politics, and philosophies in the United States today contributes to the current perception that the feminist movement is in disarray and lacks a common agenda. Some critics merely contend that feminism has outlived its usefulness: now that women have obtained "equal rights" with men, their purpose is complete and women should move on to other issues.

Other criticisms are not as gentle. Rush Limbaugh's jokes about "feminazis" and the actions of a former engineering graduate student who went on a shooting rampage in Montreal, killing eight women university engineering students "because they were feminists," demonstrates the deep-seated hatred by some elements in American culture of women who stand up for their rights. Popular descriptions of feminism as extreme, strident, and out of touch with the issues and concerns of mainstream women, have made feminism a dirty word for many Americans, including women. At the same time, the feminist movement has clearly benefited the lives of many women, and has the potential to fundamentally reshape society.

As we have seen in preceding chapters, there is no one set of principles or values, no specific perspective, that can be pointed to as "feminism." Instead, there are a number of different forms or strands of feminism, each with its own particular perspective, priorities, and set of concerns. Some of these strands are in tension or conflict with others. For example, women of color and lesbian feminists have criticized the mainstream women's movement for well over a decade for its failure to address their needs and interests (see, for example, Smith, 1982: 25–8; Molina, 1990, given as our second reading).

The plurality of feminisms can be viewed as either an asset or a liability. Some argue that there is no reason why all feminists must ascribe to the same principles or have the same agenda. For example, *Ms.* magazine devoted the lead article, entitled "No, feminists *don't* all think alike" in its September/October 1993 issue, to a debate among feminists Gloria Steinem, bell hooks, Naomi Wolf, and Urvashi Vaid. This kind of attention in a mainstream feminist publication does not negate the validity of the critique that the mainstream feminist movement has been biased, but it does demonstrate an effort by mainstream feminist leaders to listen to other women who feel alienated from the mainstream, and to attempt to find ways that all women can work together in pursuit of common causes, regardless of the class, race, and other differences that may divide them in other spheres of life. Some contend that, without some kind of organized platform that can bring women together in common cause, the women's movement will founder. Others argue that feminism has *already* foundered.

This chapter provides an introductory overview of some of the more prevalent types of feminism in American culture, and examines a couple of the recent attacks that have been made against feminism. These attacks have come from both those who claim to be feminists as well as others. Then we will turn to consider some suggestions about how feminism might make a difference for the future, both for improving the status of women as well as the rest of the world. The chapter – and the volume – concludes with Maya Angelou's inspirational poem "Still I Rise."

Feminist politics and the backlash

As we have already seen in a variety of ways in this anthology, power is not simply a matter of access to the formal institutions and processes of traditional politics. Power is exercised in a myriad of ways in US society. Thus, the feminist phrase "the personal is political." Among the many changes that have taken place within the women's movement since the early days of the second wave, feminists are struggling to develop ways of maintaining effective and robust politics without the necessity of adopting essentialist views of women.

In addition to differences among feminists about how to proceed with an effective politics, there are also outside forces seeking to fragment organized feminist action. Faludi's (1991) *Backlash* documents the many ways in which social forces have attempted to blunt the force of the women's movement through portraying feminism as the *source* of women's current suffering and unhappiness, rather than as the potential source of their liberation from oppression.

One of the many issues that fall under the rubric of feminist politics is what kind of society women would build if they had the political power to do so. There have been many utopias developed in feminist fiction, and many feminist critiques of the existing political, social, and economic systems, but not as much attention given to what a "real world" based on feminist principles would look like. In an essay entitled "Toward a woman-friendly new world order," Jones (1993b) suggests that women's vote can be a formidable political force to make women's concerns visible throughout the world. She proposes that women adopt an understanding of citizenship that focuses on the interrelationships connecting peoples of different nations rather than the boundaries that divide them, as conventional politics does.

There are a number of different forms or strands of feminism and feminist theory. These strands overlap to some extent, but each has distinctive elements as well. The following list summarizes some of the dominant characteristics of the forms of feminism that are now prominent in American culture. Their diversity reflects the fragmentation that the women's movement has been undergoing since the 1970s, a trend that has continued into the mid-1990s. Some of these forms are more political than others. But even those associated with less overtly political agendas, such as postmodernism, take on a political cast in their feminist form. They are described here roughly in terms of the chronological order of their emergence.

Liberal feminism

This form of feminism dominated the second-wave women's movement, and is probably the most prominent and well known, and is frequently regarded as representing feminists as a whole. Consequently, it is most often the target of criticism directed at "feminism." Non-liberal feminists also criticize liberal feminism as reinforcing male standards of participation and success, trying to carve out a niche for élite women in a political and economic system that is fundamentally corrupt, and ignoring the needs and interests of poor women and women of color (see Jaquette, 1992). Liberal feminism generally rests on the principles of the second wave of the women's movement: of seeking equality for women as measured by the standard of equal rights with men. Liberal feminists tend to assume that women are like men in all respects that are fundamental to women's legal status.

Socialist/Marxist feminism

These forms of feminism are generally premised on the principle that socioeconomic institutions need to be fundamentally restructured in order to end male domination and the oppression of women. Feminists in both camps stress the importance of analyzing both gender and class oppression, since both equally control women's lives. Marxist-oriented feminists place capitalism, and the gendered division of labor, at the source of human oppression (see, for example, Hartmann, 1981; Hartsock, 1983), whereas socialist feminists look to the overcoming of social and economic inequalities between the sexes as bringing about the end of women's oppression (King, 1990: 113–15; Lorber, 1994: 2; see generally Jaggar, 1983).

Radical feminism

The early second-wave feminists called "radical" include Kate Millett, Shulamith Firestone, Mary Daly, Robin Morgan, and Juliet Mitchell. Some of these early "radical feminists" are now often considered to be just as essentializing and prone to false universalism about women's experience as liberal feminists are. Radical feminists such as Catharine MacKinnon and Robin West argue that sex and gender are a worldwide system by which men dominate women through controlling their sexuality and reproductive capacities.

Cultural, gender, or different voice feminism

This form of feminism is based on work by authors like Carol Gilligan and Nancy Chodorow, who, as we have seen, make a case for women having a different moral and political sensibility. Although they have been accused of biological essentialism, their theories can be explained satisfactorily on the understanding that women's difference from men results from acculturation, not necessarily biology. Feminist political theorists like Joan Tronto (1987), Sarah Ruddick (1989), and Seyla Benhabib (1987) have argued for a more "communitarian" feminism based on principles of caring and relationality. Jean Elshtain (1981) has argued for the importance of incorporating traditional private feminine principles of nurturance and moral sensibility into the public world of politics, but without sacrificing the private sphere of the family to the "public" state.

Womanist feminism

The term "womanist" was coined by African-American writer Alice Walker as an alternative to "feminism," which she and several other writers viewed as too often failing to consider the needs and interests of women of color, while purporting to speak for *all* women. Womanist feminists have also criticized *cultural feminists* for failing to acknowledge their privileged social status as white, and thus their own complicity in the oppression of people of color.

Ecofeminism

This form of feminism takes nature, and women's relationship and identification with nature, as the central category of analysis. Ecofeminists analyze the interrelationships between the domination of nature and the oppression of women and other groups of humans, and propose a more harmonious way of living in relationship with nature rather than the conventional stance of dominating (Diamond and Orenstein, 1990).

Lesbian feminism

This type of feminism grew out of lesbian disillusionment with, and exclusion from, the mainstream women's movement in the late 1970s and 1980s. (Some lesbian feminist work is also characterized under the term "Queer theory.")

Postcolonial/Third World feminism

This form of feminism was developed by women of color who found that mainstream liberal feminism did not directly address them or the concerns that were central to their lives. While acknowledging that not all women of color are the same, the foundation of postcolonial/Third World feminism is the assumption that women of color share a visibility or invisibility based on their racial or ethnic backgrounds. This commonality joins them together in being the subjects of racial as well as gender discrimination, and provides the basis for radical and revolutionary organizing for social change (Mohanty et al., 1991). The reading by Molina in this chapter exemplifies this strand of feminism.

Postmodern feminism

Authors identifying themselves as feminist "postmodernists" or "post-structuralists" are interested in challenging universal principles, norms, and assumptions, and categories of thought that perpetuate dichotomies such as male and female, and the hierarchies of power and privilege that accompany them. This is perhaps the most recent form of feminism.

The readings in this chapter demonstrate the flavor of a couple of these strands of feminist thought. The reading entitled "Feminism: a transformational politic" by bell hooks is representative of recent work by a number of feminists, especially women of color, critical of the mainstream feminist movement for its too-facile assumptions about what all women have in common as "sisters," and what is necessary to overcome oppression in women's lives. In the reading, hooks criticizes the assumption of privileged white feminism that patriarchy and sexism are the root oppression, from which racism and class exploitation are offshoots. Instead, she suggests that the categories of "powerful" and "powerless" are more primary than those of "male" and "female." Thus, women share the capacity to be both oppressors and oppressed.

Like hooks, other feminist scholars have taken a more expansive view of politics, extending their field of vision and concern to the status and experiences of women globally. This type of feminism includes women like Cynthia Enloe, Charlotte Bunch, and participants in the 1995 United Nations Women's Conference held in Beijing, China who were concerned about the exploitation of women around the world by Western political, economic, and military power.

In *Backlash*, Faludi (1991) addresses why feminism and the women's movement, rather than the sexist and patriarchal social institutional and cultural practices that have subordinated women for centuries, have become the presumed cause of women's oppression in popular culture. She describes how feminism has been blamed for ailments ranging from the emergence of "slasher" films to rising rape rates and the feminization of poverty. While demonstrating that each of these claims about the damage the women's movement has caused are unfounded, Faludi simultaneously refutes the myth that women have achieved equality. Working women still earn far less than men, even for comparable work, are relegated more frequently to lower-paying jobs, are far more likely to live in substandard housing without health insurance or pensions, are tremendously under-represented in government, are unable to find adequate child care or child support from their children's fathers, have less reproductive freedom than a decade ago, still encounter sexual discrimination in education, and are inadequately protected against rising rates of rape, wife battering, childhood sexual abuse, and other violence.

The mass media simultaneously promote the message that women are miserable – burned out from working full time while raising children and maintaining the household – and are unable to bear children or to find a husband because they have waited too long. Faludi interprets these apparently conflicting signals as sending the same message: that it is women's very equality that is making them miserable. The backlash has succeeded, she argues, in inhibiting many women, especially young women, from calling themselves feminists, even though many of them affirm the central principles of mainstream feminism: women's rights to equal opportunity, equal pay, a satisfying career, the choice to marry or become a mother, the right to be free of sexual harassment, sex discrimination, rape, and physical abuse. A poll by *Time*/CNN taken in 1989 showed that only 33 percent of American women considered themselves feminists, even though almost all of them supported the main goals of mainstream feminism. By 1992, this percentage had dropped to 29 percent (Tanenbaum, 1995: 5).

As noted above, the backlash against feminism has also come from women, some of whom call themselves feminists. Several recent works by self-proclaimed feminists attack the feminist movement for having failed. For example, self-designated feminist Camille Paglia criticizes feminism for telling women that they have more independence and freedom than they actually do, given their existence in a society where males dominate women sexually. In her view, male dominance and sexual aggression are biologically determined, not socially constructed. Without men to protect them, women are at the mercy of other men who will take advantage of them sexually. Feminism is to blame for failing to warn women of this fact of life, and instead taking the position that sexual violence against women can be eliminated. Such attitudes, in Paglia's view, leave women even more vulnerable and defenseless (Paglia, 1992).

Christina Hoff Sommers takes a diametrically opposed line of attack on feminism, but to similar effect. Her *Who Stole Feminism* (1994) is a diatribe against what Sommers calls "gender feminism." The so-called "gender feminists" (who include Gloria Steinem, Naomi Wolf, Susan Faludi, Patricia Ireland, Marilyn French, and Catherine MacKinnon) currently dominate American feminism and "seek to persuade the public that American women are not the free creatures we think we are" (Sommers, 1994: 16).

Although Sommers contends that "I am a feminist who does not like what feminism has become" (Sommers, 1994: 18), she complains that such high-profile feminists inaccurately report statistics about the incidence of violence against women, and thus disseminate a distorted picture of the actual status of women in our society. Sommers implies that gender feminists have exaggerated or constructed male domination of society, brutality against women, structural oppression of females in schools and other social institutions, and psychological abuse of wives by husbands. Further, she argues that gender feminists are alienating the majority of American women from feminism in general, and have "stole[n] 'feminism' from a mainstream that had never acknowledged their leadership" (Sommers, 1994: 18). Thus, whereas Paglia contends that society is not as safe for women as feminists claim, Sommers argues that it is actually safer!

Katie Roiphe's *The Morning After* (1993) takes the position of a young feminist disappointed that the dominant movement she encountered in college was one of "victim feminism," which focused on expressing anger toward men and male domination, and on rape and sexual harassment to the exclusion of other issues of significance to women. Roiphe expresses the opinion that the dominant feminist movement, so described, is out of touch with the needs and interests of the majority of American women, and needs to regain its footing on ground more solidly representative of its constituency. Similarly, in *The New Victorians* (1995), Rene Delafeld contends that the "old" feminist order does not reflect the interests of the majority of younger women. In her view, "from male bashing to goddess worship, each leading feminist cause today alienates women" (Delafeld, 1995: 16). Her work reads like that of a younger Sommers. She contends that the feminist leaders have become side-tracked into causes that do not reflect the needs and interests of the majority of women, causes that reflect an attitude of victim feminism. As a result, the majority of American women reject an identification with feminism. Before the women's movement is destroyed by these feminist leaders, she argues, younger feminists need to take back the movement.

Although she characterizes the "organized, ideological form of feminism" as one represented by NOW, women's studies courses, and feminist leaders (Delafeld, 1995: 6), Delafeld chooses some of the most radical feminist thinkers – Andrea Dworkin, Catherine MacKinnon, and Robin Morgan – as exemplars of the mainstream feminist movement. But rather than also discussing the more moderate voices within the movement, Delafeld polemically contends that they have been ostracized and excluded by the more radical voices. In addition, she mischaracterizes the views of the feminists she does discuss. For example, she characterizes Faludi as attributing the backlash to an orchestrated conspiracy by males (Delafeld, 1995: 3–4)!

The twist that Delafeld's critique adds to other accounts is the claim that feminist leaders are a throwback to the Victorians in their portrayal of women as passive victims of male domination, sexual aggression, and political power, and their rejection of heterosexual sex as hopelessly sexist and the root of women's oppression (Delafeld, 1995: 10–11). Delafeld also claims that the feminist leadership has dropped the ball on political involvement, having turned inward to more psychoanalytic and spiritual responses to inequality. Delafeld's analysis is premised on the assumption that "true" or "authentic" feminism is *liberal feminism* – that its core concerns are child care, political parity, economic opportunity, abortion rights, and birth control, concerns premised on the understanding "that women can and should be equal and in full partnership with men, working together, both free from restraining sex roles" (Delafeld, 1995: 21). Her description of "real" feminism includes *no* attention to racial and ethnic differences between women or how such differences influence the appropriate way to respond to these issues. Similarly, she includes scant attention to class differences between women, and how this influences their needs.

More significantly, Delafeld totally neglects the influence of anti-feminist rhetoric on turning women away from feminism. In her description, it is the mainstream feminist movement alone that has single-handedly made feminism a dirty word for the majority of American women. She ignores the social and political conditions that have stymied feminist efforts to succeed in obtaining those goals that she characterizes as the primary concerns of women today: "helping women balance work and family" and "getting government funding for programs such as child care and maternity leave" (Delafeld, 1995: 17–18).

A final book in the "backlash" category is *Professing Feminism* by Daphne Patai and Noretta Koertge (1994). The focus of the authors' criticisms is on how women's studies is being taught in programs around the US. They contend that most women's studies programs inappropriately involve feminist politics in the teaching of courses. Such politics are just as inappropriate, they contend, as classroom advocacy of any other kind of politics. In their view, women's studies courses should be limited to presenting academic material on women, period. The bias and partiality of *Professing Feminism* has been noted by reviewers; for example, that they base their "national" survey of women's studies programs on 30 interviews, all of them anonymous (Kakutani, 1994).

Not all but a few hard-core feminists have abandoned the movement, however. A new generation of younger women are finding feminism relevant to their lives, and are unafraid to call themselves feminists (Kamen, 1991; Findlen, 1995). These younger women (mostly, although more men are also identifying themselves as feminists or as feminist "supporters" or "sympathizers") have recognized a value in the feminist causes and strategies of earlier feminists, and are determined to carry on their struggle to improve the status of women in American society and culture.

New horizons for women

What is the future for feminism and its goal of ending the oppression of women? Since there is no way to know the future, we can only speculate. There are some hints of the directions that feminism is moving toward, however, that may provide the basis for the future.

First, the trend toward greater communication among women about their differences as well as similarities will probably continue, leading to greater understanding of why some groups of women are unable to identify or join in the struggles of others against oppression. The conversations about the ways in which women's lives differ along lines of race, class, ethnicity, sexual orientation, religion, and disability will, it is hoped, continue, leading to a greater awareness of how particular groups of women have been alienated and/or marginalized by mainstream feminism, their distinctive needs and concerns unaddressed and unmet, their voices unheard. Such conversations will contribute to a greater clarity concerning how women can most effectively work to secure changes in public policy that will benefit *all* women, or at least not benefit some at the expense of others.

Secondly, despite the differences among various types and styles of feminism, feminists are learning to form alliances and work together on specific issues that they share. The reading "Recognizing, accepting, and celebrating our differences" by Papusa Molina addresses this kind of development within the women's movement. Her reading describes the anger and frustration that many women of color have experienced in being excluded from or alienated by the mainstream feminist movement. She suggests that each individual needs to recognize both how they are oppressed as well as how they oppress others as a prerequisite for being able to work together effectively.

More recently, Naomi Wolf has made a similar argument. Her book *Fire with Fire* (1993) proposes that women adopt "power feminism" by moving beyond academic feminism and embracing equal rights, regardless of differences on other issues. She argues that feminists need to work together on issues of common concern, despite whatever very real differences may divide them in other ways. She is optimistic that the basis for such collective action exists, and that women have the ability to seize the economic and political power that has been eluding them.

Thirdly, American feminists have been reaching beyond issues exclusively or primarily involving American women to address other concerns: the status of women globally, war, the environment, animal rights, and children. The United Nations Conference on Women held in Beijing, China, in September 1995, especially the Non-Governmental Forum that preceded the formal meetings, illustrated the possibility of women from many different cultures learning from one another and networking in common cause to improve the lives of all women. The reading "Healing the wounds" by Ynestra King represents an example of ecofeminism, a movement by some feminists to provide a new way of understanding and addressing the environmental crisis. As noted above, ecofeminism is premised on a fundamental connection between women and the natural world, and the way in which white males have mistreated both. Eco-feminists contend that ending oppression based on sex and race also requires ending the oppression of nature. Ecofeminists believe that women's political activism has the potential to improve the quality of the earth for the benefit of all of its inhabitants.

Finally, the poem "Still I Rise" by Maya Angelou suggests that whatever hardships and obstacles women may face, they are not about to be defeated. Rather, women's integrity, strength, intelligence, effort, and perseverance will continue to provide resources for resistance to obstacles, and the capacity eventually to overcome them. Angelou's faith and determination provide a hopeful note on which to conclude this volume on women in American culture.

Feminism: a Transformational Politic
bell hooks

We live in a world in crisis – a world governed by politics of domination, one in which the belief in a notion of superior and inferior, and its con-comitant ideology – that the superior should rule over the inferior – affects

This reading first appeared in *Talking Back: Thinking Feminist, Thinking Black* (Boston: South End Press, 1989), pp. 19–27.

the lives of all people everywhere, whether poor or privileged, literate or illiterate. Systematic dehumanization, worldwide famine, ecological devastation, industrial contamination, and the possibility of nuclear destruction are realities which remind us daily that we are in crisis. Contemporary feminist thinkers often cite sexual politics as the origin of this crisis. They point to the insistence on difference as that factor which becomes the occasion for separation and domination and suggest that differentiation of status between females and males globally is an indication that patriarchal domination of the planet is the root of the problem. Such an assumption has fostered the notion that elimination of sexist oppression would necessarily lead to the eradication of all forms of domination. It is an argument that has led influential Western white women to feel that feminist movement should be *the* central political agenda for females globally. Ideologically, thinking in this direction enables Western women, especially privileged white women, to suggest that racism and class exploitation are merely the offspring of the parent system: patriarchy. Within feminist movement in the West, this has led to the assumption that resisting patriarchal domination is a more legitimate feminist action than resisting racism and other forms of domination. Such thinking prevails despite radical critiques made by black women and other women of color who question this proposition. To speculate that an oppositional division between men and women existed in early human communities is to impose on the past, on these non-white groups, a worldview that fits all too neatly within contemporary feminist paradigms that name man as the enemy and woman as the victim.

Clearly, differentiation between strong and weak, powerful and powerless, has been a central defining aspect of gender globally, carrying with it the assumption that men should have greater authority than women, and should rule over them. As significant and important as this fact is, it should not obscure the reality that women can and do participate in politics of domination, as perpetrators as well as victims – that we dominate, that we are dominated. If focus on patriarchal domination masks this reality or becomes the means by which women deflect attention from the real conditions and circumstances of our lives, then women cooperate in suppressing and promoting false consciousness, inhibiting our capacity to assume responsibility for transforming ourselves and society.

Thinking speculatively about early human social arrangement, about women and men struggling to survive in small communities, it is likely that the parent–child relationship with its very real imposed survival structure of dependency, of strong and weak, of powerful and powerless, was a site for the construction of a paradigm of domination. While this circumstance of dependency is not necessarily one that leads to domination, it lends itself to the enactment of a social drama wherein domination could easily occur as a means of exercising and maintaining control. This speculation does not place women outside the practice of domination, in the exclusive role of victim. It centrally names women as agents of domination, as potential theoreticians, and creators of a paradigm for social relationships wherein those groups of individuals designated as "strong" exercise power both benevolently and coercively over those designated as "weak."

Emphasizing paradigms of domination that call attention to woman's capacity to dominate is one way to deconstruct and challenge the simplistic notion that man is the enemy, woman the victim; the notion that men have always been the oppressors. Such thinking enables us to examine our role as women in the perpetuation and maintenance of systems of domination. To understand domination, we must understand that our capacity as women and men to be either dominated or dominating is a point of connection, of commonality. Even though I speak from the particular experience of living as a black woman in the United States, a white-supremacist, capitalist, patriarchal society, where small numbers of white men (and honorary "white men") constitute ruling groups, I understand that in many places in the world oppressed and oppressor share the same color. I understand that right here in this room, oppressed and oppressor share the same gender. Right now as I speak, a man who is himself victimized, wounded, hurt by racism and class exploitation is actively dominating a woman in his life – that even as I speak, women who are ourselves exploited, victimized, are dominating children. It is necessary for us to remember, as we think critically about domination, that we all have the capacity to act in ways that oppress, dominate, wound (whether or not that power is institutionalized). It is necessary to remember that it is first the potential oppressor within that we must resist – the potential victim within that we must rescue – otherwise we cannot hope for an end to domination, for liberation.

This knowledge seems especially important at this historical moment when black women and other women of color have worked to create awareness of the ways in which racism empowers white women to act as exploiters and oppressors. Increasingly this fact is considered a reason we should not support feminist struggle even though sexism and sexist oppression is a real issue in our lives as black women (see, for example, Vivian Gordon's *Black Women, Feminism, Black Liberation: Which Way?*). It becomes necessary for us to speak continually about the convictions that inform our continued advocacy of feminist struggle. By calling attention to interlocking systems of domination – sex, race, and class – black women and many other groups of women acknowledge the diversity and complexity of female experience, of our relationship to power and domination. The intent is not to dissuade people of color from becoming engaged in feminist movement. Feminist struggle to end patriarchal domination should be of primary importance to women and men globally not because it is the foundation of all other oppressive structures but because it is that form of domination we are most likely to encounter in an ongoing way in everyday life.

Unlike other forms of domination, sexism directly shapes and determines relations of power in our private lives, in familiar social spaces, in that most intimate context – home – and in that most intimate sphere of relations – family. Usually, it is within the family that we witness coercive domination and learn to accept it, whether it be domination of parent over child, or male over female. Even though family relations may be, and most often are, informed by acceptance of a politic of domination, they are simultaneously relations of care and connection. It is this convergence of two contradictory impulses – the urge to promote growth and the urge to inhibit growth – that provides a practical setting for feminist critique, resistance, and transformation.

Growing up in a black, working-class, father-dominated household, I experienced coercive adult male authority as more immediately threatening, as more likely to cause immediate pain than racist oppression or class exploitation. It was equally clear that experiencing exploitation and oppression in the home made one feel all the more powerless when encountering dominating forces outside the home. This is true for many people. If we are unable to resist and end domination in relations where there is care, it seems totally unimaginable that we can resist and end it in other institutionalized relations of power. If we cannot convince the mothers and/or fathers who care not to humiliate and degrade us, how can we imagine convincing or resisting an employer, a lover, a stranger who systematically humiliates and degrades?

Feminist effort to end patriarchal domination should be of primary concern precisely because it insists on the eradication of exploitation and oppression in the family context and in all other intimate relationships. It is that political movement which most radically addresses the person – the personal – citing the need for transformation of self, of relationships, so that we might be better able to act in a revolutionary manner, challenging and resisting domination, transforming the world outside the self. Strategically, feminist movement should be a central component of all other liberation struggles because it challenges each of us to alter our person, our personal engagement (either as victims or perpetrators or both) in a system of domination.

Feminism, as liberation struggle, must exist apart from and as a part of the larger struggle to eradicate domination in all its forms. We must understand that patriarchal domination shares an ideological foundation with racism and other forms of group oppression, that there is no hope that it can be eradicated while these systems remain intact. This knowledge should consistently inform the direction of feminist theory and practice. Unfortunately, racism and class élitism among women has frequently led to the suppression and distortion of this connection so that it is now necessary for feminist thinkers to critique and revise much feminist theory and the direction of feminist movement. This effort at revision is perhaps most evident in the current widespread acknowledgment that sexism, racism, and class exploitation constitute interlocking systems of domination – that sex, race, and class, and not sex alone, determine the nature of any female's identity, status, and circumstance, the degree to which she will or will not be dominated, the extent to which she will have the power to dominate.

While acknowledgment of the complex nature of woman's status (which has been most impressed upon everyone's consciousness by radical women of color) is a significant corrective, it is only a starting point. It provides a frame of reference which must serve as the basis for thoroughly altering and revising feminist theory and practice. It challenges and calls us to re-think popular assumptions about the nature of feminism that have had the deepest impact on a large majority of women, on mass consciousness. It radically calls into question the notion of a fundamentally common female experience which has been seen as the prerequisite for our coming together, for political unity. Recognition of the inter-connectedness of sex, race, and class highlights the diversity of experience, compelling redefinition of the terms for unity. If women do not share "common oppression," what then can serve as a basis for our coming together?

Unlike many feminist comrades, I believe women and men must share a common understanding – a basic knowledge of what feminism is – if it is ever to be a powerful mass-based political movement. In *Feminist Theory: from Margin to Center*, I suggest that defining feminism broadly as "a movement to end sexism and sexist oppression" would enable us to have a common political goal. We would then have a basis on which to build solidarity. Multiple and contradictory definitions of feminism create confusion and undermine the effort to construct feminist movement so that it addresses everyone. Sharing a common goal does not imply that women and men will not have radically divergent perspectives on how that goal might be reached. Because each individual starts the process of engagement in feminist struggle at a unique level of awareness, very real differences in experience, perspective, and knowledge make developing varied strategies for participation and transformation a necessary agenda.

Feminist thinkers engaged in radically revisioning central tenets of feminist thought must continually emphasize the importance of sex, race, and class as factors which *together* determine the social construction of femaleness, as it has been so deeply ingrained in the consciousness of many women active in feminist movement that gender is the sole factor determining destiny. However, the work of education for critical consciousness (usually called consciousness-raising) cannot end there. Much feminist consciousness-raising has in the past focused on identifying the particular ways men oppress and exploit women. Using the paradigm of sex, race, and class means that the focus does not begin with men and what they do to women, but rather with women working to identify both individually and collectively the specific character of our social identity.

Imagine a group of women from diverse backgrounds coming together to talk about feminism. First they concentrate on working out their status in terms of sex, race, and class using this as the standpoint from which they begin discussing patriarchy or their particular relations with individual men. Within the old frame of reference, a discussion might consist solely of talk about their experiences as victims in relationship to male oppressors. Two women – one poor, the other quite wealthy – might describe the process by which they have suffered physical abuse by male partners and find certain commonalities which might serve as a basis for bonding. Yet if these same two women engaged in a discussion of class, not only would the social construction and expression of femaleness differ, so too would their ideas about how to confront and change their circumstances. Broadening the discussion to include an analysis of race and class would expose many additional differences even as commonalities emerged.

Clearly the process of bonding would be more complex, yet this broader discussion might enable the sharing of perspectives and strategies for change that would enrich rather than diminish our understanding of gender. While feminists have increasingly given "lip service" to the idea of diversity, we have not developed strategies of communication and inclusion that allow for the successful enactment of this feminist vision.

Small groups are no longer the central place for feminist consciousness-raising. Much feminist education for critical consciousness takes place in women's studies classes or at conferences which focus on gender. Books are a primary source of education which means that already masses of people who do not read have no access. The separation of grassroots ways of sharing feminist thinking across kitchen tables from the spheres where much of that thinking is generated, the academy, undermines feminist movement. It would further feminist movement if new feminist thinking could be once again shared in small group contexts, integrating critical analysis with discussion of personal experience. It would be useful to promote anew the small group setting as an arena for education for critical consciousness, so that women and men might come together in neighborhoods and communities to discuss feminist concerns.

Small groups remain an important place for education for critical consciousness for several reasons. An especially important aspect of the small group setting is the emphasis on communicating feminist thinking, feminist theory, in a manner that can be easily understood. In small groups, individuals do not need to be equally literate or literate at all because the information is primarily shared through conversation, in dialogue which is necessarily a liberatory expression. (Literacy should be a goal for feminists even as we ensure that it does not become a requirement for participation in feminist education.) Reforming small groups would subvert the appropriation of feminist thinking by a select group of academic women and men, usually white, usually from privileged class backgrounds.

Small groups of people coming together to engage in feminist discussion, in dialectical struggle make a space where the "personal is political" as a starting point for education for critical consciousness. This can be extended to include politicization of the self that focuses on creating understanding of the ways sex, race, and class together determine our individual lot and our collective experience. It would further feminist movement if many well-known feminist thinkers would participate in small groups, critically re-examining ways their works might be changed by incorporating broader perspectives. All efforts at self-transformation challenge us to engage in ongoing, critical self-examination and reflection about feminist practice, about how we live in the world. This individual commitment, when coupled with engagement in collective discussion, provides a space for critical feedback which strengthens our efforts to change and make ourselves new. It is in this commitment to feminist principles in our words and deeds that the hope of feminist revolution lies.

Working collectively to confront difference, to expand our awareness of sex, race, and class as interlocking systems of domination, of the ways we reinforce and perpetuate these structures, is the context in which we learn the true meaning of solidarity. It is this work that must be the foundation of feminist movement. Without it, we cannot effectively resist patriarchal domination; without it, we remain estranged and alienated from one another. Fear of painful confrontation often leads women and men active in feminist movement to avoid rigorous critical encounter, yet if we cannot engage dialectically in a committed, rigorous, humanizing manner, we cannot hope to change the world. True politicization – coming to critical consciousness – is a difficult, "trying" process, one that demands that we give up set ways of thinking and being, that we shift our paradigms, that we open ourselves to the unknown, the unfamiliar. Undergoing this process, we learn what it means to struggle and in this effort we experience the dignity and integrity of being that comes with revolutionary change. If we do not change our consciousness, we cannot change our actions or demand change from others.

Our renewed commitment to a rigorous process of education for critical consciousness will determine the shape and direction of future feminist movement. Until new perspectives are created, we cannot be living symbols of the power of feminist thinking. Given the privileged lot of many leading feminist thinkers, both in terms of status, class, and race, it is harder these days to convince women of the primacy of this process of politicization. More and more, we seem to form select interest groups composed of individuals who share similar perspectives. This limits our capacity to engage in critical discussion. It is difficult to involve women in new processes of feminist politicization because so many of us think that identifying men as the enemy, resisting male domination, gaining equal access to power and privilege is the end of feminist movement. Not only is it not the end, it is not even the place we want revitalized feminist movement to begin. We want to begin as women seriously addressing ourselves, not solely in relation to men, but in relation to an entire structure of domination of which patriarchy is one part. While the struggle to eradicate sexism and sexist oppression is and should be the primary thrust of feminist movement, to prepare ourselves politically for this effort we must first learn how to be in solidarity, how to struggle with one another.

Only when we confront the realities of sex, race, and class, the ways they divide us, make us different, stand us in opposition, and work to reconcile and resolve these issues will we be able to participate in the making of feminist revolution, in the transformation of the world. Feminism, as Charlotte Bunch emphasizes again and again in *Passionate Politics*, is a transformational politics, a struggle against domination wherein the effort is to change ourselves as well as structures. Speaking about the struggle to confront difference, Bunch asserts:

> A crucial point of the process is understanding that reality does not look the same from different people's perspective. It is not surprising that one way feminists have come to understand about differences has been through the love of a person from another culture or race. It takes persistence and motivation – which love often engenders – to get beyond one's ethnocentric assumptions

and really learn about other perspectives. In this process and while seeking to eliminate oppression, we also discover new possibilities and insights that come from the experience and survival of other peoples.

Embedded in the commitment to feminist revolution is the challenge to love. Love can be and is an important source of empowerment when we struggle to confront issues of sex, race, and class. Working together to identify and face our differences – to face the ways we dominate and are dominated – to change our actions, we need a mediating force that can sustain us so that we are not broken in this process, so that we do not despair.

Not enough feminist work has focused on documenting and sharing ways individuals confront differences constructively and successfully. Women and men need to know what is on the other side of the pain experienced in politicization. We need detailed accounts of the ways our lives are fuller and richer as we change and grow politically, as we learn to live each moment as committed feminists, as comrades working to end domination. In reconceptualizing and reformulating strategies for future feminist movement, we need to concentrate on the politicization of love, not just in the context of talking about victimization in intimate relationships, but in a critical discussion where love can be understood as a powerful force that challenges and resists domination. As we work to be loving, to create a culture that celebrates life, that makes love possible, we move against dehumanization, against domination. In *Pedagogy of the Oppressed*, Paulo Freire evokes this power of love, declaring:

> I am more and more convinced that true revolutionaries must perceive the revolution, because of its creative and liberating nature, as an act of love. For me, the revolution, which is not possible without a theory of revolution – and therefore science – is not irreconcilable with love . . . The distortion imposed on the word "love" by the capitalist world cannot prevent the revolution from being essentially loving in character, nor can it prevent the revolutionaries from affirming their love of life.

That aspect of feminist revolution that calls women to love womanness, that calls men to resist dehumanizing concepts of masculinity, is an essential part of our struggle. It is the process by which we move from seeing ourselves as objects to acting as subjects. When women and men understand that working to eradicate patriarchal domination is a struggle rooted in the longing to make a world where everyone can live fully and freely, then we know our work to be a gesture of love. Let us draw upon that love to heighten our awareness, deepen our compassion, intensify our courage, and strengthen our commitment.

Recognizing, Accepting, and Celebrating our Differences
Papusa Molina

Querida Gloria

You called me and your call takes me through an eight years' journey. *Me pides que te escriba* a piece of work about alliances, about my work with the Women Against Racism Committee. About this family of women housed in my *gringo* home, Iowa City. And Gloria, the fear kicks in. *Ese miedo* that comes late at night when I am there lying in bed without being able to sleep because I am *sola*; because everything that is familiar has stayed behind in Merida, on the beach of Isla Mujeres, in the pyramids of Uxmal. *Ese miedo* that enters me when I am afraid of not being able to express my deepest feelings because *el Ingles no da* – it's too short, too practical, not romantic enough, not soft enough for me when I want to call my lover *caracolito*. Gloria, *este es el miedo* of always being an outsider; no matter who I am with, the sense of belonging is always temporary; the fear of living in the Borderlands paralyzes and silences me. You have written about it, I know you understand. I know you know what needs to be overcome to build alliances, to trust. So I cleanse myself. I do the things that mamma Teish has taught me. I start thinking about Cindy and Joan and Mary and Rusty and *el miedo* starts disappearing. It is like magic. I just need to sit in front of the computer now. I just need to let my memory run, and my fingers will speak for my mind and soul. I will speak clear and loud so my silence does not become an accomplice of my fear. Some truths need to be said, and they will. Some experiences need to be accounted for, and they will. I will start the journey.

October of 1981. I'd been in Iowa City only three months when Rusty – a Chicana who has taught me more than anyone else about being Mexican – called to invite me to a meeting where a group of women of color expressed their rage at our invisibility in the Women's Center's programs and staff. The people working and organizing out of the Center responded and a multicultural committee was formed. We decided that one way to address the issues raised would be learning about the experience of people

This reading first appeared in *Making Face, Making Soul/Haciendo Caras: Creative and Critical Perspectives by Feminists of Color*, ed. Gloria Anzaldúa (San Francisco: Aunt Lute Foundation, 1990), pp. 326–31.

of color in the US. The Women Against Racism Committee organized its first anti-racism conference on May 2, 1982. By this date you and Cherríe Moraga had edited and published *This Bridge Called my Back*.[1] We invited Cherríe to be our keynote speaker, and she accepted. We put together a packet of readings, sent out invitations and established that our conference would be free and open to the public. It was empowering for the women of color – all 80 of us who came from the eastern part of the state. It was the first time so many of us were together in the same room, reaffirming each other with *ajas*, with hugs, with clenched fists and with tears when memories of isolation brought back the pain. For the white women, it was time only for guilt. There was no understanding of our rage, no clear sense of what we were talking about. The closing session was chaotic, to say the least. We ended up calling each other every single name in the book. A lot of tears and screaming and silencing and interrupting. The group disbanded after this conference. At the time, it seemed almost impossible that white women and women of color in Iowa City could ever be in the same room together, working for the same cause. However, some of us hung together. In September of 1983 we called former members to reconstitute the committee. Some women could not come back. Maybe *el miedo* came in, maybe the anger, the guilt or pure pain kept them away. The ones who returned once again began the process of questioning, of learning, of talking honestly and of exercising listening skills. We started reading everything that we could get our hands on: *The Combahee River Collective Statement*,[2] speeches by Audre Lorde; *This Bridge* became our bible. We organized another local conference in April of 1984. Once again, we needed to admit that we hadn't learned how to work together, hadn't learned how to work across our differences. The fact that almost all of us were lesbians and/or feminists, with an intellectual understanding of racism, classism and homophobia didn't mean a damn thing. We were stuck. We knew that something was missing but we didn't know what. *Pero Gloria*, we were hardheaded. We kept meeting each Monday, we kept reading, we kept arguing. It seems that at some intuitive level we knew that our survival on this planet depended on our ability to go beyond coalitions and form alliances.

Some time during the 1984–5 academic year, a couple of women from Iowa City attended the first national conference of the National Black Women's Health Project and they met Lillie Allen. They came back to the committee and proposed that we invite her to our next conference. We had already contacted Barbara Smith to be our keynote speaker, but we realized that we didn't have anything to lose by adding Lillie and maybe we could learn something. So an invitation went out to Lillie, and she accepted. She brought with her Ann Mackie, and for the first time since we started our

Feminism and the Future   429

work, there was something that looked a little different. A white woman and a black woman, both Southern, were working together. They were loving and respecting each other, and above all they were presenting us with a model where the individual consequences of racism were addressed and a healing process was started. They conducted workshops for the conference participants and then, after the conference, the committee got together for a session with Lillie. We weren't really prepared for what happened. From the very beginning, the purpose of having an ongoing group was to educate ourselves and others about racism. We were to serve as a laboratory. Before sharing with others we were going to explore among ourselves. It was rough. Again, Gloria, *el canijo miedo* of exploring, of exposing ourselves, of daring to be vulnerable and risk looking at each other in our totality without masks and false postures, rose up. The struggle between the intellectual and the touchy-feely approach erupted from the first moment when Lillie hugged one of us or – worst of all – encouraged our tears. This conference forever changed the life of the committee.

Years passed and we kept organizing conferences. The majority of the women – by this time we were about 25 – continued struggling in the committee. Those who left did so mainly because they moved away from Iowa City. We kept mixing the more intellectual approach – a process by which we corrected misinformation and provided new information – with what we called "personal work." Gloria Joseph, Merle Woo, Rachel Sierra, Toni Cade Bambara, Nellie Wong, Winona La Duke and you, among others, were our keynote speakers. All of you challenged our prejudices, corrected our thoughts and were vital for bringing into our small community a world existing outside the limits of our small town. Meanwhile, Barbara Love, Vivian Carlo, Lillian Roybal-Rose, Pat Roselle, and Rieki Sherover-Marcuse were taking us on an experiential journey of our personal encounters with racism. At the same time, we started to discover, as we dealt with racism, that we needed to deal with other oppressions which separated us from each other.

At the end of our 1987 conference, we realized that we had something on our hands and maybe the time had arrived to share it with other people who were doing anti-racism work in particular and liberation work in general. So, during the committee's retreat of June 20, 1987, we decided that the conference "Parallels and Intersections: Racism and other Forms of Oppression" would take place in April of 1989 in Iowa City. The other part of our resolution that day was the commitment to train ourselves more and more as facilitators in order to conduct anti-oppression workshops around the county. We accomplished both. On April 9, 1989, we held the closing session of a conference attended by 1,500 people. Many of the participants came because they had attended our workshops in their own communities or knew somebody who had done so. We had over 60 workshops, 20 speakers divided in panels and special interest sessions, concerts, dances, plays and singers. At the end of four days, 150 volunteers and the 30 committee members were exhausted but confident that a new vision had been created: that in order to dismantle the sociopolitical and economic structures of oppression, we needed to form alliances with very specific characteristics; we needed to make into reality the old adage that the "political is personal and the personal is political": and we needed to dismantle – as Angela Davis reminded us – white people's organizations and recreate them with diversity at their core and people of color as their leaders.[3] We needed to work at the personal level, unlearning attitudes and behaviors of oppression; and at the institutional level, we needed to actively dismantle the structures which privileged some by excluding and silencing others.

At this moment in the paper you may be asking yourself: "All this sounds fine, but how did they do it?" I don't know exactly how, Gloria. I don't think that exact recipes exist. I can only share what we found after eight years of searching. It is almost a matter of faith. You may smile or almost laugh, but *no te rías*. Like the words of the old Lennon song, "You may say I'm a dreamer, but I'm not the only one."[4] If I didn't believe that it is possible, I could not wake up every morning and face living in a country which practices oppression at every level, a country where internal and external colonizations follow the same patterns but *al fin y al cabo*, a country where multicultural society is an unavoidable reality. So let me share with you what I have learned.

I have learned that coalitions and alliances are different. Coalitions are intellectual/political exercises where individual needs are sacrificed for the cause. I think all of us, in one way or another, have had that experience. We all have experienced burn-out. We have acquired ulcers, alcoholism, broken hearts, insomnia, sore throats, and we have stopped smoking and have started again at least 1,000 times. We know the rewards of coalitions: a successful march, strike, rally, land preservation. But people get hurt, sick, angry, demoralized and, once in a while, might even produce a right-wing fundamentalist. When we build coalitions we forget to take care of ourselves. We dismiss our own importance because winning the battle is the goal. But don't misunderstand me: coalitions are necessary as long as we keep in mind that they are temporary, formed with specific goals in mind, and they need to be disbanded as soon as the objective is achieved. Alliances, on the other hand, are about individuals, they are about love, they are about commitment and they are about responsibility. They are about concrete manifestations of our rebellious spirits and our sense of justice. They are about shared visions of a better society for all of us.

Now I think I know what you may be saying at this moment: "*Ay Papusa, cuando vas a aprender m'hijita*, here you go again with your idealism." Well, Gloria, let me tell you how I think this is possible.

I believe there are some ways of thinking and being that we need to implement in order to be allies. Audre Lorde, in a paper delivered at the Copeland Colloquium at Amherst College in April of 1980, told us: "it is not those differences between us that are separating us. It is rather our refusal to recognize those differences."[5] In the Women Against Racism Committee we say: "It is our refusal to recognize, accept, and celebrate those differences that keeps us apart." I think, Gloria, that in the feminist movement especially, we have been very good about recognizing the differences; we have named them; we have analyzed their construction, and we have even deconstructed them. However, we have a hard time accepting and celebrating differences. Why? I think it is because we are immersed in a society where "sameness" is venerated as the most desirable quality. It is so internalized that even when we construct alternative organizations, we establish norms and regulations that create just another category of sameness – the politically correct person. We chastise each other if we do not speak the same language, look at society with the same eyes, or even dress and eat the same food. It takes an act of love, then, to recognize, accept, and celebrate our differences.

Another qualitative change consists in looking at every human being – including ourselves – as victims and perpetrators of oppression. Because we live in a society that emphasizes a dichotomous worldview, we live our lives making either/or choices, labeling each other by opposition and dividing the planet into good and bad, black and white, yes and no. Everything around us tells us that in order to affirm who we are, we need to negate the other or define it as the opposite. I think that, especially as people of color, we have a hard time seeing ourselves as oppressors. Because we look at ourselves in just one dimension – race – we aren't aware of the many times we also participate and, with our daily actions, maintain a system that distributes rewards based on gender, age, class, sexual orientation, religious/cultural background, physical and mental ability, etc., etc., etc. It is only recently that some feminists have at least started asking for an analysis based on gender, sexuality, class, and race. However, we are very quick to blame the white, upper-class, Christian, heterosexual, able-bodied man as the Oppressor with capital O. I think it is important that we start assuming some responsibility for our contribution to this patriarchal, imperialist system which ends up oppressing most of us.

Maybe the most idealistic of our proposals is the belief that because behaviors and attitudes of oppression are learned, they can be unlearned.[6]

Mary Arnold, one of the members of the committee, always talks about the smog in which we all live. We all breathe the same prejudices, the same assumptions and, with small differences, the same values. The process of clearing the air then has to be a conscious one. We have to dare to question the myths and misinformations transmitted to us by the main actors in charge of the superstructures of society. We need to challenge the teachings of our parents, religious leaders, educators, politicians, and to increase our ability to respond with an ever-clearer sense of who we are, how our prejudices get reinforced and how we create institutions to enact our collective prejudices. Understanding personal and institutional power becomes, then, the main task in the process of liberation and in this revolution where allies are struggling for life and not for death.

El miedo comes back, Gloria. I feel like I have poured my mind and my soul as I write. Maybe this will make sense to you and you would like to include it in the anthology, maybe it rambles too much and you will decide to leave it out. However, it has been good for me. I have confronted the fear of saying it as I see it. I have survived. And I serve as a testimony that change is not reached without struggle. Our journey has just begun.

En la lucha,
Papusa
Iowa City, Fall of 1989

Notes

The title of the paper is taken from the Women Against Racism Committee workshops title. It was also the title of our 1986 conference. I decided to start my paper with this title as a way to acknowledge that my voice is not an individual one. My voice is the product of a collective effort. It is my personal experience as a member of a family of women who struggle each day to get clearer and clearer about who we are and about the task in front of us.

1 *This Bridge* was first published by Persephone Press in 1981. When Persephone closed, Kitchen Table/Women of Color Press picked it up and it can be obtained from them (PO Box 908, Latham, NY 12110).
2 You can find it in Barbara Smith (ed.), *Home Girls: a Black Feminist Anthology* (New York: Kitchen Table/Women of Color Press, 1983), p. 272.
3 Closing session of "Parallels and Intersections."
4 *Imagine* by John Lennon.
5 Lorde, Audre, *Sister Outsider* (New York: The Crossing Press, 1984).

6   I would like to acknowledge the contributions of Ricki Sherover-Marcuse to the liberation movement. The incorporation of this concept in our framework derives from our work with her.

Healing the Wounds: Feminism, Ecology, and the Nature/Culture Dualism (excerpt)
Ynestra King

No part of living nature can ignore the extreme threat to life on Earth. We are faced with worldwide deforestation, the disappearance of hundreds of species of life, and the increasing pollution of the gene pool by poisons and low-level radiation. We are also faced with biological atrocities unique to modern life – the existence of the AIDS virus and the possibility of even more dreadful and pernicious diseases caused by genetic mutation. World-wide food shortages, including episodes of mass starvation, continue to mount as prime agricultural land is used to grow cash crops to pay national debts instead of food to feed people.[1] Animals are mistreated and mutilated in horrible ways to test cosmetics, drugs, and surgical procedures. The stock-piling of ever greater weapons of annihilation and the terrible imagining of new ones continues. The piece of the pie that women have only begun to sample as a result of the feminist movement is rotten and carcinogenic, and surely our feminist theory and politics must take account of this, however much we yearn for the opportunities that have been denied to us. What is the point of partaking equally in a system that is killing us all?

The contemporary ecological crisis alone creates an imperative that feminists take ecology seriously, but there are other reasons ecology is central to feminist philosophy and politics. The ecological crisis is related to the systems of hatred of all that is natural and female by the white, male, Western formulators of philosophy, technology, and death inventions. It is my contention that the systematic denigration of working-class people and people of color, women, and animals is connected to the basic dualism that lies at the root of Western civilization. But the mind-set of hierarchy originates within human society. It has its material roots in the domination of human by human, particularly of women by men. While I cannot speak for the liberation struggles of people of color, I believe that the goals of

This reading first appeared in *Reweaving the World: the Emergence of Ecofeminism*, eds Irene Diamond and Gloria Feman Orenstein (San Francisco: Sierra Club Books, 1990), pp. 106–21.

feminism, ecology, and movements against racism and for the survival of indigenous peoples are internally related and must be understood and pursued together in a worldwide, genuinely pro-life,[2] movement.

There is at the root of Western society a deep ambivalence about life itself, about our own fertility and that of non-human nature, and a terrible confusion about our place in nature. But as the work of social ecologist Murray Bookchin demonstrates, nature did not declare war on humanity, patriarchal humanity declared war on women and on living nature.[3] . . .

Ecofeminism: beyond the nature/culture dualism

Women have been culture's sacrifice to nature. The practice of human sacrifice to outsmart or appease a feared nature is ancient. And it is in resistance to this sacrificial mentality – on the part of both the sacrificer and sacrifice – that some feminists have argued against the association of women with nature, emphasizing the social dimension of traditional women's lives. Part of the work of feminism has been asserting that the activities of women, believed to be more natural than those of men, are in fact absolutely social. For example, giving birth is natural (though how it is done is very social) but mothering is an absolutely social activity.[4] In bringing up their children, mothers face ethical and moral choices as complex as those considered by professional politicians and ethicists. In the wake of feminism, women will continue to do these things, but the problem of connecting humanity to nature will still have to be acknowledged and solved. In our mythology of complementarity, men and women have led vicarious lives, where women had feelings and led instinctual lives and men engaged in the projects illuminated by reason. Feminism has exposed the extent to which it was all a lie – that's why it has been so important to feminism to establish the mindful, social nature of mothering.

It is as if women were entrusted with and have kept the dirty little secret that humanity emerges from non-human nature into society in the life of the species and the person. The process of nurturing an unsocialized, undifferentiated human infant into an adult person – the socialization of the organic – is the bridge between nature and culture. The Western male bourgeois then extracts himself from the realm of the organic to become a public citizen, as if born from the head of Zeus. He puts away childish things. He disempowers and sentimentalizes his mother, sacrificing her to nature. But the key to the historic agency of women with respect to the nature/culture dualism lies in the fact that the traditional activities of women – mothering, cooking, healing, farming, foraging – are as social as they are natural.

The task of an ecological feminism is the organic forging of a genuinely anti-dualistic, or dialectical, theory and practice. No previous feminism has addressed this problem adequately, hence the necessity of ecofeminism. Rather than succumb to nihilism, pessimism, and an end to reason and history, we seek to enter into history, to a genuinely ethical thinking – where one uses mind and history to reason from the "is" to the "ought" and to reconcile humanity with nature, within and without. This is the starting point for ecofeminism.

Each major contemporary feminist theory, liberal, social, and cultural, has taken up the issue of the relationship between women and nature. And each in its own way has capitulated to dualistic thinking. Ecofeminism takes from socialist feminism the idea that women have been *historically* positioned at the biological dividing line where the organic emerges into the social. The domination of nature originates in society and therefore must be resolved in society. Thus, it is the embodied woman as social historical agent, rather than as a product of natural law, who is the subject of ecofeminism. But the weakness of socialist feminism's theory of the person is serious from an ecofeminist standpoint. An ecological feminism calls for a dynamic, developmental theory of the person – male *and* female – who emerges out of non-human nature, where difference is neither reified nor ignored and the dialectical relationship between human and non-human nature is understood.

Cultural feminism's greatest weakness is its tendency to make the personal into the political, with its emphasis on personal transformation and empowerment. This is most obvious in the attempt to overcome the apparent opposition between spirituality and politics. For cultural feminists, spirituality is the heart in a heartless world (whereas for socialist feminists it is the opiate of the people). Cultural feminists have formed the "beloved community" of feminism – with all the power, potential, and problems of a religion. And as an appropriate response to the need for mystery and attention to personal alienation in an overly rationalized world, it is a vital and important movement. But by itself it does not provide the basis for a genuinely dialectical ecofeminist theory and practice, one that addresses history as well as mystery. For this reason, cultural/spiritual feminism (sometimes even called "nature feminism") is not synonymous with ecofeminism in that creating a gynocentric culture and politics is a necessary but not sufficient condition for ecofeminism.

Both feminism and ecology embody the revolt of nature against human domination. They demand that we rethink the relationship between humanity and the rest of nature, including our natural, embodied selves. In ecofeminism, nature is the central category of analysis. An analysis of the interrelated dominations of nature – psyche and sexuality, human oppression, and non-human nature – and the historic position of women in relation to those forms of domination is the starting point of ecofeminist theory. We share with cultural feminism the necessity of a politics with heart and a beloved community, recognizing our connection with each other – and with non-human nature. Socialist feminism has given us a powerful critical perspective with which to understand, and transform, history. Separately, they perpetuate the dualism of "mind" and "nature." Together they make possible a new ecological relationship between nature and culture, in which mind and nature, heart and reason, join forces to transform the systems of domination, internal and external, that threaten the existence of life on Earth.

Practice does not wait for theory – it comes out of the imperatives of history. Women are the revolutionary bearers of this anti-dualistic potential in the world today. In addition to the enormous impact of feminism on Western civilization, women have been at the forefront of every historical, political movement to reclaim the Earth. For example, for many years in India poor women who come out of the Gandhian movement have waged a non-violent campaign for land reform and to save the forest, called the *Chipko Andolan* (the hugging movement), wrapping their bodies around trees as bulldozers arrive. Each of the women has a tree of her own she is to protect – to steward. When loggers were sent in, one of the women said, "Let them know they will not fell a single tree without the felling of us first. When the men raise their axes, we will embrace the trees to protect them."[5] These women have waged a remarkably successful non-violent struggle, and their tactics have spread to other parts of India. Men have joined in, though the campaign was originated and continues to be led by women. Yet this is not a sentimental movement – lives depend on the survival of the forest. For most of the women of the world, interest in preservation of the land, water, air, and energy is no abstraction but a clear part of the effort to simply survive.

The increasing militarization of the world has intensified this struggle. Women and children make up 80 percent of war refugees. Lands are often burned and scarred in such a way as to prevent cultivation for many years after the battles, so that starvation and hardship follow long after the fighting has stopped.[6] And, here, too, women – often mothers and farmers – respond to necessity. They become the protectors of the Earth in an effort to eke out a small living on the land to feed themselves and their families.

There are other areas of feminist activism that illuminate an enlightened ecofeminist perspective.[7] Potentially, one of the best examples of an appropriately mediated, dialectical relationship to nature is the feminist health movement. The medicalization of childbirth in the first part of this century and, currently, the redesign and appropriation of reproduction both create new profit-making technologies for capitalism and make heretofore natural processes mediated by women into arenas controlled by men. Women offered themselves up to the ministrations of "experts," internalizing the notion that they didn't know enough and surrendering their power. They also accepted the idea that maximum intervention in and domination of nature are inherently good. But since the onset of feminism in the 1960s, women in the United States have gone quite a way in reappropriating and demedicalizing childbirth. As a result of this movement, many more women want to be told what all their options are and many choose invasive medical technologies only under unusual and informed circumstances. They do not necessarily reject these useful technologies in some cases, but they have pointed a finger at motivations of profit and control in the technologies' widespread application. Likewise, my argument here is not that feminism should repudiate all aspects of Western science and medicine. It is to assert that we should develop the sophistication to decide for ourselves when intervention serves our best interest.

Another central area of concern in which women may employ ecofeminism to overcome misogynist dualism is that of body consciousness. Accepting our own bodies just as they are, knowing how they look, feel, and smell, and learning to work with them to become healthier is a basis for cultural and political liberation. In many patriarchal cultures, women are complicit in the domination of our natural bodies, seeking to please men at any cost. Chinese foot-binding, performed by women, is a widely cited example of misogynist domination of women's bodies. But even as Western feminists condemn these practices, most of us will do anything to our bodies (yes, even feminists) to appear closer to norms of physical beauty that come naturally to about 0.2 percent of the female population. The rest of us struggle to be skinny, hairless, and, lately, muscular. We lie in the sun to get tan even when we know we are courting melanoma, especially as the accelerating depletion of the ozone layer makes "sunbathing" a dangerous sport. We submit ourselves to extremely dangerous surgical procedures. We primp, prune, douche, deodorize, and diet as if our natural bodies were our mortal enemies. Some of us living the most privileged lives in the world starve ourselves close to death for beauty, literally.

To the extent that we make our own flesh an enemy, or docilely submit ourselves to medical experts, we are participating in the domination of nature. To the extent that we learn to work with the restorative powers of our bodies, using medical technologies and drugs sparingly, we are developing an appropriately mediated relationship to our own natures. But even the women's health movement has not realized a full ecofeminist perspective.[8]

It has yet to fully grasp health as an ecological and social rather than an individual problem, in which the systematic poisoning of environments where women live and work is addressed as a primary political issue. Here the community-based movements against toxic wastes, largely initiated and led by women, and the feminist health movement may meet.

A related critical area for a genuinely dialectical practice is a reconstruction of science, taking into account the critique of science advanced by radical ecology and feminism.[9] Feminist historians and philosophers of science are demonstrating that the will to know and the will to power need not be the same thing. They argue that there are ways of knowing the world that are not based on objectification and domination.[10] Here, again, apparently antithetical epistemologies, science and mysticism, can coexist. We shall need all our ways of knowing to create life on this planet that is both ecological and sustainable.

As feminists, we shall need to develop an ideal of freedom that is neither antisocial nor anti-natural.[11] We are past the point of throwing off our chains to reclaim our ostensibly free nature, if such a point ever existed. Ecofeminism is not an argument for a return to prehistory. The knowledge that women were not always dominated and that society was not always hierarchical is a powerful inspiration for contemporary women, so long as such a society is not represented as a "natural order," apart from history, to which we will inevitably return by a great reversal.

From an ecofeminist perspective, we are part of nature, but not inherently good or bad, free or unfree. There is no one natural order that represents freedom. We are *potentially* free in nature, but as human beings that freedom has to be intentionally created by using our understanding of the natural world. For this reason we must develop a different understanding of the relationship between human and non-human nature, based on the stewardship of evolution. To do this we need a theory of history where the natural evolution of the planet and the social history of the species are not separated. We emerged from non-human nature, as the organic emerged from the inorganic.

Here, potentially, we recover ontology as the ground for ethics. We thoughtful human beings must use the fullness of our sensibility and intelligence to push ourselves intentionally to another stage of evolution: one where we will fuse a new way of being human on this planet with a sense of the sacred, informed by all ways of knowing – intuitive *and* scientific, mystical *and* rational. It is the moment where women recognize ourselves as agents of history – yes, even as unique agents – and knowingly bridge the classic dualisms between spirit and matter, art and politics, reason and intuition. This is the potentiality of a *rational re-enchantment*. This is the project of ecofeminism.

At this point in history, the domination of nature is inextricably bound up with the domination of persons, and both must be addressed – without arguments over "the primary contradiction" in the search for a single Archimedes point for revolution. There is no such thing. And there is no point in liberating people if the planet cannot sustain their liberated lives, or in saving the planet by disregarding the preciousness of human existence not only to ourselves but to the rest of life on Earth.

Notes

1 One of the major issues at the United Nations Decade on Women forum held in Nairobi, Kenya, in 1985 was the effect of the international monetary system on women and the particular burdens women bear because of the money owed the "First World," particularly US economic interests, by developing countries.
2 It is one of the absurd examples of newspeak that the designation "pro-life" has been appropriated by the militarist right to support forced child bearing.
3 See especially Murray Bookchin, *The Ecology of Freedom* (Palo Alto, CA: Cheshire Books, 1982). Of the various ecological theories that are not explicitly feminist, I draw here on Bookchin's work because he articulates a historical theory of hierarchy that begins with the domination of women by men, making way for domination by race and class, and the domination of nature. Hence the term "social" ecology. *The Ecology of Freedom* presents a radical view of the emergence, and potential dissolution, of hierarchy. Social ecology is just as concerned with relations of domination between persons as it is with the domination of nature. Hence it should be of great interest to feminists.
4 On the social, mindful nature of mothering, see the work of Sara Ruddick, especially "Maternal thinking," *Feminist Studies*, 6 (2): 342–67; and "Preservative love and military destruction: some reflections on mothering and peace," in Joyce Trebilcot (ed.), *Mothering: Essays in Feminist Theory*, pp. 231–62 (Totowa, NJ: Rowman and Allanheld, 1983).
5 Catherine Caufield, *In the Rainforest*, pp. 156–8 (Chicago: University of Chicago Press, 1984).
6 See Edward Hyams, *Soil and Civilization* (New York: Harper and Row, 1976).
7 See Petra Kelly, *Fighting for Hope* (Boston: South End Press, 1984) for a practical, feminist green political analysis and program, with examples of ongoing movements and activities.
8 I am indebted to ecofeminist sociologist and environmental health activist Lin Nelson for pointing out to me why the feminist health movement is yet to become ecological.
9 See Elizabeth Fee, "Is feminism a threat to scientific objectivity?" *International Journal of Women's Studies*, 4 (4): 378–92. See also Sandra Harding, *The Science Question in Feminism* (Ithaca, NY: Cornell University Press, 1986) and Evelyn Fox Keller, *Reflections on Gender and Science* (New Haven, CT: Yale University Press, 1985).

10   See, for example, Evelyn Fox Keller, *A Feeling for the Organism: the Life and Work of Barbara McClintock* (San Francisco, Freeman, 1983).
11   The cross-cultural interpretations of personal freedom of anthropologist Dorothy Lee are evocative of the possibility of such an ideal of freedom. See Dorothy Lee, *Freedom and Culture* (Englewood Cliffs, NJ: Prentice-Hall, 1959).

Still I Rise

Maya Angelou

You may write me down in history
With your bitter, twisted lies,
You may trod me in the very dirt
But still, like dust, I'll rise.

Does my sassiness upset you?
Why are you beset with gloom?
'Cause I walk like I've got oil wells
Pumping in my living room.

Just like moons and like suns,
With the certainty of tides,
Just like hopes springing high,
Still I'll rise.

Did you want to see me broken?
Bowed head and lowered eyes?
Shoulders falling down like teardrops,
Weakened by my soulful cries.

Does my haughtiness offend you?
Don't you take it awful hard
'Cause I laugh like I've got gold mines
Diggin' in my own back yard.

You may shoot me with your words,
You may cut me with your eyes,
You may kill me with your hatefulness,
But still, like air, I'll rise.

This reading first appeared in *And Still I Rise* (New York: Random House, 1978).

Does my sexiness upset you?
Does it come as a surprise
That I dance like I've got diamonds
At the meeting of my thighs?

Out of the huts of history's shame
I rise
Up from a past that's rooted in pain
I rise
I'm a black ocean, leaping and wide,
Welling and swelling I bear in the tide.

Leaving behind nights of terror and fear
I rise
Into a daybreak that's wondrously clear
I rise
Bringing the gifts that my ancestors gave,
I am the dream and the hope of the slave.
I rise
I rise
I rise.

Suggested activities

Questions for discussion

On feminist politics

1 How do feminist politics differ from traditional politics, if at all?
2 Do you agree with bell hooks's claim that women should support the feminist movement not because sexism and patriarchy are the root oppression, but because it insists on eradicating domination in familial and intimate relationships?
3 What is the relationship between sexism and other forms of discrimination, such as racism and classism? Are they separable, or fundamentally interrelated, as bell hooks contends?
4 Evaluate bell hooks's proposals for transforming feminism. Do you think her recommended strategies would lead to the outcome she indicates? If not, what other suggestions can you think of for transforming feminist politics to better account for both the commonalities and the differences among women?
5 Is or should political activism be a criteria in the definition of feminism?
6 If women "ran the country" do you think it would be significantly different from what it is now? If so, in what respects? Do you think women have

a "different voice" in the arena of politics? If so, what factors is your
conclusion based on?

On the backlash

1   Do you agree with Sommers, Roiphe et al. that high-profile feminists have
    co-opted the feminist movement in a direction that makes it difficult for
    more mainstream women to identify themselves as feminists? Is it *fem-
    inists*, or those like Rush Limbaugh who oppose them, that have given
    feminism a bad name? Or is it both?
2   What reasons do you think best explain the reluctance of many young
    women to identify themselves as feminists?
3   What reasons do you think best explain the backlash against feminism?
    Is it primarily being fueled by anti-feminist voices of those outside the
    women's movement, as Faludi suggests, or by frustrated voices within the
    movement, as Sommers, Roiphe, and Delafeld contend?
4   Do you find Faludi's diagnosis of a backlash against feminism in contem-
    porary society persuasive? What about the critiques of feminism by authors
    like Paglia, Roiphe, and Delafeld? Are their arguments ones that feminists
    should take seriously?

On the future of feminism

1   How important is a united feminist movement? What factors are important
    to your analysis?
2   Do you agree with Molina that not only recognizing, but also *accepting*
    and *celebrating* differences among women is necessary in order for femin-
    ists to work together effectively? Can you think of examples in everyday life
    of how social forces favor sameness rather than diversity and difference?
3   Is the ecofeminist connection between the mistreatment of women and the
    mistreatment of nature persuasive? Is this argument valid in the absence of
    essentialist assumptions that women *are* in some way closer to nature?

Films and videos

Daughters of de Beauvoir by Penny Foster (1989). VHS/55 minutes. Distrib-
    uted by Filmaker's Library. Interviews with the women who "took the
    baton" from de Beauvoir as leaders of the second-wave women's move-
    ment: Kate Millet, Marge Piercy, Eva Figes, and Ann Oakley.
The F-Word: a Video about Feminism by Marcia Jarmel (1994). VHS/color/
    10 mins. Distributed by Women Make Movies. Shows the use of and feel-
    ings evoked by the use of the word "feminism."

Its Up to Us by Bea Milwe (1986). VHS/58 mins. Distributed by Women Make Movies. Documentary of the United Nations End of the Decade for Women Conference in Nairobi, Kenya, in 1985. Shows the issues raised for women in the developing world and for an international feminism.

A Place of Rage by Pratibha Parmar (England, 1991). 16 mm/VHS/color/52 mins. Distributed by Women Make Movies. Interviews with famous African-American women such as Angela Davis and Alice Walker. Examines the role of African-American women in the women's and civil rights movements.

Some American Feminists by Luce Guilbeaut et al. (National Film Board of Canada, 1980). VHS/56 mins. Distributed by Women Make Movies. Explores the second wave of the women's movement, interviewing Ti-Grace Atkinson, Rita Mae Brown, Betty Freidan, Margo Jefferson, Lila Karp, and Kate Millett, intercut with newsreel footage of the significant events for women of the 1960s and 1970s.

Strangers in Good Company, produced by the National Film Board of Canada (1990). VHS/100 mins. Movies about seven elderly women and a female bus driver who are stranded together at a deserted farmhouse without much food or a decent place to sleep in Quebec. Non-professional actors reveal the characters' inner strengths in drawing upon survival skills and dormant feelings of enthusiasm for life and nature, and of commitment to others.

Visionary Voices: Women in Power by Penny Rosenwasser and Lisa Rudman (1992). VHS/color/22 mins. Distributed by Women Make Movies. Film of interviews from a book of the same title.

Women in Politics by Lowri Gwilym. A six-part series produced by BBC Television (England, 1989). VHS/color/6 × 40 mins. Distributed by Women Make Movies. Profiles of women in international politics, including Corazon Aquino and Benazir Bhutto.

Other activities

1   In small groups, formulate a definition of "the personal is political." Consider why this became the defining phrase of the second-wave women's movement.

2   Consider the literature on feminist utopias. This might involve students individually reading and writing reviews of books or short stories on this topic and making summary reports to the class. As a class, discuss the differences between the visions of community in these utopias and the realistic prospects for social change to end the oppression of women.

3   In small groups, discuss the impact that feminism and the women's movement has had on American culture in the past and is likely to have in the future. Can the group formulate a definition of feminism that is acceptable to all members? If not, why not?

4   Research what efforts to create social change various women's groups and feminist organizations are engaged in currently. You may want to conduct interviews with members of some of these organizations.

5   Listen to some audiotapes or radio broadcasts of Rush Limbaugh's radio program. What does he say about women, feminism, and issues of particular relevance and concern to women, like employment discrimination, affirmative action, sexual harassment, and abortion? What kind of influence do you think these statements have on views and attitudes about women?

Bibliography

Adams, Carol (ed.) (1993) *Ecofeminism and the Sacred* (New York: Continuum). A collection of essays on feminism's relation to the environment and to spirituality.

Benhabib, Seyla and Cornell, Drucilla (eds) (1987) *Feminism as Critique* (Minneapolis: University of Minnesota Press).

Castro, Ginette (1990) *American Feminism: a Contemporary History* (New York: New York University Press). History of the women's movement, description of "egalitarian" and "radical" feminisms, and alternative feminist institutions.

Collins, Patricia Hill (1990) *Black Feminist Thought: Knowledge, Consciousness, and the Politics of Empowerment* (Boston: Unwin, Hyman).

Daly, Mary (1978) *Gyn/Ecology: the Metaethics of Radical Feminism* (Boston: Beacon Press).

Delafeld, Rene (1995) *The New Victorians: a Young Woman's Challenge to the Old Feminist Order* (New York: Warner Books).

Diamond, Irene and Orenstein, Gloria Feman (1990) *Reweaving the World: the Emergence of Ecofeminism* (San Francisco: Sierra Club Books).

Echols, Alice (1989) *Daring to be Bad: Radical Feminism in America, 1967–1975* (Minneapolis: University of Minnesota Press).

Eisenstein, Hester (1983) *Contemporary Feminist Thought* (Boston: G. H. Hall). A well-regarded history and critique of American feminist thought up to 1980, including an extensive discussion of radical feminism.

Elshtain, Jean (1981) *Public Man/Private Woman: Women in Social and Political Thought* (Oxford: Martin Robertson).

Enloe, Cynthia (1989) *Bananas, Beaches and Bases: Making Feminist Sense of International Politics* (Berkeley, CA: University of California Press). Series of essays on how women are implicated in international politics and US foreign policy.

Faludi, Susan (1991) *Backlash: the Undeclared War against American Women* (New York: Crown Publishers).

Findlen, Barbara (ed.) (1995) *Listen Up: Voices from the Next Feminist Generation* (Seattle, WA: Seal Press). Stories of young women who have chosen to fight for equality, find feminism relevant to their lives, and call themselves feminists.

Firestone, Shulamith (1970) *The Dialectic of Sex: the Case for Feminist Revolution* (New York: Bantam Books).

Fox Genovese, Elizabeth (1992) "Feminist rights, individualist wrongs," *Tikkun*, 7(3): 29–34. One side of a debate, with Nancy Hewitt, on the direction that the feminist movement should be taking.

Frye, Marilyn (1983) *The Politics of Reality* (New York: The Crossing Press).

Gaard, Greta (ed.) (1992) *Ecofeminism: Women, Animals, Nature* (Philadelpha: Temple University Press). Collection of essays by ecofeminists and about ecofeminism from both activist and academic perspectives.

Garland, Anne Witte (1988) *Women Activists: Challenging the Abuse of Power* (New York: Feminist Press at the City University of New York). Women social reformers and women in politics in the US and Great Britain.

Gillespie, Marcia Ann (1992) "No woman's land," *Ms.*, November/December, pp. 18–22. Describes the plight of refugee women from other parts of the world, and the efforts of feminists to assist.

Hartmann, Heidi (1981) "The unhappy marriage of Marxism and feminism," in Lydia Sargent (ed.), *A Discussion of the Unhappy Marriage of Marxism and Feminism* (Boston: South End Press).

Hartsock, Nancy (1983) *Money, Sex, and Power: toward a Feminist Historical Materialism* (New York: Longman).

Hawkesworth, Mary E. (1990) *Beyond Oppression: Feminist Theory and Political Strategy* (New York: Continuum). Investigates the political obstacles to the achievement of feminist goals, and the strategies most likely to succeed in overcoming gender oppression by uniting men and women in political action.

Henry, Sherye (1994) *The Deep Divide: Why American Women Resist Equality* (New York: Macmillan). Like Delafeld, argues that feminism does not speak to the mainstream women it purports to represent.

Hewitt, Nancy (1992) "One feminism is not enough," *Tikkun*, 7(3): 34–6. The other side of the debate, with Elizabeth Fox Genovese, about the future of the feminist movement.

Hoff-Wilson, Joan (ed.) (1986) *Rights of Passage: the Past and Future of the ERA* (Bloomington, IN: Indiana University Press).

hooks, bell (1990) *Yearning: Race, Gender and Cultural Politics* (Boston: South End Press).

Jaggar, Alison (1983) *Feminist Politics and Human Nature* (Totowa, NJ: Rowman and Allanheld). Discusses liberal, Marxist, radical, and socialist feminist politics.

Jaggar, Alison (ed.) (1994) *Living with Contradictions: Controversies in Feminist Social Ethics* (Boulder, CO: Westview Press). Part VIB includes several essays on "Consuming animals," and Part VII, "Feminists changing the world," addresses feminist approaches to militarism and environmentalism.

Jaquette, Jane (1992) "Political science – whose common good?," in Cheryl Kramarae and Dale Spender (eds), *The Knowledge Explosion: Generations of Feminist Scholarship* (New York: Athene Press).

Jones, Kathleen (1993a) *Compassionate Authority: Democracy and the Representation of Women* (New York: Routledge).

Jones, Kathleen (1993b) "Toward a woman-friendly new world order," in Sheri Matteo (ed.), *American Women in the Nineties* (Boston: Northeastern University Press).

Kamen, Paula (1991) *Feminist Fatale: Voices from the Twentysomething Generation Explore the Future of the Women's Movement* (New York: Donald I. Fine). One of the "twenty-somethings" who explored why young women are reluctant to embrace the label "feminist" even though they support the basic principles of mainstream feminism – equal pay, employment opportunities, and so on.

Kakutani, Michiko (1994) "Examining women's studies programs," *New York Times*, December 9, p. C24. Review of Patai and Koertge's *Professing Feminism*.

King, Ynestra (1990) "Healing the wounds: feminism, ecology and the nature/culture dualism," in Irene Diamond and Gloria Feman Orenstein (eds), *Reweaving the World: the Emergence of Ecofeminism* (San Francisco: Sierra Club Books), pp. 106–21.

Kornbluh, Felicia (1992) "Feminism: still hazy after all these years," *Tikkun*, 7 (3): 34–6. Criticizes older feminists like Robin Morgan for continuing to posit a unity among women beneath a superficial affirmation of difference.

Langston, Donna (1991) "Feminist theories and the politics of difference," in Jo Whitehorse Cochran, Donna Langston, and Carolyn Woodward (eds), *Changing our Power: an Introduction to Women's Studies*, 2nd edn (Dubuque, IA: Kendall Hunt).

Larsen, Elizabeth (1991) "Granola boys, eco-dudes, and me," *Ms.*, July/August, pp. 96–7. On sexism in the environmental movement.

Lorber, Judith (1994) *Paradoxes of Gender* (New Haven, CT: Yale University Press).

Mansbridge, Jan (1986) *Why We Lost the ERA* (Chicago: University of Chicago Press).

Marshall, Susan (1991) "Who speaks for American women? The future of antifeminism," *Annals of the Association of the American Political Science Society*, 515: 50–62. Examines the anti-feminist movement in the period after the defeat of the Equal Rights Amendment.

Millett, Kate (1970) *Sexual Politics* (New York: Doubleday). A classic work of literary and cultural criticism by one of the most prominent second-wave feminists. Argues that sex has a political aspect that is generally ignored. Describes patriarchy as a political institution.

Mitchell, Juliet (1973) *Women's Estate* (New York, Vintage). On feminism and the social conditions of women.

Mohanty, Chandra, Russo, Ann and Torres, Lourdes (eds) (1991) *Third World Women and the Politics of Feminism* (Bloomington, IN: Indiana University Press). Collection of essays by feminists of color on various aspects of Third World feminist politics.

Molinà, Papusa (1990) "Recognizing, accepting, and celebrating our differences," in Gloria Anzaldùa (ed.), *Making Face, Making Soul/Hacienda Caras: Creative and Critical Perspectives by Feminists of Color* (San Francisco: Aunt Lute Foundation), pp. 326–31.

Paglia, Camille (1992) "Rape and modern sex war," in *Sex, Art, and American Culture* (New York: Vintage Books/Random House).

Patai, Daphne and Koertge, Noretta (1994) *Professing Feminism: Cautionary Tales from the Strange World of Women's Studies* (New York: Basic Books).

Phelan, Shane (1989) *Identity Politics: Lesbian Feminism and the Limits of Community* (Philadelphia: Temple University Press). Describes the problems of lesbian community, beginning with the premise that lesbian politics defines itself in opposition to liberalism.

Rowbotham, Sheila (1992) *Women in Movement: Feminism and Social Action* (New York: Routledge). History of women radicals, political activists, and social reformers.

Rocheleau, Dianne, Thomas-Slayter, Barbara and Wangari, Esther (eds) (1996) *Feminist Political Ecology: Global Issues and Local Experiences* (New York: Routledge). An examination of the intersection of politics, economics, and ecology globally.

Roiphe, Katie (1993) *The Morning After: Sex, Fear, and Feminism on Campus* (Boston: Little, Brown). On feminism in higher education in the US.

Ruddick, Sara (1989) *Maternal Thinking: toward a Politics of Peace* (Boston: Beacon Press).

Smith, Barbara (1982) "Racism and women's studies," in Gloria Hull, Patricia Bell Scott, and Barbara Smith (eds), *All the Women are White, All the Blacks are Men, but Some of Us are Brave: Black Women's Studies* (Old Westbury, NY: Feminist Press). An early voice from women of color observing the need for the mainstream women's movement to confront its racism.

Sommers, Christina Hoff (1994) *Who Stole Feminism? How Women Have Betrayed Women* (New York: Simon and Schuster).

Tanenbaum, Leora (1995) "I was a teenage 'slut'," *Ms.*, 6, p. 96.

Tronto, Joan (1987) "Beyond gender difference to a theory of care," *Signs*, 12: 644–63.

U Magazine Editorial Staff (1992) "I'm not a feminist, but . . . ," *U Magazine*, November. Reports on attitudes of college students toward the feminist label.

Wolf, Naomi (1993) *Fire with Fire: the New Female Power and How it Will Change the 21st Century* (New York: Random House). Proposes that women adopt "power feminism" by moving beyond academic feminism and embracing equal rights, regardless of differences on other issues.

Index